Pan-African Chronology

To God,
in gratitude
for granting me
enough tomorrows
to begin
this work

PAN-AFRICAN CHRONOLOGY

*A Comprehensive Reference to
the Black Quest for Freedom
in Africa, the Americas,
Europe and Asia, 1400–1865*

by
EVERETT JENKINS, JR.

McFarland & Company, Inc., Publishers
Jefferson, North Carolina, and London

ACKNOWLEDGMENTS: I cannot begin this book without acknowledging the people who have been of the greatest assistance to me in preparing the text. First, I must acknowledge my wife Monica and my children Ryan, Camille, Jennifer and Cristina for putting up with my relationship with my computer over the last year. Their loving sacrifice has, in no small measure, made this book possible.

I also wish to acknowledge my parents Everett, Sr., and Lillie. It is the heritage they gave which has inspired me to study and write African American history from this more global perspective. No words can convey the debt that I owe to them.

The people in my office also must be acknowledged for the support that they have given me over the course of this year while my mind has been, at times, preoccupied by this endeavor. Malcolm Hunter, Bill Bonnell, Wayne Nishioka, Judith Trice, Jack Judkins, Sheila Smith, Linda Thomas, and Leslie Shipp, thanks.

Additionally, while it may not be standard practice to acknowledge an editor from a competing book company, I am going to acknowledge Paul Bernabeo of Simon & Schuster. Mr. Bernabeo provided me with my first positive feedback as to the merits of this book and provided some helpful criticisms which I believe have helped to make this book better.

Finally, allow me to express my profound gratitude to all the fine people at McFarland. They have been instrumental in making what was once only a notion into this concrete reality.

To all of the above, thank you so very much.

British Library Cataloguing-in-Publication data are available

Library of Congress Cataloguing-in-Publication Data

Jenkins, Everett, 1953–
    Pan-African chronology : a comprehensive reference to the Black quest for freedom in Africa, the Americas, Europe and Asia, 1400–1865 / by Everett Jenkins, Jr.
      p. cm.
    Includes bibliographical references and index.
    ISBN 0-7864-0139-7 (lib. bdg. : 50# alk. paper) ∞
    1. Africa—History—Chronology. 2. Blacks—History—Chronology. 3. Afro-Americans—History—Chronology. 4. Slavery—History—Chronology. 5. Slave-trade—History—Chronology. I. Title.
DT17.J46 1996
909'.0496'00202—dc20   95-8294
                                     CIP

Manufactured in the United States of America

McFarland & Company, Inc., Publishers
  Box 611, Jefferson, North Carolina 28640

TABLE OF CONTENTS

PREFACE

In August of 1990, I had the opportunity to attend a family reunion in Alberta, Canada. The trip to Canada and meeting my Canadian relatives was a transformative experience for me which has led to the creation of this book.

While sitting around the dinner table at my Cousin Paulette's house in Edmonton, the conversation drifted to the reasons why and how a branch of the Sanders (Saunders in Canada) family happened to be in Alberta. Paulette's brother, Ron, gave a succinct answer. "Freedom," he said. The Saunders family immigrated to Canada in 1910 in search of freedom.

Paulette was able to dig out a book entitled *The Promised Land* by Pierre Berton which documented part of the Saunders family story. The book told of how, when Oklahoma became a state in 1907, the advent of European American control ushered in a wave of oppression for the African Americans who lived there. Previously, the African Americans had been able to enjoy a measure of freedom while Oklahoma was "Indian" Territory. The former Indigenous American territories had been the home and haven of African Americans. Many had land and had reached a certain level of prosperity. The arrival of the European Americans changed Oklahoma forever.

With the advent of European Americans, laws were passed restricting the activities and civil liberties of African Americans. Shortly thereafter, the Ku Klux Klan was present in full regalia to make sure that the laws were enforced. Oklahoma was no longer a safe haven for African Americans.

Some of the more sagacious and enterprising of the African Americans could see the writing on the wall and decided to seek greener pastures. At this same time, Canada was widely advertising the availability of land in its Western provinces. Some Oklahoma African Americans, including my great-great grandfather William Sanders, decided to try Canada. The immigrants liquidated their property and formed a caravan (trainload) of potential settlers.

Upon arrival at the Canada-Montana border, the trainload of settlers were not met with enthusiasm. While the Canadian government wanted settlers, these settlers were not quite what they had in mind. A mini–international incident developed. The resolution of the incident was that the trainload of African Americans were allowed to immigrate but afterwards the Canadians adopted a policy which severely limited the opportunity of African Americans to become Afro-Canadians.

The Saunders family traveled far north into Alberta. They found a valley some 50 miles northeast of the town of Edmonton—a place called "Amber Valley," and it was there that they once again tried to lead peaceful lives.

Hearing the story of the Saunders family perked my interest in African American history in general. I began reading books on African American history for the first time in some fifteen years. I discovered the trek that the Saunders family took was not the first taken by African Americans. I discovered that even before the first Englishman ever lived in America, people of African descent were living here amongst the Indigenous Americans. I discovered that contrary to previously held notions, African slaves were not the passive beings so commonly depicted in old movies but often courageous resisters of their oppression. I discovered that an uncommon bond has existed between African and Indigenous American people which goes back perhaps as much as three thousand years. I discovered there was much about my history I simply did not know and, as a consequence, there was much about myself that I did not know as well.

I became fascinated by the subject and as my fascination grew into knowledge I became a bit disappointed. I was disappointed because I found the history books wanting in setting forth what I perceive to be the totality of African American history.

For me, African American history is not simply the telling of the African experience in America. While the African experience in America is important, it is not the totality of African American history. African American history is, or should be, a tale of the dynamic interactions among three cultures—the African, the Indigenous American and the European. African American history is also a tale of a compelled African diaspora which includes Chinese, East Indian, Portuguese, Spanish, Dutch, British, Mexican, Canadian and other branches. As an African American, a person with African, Indigenous American, and European blood flowing through my veins, I hungered for a book that would tell my forebears' story. Despite an assiduous search, I have not been able to find such a book.

These are some of the reasons why I have written and compiled this book. This book is a chronology of, and commentary on, the history of African people throughout the world. It is truly a Pan-African chronology.

It is my belief that this chronology is one of the most comprehensive (and culturally sensitive) chronologies of the African (and African American) experience ever compiled. I leave it to you, the reader, to attest as to whether or not my belief has been confirmed.

EVERETT JENKINS, JR.
Fairfield, California
Fall 1995

INTRODUCTION

Europeans did not invent slavery. Slavery has existed since prehistoric times and has been practiced by all races, including Africans.

The word "slave" is derived from the word "slav." In the Middle Ages, men and women from the Balkans (a region where Slavic people predominate) were abducted in large numbers to work on the sugar plantations located on islands in the eastern Mediterranean. When sugar cultivation was introduced to the Madeira Islands, and later to the Americas, the idea of using slaves was a natural carryover from historical practices.

In the fifteenth century, slavery was an almost universal fact of life. There were European slaves in the Middle East, Moorish slaves in Europe, African slaves in India and a well-established slave system within the kingdoms of Africa.

When the Portuguese encountered the West African societies, they encountered peoples who already practiced slavery on a considerable scale. Often tribal wars were fought not for land but for slaves, since a man's (a chieftain's) wealth was measured by the number of people he controlled, not by the amount of territory he dominated. Additionally, many societies operated a legal system in which one form of punishment for criminals was to make them slaves. For many centuries, Arab traders in particular had been able to acquire slaves which they took with them to all parts of the world.

Initially, the Arab and European trade in African slaves was limited in scope. However, with the European "discovery" of the Americas, the growth in the trade of African slaves increased tremendously. In the 1400s only a few thousand slaves were taken from West Africa to Europe and the Atlantic islands such as Madeira. But with the need to colonize the Americas, the demand for African slaves reached monumental proportions: during the 1700s some six to seven million Africans were shipped to the Western Hemisphere to work as slaves.

This *Pan-African Chronology* is a record of the most significant events in African, African American and Pan-African history. This book covers the time period of 1400 to 1865. It begins with the roots of the European exploration of the African continent and ends with the passage of the Thirteenth Amendment to the United States Constitution making slavery unconstitutional. While it must be noted that not all African people have had slavery as part of their history, nevertheless, it was roughly during this time period that slavery became a dominant institution touching the lives, in one way or another, of the majority of African people throughout the world.

This volume is divided into five principal chapters, covering the 1400s, the 1500s, the 1600s, the 1700s and the years from 1800 to 1865.

In each of the chapters, divisions are made which track the history of Africans in Africa, Europe, Asia, the Americas, and the United States. In addition, pertinent Related Historical Events are noted.

Beginning in the late 1700s, the history of African Americans (African people located in the land that came to be known as the United States) is compartmentalized into such categories as The Abolition Movement, The Colonization Movement, The Civil Rights Movement, The Labor Movement, The Socialist Movement, Notable Births, Notable Deaths, Miscellaneous State Laws (or Legislation), Miscellaneous Cases, Publications, Scholastic Achievements, The Black Church, The Arts, The Sciences, Black Enterprise, and Sports.

Before embarking upon reading the entries contained in *Pan-African Chronology*, it is advisable to understand a bit more concerning the language used and the references made in the text.

When reading history from an African American perspective, one is frequently confronted with a vocabulary which reflects the racial biases and misunderstandings of the times. Columbus, believing he had landed in the East Indies, called the people he encountered "Indians." His error became a part of the language. Africans were called "Negroes" because "negro" is the Spanish word for "black" and that was perceived to be the color of the skin of most Africans. Today the term "Negro" is in disrepute but its English equivalent "black" is still commonly used even though the skin color of most African Americans is obviously not black.

In this book, I have used the terms "African" or "person of African descent" when referring to a person with some measure of African blood in their veins. As for the term "African American," I have refrained from applying this term in describing individuals until later on in the chronology, when the term "African American" begins to coincide with the founding of the British American colonies and the creation of the United States.

In the spirit of frank disclosure, I must admit that I have used the term "African American" in this volume because, in 1994, it is the phrase preferred by most. However, in all honesty, for me the phrase "African American" is also inaccurate. In researching history, one finds that most persons of African descent in the United States also have European genes and many have an Indigenous American heritage as well. By labelling these individuals as "African" Americans, I fear that society may be denying an essential element of their being. Nevertheless, as part of the language of the day, the term "African American" is used in this book.

In this book, I have also liberally used the phrase "Indigenous American." The use of the phrase "Indigenous American" reflects this author's discomfort with the terms "Indian" and "Native American." For me the phrase "Indigenous American" most aptly describes the people the Europeans found inhabiting North America.

In addition to, or in lieu of, the general term "Indigenous American," wherever possible I have used the specific name of the Indigenous American Nation when describing the people the Europeans encountered.

As for the terms "whites" or "white people," I have resisted using those phrases because they too are inaccurate and have certain racial and psychological connotations. Instead, I have used the term European or Euro-American.

With regard to slaves and their conditions, I have adopted terms which I view as less pejorative than those commonly placed in American history books. For me, a slave was never a "runaway" or a "fugitive." Any slave who had the courage and ability to escape from enslavement should be viewed in a positive light, which the words "runaway" and "fugitive" do not connote. Therefore, self-liberated slaves are generally referred to in this book as "escaped slaves."

I also personally object to the use of the term "master" to describe a slave owner. In this text, the slave owners are called "slave owners" or "slave holders."

One of the more difficult terminological problems confronted in writing this book had to do with the description of acts of violence committed by slaves against their owners or by Indigenous Americans against the encroaching Europeans. Given the genocide and oppression that were suffered by African Americans and Indigenous Americans, I found it difficult to condemn acts of violence that may have been used by African Americans and Indigenous Americans to secure and maintain their freedom. Such acts, from a theological perspective, may have been justifiable given the perpetual warfare and acts of brutality which were being perpetrated upon Africans, African Americans and Indigenous Americans during the 465 years covered by this book.

The reader will notice that occasionally herein there is a phrase instructing the reader to see another year. These italicized references are provided to assist the reader in finding another reference in the book which may offer a fuller explanation of a certain topic.

The information in this book has primarily been compiled using secondary sources such as other chronologies. Without meaning any disrespect to the sources I have relied upon, I must state that they contain a number of errors or pieces of outdated information. To the best of my ability, I have attempted to correct the errors and to update the information. However, it is inevitable that errors and outdated information continue to exist within this text.

For any errors or outdated information appearing herein I take full responsibility. I do, however, make a special request of the reader. If errors are found, I would greatly appreciate being informed of them by letter sent to me in care of the publisher. As I envision the life of this book, it will be subject to additional editions and revisions. Therefore, the assistance of critical readers would be most appreciated in correcting any deficiencies.

Additionally, the reader will find throughout this book certain interpretations of historical events. Descriptions of historical events are highlighted in the text with bullets and are indented so that they may be easily found and identified. Interpretations of the events follow the descriptions. From the outset, it must be noted that these interpretations are based upon my own particular African American perspective, which may not necessarily comport with the perspective others have placed on the same event. After all, given the complexity of history, the uncertainty of numbers, and the contestability of facts, it is quite understandable that differing viewpoints may arise concerning the same historical event. The comments I have made simply set forth my particular opinion as to the significance of the event. The reader is encouraged to read and develop independent opinions.

There is, however, one area of criticism which I do wish specifically to address. While I expect and encourage the occasional disagreement with my interpretations or opinions, the one criticism I am particularly sensitive to is that my interpretations are unfair or are too pejorative without being based on facts. Having lived in a country where the history of African American people has largely been ignored, where even today, erroneous facts and historical interpretations are presented as the truth, I am loath to perpetuate the evil that I am endeavoring to cure. A reader who finds that a certain unfair or unwarranted bias has interfered with the presentation of the truth is implored to convey that criticism to me.

As a student of history, the most important lesson I have learned is that history is not written in stone. After all, even some of the more basic facts are often contested, numbers are frequently merely estimates, and the historical records almost invariably reflect the interests and biases of the historian.

Given all this, the study of history must be an evolving process which, if done appropriately, is approached from different perspectives as well as from different times. The study of history must be a never ending search that examines the ramifications of historical events not only for the conquerors but also for the conquered.

In this book, I have endeavored to present a chronological study of African and African American history as I believe it should be presented. However, I know all too well that this book is not finished — that my work is not yet done. After all, the essence of what I have learned and discovered in compiling and writing this book is that the "quest for freedom" *must* be synonymous with the never ending quest for truth.

1400–1499

The 1400s were a pivotal time in the history of Africans and African Americans. In Africa itself, these years saw the rise and dominance of the Songhai Empire. But there were other developments as well. New city states arose in Hausaland (northern Nigeria), Yorubaland (southwestern Nigeria) and Benin. A strong chieftainship was established among the Karanga of the southwestern lands south of the Zambezi River, leading to the prominence of Great Zimbabwe. Ntemi kingships spread throughout western Tanzania.

All in all, the coastal cities flourished; older cities became richer; and newer cities, such as Gedi in what is today Kenya, erected impressive stone structures.

Among the most significant developments of the 1400s was, however, the exploration of Africa by Asian and European explorers. More specifically, the Chinese and Portuguese would send noteworthy naval expeditions to explore the coasts of Africa.

Another significant development of the 1400s was the expansion of the slave trade. By the end of the 1400s, African slaves could be found from India to the Indies and a foundation would be laid for a peculiar institution that would last well over four hundred years.

1402

AFRICA

• Jean de Bethencourt led an expedition to the Canary Islands.

The Canary Islands are a group of thirteen islands in the Atlantic Ocean about sixty miles (97 kilometers) off the northwest coast of Africa. The islands cover 2,796 square miles (7,242 square kilometers) and have 626 miles (1,007 kilometers) of coastline.

The ancients named the Canary Islands (Canaria) from the Latin word "canis" (dog) because they found large, fierce dogs on the islands. Canary birds are called "canaries" because the birds were first found on the Canary Islands.

1405

AFRICA

• Jean de Bethencourt captured Lanzarote of the Canary Islands.

1410

AFRICA

• Abu Faris captured Algiers.

—— 1 4 1 4 ——

AFRICA

• In Ethiopia, Yeshaq (Yeskaq) of Ethiopia began war with Zaila (Zeila).

—— 1 4 1 5 ——

AFRICA

• An expedition sponsored by Prince Henry of Portugal sailed to Morocco and captured Ceuta, the first of a series of Portuguese conquests and successful voyages of exploration in Africa.
• The Spanish captured Tenerife in the Canary Islands.
• Yeshaq of Ethiopia conquered and occupied Zaila.

ASIA

• In 1415, the kingdom of Malindi sent a diplomatic mission to China.

—— 1 4 1 6 ——

AFRICA

• A Chinese fleet under the command of Zheng He reached Aden on the southern tip of the Arabian peninsula.

When the Portuguese became the first Europeans to reach the Indian Ocean by sea, they found themselves in waters well traversed by Asian and Arab traders and seafarers. Almost a century before the Portuguese arrived in a rather pitiful fleet of four ships, the Chinese sponsored a series of expeditions which reflected the prominence of China in the world of the 1400s.

Under the command of Zheng He, a eunuch admiral in Emperor Yung Lo's navy, seven expeditions were sent westward. For the first expedition in 1405, Zheng He assembled a fleet consisting of 63 junks and 100 smaller ships bearing nearly 30,000 crew members. The junks commanded by Zheng He were massive in size. The largest of his ships displaced more than 1600 tons and were almost 450 feet long. Such a ship required a crew of almost 500 men. By comparison, Vasco da Gama's entire crew numbered only 170 men and the ships he captained would have been lesser vessels in the fleet of Zheng He.

On the fourth of the seven expeditions, in 1417, Zheng He sailed along the eastern coast of Africa to the kingdom of Malindi (Kenya).

The people of Malindi greeted Zheng He warmly. Upon his departure, they gave him a giraffe to present to his emperor. When Zheng He returned to China in 1419, he was received in person by a delighted Yung Lo who marveled at the giraffe and other African wonders brought home by Zheng He. The giraffe was placed in the imperial zoo, was called a "celestial unicorn," and was treated as a symbol of the esteem held by Yung Lo.

With the seaworthiness of the Chinese vessels, the ability of Zheng He, and the wealth of imperial China, it is conceivable that the Chinese could have sailed around the world if they had chosen to do so. But the last voyage of Zheng He occurred in 1433. As has happened so often in Chinese history, certain elements of Chinese society criticized foreign explorations as being expensive and unnecessary. After Zheng He's last voyage, the Chinese would look inward avoiding foreign ventures.

• The Walasma dynasty was revived as the Sultans of Adal (Djibouti, Eritrea and Ethiopia).

—— 1 4 1 7 ——

AFRICA

• Benedetto Dei, a Florentine agent of Portinari, told of his travels to land we today call "Nigeria." He reported on his visit to a place called Timbuktu, a place south of the kingdom of Barbary (a North African coastal and desert kingdom). He mentioned the trade that occurred there—a trade in the sale of cloth, serges, and other precious items.
• The Chinese fleet of Zheng He after visiting Mogadishu (Somalia) and Barawa (Baraawe, Somalia), arrived in Malindi (Kenya).

Two thousand years ago, much of East Africa was inhabited by relatively simple farmers and hunters. Only a few areas had acquired the ability to work iron. However, by A.D. 800, the peoples of East Africa began to indulge in long distance trade. The products of the region—frankincense, exotic animal skins, ivory and, a little later, slaves and gold, were brought to the cities of the East African coast where these "products" were transported to Arabia and to India, utilizing the monsoon winds of the Indian Ocean to establish regular seasonal trade routes. In return for the East African products, such imports as carpets from Isfahan and Gujarat, ceramics from China and

Persia, horses from Arabia, and cotton from India were sent to the great East African city states of Gedi (Kenya), Malindi (Kenya), and Kilwa (Tanzania).

According to official documents, the earliest recorded African kingdom known to China was Shunai, located in the southern part of present day Somalia. In 629, Shunai sent a diplomatic mission to Chang'an. It is believed that Shunai was one of the group of African people that the Tang called "Kunlun." The term "Kunlun" referred to African servants, but may also have included Southeast Asians and other foreigners. During the Tang dynasty (608–916), China engaged in sea trade with Africa from the commercial port of Canton where domestic merchandise was traded for products like ivory and incense. In Africa, in places such as Zanzibar (Tanzania), many Chinese coins and ceramics have been unearthed.

The Kunlun people introduced the "Kunlun dance" to Chang'an. In one of the surprise archaeological discoveries of the 20th century, the discovery of the tomb treasures of Xi'an and Chang'an revealed not only the remarkable terra cotta army of 7,000 soldiers, 100 chariots, and 600 horses, it also revealed a varied and rich interchange between the African city states and China. Sprinkled throughout the tombs from the Tang dynasty are many figurines of African men signifying that their presence at the Tang court had left an indelible impression.

By the time Zheng He arrived in Malindi in 1417, the trade between Africa and China had been going on for some 800 years. In addition to the contacts with the Tang dynasty, it is recorded that in 1071, the trading cities of East Africa sent an ambassadorial delegation to China. Additionally, recent archaeological excavations reveal that copious quantities of Chinese porcelain from the early Ming (1368–1644) period have been found at the ruins of the ancient East African city states. It was the long established existence of the trade between the Indian Ocean African nations and the Emperors of China which led to the Chinese fleet of Zheng He visiting the East African coast.

1418

AFRICA

• Portuguese explorers landed on the Madeira Islands in the Atlantic Ocean off the west coast of North Africa. The Portuguese planted sugar cane from Sicily on the islands. *See 1456 and 1460.*

The inhabitants of the South Pacific islands grew sugar cane more than 8,000 years ago. The plants were also widely grown in ancient India. Sugar cane is specifically mentioned in records of an expedition by the Macedonian king Alexander the Great in what is now Pakistan in 325 B.C.

The cultivation and refining of sugar cane spread east from India to China about 100 B.C. but did not reach Europe until about A.D. 636. During the early 1400s, Europeans planted sugar cane in northern Africa and on islands such as the Madeira Islands.

In 1493, Christopher Columbus brought sugar cane cuttings to the islands in the Caribbean. The first sugar mill in the Western Hemisphere was built in 1515 in what is now the Dominican Republic (Hispaniola).

By 1520, there were more than twenty-eight sugar mills on Hispaniola. However, the Portuguese in Brazil were the first to recognize and develop the possibilities of sugar cane as a commercial plantation crop produced by black slaves. Before the sixteenth century, sugar had long been known in Europe as an expensive luxury, sometimes prescribed in small quantities as medicine. This changed when the Portuguese planters of Pernambuco began to put sugar on the market at lower prices. At lower prices and in greater quantity, sugar soon became a popular commodity. Europeans developed a sweet tooth and the economic basis for the growth in slavery was established.

Sugar cane became the main agricultural product of the islands of Puerto Rico, Jamaica, and Cuba. The sugar economy of the seventeenth and eighteenth centuries was based on the institution of slavery, and as the markets and demand for sugar grew, so too did the markets and demand for slaves.

Thus, the introduction of sugar along with the decimation of the Indigenous American populations were two of the key factors leading to the establishment of African slavery in the Americas.

• The Canary Islands were ceded to Castile.

1421

AFRICA

• The Portuguese prince, Henry the Navigator, assembled Europe's leading mariners, cartographers, astronomers, scholars, and instrument makers at Sagres on the Cape Saint Vincent where a new method of navigation was developed. Another innovation would be the development of the lateen-rigged caravel with three masts—a highly maneuverable vessel able to withstand the winds and waves of the open sea. The caravel would be the ship used during the 1400s to explore the coastline of Africa leading to the rounding of Cape of Good Hope in 1488 and the venturing into the Indian Ocean in 1497.

• The Chinese fleet under Zheng He revisited Mogadishu (Somalia).

• Sulaiman ibn Muhammed became the sultan of Kilwa (Tanzania).

---

1 4 2 3

EUROPE

• Alice Kyteler was tried for witchcraft in Kilkenny, Ireland. As part of the evidence against her, she was accused of having intercourse with an "Ethiop" who could also turn into a black cat or black shaggy dog.

---

1 4 2 5

AFRICA

• The Canary Islands, less than 70 miles off the northwest coast of Africa fell to the forces of Portugal's Henry the Navigator, who captured them from Castile (Spain).

• Mutota, king of the Karanga, mounted a successful campaign of conquest which extended his rule over the whole inland plateau between the Zambezi and the Limpopo—the main gold bearing area of south central Africa. This conquest would lead to the emergence of the Great Zimbabwe as a major political and religious center. Mutota would adopt the praise name of Mwanamutapa—"the explorer." This praise name would become affixed to both his empire and his heirs.

Bushmen paintings and tools have been found in Zimbabwe which indicate that Stone Age people lived in Zimbabwe. By the 800s, people were mining minerals for trade purposes.

The Shona people established their rule over Zimbabwe in A.D. 1000. They built a city called Zimbabwe, or Great Zimbabwe. The word "zimbabwe" means "house of stone" in the Shona language.

During the 1400s, a branch of the Shona, called the Karanga, established the Mwanamutapa Empire. This empire included what is today's Zimbabwe. At eastern African ports, the Karanga traded ivory, gold, and copper for porcelain from China and cloth and beads from India and Indonesia. The Rozwi, a southern Karanga group, rebelled in the late 1400s and founded the Changamire Empire. The Changamire Empire became stronger than the Mwanamutapa Empire. The Rozwi soon gained control over the city of Zimbabwe. It was the Rozwi who built the city of Zimbabwe's largest stone structures.

• Civil disturbances beset the kingdom of Kilwa (Tanzania). *See 1421.*

Not long after the Chinese visited the East African coast, the East African city states entered a period of decline. This decline was hastened by the arrival of the Portuguese after 1498 who usurped the maritime commerce of the city states. However, the demise of the city states was principally due to internal conflicts and tribal wars not necessarily to European imperialism.

---

1 4 2 7

AFRICA

• The king of Cyprus recognized Egypt as the overlord of Cyprus.

• Ethiopia established a diplomatic mission in Aragon (Spain).

---

1 4 2 8

AFRICA

• Yeshaq of Ethiopia conquered Enarya.

---

1 4 3 0

AFRICA

• A great stone enclosure was constructed at Great Zimbabwe.

The granite walls at Great Zimbabwe cover an area of over 100 acres, and constitute probably the largest ancient archaeological ruins in sub–Saharan Africa. In its prime, the stone works included a tower 30 feet high and part of a wall 800 feet around. The ruins lie off the southern edge of the high plateau (near today's Masvingo next to Lake Kyle) that forms the watershed between the Zambezi and Limpopo rivers, in a fertile basin midway between an area rich in gold and an area of extensive grasslands. Due to its prosperity, Great Zimbabwe became a major political and religious center.

1431

AFRICA

• The Portuguese discovered the Azore Islands.

The Azore Islands are a group of nine islands that are located in the North Atlantic Ocean about 800 miles (1,300 kilometers) west of Portugal.

Navigator Gonzalo Cabral claimed the Azores for Portugal in 1431. At the time, the islands were uninhabited.

1433

AFRICA

• Timbuktu, the ancient learning center of the Mali Empire, fell to Berber forces led by Akil. *See 1310.*

Berbers are a people of Northwest Africa and the Sahara Desert region. During Roman rule (600 B.C. to A.D. 400), Berber traders linked the Mediterranean coast to the gold, ivory, and slave markets of West Africa. Arab invasions of North Africa began in the 600's. Under Arab influence, many Berbers converted to Islam and became Muslims. During the 700s, Muslim Berbers joined with Arabs to conquer Spain.

The demise of the Mali Empire and the advent of Arab (Berber/Muslim) expansionism, led to the enslavement of many sub-Saharan African peoples. Indeed, it was the enslavement of Africans by Muslim Arabs and Berbers which would be responsible for part of the expansion of African slavery into Europe and Asia. *See 1442.*

In later years, the Berber people would become closely associated with the Barbary pirates who terrorized the Mediterranean sea lanes. It is of interest to note that the terms Berber and Barbary come from the same Latin word—barbari. Barbari was the name given in Roman times to the people who lived on the fringes of the Roman Empire.

• Africa's Cape Bojador, south of the Canary Islands, was rounded for the first time by Portuguese navigator Gil Eannes (Gil Eanes or Guillanes?), a captain in Prince Henry's navy. *See 1460.*

RELATED HISTORICAL EVENTS

• Zheng He, the great Chinese admiral, returned from his seventh (and final) expedition.

1434

AFRICA

• Gil Eanes reached Cameroon.
• Zara Yaqub (Zara Yaqob [Jacob]) came to power in Ethiopia. During his reign, the Solomonic dynasty reached its apex in terms of power and culture.

Ethiopia's Solomonic emperor Zara Yaqub reigned for 34 years. During his reign, Zara Yaqub defeated Muslim armies to protect the freedom of his country's Coptic Christians. Yaqub brought all of the Ethiopian highlands under his rule.

1437

AFRICA

• Portuguese forces were defeated at Tangier at the hand of the Moors. King Duarte's youngest brother, Fernando, was taken as a hostage. Five years later, Fernando would die in the dungeons of Fez after enduring years of cruel punishment.

Moors are a Muslim people of mixed Arab and Berber stock living in northwestern Africa. The Moors invaded and conquered Spain in the A.D. 700s. They were driven out in 1492. *See 1433 and 1492.*

• In 1437, a Portuguese expedition to Ceuta was destroyed. Subsequently, the Portuguese abandoned Ceuta.

ASIA

• African slaves were introduced in large numbers into western India. *See 1486.*

1438

AFRICA

• Portugal's King Duarte I died of plague at age 47 with his brother Fernando (Fernao) still unransomed in a Fez (Morocco) dungeon. Duarte's 6-year-old son inherited the crown.

1440

AFRICA

• The Rozvi King Mutota launched a campaign to set up an empire. Mutota became Mwene Mutapa (also known as Monomotapa).
• Around 1440, Benin became a powerful kingdom under the leadership of Oba Ewuare.

"Oba" is the title given to the ruler of the Edo speaking kingdom of Benin. "Oba" is also the term for "king" among the Yoruba peoples. Both the Benin and Yoruba "oba" were "divine kings" who exercised great power and influence.

Oba Ewuare is remembered as one of Benin's greatest rulers who employed both force and magic to extend the Benin Empire beyond the Edo-speaking peoples.

• Joao Fernandes of Portugal visited the Sahara. Fernandes reported on the extensive salt and gold trade.

1441–1442

AFRICA

• Antam Goncalvez (Antao Goncalves), a captain in the navy of Henry the Navigator, captured two or three Moors of noble birth on the African coast (1441). The Moors offered as ransom "ten blacks, male and female." The ransom was accepted and the Africans were brought to Lisbon, Portugal, where they were sold at a market (1442). These ten Africans represent the beginning of the African slave trade which up until the year 1517 was, pursuant to a papal grant, monopolized by the Portuguese crown. One of the captives was a chieftain named Adahu, who told Henry the Navigator about lands in Africa that were farther south and inland of the area explored by the Portuguese.

1443

AFRICA

• The coast of Rio de Oro was explored by Portuguese navigators Affonso Goncalves Baldaya and Gil Eanes. A settlement was established on Arguin Island just south of Cape Blanco near the site of modern day Port Etienne (Mauritania).

1444

AFRICA

• Portuguese explorer Nino Tristram (Nuno Tristao) reached the Senegal River in West Africa. *See 1460.*

1445

AFRICA

• Portuguese explorer Dinis Diaz rounded Africa's Cape Verde for the first time in modern history. *See 1460.*
• Ethiopia went to war against Mogadishu (Somalia) and Adal.
• The Portuguese built a trading fort at Arguin Island. *See 1443.*

EUROPE

• In 1445, some 25 caravels per year were employed in trade between Portugal and West Africa. One of the principal cargos carried in the caravels was African slaves.

In 1445, a great slave auction was held in Lagos, in the Algarve. In the words of the chronicler Azurara: "Some held their heads low with their faces bathed in tears; ... others stood very dolorously, looking up to the height of heaven and crying out loudly as if asking help from the Father of Nature; others still made their lamentations in the manner of a dirge, after the custom of their country. And though we could not understand the words of their language, the meaning was clear enough ... And then, to increase their suffering still more, those who had charge of the division of the captives now arrived, and began to separate one from another. They parted husbands from wives, fathers from sons, brothers from brothers. No respect was shown either to friends or relations. It was a terrible scene of misery and disorder..."

1446

AFRICA

• The Portuguese explorer Alvaro Fernandes reached Sierra Leone.

1447

AFRICA

• Malfante, a Genoese traveler, reached Touat.

EUROPE

• By 1447, 900 African slaves had been introduced into Portugal by way of the fledgling slave trade.

1448

AFRICA

• Prince Henry established a fort (and a slave market) on Arguin Bay, south of Cape Blanco. *See 1445.*
• Dinis Dias reached Sierra Leone. *See 1446.*

1450

AFRICA

• In Zimbabwe, an envigorated society began a building program which promoted the building of large stone structures. *See 1430.*

In 1450, Matope succeeded his father, Mutota, and became the second Monomotapa. Matope completed the conquests begun by Mutota and established his authority over the Zimbabwe plateau. *See 1425 and 1440.*

• The Empire of Kanem was reorganized.

Kanem was one of the longest lasting empires in history. It began on the northeast side of Lake Chad in Africa during the 700s and lasted until the late 1800s. At its height, Kanem included parts of what are now Cameroon, Chad, Libya, Niger, Nigeria, and the Sudan. The prosperity of Kanem depended on trade. Copper, horses, metalware, and salt from North Africa, Europe and Asia were traded in Kanem's markets for ivory and kola nuts from the south. The rulers of Kanem maintained a powerful army that kept the trade routes safe and collected a tax from traders.

The Sefuwa (Sefawa) royal family ruled Kanem from the 800s to the 1800s (the longest dynastic reign in African history). The rulers converted from tribal beliefs to Islam, the Muslim religion, in 1086. The Sefuwa royal family began to expand their territory at about the same time. After Bornu, a kingdom on the southwest side of Lake Chad, became a province of Kanem, the empire was called Kanem-Bornu.

• In 1450, the Portuguese transported some 200 Africans from Arguin Bay to Portugal as part of the growing slave trade.

1451

RELATED HISTORICAL EVENTS

• Christopher Columbus, the European "discoverer" of the Americas, was born. *See 1492 and 1506.*

Christopher Columbus (1451–1506) was born in Genoa, Italy. While still a teenager, he began to sail the Mediterranean and the Atlantic as far as Iceland.

In 1485, Columbus went to Spain in search of support for a novel idea. He asked Spain's King Ferdinand and Queen Isabella to finance his attempt to find a sea route to China by sailing westward. Columbus, unlike the more knowledgeable (and correct) scholars of the day, thought that India was only 4,000 kilometers (2,500 miles) west of Portugal.

In 1492, Queen Isabella finally agreed to provision Columbus' expedition. Three ships were provided, the Nina, the Pinta, and the flagship, the Santa Maria. On August 3, the fleet set sail and, after a short stopover in the Canary Islands, reached an island believed to be in the country known today as the Bahamas on October 12.

Columbus named the island upon which he landed San Salvador. Still believing that he was near China, Columbus continued to explore the northern Caribbean, encountering the shores of Hispaniola and Cuba. Columbus returned to Spain in March 1493 with some Arawaks—the people Columbus called "Indians"—, gold and trinkets.

During his second voyage (1493–1496), Columbus explored a number of other islands in the Caribbean and established the first European colony in the Americas—the colony of Isabella on the northern coast of Hispaniola. Columbus also ventured to the southern coast of Cuba, which Columbus thought might be the mainland of Asia.

During his third voyage (1498), Columbus reached Trinidad and the coast of Venezuela, but failed to realize that the lands that his eyes surveyed were new lands unknown to Europeans. It was also during this third voyage that Columbus returned to the island of Hispaniola. It was during this return that Columbus was seized by the new governor of the island and sent back to Spain in chains.

Once in Spain, Columbus' patroness, Queen Isabella, had him freed. Not long later, Columbus began his fourth voyage—his last trip to the Americas. On this voyage, Columbus sailed along the coast of Central America and learned that there was another ocean beyond the mountains, but he was unable to find a passage to this new sea.

During this voyage, Columbus also sailed eastward into the Caribbean. It was at this time that Columbus was forced to abandon his rotting vessels and spend a year marooned on the island of Jamaica.

Columbus finally returned to Spain in November 1504 and died there two years later, still believing that he had reached Asia.

The tale of Columbus' "discovery" of the Americas is perhaps the greatest case of serendipity to have ever occurred. While searching for the East, he found the West and initiated an Age of Discovery which continues to this day.

With regards to African and African American history, Columbus set in motion certain creative and destructive forces emanating from the expansion of the slave trade and African slavery from which Africans and African Americans continue to reverberate.

1 4 5 2

AFRICA

• Ethiopia (Abyssinia) established embassies in Aragon (Spain) and Lisbon (Portugal).

1 4 5 5

AFRICA

In 1455, Henry the Navigator tried to stop the abuses of the slave trade by forbidding the capture of Africans. However, by this time, the slave trade had become a profitable and entrenched enterprise in Portuguese society. Between 1455 and 1460, 700 to 800 Africans were brought from Arguin Bay to Portugal on an annual basis.

• The Venetian navigator Alvise da Cadamosto discovered the Cape Verde Islands off the coast of Africa. Cadamosto went on to explore the Senegal and Gambia rivers over the next two years in service to Portugal's Prince Henry the Navigator.

The Cape Verde Islands are an African country that consists of 10 main islands and 5 tiny islands. The Cape Verde Islands lies in the Atlantic Ocean, about 400 miles (640 kilometers) west of Dakar, Senegal, on the African mainland.

When the Portuguese discovered the Cape Verde Islands, the islands were uninhabited.

1 4 5 9

AFRICA

• The realm of an African king named Prester John appeared on a map drawn by the Venetian monk Fra Mauro. *See 1487.*

The legend of "Prester John" dates from the 1100s. The legend arose when stories of a powerful Christian monarch around Arabia filtered back to Rome. Such stories intrigued the papal powers because, at the time, Christendom was engaged in the Crusades—a concerted attempt to wrest control of the Holy Land from the Muslims.

By the 1300s, Europeans were well aware of the fact that Ethiopia was ruled by Christians. It was at this time that the legend of Prester John became firmly associated with this African kingdom and an assiduous search by the Portuguese for this kingdom began.

1 4 6 0

RELATED HISTORICAL EVENTS

• Henry the Navigator died (November 13).

Henry the Navigator (1394–1460): Henry the Navigator was a Portuguese prince who promoted explorations of the west African coast during the 1400s. These explorations helped advance the study of geography and made Portugal a leader in navigation among European nations of that time. Henry sent out more than 50 expeditions but went on none of these voyages himself.

Henry was the son of King John I (Joao I) and Queen Philippa. He was a serious, studious youth with a special interest in mathematics and astronomy. Henry and two older brothers, Duarte *see 1438* and Pedro, wanted to prove that they were worthy to be knighted. With their father's approval, they organized an army and captured Ceuta *see 1415,* an important commercial town in Morocco. The brothers were knighted, and Henry was made governor of Ceuta.

The commercial routes between Ceuta and inner Africa stirred Henry's interest in the geography of Africa. Henry wanted to expand Portugal's trade and influence along the

African coast. He also hoped to find the source of the gold that Muslim traders had been carrying north from central Africa for hundreds of years.

Henry's skill in mathematics and astronomy helped him to organize expeditions along the northwest African coast. In 1418, two Portuguese explorers sent by Henry reached Porto Santo, one of the Madeira Islands. *See 1418.* These explorers, Joao Goncalves and Tristao Vaz, sailed to the island of Madeira itself in the early 1420s. Portugal colonized both islands.

One of Henry's goals was to send explorers beyond Cape Bojador (Cap Boujdour), in what is now Western Sahara. The cape was the southernmost point known to Europeans at that time. After several unsuccessful attempts, an expedition led by Gil Eanes finally passed the cape in 1433. *See 1433.* Eanes reached Rio de Oro (River of Gold), also in Western Sahara, in 1436.

One of Henry's explorers, Antao Goncalves, returned to Portugal with some Africans he had captured on an expedition in 1441. Among the captives was a chieftain named Adahu, who told Henry about lands farther south and inland. In 1444, Nuno Tristao sailed as far south as Cape Blanc (Cap Blanc), on the border of Western Sahara and Mauritania. *See 1444.* Diniz Diaz reached Cape Verde, in present day Senegal, in 1445. *See 1445.* By the time of Henry's death in 1460, Portuguese ships had reached the coast of Sierra Leone.

Henry planned and raised money for the expeditions. He was aided by mapmakers, astronomers, and mathematicians of many nationalities, whom he gathered together at Sagres, near Cape Saint Vincent (Cabo de Sao Vicente), Portugal. The navigational knowledge gained under Henry's direction led to several historic voyages within 50 years after his death. They included the voyages of the Portuguese explorers Vasco da Gama and Bartolomeu Dias around the southern tip of Africa. *See 1488.*

Under Henry the Navigator, Portugal established itself as a great power of sea navigation. Henry the Navigator sacrificed his right to the crown of Portugal to study maps and the stars and to teach others the ways of the sea. *See 1438.* While never embarking on a maritime voyage of his own, Prince Henry sponsored many expeditions that spurred the European exploration of many foreign lands. Henry also developed the advanced style caravel (a small, fast sailing ship of the type used by Columbus

and other early explorers), improved the science of cartography and enhanced sea trade, including commerce beyond Morocco. In 1418, Henry began to promote ocean voyages along the coast of Africa. Under his auspices, Portuguese sailors explored, and began the colonization of, the Madeira and Azores Islands. Perhaps his biggest achievement came in 1434 when he persuaded Gil Eanes to defy tales of evil sea monsters and sail beyond the Cape of Bojador. *See 1433.* This voyage inspired Portugal's sailors to venture further down the coast to Cape Verde and Sierra Leone, returning with gold and slaves. The one dream that Prince Henry left unrealized was the establishment of a sea route connecting Europe to India. However, this dream was realized posthumously when Vasco da Gama sailed from Portugal to India at the end of the 1400s. *See 1488, 1492, and 1497.*

Some commentators have argued that the responsibility for the slave trade lies at the feet of Henry the Navigator because it was at his instigation that Africans were first kidnapped and brought to Portugal. Ostensibly, this was done to acquire more information that would facilitate the exploration of the African coast and also to "save the souls" of the Africans by subjecting them to Christian doctrine. And indeed, the slavery of Africans in Portugal during Henry's time was milder than the form of slavery instituted by the Spanish and later the British. In Portugal, often the slaves were incorporated and adopted into the families which they originally served. Once converted to Christianity, the Africans were often set free and allowed to become integrated into Portuguese society. However, despite the relative mildness of the Portuguese practice of slavery, the institution nevertheless created untold human misery (*see 1445*). It destroyed families. It resulted in untimely deaths. It undermined civilizations. It was an evil thing. Accordingly, as we credit Henry the Navigator with his great nautical accomplishments, we must also note that to his discredit, Henry the Navigator not only perpetuated but greatly expanded an evil the vestige of which haunts us to this day.

AFRICA

• The Blessed Anthony Noyrot was martyred at Tunis.

ASIA

• From 1460 to 1474, the sultan of Bengal, Rukn ud Din Barbak Shah, acquired some

8000 African slaves. Many of these slaves became employed in the sultan's army where a number achieved great stature and a correspondingly appropriate rank. The sultan ruled his domain from the Bengali capital of Gaur.

1 4 6 2

AFRICA

• Factories were founded at Cacheu (Guinea-Bissau) and the district became a center for the slave trade in the 17th and 18th centuries.
• The Bissagos Islands were discovered.

1 4 6 4

AFRICA

• Sunni Ali ascended to the throne of the Songhai (Songhay) Empire.

The Songhai Empire was an African empire that reached its peak in the 1400s and 1500s. Songhai began in the 700s, and by the 1400s had eclipsed the great Mali Empire as the dominant state on the African continent. At its height, Songhai possessed more wealth and wielded more power than any other African empire.

Songhai extended from the central area of what is now Nigeria to the Atlantic coast and included parts of what are now Burkina Faso, Gambia, Guinea, Mali, Mauritania, Niger, and Senegal. Gao, the capital of the Songhai Empire, stood on the Niger River.

Songhai became powerful principally by controlling trade across the Sahara. Most of Songhai's people were farmers, fishermen, or traders. The traders exchanged gold and other West African products for goods from Europe and the Middle East.

Two kings, Sunni Ali and Askia Muhammed, strengthened the empire more than any other rulers. Sunni Ali ruled from 1464 to 1492 and began a unified system of law and order, central government, and trade. His army conquered Timbuktu and Jenne, two West African trading centers. Askia Muhammed, also known as Askia I or Askia the Great, became king in 1493. Songhai reached its peak under his rule. Askia reorganized the government, expanded trade, and encouraged the people to practice Islam, the religion of the Muslims. His three sons deposed him in 1528. The empire itself came to an end in 1591 when a Moroccan army defeated the Songhai in the Battle of Tondibi. *See 1591.*

1 4 6 5

AFRICA

• Sunni Ali began his campaign of conquest. *See 1464.*

1 4 6 6

AFRICA

• The Portuguese royal government formally set up a charter for the trade in Guinea and on the Cape Verde Islands (June 12).

1 4 6 8

AFRICA

• Ethiopia's Solomonic emperor Zara Yaqub died after a 34 year reign during which he defeated Muslim armies to protect the freedom of his country's Coptic Christians. Yaqub brought all of the Ethiopian highlands under his rule.
• Baeda Mariam (Maryam) succeeded Zara Yaqub in Ethiopia. Mariam reorganized the provinces and rotated the capital of his kingdom among various cities.
• The Songhai king Sonni Ali (Sunni Ali) captured Timbuktu by defeating the Tuaregs (a Muslim nomad people of the Sahara—Berbers).

1 4 6 9

AFRICA

• The Portuguese captured Anfa.

1 4 7 0

AFRICA

• Portuguese explorers reached Africa's Gold Coast. Fernao Gomes dispatched Joao de Santarem and Pedro de Escolar to Africa in accordance with terms of a 5-year lease on the Guinea trade granted to Gomes in 1469 on condition that he, Gomes, carry explorations forward by at least 100 leagues per year.
• Benedetto Dei visited Timbuktu. But see 1417.
• Ngazargarmu was founded as the capital of Bornu. *See 1450.*

1 4 7 1

AFRICA

• San Jorge d'el Mina was founded by the Portuguese as a port to trade in gold on what would come to be called Africa's Gold Coast (Ghana). *See 1482.*

• Tangier (along with Arzila and Larache) was captured by Portugal, following the earlier conquest of Casablanca. These conquests were part of a campaign against the North African kingdom of Fez.

• Joao de Santerem and Pedro d'Escobar reached the river Niger estuary.

• Gao (the forces of Sunni Ali) besieged Jenne.

1 4 7 2

AFRICA

• Portuguese explorers continued to explore the west coast of Africa. Fernando Po discovered islands off the coast of Africa that would come to bear his name. Lopo Gonsalves crossed the equator. Ruy de Sequeira reached a latitude 2 degrees south of the equator (the Bight of Benin).

• Ali Ghadji (Gaji) became king of Kanem-Bornu. His capital was Ngazargarmu (Birni Gazargamu).

Ali Ghadji is considered to be one of the three greatest rulers during the millenia long rule of the Sefawas over Kanem-Bornu. Under Ali Ghadji, the internecine strife that had wracked the kingdom was subdued, the external threat from the Bulala nomads was eradicated, and the great capital city of Ngazargarmu was founded in a location far away from enemies but close enough to extract tribute from the neighboring Hausa states.

1 4 7 3

AFRICA

• Sunni Ali conquered Jenne and took away from the authority of the mansa a good part of the Massina. Sunni Ali made himself the master of Jenne (Mali) and of Massina, after having annexed to his kingdom the region of the lakes (Mali) and Walata (Mauritania).

• Ethiopia was twice defeated by Adal.

EUROPE

• A formal exchange of gifts, messages, and ambassadors occurred between the Mandingo emperor (Mamoud or Mamudu) and the king of Portugal, John (Joao) II.

1 4 7 4

EUROPE

• The ecclesiastical annals of Ortiz de Zuniga noted that African slaves abounded in Lisbon, Portugal, and that the tithes levied on the Africans produced considerable revenue for the royal treasury.

• African slaves were also common in Spain at this time. It was noted that African slaves abounded in Seville. Indeed, Ferdinand and Isabella recognized the presence of the Africans in Seville by sending a letter to an African named Juan de Valladolid (also known as El Conde Negro) in which they nominated him to the office of mayor of the Africans in Seville.

Meanwhile, the population of Algarve (Portugal) was almost completely African.

The increase in the number of African slaves in Portugal and Spain would accelerate during the 1400s and 1500s. At one point in the mid–1500s, there were more Africans in Lisbon than there were Portuguese. This was perhaps due to the fact that, at the time, Portugal was the nation granted a virtual monopoly over the slave trade by papal decree.

1 4 7 5

AFRICA

• Ruy de Sequeira reached Saint Catherine (November 25) and Sao Tome (December 21).

1 4 7 6

AFRICA

• Spain occupied the Canary Islands.

1 4 7 7

AFRICA

• A revolt in the Canary Islands was put down by the Spanish.

• The king of the Mossi of Yatenga invaded Massina and advanced as far as Walata in the Songhai Empire.

1 4 7 8

AFRICA

• Eskender became Emperor of Ethiopia.

1 4 7 9

AFRICA

• The Mossi captured Walata.

Today the Mossi are a people who live in the northern and upper regions of Burkina Faso and in smaller numbers in northern Ghana and Togo.

1 4 8 0

AFRICA

• Ferdinand and Isabella made peace with Portugal at Alcacovas on September 4 after four years of bitter fighting. Portugal acknowledged Spanish rights to the Canary Islands and in return secured a monopoly in trade and navigation on Africa's west coast.

• Changa, later Changamire, and Torwa, began to make themselves independent of the Monomotapa. *See 1450.*

1 4 8 1

AFRICA

• The declining Mali Empire established the first direct Sudanese contact with Europeans through Portuguese sailors who had arrived on Mali's Atlantic coast. Mali sought an alliance with the Europeans to hold back the advance of the forces (and influence) of the Songhai Empire.

• John Tintam and William Fabian became the first English adventurers to venture along the West African coast.

• Jem, brother of the Ottoman Bayazid II, was given refuge by Qait Bay.

1 4 8 2

AFRICA

• The Portuguese built the first slave-trading port (fort), Sao Jorge de Mina, at Elmina on the African Gold Coast (Ghana). The Portuguese would extend this trade down the west coast of Africa and up the east coast of Africa. The traffic in people became so pervasive and so important that it soon came to dominate all commerce on the African coast. *See 1471.*

• Portuguese explorers on Africa's west coast found bananas growing and adopted a version of the local name for the fruit.

RELATED HISTORICAL EVENTS

• Pope Pio II condemned the slave trade.

1 4 8 3

AFRICA

• The Portuguese captain Diogo Cao (Diego Cano) anchored in the waters of the Congo River. The Kongo people had established a large and closely articulated state in the northern region of modern Angola. The king of the Kongo people willingly entered into trade with the Portuguese, exchanged ambassadors with Lisbon, and received Christian missionaries.

• The Mossi raided Walata. They were routed by Sunni Ali and the forces of the Songhai Empire.

1 4 8 4

AFRICA

• Portuguese explorer Diogo Cao (Diego Cano) reached as far south as the 22nd parallel (the coast of modern day Namibia).

1 4 8 5

AFRICA

• Sao Tome was colonized by the Portuguese.

1 4 8 6

AFRICA

• Joao Afonso d'Aveiro visited Benin. After this visit, Benin began to trade regularly with Portugal. The king of Benin even sent an emissary to King John II of Portugal to request the dispatch of missionaries to Benin.

Benin was a West African kingdom that flourished from the mid–1400s to the mid–1600s. It was the largest and most powerful state in the forest region of what is now Nigeria. At the height of its power, Benin controlled several states along the coast of the Gulf of Guinea, from Lagos in the west to Bonny in the east. The largest group of people in Benin were the Edo, also called the Bini.

Benin probably became rich because it lay on trade routes between the forest and the northern plains. At first, cotton goods were traded for copper, dates, figs, ivory and salt. Soon after the Portuguese came in 1486, Benin also began to sell slaves and to buy European firearms and other goods. The port of Gwato was a center for the export of slaves from West Africa.

Warfare with other slave-selling states and revolts by states that Benin had conquered led to the kingdom's decline. The British conquered Benin in 1897.

Today the kingdom of Benin is best known for the sculptures that were crafted during the height of Benin's influence and power. Benin sculptures dating from the 1400s to the 1600s are world famous. Many of these works—made of brass, bronze, and ivory—honored the king of Benin.

- Diogo Cao led a second expedition to the Congo. Upon his return to Portugal, Diogo Cao brought specimens of ivory sculpture from the King of the Kongo to the Court of Portugal.
- The Wolof ruler of Bemoim visited Lisbon (Portugal) and presented King Joao II a gift of 100 slaves.

ASIA

- African slaves in the kingdom of Bengal in India rebelled and placed their own leader on the throne.

In 1486, African slaves in the kingdom of Bengal in India rebelled. They killed the Sultan of Bengal, Jalal ud Din Fateh Shah (Fath Shah), and installed their leader as the new sultan. Their leader became known as Sultan Shahzada Barbak Shah (Barbah Shah). However, another African, Indil Khan, remained loyal to the deceased Fateh Shah. Upon his return from a distant expedition, Indil Khan, defeated Barbak Shah and executed him. Indil Khan then assumed the sultanate under the name of Saif ud Din Firuz Shah.

Firuz Shah quelled the disorders of the kingdom and restored discipline. He ruled for three years (1487-1490). He was succeeded in 1490 by Fateh Shah's young son, Nasir ud Din Mahmud Shah, under a regency exercised by another African. However, within a year, still another African, Shams ud Din Musaffar Shah (Sidi Badr), murdered both the child-sultan and the regent and usurped the throne.

Shams ud Din Musaffar Shah reigned in Bengal for three years (1491–1494). His reign ended when he was killed at the head of a sortic against rebel forces that were besieging Gaur, the capital of Bengal. With the death of Shams ud Din Musaffar Shah, the black regime (the line of Habashis) came to an end. An Asiatic, Sayyid Ala ud Din Husain Shah, from the Oxus country was elected to the throne and one of his first acts was to expel all the Africans from the kingdom. The exiles, many thousands in number, were turned back from Delhi and Jaunpur and finally drifted to Gujarat and the Deccan, where the slave trade had established a considerable black population. *See 1550.*

1487

AFRICA

- Portugal's Joao II (John II) sent explorer Pedro de Covilhao to the Levant (the Middle East) in search of spices and the land of the legendary Prester John mentioned by Fra Mauro in 1459. Covilhao crossed the Red and Arabian Seas to India. He also visited Madagascar. Covilhao sent back to Portugal word that if ships could round southern Africa they would find pilots who could guide them to India. *See 1497.*
- The Portuguese established a factory at Wadan.

ASIA

- Firuz Shah, an African, ruled the kingdom of Bengal (India) for three years (1487–1490). He was succeeded in 1490 by Nasir ud Din Mahmud Shah, under a regency exercised by another African. However, within a year still another African, Shams ud Din Musaffar Shah (Sidi Badr), murdered both the child-sultan and the regent and usurped the throne.

1488

AFRICA

- Sailing to the bottom of the African continent, the Portuguese explorer Bartolomeu Dias explored the Cape of Good Hope (May).

Going where no "European" man had gone before, Dias verified that there was a sea route from Europe to India via the tip of Africa. The commercial potential excited the European sailing community. On assignment from King Joao II, Dias set sail on the Sao Cristovao from Lisbon in August 1487. The king spared no expense for this mission, commissioning some of Portugal's finest sailors to accompany Dias, including Joao Infante on the *San Pantaleao.* Heavy storms hit the fleet in January, pushing it away from the African coast, into unknown regions of the South Atlantic. But Dias guided the ships north and east. On February 3, he sighted land and realized it was the east coast of the African continent and that the flotilla had unknowingly rounded the cape. Dias named the cape, the Cape of Storms, and then turned back, satisfied that the expedition had realized the dream of the late Prince Henry the Navigator: to find a Europe to Asia seaway. On the return voyage, Dias went ashore and erected a stone pillar, claiming the land for Portugal. Upon his return to Portugal in December of 1488, Dias reported his adventures to King Joao II. The king saw hope of a sea route to India and suggested that Dias's Cape of Storms be called the Cape of Good Hope.

• Pedro da Covilhao visited the Red Sea and eastern Africa, returning to Portugal via Cairo.

EUROPE

• A gift of 100 slaves was made by the Catholic kings to Pope Inocencio.

1490

AFRICA

• The Portuguese planted sugar cane on the island of Sao Tome off the west coast of Africa and brought in slaves from the kingdom of Benin and other African countries to work in the canefields.
• Portuguese explorers traveled up the Congo River for some 200 miles and converted the king of the Kongo Empire to Christianity. The Portuguese established a post at Sao Salvador.
• Changamire became independent of Monomotapa. The Changamire dynasty was thus founded in the Bulawayo area.

1491

AFRICA

• The Portuguese sent an expedition to Angola.
• The Kongo diplomatic mission, which had been sent to Lisbon in 1489, returned with missionaries and artisans. King Nzinga a Nkuwa was baptized as Afonso I.

Afonso I is considered to be the greatest of the rulers of the Kongo kingdom. Under his rule, Catholicism was brought to the Kongo along with European technology. However, the relationship between the Portuguese and Afonso I became an exploitative one which by the end of his reign had made Afonso relatively powerless to rid his country of the Portuguese.

ASIA

• Shams ud Din Musaffar Shah, an African reigned as the sultan in Bengal for three years (1491–1494). His reign ended when he was killed at the head of a sortie against rebel forces that were besieging Gaur, the capital of Bengal. With the death of Shams ud Din Musaffar Shah, the black regime (the line of Habashis) came to an end. An Asiatic, Sayyid Ala ud Din Husain Shah, from the Oxus country was elected to the throne and one of his first acts was to expel all the Africans from the kingdom. The exiles, many thousands in number, were turned back from Delhi and Janupur and finally drifted to Gujarat and the Deccan, where the slave trade had established a considerable African population. *See* 1486 and 1550.

1492

THE AMERICAS

• Christopher Columbus weighed anchor on August 3 with 52 men aboard his flagship the 100 ton *Santa Maria*; 18 aboard the 50 ton *Pinta* commanded by Martin Alonso Pinzon and another 18 aboard the 40 ton *Nina* commanded by Vicente Yanez Pinzon. The *Pinta* lost her rudder on August 6 causing the fleet to put in to Tenerife on the Canary Islands. The three caravels put out to sea again on September 6 and sighted land on October 12.
• Pedro Alonzo Nino, said by many scholars to have been of African descent, arrived with Christopher Columbus as one of his pilots (October 12).
• Financed by Castile's Isabella, who borrowed the funding for the expedition from Luis de Santangel by putting up her jewels as collateral, Columbus crossed the Atlantic to make the first recorded European landing in the Western Hemisphere. Columbus and his crew disembarked on an island in the Bahamas which he named San Salvador under the impression that he had reached the East Indies.
• Columbus landed in Cuba on October 28 and, on December 6, he landed on the island of Quisqueya which he renamed Hispaniola. At Hispaniola, the *Santa Maria* ran aground and had to be abandoned.

The True Discoverers of America: From a Euro-centric perspective, Columbus is deemed to have "discovered" America. But the word "discovered" is not a wholly accurate description of what Columbus accomplished.

As is evident by the archaeological and demographic facts, the Americas were "discovered" tens of thousands of years ago by people of Asiatic origin. It is theorized that at least two great migrations of Asiatic peoples were made possible by temporary land bridges which periodically connected Asia to North America. It is believed that Asiatic people "discovered" the Americas some 40,000 years ago and that, by the time Columbus arrived, there were some 80 million indigenous inhabitants living throughout the Americas.

Additionally, there is considerable evidence that other people may have preceded Columbus to the shores of America. There is no question that the Vikings explored the coast of North America some 400 years before Columbus arrived. However, as the voyages of Thor Heyerdahl have shown, contact between the indigenous people of the Americas and the people of other continents (particularly Asia and Africa and the islands of Micronesia) is quite probable and that such encounters predated even the Vikings.

Of particular interest is Heyerdahl's 1970 voyage. In 1970, Heyerdahl and a crew of seven sailed a papyrus reed boat named *Ra-2* from Morocco to Barbados in the West Indies. Heyerdahl claimed that this voyage proved that the ancient Egyptians could have sailed similar boats to the New World and, conceivably, have influenced the Olmec, Mayan, Incan, and Aztec cultures. However, unintentionally, Heyerdahl's voyage also proved that African people could have sailed between their native continent and the Americas.

The Olmec civilization (1200 B.C.–100 B.C.)—the most ancient Indigenous American civilization in Mexico and the civilization upon which the Aztec and Mayan civilizations were based—provides some startling evidence for the supposition that there was a pre–Columbian African presence in the Americas. Ruins of an Egyptian-like Olmec ceremonial center have been discovered at La Venta on Mexico's southern Gulf Coast. The La Venta site featured an enormous pyramid and was surrounded by platforms and mounds. Of significance to the history of Afro-Americans is the presence, at the site, of four huge heads carved from basalt which have markedly African features. The largest of these heads is about eight feet tall and weighs about 40 tons. The nearest source for the basalt lies some 80 air miles to the north. The scale of the operation required

to bring the basalt to La Venta dwarfed the erection of Stonehenge. The inspiration for this effort appears to have been the African-like beings whose likenesses boldly, arrogantly adorn the Colossal Heads. Some archaeologists believe these likenesses to be those of "rain spirits." But just as plausible a case can be made that the likenesses are of real people who brought aspects of African and Egyptian culture to the Americas.

In his seminal, albeit sometimes speculative, work, *They Came Before Columbus*, Ivan Van Sertima bolsters the case for a pre–Columbian African presence in America. Professor Van Sertima notes that a February 1975 Smithsonian Institution archaeological team found two African male skeletons in a grave in the United States Virgin Islands which appear to have been interred around A.D. 1250. This find was, at that time, just the latest in a series of archaeological finds.

Other such finds were reported in pre–Columbian layers in the valley of the Pecos River, a river in northern Mexico and Texas which empties into the Gulf of Mexico. Additionally, in September 1974, a Polish craniologist, Andrzej Wiercinski, disclosed to the Congress of Americanists that skulls from Olmec and other pre–Christian sites in Mexico showed a clear prevalence of the total African cranial pattern. The carbon dating of artifacts taken from the Olmec ceremonial center indicates that the Olmecs rise (circa 800 B.C. plus or minus 150 years) coincided with the rise of the Afro-Nubian military as the dominant force in Egyptian politics. The period also coincided with the period of an alliance between Phoenicia and Egypt which enabled the Phoenicians to continue, and to expand upon, their maritime activities.

Van Sertima's book also details the work of Alexander von Wuthenau, an art historian, who brought to public attention numerous African portraits in clay, gold, copper and copal from ancient and medieval Central and South America. The African portraits captured not only the dense close curl and kink of African hair but also the occasional African goatee beard which was unknown among the indigenous people of the Americas. Additionally, the portraits portrayed a people with projecting jaws, broad noses, full fleshed lips, African ear pendants, headdresses, coiffures, facial tattoos and scarification.

It is theorized that African voyages to the

Americas probably began as early as 4000 B.C. as accidental driftings and continued on through the centuries up to the planned expeditions of the Mali King Abu Bakara II in the early 14th century. Whether by design or by accident, the evidence is rather substantial that Africans visited the Americas long before Columbus set sail and that those intrepid African explorers were able to make a long lasting impression upon the indigenous peoples they encountered.

AFRICA

• Sonni Ali (Sunni Ali) died (disappeared?) under mysterious circumstances after a 28-year reign during which he enlarged Gao from a small one-city kingdom into the vast Songhai Empire. During the reign of Sunni Ali, the mullahs of Timbuktu were executed for defying the authority of Sunni Ali.

Sunni Ali ruled the Songhai Empire in West Africa from 1464 to 1492. Sunni Ali began to absorb the Mali Empire about 1464 and developed Songhai into the most powerful state in the western Sudan. Sunni Ali conquered many neighboring countries. He captured Timbuktu in 1468 and threw out the Tuaregs who had held the city since 1433. About 1475, he conquered Jenne, another center of trade.

Sunni Ali established law and order in the Songhai Empire and encouraged trade. He disappeared mysteriously in 1492. Historians believe he may have drowned in a flood.

• Cairo (Egypt) was devastated by plague. 12,000 persons were said to have died in one day.
• Muhammadu Koran became the first Muslim king of Katsena.

EUROPE

• Granada, the last great stronghold of the Moors, surrendered to Castile's Isabella and Aragon's Ferdinand. The fall of Granada on January 2 completed la reconquista — the reconquest of Spain by Christian forces after 700 years of Muslim domination.

After the fall of Granada, about 100,000 Spanish Moors left Spain and went to Africa. However, after centuries of habitation in Spain, the Spanish Moors were not warmly welcomed back. They were consigned to live in and rebuild the ruined and deserted cities of the Moroccan coast. But in essence, they were strangers in a strange land. These Spanish Moors were called Tigarins (Andalucians) by the African Moors and were known as Moriscos by the Europeans.

RELATED HISTORICAL EVENTS

• Ferdinand decreed on November 23 that all property and assets left by the Jews belonged to the Crown even if the property had since found its way into Christian hands.

The expulsion of the Jews from Spain and the confiscation of their property was a key event in African American history because it was the funds derived from the sale of this confiscated Jewish property which financed the second voyage of Columbus to the New World in 1493. During this second voyage, African slaves were first introduced to the Western Hemisphere along with sugar cane, a principal commodity upon which an economic enterprise would be based—an enterprise which would result in the deaths and enslavement of millions of Africans.

—— 1493 ——

THE AMERICAS

• Christopher Columbus built a fort on the island of Hispaniola using wreckage from the *Santa Maria*. He left 44 men at Fort La Navidad and set sail for Spain on January 4 on board the *Nina*. Two days later, the *Pinta* under Martin Pinzon rejoined Columbus but they were soon separated by a storm.
• Columbus reached Lisbon on March 4 after having been delayed for 6 days by the Portuguese governor of the Azores. He arrived in Palos, Spain on March 15.
• At his royal reception, Columbus presented Isabella with "Indians," parrots, strange animals, and some gold. Columbus then demanded (and received) the reward which rightfully belonged to the sailor, Rodrigo de Triana, of the *Nina* who first sighted land. Isabella granted Columbus enormous privileges in the territories he had claimed for Spain and she sent him back as governor with 1,500 men in a fleet of 17 ships which weighed anchor on September 24.
• Doctors used some of the peppers brought back from the "Indies" by Columbus in a medicinal preparation to treat the ailing Isabella.
• The financing for Columbus' second voyage was made possible by the sale of assets formerly owned by the Jews. *See 1492.*
• As part of the cargo on this second

voyage, Columbus brought along African slaves. These slaves were eventually enslaved on the island of Jamaica.

Columbus landed on Sunday, November 3, on an island Columbus named Dominica. On November 22, Columbus sighted Hispaniola but, upon his return, he found that the fort which he had built had burned down and the colony had been dispersed.

• The sugar cane and cucumbers planted by Columbus at Santo Domingo came from the Canary Islands. Columbus had a special interest in sugar—his first wife's mother owned some Madeira Island canefields. This introduction of sugar cane will lead to the institutionalization of slavery in the Americas.

AFRICA

• Askia Mohammed assumed the leadership of the Songhai Empire in the wake of the death of Sunni Ali. Askia Mohammed was a Sarakolle general named Mamadu (Mohammed Toure). Upon his ascension to the throne, he assumed the title Askia and affixed it to his name to become Askia Mohammed. *See 1492.*

RELATED HISTORICAL EVENTS

• A papal bull (an edict of the pope) issued by Alexander VI on May 4 established a line of demarcation between Spanish discoveries and Portuguese. The Spanish were granted dominion over any lands they discovered west of the line, the Portuguese would have dominion over land east of the line.

With the discovery of "new" lands by the Portuguese and Spanish explorers, various problems arose concerning the ownership of the lands so discovered. The Spanish pope, Alexander VI, intervened to solve the problem of ownership of the New World. The Papal Bull of Demarcation (Papal Donation) gave the New World to Spain and Africa and the East (India) to Portugal. The pope's edict barred Spain from any African possessions and, thereby, compelled Spain to contract with other nations for slaves. The slave trade contract with the Spanish was in the hands of the Portuguese in 1600; in 1640 the Dutch received it; and in 1701 the French. The War of the Spanish Succession was partly motivated by the desire to bring the slave trade monopoly to England.

1494

THE AMERICAS

• The Treaty of Tordesillas divided the world between Portugal and Spain along lines similar to those established in 1493 by Pope Alexander VI.
• Columbus discovered the island of Jamaica on May 14 and named it Santiago. Columbus then proceeded to land on islands that eventually would be called Guadeloupe, Montserrat, Antigua, St. Martin, Puerto Rico, and the Virgin Islands.

AFRICA

• Naod became Emperor of Ethiopia.
• Pedro da Covilha reached Ethiopia. He was detained at court.
• War erupted between the Monomotapa and Changamire.

1495

THE AMERICAS

• Queen Isabella of Castile suspended a royal order for the sale of more than 500 Arawak "Indians" into slavery. Christopher Columbus brought the Arawaks to Spain from the West Indies. Queen Isabella ordered the release after theologians disagreed on the lawfulness of Indian slavery.
• Columbus ordered every Hispaniola native (Arawak) over 14 to pay tribute in gold to the king of Spain.

Columbus and the Annihilation of the Arawaks (1495-1540): In the year 1495, on the island of Hispaniola, Columbus rounded up 1500 Arawaks—men, women and children—and imprisoned them in pens guarded by men and dogs. Of these 1500, 500 were selected for shipment to Spain as slaves. Three hundred of the original five hundred Arawaks arrived in Spain where they were sold into slavery. However, even these surviving slaves did not fare well. Most of the 300 soon died under the harsh conditions of slavery in Spain and the trade in Arawak slaves was soon deemed an "unprofitable" enterprise.

With the demise of the Arawak slave trade, Columbus decided to concentrate on the acquisition of gold and that is when the reign of terror on the island of Hispaniola truly began. Columbus required every man and woman, every boy or girl of fourteen or older, to collect gold for the Spaniards. Every three months, every Arawak had to bring to one of the

Spanish forts a bell filled with gold dust. The Arawak chieftains had to bring in about ten times that amount. In exchange, the Arawaks were given copper tokens which were stamped with the month of issuance and which were designed to be hung around the neck.

Under Columbus' rule, any Arawak found without a copper token was killed by having his or her hands cut off. Many Arawaks met their deaths in this way because the island had very little gold. Many others tried to escape but they were hunted down with dogs and killed. Armed resistance was impossible because of the superior weaponry (armor, muskets, swords, horses, and dogs) of the Spaniards.

Life on Hispaniola for the Arawaks became a living hell. Many Arawaks tried to escape their condition by committing suicide. The Arawaks used casava poison to kill themselves. During the two years (1495–1496) of Columbus' initial administration of Hispaniola, it is estimated that one half of the entire population of Hispaniola was killed by the Spanish or killed themselves by committing suicide. It is estimated that there were 240,000 Arawak people on Hispaniola in 1492. Columbus and his brother Diego, as chief administrators of the island, essentially oversaw the deaths of some 120,000 people.

The decimation of the Arawak people did not cease with the death of Columbus in 1506. Of the 250,000 Arawaks on Hispaniola in 1492, only 60,000 remained in 1510; 10,000 in 1515 and 0 in 1540.

It was the rapid demise of the Arawak people due to the genocidal practices of the Spanish, along with the Arawak's susceptibility to European diseases, the introduction of sugar cane to Hispaniola and the economic benefit associated with slave labor which led to the mass introduction of African slaves to the New World.

AFRICA

• Askia Mohammed, the emperor of Songhai, made a pilgrimage to Mecca accompanied by many scholars and court attendants. Askia Mohammed was made Caliph of the Sudan by the authorities of Mecca. During the reign of Askia Mohammed, the Songhai Empire was enlarged to a point where it was 2,000 miles long and 1,000 miles wide—an area equivalent to all of Europe.

1496

AFRICA

• Spain captured Melilla.

RELATED HISTORICAL EVENTS

• England's Henry VII refused to recognize Spanish and Portuguese claims under the 1493 papal bull (order of the pope). Henry VII granted a patent to John Cabot to search for new lands and to rule any he might find. Born Giovanni Caboto, Cabot was a Venetian merchant who settled in England with his sons.

1497

AFRICA

• Portuguese explorer Vasco da Gama departed from Lisbon with four ships to investigate the possibility of a sea route to India as suggested by the voyage of Bartholomeu Dias in 1487. Da Gama sailed around the Cape of Good Hope on November 22. On Christmas Day he sailed along the east coast of Africa and gave Natal its name.

The success of Vasco da Gama's voyage was directly dependent upon the goodwill of the king of Malindi (Kenya). After rounding the Cape of Good Hope, Vasco da Gama entered what was essentially a hostile Muslim world. In Malindi, however, da Gama was lucky enough to find a friendly king who saw the Portuguese as potential allies against his rivals. The king of Malindi helped da Gama obtain the services of an experienced navigator named Ahmed-ibn-Majid for the most perilous portion of the expedition—the eastward voyage across the unknown (to the Portuguese) Indian Ocean to India.

With ibn-Majid's guidance and good following winds, the 2,500 mile journey took just over a month. The fleet—the first European ships to reach India—arrived in Calicut, India in mid–May of 1498.

Da Gama's stay in Calicut was a difficult one. He was met by hostility by the Muslim merchants whose monopoly he threatened and by indifference by the Hindu ruler of Calicut who was unimpressed by the gifts the Portuguese brought with them to trade for spices and jewels. Additionally, da Gama's navigator, ibn-Majid disappeared during the crew's stay in Calicut.

It took da Gama three months to cross the Indian Ocean on his return trip. Low on provisions, the Portuguese experienced, for the first time, the horrors of long voyages over open seas. Rotting food and excrement gathered in the bilges to form a cesspool which bred rats, lice, and maggots. The crew survived on freshly caught fish, salted pork heavily laced with garlic to disguise the decay, and biscuits crawling with worms. Deprived of fresh fruit and vegetables, the crew eventually fell prey to scurvy. Gums swelled, bled, and decayed; joints became swollen; seamen fell into comas; and many died.

But the fleet did, somehow, manage to make it back to Malindi where the same friendly king saved the lives of da Gama and his crew by nursing them and supplying them with supplies of oranges, eggs, meat, and poultry. Thus nourished, the fleet was able to continue on its voyage home to Portugal, where da Gama was declared a hero by King Manuel.

1498

AFRICA

• Vasco da Gama visited Mozambique (March 2), Mombasa (April 7) and Malindi (April 14) and arrived in Calicut, India (May 20), where Arab spice dealers provided him with a rude reception. By discovering a sea route to India, da Gama freed Europe from its dependence on Venetian middlemen and destroyed the Arab monopoly on the Indian spice trade. *See 1497.*

• Great Zimbabwe became the capital of the Karanga kingdom of Urozwi (Rozwi), ruled by kings (mambos) who took the dynastic title of Changamire.

RELATED HISTORICAL EVENTS

• The Spanish shipped some 600 cannibal Caribs to Spain to be sold into slavery.

• Christopher Columbus embarked on June 7 on a third voyage to the New World. He commanded a fleet of six ships. Columbus landed on St. Vincent on July 22 and on Grenada on August 15. He also discovered Trinidad and landed at what was probably the mouth of the Orinoco River on the South American mainland.

• The Spanish government permitted Columbus to take criminals with him on his third voyage to the Americas, a group which included murderers who were sentenced to death. In the New World, the criminals were set free, huge parcels of land were given to them, and they were granted the right to treat everybody who was not a Christian (and European) as a commodity and as an animal.

• The Spanish settled some 200 colonists on the island of Hispaniola.

1499

AFRICA

Vasco da Gama completed his two-year voyage around the Cape of Good Hope to India, bringing back spices (pepper, nutmeg, cinnamom and cloves), gems and silks to King Manuel (September 9). The voyage was the first of its kind, opening a sea trade route between Europe and the Indian subcontinent. The three ship fleet encountered hostile Muslim merchants, blustery winds at the tip of Africa and an outbreak of scurvy that killed so many (116 out of 170) men that da Gama, lacking crewmen, burned one of the ships. The other two vessels completed the voyage, paving the way for commercial exchanges between the two cultures and the exploitation of the African continent. Appropriately, Bartolomeu Dias, the man who discovered the Cape of Good Hope, accompanied da Gama as far as the Cape Verde Islands.

Before returning to Portugal, Vasco da Gama bombarded Mogadishu (Somalia).

The "Oriental" spices brought back by Vasco da Gama were important because such spices were widely used to preserve meat and to disguise the bad taste of spoiled meat which comprised the bulk of human diets in late winter and spring.

EUROPE

• Granada's Moors stage a massive revolt as the Spanish Inquisitor-General Francisco Jimenez de Cisneros introduced forced conversion to Christianity on a wholesale basis.

1500–1599

The 1500s saw the rise of the Luba Empire in Katanga. The Ngola dynasty of Ndongo was founded. Mapungubwe was abandoned. And, in what is today Uganda, the first Bito dynasties arose.

In the 1500s, the Wolof Kingdoms emerged around Senegambia and the Kongo people began to move into Zambia and Zimbabwe. The Fung (Funj) sultanate would be founded at Sennar on the Blue Nile as a Muslim successor to the Christian Nubian kingdom of Alwa.

As for outside Africa, the 1500s were a decidedly Spanish century. The Spaniards, through the inheritance and auspices of Charles I, created the most extensive empire that the world has ever seen.

In addition to being King of Spain and the ruler of the Netherlands and Burgundy, Charles I, who is better known by his title as Holy Roman Emperor Charles V, was the heir to the Hapsburg dynasty, the greatest ruling house in Europe. As such, his possessions were immense. They included Germany, Naples, Sicily, Sardinia, portions of Africa, the Americas, and the Spanish lands of the Pacific. Charles V ruled the greatest of all empires. No one before him, not even the Roman emperors had controlled so much territory, such a variety of people, and such enormous material wealth.

However, while kingdoms and empires were being created in both Africa and elsewhere, a peculiar institution was also being created which would endure longer than any of the empires of which it was so often an integral part. This institution—this peculiar institution—was the institution of slavery.

With regards to the Spanish Empire, wherever the intrepid Spanish conquistadores ventured, their African slaves and compatriots ventured also. Indeed, it was often the Africans who cut the path through the jungle or scouted the trail through Indian territory in advance of the Spanish who followed.

It was the slaves who cut the sugar cane and who plunged into the mines in search of silver and gold. It was the slaves who built the cities and it was the slaves who "civilized" the wilderness. Indeed, in many Spanish colonies, it was the slaves who eventually became the colonists—the settlers and inheritors of the land.

1 5 0 0

THE AMERICAS

• Portuguese explorer Pedro Alvares Cabral claimed Brazil for Manoel I.

Pedro Alvares Cabral (1467–1528) was born near Covilha, Portugal. He was educated at the royal court and became a member of the King's Council. In 1499, King Manoel I named Cabral the commander of the second Portuguese fleet to sail to India. Oddly enough, it is believed that Cabral had never sailed a ship before his appointment.

Cabral and his fleet of 13 caravels sailed from Belem, near Lisbon, on March 9, 1500. The course charted for the fleet was the same route followed by Vasco da Gama *see 1497 and 1498*. First the fleet sailed southwest and passed the Canary and Cape Verde Islands. Cabral hoped for winds that would carry the fleet around the Cape of Good Hope (the southern tip of Africa). However, strong winds drove the fleet westward.

On April 22, Cabral's men sighted what is now southwestern Brazil. Cabral landed on Good Friday and, on Easter Monday, he claimed the land for Portugal.

By the time he reached Brazil, Cabral had already lost one ship. However, because of his discovery, Cabral authorized one of his remaining ships to return to Portugal with news of the landing. The remainder of the fleet stayed in Brazil for eight days and then continued on the voyage to India.

On May 24, 1500, after rounding the tip of Africa, the fleet encountered a storm. The storm scattered the fleet. Four ships were lost at sea while another was permanently separated from the fleet. (The separated ship did manage to reach Madagascar.) The six surviving ships of the fleet reassembled at Mozambique and followed the African coast northward.

Cabral continued on his voyage to India stopping along the way at Kilwa in what is today Tanzania. In the years following Cabral's visit to Kilwa in 1500, the Portuguese would begin extracting a tribute from Kilwa on a regular basis. But when Cabral first sailed into Kilwa's harbor, he and his crew first marveled at Kilwa's fine houses of coral stone, many of them three and four stories high. Kilwa was described as being a place where there were rich merchants and there was much gold, silver, amber, musk and pearls.

The fleet then crossed the Indian Ocean and arrived in Calicut, India, on September 13.

While in India, hostilities erupted between the Portuguese and the Arab merchants whose trade monopoly was now threatened. A pitch battle ensued and many of Cabral's men were killed.

Cabral's fleet left Calicut. The fleet sailed to the Indian towns of Cochin and Cannanore where the ships were loaded with spices. These spices were the beginning of the lucrative Portuguese spice trade.

Cabral, who was accompanied by Bartholomeu Dias *see 1488* and Duarte Pareira, completed the return voyage to Portugal. The fleet arrived in Lisbon on June 23, 1501.

• Estevanico, the famed explorer of the American Southwest, was born in Azamore, Morocco. *See 1527.*

AFRICA

• The first sub–Saharan African city to be attacked by European forces was Mozambique. Mozambique (which is located in the country of the same name) was attacked by Portuguese forces.

Mozambique lies on the southeastern coast of Africa. People have lived in what is now Mozambique since 4000 B.C. Bantu speaking people settled there before A.D. 100. Arabs arrived in the area by A.D. 800.

The Portuguese explorer Vasco da Gama first visited Mozambique in 1497. However, the reception for the Portuguese in 1497 was quite hostile. The Arab traders who had an established presence in Mozambique showed their contempt of the Portuguese at every turn. The Arabs even tried to seize Da Gama's ships.

The Portuguese did not forget the reception received by da Gama, nor did they forgive. In 1500, when a second Portuguese fleet arrived — the fleet commanded by Pedro Alvares Cabral —, Mozambique was attacked. The European assault upon Africa was clearly under way.

In 1505, the Portuguese established a trading post in Mozambique and the country became a slave trading center.

• A *kanta* reigned who was considered master of Katsena, Kano, Zaria, the Gober, and the Zanfara (northern Nigeria and southern Niger). The kanta also extended his power over Air, a strategic market town.
• By 1500, the southern Bantu peoples were well established throughout the region south of the Limpopo River. The Bantu

people would form the basis for the Swazi, Ngoni, and Xhosa kingdoms that were to come.
• The Luba Empire was founded.

The Luba people live in the Kasai and Shaba (Katanga) regions of Zaire. From the fourteenth to eighteenth centuries, the Luba controlled a large empire in the southeastern part of present-day Zaire.

• The Ngola dynasty of Ndongo (Angola) came to power.
• Mapungubwe was abandoned.
• The first Bito dynasties arose in Uganda.
• The Wolof kingdoms began to decline in Senegambia.

Today the Wolof live in northwestern Senegal, the Gambia, and Mauritania. It is believed that the Wolof originated in Mauritania and migrated southward under pressure from the Berbers of North Africa. Arriving in the region of today's Senegal, the Wolof started a dual process of driving the Serer farther south and "assimilating" them. By the thirteenth century, distinct Wolof states appeared, but they were conquered, like the rest of the Senegambia region, by the expanding Mali Empire.

According to Mali oral traditions the Wolof were under Mali's rule for about a century. In the mid-fourteenth century, the Wolof broke away from Mali and formed the Jolof Empire, providing them with political, cultural, and linguistic unity. The empire included the Wolof states of Kajoor, Bawol, and Waalo; the Serer states of Siin and Salum; and western and central Futa Toro, home of the Tukulor people.

Toward the end of the fifteenth century, the Jolof Empire began to disintegrate. The revolt of Kajoor in the mid-sixteenth century marked its downfall. However, some Wolof states with a similar social and political system continued to exist until conquered by the French in 1886.

• The Kongo people began to move into Zambia and Zimbabwe.

EUROPE

• Reference was made to an African presence at the Scottish court shortly after 1500. The women mentioned were Ellen (Helenor) More and Margery Lindsay and the men mentioned were Peter, Nageir and Taubronar. Taubronar was listed as a married man with a child at the Court. These Africans most likely came to Scotland from Portugal.

——— 1 5 0 1 ———

THE AMERICAS

• Amerigo Vespucci made a second voyage to the New World, this time in the service of Portugal. Vespucci's account of the Brazilian coast would express his conviction that Brazil was not part of Asia but indeed a New World. It was this bold assertion which would lead to the lands being called the Americas. *See 1507.*

Amerigo Vespucci (1454–1512) was born in Florence, Italy. As a youth, he studied navigation. In 1491, Vespucci moved to Seville, Spain. In Spain, he became associated with a company that equipped ships for long voyages.

Vespucci claimed to have made four voyages to the New World. His first voyage was supposedly made in 1497. After this voyage, Vespucci said that he had sighted a vast continent.

What is known for certain is that in 1499 and 1500, Vespucci accompanied a Spanish expedition led by Alonso de Ojeda. During this voyage, Ojeda's expedition traveled along the coast of Venezuela.

In 1501 and 1502, and again in 1503 and 1504, Vespucci sailed with the fleet of Goncalo Coelho for Portugal. On these expeditions, the Portuguese explored the southern coast of Brazil.

While never commanding an expedition of his own, Vespucci's claim to fame came largely from a letter he wrote to Lorenzo di Pier Francesco de Medici in 1502 or 1503. In the letter, Vespucci told of "his discovery" of a new continent and vividly described his discovery in great detail. Vespucci's letter was published the following year under the title *Mundus Novus (New World)*.

Vespucci's letter was a marvel much akin to Marco Polo's remarkable tales. The letter became extremely popular and later was published in several editions and translations. Based on this one letter, Vespucci was lionized as a great explorer.

Vespucci became a Spanish citizen in 1505 and served in governmental posts until his death in 1512.

Soon after Vespucci's death, scholars began to question his claims of discovery. The scholars found little evidence to support Vespucci's claim of a 1497 voyage. The scholars also "discovered" that Vespucci never led any of the expeditions he was on.

It is one of the true ironies of history, that the man whose name is affixed to two continents and whose name is so proudly proclaimed by those who call themselves "Americans" was, in many ways, a self-important fraud.

• A royal ordinance gave official sanction to the introduction of African slaves into the Spanish colonies.
• Spain initially imported European rather than African slaves to Hispaniola because the Africans were considered rebellious and difficult to manage.

AFRICA

• Ascension Island was discovered.

EUROPE

• The Spanish attempt to make Granada a Christian kingdom encountered resistance from the Moors.

1502

THE AMERICAS

• Amerigo Vespucci returned to Portugal in September after a voyage which took him to the Brazilian coast. Vespucci's account of this voyage and his claim that the new lands were a new world distinct from Asia would lead to the naming of the new lands "America." *See 1501 and 1507.*
• Some 2,500 new colonists arrived in Hispaniola. Nicolas Ovando (Nicholas de Ovando) was installed as governor of the new colony.

Queen Isabella's royal commission to colonial Governor Nicolas Ovando prohibited the passage to the West Indies of Jews, Moors, or recent converts, but authorized Ovando to take over African slaves that had been "born in the power of Christians." Ovando set sail in February, 1502. In 1503, Ovando would protest the restriction on the importation of non–African slaves because the African slaves tended to escape and often demoralized the local indigenous (Indian) population.

The Spanish brought the first group of African slaves to the island of Hispaniola. These first Hispaniola slaves were carried by way of Europe so that they might be "Christianized" before being sent to the colonies. In the New World of Hispaniola, some of the Spanish began to intermarry with the African slaves.

• Between 1502 and the year 1600, it is estimated that 900,000 African slaves were brought to Latin America alone.

Between 1502 and the year 1888, when slavery was abolished in Brazil, approximately five million Africans were imported for work on the sugar plantations. These Africans, who were erroneously considered resistant to malaria and yellow fever, were concentrated in Minas Geraes, Bahia, Rio de Janeiro and Maronhao. Most of the African slaves shipped to Latin America came from the Guinea coast, Angola, and the Congo River basin. Each group of African slaves had a distinct culture and language and often specific tribal groups would be sought for enslavement because of their special skills. Later on, with the expansion of the slave trade, Africans would be kidnapped from Guinea and the Western Sudan.

AFRICA

• The last of the armed forces of the Berbers and Moors in Castile (Spain) were expelled and driven back into Africa. *But see 1610.*
• Vasco da Gama won control of the spice trade for Lisbon. He set out with a fleet of 20 caravels to close the Red Sea and he cut off the trade route through Egypt to Alexandria, where Venetian merchants had been buying spices.
• Saint Helena was discovered.

Saint Helena is an island in the Atlantic Ocean. It lies about 1,200 miles (1,930 kilometers) off the southwest coast of Africa, and about 700 miles (1,100 kilometers) southeast of Ascension Island.
Saint Helena is famous because Napoleon Bonaparte was forced to live there from 1815 until his death in 1821.

• Kilwa (Tanzania) began paying tribute to Portugal.

1504

THE AMERICAS

• The license of Medina del Camo to Ojeda provided for the utilization of white slaves—not black slaves—in the Americas.

AFRICA

• Around 1504, "Oba" Esigie began his reign in Benin. Esigie's reign would be a long and prosperous one which would see Idah annexed to the Benin kingdom and would find the Portuguese accepted as residents in the city of Benin.

RELATED HISTORICAL EVENTS

In 1504, Queen Isabella I of Spain died. In 1469, Isabella married Ferdinand of Aragon. The marriage led to the union of Spain's largest kingdoms — Castile and Aragon in 1479.

During the reign of Ferdinand and Isabella, new roads were built and the coinage was made standard. Spanish law was codified and the rulers presided over the administration of justice.

Most importantly, during the reign of Ferdinand and Isabella, the Moors were defeated which made possible the unification of Spain. During their reign, the Jews were expelled or forced to convert to Catholicism. And during their reign, Columbus sailed westward and "discovered" the Americas.

Queen Isabella was one of the principal supporters of Columbus. She was one of the few people who saw merit in Columbus' plan to sail to the Indies by sailing west. It was Isabella's financial support which made Columbus' initial voyage possible and it was this initial voyage which led to the creation of a Spanish Empire which has been unrivaled in history.

1505

THE AMERICAS

• Nicolas Ovando, the Governor of Hispaniola, sailed from Seville with seventeen African slaves and some mining equipment to be used in the copper mines of Hispaniola.

In 1505, King Ferdinand sent a letter to Governor Ovando. The letter read: "I will send more black slaves as you request; I think there may be a hundred. At each time a trustworthy person will go with them who may have some share in the gold they may collect and may promise them ease if they work well."

There is no record that King Ferdinand ever fulfilled his promise.

AFRICA

• Sofala (near modern day Beira, Mozambique) was occupied by the Portuguese, the Portuguese constructed a fort at Sofala, and the Portuguese East African Empire began.

• Portuguese forces under the command of Francisco d'Almeida attacked and sacked Kilwa (Tanzania) and Mombasa (Kenya). The Portuguese extended their domination along the East African coast, but concentrated their trade operations at the key cities of Kilwa, Mombasa, and Malindi (Kenya). In Kilwa, the Portuguese erected Fort Santiago.

• In Malawi, the people formed a strong confederation under separate chieftainships of Undi, Karonga, Mwase, and others. This confederation of African peoples was strong enough to keep the Portuguese in check within their regions.

• The Spanish captured Mers el-Kebir.

• The Portuguese captured Agadir.

1506

THE AMERICAS

• By a royal decree, Berber slaves, free Africans and new African converts to Christianity along with unruly African slaves and Moorish servants were not permitted to enter Hispaniola.

AFRICA

• The Portuguese landed on the island of Madagascar.

The Mystery of Madagascar: When the Portuguese landed on the island of Madagascar, they landed in a place like no other.

The island of Madagascar was created some 250 million years ago when the island broke away from the continental mainland. After breaking away, the island slowly drifted away from Africa to a point some 240 miles due east. There it remained isolated, uninhabited and unknown.

But then came the Indonesians.

Some two thousand years ago, before Jesus of Nazareth began his ministry, a group of intrepid Indonesians discovered the island of Madagascar. These Indonesians, finding the island uninhabited, decided to make the island their home.

The Africans and Arabs who today also inhabit the island came later.

The Mystery of Madagascar centers on the origins of the Indonesian presence and dominance of the island. Why did the Indonesian people travel thousands of miles to settle upon Madagascar? How did they get there? Why was Madagascar chosen as opposed to the African mainland?

All of these questions are mysteries which have yet to be solved. But what is known is that for some two thousand years the African island nation of Madagascar has been inhabited and dominated by a people of Asian origin.

• Tristan da Cunha Island was discovered.

RELATED HISTORICAL EVENTS

• Columbus died (May 20).

The Legacy of Columbus: In the United States, a national holiday has been created in honor of Columbus. However, for Indigenous (Native) Americans and for African Americans the day should be a day of somber reflection. While Columbus may have been a courageous and bold explorer, he was also a petty, greedy, and sometimes barbaric man. Under his administration of Hispaniola, some 120,000 Arawaks were killed or compelled to kill themselves. Under Columbus' administration, the Spaniards made low, wide gallows on which they strung up the Arawaks, their feet almost touching the ground. The Spaniards would then put burning green wood at their feet. These executions took place in lots of thirteen. Why thirteen? Thirteen was the number chosen "in memory of Our Redeemer and His twelve Apostles."

Under Columbus' administration, Arawak chiefs and nobles were burned to death like slabs of meat on grids of iron rods. Arawak men, women and children were often hacked to pieces and the pieces were subsequently fed to the Spaniards' dogs. After all, it was deemed to be good military policy to give the dogs a taste for Arawak flesh.

Of the 250,000 Arawaks on Hispaniola in 1492, only 60,000 remained in 1510; 10,000 in 1515 and 0 – yes, 0 – in 1540. The entire Arawak nation had vanished from the face of the earth. In their place, the Spanish brought in millions of Africans, who but for the sheer magnitude of their number and their durability, would have met a similar fate as the Arawaks.

In light of the atrocities directly inflicted upon the Arawaks at Columbus' direction, and the subsequent holocaust of indigenous peoples in both America and Africa caused by Columbus' "discovery," it would be easy to understand a certain hostility emanating from Indigenous Americans and African Americans regarding "celebrating" Columbus Day. Nevertheless, despite the horrors connected with the man, it must not be overlooked that it is because of Columbus that African Americans as a people exist.

In Latin America, in lieu of Columbus Day, the people celebrate *La Dia de la Raza*, the Day of the Race. On this day, the people celebrate the fact that Columbus' "Discovery" brought into being a new racial entity—a new people from the Spanish, Indigenous American, and African races. From the perspective of the Latin Americans, Columbus' "Discovery" was not a single historical event but is rather an ongoing contemporaneous encounter. This mutual discovery was horrendous for the Indigenous Americans but for the mestizos of today the day recognizes their dual heritage and history.

In many ways, the African American who looks in the mirror will see one of the direct benefits of Columbus' discovery. With so many African Americans having not only European but also Indigenous American blood flowing through their veins, the birth of the African American people, while initiated in pain, is nevertheless, attributable to Columbus.

1 5 0 7

THE AMERICAS

• The term "America" was used for the first time as a label for the New World. The reference was made in Martin Waldseemuller's *Cosmographiae Introductio.*

Waldseemuller apparently had believed the claims of Amerigo Vespucci that he, Vespucci, had "discovered" the Americas and not Columbus. Indeed, Vespucci would often claim to have discovered the New World in 1491, a full year before Columbus. But historians have obviously discounted this claim.

Waldseemuller wrote: "[N]ow that these parts have been more extensively examined, and another fourth part has been discovered by Americus Vespuccius.... I do not see why anyone should by right object to name it America ... after its discoverer, Americus, ..."

AFRICA

• Leo Africanus visited the Songhai Empire. He would later report on the kingdom ruled by Mohammed Askia and the intellectual centers at Gao, Timbuktu, and Jenne. *See 1518.*

At the intellectual centers of Gao, Timbuktu, and Jenne, writers and students from North Africa came to study. During the sixteenth and seventeenth centuries, a literature was developed in Timbuktu. The University of Sankore became a center of learning in correspondence with Egypt and North Africa. There were a large number of Sudanese students in attendance at the university.

• The Portuguese established a fort at Sofala, Mozambique.
• 1507 saw the reinvigoration of the Kanem-Bornu Empire. Mai Idris Katakar-mabe reoccupied Njimi, the old Kanem capital.

1 5 0 8

THE AMERICAS

Following the lead of the Portuguese, who had planted sugar cane in Madeira, on the Cape Verde Islands and on the Canary Islands, and of Columbus, who brought the plant to the Indies on his second voyage, the Spanish on the island of Hispaniola switched from unsuccessful mineral mining to profitable sugar cane plantings, initially using indigenous people as slave labor.

However, as sugar cane cultivation prospered, the indigenous slave force became more and more subject to decimation. Within the span of eighteen years, it is estimated that the indigenous population was reduced by some 190,000 people. Because of this susceptibility, the Spanish felt compelled to import ever increasing numbers of African slaves to work the sugar cane plantations.

In other areas of the West Indies, the Spanish importation of Africans to work in the mines continued.

AFRICA

• Vasco Gomes d'Abreu completed a church, fort, factory and hospital in Mozambique.
• In 1508, annual expeditions between Portugal and the Congo began.

1 5 0 9

AFRICA

• Oran was taken by Cardinal Ximenes. It would be held until 1708.
• The Portuguese established a factory in Malindi.

1 5 1 0

THE AMERICAS

• King Ferdinand of Spain ordered the "La Casa de Contratacion" and sent 250 Africans to the New World to work as slaves. These Africans were imported to Hispaniola to work the sugar fields and the gold mines.

By 1510, the enslavement of Moors, Jews and other white (European) people was a common practice in Spain. However, along with slavery the voluntary emancipation of slaves was also a fairly common occurrence. Among the slaves manumitted were African slaves. Early on, these manumitted African slaves began to appear on the lists of persons licensed by "La Casa de Contratacion" to go to the New World as free Spanish colonists.

In the New World, there was a great demand for laborers. The first considerable response which King Ferdinand made to the appeal for laborers was his ordering La Casa de Contratacion to send out 250 Africans. These Africans were "Christianized" African slaves which were purchased in Lisbon.

One of the last acts that King Ferdinand was to make was to urge that no more Africans be sent to the New World. However, his successor, Charles V, at the pleading of Bishop Las Casas drew up a plan of assisted Spanish immigration to the New World under which each immigrant was allowed to import twelve African slaves in return for which the decimated Indigenous peoples (Native Americans) were to be set free.

• An order of African monks was inaugurated by the Catholic Church in Spanish America early in the 1500s. By the middle of the 1600s, a freed African would see the day when his son, Francisco Xavier de Luna Victoria, would become Bishop of Panama, the first indigenous Catholic Bishop and the first Catholic Bishop of African descent in the Americas.
• In 1510, the first slaves from Guinea arrived in Hispaniola.

AFRICA

• In Africa, certain African kingdoms (such as Ndongo—in modern day Angola) flourished on the European stimulated slave trade.

It is relatively rarely discussed that Africans themselves were participants in the slave trade and profited from it. The participation varied. Sometimes internecine warfare led to captured prisoners being sold into slavery, other times the greed of certain chieftains resulted in Africans from rival clans (tribes) or from the same clan being sold into slavery, and still later on, Africans in the Americas would own other Africans. It is a shameful, hurtful fact of history that the enslavement (and deaths) of so many Africans, was in no small measure, caused by their fellow Africans.

• Francisco d'Almeida was killed in a battle at Table Bay.

• Spain captured Bougie, Tunis and Tripoli.

EUROPE

• Alessandro de Medici (1510–1537) was born. Alessandro is believed to have been the son of Pope Clement VII (the Cardinal de Medici) and Anna, an African servant. After the death of Pope Clement VII, Alessandro headed the famous de Medici family and was made Duke of Florence. Alessandro married Maria, the daughter of Charles V (the Holy Roman Emperor *see 1500 above*) and the sister of Philip II *see 1588.* Alessandro was assassinated before his full potential had been reached.

1511

THE AMERICAS

• The first 50 African slaves arrived in the Antilles.

• Cincuenta piezas de ebano (fifty black slaves) were brought to work in the mines of Santo Domingo, Hispaniola.

AFRICA

• In 1511, Spanish expansion into Morocco was halted.

• The Portuguese abandoned Socotra.

1512

THE AMERICAS

• Bartholome de Las Casas became a missionary to the indigenous people of Cuba. Upon his assumption of his missionary duties, he began to write about Spanish mistreatment of the Indigenous Cubans.

• The Laws of Burgos were passed in Spain giving the indigenous people (the Indigenous Americans) of the New World protection against abuse while still authorizing their enslavement. (December 27).

AFRICA

• Askia Muhammed (Askia the Great) of the Songhai Empire captured Katsena, Kano and Zaria.

• The Portuguese fort at Kilwa was dismantled.

• Simao da Silva was dispatched to the Kongo to serve as the resident Portuguese ambassador.

ASIA

During the period from 1512 through 1515, the Portuguese trader, Tome Pires, traveled throughout the Far East. He reported that he found a number of Africans in Malacca (Melaka) [what is today known as Malaysia]. The Africans were there along with a large number of Indians and Asians. Pires specifically mentioned that, among the Africans, representatives from the East African city states of Kilwa, Malindi, Mogadishu, and Mombasa were identifiably present.

The presence of Africans in far off Malaysia, Singapore and Java should not have been a surprise. By 1512, contacts between the great Chinese Empire and East African people had existed for almost nine hundred years *see 1417;* Africans, in significant numbers, had been in India for over one hundred years; and Arab (Muslim) traders with their African slaves had been traveling throughout the region for hundreds of years.

It is important to remember that for many centuries before the arrival of the Portuguese in 1497, the Indian Ocean was an Arab ocean dominated by the Arab traders who traversed the seas implanting their religious beliefs (the Muslim faith) in the same lands where they exchanged their material wares. And since so many Arabs traded in slaves, it was only natural that wherever Arabs may have gone, their African slaves (and companions) were bound to go also.

EUROPE

• In Spain, a female mulatto, Juana, who declared herself to be the daughter of a Francisco Martin de Cazell and a freedwoman named Christina (along with Christina's three year old daughter) received permits under the Casa de Contratacion to go to the West Indies. *See 1510.*

RELATED HISTORICAL EVENTS

• Selim I (Salim I) became the ruler of the Ottoman Turks.

1513

THE AMERICAS

• By 1513, licenses for importing Africans were sold by Spain, and were considered an excellent source of government revenue.

• The expedition of Vasco Nunez de Balboa crossed Middle America and sighted the Pacific Ocean. This expedition to the Pacific included thirty persons of African descent who were instrumental in clearing the way between the two oceans. One of the Africans was Nuflo de Olano. De Olano and the other Africans also assisted in building the first ships constructed on the Pacific coast of the Americas.

• Africans found in the New World at Qugre-qua by Vasco Nunez were thought to have been survivors of a shipwreck.

• The Spanish Real Cedula of 1513 permitted the transfer of slaves to Cuba. Between 1513 and 1865, Cuba imported 527,828 Africans as slaves. 60,000 of the half-million imported Africans were brought in between 1513 and 1763. The remainder, some 470,000, were brought in between 1764 and 1865.

While it is not possible to give an exact number of how many Africans came to the Americas via the Atlantic slave trade, a conservative estimate is that between 7 and 11 million slaves were transported to the New World — alive. However, because of the brutal treatment on transport and the conditions of crossing, the total number of people of which the African continent was depleted amounted to at least a million more than the 7 to 11 million number.

Whatever the number of millions may be, what cannot be overstated is the devastating impact the slave trade had upon the people of Africa. Not simply families were destroyed but rather entire cultures were destroyed, and while Africans themselves were partly responsible for creating the misery endured by their brothers and sisters through their own active participation in the slave trade, eventually this complicity was overshadowed by the sheer exploitative volume of the trade in the "fruit of Africa" that was taken by Europeans from African lands to be sold in markets located on American shores.

AFRICA

• Portugal's King Manoel seized the city of Azamore, Morocco, the birthplace of Estevanico. Many of the city's residents were enslaved.

It is theorized that during this seizure of Azamore, Estevanico was taken captive and enslaved. Thus, in a truly ignominious fashion the great mythic epic that was the life of Estevanico began. *See 1527.*

• The Hausa people made alliance with Askia Mohammed of Songhay in a position of subservience, but afterwards regained their independence.

The Hausa are a widespread and numerous African people who inhabit the area from northern Nigeria to the Sudan.

• Reunion and Mauritius were discovered by the Portuguese.

Reunion is an island in the Indian Ocean about 400 miles (640 kilometers) east of Madagascar. When discovered by the Portuguese in 1513, Reunion was uninhabited. It would not be settled until the French took possession of it in 1642. The French would name the island Bourbon. This name would last for two hundred years. In 1848, the island was renamed Reunion. Today it is still considered a French possession.

Mauritius is an island nation in the Indian Ocean about 500 miles (800 kilometers) east of Madagascar. When discovered by the Portuguese in 1513, Mauritius was uninhabited. It would remain so until 1598 when the Dutch took possession of the island. It was the Dutch who renamed the island Mauritius after Prince Maurice of Nassau.

EUROPE

• 565 slaves were sent from Guinea to Portugal.

1514

THE AMERICAS

• The Spanish priest, Bartolome de Las Casas, began his opposition to the use of the indigenous people of the Americas (Indigenous Americans) as slaves. He condemned their treatment in his writings and, in his anxiety to help the indigenous people of the Americas, Las Casas suggested to the king of Spain that African slaves be used instead.

Las Casas was the first priest ordained in the Western Hemisphere. He was ordained in 1510. Two years after his ordination, Las Casas witnessed a routine "pacification" mission in Cuba. The mission was led by a Panfilo de Narvaez *see 1527* who turned it into a bloody massacre. Las Casas wrote that there "was a river of blood, as if a multitude of cows had been slaughtered." In 1514, Las Casas turned away from the enslavement of the indigenous people of the Americas and endorsed African slavery.

AFRICA

• Antonio Fernandes explored the Sofala hinterland.

• The king of the Kongo (Afonso I) sent a formal protest to the king of Portugal concerning the devastation being caused by the slave trade.
• The Portuguese captured Mazagan.
• Ottoman (Turkish) forces under the command of Barbarossa captured Djidjelli.

Barbarossa (1466–1546) was a Barbary pirate. Also known as Khair-ed-Din (Khair-al-Din), he was the younger of two red-bearded brothers who wreaked havoc on the western Mediterranean in the 1500s.

Khair-al-Din succeeded his brother Arouj (Aruj) as commander of organized fleets of pirate ships. Because of his success, Khair-al-Din became a high admiral of the Turkish navy. He devoted his life to launching ferocious and vengeful attacks on Christian ships and towns on the Mediterranean coast.

Khair-al-Din captured Tunis and Algiers. He ravaged the shores of Italy, France, and Spain. He enslaved thousands of European Christians.

Twice Khair-al-Din defeated the great European navies. His successful engagements against the Genoese admiral Andrea Doria enabled the Turks to maintain their dominance of the Mediterranean Sea. Turkish dominance of the sea would not be abated until 1571 at the Battle of Lepanto—a battle which occurred after Khair-al-Din's death. As for the Turkish dominance of Tunisia and Algeria, it would not be abated for over three hundred years.

EUROPE

• King Ferdinand of Spain restricted the importation of African slaves into Spain because the ratio of Spaniards to Africans had become three to one which threatened the security of the nation.
• 978 slaves were sent from Guinea to Portugal.

1515

EUROPE

• 1,423 slaves were sent from Guinea to Portugal.

1516

AFRICA

• Barbarossa captured Algiers. *See 1514.*

EUROPE

• Juan Latino, the author of *Ad Catholicum*, was born.

Juan "de Sesa" Latino (1516–1597) was a Spanish scholar. He was born in Africa on the Barbary Coast. When he was twelve years old, he was captured and taken to Seville, Spain. Latino was sold into slavery and was purchased by a famous Spanish family—the family of Fernando Gonzalo de Cordoba.

Juan was given to the heir of the Cordoba family, the third Duke de Sesa. Juan became the companion of the young duke. He went with him wherever he went, even to school. While carrying and tending to the duke's books, Juan would often peep into them and would sometimes ask the duke what the books were about. The curiosity of the young slave intrigued the duke's family who eventually approved of Juan's studying along with the young duke.

As fortune would have it, the Archbishop Pedro Guerrero authorized the acceptance of a slave into classes with his owner. Juan accompanied the duke to Spain's main learning center at Granada. Juan began to master Latin. He became quite proficient and even wrote Latin poetry. Because of his excellence in Latin, Juan became known as Juan "Latino" instead of Juan "de Sesa."

Juan Latino continued with his studies. He learned Greek and soon taught both languages. In 1546, Juan Latino earned a degree from the University of Granada.

Noted for his quick wit, his musical talent, and his charm, Juan received a master of arts degree in 1556. In 1565, Juan was honored when he was selected to open the school year with a Latin oration.

In 1635, a presentation of Encisco's play of Latino's career revived interest in the life of the Afro-Spanish scholar. The play focused on the romance between Juan Latino and a Spanish noblewoman, Dona Ana—the love of his life whom Juan Latino eventually married.

RELATED HISTORICAL EVENTS

In 1516, King Ferdinand of Spain died. Ferdinand (1452–1516), along with his cousin-wife, Isabella united the kingdoms of Castile and Aragon through their marriage. This union was essential because with their kingdoms united Ferdinand and Isabella were able to concentrate upon fighting the Moors, the African Muslims who had ruled Spain for 700 years. La reconquista, the expulsion of the Moors and the unification of Spain occurred in 1492—the same year that Columbus "discovered" the Americas.

During Ferdinand's reign, Spain became a dominate European power. Upon Isabella's death in 1504, Ferdinand expanded his kingdom by adding Italy's Naples and the province of Navarre to his realm.

Ferdinand's greatest triumphs and greatest mistake all occurred during the same year— 1492. The greatest triumphs were the reconquest of Spain and sponsoring Columbus' initial voyage to the Americas. Ferdinand's great mistake was the expulsion of the Jews.

The expulsion of the Jews, while in the short run enriching the monarchy through the confiscation of Jewish property, in the long run led to the ruin of Spain.

In 1492, there were approximately seven million people in Spain. Out of these seven million, only a half million were Jews. However, this was an important half million because the Jews were a predominantly urban people and the urban economy of the nation was dependent upon them.

One year after the edict which expelled the Jews was issued, the rents in Seville dropped by one half and, in Barcelona, the municipal bank went bankrupt.

But even more significantly was the loss of expertise that the expulsion caused. The Jews of Spain were a highly skilled people. They were the doctors of Spain—the bankers, the merchants, and the tax collectors. Their expulsion hurt Spain and benefited Spain's enemies since many of the expelled Jews fled northward to the Protestant nations or eastward to the Ottoman Empire.

1517

THE AMERICAS

• Bishop Las Casas persuaded the Spanish government to allow Spanish colonists to individually import up to twelve persons of African descent as a means of encouraging immigration to the New World. In later years, Las Casas would come to regret his proposal and began to speak out vehemently against African slavery. At the time of his death, in 1566, the annihilation of the indigenous people of the Americas had progressed despite Las Casas' protestations, while the African slave trade, which Las Casas had advocated as a substitute for the enslavement of the indigenous population, had greatly increased.

As soon as the Las Casas plan to import twelve African slaves per immigrant to the West Indies was proposed, Lorens de Gomenot, a Savoyard (Frenchman) and governor of Bresa, obtained a monopoly over the proposed trade and shrewdly sold it to the Genoese (Italians) for 25,000 ducats.

Las Casas was soon joined in his call for African slaves to be introduced into the Americas by his fellow clergymen from the Order of San Jeronimo. The Jeronimite Fathers actually requested to be allowed to purchase African slaves. As for their petition for the introduction of African slaves, unlike Las Casas, they preferred that the slaves come directly from Africa—that the Africans *not* be Christianized before being sent to the Americas. Demographers believe that of the estimated 80 million indigenous people in the Americas in 1492 when Columbus initiated the European colonization of the Americas only 10 million remained by the year 1600. The primary cause of death for the Indigenous Americans was disease. Indigenous Americans found themselves highly susceptible to diseases such as smallpox (which was brought to the Americas by the Europeans) as well as other diseases such as measles, dysentery, typhoid, and tuberculosis. Other causes of death were genocide and starvation caused by the colonization policies of the Europeans. *See 1495.*

The initial employment of Indigenous Americans as slaves severely disrupted their societies. So much effort was put into mining gold or otherwise working for the Spaniards, that many of the basic needs such as food production and procurement suffered. Malnutrition and outright starvation followed, helping to further decimate the already diminished Indigenous American populace and to hasten the mass employment of Africans as slaves.

• Emperor Charles V granted a charter to a Flemish merchant for the exclusive importation of African slaves into Spanish America.

Charles V and the Slave Trade: Charles V (1500–1558) was an integral figure in the development of the slave trade. Charles was the king of Spain from 1516 to 1556. A little known fact of history is that Charles V ruled over more countries than any other European monarch in history. As such his decisions had a far reaching impact not only in Europe but in the Americas.

Charles V was the grandson of Ferdinand and Isabella. He was also the grandson of Maximilian and Mary of Burgundy (eastern France). Charles V was born in Ghent, Belgium. In 1506, at the age of six, Charles V inherited the Netherlands and the Burgundian lands. Upon the death of Ferdinand in 1516, Charles became Charles I, the sixteen year old King of Spain.

Charles became king at such a young age because of the tragedy which befell his parents. His mother was Queen Joanna, the daughter of Ferdinand and Isabella. Queen Joanna was married to Philip the Fair. Philip the Fair died a premature death after strenuously playing ball and then drinking cold water. Queen Joanna was distraught over his death. She refused to bury Philip the Fair. Instead she took his corpse from monastery to monastery always avoiding convents lest Philip should seduce the nuns from his coffin. Finally persuaded to let her husband lie in peace, Queen Joanna was herself locked up in Tordesillas Castle.

In addition to being king of Spain and the ruler of the Netherlands and Burgundy, Charles I, who is better known by his title as Holy Roman Emperor Charles V, was the heir to the Hapsburg dynasty, the greatest ruling house in Europe. As such, his possessions were immense. They included Germany, Naples, Sicily, Sardinia, portions of Africa, the Americas, and the lands of the Pacific. Charles V ruled the first and the greatest of all empires. No one before him, not even the Roman emperors had controlled so much territory, such a variety of people, and such enormous material wealth.

And yet one of the oddities of this great king of Spain is that he could not speak Spanish. Charles V, having been born in Belgium, maintained allegiances with the Flemish people. He surrounded himself with Flemish court attendants and appointed Flemish courtiers to high Spanish posts. Of his fifty-eight years on earth, Charles V spent 28 years in Flanders (the western part of Belgium), nine years in Germany, and eighteen years in Spain.

Under Charles V, the long-standing policy of having Africans first go to Spain to be "Christianized" was discontinued. This change in policy was ostensibly necessitated by the rapid decimation of the Indigenous American populations in the Caribbean. However, it must be noted that the Spanish Crown, at that time, regulated the slave trade to its own profit. Obviously, requiring the middle step of Christianizing Africans by taking them first to Spain made the slave trade a more expensive enterprise. Eliminating the stay made the enterprise more profitable.

In 1518, Charles V awarded a concession to a of Flemish merchant which allowed the merchant to introduce four thousand African slaves into the Spanish colonies *without* first bringing them to Spain. From that moment, the African population in Spanish America grew from the initial rate of eight thousand people a year to thirty thousand per year in 1620.

The change in Spanish policy under Charles V also had a tremendous psychological effect. No longer were Africans initially deemed to be a people with souls worth saving. Instead, they became a commodity—economic objects which, all too often, could be discarded at will.

AFRICA

• Salim I captured Syria and Egypt.

On January 22, the Ottoman Turks, led by Salim I defeated Sultan Tumanbay outside Cairo. Cairo was subsequently besieged by Salim I.

On April 14, Sultan Tumanbay was hanged. With the execution of Sultan Tumanbay, Egyptian opposition to the Turks ceased. The Turks would dominate Egypt until 1798.

• Zaila was burned by the Portuguese.

1518

THE AMERICAS

• Emperor Charles V of Spain confirmed the legal status of the African slave trade. The slave trade system was institutionalized as the asiento, and not more than 4,000 Africans were to be imported each year.
• The first cargo of African slaves shipped directly from Africa (the coast of Guinea) arrived in the West Indies thereby bypassing the previously required "Christianizing" stay in Spain.
• Gold was discovered in Jamaica.
• Africans from Cuba were used in the conquest of Mexico.

AFRICA

• Aruj, the brother of Barbarossa, was killed. *See 1514.*
• Barbarossa offered Algiers to the Turks. The Turks accepted the offer and conveyed upon Barbarossa the title of Beylerbey. *See 1514.*
• Berbera (Somalia) was razed by the Portuguese.

EUROPE

• Papal permission was granted for Portuguese bishops to consecrate any Ethiopians, indigenous people of the Americas or Africans who might reach the educational and moral standards required of the priesthood.
• In 1518, Leo Africanus, a Moor, was captured by pirates while traveling on the Mediterranean Sea. The pirates, finding that the Moor knew a great deal about Africa, gave him to Pope Leo X as a gift. The pope set him free and as a special favor gave him his own name, Leo. *See 1507.*

1519

THE AMERICAS

• Six Africans were with Cortez as he marched into Mexico. The Africans were used to harvest the first wheat crop grown in the Americas.

In 1519, when the Spaniards arrived, Mexico had an indigenous population of 25 million. By the end of the century (1599), only a million were still alive.

AFRICA

• In 1519, the oldest literary work written by a West African was begun. The *Tarikh al-Fettach* by Mahmout Kati of Timbuktu was a recitation of Sudanese oral traditions and a compilation of histories of the royal houses and dynasties of the sixteenth century. The text of the book contains the myths of the origins of the Songhai, Mandingo, and Sarakole peoples. The book also relates the history of the kings of Ghana, the Kaymagas, and the Mali Empire.
• The Spanish aborted an attack on Algiers.

1520

THE AMERICAS

• Two hundred African slaves traveled with Alvarado on his expedition to Quito in Peru.

AFRICA

• Khair-al-Din (Barbarossa) was defeated by the Hafsids. *See 1514.*
• A chronicle of Kilwa was written in Arabic.
• The Funj defeated the Turks at Hannak.
• The Luba states in the region of Katanga began to expand.

• The capital of Adal was moved to Harar.
• The sultanate of Bagirmi (Baghirmi), southwest of Lake Chad, was established.
• Massawa was occupied by the Portuguese.

RELATED HISTORICAL EVENTS

• Suleyman "the Magnificent" became ruler of the Ottoman Turks.

1521

AFRICA

• Henrique, the son of Afonso, was made the first bishop of the Kongo and returned to Mbanza after spending thirteen years in Europe.
• Khair-al-Din (Barbarossa) captured Collo. *See 1514.*
• Lamu paid tribute to Portugal in Venetian currency.

1522

THE AMERICAS

• African slaves staged a revolt in Hispaniola.

The slave revolt on the island Hispaniola began in the town of Santo Domingo. The slaves were owned by Diego Columbus, Christopher Columbus' son. Diego Columbus was at the time serving as the governor of Hispaniola.

The slave revolt was put down with great severity. Indeed, some of the measures taken against the slaves were barbaric. Some of the Spaniards employed the mutilation of sex organs as a means of torturing the rebellious slaves. This practice so outraged the authorities that, in the aftermath of the rebellion, a law was passed which prohibited the "cutting off" of parts, "which out of decency cannot be named." *See 1540.*

AFRICA

• The Mamluks revolted in Fayoum and West Delta.

1523

THE AMERICAS

• African slaves accompanied Don Pedro de Alvarado in the conquest of Guatemala.

1524

AFRICA

• There was a rebellion against the Turks in Egypt.

1525

AFRICA

• African slaves were credited with saving their Spanish captors from the indigenous people of Chile while accompanying the explorers Almagro and Valdivia in Chile.
• Silver deposits were discovered at Tasco spurring the additional use of African slaves in American mines.

AFRICA

• Banu Saad captured Marrakesh (Morocco).
• Khair-al-Din (Barbarossa) extended the Turkish dominions in northern Africa.
• Mai Muhammed of the Kanem-Bornu Empire continued the war against the Bulala.

1526

THE AMERICAS

• The first slave revolt in the territory which would eventually be part of the United States took place in a Spanish settlement in what is present-day South Carolina (April 22). Lucas Vasquez de Ayllon, a Spanish explorer, had tried to establish a settlement in the Carolinas (San Miguel de Guadalupe near the mouth of the Pedee River). African slaves had been brought along to erect the settlement. They also took part in helping to build the first European ship built in the Americas. These African slaves are today considered to be the first known persons of African descent to have come into what is now the United States. Many of the settlers died of fever, including Allyon. After Allyon's death, the settlers returned to Hispaniola. However, a number of the African slaves fled the colony in November and lived with the Indigenous Americans.

While there is no recorded history of what happened to the African slaves who fled the Spanish colony, it is quite conceivable that they succeeded in living with the Indigenous Americans. The history of African and Indigenous American peoples is long and intertwined. Almost from the moment of introduction of the two peoples, a commonality of interest existed between them, namely fighting the oppression of the Europeans. This led to the establishment of a multitude of maroon communities throughout the Americas. "Maroons" was a loose description of self-liberated slaves who established camps amongst the Indigenous Americans or by themselves. From the perception of the Europeans, the maroons were outlaws who engaged in unlawful attacks upon plantations and towns. But from the perception of the Africans, they were "freedom fighters"—fighting to maintain their own freedom and to secure freedom for other Africans held in captivity. The word "maroon" is derived from the Spanish word "cimarrones," a term for self-liberated slaves.

• Africans accompanied Francisco Pizarro to Peru.

AFRICA

By the year 1526, the slave trade had begun to have a dramatic impact upon some of the African kingdoms which supplied the slaves. In 1526, the Kongo king, King Afonso, wrote a letter to his brother who was serving as a liaison to the Portuguese in Lisbon. In the letter, King Afonso noted that "we cannot reckon how great the damage is ... and so great ... is the corruption and licentiousness that our country is being completely depopulated."

EUROPE

• The Real Cedula prohibited the introduction into Nueva Espana (New Spain) of "Negros ladinos" (Africans who had lived for two years in Spain or Portugal).
• Saint Benedict the Black was born in San Fratello (near Messina) in Italy.

Saint Benedict the Black (1526–1589) became the patron saint of persons of African descent in the Americas. He was born to African parents who were slaves to a rich landowner. As was the custom throughout slavery, the parents of Saint Benedict took the name of their owner (Manasseri) as their own.

Saint Benedict's parents were Christians. Benedict's father was named Christopher. The Manasseris made Christopher the foreman over their other servants and promised him that his eldest son, Benedict, would be free. The baby Benedict grew up a sweet tempered, devout child. When he was ten years old he was called "The Holy Black" ("Il moro santo"), a nickname which stuck with him throughout his life.

One day, when Benedict was about twenty-one, he was hatefully abused by some of his neighbors who taunted him about his color and the status of his parents. Just at that time, a young man named Lanzi happened by. Lanzi had recently retired from the world to live the life of a monk in imitation of Saint Francis of Assisi. Lanzi was greatly impressed by the gentleness of Benedict's replies to his tormentors. Lanzi intervened and rebuked the mockers. He said, "You make fun of this poor black man now; but I can tell you that ere long you will hear great things of him." Lanzi befriended Benedict and soon thereafter, at Lanzi's invitation, Benedict sold his meager possessions and joined Lanzi and his fellow hermits.

Over the years, the hermits' domicile shifted from place to place until the hermits finally settled upon Montepellegrion near Palermo. It was here that Lanzi died. Upon his death, the hermits chose Benedict as their superior. It was an honor that Benedict did not seek and did not want but which he dutifully accepted.

When Benedict was thirty-eight, Pope Pius IV decreed that the hermits would have to disperse and join another order. Benedict chose to join the Friars Minor of the Observance, and was welcomed as a lay brother in the convent of Saint Mary near Palermo.

At first, Benedict was employed as a cook. He thoroughly enjoyed this position because it suited his retiring nature and gave him opportunities for little deeds of kindness. However, even in this obscure position, Benedict's extraordinary goodness could not long be hidden. According to Catholic authorities, Benedict's "face when he was in chapel often shone with an unearthly light, and food seemed to multiply miraculously under his hands."

In 1578, when the Friars Minor of the Observance held their meeting at Palermo, it was decided that the house of Saint Mary would be converted into a convent of the reform. The conversion necessitated the appointment of a very wise guardian. The choice of the friars was Benedict, even though he could neither read nor write. Once again, Benedict found himself appointed to a task which he did not seek and did not want but, in obedience to God, was obliged to accept.

The friars' choice turned out to be a wise one. Benedict proved to be an ideal superior. His judgment was sound and his admonitions were so tactfully and wisely given that while never resented they were always taken to heart.

Benedict's reputation for sanctity and miracles grew and spread throughout Sicily. When Benedict happened to venture out among the people, he found himself surrounded. Men and women struggled to touch his hand or to obtain a fragment of his habit as a relic.

Saint Benedict was made vicar of the convent and novice master. In these positions, Saint Benedict infused a sacred science which enabled him to expound upon the Holy Scriptures to the edification of priests and novices alike. His intuitive grasp of deep theological truths often astonished learned inquirers. According to the Church, it was known that he could read men's thoughts, and this power, coupled with great sympathy, made him a successful director of novices. Nevertheless, he was grateful when he was occasionally released from his duties and allowed to return to the kitchen. Even though it was clear that he was not just a cook any more.

Benedict's days were filled. All day long, he was besieged by visitors of all conditions—the poor demanding alms, the sick seeking to be healed, and distinguished persons requesting his advice or prayers. Though he never refused to see those who asked for him, he shrank from the praise and adulation. Benedict became so popular and so well known that it soon became difficult for him to travel without attracting a crowd. To conceal his identity when traveling about the countryside, Benedict began covering his face. He also began to confine his ventures outside the convent to the nighttime.

Throughout his life, Benedict continued the austerities of his hermit days. His one relaxation centered around food. On the subject of food, Benedict believed that the best form of mortification was not to deprive oneself of it, but rather to desist after eating a little. He also remarked that it was right to partake of food given in alms, as a token of gratitude and to give pleasure to the donors.

Upon his death, Saint Benedict was buried in the friary church in Palermo. In 1611, King Philip III of Spain donated a new shrine to the church in Palermo in order to house the remains of Saint Benedict. In 1743, Benedict the Black was beatified by Pope Benedict XIV and, in 1807, he was canonized by Pope Pius VII.

The feast day for Saint Benedict the Black is April 4. Saint Benedict the Black is the patron saint for all African Americans in North America and is the protector saint of Palermo, Italy.

1 5 2 7

THE AMERICAS

• Estevanico (Little Stephen), a Spaniard of African descent, accompanied the Narvaez expedition to Florida and the Mississippi region. Estevanico lived with Alvar Nunez Cabeza de Vaca among the Indigenous Americans for several years, and then travelled with de Vaca across Texas and Mexico to the Gulf of California, finally returning to Mexico City in 1536.

The Legend of Estevanico: In June 1527, Panfilo de Narvaez set sail from Spain with five ships and 600 men. He planned on an expedition which would explore and settle lands between Florida and Mexico. The expedition landed in Florida on April 14, 1528.

Seven months later, the expedition was deemed a bonafide failure. Narvaez, while dreaming of empire, was ineffectual at making decisions. After finding traces of gold, Narvaez split his party, sending the ships to the River of Palms (Rio Grande), while appointing a land force to find the allegedly rich city of Apalachen (near modern day Tallahassee, Florida).

Pressing on through "vast forests with astonishingly high trees," Narvaez's expedition found only tiny villages with naked Indigenous Americans, scantily fed on corn. Because supplies were running low, it soon appeared that the explorers would leave the "new world" only by dying.

After 16 days of labor without tools, some 260 survivors set out on makeshift boats with shirts for sails and stones for ballast. Worn out by bailing and half-crazed from drinking salt water, only one boat load made it ashore, far from the safety of the Spanish colonies. Narvaez himself was lost at sea.

*****

On July 24, 1536, four stragglers were brought to Mexico City by a Spanish slaving party. The four stragglers claimed to be members of the Narvaez expedition of 1527–28. The four self-proclaimed survivors included Cabeza de Vaca, Estevanico (also known as Esteban Dorantes) and two others.

The four men claimed to have survived slavery under the Indigenous Americans and starvation while 80 of their compatriots succumbed to cannibilism and disease. After six years of living naked and following seasonal foods as bearers for the Indigenous Americans, the four survivors escaped (1534). Posing as shamans (medicine men), they crossed the country, curing Indigenous Americans and attracting a crowd of followers looking for enlightenment from the "children of the sun."

The diary kept by de Vaca of the journey credited Estevanico as being the key member of the expedition who served as principal healer and as the liaison between the Spaniards and the Indigenous Americans the expedition encountered.

The survivors also told of a land north of Mexico that was "the best and all the most opulent countries"—a land that would come to be known as the "Seven Golden Cities of Cibola."

Despite their fabulous tale of golden cities, de Vaca and his Spanish companions were not so enamored as to want to return to the golden lands. As soon as they had recovered, they returned to Spain. However, Estevanico was not so fortunate. For all his efforts, Estevanico was rewarded by being sold to the Viceroy of Hispaniola, Antonio de Mendoza.

The viceroy kept Estevanico employed as a storyteller relating adventures and talking about the riches of Cibola. In 1538, Viceroy Mendoza organized an expedition to find the land of Cibola of which Estevanico spoke.

In 1539, while serving as an advance scout for the expedition led by Marcos de Niza near the Hawikuh Pueblo in what is today New Mexico, it was reported that Estevanico was killed by members of the Zuni Nation—but his body was never found. There are some who believe that Estevanico may have simply liberated himself to live among the Indigenous Americans in the new land he had explored for so long.

Regardless of his fate, Estevanico is today credited with being the first non–Indigenous American to traverse what is today the American Southwest.

• There was an African slave revolt in Puerto Rico.

• A Spanish law was enacted which required Africans to marry Africans.

• A major slave insurrection threatened Spanish headquarters in Mexico City. Viceroy Antonio de Mendoza reported that Africans "had chosen a King, and had agreed . . . to kill all the Spaniards . . . and that the Indigenous Mexicans were also with them." Concerned Spanish officials agreed to halt any further importation of Africans into Mexico pending the suppression of the revolt. For the time being, slave resistance had halted the African slave trade in at least one part of the Americas.

AFRICA

• Ahmad Gran (Ahmad Ibn Ibrahim) defeated the Ethiopian army of Lebna Dengel (Dauti [David] II) in Adal. Over the next few years, Lebna Dengel would become a virtual exile in the northern part of his own country while the Muslim armies ravaged Ethiopia.

EUROPE

• A former slave of the Archbishop of Tarragona crossed the Atlantic with his wife Francisca. *See 1510.*

1528

THE AMERICAS

• A Spanish expedition led by Panfilo de Narvaez landed near modern day Tampa Bay, Florida with 400 colonists, including the legendary Estevanico (April 14). By November 6, only a handful of stragglers would be alive and able to make it to Galveston Island in the Gulf of Mexico. *See 1527.*

By 1528, it is estimated that there were some 10,000 African slaves in the New World.

• A charter was granted to Enrique Eynger and Jeronomi Sayller for the purpose of allowing them to import up to 4,000 slaves to the West Indies over a four year period of time.

AFRICA

• There was an uprising against the Portuguese in eastern Africa. In retaliation, the Portuguese sacked Mombasa (Kenya).

1529

THE AMERICAS

• Slaves set fire to Santa Marta, the capital of Magdalena (northern Colombia).

AFRICA

• Askia Mohammed, of the Songhai Empire, was dethroned by his son Mussa.
• In 1529, Navarre (a kingdom of northeastern Spain) made a treaty with Morocco.
• Khair-al-Din (Barbarossa) recaptured Algiers. During his administration, a new port was constructed and the administration of the state was reorganized.

By 1529, the influence of the Ottoman Empire had reached as far as Algiers and the Ottoman Turks had come to dominate northern Africa.

1530

THE AMERICAS

• An Englishman, William Hawkins, visited the coast of Guinea and, after capturing several Africans, sailed for Brazil. In Brazil, Hawkins sold the Africans into slavery to become the first known English slave trader.

In 1530, the Portuguese began the colonization of Brazil.

• In 1530, there was a slave revolt in Mexico. In the aftermath of the revolt, the followers of the African insurgent, Ba ya No, were captured and sent back to Spain.

AFRICA

• By 1530, the Ottoman Turks had achieved a dominance over the Red Sea trade, threatening Ethiopia and the interests of the Portuguese traders.
• William Hawkins visited the coast of Guinea, capturing several Africans. *See above.*

By 1530, it is estimated that four to five thousand slaves were being shipped from the Kongo on an annual basis.

EUROPE

• By royal decree, only African slaves were to be sent to America. Mulattos, mestizos, Turks and Moors were prohibited from being sent from Spain as slaves.

1531

THE AMERICAS

• African slaves revolted in Panama.
• The Real Cedula, the royal Spanish edict which made the enslavement of IndigenousAmericans illegal, was proclaimed at Santiago.

AFRICA

• Ahmad Gran occupied Dawaro and Shoa.
• The Portuguese opened a market at Sena.

1532

THE AMERICAS

• Africans were with Pizarro in Peru during his conquest of the Incas. The African slaves carried Pizarro to the cathedral after he was assassinated.

Francisco Pizarro (1478–1541) was a Spanish conquistador. His conquest of the Inca Empire enabled Spain to colonize the major part of South America.

Pizarro was born in Trujillo, Spain. His father was a royal captain of infantry. Francisco's parents were never married and Francisco was raised by poor relatives of his mother.

In 1502, Pizarro left for the West Indies. He lived for a while on the island of Hispaniola, the main Spanish outpost in the New World.

In 1509, Pizarro left Hispaniola to take part in the exploration of the Caribbean coast of northern South America and southern Central America. He served as Vasco Nunez de Balboa's chief assistant when Balboa marched across the Isthmus of Panama to the Pacific Ocean see 1513.

For a time Pizarro remained in Panama and eventually became one of its wealthiest and most powerful citizens.

After a while, the Spaniards of Panama began hearing reports of a great Indigenous American kingdom located on the southern continent. In 1524, Pizarro went in search of this kingdom.

With the assistance of another Spaniard, Diego de Almagro, Pizarro began by sailing down the Pacific coastline. At first, bad weather and attacks from the Indigenous Americans prevented the voyagers from finding the great kingdom. But eventually, in the winter of 1527 (the summer of 1527 in the Southern Hemisphere) Pizarro found the kingdom in the highlands of what is today Peru.

The kingdom that Pizarro found was the great empire of the Incas. The Incas were the dominant people of the Southern Hemisphere. Their wealth of material goods attested to the Incas' power and their greatness.

Pizarro saw the wealth but did not respect the greatness of the Incas. Pizarro had a hunger for gold and gold is what the Incas possessed. Pizarro returned to Spain to report on his find, but he planned on a return to conquer the golden land.

The emperor Charles V appointed Pizarro governor of Peru. In 1531, Pizarro sailed from Panama City with about 180 men. They landed in what is now Ecuador. In 1532, Pizarro and his men founded the town of San Miguel (now Piura) in northern Peru.

Pizarro next advanced to Cajamarca, where the Inca ruler Atahualpa had gathered his forces. In a surprise attack with swords, horses, and a few guns, Pizarro's men captured Atahualpa and killed thousands of Incas. Pizarro promised to spare Atahualpa's life in return for vast riches.

The Incas were able to agree to the ransom because Peru had more silver and gold than any other part of the Americas. However, in 1533, despite receiving a large treasure as a ransom payment, Pizarro executed Atahualpa.

After the defeat of the Incas at Cajamarca, Pizarro marched southward to Cusco, the mountain capital of the Incas. After a brief struggle, the Spaniards took control of the city in 1533.

In 1535, Pizarro founded the city of Lima and made it Peru's capital. While Pizarro was governor many Spaniards settled in Peru in search of their own fortune. These settlers began mining great amounts of silver and gold and began to build many cities. However, the actual work of laboring in the mines and building the cities often rested on African slaves. While Pizarro was governor, African slaves were introduced to work the lucrative silver and gold mines of the region.

Using Peru as its base, Spain was able to conquer the rest of South America.

In the late 1530s, a dispute arose between Pizarro and Diego de Almagro over control of the mining area of Cusco. The dispute led to armed hostilities between the two Spanish camps. Pizarro's forces prevailed and, in 1538, executed Almagro. In 1541, the followers of Almagro's son killed Pizarro in retaliation.

1533

THE AMERICAS

• African slaves revolted in Cuba. The revolt occurred in the mines of Jobabo.
• The Germans Ehinger and Cuon imported African slaves into Mexico.

AFRICA

• Ahmad Gran captured Amhara, Lasta and other parts of Ethiopia.
• The French established an embassy in Morocco.

1 5 3 4

THE AMERICAS

• 200 Africans went with Alvarado on his expedition from Nicaragua to Quito in equatorial South America.
• Cabeza de Vaca, Estevanico and two other survivors of the Narvaez expedition escaped from six years of captivity among the Indigenous Americans.
• Rodrigo Contreras, governor of Nicaragua, received permission by a special decree to import two European (white) slaves.

In 1534, the Real Cedula authorized twenty licenses to import European (white) slaves into the West Indies. One of the licenses was granted to Domingo de Irala. The license also permitted him to carry with him 200 Africans to the Rio de la Plata.

AFRICA

• The Ottoman Turks seized Tunisia.

1 5 3 5

THE AMERICAS

• Pizarro was permitted to bring with him four European (white) slaves. *See 1534.*

AFRICA

• Charles V led the Spanish forces in taking Tunis. The Turkish garrison in control of Tunis escaped to Algiers—the domain of Barbarossa.
• A military agreement was reached between Algiers and France.
• Ahmad Gran seized Tigrai (Tigrey—a province in northern Ethiopia). In desperation, the ruler of Ethiopia appealed to Portugal for assistance.

EUROPE

• Luis Molina (1535–1600), a person of African descent, was born. Molina held the chair of moral theology at the University of Evora in Portugal. He is famous for his publication of *Liberi Arbitrii cum Gratiae Donis, Divina Praescientia, Providentia, Praedestinatione et Reprobatione Concordia* in 1588. In this work, Molina presented a novel approach to resolving the apparent contradiction between the doctrine of grace and free will.

1 5 3 6

THE AMERICAS

• Cabeza de Vaca, Estevanico and their two fellow survivors of the Narvaez expedition were found by a Spanish slaving party and returned to Mexico City where they told of their adventures and of the fabled Seven Cities of Gold of Cibola (July 24).

On July 24, 1536, four stragglers were brought to Mexico City by a Spanish slaving party. The four stragglers claimed to be members of the Narvaez expedition of 1527–28. The four self-proclaimed survivors included Cabeza de Vaca, Estevanico (also known as Esteban Dorantes) and two others. The four men claimed to have survived slavery under the Indigenous Americans and starvation while 80 of their compatriots succumbed to cannibalism and disease. After six years of living naked and following seasonal foods as bearers for the Indigenous Americans, the four survivors escaped (1534). Posing as shamans (medicine men), they crossed the country, curing Indigenous Americans and attracting a crowd of followers looking for enlightenment from the "children of the sun." The diary kept by de Vaca of the journey credited Estevanico as being the key member of the expedition who served as principal healer and as the liaison between the Spaniards and the Indigenous Americans the expedition encountered. *See 1527.*

• "Maestre Jorge" and his wife, Maria Lopez, and his son Jeronimo, received permission to return to Santo Domingo, where he had been a slave of the bishop.

Not all Africans who came to the Americas came in the holds of slave ships. Some came as willing immigrants seeking their fortunes in a new land. It is important to remember that by 1536, African slavery as an institution had existed in Portugal and Spain for almost one hundred years. Indeed, it is estimated that for a time during the mid–1500s, Africans constituted more than half of the population of Lisbon. *See 1474.* During this initial century of massive African slavery, it was inevitable that the color line between Africans and Europeans would be repeatedly crossed. By 1536, a number of Africans and persons of African descent (mulattoes) lived in Spain as free persons. However, having lived all their lives in Spain and having been Christianized, their culture was no longer African. They were the beginning of a new people—a new people who would perhaps find their destinies fulfilled in the new land.

• The first Africans arrived in Chile in the company of Diego de Almagro.

From 1536 to 1545, a series of slave insurrections occurred in Cartagena.

AFRICA

• Khair-al-Din (Barbarossa) was recalled to Constantinople to become commander-in-chief of the Turkish navy. Barbarossa was succeeded in Algiers by Hasan Agha.

1537

THE AMERICAS

• African slaves, used in the mines of Mexico, rebelled.

Between 1537 and 1670, a number of major slave rebellions would take place in Mexico. Rebellions would occur in 1546, 1548, 1570, 1608, and 1670.

In 1537, Africans in Mexico City were rumored to have a "king" who was enlisting Indigenous Mexicans to aid the slaves overthrow the Spanish.

• Pope Paul III declared that the indigenous people of the Americas were not to be enslaved.

EUROPE

• Alessandro de Medici, the mulatto duke of Florence believed to have been the son of Pope Clement VII, was assassinated. *See 1510.*

1538

THE AMERICAS

• Estevanico (Little Stephen), a Spaniard of African descent, served as a guide for Friar Marcos on an expedition searching for the Seven Cities of Cibola. Estevanico led the expedition from Mexico to the lands which now make up Arizona and New Mexico. In 1539, while leading an advance party of the expedition, Estevanico was reportedly captured and killed by Zuni Indigenous Americans who did not believe him when he said that he was the emissary of two Spanish explorers.

In 1538, the viceroy of Hispaniola organized an expedition to find the land of Cibola of

which Estevanico spoke. In 1539, while serving as an advance scout for the expedition led by Marcos de Niza, it was reported that Estevanico was killed by members of the Zuni Nation—but his body was never found. There are some who believe that Estevanico may have simply liberated himself to live among the Indigenous Americans in the new land he had explored for so long.

• The first Africans arrived in Bahia (Brazil). Father Nobrega protested their arrival and enslavement. But see 1557.

1539

THE AMERICAS

• Persons of African descent accompanied Hernando De Soto on his journey to the Mississippi. De Soto would claim Florida for Spain and would explore the Southeast. During his travels, de Soto made contact with (and made enemies of) the Creek, Hitchiti, Chickasaw, Chakchiuma, Choctaw, Tunica, Yuchi, Cherokee, and Alabama people. In 1541, De Soto died on the Mississippi River and Luis de Moscosco assumed command. De Soto was buried in the Mississippi River. It is reported that one of the Africans who accompanied De Soto stayed to live among the indigenous people of Alabama, thereby becoming one of the first permanent settlers of the Old World in what was to become the United States.

• Father Marcos de Niza, with Estevanico, led an expedition north of Mexico in search of the Seven Cities of Gold of Cibola (March 7). In June, Father Marcos received word that Estevanico had been killed while leading an advance scouting party. See 1527.

RELATED HISTORICAL EVENTS

• Lectures by Francisco de Vitoria in Spain advocated that Indigenous Americans were free men and should be exempted from slavery.

1540

THE AMERICAS

• The second settler in the Spanish territory which now comprises the State of Alabama was a person of African descent who was previously with DeSoto's expedition. The settler decided to live among the Indigenous Americans.

• In 1540, the Real Cedula again

prohibited the importation of mulatto and mestizo slaves. *See 1530.*

In 1540, the mutilation of the sex organs of cimarrones was prohibited in the West Indies. *See 1522.*

• Africans accompanied Alarcon and Coronado during their explorations of New Mexico and the American Southwest. Coronado was in search of the mythic Seven Cities of Cibola. During this expedition, Coronado encountered Hopi, Apache, Pawnee, Zuni, and Wichita people. The slaves often served as messengers to the indigenous people for the Spaniards.

By 1540, the annual importation of African slaves to the West Indies had reached 10,000 per year.

AFRICA

• In 1540, the Ottoman Turks increased their attacks on the coastal kingdoms of East Africa.
• Galawdewos (Claudius) became emperor of Ethiopia.

1541

AFRICA

• A Portuguese force of 400 men under the command of Cristovao da Gama (the son of Vasco da Gama) reached Massawa to aid Ethiopia in its war against the Turkish forces led by Ahmad Gran, the sultan of Adal, an ally of the Turks. The arrival of the Portuguese forces helped to equalize the use of firearms and the Muslim conquest of Ethiopia was temporarily repulsed.

1542

THE AMERICAS

• A Spanish law was enacted which prohibited Africans from going out at night.
• In 1542, it is estimated that ten percent of the African slaves on Hispaniola were living in maroon communities. At the time, there were 30,000 Africans on the island.

The Africans and the Arawaks: In recent years it has been discovered that the Arawak people did not entirely disappear from the face of the earth. Instead their destiny became combined with the destiny of the Africans who were brought to the Indies to replace them. Through a commingling of Arawak blood with the blood

of escaped African slaves, a remnant of the Arawak people and the Arawak culture still lives.

• It is estimated that, by 1542, there were over 100,000 African slaves in the West Indies.
• In Peru, Africans were used by the army against Diego Almagro.
• An agreement was reached between Hernando Cortes and the Genoese slave trader Leonardo Lomelin signed in Valladolid for 500 slaves.

AFRICA

• The occupied provinces of Ethiopia rose against Ahmad Gran. An indecisive battle was staged at Anasa. Cristovao da Gama, the leader of the Portuguese forces assisting the Ethiopians, was captured and executed. In October of 1542, the forces of Emperor Galawdewos, along with their Portuguese allies, would take the offensive against Ahmad Gran.

1543

AFRICA

• On February 21, Ahmad Gran was killed in a battle with the Portuguese and Ethiopian forces near Lake Tana. In the aftermath of the hostilities, 100 Portuguese families settled at Fremonat.
• The Wazir Abbas tried to form a Muslim state in Ethiopia.

EUROPE

• A royal decree prohibited the importation of Moors who had been converted from Islam to Christianity into the West Indies.

1544

AFRICA

• The Portuguese established a factory in Quelimane (Mozambique).

Quelimane is a port on the central part of the Mozambique coast. In the 18th and 19th centuries, Quelimane was notorious for being a major slave trading port.

• Hasan Pasha, the son of Barbarossa, became the governor (Beylerbey) of Algiers.

1545

AFRICA

• Morocco claimed the principal salt mines at Tegazza but the reigning emperor of the Songhai Empire refused to recognize the claim.

• Galawdewos (Claudius), the emperor of Ethiopia, defeated Wazir Abbas, thus preventing the conversion of Ethiopia to Muslim influences.

1 5 4 6

EUROPE

• In 1546, Juan Latino earned a degree from the University of Granada. *See 1516.*

1 5 4 8

THE AMERICAS

• In 1548, there was a slave revolt in the mines of Colombia. Twenty Spaniards were killed and hostages were taken. Another slave insurrection erupted in Honduras.

AFRICA

• The Portuguese established a settlement in Madagascar.
• In the Congo, the first Jesuit missionaries arrived. The missionaries consisted of three priests and a lay teacher.

1 5 4 9

AFRICA

• From 1549 to 1583, Daoud reigned as the Askia (Emperor) of the Songhai Empire. During his reign, the Songhai Empire extended from the Atlas Mountains to the forests of Cameroon. Daoud renewed agriculture and science but despite his efforts, the empire had entered a period of steady decline.
• The Saadi dynasty of Morocco began.

1 5 5 0

THE AMERICAS

• In Peru, there was another slave revolt. Slaves burned the town of Santa Marta on the Peruvian coast. In the wake of this uprising, an edict was issued which prohibited African slaves from being on the streets from 10:00 a.m. to 4:00 p.m.
• In Nicaragua, 250 African slaves were used in a rebellion against Spain.

AFRICA

• In 1550, the Songhai Empire continued its decline. Kanem-Bornu (the Bornu Empire in modern day Nigeria) captured the strategic market town of Air (located on the fringe of the Sahara) from the Songhai Empire. Additionally, the Hausa tributary states (in modern day Nigeria) staged a successful revolt.
• By 1550, 1500 slaves were being sent annually to Portugal from Guinea.
• Around 1550, the Lunda Empire was founded by Kibinda Ilunge.

Today, the Lunda people live in eastern Angola, the northwest region of Zambia and in southwestern Zaire. The Lunda Empire was noted for its collaboration with the Portuguese and its participation in facilitating the slave trade.

ASIA

• Malik Ambar, one of the great men of India, was born.

Malik Ambar (1550–1626) was born around 1550 in Harar, a province of Ethiopia. His Ethiopian name was Shambu and, aside from his Ethiopian name, little is known of his youth except that he was sold into slavery by Arabs. During his youthful enslavement, Shambu would be sold several times in such Arab cities as Hejaz, Mocha and Baghdad.

While in Mocha, Shambu's Arab owner, Kazi Hussein, came to recognize that his slave had certain intellectual abilities and decided to train him in the areas of finance and administration. As the relationship between Shambu and Hussein became stronger, Shambu became a Muslim and Hussein gave him the name Ambar.

When Hussein died, Ambar was sold to a slave dealer, who took him to India. Around 1575, Ambar was purchased by Chingiz Khan, the prime minister to Nizam mul-Mulk Bani — the king of Ahmadnagar. It is reported that Chingiz Khan was also of African origin and may very well have been a descendant of African mercenaries who served in India as early as the 1200s.

Chingiz Khan was impressed by Ambar's knowledge of Arabic, his loyalty, and his general intelligence. Seeking to solidify his control of the rather prominent (and mercenary) contingent of African (Habshi) slaves in the Deccan region, Chingiz Khan appointed Ambar as a key lieutenant with significant military and administrative responsibilities.

Ambar's future was for a time hopeful.

However, Chingiz Khan unexpectedly died, and Ambar was once again sold.

First Ambar was sold to the Shah of Golconda and later to the king of Bijapur. (Golconda and Bijapur were both kingdoms in the Deccan area of India.) Because of the training he had received from Kazi Hussein and Chingiz Khan, Ambar soon found favor with the king of Bijapur. So impressed was the king that he gave Ambar the title of Malik ("like a king").

While at Bijapur, Malik Ambar became a military commander. As a military commander, Malik Ambar was well respected by the Arab and African troops which were subject to his commands. Contrary to policy, Malik Ambar habitually promoted Arabs (as opposed to Indians) to position of authority. This practice led to a dispute between Malik Ambar and the king of Bijapur which resulted in Malik Ambar's desertion in 1590 from the service of the King.

Malik Ambar became a wild card mercenary. He attracted not only independent Arab and African warriors but also Deccani (Indian) warriors. Eventually, Malik Ambar built a personal (private) army of over 1,500 well-trained cavalrymen and infantrymen. These soldiers of fortune were employed in various conflicts by various rulers in India.

In 1595, the king of Ahmadnagar organized a Habshi (African) army and his wise counselor, the Habshi (African) prime minister Abhangar Khan, invited Malik Ambar and his men to join him.

The return of Malik Ambar to Ahmadnagar was providential. Malik Ambar's return provided the opportunity for him to become a great champion of the Deccanis (Hindu Indians) against the Mughuls (Muslim Indians). Malik Ambar and a Deccani, Mian Raju Dakhani, combined their military efforts on several occasions to repel attacks by the Mughuls. Although Malik Ambar and Mian Raju Dakhani would become political and military rivals, on this occasion they worked together to defend the province of Ahmadnagar from the Mughuls.

After repulsing the Mughuls, the rivalry between Malik Ambar and Mian Raju Dakhani came to the fore. Both men sought to usurp the throne of King Murtaza II. In 1602, Malik Ambar imprisoned Murtaza and named himself regent-minister. As regent minister, Malik Ambar repelled a series of Mughul attacks and prevented the Great Mughul, Emperor Akbar, from fulfilling his aim of conquering the Indian subcontinent.

By the time that Jahangir had succeeded Akbar as the Mughul emperor in 1605, Malik Ambar had established a capital at Kirkee and had become well entrenched in the Deccan. During all this time, Malik Ambar also fought off the ventures of his rival Mian Raju Dakhani. In 1607, Malik Ambar captured Raju and had him executed. After this act, Malik Ambar was the supreme lord of Ahmadnagar.

Upon consolidation of his power, Malik Ambar organized an estimated 60,000 horse army. His light cavalry was very effective as a mobile unit. Malik Ambar also enlisted the naval support of the Siddis (fellow Africans) of Janjira Island in 1616 in order to cut the Mughul supply lines and to conduct harassing missions.

The guerrilla tactics employed by Malik Ambar proved to be very successful against the Mughuls. On one occasion, the Mughul emperor Jahangir was moved to remark: "Ambar, the black-faced, who had himself in command of the enemy, continually brought up reinforcements till he assembled a large force. . . . It was deemed expedient to retreat and prepare for a new campaign."

Ambar built his greatest fortifications at Daulatabad to protect his kingdom from Prince Shah Jahan—the prince destined to become the next Mughul emperor. In 1621, Shah Jahan's forces launched an attack on Daulatabad. Surprisingly, the Mughul forces were defeated and forced to retreat after suffering heavy losses at the hands of Malik Ambar.

However, while this victory over the Mughuls was welcomed by Malik Ambar, it also brought the realization that he could not continue to resist without reinforcements. Seeking the support of the Deccani ruler, Ibrahim Adil Shah II, Malik Ambar had his daughter married to the Shah's favorite courtier. Additionally, his long and distinguished service in Golconda and Bijapur (along with their realization that Malik Ambar provided a buffer from the Mughuls for them) brought support from those kingdoms. For a time, Malik Ambar was able to continue to resist the power of the Mughuls.

Nevertheless, by the 1620s, Malik Ambar was having difficulty in maintaining the loyalty of his officers and forces. Almost continuous warfare for over a twenty-year period of time had demoralized the army and drained the local economy. Although he was never defeated, Malik Ambar died a besieged man in 1626.

Malik Ambar was succeeded as regent minister of the kingdom of Ahmadnagar by his son Fettah Khan. But Fettah Khan was not Malik Ambar. He was deposed in 1629. Thus ended the short but glorious reign of the Africans in the Deccan.

EUROPE

• The report of Leo Africanus (also known as Hassan Ibn Muhammed) to Pope Leo X was published in 1550. This report chronicled the travels of Leo Africanus throughout the African continent. It was published by Giovanni Battista Ramusio, a secretary in the Venetian government. Until the appearance of this report, most Europeans knew very little about the continent or its people. This ignorance was due to the fact that the Portuguese not only monopolized the slave trade but also monopolized any information concerning the continent. For various economic and political reasons, the Portuguese considered their knowledge of Africa to be a state secret and their African records were maintained in confidence in the state archives.

1551

THE AMERICAS

• Spanish Colonial Law No. 7 was enacted. The law read: "We prohibit ... free or enslaved (persons of African descent from using) the services of the indigenous people. This prohibition rises from the fact that many (persons of African descent) have mistreated their (Indigenous American) mistresses. The punishment for a slave will firstly be 100 lashes; secondly, have their ears cut off. If free, they will receive 100 lashes and secondly be perpetually exiled from the Spanish dominions. Those officials who denounce (betray) these (persons of African descent) will be given 10 pesos for their efforts."
• Spanish Colonial Law No. 15 was enacted. The law stated that no person of African descent, slave or free, would be allowed to carry any type of arms. The punishment for a first offense was the confiscation of the arms; for a second offense, 10 days in jail; and for a third offense, 10 lashes. If free, the person of African descent carrying arms would be expelled from the province.
• Afro-Cubans were prohibited from selling certain articles on the streets of Havana.

AFRICA

• The Ottoman Turks captured Tripoli (Libya).

• The first English merchants settled in Morocco.

1552

THE AMERICAS

In 1552, a new book was published which supported the claim made by the historian Pietro Martire d'Anghiera that a boat could travel from the Bahamas to Hispaniola "without compass or chart, guiding itself solely by the trail of dead [*indigenous people*] who had been thrown from ships." The new evidence appeared in *Brief Relations of the Destruction of the Indies*, a stinging attack on colonial practices in the New World written by Bartolome de Las Casas, a member of the Dominican Order of Friars. De Las Casas was best known for drafting Spain's New Laws (1542–43), which called for the eventual abolition of encomienda—the colonial system of enslaving the indigenous populations. However, by 1552, the practice of encomienda had crept back into favor, and the new Las Casas book was a plea for its end.

Las Casas wrote from firsthand experience. The son of a merchant who traveled on Columbus' second voyage to the New World, Las Casas joined Spain's 1502 expedition to the West Indies. In the West Indies, Las Casas became so appalled by the cruelty the Spanish troops showed toward the indigenous people that he began the campaign for reform that became his life's work. After entering the Dominican order in 1523, Las Casas sought to convert Indigenous Americans to Christianity and to improve their status in the eyes of their conquerors. His efforts earned Las Casas the title of "protector of the Indians."

However, from an African American perspective, Las Casas was an initiator of great misery rather than a benefactor. Las Casas' efforts to liberate the indigenous people of the Americas led to the institution of African slavery and the mass importation of African slaves. The African slaves were needed to replace the indigenous labor force Las Casas befriended and liberated. The mass importation of African slaves ultimately led to the untimely termination of millions of innocent African lives, the decimation of cultures, and the devastation of the indigenous cultures of three continents (Africa and North and South America).

• There was a slave insurrection in Panama and a slave uprising in Venezuela.

AFRICA

• The first Jesuit mission departed from the Congo. *See 1548.*
• Salah Rais became the Beylerbey of Algiers.

1 5 5 3

THE AMERICAS

• In the woods near Nombre de Dios, Panama, a number of maroon communities arose. The population of cimarrones (escaped slaves) was estimated at about 800.
• In Peru, an uprising of African slaves lasted for over a year. The main event associated with the uprising was the Battle of Pucara.
• By 1553, there were an estimated 20,000 Africans in Mexico.

AFRICA

• A fleet of British ships arrived in Africa. The British, under the command of Captain Windham, came in contact with the people of Benin. In Benin, they traded for ivory, palm oil and other goods. Also in Benin, the Dutch began their participation in the slave trade.

EUROPE

• Africans were utilized during the Spanish Civil War.

The use of Africans in the Spanish Civil War would be the forerunner for an expanded use of African people in European wars—a use which would continue through modern times.

1 5 5 4

THE AMERICAS

• Africans participated in rebellions in Honduras and Guatemala.

AFRICA

• A Songhai expedition to take Katsina (a town in northern Nigeria) was aborted.
• Fez (a city in northern Morocco) was captured by the Sharifs of Morocco.

1 5 5 5

THE AMERICAS

• Three expeditions were carried out against the cimarrones of Panama. *See 1553.*
• In Peru, a slave revolt was led by Bayano.
• In Santiago, Chile, a free African Spaniard was reported as owning land within the town.

AFRICA

• An English expedition to West Africa returned with a cargo of 400 pounds of gold and 250 ivory tusks. This cargo represented a windfall profit for the English as it multiplied the investment in the expedition many times over. The success of expeditions such as this one, soon prompted other English mariners to voyage to Africa to seek their fortunes. Indeed, in 1561, Queen Elizabeth I herself invested in the African trade and made a profit of 1000 pounds. *See 1562.*
• Fremonat was founded by Father Andrea de Oviedo.

1 5 5 6

THE AMERICAS

• In Panama, the Spaniards were forced to travel in groups of twenty men out of fear of the African slaves. At the time, the ratio of Africans to Europeans was approximately 15 to 1.
• In Mexico, the viceroy complained that the presence of 20,000 Africans, together with the mestizos (people of European and Indigenous American blood or African and Indigenous American blood), endangered the safety of the Spaniards.

AFRICA

• The Ottoman Turks captured Tripoli, defeating the Knights of Malta.
• Diogo I of the Kongo was defeated by the Ngola.

Diogo I was the grandson of Afonso I. Afonso I was succeeded by Pedro I but Pedro I was overthrown and Diogo assumed the throne. Upon his ascension, Diogo immediately attempted to restrict the activities of the Portuguese within his realm.

In 1555, Diogo I evicted the Portuguese traders but this eviction had little effect because the traders merely relocated to nearby Sao Tome.

• The Ngola sent an ambassador to Portugal requesting missionaries.

EUROPE

• Noted for his quick wit, his musical talent, and his charm, Juan Latino received a master of arts degree from the University of Granada in 1556. *See 1516.*

——— 1557 ———

THE AMERICAS

• Manuel de Nobrega, a Jesuit priest, denounced Indigenous American slavery upon his arrival in Brazil, but eventually accepted African slavery for the good of the colony, and the good of the Jesuit order.

AFRICA

• The Turks seized Massawa (Mits'iwa) and Arkiko (in today's Eritrea). The monks at Debra Damo were massacred. The people of Tigre (a northern province of today's Ethiopia which borders on Eritrea) staged a mass resistance and succeeded in driving the Turks back.
• The Portuguese captured Zaila (Zeila).

——— 1558 ———

AFRICA

• By 1558, Barbary piracy had become a well established institution. In 1558, thirty-five galleys and twenty-five brigantines were engaged in piracy operating out of the port of Algiers.
• Mozambique replaced Sofala as the Portuguese East African capital.

——— 1559 ———

AFRICA

• Phillip II of Spain sent a fleet of German, Italian and Spanish ships to take Algiers. The fleet was utterly destroyed by the Turks.
• Harar attacked Ethiopia. The Ethiopian Emperor Galawdewos (Claudius) was killed in battle. Galawdewos was succeeded by Minas.

——— 1560 ———

THE AMERICAS

In the 1550s, maroons frequently attacked the treasure caravans which traveled across the Isthmus of Panama. Indeed, during this time a de facto government developed amongst the self-liberated Africans. The leader of this rebel government was Bayano and one of the cities which his followers founded is San Diego de Principe.

In 1560, the Spanish colony started a campaign against the maroon communities. The Spaniards eventually captured Bayano and sent him to Spain.

• By 1560, on the island of Hispaniola, the ratio of Africans to Europeans had become 15 to 1.
• In 1560, there were 17,000 Africans in Mexico about the same as the number of Europeans.

AFRICA

• Around 1560, the first Jesuit missions were established in Mozambique.
• Farima, the first Mani king of Loko, began his reign.

——— 1561 ———

AFRICA

• In 1561, an Anglo-French fleet began trading on the West African coast.

——— 1562 ———

THE AMERICAS

• John Hawkins, an Englishman, visited Guinea (Sierra Leone today), loaded his ship with 300 African slaves, and carried the slaves from Portuguese Africa to Spanish America (Hispaniola). Despite the existence of a Spanish law which restricted the slave trade to Spanish ships, Hawkins was able to sell the slaves to the Spanish planters. Hawkins returned to England with a rich cargo of sugar, ginger, hides and pearls. The large profits Hawkins (and Queen Elizabeth I) reaped from this voyage sparked England's involvement in the slave trade.

In 1562, the English passed an act which legalized the purchase of Africans. The passage of this act is deemed to be the first official English sanction of the slave trade.

The initial sanction of an institution of slavery did not immediately result in the wholesale participation of the English in the slave trade. At the time, England did not have any American colonies and the Spanish and Portuguese were hostile to the notion of English interference with their enterprise. Thus, during the better part of the 1500s,

England's participation in the slave trade was sporadic.

AFRICA

• The Mossi Empire attained a level of sophistication in governance.

The Mossi began as a people who lived inland from the Gulf of Guinea. In the eleventh and twelfth centuries the Mossi formed two kingdoms which developed into a rather unique form of governance.

The Mossi are of interest because their form of government was widely repeated throughout Africa—even up to this day. The Mossi Empire had four vassal kingdoms in addition to the main kingdom of the emperor. In the emperor's kingdom, there were five provinces whose governors made up the imperial council and were the chief officers of state. Associated with the council were eleven ministers who administered the army, religious ceremonies and practices, musicians and tax collecting. The Mossi Empire did not make extensive conquests, but at one time the Mossi did attack Timbuktu and resisted the expansionism of Sonni Ali.

Today, the Mossi people reside in the nation of Burkina Faso, one of Africa's poorest and least developed countries.

• Beginning in 1562, there were annual voyages from England to the coast of West Africa by "interlopers."
• Between 1562 and 1591, the Ottoman Turks conducted a series of raids on the coastal kingdoms of East Africa.

1563

THE AMERICAS

• Pursuant to a Spanish colonial law, those Spaniards who had children by African slaves and who now wished to purchase their children in order to grant them manumission, were to be given preference over other buyers.

AFRICA

• By 1563, the Galla controlled a third of Ethiopia.

The Galla (also called the Wallo Galla) are considered part of the Oromo ethnic group of Ethiopia. The Galla are a northern subgroup of the Oromo who during the 1700s came to dominate the imperial court of Ethiopia.

• Sarsa Dengel became king of Ethiopia.

Sarsa Dengel was merely a child when he succeeded his father as Emperor of Ethiopia and his country was in turmoil as the Galla insurgents staged a massive rebellion. Such turmoil would mark the reign of Sarsa Dengel throughout his thirty-four year reign.

• Father Gouveia of the Society of Jesus (the Jesuits) recommended that Portugal annex Ndongo (Angola) in order to convert it to Christianity.

1564

THE AMERICAS

• On John Hawkins' voyages in this year and in 1567, Hawkins again acquired slaves in Africa, transported them to Spanish America, and illegally sold them to Spanish planters in the West Indies. Although she officially denied approval of any English participation in the slave trade, Queen Elizabeth I appears to have financially benefited from Hawkins' voyages. The queen even authorized Hawkins to include the figure of a bound African in his coat of arms.

AFRICA

• The French established a consulate at Algiers.

1565

THE AMERICAS

Persons of African descent were present for the founding of St. Augustine, Florida. The introduction of 500 African slaves was specifically authorized by King Felipe II (Philip II). The African slaves comprised a group of artisans and agriculturists who accompanied Spanish Admiral Pedro Menendez de Aviles when he founded the new settlement (August 28). St. Augustine would grow to become the first permanent European settlement in North America.

• In 1565, the smoking of tobacco was introduced to England by John Hawkins. Hawkins was a slave trader. Most of his dealings were with the Spanish in the West Indies. However, in 1564, he visited the French colony on the St. Johns River in Florida. It was there he learned to smoke tobacco from the French colonists who themselves had learned from the Native Americans. Hawkins returned to England with a shipload of tobacco.

AFRICA

• East Africa was claimed by Portugal as Portuguese Territory.

ASIA

• Beginning in 1565, there was regular trade between the Spanish colonies of Mexico and the Philippines. This trade would be conducted for 250 years during which time, inevitably, the Spanish would introduce the people of the Philippines to Africans.

EUROPE

• In 1565, Juan Latino was honored when he was selected to open the school year at the University of Granada with a Latin oration. *See 1516.*

1 5 6 7

THE AMERICAS

• The City of Rio de Janeiro (Brazil) was founded.

AFRICA

• The Galla, the conquerors of Ethiopia, devastated Harar.

1 5 6 8

THE AMERICAS

• A Spanish colonial law was enacted which forbade mulattoes (persons of African and European lineage) from carrying arms.

AFRICA

• Jaga (Yaka) warriors invaded the Kongo.

The invasion of the Kongo by the Jaga warriors prompted the Kongo King Alvere I to request assistance from the Portuguese traders who had been exiled to Sao Tome. The Portuguese responded by sending 600 soldiers who helped to drive out the Jaga. However, after the task was completed the Portuguese refused to leave. In essence, the Portuguese traders came to control the kingdom. This usurpation of his authority led Alvere I to request that his kingdom be incorporated into Portugal. This request was denied. Alvere also asked for missionaries in an effort to ameliorate the detrimental impact of the Portuguese traders. However, these requests also met with little success.

• The Turks raided Cambo in East Africa.

1 5 6 9

THE AMERICAS

• Audencia Real of Lima, Peru, ordered a curfew for African slaves. African slaves were not permitted to carry arms. They were also prohibited from being served by either male or female Indigenous Americans. There were severe penalties (lash and pillory) for violation of the rules.

AFRICA

• Francisco Barreto led an abortive expedition against Monomotapa (Zimbabwe).
• The English established a consulate in Algiers.
• The Portuguese began construction of a fort at Mombasa.
• Cambo, after a series of Turkish raids, agreed to accept Turkish "protection."
• There was a revolt in Harar (Ethiopia).

RELATED HISTORICAL EVENTS

In 1569, Gerardus Mercator developed a map of the world which was deemed indispensible to explorers. Mercator's map was a cylindrical projection which showed all lines of longitude as parallel. Although the map distorted the size of land masses in the far north and south, it simplified navigation by showing a constant compass direction as a straight line.

However, from an Afro-centric perspective, Mercator's map gave Europeans a false understanding of the world and their relationship to it. The distortions created by the map center on two aspects (1) the exaggeration of the land area of the Northern Hemisphere and (2) the concept that the Northern Hemisphere is the top of the world when in actuality the position of the Northern Hemisphere is relative to one's position in space.

The distorted perceptions created by the Mercator map may have psychologically contributed to the false sense of self importance found throughout much of Euro-centric thought.

1 5 7 0

THE AMERICAS

• The maroons of Panama founded the town of Santiago del Principe. *See 1560.*
• The Real Cedula prohibited African slaves that had been married in Spain from being carried to the Americas without their wives and children.
• Accompanying Juan Ortiz de Zarate on

his expedition to the Rio de la Plata in Argentina was "un portuguese mulato marinero"—a mulatto Portuguese sailor.

• In 1570, there were 18,535 Africans and 1,465 Afro-mestizos in Mexico. However, it was also believed that there were some 2,000 cimarrones who were living outside the law and were, therefore, uncountable.

AFRICA

• The most famous of the kings of Bornu, Idris Alooma (Aloma), ascended to the throne. Under Idris, who ruled as Idris III, the empire of Bornu would reach its heights. Mai (King) Idris Alooma, "the learned, just, courageous, and pious Commander of the Faithful," ruled over Kano, the Air, Kanem, and land south of Lake Chad.

• Zimba ravaged the country near the river Zambesi.

• The Galla continued their march through Ethiopia, taking Amhara and Begember.

• For the next hundred years, Katsina and Kano would be engaged in a bitter struggle for control of the Saharan trade.

1571

THE AMERICAS

• A Spanish colonial law was enacted which listed punishments for escaped slaves. The punishments were: (1) absent four days, 50 lashes; (2) absent eight days, 100 lashes and compulsory wearing on his neck for two months a ball and chain weighing 12 pounds; (3) four months absence, 200 lashes; (4) a second long absence, exile. Additionally, those finding an escaped slave were obliged to declare the slave's presence within three days or be fined 20 gold pieces. The principal leaders of escaped slaves were to be put to death. The owners of escaped slaves were obligated to pay the costs of recapture.

By the 1570s, one in every ten slaves in Mexico was living a free life in hiding, usually amongst the Indigenous Mexicans. Alarmed by the situation, Viceroy Martin Enriquez wrote to the king of Spain: "Your Majesty, . . . the time is coming when these *African* people will have become masters of the *Indigenous Mexicans,* inasmuch as they were born among them and their maidens, and are men who dare to die as well as any Spaniard in the world. . . . I do not know who will be in a position to resist them."

• In 1571, a Spanish law was enacted which imposed a dress code upon women of African descent. The law prohibited both free and slave African women (as well as mulatto women) from wearing gold, pearls, or silk. However, if an African woman was married to a Spaniard she was allowed to wear gold earrings with pearls, and a small necklace.

AFRICA

• The Portuguese campaigned in the Congo against Jaga. This campaign led to the virtual military occupation of the Congo by the Portuguese.

• Francisco Barreto conducted a military expedition against Manica of Monomotapa (Zimbabwe).

• Idris Alooma, the Mai of Kanem-Bornu, introduced firearms as an instrument of warfare between African people.

EUROPE

• A French royal declaration, reconfirmed in 1607, prohibited slavery: "All persons are free in this kingdom; as soon as a slave has reached these frontiers and becomes baptized, he is free."

1572

THE AMERICAS

• Pursuant to Spanish colonial law, African mestizos (persons of African and Indigenous American lineage) were compelled to pay the same tribute as "pure-blood" indigenous people of the Americas.

AFRICA

• An epidemic in Algiers killed one third of the population of the city.

• The Portuguese Augustinians opened a school at Elmina (Ghana).

• The Jaga, the invaders of the Kongo, were routed by the Portuguese.

1573

THE AMERICAS

• Bartolome de Albornoz, professor of law at the University of Mexico, wrote an attack on the methods of enslavement of persons of African descent and on the injustice of selling them.

AFRICA

• Don John of Austria attacked Tunis.

EUROPE

• Juan Latino, professor of poetry at the University of Granada during the reign of Philip II published a poem praising the king upon his return from the Battle of Lepanto. This historical poem would predate the historical poetry of Shakespeare by twenty years.

———— 1574 ————

THE AMERICAS

• A Spanish colonial law was enacted which required all free Africans and mulattoes to pay tribute to the king of Spain. Provincial officials determined the amount according to the wealth of the estates of the Africans and mulattoes.

In 1574, a Spanish colonial law was enacted concerning escaped slaves. The law provided that "(1) if the apprehender of an escaped slave was himself a slave, the apprehender's enslaver acquired the escaped slave; (2) if the informer was a cimarrone (an escaped slave), the local justice owed the cimarrone a reward; (3) if an escaped slave was killed, the person who killed the slave would receive 50 pesos; (4) if the slave could prove that he accompanied another slave involuntarily, the slave was merely sent back to his enslaver; (5) an escaped slave who fled but later brought another escaped slave back with him when he returned was freed; (6) for each additional slave an escaped slave brought back with him, he would receive 20 pesos per slave; (7) if an African or a mulatto counseled a slave to hide for four months so that the African or mulatto could bring in the escaped slave for a reward, the African or mulatto would be put to death; (8) those Africans or mulattoes who hid slaves received the same penalty as the escaped slave; and (9) a slave could be a bounty hunter provided that he had the permission of the local justice as well as the permission of his owner."

AFRICA

• The Portuguese aborted their military campaigns to seize Ceuta and Tangier.
• Vasco Fernandes Homem staged an expedition to Manica (Zimbabwe).
• Mozambique, a Portuguese stronghold, was razed by African forces.
• Tunis was captured by the Turks.
• Paulo Diaz, grandson of Bartolomeo Diaz, the explorer, visited Angola and was deeply impressed with the high culture of the inhabitants. In this same year, the Portuguese established a colony in Angola.

The Portuguese establishment of a colony in Angola would result in a thirty-year war with the native Angolans. Abundu and Imbangala resisted Portuguese attempts to seize fertile lands and silver mines along with the abduction of thousands for the slave trade.

———— 1575 ————

THE AMERICAS

• Between 1575 and 1591, 52,053 slaves were exported to Brazil from Angola.

AFRICA

• Ralamba, the Merina (Indonesian heritage) ruler of Madagascar, increased his dominions.

———— 1576 ————

THE AMERICAS

• By 1576, there were an estimated 40,000 African slaves in South America.

AFRICA

• African forces destroyed the Portuguese fort at Accra (Ghana).

Today Accra is the capital and main port of Ghana.

———— 1577 ————

THE AMERICAS

• In Chile, a slave code was decreed.

AFRICA

• Ethiopians recaptured Harar thereby ending the Harari sultanate. A new sultanate would arise in Aussa.
• The first Dominican mission was dispatched to Mozambique.

———— 1578 ————

THE AMERICAS

• English sea captain, Francis Drake, explored the California coast, making contact with the Miwoks.

During this voyage of Sir Francis Drake, Drake stopped in Lima, Peru. Drake's visit terrorized the Spanish authorities and also inspired the African slaves to stage a revolt.

AFRICA

• In June of 1578, Dom Sebastiao, the King of Portugal, led a force of 500 ships and 17,000 men against Morocco. On August 4, Dom Sebastio was defeated and killed at the Battle of Kasr-al-Kabir (Alcazar). Along with Dom Sebastio, 8,000 Portuguese lost their lives. Of the total contingent of 17,000, only 100 would return to Portugal. After this battle, the Portuguese domination of Morocco rapidly declined.

In an exercise of global politics, Queen Elizabeth I supplied the Moroccan forces of Abu al-Abbas Ahmad I with arms in their fight against the Portuguese.

The provision of these arms, led to a commercial treaty between England and the Ottoman Turks. Additionally, England was granted certain privileges by Ottoman Sultan Murad III.

• Ahmad al-Mansur became Sultan of Morocco.
• From 1578 through 1585, Sir Francis Drake not only wreaked havoc on the Spanish seas of the Americas, he also caused chaos on the Portuguese dominated west coast of Africa. He was, with little dispute, the most prominent pirate of his time.
• The Ethiopians defeated the Turks by taking the fortress at Dabarwa.

EUROPE

• In 1578, when the Friars Minor of the Observance held their meeting at Palermo, it was decided that the house of Saint Mary would be converted into a convent of the reform. The conversion necessitated the appointment of a very wise guardian. The choice of the friars was Benedict, an African who could neither read nor write. This Benedict would later become known as Saint Benedict the Black. *See 1526.*

────── **1 5 7 9** ──────

AFRICA

• War erupted between the Ngola and the Portuguese in Angola.

────── **1 5 8 0** ──────

THE AMERICAS

• The Dutch visited the coast of Guiana.

This visit was a precursor to the establishment of a Dutch colony in South America.
• In 1580, there were 18,500 Africans and 1,500 Afro-mestizos counted in Mexico.

AFRICA

• The Portuguese launched an offensive against the Ngola using an army comprised mostly of Africans.
• From 1580 to 1590, in Mozambique, the Makua revolted.

Today, the Makua are an ethnic group comprising two groups living along the lower Zambezi River and on the northeastern coasts of Mozambique. The Makua have adopted many Arab customs.

In 1582, the Makua defeated the Portuguese along the Mozambique coast.

Today there is considerable animosity between the Makua and the Makonde who, during colonial times, raided the Makua for slaves. This animosity was used by the Portuguese during Mozambique's War of Independence (1964–1974) to deprive the FRELIMO (Liberation Front of Mozambique) army of members by claiming that FRELIMO was dominated by the Makonde.

RELATED HISTORICAL EVENTS

In 1580, Spain invaded and conquered Portugal. The Spanish conquest of Portugal was a significant event in African American history because it placed the source and the market for slaves under the auspices of Spain, thereby eliminating the all too often expensive intermediary middlemen and making the expansion of the slave trade more economically feasible.

Nevertheless, given the knowledge and contacts possessed by the Portuguese concerning the African slave market, the privilege of importing slaves to the New World continued to be the province of Portuguese slave traders.

────── **1 5 8 1** ──────

RELATED HISTORICAL EVENTS

On July 26, 1581, the Federal Republic of the United Provinces (of Holland) formally declared their independence from Spain. The emergence of the Dutch would have a profound impact upon Africans and African Americans throughout the world. *See 1619.*

1584

AFRICA

• The Ottoman Empire (the Turks) attempted to seize the Zanzibar Coast from Portugal. However, the Turkish forces were defeated by the Portuguese Admiral Thome de Sousa Coutinho.

Africa and the Continuation of the Crusades: The Crusades were Christian military expeditions organized mainly to recapture Palestine during the Middle Ages. Palestine, also called the Holy Land, was important to Christians because it was the region where Jesus Christ had lived. Palestine lay along the eastern coast of the Mediterranean Sea, and Muslims had taken control of it from Christians.

The crusaders, who came from Western Europe, organized eight major expeditions between A.D. 1096 and 1270. This was also a period when Western Europe was expanding its economy and increasing its military forces. The Crusades were, therefore, a part of a broad Christian expansion movement.

Despite two hundred years of effort, the Western European forces were unsuccessful in wresting Palestine from the Muslims. Then, in 1453, the Muslim Ottoman Empire established itself as the dominant power not only in the Middle East but also on the Mediterranean. The struggle between the forces of Christianity and the forces of Mohammed was once again a focus of Western Europe. In a very real sense, the Crusades lived on albeit with a different objective.

The new objective was the markets of the Far East. In the 1400s, access to the markets of the Far East were controlled by Muslims. It was this lack of access to the markets of the Far East which prompted Columbus to sail west in search of the Indies and which prompted the Portuguese to explore the coastline of Africa.

By the 1500s, the east coast of Africa had become the battlefield for the continuation of the Crusades. Up and down the coastline of East Africa, first Arab Muslims and later Ottoman Turks would battle first Portuguese and later other "Christian" Europeans for control of the African seaports which made possible European access to the Far East. In a number of encounters which hauntingly remind us of the Cold War conflicts on the African continent that were to follow in the late 1900s, the Muslim and Christian forces would fight proxy wars for control of the East African seaboard.

1585

AFRICA

• The Ottoman Empire and the Bornu Empire (Kanem-Bornu) exchanged diplomats and military personnel. In this year, Kanem-Bornu, under Mai Idris Alooma would be at the height of its influence.
• The sultan of Morocco seized the salt mines of Taghaza from the Songhai Empire.
• Swahili towns of East Africa revolted against the Portuguese in alliance with the Turkish adventurer Amir Ali Bey.
• The Portuguese moved inland up the Zambesi River and penetrated the empire of Mwanamutapa in the northern part of the country. The Portuguese founded settlements on the Middle Zambesi at Sena and Tete, and used these sites increasingly as bases from which to interfere with the affairs of the Mwanamutapa king.
• The warfare between the Angolans and the Portuguese continued. In 1585, the Angolans would badly defeat the Portuguese. But the victory was short lived. The continuous nature of the Portuguese conflicts with the Angolan kingdom of Ndongo would lead to Ndongo's ruin.

By 1585, the Dutch, English, and French began to compete with the Portuguese and Spanish for overseas treasure, trade and conquest. The addition of these European nations would add to the mosaic of both Africa and the Americas.

1586

THE AMERICAS

Between 1586 and 1655, more than 13,000 Africans slaves would be imported into Buenos Aires, Argentina. However, this number did not satisfy the demand. Throughout the 1600s, appeals from Argentinian officials for additional African slaves would be repeatedly voiced.

The influence of Africans upon Argentina can not be underestimated. By the end of the 1600s, one third of the population of Argentina was composed of African slaves.

• Sir Francis Drake attacked San Domingo City and secured an enormous ransom. The attack of Drake and other "adventurers" ("pirates") would eventually destroy the commerce between San Domingo (Hispaniola) and Spain.

AFRICA

• In Ethiopia, Sarsa Dengel led an expedition against Enarya.

1 5 8 7

AFRICA

• A Zimba horde wrecked Kilwa. 3,000 of the 4,000 inhabitants of Kilwa were killed and some were eaten. The Portuguese fleet was called in to put down the rebellion.

The Zimba are a subgroup of the Chewa people. Today the Chewa people live in eastern Zambia, the Tete district of Mozambique and southern Malawi.

1 5 8 8

AFRICA

• The Zimba reached Mombasa. The Amir Ali Bey of the Ottoman Turks attacked Mombasa by sea. Tome de Sousa repelled the attack by the Turks but failed to stop the Zimba. Mombasa fell and was sacked. The Zimba then attacked Malindi. At Malindi, the Zimba forces were annihilated by the Portuguese and the Segeju.
• By 1588, Portuguese factories were established at Cacheu, Lagos, Warri, New and Old Calabar and on the Cameroon River.

EUROPE

• Luis de Molina, an Afro-Portuguese theologian, published *Liberi Arbitrii cum Gratiae Donis, Divina Praescientia, Providentia, Praedestinatione et Reprobatione Concordia*, a body of work in which the term "scientia media" was first formulated. *See 1535.*

RELATED HISTORICAL EVENTS

• The Spanish Armada was defeated. Out of an original 130 ships and 30,000 men only 65 vessels and 10,000 men would return to Spain.

The defeat of the Spanish Armada was a pivotal point in world history and in the history of African Americans. The defeat of the Spanish Armada opened the way for the English colonization of the American continent and the English colonization of the American continent, in turn, led to the development of the peculiar institution of American slavery.

1 5 8 9

AFRICA

• Morocco ceded Arzila to Spain.

EUROPE

• Saint Benedict the Black, the patron saint of African Americans in North America and the protector of Palermo, died. Upon his death, Saint Benedict was buried in the friary church in Palermo. *See 1526.*

1 5 9 0

THE AMERICAS

• Simon Bolivar obtained authorization to import 3,000 African slaves.

AFRICA

• The Moroccan army under Judar Pasha invaded and seized Songhai.
• The Portuguese were defeated by the allied forces of the Jaga, Kongo, Matamba and Ndongo.

1 5 9 1

AFRICA

• The Songhai Empire was defeated by a Moroccan army at the Battle of Tondibi.

The Moroccan army which defeated the Songhai Empire at the Battle of Tondibi included a contingent of 3,000 Spanish mercenaries carrying muskets. Led by a man named Judar (Judar Pasha), the Spanish used their superior firepower to deadly effect. The forces of the Songhai, using bows and arrows, were helpless against the powder and shot and armor of the Moroccan forces.

Askia Ishak, the Askia (emperor) of Songhai, offered his terms of surrender. The terms were referred to Morocco by Djouder (Judar) Pasha.

The Songhai Empire was soon to be no more.

The greatest concession was that Timbuktu, the great learning center of the Songhai which was founded in the eleventh century became Muslim under Moroccan rule.

Between 1591 and 1748, the Moroccan Pashas ruled the once great Timbuktu. During their 157-year reign, there would be some 150 pashas to rule over Timbuktu.

• 1591 saw the beginning of a period of Portuguese raids on the kingdoms of Angola.

Duarte Lopes, an emissary from Philip II of Spain and Portugal, was sent to the Congo. Upon his return, he related his experiences to both the king and a papal official by the name of Filippo Pigafetta. Pigafetta subsequently published Lopes' account.

1 5 9 2
AFRICA

• A Portuguese factory was established in Zanzibar.
• A Portuguese force from Sena and Tete was routed by the Zimba.

1 5 9 3
AFRICA

• Fort Jesus at Mombasa (Kenya), the greatest of all the Portuguese citadels on the east coast of Africa, was begun. It would be completed in 1639.
• The Portuguese were once again routed by the Zimba.
• 1,200 slaves were sent across the Sahara to join the Moroccan army.

1 5 9 4
AFRICA

• The Portuguese established a customs house in Mombasa.

1 5 9 5
THE AMERICAS

• In 1595, a license to import slaves was granted to Gomez Reynal. Over the course of nine years, Reynal was to deliver 38,250 slaves, at a rate of 4,250 per year. For his efforts, Reynal was to be paid 900,000 ducats but, for every slave short of the quota, Reynal would forfeit 10 ducats. The slaves that were to be imported were not to include mestizos, Turks or Moors. The slaves were to be African slaves from the Sub-Sahara.

AFRICA

• A Dutch expedition explored the coast of Guinea (the Gold Coast).

1 5 9 6
EUROPE

• In 1596, Queen Elizabeth I wrote to the mayors of various English cities requesting that persons of African descent be deported from England. The queen's request was based upon her perception of the need to rid England of Africans because of the hard economic times that the country was undergoing and because the Africans were considered to be "infidels, having no understanding of Christ or his Gospel."

1 5 9 7
AFRICA

• A monastery of Augustinian friars was established in Mombasa (Kenya).
• Yaqub became Emperor of Ethiopia.

EUROPE

• Juan Latino, the noted Afro-Spanish scholar, died. *See 1516.*

1 5 9 8
AFRICA

• Several thousand African slaves who worked the gold mines near Zaragosa in Nueva Granada (now Colombia) wrecked the mines and killed the Spanish administrators of the mines. The rebellious slaves then defied the Spanish authorities from behind palisades that the slaves had erected. The uprising was only suppressed by ruthless actions taken by Spanish authorities.

AFRICA

• The Dutch established four factories in West Africa.
• The Portuguese made al-Hassan king of Mombasa.

1600–1699

During the 1600s, the Portuguese continued their military campaigns in Angola and Zaire; the Lwoo chieftainship was established among the Alur in Uganda; the Lozi kingdom was founded in Zambia; Coptic ceased to be the spoken language in Ethiopia; the Lunda Empire was founded in Angola; and the first Sakalava dynasty arose in Madagascar.

Meanwhile, in the Americas, the English established their first permanent footholds on the American continent. In their struggle to carve out a place for themselves, the English began to utilize a practice which the Portuguese and Spanish had been using for nearly two hundred years—they began to use African slaves.

1600

THE AMERICAS

Between 1600 and 1700, approximately 2,750,000 slaves were brought to Latin America via the slave trade. A significant factor contributing to the mass importation of African slaves was the "invention," in 1600, of a new alcoholic beverage called "rum" (also known as "demon rum" by its detractors and admirers alike). In 1600, the Spanish colony of Barbados began making rum from sugar cane. The rum was made by refining the sugar by-product molasses, thereby developing a high-alcohol liquor that was cheaply made. Rum was an exceptional commodity. Its color was a deep brown, its taste was unique and highly addictive, and its production easily fit in with the slave farm system of the Spanish plantations which were rich in sugar cane. Because so much of the Indigenous (Native) American population had been decimated, the Spaniards were compelled to enslave Africans to provide the cheap labor force needed to work the plantations, turn the sugar cane into molasses and then turn the molasses into rum.

The importance of rum in the establishment and perpetuation of slavery should not be underestimated. Rum was a key consumable commodity which was used in trade with Europe and Africa both. In exchange for rum, Europe sent the colonies cloth and other material goods—Africa sent the colonies slaves. The more slaves a person had, the more rum that could be produced. The more rum that could be produced the more cloth and other material goods could be purchased from Europe and the more slaves could be bought and stolen from Africa.

Another essential quality of rum was the debilitating impact it had upon indigenous populations such as African and Indigenous (Native) American peoples. A culture impacted by rum became a culture which had a difficult time organizing resistance to exploitation by the European cultures.

In examining history, one often cannot escape the analogy that can be made between historical times and present times.

• In 1600, there were 140,000 Afro-mestizos in Mexico.

AFRICA

• The first known king of the Ashanti, a part of the Akans, reigned.

The Akan people are a major group of peoples of West Africa centered around what today is the country of Ghana. According to tradition, the Akan people originated in the Adanse region around Lake Bosumtwi. The Akan people speak Akan and are divided into numerous and distinct subgroups including the Akim, Akuapem, Akyem, Kwahu, Ashanti, Brong, Denkyira, Assin, Nzema, and Fante.

Among the Akan people, the Ashanti are the largest and most powerful ethnic group in the West African country of Ghana. The Ashanti are also known as the Asante. Most of the nearly two million Ashanti live in south central Ghana in a region which bears their name. The Ashanti Region is one of Ghana's nine political subdivisions. The capital of the Ashanti Region is Kumasi, the second largest city in Ghana.

Most Ashanti make their living as farmers, raising cocoa and other crops. Others work in the mining or forestry industries. The Ashanti weavers of today are famous for producing the colorful *kinte* cloth.

The Ashanti language is called Twi, but many Ashanti also speak English. A number of Ashanti are Christians, and some are Muslims. The traditional Ashanti religion focused upon a supreme being named Nyame. Nyame converses with the people by communicating through lesser gods. The Ashanti also honor their ancestors at ancestral shrines.

In the late 1600s, a leader named Osei Tutu united the Ashanti into a single state and became the first *Asantehene* (king) of the unified kingdom. Osei Tutu made Kumasi the capital of the newly united kingdom.

With unity came prosperity and power. The Ashanti built a powerful army. During the 1700s this army conquered many neighboring states. At its height in the early 1800s, the Ashanti Empire included much of what are today the nations of Ghana, the Ivory Coast and Togo.

During the 1800s, the Ashanti and the British fought each other for control of trade in West Africa. In 1901, the British defeated the Ashanti and made the Ashanti lands a British colony. The colony, called Ashanti, was subject to the authority of another British colony which at the time was named the Gold Coast.

In 1957, Ashanti, the Gold Coast, and other nearby areas controlled by Great Britain became the independent country of Ghana. Since the independence of Ghana, and indeed, throughout Ghana's recent history, the Ashanti have been a major factor in Ghana's economic and political development.

• The Wallo Galla continued their march southward, reaching the Kenyan coast.

1601

AFRICA

• English navigator James Lancaster made a last foray to the Cape of Good Hope. On this last voyage, he once again bartered with the Khoikhoi (indigenous South Africans) exchanging iron for sheep and cattle.
• In Egypt, the army mutinied against the Turks.
• Benin was visited by De Bry.

1602

THE AMERICAS

• According to Spanish colonial law, criminals and idle persons of African descent were to be sent to work in the mines of Latin America. Their pay was to be given to the Spanish crown. Many of the Africans sent to the mines died from cave-ins, rock slides or unexpected tropical storms.

AFRICA

• The Dutch East India Company received a charter for trade with the East Indies.

The Dutch East India Company was a powerful trading company which eventually established Dutch control of the lands now known as Indonesia.

In 1602, the Dutch government granted the Dutch East India Company a monopoly on trade between Asia and the Netherlands. The Dutch East India Company also received broad governmental and military powers, including the right to rule territories and the right to wage war in Asia.

In 1652, the Dutch East India Company established an outpost settlement at the Cape of Good Hope (Cape Town) in what is today South Africa. This outpost served as a midway stopping point for the Dutch vessels plying the East Indies trade routes.

By 1700, the company had gained control of the cinnamon, clove, and nutmeg trade in the East Indies. Also by this time, the company effectively controlled and ruled what are today the countries of South Africa, Sri Lanka and Indonesia.

In the 1700s, the demand for textiles from India, tea from China, and coffee from Arabia and Java exceeded the demand for spices and caused competition for the Dutch trading routes to increase. A strong competitor emerged from England. The English East India Company soon began to take over the business. The Dutch East India Company lost money. By 1799, it was no more.

• The Dutch established a settlement at Cape Mount in Sierra Leone.

• The French made their first expeditionary visit to Madagascar.

ASIA

• In the Deccan region of India, after repulsing the Mughuls, Malik Ambar, an African mercenary, sought to usurp the throne of King Murtaza II. In 1602, Malik Ambar imprisoned Murtaza and named himself regent-minister. As regent minister, Malik Ambar repelled a series of Mughul attacks and prevented the Great Mughul, the Emperor Akbar, from fulfilling his aim of conquering the Indian subcontinent. *See 1550.*

1603

THE AMERICAS

AFRICA

• The Keira (Kera) dynasty was founded in Darfur (western Sudan and Chad).

• Beginning in 1603 until 1624, Father Paris of the Jesuits ministered in Ethiopia and there was missionary activity centered around Tigre (Ethiopia/Eritrea).

1604

AFRICA

• The harsh rule of Ibrahim Pasha, the Turkish governor of Egypt, provoked a military revolt.

• Between June 17 and August 25 of 1604, the Dutch blockaded Mozambique.

RELATED HISTORICAL EVENTS

• William Shakespeare wrote *Othello.*

Othello is a classic story which portrays the growth of unjustified jealousy in the title character who happens to be an African Moor serving as a general in the Venetian army. The object of Othello's jealousy is his European wife, the beautiful Desdemona. In this tale of domestic tragedy, Othello's evil European aid (his "ancient") Iago plants the seed of jealousy in Othello's heart and nourishes it until Othello is consumed by jealousy to his fatal ruin.

Othello is an important literary achievement for African Americans because for the last four hundred years it has provided some of the rare opportunities for actors of African descent to act in a substantial and serious role in the theatre.

Othello is also an important literary work because it is one of the few accepted, and widely read, literary works which portrays the relationship of an interracial couple. As such, the impression that this play has had upon the psyche of Europeans and European Americans with regard to interracial marriage should not be underestimated. And the fact that the play is a tragedy in which the African kills his European wife and then kills himself speaks volumes as to how interracial matings are often perceived to be destined for trouble and failure.

1605

THE AMERICAS

• Henrique Dias, the great Afro-Brazilian general, was born in Pernambuco, Brazil.

Henrique (Henry) Dias (1605–1662) is one of the great African military leaders in history. Under his leadership, the Portuguese were able to secure control of Brazil.

After establishing its colony at New Amsterdam (New York), the enterprising expansionist Dutch looked southward for new territories. They decided upon the Portuguese territory of Brazil.

In the 1630s, the Dutch landed in Brazil with a substantial force under the command of Count Maurice. The Dutch forces perfunctorily defeated the Portuguese in a series of battles which established their control over the northern portion of Brazil.

However, while the Portuguese were suffering these defeats, the heroism of one of the African slaves came to the fore. Henrique Dias distinguished himself in the defeats and because of this distinction was able to convince the Portuguese generals to allow him to form a company of Africans to fight under his command.

The forces of Henrique Dias proved instrumental in turning the tide against the Dutch. Where the Portuguese generals had met only failure, Dias succeeded. At Arccise, he met and defeated the feared Count Maurice resulting in the recall of the Count.

At Pernambuco, Dias met Maurice's successor, Count Sigismond, and literally destroyed the Count's vaunted Dutch forces.

At the siege of Cinco Pontus, the masterful Dias used the cover of night and the ingenious use of blocks of wood to bridge a moat and climb the fortress walls. At close quarters, Dias received a wound to his wrist, but rather than allowing his injury to interfere with the progress of the battle, Dias had his hand cut off and proceeded to win the day.

It was this rousing victory which led to the eviction of the Dutch from Brazil.

For his service, Dias received great praise and was taken to Portugal to be commended by King John IV.

Unfortunately, the heroism of Dias and his fellow slave warriors was soon relegated to fading memories as Brazil struggled to recover from the ravages of the war with the Dutch. Despite their valor, the slave warriors were once again enslaved.

As for Henrique Dias, the noble warrior died on June 8, 1662, in poverty—neglected by the country he had helped to create.

AFRICA

• In Egypt, the troops killed Ibrahim Pasha, the Turkish governor of Egypt.

1 6 0 6

THE AMERICAS

• In 1606, Spain ordered all Spanish settlers to move to the Santo Domingo area to strengthen the defense of Santo Domingo and increase trade for Spanish merchants who were already located there. This plan failed because non-Spanish settlers (including escaped African slaves) moved into the abandoned lands in the interior and on the northern coast. The Spanish abandonment of the interior of the island led to the Treaty of Ryswick of 1697. In the Treaty of Ryswick, Spain turned over the western third of the island—what we today call "Haiti"—to France.

AFRICA

• In 1606, Adlan became king of the Fung (Funj). His court would be distinguished by the numerous holy men that attended it.

The Fung are an ethnic group found in the northern Sudan who inhabit the land on either side of the Blue Nile River.

1 6 0 7

AFRICA

• Dutch forces attacked the Portuguese outpost at Mozambique. The attack failed but it did signal the beginning of the erosion of Portuguese control of the Indian Ocean trade.
• The warfare between the Moroccan forces and the remnant forces of the once great Songhai continued.
• Muhammed Pasha became governor of Egypt.

ASIA

• By the time that Jahangir had succeeded Akbar as the Mughul emperor in 1605, Malik Ambar, the African mercenary, had established a capital at Kirkee and had become well entrenched in the Deccan region of India. During this time, Malik Ambar also fought off the ventures of his rival Mian Raju Dakhani. In 1607, Malik Ambar captured Raju and had him executed. After this act, Malik Ambar was the supreme lord of Ahmadnagar. *See 1550.*

1 6 0 8

THE AMERICAS

• The governor of New France, the Sieur Du Gua de Monts, was reported to have had an African servant named Mathieu de Coste working in Acadia (Nova Scotia, Canada).

AFRICA

• Dutch Admiral Cornelis Matelief bartered with the Khoikhoi (indigenous South Africans) near Table Bay (Cape of Good Hope).
• In July and August, the Dutch again besieged the Portuguese outpost at Mozambique.
• On August 1, 1608, the Portuguese entered into a treaty with the Monomotapa.

EUROPE

• Antonio Vieira (1608-1697), an Afro-Portuguese clergyman and statesman who, for a time, effectively governed Portugal, was born.

———— 1 6 0 9 ————

THE AMERICAS

• There was a slave uprising in Mexico led by Yanga.

In the early 1600s, a growing maroon threat arose in the area around Veracruz. In Veracruz, an elderly former slave named Yanga along with his followers had escaped to the nearby mountains and had lived in freedom for some thirty years. In 1609, the viceroy of Mexico sent a force of 600 men against Yanga's encampment. Yanga only had 80 men along with some women and children. Nevertheless, using guerrilla tactics, Yanga eluded the Spaniards and after a number of inconclusive skirmishes, forced them to negotiate. In the resulting treaty, Yanga and his followers were guaranteed their freedom. Not long afterwards, an independent Afro-mestizo town, San Lorenzo de los Negros, was founded near what is today the city of Cordoba.

AFRICA

• In 1609, some 80,000 Moriscos (Spanish Moors) were reported to have arrived in Tunis.
• There was a general uprising against the Turks in Egypt.
• The treaty between the Monomotapa Gatsi Rusere and Portuguese went into effect.

Around 1597, the kingdom of Gatsi Rusere was invaded by the Zimba. The army of Gatsi Rusere was able to defeat the Zimba but Gatsi Rusere was displeased with the performance of his generals. Gatsi Rusere had a number of his military commanders executed.

The execution of these military commanders touched off a civil war which forced Gatsi Rusere to seek assistance from the Portuguese to subdue the rebel forces. In the treaty which formalized the relationship between the Monomotapa and the Portuguese, the Portuguese were granted land and control over the kingdom's gold mines. This concession led to Portuguese domination of the area because while the Portuguese profited from the gold, they refused to adequately pay the taxes (the tribute) which the kingdom needed to function.

———— 1 6 1 0 ————

THE AMERICAS

• Saint Peter Claver, a Spanish Jesuit priest, went to Colombia. Claver is considered the "Friend of the Blacks" among the Saints of the Catholic church. It is said that during his stay of more than 40 years in Latin America, Claver baptized about 300,000 African slaves.

Saint Peter Claver (1581–1654) was born in Verdu, in Catalonia, Spain. As a youth, Peter demonstrated fine qualities of mind and spirit. His mental acuity led him to study at the University of Barcelona.

Peter graduated with distinction from the University and, after receiving minor orders, decided to join the Society of Jesus (the Jesuits). Peter was received into the novitiate of Tarragona at the age of twenty, and was sent to the college of Montesione at Palma, in Majorca.

In Majorca, Peter met Saint Alphonsus Rodriguez, who was then a porter in the college, though with a reputation far above his humble office, and this meeting was to set the direction of Peter Claver's life.

Peter studied the science of the saints at the feet of the Alphonsus, and Alphonsus developed a corresponding regard for the capabilities of young Peter. In Peter, Alphonsus soon began to think that he had found the right person for a very difficult and arduous calling. Alphonsus commissioned Peter to go to the New World to minister amongst the many who were without spiritual guidance.

In later years, Peter would often recall that Alphonsus had actually foretold not only that Peter would go to the New World but also the precise location where he would work. Moved by the inspirational fervor of Alphonsus, Peter approached his superiors and offered himself for the West Indies. His superiors told him that his vocation would be chosen for him, in due course.

Peter returned to Barcelona to study theology. After two years, and after additional requests from Peter, his superiors chose Peter to represent the province of Aragon on the Jesuit mission to New Granada.

Peter left Spain forever in April of 1610. After a wearisome voyage, Peter landed with his companions at Cartagena, in what is now the Republic of Colombia.

The first five years of Peter's mission in Colombia were spent performing various tasks associated with the Jesuit mission located outside of Cartagena. However, in 1615, Peter returned to Cartagena, was ordained a priest, and began the calling for which he is today remembered.

By 1615, the slave trade had been established in the Americas for over a hundred years and the port of Cartagena was one of the principal centers of slave debarkation. By 1615, the enslavement of Indigenous Americans had subsided due to the inability of the Indigenous Americans to withstand the harsh environment of the silver and gold mines along with the debilitating European diseases. Thus, African slaves from Angola and the Congo were in great demand.

The conditions under which the African slaves were transported to the colonies were truly hellacious. It was estimated that in each cargo of slaves up to one third of the slaves would die during the six- or seven-week voyage. Nevertheless, each year some ten thousand slaves survived the trip and landed in Cartagena.

Slavery had been condemned by Pope Paul III as being a great crime and was termed a "supreme villainy" by Pope Pius IX. Nevertheless, slavery in Catholic America continued to flourish.

Despite the papal decrees and the ameliorating implorations of the Catholic clergy, most slave owners limited their religious instruction of their slaves to simply having them baptized. The slaves received no religious instruction and no religious ministration. Indeed, over time the very act of the slaves' religious conversion their baptism—became synonymous to their oppression.

For the most part the Catholic clergy were ineffective at changing the conditions of the slaves. The best that they could do was to express some compassion for the misery being suffered by the Africans.

At the time of Peter Claver's ordination, the leader in the field work among the African slaves was Father Alfonso de Sandoval, a great Jesuit missionary who spent forty years in the service of the slaves. After working with Father Alfonso, Peter declared himself "the slave of the Negroes for ever."

Although by nature shy and without self-confidence, Peter, nevertheless, threw himself into the work. He pursued it not with unbridled enthusiasm but with methodical organization. Peter enlisted bands of assistants. As soon as a slave ship entered the port of Cartagena, Peter would go to the docks. After the slaves had disembarked and were shut up in the yards, crowds of locals would gather to gape at them. These "idle gazers" were drawn by a morbid curiosity but were careful not to come too close. After all, when hundreds of men are transported like sardines in the hole of a slave ship for weeks on end, the "unpacking" of the slaves was not a particularly pretty sight.

The misery of the slaves did not end with their disembarkation. Despite the fact that they may have been malnourished, ill or dying, they were all herded together and confined in a crowded pen. The misery of the situation was increased by the damp heat and humidity. So horrible was the scene and revolting the conditions that a friend who came with Father Claver once could never face it again, and of Father Sandoval himself it was written in one of the "relations" of his province that, "when he heard a vessel of Negroes was come into port he was at once covered with a cold sweat and a deathlike pallor at the recollection of the indescribable fatigue and unspeakable work on the previous like occasions. The experience and practice of years never accustomed him to it."

Father Claver would venture into the yards to minister to the huddled masses of slaves. He would take medicines and food, bread, brandy, lemons and tobacco to distribute among the Negroes, some of whom were too frightened, others too ill, to accept them.

"We must speak to them with our hands, before we try to speak to them with our lips," Claver would say. When he came upon any slaves that were dying, he baptized them. During the time that the Africans were confined in the shed, penned so closely that they had to sleep almost upon one another and freely handed on their diseases, St. Peter Claver cared for the bodies of the sick and the souls of all.

Unlike many of his brethern, Claver did not consider that ignorance of the African languages absolved him from the obligation of instructing the Africans in the matters of the Catholic religion. Claver considered it his duty to bring to the abused Africans the consolation of the words of Christ.

Claver employed seven interpreters, one of whom spoke four African dialects. With the aid of his interpreters, Claver prepared the slaves for baptism, not only in groups but also individually. Often Claver would use pictures to get his message across. These pictures usually depicted Jesus suffering on the cross for the slaves or showed popes, princes and other great Europeans rejoicing at the baptism of an African.

Claver's aim was always to instill in the slaves some degree of self-respect — to give them at least some idea that as redeemed human beings they had dignity and worth, even if as slaves they were outcast and despised. Claver showed the slaves that they were loved even more than they were abused and that the divine love of God must not be outraged by the slaves doing evil deeds.

It is estimated that in forty years St. Peter Claver instructed and baptized over 300,000 slaves. Claver never tired of preaching to the Africans to turn away from sin and he repeatedly urged the slave owners to care for the souls of the slaves.

When the slaves were sent off to the mines and plantations, St. Peter would appeal to them for the last time with renewed earnestness, to not sin. Claver had a steady confidence that God would care for the slaves.

Claver also believed that God would care for the slave owners. Claver did not regard the slave owners as despicable barbarians, beyond the mercy or might of God. Peter believed that slave owners also had souls that needed to be saved. Peter appealed to the slave owners and urged them to exercise physical and spiritual justice with the slaves — for their own sake if not for the sake of the slaves.

Of course, Peter's faith in his fellow human beings would often prove to be unfounded. Thousands of slaves would die in the mines and on the plantations of Colombia. In that respect, Peter was naive.

However, in some respects, Peter's work was ameliorative. It must be stated that while Spanish slavery was a most vile institution, it paled in comparison to the barbarity of the English practice of slavery. At least under the Spanish, the laws of the government and the auspices of the church provided for the marriage of slaves, prohibited the separation (disintegration) of slave families, and protected freed slaves from unjust seizure after liberation. In comparison, the moral indifference of the British (and later the Americans) was simply evil.

As the messenger of the church, Claver did all he could to provide for the observance of the laws. Every spring after Easter, he would make a tour of the plantations near Cartagena in order to see how the Africans were being treated.

Father Claver was not always well received by the slave owners. The slave owners complained that Father Claver wasted the slaves' time with his preaching, praying and hymn singing, and when the slaves misbehaved, the owners blamed Father Claver for the slaves' bad behavior. But Father Claver was not deterred, not even when his superiors lent too willing an ear to the complaints of his critics.

Many of the stories of the heroism and of the miraculous powers of Saint Peter Claver concern his nursing sick and diseased Africans, in circumstances often that no one else, black or white, could face. However, Saint Peter Claver also cared for others besides slaves.

There were two hospitals in Cartagena, one for general cases, served by the Brothers of Saint John-of-God — Saint Sebastian's — and another — Saint Lazarus' — for lepers and for those suffering from the complaint called "Saint Anthony's Fire." Father Peter visited both of these hospitals every week.

Claver also ministered to the traders and travelers who often visited Cartagena. He is credited with having converted an Anglican archdeacon but was less successful with the Muslim Turks and Moors who came to port.

Father Claver was also frequently requested to attend condemned criminals. It is reported that not one prisoner was executed in Cartagena during Claver's lifetime without his being present to console him. Under Claver's guidance, the most hardened and defiant criminals would spend their last hours in prayer and sorrow for their sins.

During his spring forays into the countryside, Claver would often refuse the hospitality of the slave owners in order to reside with the slaves.

In 1650, Claver went to preach the jubilee among the slaves, but illness attacked his emaciated and weakened body. He was forced to return to Cartagena. In Cartagena, a virus epidemic was raging through the city. Claver in his weakened state soon contracted the virus. His death was near.

However, after receiving the last rites, Father Peter recovered, but he was never the same. For the rest of his life, pain hardly left him, and a trembling in his limbs made it impossible for him to celebrate Mass.

Father Claver became almost entirely inactive, but would sometimes hear confessions, especially of his dear friend Dona Isabella de Urbina, a generous patron. Occasionally, Father Claver would be carried to a hospital, a condemned prisoner, or some other sick person. Once when a slave ship arrived carrying slaves from an area of Africa which had not been contacted for thirty years, Father Peter became excited and shook off his infirmities. He was carted around until he found an interpreter and then went to the pens to minister to the newly arrived slaves. He baptized the children and gave brief moral instructions to the adults.

As his health declined and his activities became curtailed, the citizens of Cartagena and even his fellow brothers began to forget about him. At times, Father Peter would be left unattended for days on end. The treatment of Father Peter was simply deplorable.

In the summer of 1654, Father Diego Ramirez Farina arrived in Cartagena from Spain with a commission from the King of Spain to work among the slaves. Father Peter was overjoyed and dragged himself from his bed to greet his successor. Shortly afterwards, he heard the confession of his good friend Dona Isabella and told her it was for the last time. On September 6, after assisting at Mass and receiving communion, Father Peter confided to Nicholas Gonzalez, "I am going to die." That same evening, he became very ill and slipped into a coma.

The news of the impending death of the priest spread like wildfire through Cartagena. Suddenly, everyone remembered the saint again. Scores came to kiss his hands before it was too late. Some of the more greedy citizens stripped his meager cell of everything that could be carried off as a relic.

Saint Peter Claver never recovered. He died on September 8, 1654.

After his death, the civil authorities who had looked with disdain at his solicitations amongst the slaves and his fellow clergy who had criticised his zeal, now vied with one another to honor his memory. The city magistrates ordered that he should be buried at public expense with great pomp, and the vicar general of the diocese officiated at the funeral. The slaves and the Indigenous Americans arranged for a Mass of their own. Father Peter's church was ablaze with lights, a special choir sang, and an oration was delivered which eloquently spoke of the virtues, holiness, heroism, and stupendous miracles of Father Claver.

Saint Peter Claver was never again forgotten and his fame spread throughout the world. He was canonized in 1888 and he was declared by Pope Leo XIII the patron of all missionary enterprises among persons of African descent, in whatever part of the world.

The work performed by Saint Peter Claver is simply unparalleled in the annals of African or African American history. In one way or another, he touched the lives of over 300,000 persons of African descent at a time when they were at their most vulnerable. His greatness cannot be denied and his memory should never be forgotten.

• Officials in Buenos Aires were denounced by the King of Spain (Philip III) for smuggling slaves.

AFRICA

In 1492, the Moors were defeated and Spain became united. In the aftermath of "la reconquista," Spain went through a period of "ethnic cleansing" which resulted in the expulsion of not only the Moors but also the Jews. However, the expulsion of the Moors was not an immediate occurrence. After dominating Spain for seven hundred years, Moors had become an integral part of Spanish society. Consequently, after their defeat, the Moors lingered in Spain for another hundred years.

Nevertheless, by 1610, through expulsion and migration, over a million Moors—among them thousands of Jews had returned to North and Northwest Africa. *See 1609.*

• Between 1610 and 1613, intermittent hostilities erupted between the Portuguese and the Monomotapa.
• Tananarive became the Merina capital of Madagascar.

The Merina are the largest ethnic group among the Malagasy. The Malagasy are a hybrid group of mixed African-Indonesian descent. It is generally believed that the Malagasy first migrated from Indonesia some 2,000 years ago. Some may have reached the African coast where a hybrid Indonesian-African culture is thought to have flourished until it displaced was during the Bantu expansion in the seventh and eighth A.D. centuries. Over the centuries, the African and Arab immigrants to the island intermingled with the Malagasy, but by that time the Malagasy culture was firmly established.

A well-developed hereditary class system of nobles, commoners, and slaves led to the emergence of numerous city-states on the island. From the sixteenth to eighteenth centuries, the Merina began a series of conquests from which a unified Madagascar emerged.

• Yusuf, the Dey of Tunis, began to organize the pirates along the Barbary Coast.
• Abu Mahalli, claiming to be the Mahdi, seized Marrakesh, Morocco.

"Mahdi" is an Islamic title meaning "the divinely guided one"—the long awaited deliverer and restorer of pure Islam. The concept of the Mahdi does not appear in the Koran but the belief in the coming of the Mahdi was, and is, widespread among Muslims. Since the 900s, several self-proclaimed Mahdis have appeared in northern Africa.

1611

EUROPE

• In 1611, King Philip III of Spain donated a new shrine to the church in Palermo in order to house the remains of Saint Benedict the Black, the patron saint of African Americans and the protector of Palermo. *See 1526.*

1612

THE AMERICAS

• Around 1550, there were 20,000 African slaves in Cuernavaca and Veracruz, Mexico. The African slaves were a source of great consternation for the Spaniards. Indeed, keeping the African slaves subdued often proved to be more problematic than the subjugation of the Indigenous Americans. Around 1612, a rumor spread throughout Mexico City that the Africans were planning to stage a revolt and massacre the Spaniards. One night during this same time period, the Spaniards mistook the noise of a herd of runaway hogs in the streets for the sound of barefoot Africans bent on destruction. The next day, the Spaniards executed more than thirty Africans in sheer paranoid panic.

AFRICA

• By 1612, 10,000 slaves were being shipped from Angola on an annual basis.
• Pemba, a clove-growing island in the Indian Ocean off the coast of Tanzania, was brought under the control of the king of Malindi.

1613

AFRICA

• A Khoikhoi (an indigenous South African) named Gorachouqua was kidnapped and taken to London aboard the *Hector*. Gorachouqua returned to South Africa as an English "trading agent" but, as such, he required that the English pay a fair price for the livestock they purchased.

RELATED HISTORICAL EVENTS

• The British established a settlement on the Bermuda Islands.

The Bermuda Islands are the most northerly group of coral islands in the world. The group of over 300 islands was named for the Spanish explorer, Juan de Bermudez, who discovered them in the early 1500s. The *Sea Venture*, a ship carrying colonists destined for Virginia, was shipwrecked near the islands during a storm on July 28, 1609. For a time, the colony was called Somers Islands after Admiral Sir George Somers, the captain of the *Sea Venture*. The town of St. George was also named in his honor.

The passengers of the *Sea Venture* remained for a time, but all except two of the group sailed to Virginia in 1610. These two settlers became Bermuda's first permanent inhabitants. The settlers who left for Virginia were part of the rescue party which found the Jamestown settlers on the brink of starvation.

Around 1610, King James I of England awarded Bermuda to the Virginia Company. The Virginia Company sold its rights in 1613 to a group of British merchants who were active in the slave trade. These merchants were the ones who established a permanent settlement on Bermuda.

1614

THE AMERICAS

• Spanish colonial law forbade the buying of goods from slaves. It was assumed that such transactions caused the slaves to rob and become unruly.

AFRICA

• Portuguese ships bombarded al-Hasan, the sultan of Mombasa, while he was in his palace. To protest the insult, the sultan traveled to Goa (India) to formally lodge his complaint with the Portuguese authorities.
• There was a struggle for succession in the kingdom of the Kongo.

1615

AFRICA

• The sultan of Mombasa (al-Hasan) was murdered by the Nyika (Nyiha/Nyoka) at the instigation of the Portuguese. The sultan's successor Yusuf al-Hasan, was sent to Portuguese Goa (India) for his education.

The Nyika are an ethnic group living in Zambia.

1616

THE AMERICAS

By 1616, the Dutch had begun to supplant the Portuguese as the principal slave traders on the African coast. Indeed, it was the Dutch who brought the first slaves to the British North American colonies.

In 1616, the Dutch settled Guiana, in northern South America, and began the cultivation of sugar cane. Later, to curb the rebellious slaves, the Dutch imported East Indians. The so-called "Bush Negroes" in the interior of Guiana were descendants of runaway slaves who had established villages and organized a form of government.

By the end of the seventeenth century, the maroons of Guiana had large settlements on the Surinam River and, by 1750, these maroons were making repeated raids on the neighboring plantations.

AFRICA

• A group of Dutchmen assisted the Khoikhoi (indigenous South African) Gorachouqua by attacking his inland enemies the Cochoqua.

ASIA

• Upon consolidation of his power, Malik Ambar, the African lord of India's Ahmadnagar, organized an estimated 60,000 horse army. His light cavalry was very effective as a mobile unit. Malik Ambar also enlisted the naval support of the Siddis (fellow Africans) of India's Janjira Island in 1616 in order to cut the Mughul (Muslim) supply lines and to conduct harassing missions. *See 1550.*

1618

THE (FUTURE) UNITED STATES

In 1618, a smallpox epidemic raged throughout New England from Maine to Virginia. The epidemic hit the Indigenous (Native) Americans the hardest. It is estimated that as many as 9 out of every 10 Indigenous (Native) Americans in the New England area died of the disease. In 1618, the disease struck and killed Powhatan, the proud Indigenous (Native) American chief in Virginia whose fabled daughter was Pocahontas. Pocahontas, by the way, predeceased her father. She died in 1617 from smallpox. Pocahontas was 21 when she died.

The impact of smallpox and other European diseases upon the Indigenous (Native) Americans is very important in African American history for three reasons: First, the susceptibility of the Indigenous (Native) Americans to European diseases made Indigenous (Native) Americans generally unsuitable for slave labor thereby necessitating the introduction of "hardier" African slaves. Secondly, the decimation of the Indigenous (Native) Americans from disease weakened the Indigenous American resistance to the European colonization of America and, consequently, facilitated the expansion of not only the American colonies but also the institution of African slavery. Thirdly, the decimation of the Indigenous population essentially served to depopulate the land, leading to the impression that the wilderness was less populated than it was and thereby encouraging colonial expansion.

AFRICA

• In 1618, the source of the Blue Nile was discovered by Pedro Paez.
• The Portuguese campaigned against the Ndongo (in Angola).
• Morocco relinquished control of Timbuktu. Thereafter, the ruling pashas of Timbuktu were elected by the armed forces.
• Fort James was built by the English at Bathurst, Gambia.

EUROPE

• In England, the government granted monopolies to special companies to trade in slaves.
• King James I granted an exclusive charter to Sir Robert Rich and others to organize a stock company for trade with Guinea, and the Company of Adventurers of London established an outpost on the Rio Gambia.

1 6 1 9

THE (FUTURE) UNITED STATES

• A Dutch ship anchored at Jamestown, Virginia, with a cargo of twenty Africans. This was the beginning of the African presence in Anglo-America. These first persons of African descent were treated as indentured servants who were freed upon completion of their terms of servitude (August 20). *See 1621.*

THE AMERICAS

• In the Spanish colonies, a summary trial could be used in actions against fugitives of African descent.

AFRICA

• In 1619, pestilence killed 330,000 people in Egypt.
• The Portuguese initiated an unsuccessful attempt to develop silver mines in Chicoa, Mozambique.

1 6 2 0

THE (FUTURE) UNITED STATES

• The first public school for persons of African descent and Indigenous (Native) Americans was established in Virginia.

1 6 2 1

THE AMERICAS

• The Dutch West India Company was organized with a monopoly of both the African slave trade and trade with the Dutch colonies in the New World. This company challenged the right of the Portuguese to trade on the coast of Africa, and by 1650 the Dutch had a stronghold there. Following the English Civil War (c. 1650), England tried to close the slave trade to the Dutch.

In 1621, the private companies trading in the west were all merged into the Dutch West India Company. Over the next four years, the Dutch West India Company would transport some 15,430 Africans to Brazil, carry on a war with Spain, supply British plantations and gradually become the great slave carrier of the day.

Under the Dutch West India Company, the slave trade reached new heights. The Dutch, in essence, perfected the overseas slave trade as an institution. By 1621, the Dutch had captured Portugal's various slave forts on the West Coast and then proceeded to open sixteen forts along the coast of the Gulf of Guinea. Dutch ships sailed from Holland to Africa, got slaves in exchange for their goods, carried the slaves to the West Indies or Brazil, and returned home laden with New World produce.

The Dutch perfection of the slave trade is directly responsible for what is now known as the Golden Age of the Netherlands. With the slave trade, the Dutch became the leading sea power in the world. Between 1600 and 1650, the Dutch merchant fleet tripled in size and Dutch ships supplied about half of the world's shipping.

The affluence acquired from such lucrative ventures as the slave trade, helped to make Amsterdam the world's major commercial city and gave the Dutch the highest standard of living. It was this high standard of living which enabled the Dutch to finance the great artists of the day. Pieter de Hooch, Frans Hals, Rembrandt, Jacob van Ruisdael and Jan Vermeer all achieved prominence during this Golden Age.

During the Golden Age, the Dutch developed a great colonial empire in many parts of the world. In 1602, Dutch firms trading with the East Indies combined to form the Dutch East India Company. The company founded Batavia (now Jakarta, the capital of Indonesia) as its headquarters.

Later, Dutch forces drove the British and the Portuguese out of what later became the Netherlands Indies (now Indonesia). The company also took control of Ceylon (now Sri Lanka) and colonized the southern tip of Africa (South Africa). Additionally, from the 1600s to the 1800s, the Dutch were the only Westerners who were allowed to trade with Japan.

In the pantheon of imperialistic powers who participated in the slave trade and the oppression of indigenous peoples around the world, the Dutch also must be included to their glory and to their shame.

• In Cartagena, a Spanish landing point in Colombia, a Spanish colonial law forbade persons of African descent, even if accompanied by their owners, from bearing arms without a license.
• In Brazil, royal decrees prohibited the participation of non–Europeans in the

industrial arts, the goldsmith's trade, and weaving.

AFRICA

• A Dutch station was established at Goree.

ASIA

Malik Ambar, the African lord of India's Ahmadnagar, built his greatest fortifications at Daulatabad to protect his kingdom from Prince Shah Jahan—the prince destined to become the next Mughul emperor. In 1621, Shah Jahan's forces launched an attack on Daulatabad. Surprisingly, the Mughul forces were defeated and forced to retreat after suffering heavy losses at the hands of Malik Ambar. *See 1550.*

1 6 2 2

THE (FUTURE) UNITED STATES

• Anthony and Mary Johnson, persons of African descent, were reported as being free in Old Accomack (Northampton County) in the Virginia colony.

AFRICA

• The English bombarded Algiers.
• Susenyos of Ethiopia was submitted to the Holy See.
• The Wallo Galla raided Amhara.
• A combined fleet of English and Dutch ships blockaded the Portuguese held port of Mozambique.

By 1622, some 3,000 slaves were being sent from Guinea to Portugal on an annual basis.

1 6 2 3

THE AMERICAS

• In Cuba, peaceful and industrious free Morenos (persons of African descent) were not to be molested or disturbed, according to Spanish law. In particular, those Morenos used by the governors for defense rather than agriculture were to be treated fairly by colonial officials.

AFRICA

• The Xhosa and the Tembu (Tembo) crossed the Umzimvutu River.
• In 1623, the Jesuits established a training college for missionaries at Sao Salvador in Angola.

RELATED HISTORICAL EVENTS

Between 1623 and 1638, the Dutch seized 500 Portuguese and Spanish vessels off the coast of the Americas.

1 6 2 4

THE (FUTURE) UNITED STATES

• William Tucker became the first child of African descent born and baptized in Anglo-America at Jamestown, Virginia. Tucker was the child of Africans who were sold to the British colony in 1619 as indentured servants. Tucker's birth raised an interesting dilemma for the colonists: Was the child of an indentured servant an indentured servant as well or was the child a free person?

The baptism of William Tucker began a tradition that would later prove to be of immeasurable importance for African American genealogists. Upon his baptism, William Tucker's name was entered upon the register of the Church. These registers became the official records of not only the church but also the community, recording births, deaths, and marriages of African Americans for whom all too few records were kept. [Note: Some historians contend that William, the son of Isabella and Anthony Johnson, was actually the first baptized African in Jamestown, Virginia, and that the baptism occurred in 1623.]

• John Phillip, a person of African descent, testified in a Jamestown court against an English colonist. Phillip's testimony was admitted. Phillip had been baptized in England 12 years before.
• In 1624, the Dutch West India Company colonized New Netherland, which consisted of parts of present-day New York, New Jersey, Connecticut, and Delaware. The Dutch in the area of modern day New York imported African workers from Angola and workers of African descent from Brazil to work on Hudson Valley farms. Under the Dutch in New York, the children of a manumitted slave were bound to slavery.
• There were 23 persons of African descent in Virginia.

AFRICA

• By 1624, there were eight Jesuit missions on the Zambezi River.

The Zambezi River is a river located in southern Africa. It originates in Zambia and flows through Zimbabwe and Mozambique to empty into the Indian Ocean.

Around 1624, the Ajuran and Madaule Somali migrated from the El Wak region. This mass migration coincided with the end of the Muzaffaric dynasty in Mogadishu.

---

1 6 2 5

THE AMERICAS

• The French took possession of Haiti.

As the gold fields of Hispaniola became depleted, the Spaniards began to drift away to the more alluring and prosperous Spanish settlements of Mexico and Peru. Thus, by 1606, there were so few Spaniards left on Hispaniola that the king of Spain ordered all of them to relocate to the city of Santo Domingo in what is today the Dominican Republic.

The abandonment of the western half of the island led to a rather colorful phase of island history. The western part of the island became a stronghold for maroon communities. It also became a haven for French, English, and Dutch pirates. The pirates used the small island of Tortuga as a base and attacked ships carrying gold from Mexico and Peru to Spain.

The Spanish would often try to control the maroons and would try to drive out the pirates. However, both efforts failed.

By 1625, the French were exercising a great influence over the area. This influence was formally recognized by Spain in 1697 when it granted to France the control over the western third of the island—the portion of the island which is today known as "Haiti."

AFRICA

• In 1625, the Abomey were conquered by Tacoodounu, the chief of the Fons (Fon). Afterwards, the kingdom of Dahomey was founded.

The Fon are a major people of Benin. They are found throughout central and southern Benin and in Togo along the southern border area. The Fon speak Fon and practice traditional religions. The Fon are famous for their art, especially distinctive sculpture.

During the precolonial period of the 1600s, the Fon were the foremost ethnic group of one of West Africa's most powerful and well-organized kingdoms, the kingdom of Dahomey.

Established in the 1600s, Dahomey expanded to the coast in the 1700s, gaining access to European trade, especially the slave trade.

• The Kasanje Empire in present day Kinshasa emerged to become one of the principal African states.

---

1 6 2 6

THE (FUTURE) UNITED STATES

• There were eleven Africans reported in Dutch New Amsterdam (New York City). Four of the Africans were Paul d'Angola, Simon Congo, Anthony Portuguese, and John Francisco.

AFRICA

• The French established their first outpost in West Africa—a small settlement at what would become Saint Louis—on the Senegal River.
• The Khoikhoi (indigenous South African) Gorachouqua was killed by the Dutch for refusing to trade with them.
• Yusuf al-Hasan was enthroned as sultan in Portuguese-held Mombasa. As the new sultan, Yusuf al-Hasan became a Christian and assumed the name Dom Hieronimo Chingulia. Dom Hieronimo Chingulia sent a letter of obedience to the pope.

ASIA

During the early 1620s, Malik Ambar, the African lord of India's Ahmadnagar, experienced difficulty in maintaining the loyalty of his officers and forces. The almost continuous warfare for over a twenty year period of time against internal and external enemies had demoralized the army and drained the local economy. Although he was never defeated, Malik Ambar died a besieged man in 1626.

Malik Ambar was succeeded as regent minister of the kingdom of Ahmadnagar by his son Fettah Khan. But Fettah Khan was not Malik Ambar. He was deposed in 1629. Thus ended the short but glorious reign of the Africans in the Deccan. *See 1550.*

---

1 6 2 7

AFRICA

• There was an incipient revolt in Kilwa.
• Bou Regreg became an independent republic.

---

1 6 2 8

THE (FUTURE) UNITED STATES

In 1628, the English colonists began a new enterprise. The new enterprise was gun-running. Indigenous (Native) Americans in Dover, New Hampshire, were reported to have been found hunting with rifles. Selling firearms to Indigenous (Native) Americans was illegal but, on the frontier, enforcement was lax.

Along with the introduction of epidemics, of diseases and rum-induced alcoholism, the introduction of guns to the Indigenous (Native) Americans was to play a significant role in their subjugation. After all, the gun was a weapon which was far more advanced (and far more destructive) than any weapon the Indigenous Americans had ever known. Accordingly, those Indigenous (Native) Americans who possessed guns obviously held an advantage over those who did not and this advantage was often exploited in the internecine struggles between various Indigneous American Nations. The tragic result was that those Indigenous (Native) Americans who did not succumb to disease or were not directly killed by the European Americans often wound up killing each other (or their Indigenous (Native) American cousins) in perpetuation of indigenous rivalries which preceded the European presence.

The fratricidal tendencies of Indigenous (Native) Americans would be used over and over again by the Europeans to their advantage. The practice of promoting such fratricide would time and time again lead to the decimation of Indigenous (Native) American populations and the eventual dispossession of Indigenous (Native) American lands.

The practice of promoting fratricide among Indigenous (Native) Americans was also carried over to Africans to gain control of African lands and, eventually, to African Americans. By 1650, the gun had come to be an integral part of the African trading scene and by 1700 had developed into a social factor affecting the fortunes of African kingdoms.

The legacy of the gun is evident in the often autocratic structure of most African nations and in the wholly tragic situation confronting the all too many urban areas inhabited by African Americans in the United States to this day.

THE AMERICAS

• An African slave who would become known by the name of Olivier Le Jeune was the first person of African descent to be enslaved in Canada. Le Jeune was brought to New France from Madagascar. Le Jeune was only a child at the time. When Le Jeune died in 1654, he was approximately 30 years old and he would be the only recorded

African slave in Canada until near the end of the century.

• Pursuant to Spanish colonial law, no Spanish official was to give a license to any person to supply persons of African descent with arms.

AFRICA

• A battle took place in 1628 which resulted in the defeat of the Monomotapa people (in what is today Mozambique). The defeat of the Monomotapa enabled the Portuguese to install a puppet king over the Monomotapa. In 1629, this puppet king, Mavura, signed a concession treaty with the Portuguese which essentially gave the Portuguese the mineral rights of the Monomotapa people.

• By 1628, eleven Jesuit missions had been established in Ethiopia.

• The French founded a factory at St. Luce, Madagascar.

• The French took control of the coral market in Algiers.

1629

THE (FUTURE) UNITED STATES

• Slavery was introduced into the Connecticut colony.

THE AMERICAS

• Among the freedoms and exemptions granted by the Dutch West India Company was the first recorded promise to return escaped slaves or bound servants.

AFRICA

• Beginning in 1629, the first attempts were made to cultivate in Africa certain foods from the Americas and beyond. Maize, manioc (cassava), sweet potatoes, pawpaw, guavas, coconuts and groundnuts would all be introduced to small farms near Luanda (Angola).

ASIA

• In 1626, Malik Ambar, the African lord of India's Ahmadnagar, was succeeded as regent minister of the kingdom of Ahmadnagar by his son Fettah Khan. But Fettah Khan was not Malik Ambar. He was deposed in 1629. Thus ended the short but glorious reign of the Africans in the Deccan. *See 1550.*

1630

THE (FUTURE) UNITED STATES

• The Massachusetts colony instituted a

broad fugitive law which included escaped slaves. As in New Netherlands, the law included a provision to protect those who fled because of ill treatment "till due order be taken for their relief."

THE AMERICAS

• In 1630, the Dutch captured Olinda and Recife in an attempt to conquer Brazil.

In 1630, the Dutch gained control of the Pernambuco region (near modern day Recife) of Brazil. The resulting political and social upheaval created an opportunity for many African slaves to escape into the surrounding forests. In these forests, the slaves formed a number of maroon communities.

During the period from 1630 to 1694, the various maroon communities of Pernambuco, Brazil attempted to organize their own state, the state of Alagoas or Palmares. In 1640, a Dutch citizen named Lintz reported eleven thousand people living in the three villages which made up the "Republic of Palmares." The Dutch West India Company repeatedly tried to eradicate Palmares but with little success.

The principal village of Palmares was half a mile long, with streets six feet wide, and had hundreds of homes, churches, and shops. Its well kept lands produced cereals and other crops irrigated African style with streams. It boasted courts that carried out justice for its thousands of citizens, and was ruled over by King Ganga-Zumba. ("Ganga-Zumba" combined an Angolan African word for "great" with a Tupi (Indigenous Brazilian) word for "ruler.") Christianity was commonly practiced, including elaborate marriage and baptism ceremonies that drew large crowds.

In 1654, the Portuguese reacquired Brazil and began a systematic campaign to destroy the Republic of Palmares. Despite the persistent campaign, the Republic survived intact until 1694 when a force of some 6,000 mercenary Indigenous Brazilians were brought in, and along with Portuguese soldiers and weapons, laid siege to Palmares for forty-two days. On February 5, 1694, Palmares was overrun. According to legend, many of Palmares bravest warriors hurled themselves over a cliff rather than surrender.

AFRICA

• Queen Nzinga (Nzinga Mbande/Ann Zingha) tried in vain to save the Ndongo people (in what is today Angola) from the oppressive forces of the Portuguese. Queen Nzinga would later conquer and organize the state of Matamba. From her position as Queen of Matamba, Nzinga came to control the supply of slaves to the Portuguese trading posts in Angola. Of the thousands of slaves that were supplied to the Portuguese during this time for shipment to Brazil, many were enslaved due to the efforts of Queen Nzinga.

• By 1630, many Capuchins had gone to Cairo (Egypt) to evangelize Ethiopia.

Capuchins are members of the Order of Friars Minor Capuchin, a Roman Catholic religious order. The Capuchins are an independent branch of the Franciscans. The name "Capuchin" is derived from the word "capuche"—the word for the long pointed hood that the Capuchins wore.

• 1630 marked the beginning of the ascent of the Bakuba culture.

1631

AFRICA

• Charles I of England granted a charter to Richard Young and others giving them the exclusive trade rights to the coast of Guinea, between Cape Blanco and the Cape of Good Hope, for a period of thirty years.

• Musa Pasha, the Viceroy of Egypt, was suspended by the Turkish grandees. For the next twenty-five years, Egypt would be ruled by an elected viceroy rather than an appointed one. Faqariyyah was deemed the most influential group of grandees.

• In August, in Mombasa (Kenya), Muslim forces under Yusuf bin Hasan, recaptured the city from the Portuguese. 250 Portuguese, Goans (Indians), and Africans were martyred following the execution of the Portuguese governor. This Muslim resurgence would adversely affect European interests all along the east coast of Africa. *See 1505.*

By 1631, the Kamba were trading on a regular basis with Mombasa. The Kamba were, and are, a people living in the Congo. They are related to the Kongo people and speak the Kongo language.

• By 1631, the Bunyoro kingdom (of northern Uganda) reached the height of its powers. At the same time, the Buganda began their ascent to power in what is today southern Uganda.

• The Strandloper leader Autshumao (also known as Harry) sailed to Java. He would return to South Africa and serve as an interpreter and as an unofficial postmaster for English sailors.

The Strandlopers were outcasts of the Khoikhoi (indigenous South African) people. They had very little in the way of possessions and were bound together not by kinship, but rather by common misfortune.

1632

AFRICA

• On January 8, the Portuguese attacked Mombasa in an attempt to retake the city. The attempt failed. On May 16, Sultan Yusuf ibn Hasan abandoned Mombasa and took to the seas as a pirate. On August 5, the Portuguese reentered and reclaimed Mombasa.

• In Ethiopia, the Emperor Susenyos (Basilides?) broke with Rome. Subsequently, the Jesuits were expelled and other Catholic missionaries were banned and warned that they would be sentenced to death if found in the country.

During the 1620s, a zealous Spanish priest, Alfonso Mendes, converted Susneyos, the Ethiopian emperor, to Catholicism. Using his influence over the emperor, from 1626 to 1632, Mendes purged the Ethiopian Coptic Church of opponents of the Catholic Church. This purge created clerical and popular dissension. It was this uproar which led Susneyos to renounce Catholicism and to expel the Catholic missionaries.

1633

AFRICA

• Between 1633 and 1635, war was waged between the Portuguese and the Dembo.
• Gondar was established as the imperial capital of Ethiopia.

1634

THE (FUTURE) UNITED STATES

• Slavery was introduced into the Maryland colony.
• French Catholics in Louisiana argued for educational opportunities for persons of African descent, including slaves.

THE AMERICAS

• By 1634, there were some 6,000 slaves in Barbados.

1635

AFRICA

• England and Morocco entered into a treaty.
• England initiated a military expedition against Algiers (Algeria).

EUROPE

• In 1635, a presentation of Encisco's play of Juan Latino's career revived interest in the life of the Afro-Spanish scholar. The play focused on the romance between Juan Latino and a Spanish noblewoman, Dona Ana—the love of his life whom Juan Latino eventually married. *See 1516.*

1636

THE (FUTURE) UNITED STATES

• Slavery was introduced into the Delaware colony.

AFRICA

• Francisco de Seixas de Cabreira became the Portuguese governor of Mombasa. Under his leadership, the Portuguese initiated a number of savage, punitive raids on the coastal towns along the East African coast in retaliation for the support of the Muslims.
• Between 1636 and 1643, the North African city state of Algiers would wage war against France.

1637

THE (FUTURE) UNITED STATES

• Slaves were imported into Massachusetts from Barbados. The slaves were part of a cargo that also included tobacco and cotton.
• Slaves were reported in Boston and in New Netherland (New York).

AFRICA

• French merchants of Dieppe constructed Fort St. Louis in Senegal and obtained privileges (charters) to conduct trade for ten years.
• The Portuguese plan to colonize Mozambique was abandoned.
• The Portuguese castle at Elmina (Ghana) was transferred to Dutch control.

Soon after the Dutch gained control of the key slave trade port of Elmina, the rent agreement for the settlement—a document called "the Note"—became the possession of the king of Denkyira. The king of the Denkyira had made the Dutch his trading partners.

The Denkyira were an Akan speaking group living in what is today western Ghana. For a time the Denkyira were the most powerful group in the region. However, in 1701, the Denkyira were defeated, and supplanted, by the Ashanti.

Among the spoils that the Ashanti acquired by defeating the Denkyira was "the Note." Thus, the Ashanti became the principal trading partners (and slave providers) of the Dutch and the English.

RELATED HISTORICAL EVENTS

• In France, the Huguenot synod decreed that slavery was not condemned by the law of God.

The Huguenots were a group of Protestants who became the center of political and religious quarrels in France in the 1500s and 1600s. The Huguenots believed the teachings of John Calvin and belonged to the Reformed Church. The French Roman Catholics named these Protestants "Huguenots." It is believed that the name is derived from Besancon Hugues, a Swiss religous leader.

Because of religious persecution in France in the 1600s, thousands of Huguenots fled France for new homes in the Americas. Many of these Huguenots settled in such places as South Carolina, Virginia, Massachusetts and New York. Among these American immigrants were such proud families as the Legare, Petigru, Maury, Revere, Jay, and DeLancey.

1638

THE (FUTURE) UNITED STATES

• New England became involved in the slave trade. Captain William Pierce of Salem, Massachusetts, sailed the *Desire* to the West Indies and exchanged Pequot [Indigenous (Native) American] slaves for goods and slaves of African descent.

AFRICA

• The Dutch occupied Mauritius.
• The English constructed a fort at Cormantin.

1639

AFRICA

• The Dutch blockaded the mouth of the Zaire River.

RELATED HISTORICAL EVENTS

• Pope Urban VIII excommunicated all Catholics who were engaged in the slave trade.

1640

THE (FUTURE) UNITED STATES

• Around 1640, a certain Captain Smith attacked an African village and brought some of the Africans to Massachusetts. Captain Smith was arrested and the Africans were sent home at the colony's expense.
• Three Virginia escaped indentured servants were captured and tried. The Dutch and Scottish servants were sentenced to serve four extra years while the servant of African descent, John Punch, was sentenced to serve "for the time of his natural life."
• In Virginia, a European man who had "associated" with a woman of African descent was compelled to do penance in church. The woman was whipped.

Between 1640 and 1699, fugitive laws were instituted in the following colonies: Connecticut, Maryland, New Jersey, Virginia, and South Carolina. These fugitive laws applied primarily to indentured servants, but were most harshly enforced against persons of African descent.

THE AMERICAS

Slaves of African descent were first used on the English tobacco plantations of the Caribbean Islands. As the European tobacco market became saturated, Caribbean planters turned to sugar as a money crop. With this development, the importation of Africans into the Caribbean began in earnest. Spurred by the increasing use of sugar as a money crop, the African slave population in the West Indies multiplied rapidly. For example, the African slave population of Barbados grew from a few hundred in 1640 to 6,000 in 1645.

As a result of sugar cane cultivation and the slave trade, the wealth of Barbados increased fortyfold between 1640 and 1667.

AFRICA

• Sweden became a participant in the slave trade.

• All Portuguese missionaries were expelled from Ethiopia.

1641

THE (FUTURE) UNITED STATES

• Massachusetts became the first colony to recognize slavery as a legal institution. The Massachusetts *Body of Liberties* legally recognized slavery, but allowed the enslavement of both Africans and Indigenous Americans only if they were "lawful" captives. Capture by "unjust violence" was illegal. This law was later incorporated into the Articles of the New England Confederation and became law for all of the New England colonies (December).

In 1641, the Bouweire Chapel in the New Netherlands had forty members of African descent.

THE AMERICAS

• The French landed on Santo Domingo and established the settlement of Port Margot. Lacking women, they brought in women of African descent purchased from traders or abducted from English or Spanish settlements.

AFRICA

• The Dutch attempted to conquer Angola.

By 1641, 13,000 to 16,000 slaves were being exported from Angola annually.

• The Jaga state of Kakonda was established.

1642

THE (FUTURE) UNITED STATES

• The Virginia Fugitive Law of 1642 stated that people who harbored escaped slaves and servants of any variety were to be fined 20 pounds of tobacco for each night of sanctuary. A second escape attempt by a slave was to be punished by branding the slave.

THE AMERICAS

• The French introduced African slaves into the Caribbean island of Martinique.

AFRICA

• The French organized the Compagnie de l'Orient for the purpose of colonizing Madagascar.
• The Dutch seized the Portuguese fort at Axim and commenced a series of raids against the English African positions. The Dutch would be successful and would secure all English forts except Cape Castle.
• An Ethiopian diplomatic mission was sent to Yemen.

1643

THE (FUTURE) UNITED STATES

In Virginia, before this year, servants without contracts generally became freedmen after terms of service varying from two to eight years. After 1643, the terms of service for such immigrants was fixed by law at four to seven years, the period varying somewhat with the youthfulness of the servant. The variations in the terms of service for servants of African descent appear to have been greater than for European servants.

• An intercolonial agreement on fugitives of the New England Confederation formed the basis of the United States Fugitive Laws of 1787, 1793 and 1850. It made the certificate of a magistrate the only evidence necessary to convict an escaped slave.

1644

THE (FUTURE) UNITED STATES

• The marriage of Antony van Angola and Lucie d'Angola in the New Netherlands (on Manhattan Island) became the first marriage between persons of African descent to be recorded in the area that would come to be known as the United States. The Angolas were married in the Boulweire Chapel, a Dutch chapel with an integrated congregation. *See 1641.*

In 1644, the Dutch authorities granted land to the first eleven persons of African descent who had been brought to the New Netherlands. The land given to the black settlers included property that today comprises Brooklyn and Greenwich Village.

AFRICA

• The Pemba were at war with the Faza.
• The Dutch began armed hostilities against the Portuguese in alliance with Queen Nzinga of Matawba.
• The Monomotapa acknowledged Portuguese suzerainty.

1 6 4 5

THE (FUTURE) UNITED STATES

• The *Rainbowe*, the first slave ship built in Anglo-America, set sail.

The profitable but "unpleasant" trade of slaving became an American industry with ships frequently leaving Boston harbor for raids along the West African coast. There, Africans were purchased by the New Englanders and taken to Barbados, where they were traded for salt, tobacco, sugar, wine, and rum. These valuable commodities were then sold in Boston at a huge profit. In fact, the profits were so great as to encourage the continuation and growth of this trade in other British ports in North America. The market in Barbados shipped slaves throughout the Americas. Between 1640 and 1667 the wealth of Barbados increased fortyfold.

• There were slaves of African descent reported in New Hampshire colony.

THE AMERICAS

• The Portuguese exported slaves from Mozambique to Brazil for the first time.

During the 1640s, the primary source for slaves for the Portuguese, Angola, was under Dutch control. As a result, the Portuguese began to utilize other slave markets such as the long established slave market of East Africa.

AFRICA

• Sweden constructed Fort Christianborg on the Gold Coast (Ghana) of Africa.

1 6 4 6

THE AMERICAS

• In 1646, there were 35,000 Africans and over 100,000 Afro-mestizos in Mexico.

AFRICA

• There was an uprising in Cacheu (Guinea-Bissau).

1 6 4 7

THE AMERICAS

• An African slave proclaimed himself king of Guinea in Santiago de Chile.

AFRICA

• The Dutch ship *Haarlem* wrecked in Table Bay (South Africa). The crew under Leendert Jansz built a fortress on the beach.

• A Carmelite mission was established in Madagascar.

• The uprising in Cacheu (Guinea-Bissau) was suppressed.

• Harar was made an independent sultanate by Ali Daud.

• An Ethiopian diplomatic mission was sent to Yemen.

1 6 4 8

THE (FUTURE) UNITED STATES

• In 1648, the governor of the Virginia colony decided to plant rice. The planting of rice was based upon a suggestion from the governor's slaves who believed the crop would grow in Virginia because the land was so similar to the slaves' homelands in Africa.

THE AMERICAS

• A unit of soldiers of African descent under General Henrique Diaz participated in a battle against the Dutch at the First Battle of Guararapes, near Recife, Brazil.

AFRICA

• Beginning 1648 and lasting until 1655, Ceuta was besieged by Ahmad Gailan, a rebel Moroccan chieftain.

• Luanda fell to fifteen ships and 1500 men from Brazil, and with this victory, the Portuguese were successful in evicting the Dutch from Angola.

Luanda is the capital and largest city of Angola. The Portuguese ruled Angola for over 400 years. The Portuguese founded Luanda in 1576. It soon became the main center for Portuguese settlement in Angola.

In Luanda, the Portuguese built many impressive European-style structures, including a fortress, churches, libraries, and government buildings.

RELATED HISTORICAL EVENTS

• In 1648, the Society of Friends (the Quakers) was founded by George Fox.

1 6 4 9

THE (FUTURE) UNITED STATES

• By 1649, there were 300 indentured servants of African descent in Virginia.

• In 1649, the Society for Propagating the Gospel in New England was incorporated by the British Parliament after John Eliot's success at converting Indigenous (Native) Americans (July 19). This Society would later expand its operations to include converting and educating persons of African descent.

RELATED HISTORICAL EVENTS

• The first English translation of the *Koran* was published.

1650

THE (FUTURE) UNITED STATES

• Connecticut gave statutory recognition to slavery.

THE AMERICAS

• By 1650, there were 18,000 African slaves in Barbados.
• In 1650, there were 35,000 Africans and 130,000 Afro-mestizos in Mexico.
• Sugar planting began on the Caribbean island of Martinique. Within a century, there would be 60,000 slaves on the island. It would take three revolts and a civil war to free these slaves.

Christopher Columbus reached Martinique in 1502. The French began to colonize the island in 1635. The Empress Josephine, the first wife of Napoleon Bonaparte, was born at Trois-Ilets on the island of Martinique.

AFRICA

• The kingdom of the Akwamu (a predecessor of the Ashanti kingdom in the region of Ghana) came to prominence.
• Omani Arabs recaptured Muscat from the Portuguese and began to build a new empire based on strength at sea in the Indian Ocean.

In 1507, the Portuguese captured Muscat and several other seaports in Oman and remained for the next 150 years. However, in 1650, the Omani Arabs forced the Portuguese out of Oman. Oman gradually took over much of the east coast of Africa and established trading posts there. The Arabs would maintain their presence there for the next two hundred years.

The Arab presence in East Africa is of great significance to both Africans and African Americans because for nearly two thousand years the two cultures have interacted and enriched each other. Historians believe that Arab traders began to settle in coastal communities of East Africa as early as the time of Christ. The African and Arab cultures gradually mixed and developed into the Swahili civilization which gave birth to the Swahili language.

The word "Swahili" means "coast people." The Swahili language was developed on the coast of East Africa for business purposes and to facilitate communication between the Arabs and the various East African peoples. Today Swahili is the official language of Kenya and Tanzania. Almost all Swahili people are Muslims.

• During the 1650s, inland trade between peninsular Khoikhoi in South Africa and the inland chiefdoms was reopened. The peninsular Khoikhoi were able to maintain their monopoly on trade with the Dutch.
• The Yoruba seized Dahomey (Benin).
• By 1650, the introduction of firearms into the African trading societies of the African west coast began to have significant political and social effects.
• Around 1650, Jenne (Mali) became one of the principal markets of the Muslim world.
• Beginning in 1650, the Portugal began exporting slaves from Mozambique on a regular basis to its American colonies.
• Kabaka Kaberega (Kabelega) of Buganda (Uganda) attacked the Bunyoro. The success of the campaign enabled Buganda to double in size.

"Kabaka" is the title given to the rulers of the Ganda kingdom (Buganda/Uganda).

• During the mid-1600s, the Jie, Karamojong, Lango and Teso expanded in the region of Uganda.

Today the Jie live in Uganda between the Dodoth people of the north and the Karamojong of the south. The Jie regard both the Dodoth and the Karamojong as their enemies. The Jie are noted for their inclusion of a rainmaking ritual in their religious beliefs. All the initiated men take part in the rainmaking ritual in March when the rainy season is expected to begin.

The Karamojong are a large ethnic group which resides on the plain which carries their name in Uganda. The Karamojong were the original people from which came the Dodoth, Jie, and Turkana. These splinter groups, along with the Karamojong, are all considered to be part of the Karamojong cluster. The Karamojong are cattle herders. Their love of cattle has prompted them to raid their neighbors—the Jie and the Teso—for centuries.

The Lango live in the area north of Uganda's

Lake Kyoga. The Lango are noted for their ancestor worship. The Lango believe that ancestor spirits can intervene in everyday life, especially when they are perceived as being angry. Contact with the ancestors is established through rituals at the ancestor shrines without the aid of a religious specialist. However, other spheres require the services of a religious specialist—an "ajoka"—who interprets the will of Jok—the will of the Creator. Among the more notable sons of the Lango was Milton Obote, the prime minister of Uganda during the late 1960s.

The Teso live in central Uganda. Teso tradition claims that they once lived in the region now occupied by the Karamojong. However, over a period of 250 years, the Teso moved into their present location in Uganda and northern Kenya. In this new location, the Teso transformed from being cattle herders to farmers due to the fertility of the land and the abundance of the rain. Like the Jie, the Teso consider the Karamojong to be their historic enemies.

• Around 1650, the Fon state rose to prominence in Dahomey under the leadership of Wegbaja.
• Beginning in 1650, the introduction of firearms into the African trading societies of the African west coast began to have a significant political and social effect.

1651

THE (FUTURE) UNITED STATES

To curtail the activities of the Dutch West India Company, the English Navigation Act of 1651 limited England's colonial slave trade to English merchants: "No goods or commodities of Asia, Africa or America . . . or of any . . . of the English plantations . . . shall be imported or brought into this commonwealth of England . . . or any other lands, islands, plantations or territories to this commonwealth belonging . . . in any other ship or ships . . . but only such as do . . . belong only to the people of this commonwealth or the plantations thereof.

Under the terms of the new legislation, all goods brought into England or its colonies from countries outside Europe had to be carried in ships owned by Englishmen or colonials. Further, at least half of the crews of these ships had to be of English nationality. Imports into England or its colonies from any part of Europe had to be carried either in English or colonial vessels, or vessels belonging to the country in which the imported goods were made. Most of the commodities that were produced in the colonies were to be shipped to England only.

This Act was aimed at promoting English maritime activities at the expense of the Dutch. Over the next fifty years, two wars would be fought to wrest the slave trade from the Dutch and place it in the hands of the English. The final terms of peace, among other things, surrendered New Netherlands to England and opened the way for England to become the world's greatest naval power—and the world's greatest slave trader.

• Anthony Johnson, a person of African descent, imported five servants and received head rights (a grant of land for each servant imported). Johnson was given 200 acres along the Pungoteague River in Northampton County, Virginia. Other persons of African descent followed Johnson and soon a community developed. At its height, this Anglo-African settlement had perhaps 12 homesteads with extensive holdings. Dissension plagued the community and much litigation ensued over contract infringement and property disputes.

Anthony Johnson came to Virginia from England in 1621 as an indentured servant. After working off his years of servitude, Johnson saved his money, bought land, and began to bring in other indentured servants, both European and African.

After Johnson received the initial 200 acres in 1651, his sons were able to add an additional 650 acres.

AFRICA

• The Dutch blockaded Bou Regreg in an attempt to curtail piracy.
• Courlanders constructed James Fort on an island in the Gambia estuary.
• A delegation from Mombasa requested aid from the Omanis in their effort to expel the Portuguese.
• The British East India Company took the island of St. Helena from the Dutch.

Saint Helena lies about 1,200 miles (1,930 kilometers) off the southwest coast of Africa. Saint Helena is famous because Napoleon Bonaparte was forced to live in exile on the island from 1815 until his death in 1821.

1652

AFRICA

• Between 1652 and 1674, the Dutch

fought three naval wars with England. The English aspired to gain supremacy over the seas which, at the time, was held by the Dutch. The naval wars were fought by the English in order to seize the shipping and trading routes of the Dutch, but the English were not successful in these wars. As a consequence of their failure, the English were forced to give up their principal South American territory (modern day Suriname). In consolation, the English received the relatively small and insignificant Dutch possessions in chilly North America. The English received New Netherland, — a place we know today as New York.

• Massachusetts law required persons of African descent and Indigenous (Native) Americans to train for the militia.

• Rhode Island's General Court of Election passed a law which prohibited bondage of more than ten years for both Europeans and persons of African descent. However, this law was not uniformly enforced (May 18).

AFRICA

• By 1652, a number of new kingdoms arose on the Congo grasslands. Of particular note, the Lozi and Bemba entered Zambia at about this time.

The Lozi and Bemba: The Lozi are a people who today live in southwest Zambia. The Lozi speak the Lozi language and, today, are predominantly Christians. Lozi agriculture is centered around the Kafue River flood plain. The Lozi people also engage in fishing, cattle raising and trade.

The Bemba are a people who today live in the northeastern part of Zambia. The Bemba speak the Chibemba language. The early Bemba were renowned as hunters and warriors. They often raided their neighbors and absorbed them to expand their realm. The militaristic tendency of the Bemba led to their involvement in the ivory, copper and slave trade in East Africa and along the Indian Ocean.

• The Angolan kingdoms of the Kongo and Ndongo were thoroughly defeated and devastated by Portuguese invasions and the perpetuation of the slave trade.

The Kongo are a people who today live in the western part of Zaire and the northwestern part of Angola. The Kongo speak the Kikongo language.

The Kongo formed a great kingdom that reached its zenith in the fifteenth and sixteenth centuries. However, during the seventeenth century the kingdom disintegrated because of the devastation wrought by European invasions and the perpetuation of the slave trade. Nevertheless, the Kongo linguistic and cultural dominance of the region continued to be felt and is still felt to this day.

• The Dutch founded a settlement at the Cape of Good Hope.

In 1652, a Dutch expedition consisting of three ships was sent by the Dutch East India Company to the southern tip of Africa. Under the command of Jan van Riebeeck, the expedition landed at Table Bay and erected a supply base at the present site of Cape Town. The base was to serve as a halfway station where ships of the Dutch East India Company could pick up food and water on the way to and from the East Indies. Not long after the Dutch established their Cape Town base settlement, they imported slaves from tropical Africa — and later from the East Indies — to work on the Cape Town farms.

• The Omani raided the East African coast as far south as the island of Zanzibar.

• The Bambara on the middle Niger River, and the Yoruba of Oyo in southwestern Nigeria came to prominence.

Today the Bambara people occupy the central part of the country of Mali and the northern part of the Ivory Coast (Cote d'Ivoire). The Bambara speak the Bamana-ka language. The Bambara are primarily farmers. Agriculture is their main occupation and is considered to be the most highly valued work among the Bambara people.

The Yoruba are found in Nigeria, Benin and Togo. The Yoruba speak the Yoruba language. In precolonial times, the Yoruba were divided into many independent groups. Each group was ruled by a king who was considered to be a friend of the gods and to have spiritual powers which set him apart from his people. Great power was also in the hands of commoner chiefs who formed a council of state which could choose the next king.

One of the earliest and most important Yoruba kingdoms was Oyo which was founded around 1100. The Oyo kingdom reached its zenith in the sixteenth through the eighteenth centuries.

• March 9, 1652, is recorded as the probable cipher date for the *Hamziya*, the earliest known poem composed in Swahili.

The first Swedish voyages to the Gold Coast occurred. The Swedes set up trading lodges at Takoradi, Cape Coast, Osu and Accra (in Ghana).

1 6 5 3

THE (FUTURE) UNITED STATES

• In 1653, Anthony Johnson became the first person of African descent to be on record as owning slaves.

AFRICA

• Kwararafa besieged Katsina.
• An armed Dutch expedition was sent against the Khoikhoi.

1 6 5 4

THE AMERICAS

In the summer of 1654, Father Diego Ramirez Farina arrived in Cartagena from Spain with a commission from the king of Spain to work among the slaves. Father Peter Claver was overjoyed and dragged himself from his bed to greet his successor. Shortly afterwards, Father Peter heard the confession of his good friend Dona Isabella and told her it was for the last time. On September 6, after assisting at Mass and receiving communion, Father Peter confided to Nicholas Gonzalez, "I am going to die." That same evening, he became very ill and slipped into a coma.

The news of the impending death of the priest spread like wildfire through Cartagena. Suddenly, everyone remembered the priest again. Scores came to kiss his hands before it was too late. Some of the more greedy citizens stripped his meager cell of everything that could be carried off as a relic.

Saint Peter Claver never recovered. He died on September 8, 1654.

After his death, the civil authorities who had looked with disdain at his solicitations amongst the slaves and his fellow clergy who had criticized his zeal, now vied with one another to honor his memory. The city magistrates ordered that he should be buried at public expense with great pomp, and the vicar general of the diocese officiated at the funeral. The slaves and the Indigenous Americans arranged for a Mass of their own. Father Peter's church was ablaze with lights, a special choir sang, and an oration was delivered which eloquently spoke of the virtues, holiness, heroism, and stupendous miracles of Father Claver.

Saint Peter Claver was never again forgotten and his fame spread throughout the world. He was canonized in 1888 and he was declared by Pope Leo XIII the patron of all missionary enterprises among persons of African descent, in whatever part of the world.

The work performed by Saint Peter Claver is simply unparalleled in the annals of African or African American history. In one way or another, he touched the lives of over 300,000 persons of African descent at a time when they were at their most vulnerable. His greatness cannot be denied and his memory should never be forgotten.

• The Dutch established new settlements in Guiana and on some neighboring islands.

1 6 5 5

THE AMERICAS

• British forces seized Jamaica and the Cayman Islands, wresting them from Spanish control (May 10).

Following a pattern that would repeat itself throughout history, the conflict between the European powers provided a window of opportunity for oppressed people of African descent. In 1655, when the British wrested control of Jamaica from the Spanish, the African slaves in Jamaica seized the day to stage a revolt against the slave owners. The successful rebels found sanctuary amongst the already extant maroon communities in the hills of Jamaica.

The English expedition sent by Oliver Cromwell to take San Domingo (the island of Hispaniola) had been repulsed by the Spanish there. However, in Jamaica, they overpowered the relatively small Spanish contingent. Not so with the Jamaica maroons.

After defeating the Spanish, the English found the Jamaican mountains populated by more than 1500 self-liberated Africans. These Africans refused to submit to English authority. While the English were able to gain control over most of the island by 1660, they could never quite gain control over the entire island — they could never quite gain control over the maroons.

For seventy years, the maroons refused to be subjugated. Not until 1738 were the British able to say that Jamaica was British. In that year, the British and the maroons signed a peace treaty which temporarily brought to an end their formal, armed hostilities.

The record of maroon uprisings in Jamaica is a rather lengthy one. There were slave or maroon uprisings in Jamaica in 1669, 1672, 1673, twice in 1678, 1682, 1685, 1690, 1733, and 1734. There were other revolts in Jamaica in 1760, 1765, 1766, 1807, 1815, and 1824. The Christmas Rising of 1831 is estimated to have involved possibly 20,000 slaves and maroons. *See 1663.*

AFRICA

• In Angola, the plague struck. Half of Angola's population succumbed to the epidemic.
• The first of many Khoikhoi (indigenous South African) protests against the land seizure by the Dutch was staged.
• A Tunisian (Barbary pirate) corsair fleet was destroyed by Blake. The English then proceeded to bombard Algiers.

1656

THE (FUTURE) UNITED STATES

• Benjamin Doyle, a person of African descent, received a land grant of 300 acres in Surrey County, Virginia. Other persons of African descent also had land holdings, many in integrated communities.

AFRICA

• In what is today South Africa (but what was then the Dutch Cape settlement), a slave was freed in order to marry a Dutch man.

When the Dutch first began to settle what is today South Africa, it was imperative to them to maintain good relations with the Khoikhoi (the indigenous South Africans). The Khoikhoi were important to the Dutch because the Dutch relied upon the Khoikhoi to furnish their ships with cattle and sheep on their long voyages to the East Indies. With maintaining good relations with the Khoikhoi in mind, the Dutch East India Company prohibited the Dutch settlers of the Cape from enslaving the Khoikhoi. However, this prohibition on enslaving the local Africans did not prohibit the importation of slaves from other places.

The first slaves brought to the Cape settlement were mainly from West Africa—particularly Guinea and Angola. However, the South African importation of slaves was not limited to African slaves. Later expeditions brought slaves from Mozambique and Madagascar. Indeed, even more "prized" than African slaves, were the slaves imported from Java, Bali, Timor (Indonesia), the Malay Peninsula, and China. Over the next century, slaves would also be imported from India and the Philippines.

1657

THE (FUTURE) UNITED STATES

• George Fox, founder of the Quakers, impressed upon his followers in America "the duty of converting the slaves" and Fox himself practiced what he preached by ministering to the slaves in the West Indies.

AFRICA

• The Dutch East India Company began to allow some of its Cape Town settlers to leave the settlement and start their own farms further inland (in the area known as the Liesbeeck Valley). These settlers would come to be known as Boers (farmers).
• The Goringhaiqua (indigenous South African) Doman was sent to Batavia (Indonesia) to become an interpreter. Doman's Batavia experiences would engender his opposition to the Dutch when he returned to the Cape settlement.
• Slaves from Angola and West Africa arrived at the Cape settlement of the Dutch.
• The Danes took possession of Fort Christianborg on the Gold Coast of Africa (Ghana), thereby displacing the Swedes.

1658

THE (FUTURE) UNITED STATES

• Africans and Indigenous Americans staged a revolt in Hartford, Connecticut.

AFRICA

• The first Khoikhoi-Dutch (Hottentot) War began as a result of conflicts between the Boers (Dutch farmers) and the Khoikhoi (indigenous South Africans) over cattle raids and Dutch land seizures. Doman *see 1657* led the Khoikhoi in their "War of Liberation" by raiding the herds of the Dutch who had seized land outside of the Cape settlement.
• There was an army revolt in Cairo, Egypt.
• The Dutch abandoned Mauritius.

EUROPE

• African ambassadors from Togoland were sent to the courts of Spain and France. Bans was sent to the court of King Philip IV of Spain in 1658, while Don Matthew Lopes was sent to the court of Louis XIV at Versailles in 1670. *See 1670.*

---------- **1 6 5 9** ----------

AFRICAN HISTORY

• Saint Louis, Senegal, was founded.

---------- **1 6 6 0** ----------

THE (FUTURE) UNITED STATES

Up to 1660, it was an accepted practice in most American colonies and in the British West Indies that baptism into a Christian Church would legally free an African slave.

• Connecticut barred persons of African descent from serving in the militia.
• A statute was passed in Virginia which limited the tax on the sale of slaves. This statute was the first indicator that slavery had become institutionalized in Virginia (March 13).
• The plan for colonial government for South Carolina was drafted by John Locke and included provisions which granted slave owners absolute authority over their slaves.

THE AMERICAS

• By 1660, 4,000 to 5,000 slaves were brought to Barbados annually. These slaves were sold for a price of about seventeen pounds each.

AFRICA

• From 1660 to 1780, the Pashas ruled at Timbuktu. These Pashas often were of interracial heritage. After 1780, the title of Pasha was replaced by "mayor." The mayors of Timbuktu were alternately chosen by the Bambara, the Tuareg, and the Fulani.

Today the Bambara people occupy the central part of the country of Mali and the northern part of the Ivory Coast (Cote d'Ivoire). The Bambara speak the Bamana-ka language. The Bambara are primarily farmers. Agriculture is their main occupation and is considered to be the most highly valued work among the Bambara people.

The Tuareg are a Berber people living in the southern Sahara Desert region which includes portions of Algeria, Libya, Mali, Niger and Chad. The Tuareg are a mobile (nomadic) tent-dwelling people. The Tuareg make their living by breeding camels and serving as guides and guardians for desert caravans. The reputation of the Tuaregs rested upon their legendary raids against their more sedentary neighbors and upon caravans. Their success at these raids enabled the Tuaregs to increase their cattle

herds. Due to their swift camels and their often superior weaponry, the Tuaregs were always a formidable foe.

The Fulani live in northern Nigeria, Mali, Guinea, Cameroon, Senegal, Niger, Burkina Faso, Guinea-Bissau and many other West African nations. The Fulani speak Fulfulde and were among the first African people to embrace Islam.

• The first war between the Dutch and the Khoikhoi came to an end. The conclusion of the war, while providing the Khoikhoi with a short term victory, insured the eventual loss of independence because the war failed to eradicate the Dutch from Khoikhoi lands. In response to the Khoikhoi resistance, the Dutch built more, better fortified posts and erected almond hedges to prevent the unauthorized taking of cattle. In this year, the Dutch also began to send exploration parties further inland in an attempt to bypass the Khoikhoi as their principal trading partners.

In the 1660s, the Dutch introduced the first horses into South Africa. The introduction of horses also evidenced and solidified the Dutch military superiority over the Khoikhoi.

• The Omanis continued their raids upon the East African coast.

---------- **1 6 6 1** ----------

THE (FUTURE) UNITED STATES

• The first individual petition of a person of African descent requesting his freedom and addressed to the colony of New Netherlands was granted.

In the New Netherlands (what is today New York), Emanuel Pieterson and Reytory, free African husband and wife petitioned the Noble-Right Honorable Director-General and Lords Councillors to declare Anthony, an African orphan born of free persons, to be free as well. The petition was eventually granted.

• Slavery was officially recognized in Virginia by a slave law which stated: "In case any English servant shall run away in company with any *persons of African descent* who are incapable of making satisfaction by addition of time, be it enacted that the English so running away in company with them shall serve for the time of the *absence of the persons of African descent* as they are to do for their own by a former act."

Two other measures passed in Virginia in 1661 effectively made African slaves slaves for life. One measure stated that Africans and their children would be slaves for life, the other declared that all servants not being Christians when brought in by sea were declared slaves for life.

AFRICA

• The Omani, the main Indian Ocean rivals of the Portuguese, once again seized the Portuguese outpost at Mombasa.
• A French expedition was launched to take Algiers.

—————— 1 6 6 2 ——————

THE (FUTURE) UNITED STATES

• Virginia enacted a statute making slavery hereditary, following the status of the mother (December).

The law enacted by Virginia read: "Whereas some doubts have arisen whether children got by any Englishman upon [an African] woman should be slave or free, be it therefore enacted and declared by this present Grand Assembly, that all children born in this country shall be held bond or free according to the condition of the mother; and that if any Christian shall commit fornication with [an African] man or woman, he or she so offending shall pay double the fines imposed by the former act."

This law is important because it is statutory recognition of the English denial of responsibility for individuals who were, in fact, their own children. Unlike in Spain and France, where the products of liaisons with slaves were often taken into the family, in Anglo-America it was as if the blood relationship between the father and the child did not exist.

Some historians contend that this statute was the most important piece of legislation in African American history prior to the passage of the Thirteenth Amendment. What is certainly unarguable is that this law had ramifications which deleteriously impacted the psyche of both European Americans and African Americans in ways which have not been healthy or conducive to resolving the nation's race problem. What this law did was to institutionalize rejection and denial and to create the foundation for a society in which dysfunction and racial animosity have become ingrained.

AFRICA

• A British Royal African Company chartered by Charles II seized a fort (Cape Coast Castle) at James Island at the mouth of the Gambia River in West Africa. The British Royal African Company was composed of numerous persons of high rank including the king's brother, the duke of York. Taking advantage of the war declared against the Dutch, the Company seized and retained several Dutch forts on the Gold Coast between 1665 and 1672.
• Jan van Riebeeck, one of the European founding fathers of South Africa, moved from the Dutch Cape colony to Malacca.

RELATED HISTORICAL EVENTS

• Colbert's mercantilist theory proposed the establishment of a French-controlled slave trade to rival Spain's.

—————— 1 6 6 3 ——————

THE (FUTURE) UNITED STATES

• Governor Calvert of Maryland wrote to Lord Baltimore that the colony needed African slaves, but was too poor to guarantee a large annual sale to the Company of Royal Adventurers.
• In Maryland, by law, all imported persons of African descent were to become slaves *durante vita* (for life). Any free European woman who married a man of African descent would become a slave during the life of her husband, and her children were to be slaves. This law gave legal recognition to slavery in the Maryland colony. A 1681 revision of this law stated that the children born of European servant women and men of African descent would be free.
• The first major slave rebellion in colonial Anglo-America took place in Gloucester, Virginia. The slave rebellion consisted of a conspiracy between European indentured servants and slaves of African descent. The conspiracy was betrayed by a house servant (September 13).
• The settlers in the Carolinas were offered 20 acres of land for every male slave of African descent brought to the colony in the first year of settlement, and 10 acres for every female slave of African descent.

THE AMERICAS

• In Hispaniola, the French annexed the eastern part of the island, thereby, briefly ending the division of the island between France and Spain.
• In Jamaica, the freedom of the maroons

of Jamaica was formally acknowledged. Land was given to the maroons and their leader, Juan de Bolas, was made a colonel in the militia. In 1664, Bolas would be killed. *See 1655.*

AFRICA

• In 1663, two of South Africa's most colorful indigenous leaders died. Both Doman, the Khoikhoi leader during the first Khoikhoi-Dutch (Hottentot) War, and Autshumao (Harry, the Strandloper) died.

• A school for the Dutch and the Khoikhoi opened in Cape Town (South Africa).

• The first English settlement was built in Sierra Leone.

EUROPE

• King Charles II of England granted a charter to the Company of Royal Adventurers which allowed the Company to establish forts and factories to facilitate English participation in the slave trade (June 10).

The Duke of York, King Charles II of England, the dowager queen and prominent merchants organized the Company of Royal Adventurers. In 1672, the company was renamed the Royal African Company. The Royal African Company enjoyed a monopoly on the slave trade that serviced the English colonies.

• The Italians, Grillo and Lomelin, obtained an asiento from the government of Spain for transporting 24,000 African slaves to the Americas.

1664

THE (FUTURE) UNITED STATES

• A Maryland colonial law stated that baptism had no effect on the status of a slave. The statute was passed to end judicial decisions that had freed slaves after baptism. Similar acts were subsequently passed in North Carolina, New Jersey, New York, South Carolina and Virginia.

• Maryland passed a statute preventing marriages between English women and men of African descent. This statute established a precedent which was soon adopted by several of the other colonies (September 20).

The Maryland statute preventing interracial marriage between Anglo women and African men was ostensibly enacted because the legislators deemed the marriage of English women to African men to be a disgrace but, in actuality, the law addressed a more profound issue.

At this time in colonial history, a problem arose over the status of the children born in a marriage between slaves and free persons. Under English law, the status of the child was determined by the status of the father. Devious slave owners would therefore sometimes mate African male slaves to Anglo female servants. By doing so, they knew that the offspring of such a union would have the same status as their father—that the offspring of such a union would be slaves for life.

The new Maryland law made the mating of African males to Anglo females a violation of the law. However, the law went one step further by declaring that any child born of such a union would be enslaved. (September)

• New York and New Jersey officially and legally recognized the institution of slavery.

It is important to note that prior to 1664, New York and New Jersey were Dutch possessions, and that slavery flourished in them. However, the legislation of 1664 referred to herein, was the first official Anglo-American pronouncements on the issue of slavery in the newly acquired colonies.

THE AMERICAS

From 1664 to 1788, up to 3,000 Jamaican maroons would wage a continual guerrilla war against the British. Soldiers, indigenous Jamaicans, and dogs would be sent against them. But success was limited. Eventually, in 1738, Captain Cudjo and other maroon chiefs would make a formal treaty of peace with Governor Trelawney. Under the treaty, the maroons were granted 2,500 acres, their freedom was recognized, and they were promised bonuses for the return of escaped slaves. *See 1655 and 1663.*

AFRICA

• War erupted between the English and the Dutch in West Africa.

As an extension of the growing hostilities between the English and the Dutch, on August 29, 1664, the Dutch held city of New Amsterdam was captured by a fleet of three English warships. Upon its capture, the English renamed the city. The English named their prize New York.

• The Dutch reoccupied Mauritius.

RELATED HISTORICAL EVENTS

• The French West Indian Company was organized by Colbert.

• An English Puritan, Richard Baxter, in his *Christian Directory,* called slave traders "common enemies of mankind" and said it was a sin to buy their captives except to free them. Baxter later called the slave trade "one of the worst kinds of thievery in the world."

1 6 6 5

THE (FUTURE) UNITED STATES

• Duke's laws for the government of New York did not exempt Christian Africans and Indigenous Americans from slavery.

THE AMERICAS

• In the Spanish colonies, slaves, mestizos and mulattoes who served the government were allowed to carry arms.

AFRICA

• On October 29, the battle of Mbwila took place. After the battle, the Portuguese reigned supreme in Angola.
• Bourbon (now known as Reunion) was seized by France.
• There was a French expedition against Algiers.

RELATED HISTORICAL EVENTS

• In March of 1665, war erupted between England and Holland (the Dutch). On June 3, the Dutch would be defeated at South wold Bay. In November, the Dutch blockaded the Thames.

One of the dire consequences of the war between the English and the Dutch was the spread of the Great Plague. The Plague had ravaged Amsterdam and was brought to England upon Dutch ships. In the summer of 1665, it struck with full force in England. Altogether some 70,000 Londoners (one-seventh of the total population) fell prey to the disease.

In desperation to alleviate the devastation caused by the Plague, the doctors of the day tried a number of cures and preventive measures. One of the preventive measures which seemed promising was a certain plant from the Americas. It was thought that when the plant was smoked the vapors had certain curative properties. The plant was tobacco and its use in England soon became commonplace. Indeed, during the height of the Great Plague, school-children were *required* to smoke pipe tobacco in an effort to ward off the disease.

As a consequence of the Great Plague, the use of tobacco spread throughout England. The popularity of smoking tobacco created a demand which, in turn, led to an emphasis be-

ing placed on the English American colonies' increased production of the plant. With the increased demand, tobacco plantations soon arose in the colonies of Virginia, North Carolina and South Carolina.

The tobacco plantations of the 1600s were labor intensive operations requiring a large number of field hands. Of course, as an additional consequence of its many European wars and of the devastation wreaked by the Great Plague, England during the late 1600s did not have many spare laborers. A cheap alternative labor force had to be acquired to work the tobacco plantations and, for the source of this cheap labor, the English looked to Africa.

1 6 6 6

AFRICA

• Construction on Cape Town Castle was begun.

1 6 6 7

THE (FUTURE) UNITED STATES

• Virginia passed a law which declared that conversion of slaves to Christianity did not affect their slave status (September 23). Another Virginia law declared that the killing of a slave by "extremity of correction" would not be considered a felony.

England passed the "Act to Regulate the Negroes on the British Plantations." The act referred to persons of African descent as having a "wild, barbarous and savage nature, to be controlled only with strict severity." Slaves were forbidden to leave the plantation without a pass; they were never allowed to leave on Sunday; and they were forbidden to carry weapons. The punishment for a slave striking a Christian was severe whipping, and for a second offense, branding on the face with a hot iron. No punishment was provided for an owner who "accidentally" whipped a slave to death. The act also forbade slaves from possessing horns or other signaling devices. The punishment for an owner's "wanton" killing of his or her own slave was a fifteen pound (English currency) fine and for killing the slave of another was twenty-five pounds.

THE AMERICAS

• The Cabildo of Buenos Aires informed the king of Spain that there was a scarcity of slaves due to the ravages of pestilences and diseases.

AFRICA

• England took possession of the Cape Coast Castle as a condition of the Treaty of Breda. At this time, Indians began to arrive at the Cape as laborers and slaves.
• In 1667, Yohannes I came to power in Ethiopia. During his reign, Yohannes effected numerous ecclesiastical reforms and was responsible for building the first royal library and the chancery of Gondar.

RELATED HISTORICAL EVENTS

• After years of an inclusive war, on July 31, England and Holland (the Dutch) negotiated the Treaty of Breda. The Treaty of Breda gave New Amsterdam (New York) to England while the Dutch were given Guiana (Guyana).

1668

THE (FUTURE) UNITED STATES

• A Virginia colonial law said: "...women (of African descent) set free, although permitted to enjoy their freedom, yet ought not in all respects to be admitted to the full fruition of the exemptions and impunities of the English."

AFRICA

• The Council of Gondar (Ethiopia) required all resident Frenchmen to adhere to the Ethiopian (Coptic) Church and required all Muslims to reside in segregated villages.

RELATED HISTORICAL EVENTS

• Josiah Child, future governor of the East India Company, argued for African slavery and against the settlement by European laborers in the West Indies. The emigration of Europeans, he explained, deprived England of consumers and laborers, while with slavery a few Europeans could produce goods and beneficially stimulate English trade.

1669

THE (FUTURE) UNITED STATES

• Virginia passed a law which acquitted masters who killed their slaves because "it cannot be presumed that premeditated malice (which alone makes murder a felony) should induce any man to destroy his own estate" (October).

THE AMERICAS

• There were slave uprisings in Jamaica in 1669, 1672, 1673, twice in 1678, 1682, 1685, 1690, 1733, and 1734. There were other revolts in Jamaica in 1760, 1765, 1766, 1807, 1815, and 1824. The Christmas Rising of 1831 is estimated to have involved possibly 20,000 slaves and maroons. *See 1655 and 1663.*

1670

THE (FUTURE) UNITED STATES

• The Body of Liberties of Massachusetts was amended to close an unintentional legal loophole that had allowed children of slaves to sue for freedom.
• A Virginia law declared that "all servants not being Christians imported into this colony by shipping" were to be slaves for life, but such servants as came by land were to "serve, if boys and girls, until 30 years of age, if men and women, 12 years and no longer." This law in effect made all African slaves, slaves for life, while European servants were servants only for a period of time.

In 1670, Sir William Berkeley estimated that there were 2,000 African slaves and 6,000 European servants in Virginia out of an overall population of 40,000.

• In Virginia, the principle and practice of universal suffrage were abandoned. Voting privileges were restricted to freeholders and housekeepers of certain qualifications, with the avowed purpose of disenfranchising persons recently freed from servitude.
• Virginia enacted a statute which banned slavery for persons of African descent who arrived in the colonies as Christians (October 13). However, twelve years later, in 1682, the law was repealed.

THE AMERICAS

• A French royal order opened the slave trade to Frenchmen to promote "the trade in [Africans] from Guinea to the Islands," as "there is nothing that does more to help the growth of those colonies ... than the labor of [Africans]."

Between 1670 and 1672, the French imported more than 3,000 slaves per year into their Caribbean colonies.

• A treaty between England and Spain recognized England's right to Jamaica and its other possessions in the Americas. In return,

England promised to stop its sanction of piracy.

Despite the assurances made by the English government during the 1670s, English pirates continued to use Jamaica as a base from which attacks on Spanish ports and ships could be staged.

AFRICA

• Timbuktu was overrun by the Bambara.
• Kwararafa sacked Kano and attacked Katsina.
• The Omani continued their raids on the East African coast as far south as Mozambique. As part of the raid, the town of Mozambique was sacked and burned.
• In 1670, the Dutch began construction of a fort at Sekondi.

Today Sekondi-Takoradi is the main port of Ghana.

EUROPE

• Don Matthew Lopes, from Togoland, was sent as an ambassador to France and the court of King Louis XIV at Versailles.

Southern Europe began to see a number of diplomatic visitors from Africa in the fifteenth and sixteenth centuries. In the seventeenth century, African emissaries began to reach the nations of northern Europe. One of the earliest was Don Matthew Lopes (Matteo Lopez), the royal interpreter to Kpoyizoun, the king of Ardra (modern day Dahomey).

Don Matthew Lopes was presented at the court of Louis XIV and was lionized briefly by the French aristocracy but the projected treaty of alliance between France and Ardra was never ratified.

Don Matthew Lopes was followed a few years later by Aniaba from the Ivory Coast. Aniaba succeeded in passing himself off as the son of the reigning king when, in fact, he was only a slave to the courtier of the king.

Aniaba stayed in France from 1687 to 1701, serving as an officer in the French cavalry. So well received was Aniaba, that he was eventually baptized with the king, Louis XIV, serving as his godfather.

———— 1671 ————

THE (FUTURE) UNITED STATES

• Governor Berkeley of Virginia estimated that more than 2,000 slaves were in the colony.

• A Maryland act extending the scope of the slavery law passed in 1664 declared that conversion or baptism of slaves before or after their importation did not entitle them to freedom. The act was passed to quell fears of slave owners who hesitated to import slaves for fear of losing their investment through prior or subsequent conversion, and also to encourage slave owners to convert their slaves to Christianity.

THE AMERICAS

• George Fox, the English Quaker, included Africans in Christ's martyrdom in sermons made on a missionary trip to Barbados.

AFRICA

• The French built a fort at Whydah.
• Madagascar was declared a French royal property.
• Louis XIV dispatched Vansleb to visit churches in the Nile Valley.
• The first dey came to power in Algiers. "Dey" was the title given to the commanding officer of the Janissaries, an elite corps of Turkish troops. However, with the ascension of the dey, Turkish authority over Algiers actually began to subside instead of increase.

———— 1672 ————

THE (FUTURE) UNITED STATES

• Virginia passed a law urging and rewarding the killing of maroons. "Maroons" was a loose description for self-liberated (escaped) slaves who had established communities in which they lived a primarily nomadic life due to the persistent harassment of European bounty hunters. The maroons formed communities in the mountains, swamps and forests of the frontier fringe areas. The term "maroon" was derived from the Spanish "cimarrones," a term for self-liberated (escaped) slaves.

Between 1672 and 1864, there was evidence of at least 50 maroon communities in or near the English colonies (later American states), mainly in the mountain forests and swamps of South Carolina, North Carolina, Virginia, Louisiana, Florida, Georgia, Mississippi, and Alabama.

In the 1800s, the maroon colonies established in Florida fought along with the Indigenous (Native) Americans against Americans who wanted the United States to annex Spanish Florida and to eliminate the presence of the maroon havens for escaped slaves.

Soon after the maroons began to settle in Florida, refugees from the Creek nation also settled there. This group of Indigenous (Native) Americans called themselves "Seminoles," and their Muskogee culture accepted a variety of Indigenous (Native) American ethnic groups.

The African settlers proved far more familiar with Florida's tropical terrain than Spaniards or Seminoles and, because of the Africans' adaptability to the Florida environment and their knowledge of Europeans, the Seminoles grew to rely upon them. Soon there was a great deal of interdependence and intermarriage between the two groups of oppressed people. As time passed and the oppression became stronger, so did the bond between the two people. *See 1837.*

THE AMERICAS

• The king of England (Charles II) chartered the Royal African Company which came to dominate the world slave trade. One of its contracts was to supply 3,000 slaves a year to the British West Indies.

The charter granted to the Royal African Company covered the area from Sallee on the coast of Morocco down to the Cape of Good Hope. The company was supported by recently raised capital of more than 100,000 pounds (English currency). The Royal African Company announced that it would place great emphasis on promptness of sale, and that if those interested would contract to receive whole cargoes, then any slave between 12 and 40 years of age "able to go over the ship's side unaided" would be supplied for 15 pounds per head in Barbados, for 16 pounds in Nevis, for 17 pounds in Jamaica, and for 18 pounds in Virginia (September 27).

• There were slave uprisings in Jamaica in 1672, 1673, twice in 1678, 1682, 1685, 1690, 1733, and 1734. There were other revolts in Jamaica in 1760, 1765, 1766, 1807, 1815, and 1824. *See 1655 and 1663.*

AFRICA

• In 1672, the Dutch attempted to formalize their seizure of the Khoikhoi land by drafting purchase agreements and having two Khoikhoi chieftains sign the agreements. However, it is doubtful that the Khoikhoi knowledgeably consented to the content of the agreements because for the Khoikhoi the concept of individual land ownership was an unknown, unfathomable concept. For the Khoikhoi, the land belonged to the people—to the community—and could not be individually owned.

• Denmark established forts on the Gold Coast.

• The English bombarded Algiers.

• The English established a fort at Sierra Leone.

• Beginning in 1672, Morocco conducted a series of slave raids by raiding the peoples of the Sub-Sahara.

1673

THE AMERICAS

• There were slave uprisings in Jamaica in 1673, twice in 1678, 1682, 1685, 1690, 1733, and 1734. There were other revolts in Jamaica in 1760, 1765, 1766, 1807, 1815, and 1824. *See 1655 and 1663.*

AFRICA

• In 1673, the second Khoikhoi-Dutch War began. The war was initiated when Jeronimus Cruse mounted a raid stealing livestock from the Cochoqua (another indigenous South African people).

• The French Senegal Company was organized for the purpose of facilitating France's participation in the slave trade.

1674

THE (FUTURE) UNITED STATES

• John Eliot, having worked to educate Indigenous (Native) Americans, turned his attention to the education of persons of African descent.

THE AMERICAS

• Barbados developed a savage slave code which led to a number of attempted slave insurrections. In 1674, 1692, and 1702, slave uprisings occurred, but they were not successful. However, the slave uprising of 1816 was successful. In the 1816 insurrection, a great deal of property was destroyed. The slaves, under the leadership of a mestizo, Washington Franklin, were successful in securing a repeal of the slave laws and, eventually, the slaves became recognized as full citizens with the right to vote.

Barbados is an island country in the West Indies. Barbados is the easternmost island of the

West Indies archipelago. It lies about 250 miles (402 kilometers) northeast of Venezuela.

It is believed that the first inhabitants of Barbados were the Arawaks who were driven off the island by the Caribs in the 1500s.

The English reached Barbados in 1625, and the first permanent English settlement was begun in 1627. From 1629 to 1652, Barbados was the site of an interfamilial struggle between several English families. These families fought to gain control of the island for themselves.

In 1652, the English sent an expeditionary force which seized the island and quelled the factional fighting.

• The Dutch took possession of Martinique.

In 1672, hostilities between the English and the Dutch erupted once again. Along with Martinique, the Dutch also reoccupied New York for the period of 1672 to 1674.

AFRICA

• The sultan of Morocco attempted to take Ceuta from Spain.
• The French evacuated Madagascar.

1675

THE (FUTURE) UNITED STATES

• In Virginia, Philip Corven, an African slave, petitioned for his freedom on the basis that his original owner's will had limited his time of enslavement to eight years after her death. However, under coercion, Corven's new owner forced him to sign an indenture for an additional twenty years. The record is unclear as to the disposition of the petition.

AFRICA

• In 1675, the Masai began their descent into Kenya.

Today the Masai (Masaai) live in southern Kenya and northern Tanzania. The Masai are pastoral nomads. Their lives and their culture revolve around their cattle, which are the only wealth they recognize, and they move to wherever conditions are best for their herds.

The dominance of cattle in Masai culture cannot be underestimated. The Masai religion is centered around mystical beliefs concerning the Masai, their cattle and God. The cattle are sacred, and therefore their land and all other elements concerning cattle are sacred.

Cattle provide all the needs of the Masai. The milk, blood, and meat of their cattle comprise the diet of the Masai while the hides and skin provide their clothing. The Masai are one of the truly remarkable people of the world.

1676

THE (FUTURE) UNITED STATES

• William Edmondson, an English Quaker, sent a general letter to colonial slave holders, implying that Christianity and slave holding were incompatible.
• Slavery was prohibited in the western portion of what is today New Jersey.

AFRICA

• Because of the military and naval strength of the Dutch West India Company and the English Royal African Company, the New England slave traders bypassed the west coast of Africa and began slave trading on its east coast. The New England slave traders were based on the island of Madagascar.

1677

AFRICA

• The second Khoikhoi-Dutch War came to an end. The conclusion of the war led to a rapid expansion of the Dutch Cape settlement. *See 1673.*
• Slave children under twelve were required to attend school in the Dutch Cape colony.
• An expansion of Akwamu (southeastern Ghana) under Ansa Sasraku began when Ansa Sasraku defeated the coastal kingdom of Accra and beheaded its unpopular king, Okai Koi. The expansion would continue until 1702 when Akwamu briefly occupied Ouidah.
• The capital of Morocco was moved to Meknes.

Meknes is no longer the capital of Morocco, but today it is still known for the royal palace which was constructed in the 1600s when it served as the home of the sultan.

1678

THE AMERICAS

• There were slave uprisings in Jamaica in 1678, 1682, 1685, 1690, 1733, and 1734. There were other revolts in Jamaica in 1760, 1765, 1766, 1807, 1815, and 1824. *See 1655 and 1663.*

AFRICA

• The French took Arguin from the Dutch.
• The Portuguese sent punitive expeditions against the Lamu, Manda, Pate, and Siu.

---

1 6 7 9

THE AMERICAS

• In 1679, and again in 1691 and 1718, there would be slave uprisings in Haiti. In the middle of the eighteenth century an African named Macandel would poison a number of people. Macandel's poisonings would cause a near panic to exist on the western part of Hispaniola.

In 1679, western Hispaniola (today's Haiti) was ceded by Spain to France.

• Charles II abolished slavery in Chile.

AFRICA

• The Dutch East India Company began to offer free passage and land to new settlers from Europe who were willing to colonize the Cape colony in what is now South Africa. The settlers were Dutch, as well as French and German colonists. Simon van der Stel became governor of the Cape colony with the express orders to expand the colony. During his tenure, van der Stel would extend the colony into the area known as the Stellenbosch (Van Der Stel's Bosch) and Dutch settlers would begin to settle along the Eerste River.
• An Omani fleet temporarily compelled the Portuguese to withdraw from Pate (Pate Island, Kenya).
• The French Senegal Company was refounded.

---

1 6 8 0

THE (FUTURE) UNITED STATES

• In Virginia a law was enacted which prohibited persons of African descent from meeting in considerable numbers, walking abroad, bearing arms, carrying clubs, staves or other offensive weapons or instruments.
• In New York, the authorities declared that no more than four slaves could meet at any time unless in the presence of a slave owner. The authorities also declared that slaves could not carry arms.

THE AMERICAS

• In Haiti, Maroons formed into separate bands, raided plantations and established their own settlements in the mountains.

Between 1680 and 1786, the British West Indies and the American colonies imported 2,130,000 slaves. The thirst for slaves was at times unquenchable. Even young Irish peasants were "hunted down as men hunt down game, and were forcibly put aboard ship, and sold to the planters in Barbados.

Between 1680 and 1688, the English African Company alone would attempt to transport 60,000 slaves to the British West Indies. Sadly, the records of the 249 ships involved indicate that out of the 60,000 slaves shipped to the Americas, only 46,000 (46,396) arrived. The remaining 14,000 died en route.

AFRICA

• Beginning in 1680, the Ga migrated from the Accra plain to Anecho, Dahomey.

Today the Ga live in Ghana, mostly in the capital, Accra, and the towns of Labadi, Nungua, Teshi, and Tema. In the precolonial era, the Ga had a thriving trade with the Europeans.

• The Akwamu took over the Accra plain.
• The rise of the Ashanti began. *See 1690.*
• By 1680, the Ewe state of Anlo was firmly established.

The historic homeland of the Ewe lies between the Volta River in Ghana and the Mono River in Togo. The Ewe separated from the Adja in the early 1600s when they began migrating southward.

---

1 6 8 1

THE (FUTURE) UNITED STATES

• A Maryland law declared that children of African descent who were born of European mothers and children born of free women of African descent were to be free.

Prior to this legislative action, planters would sometimes marry their European women servants to their African male slaves. This was done to transform the offspring of the European women into slaves for life. Such was the case of Irish Nell, a servant woman brought to Maryland and sold to a planter when her former owner returned to England. The proceedings to obtain freedom for her offspring by her African husband occupied the courts of Maryland for a number of years. The petition was finally granted and Irish Nell's children were set free.

The case of Irish Nell, and other similar situations, caused the Maryland authorities to change the common law tradition of having the status of the father determine the status of the child.

AFRICA

• Civil war erupted in Monomotapa.

1 6 8 2

THE (FUTURE) UNITED STATES

• South Carolina gave statutory recognition to slavery.

After 1682, persons of non–Christian nationalities could enter Virginia only as slaves. Virginia also repealed the law passed in 1670 which freed Christian persons of African descent upon their arrival in the English colony (November 10).

• In Pennsylvania, William Penn forwarded plans for the creation of a city to be named "Philadelphia." Working closely with his surveyor general, Thomas Holme, Penn planned a city which would serve as a place of refuge for the persecuted as well as a meeting place for the neighboring Indigenous (Native) Americans. In short, Penn planned on creating a "city of brotherly love" to be unlike any other city in the known world (September).

However, in the same year of 1682, the charter of the Free Society of Traders in Pennsylvania recognized the slavery of blacks. Slaves were to be freed after fourteen years of service, upon the condition that they cultivate land allotted to them, and surrender two-thirds of the produce annually.

THE AMERICAS

• There were slave uprisings in Jamaica in 1682, 1685, 1690, 1733, and 1734. There were other revolts in Jamaica in 1760, 1765, 1766, 1807, 1815, and 1824. *See 1655 and 1663.*

AFRICA

• Algiers was bombarded by the French fleet for alleged acts of piracy.
• In 1682, expeditions were initiated from the Cape colony to Namaqaland in search of copper.

RELATED HISTORICAL EVENTS

• In 1682, the Dutch East India Company acquired a commercial monopoly in the East Indies.

1 6 8 3

RELATED HISTORICAL EVENTS

• The Royal African Company went bankrupt.

1 6 8 4

THE (FUTURE) UNITED STATES

• By 1684, a tremendous expansion in sugar and tobacco production and consumption prompted a great demand for African slaves in the Caribbean and on the American mainland. Due to this increased demand, the Atlantic slave trade flourished. Indeed, by 1713, British colonies would be the largest buyer of Africans for enslavement.

AFRICA

• By 1684, the Portuguese had lost all of their posts on the coasts of Kenya and Tanzania, but still retained some of their posts and influence along the coast of Mozambique.
• The English abandoned Tangier after destroying its fortifications.
• The Royal African Company was reformed.

EUROPE

On March 6, 1684, the General Congregation of Propaganda Fide and the Holy Office, two of the most powerful organs of the Papacy, handed down a set of decisions which if they had been adhered to would have halted almost all the excesses of the slave trade a century before the great abolitionist movement of the eighteenth century.

The initiatives leading to these decisions were made by an African, Lorenzo de Silva e Mendoza. Lorenzo de Silva e Mendoza was the procurator general for a religious association of Africans, "Africans of mixed ancestry," and for many other institutions.

The failure of the decisions to affect the

growth in the slave trade is perhaps due to the fact that the principal parties involved in the slave trade—the British and the Dutch—happened to be of the Protestant sect and, therefore, not subject to papal edicts.

The slave trade produced great profits for the Dutch and the British. The wealth accumulated by the Dutch during the seventeenth century is aptly chronicled in the paintings of the great Dutch masters of the day. As for the British, they too benefited from the profits of the slave trade. Indeed, it is propositioned that the trade in the flesh of men is what made possible the British Industrial Revolution.

1685

THE (FUTURE) UNITED STATES

• In 1685, Virginia law prohibited slaves from attending meetings of the Quakers which were held for educational purposes.

THE AMERICAS

By 1685, the French West Indian Company had begun to occupy San Domingo (Hispaniola) and their right to the western portion of the island (Haiti) was formally recognized by the Treaty of Ryswick. By this time, the island was dominated by Africans or persons of African descent. There were so many slaves and "coloreds," that the Catholic French King Louis XIV felt compelled to issue the celebrated *Code Noir*. The French *Code Noir* (the "Black Code") required baptism and religious instruction for slaves. The code promoted interracial marriage when children were already present and forbade the working of slaves on Sundays and holidays.

The French colonists in the West Indies ignored the code because they believed that they were safer if the slaves were kept ignorant and because they preferred their illicit relationships with African women. Prior to the Code Noir, French colonists in the West Indies traditionally freed their mulatto children at 21 years of age. The code prohibited such manumission if the mother was not free. This code provision was also ignored by the planters.

However, in Canada, the Code Noir was generally followed and had an ameliorating effect on the institution of slavery as practiced in French Canada.

• Monsieur de Cussy, the governor of French settlements in Santo Domingo (Hispaniola), warned the French government that the continued importation of African slaves would soon result in a non–European majority on the island. The African slaves that were imported to Santo Domingo generally came from Senegal, Sierra Leone, and the Gold Coast (Ghana).

• Baltasar Coyman received an asiento (charter) from the government of Spain for transporting 10,000 African slaves to America.

The history of the Saramakan people of Surinam in South America started around 1685 when African and Indigenous (Native) American slaves escaped and formed a maroon society. For eighty years, Dutch armed forces tried to crush the Saramakan community, but it persists to this very day and now boasts some twenty thousand members. For the Saramakans, freedom was assured in 1761 when the Dutch abandoned their wars and sued for peace.

AFRICA

• Commissioner Hendrik van Reede visited the Cape Colony and decreed that certain male slaves could buy their freedom at age 25 and females at 22. The slaves to which this decree was targeted were those slaves whose fathers were obviously Europeans and those slaves who had been confirmed in the Dutch Reformed Church.

• Successful wine growing was started in the Cape colony.

• The French Guinea Company was founded to facilitate France's participation in the slave trade.

• Akaba assumed leadership of the Fon state (Dahomey) and continued its efforts at expansion.

1686

THE (FUTURE) UNITED STATES

• The Carolina colony (North and South Carolina) prohibited Africans from engaging in any kind of trade or from leaving their owner's plantation without written authorization.

AFRICA

• The inhabitants of Pate (Kenya) rebelled against the Portuguese. The sultan of Pate was captured and taken to Goa (India).

1687

AFRICA

• During a funeral, a group of slaves on the northern neck of Virginia planned an uprising, but it was discovered before it could be carried out. A period of general disobedience and lawlessness followed.

• Antoine Court, a French Huguenot traveling in New England, reported that for a small reward Indigenous (Native) Americans would recapture escaped slaves and return them to their owners.

AFRICA

• Settlers from Brandenburg, Prussia (Germany) established a settlement at Arguin Island off the coast of French West Africa (Mauritania), just south of Cape Blanco. The Prussians established a slave market on Arguin Island.

• By 1687, the Stellenbosch farming district of Cape colony was fully settled by Dutch colonists.

• The Rif attacked Melilla.

RELATED HISTORICAL EVENTS

• In 1687, the unconverted French Huguenots were banished from France.

1688

THE (FUTURE) UNITED STATES

The newly settled Mennonites of Germantown, Pennsylvania, made the first formal protest against slavery in the Western Hemisphere. Their leader, Franz Daniel Pastorius, addressed the petition to the Monthly Meeting of the Quakers. The petition was particularly noteworthy because it came from immigrants who had felt persecuted for conscientious reasons in Holland and Germany and who were then brought to the British colony from Crefeld (the Rhine) on invitation of William Penn.

The Mennonites were a radical Protestant sect whose members first settled at Germantown, near Philadelphia, in 1683. In 1688, after a regular monthly meeting, held at the home of Rigert Worrels, the Mennonites issued a public statement condemning slavery. This condemnation was the first time any religious group in the colonies had condemned the rapid growth in what the Mennonites called the "traffic of mensbody." Many reasons were given for the condemnation, but primarily it was a matter of liberty: "Now, though they are black, we cannot conceive there is more liberty to have them as slaves as it is to have the other white ones." The Mennonites saw slavery as theft and evoked a principle they called "liberty of body," which they saw as everyman's due except those who

had done evil. The German sect was also critical of its Quaker neighbors who they claimed handled men like cattle.

The Mennonites evolved out of the Anabaptist movement of the 16th century, although their name derived from Menno Simons, a Dutch priest who joined the movement in 1536. The sect's stand on slavery was consistent with its views opposing militarism and in favor of nonconformity. From a theological standpoint, the Mennonites were influenced by Pietism, a Lutheran-based movement that emphasized personal religious belief.

The petition of the Mennonites condemning the slave trade was forwarded by the Quakers to the "Quarterly Meeting" and finally to the "Yearly Meeting" where it was filed away. Only some 23 years later, in 1711, did the protests of the German Mennonites move the Quakers in Pennsylvania to take a stand against the slave trade (February 18).

THE AMERICAS

• The slave trade from Angola to Brazil ranged from 6,000 to 7,000 Africans yearly.

• After years of pleading for the introduction of African slaves by the administrators of Canada, King Louis XIV finally gave his approval to Governor Denonville.

• The Barbados Legislature enacted Statute No. 82 for the government of persons of African descent. The law provided no penalty for loss of life or limb by a slave under punishment; imposed a 15-pound (English currency) fine for wanton killing of a slave; imposed a 25-pound fine for the intentional killing of another's slave; and imposed no penalty for killing a person of African descent caught stealing at night. The penalty for a slave striking a Christian was severe whipping, and, for a second offense, whipping and having the nose slit and the face branded. Persons of African descent were not allowed to give evidence against Europeans.

AFRICA

• In 1688, French Huguenot refugees arrived to swell the number of settlers at the Cape colony. Many of the Huguenots settled on land at Franschhoek. By this time, the settlers had gone far beyond the original Cape colony boundaries.

• The French launched an expedition against Algiers.

• The Omani temporarily occupied Pate (Kenya).

In 1688, the systematic breeding of Africans for the supply of the Moroccan army began.

1689

THE (FUTURE) UNITED STATES

• In 1689, King William's War began. Among the first casualties of the conflict was a person of African descent who was killed at Falmouth, Massachusetts.

AFRICA

• The French entered into a treaty with Algiers.
• Port Natal was "purchased" from a Bantu chief for 1,700 pounds, but was not immediately occupied.

ASIA

• The Sidis attacked and captured British held Bombay, India (February 14).

In India, there were two terms which were applied to persons of African descent. There were the "Habshis" and the "Sidis." The term "Habshi" generally applied to Africans who lived in the interior of the Indian subcontinent. Such African Indians as the sultans of Bengal of the late 1400s and Malik Ambar of the early 1600s were considered to be Habshis. The term "Sidi" generally applied to Africans who lived in seafaring communities on the west coast of India.

In the 1680s, the Sidis of West India exercised a great deal of influence in Indian political affairs because the Sidis were mercenaries and pirates who wreaked havoc upon the seas. In the 1680s, the Sidis had two fleets—one, consisting of their own ships and based on Janjira Island, and another, based on Surat, and consisting of ships provided by the Mughals. The commander of the Surat fleet liked to winter his ships in the Bombay Harbor. This practice led to friction between the British and the Sidis, especially given the Sidis tendency to engage in riotous behavior while on "shore leave."

It is not known what prompted the Sidi attack on Bombay in 1689. However, the occupation of Bombay by the Sidis would last throughout 1689 until 1690.

RELATED HISTORICAL EVENTS

• Peter the Great came to power in Russia.
• In 1689, John Locke published *Treatise on Civil Government*. In *Treatise*, Locke condemned slavery.
• On May 3, 1689, William III declared war on France. This war became known as King William's War.

1690

THE (FUTURE) UNITED STATES

John Eliot (1604–1690) died. Eliot was a member of the clergy and a missionary who was called the "Apostle to the Indians." Eliot came to the American colonies from England in 1631, and was made the teacher of a church in Roxbury, Massachusetts.

Eliot organized his first village of Indigenous (Native) American converts at Natick (near Boston), Massachusetts, in 1651. By 1674, Eliot had organized fourteen villages with more than 1,000 Indigenous (Native) Americans. However, King Philip's War (1675–1676) virtually ended his experiment. Eliot's converts were scattered and the remaining Indigenous (Native) Americans in New England became skeptical of the evangelical promises of the English. Eliot's principal notoriety, aside from his missionary work, lies in his publication of *A Primer or Catechism in the Massachusetts Indian Language* (1653) and a translation of the Bible into the language of the Indigenous (Native) Americans of New England—the first Bible to be printed in North America (May 21).

The significance of John Eliot from an African American perspective is that in 1674 Eliot turned his attentions to the education of African slaves. By doing so, Eliot began a New England tradition which persisted throughout the history of the United States and produced many of the leaders of Afro-America.

THE AMERICAS

The mortality rate among persons of African descent on Jamaican plantations was very high. There were 40,000 slaves in 1690. Between 1690 and 1820, 800,000 slaves were imported. However, in 1820 there were only 340,000 slaves in Jamaica.

AFRICA

• Around 1690, a leader named Osei Tutu united the Ashanti people into a single state and became the Asantehene (king) of the Ashanti kingdom. Osei Tutu made Kumasi the capital of the new kingdom. The new kingdom was located at the junction of two northern trade routes. This location allowed the Ashanti to accumulate great wealth. Gold flowed through the kingdom and the Golden Stool of the Asantehene became the symbol of Ashanti power and unity.

In the 1690s, the South African trekboers came to be. By 1690, the Cape colony was well settled. However, European immigrants continued to arrive. With limited opportunities available at the Cape colony, many of the European immigrants began to seek their fortunes in the hinterland of South Africa.

These intrepid immigrants came to be known as trekboers. Trekboers were the surplus people of the then Cape economy. Impoverished and without property, the early trekboers left the boundaries (and the jurisdiction) of the Cape colony to live amongst the indigenous peoples of South Africa. The trekboers survived by trading with (and often stealing from) the indigenous people they encountered. In both trading and stealing, the trekboers proved to be quite adept.

The history of the trekboers is quite significant in African history because, in many respects, trekboers—the vagabond European settlers of South Africa—became a new people. The trekboers became Africans and they would forever be distinct from any other Europeans on the African continent.

- In 1690, a rare slave uprising occurred in South Africa. In Stellenbosch, four slaves attacked a farmhouse, killing one farmer and wounding another. Dutch authorities responded by assembling a force composed of farmers, soldiers and Khoikhoi (indigenous South Africans). A gunfight ensued. Three of the slaves were wounded and a fourth was wounded and taken prisoner. Interrogated, the slave prisoner offered that the rebels planned to murder a number of settler families and set fire to their fields. It was hoped that other slaves would join in the rebellion and that the combined forces might somehow make their way to Madagascar.
- During the 1690s, the Portuguese were driven out of Mashonaland (Zimbabwe) by Changamire Dombo. Changamire Dombo fortified the Rozwi state. The Portuguese were never able to retake the land.
- The tenth dey of Algiers, Ali Chaouch, assumed the title of pasha (provincial governor) and the autonomy of Algiers from the Ottoman Empire increased.
- The Emperor Iyasu I (Iyasu the Great) visited the Ark of the Covenant in Axum.

1691

THE (FUTURE) UNITED STATES

- By 1691, free persons of African descent had become an object of suspicion and fear in Virginia. The preamble of a restrictive act enacted in 1691 declared that a law was necessary to prevent manumissions because "great inconvenience may happen to this country by setting [persons of African descent] free, by their either entertaining ... slaves or receiving stolen goods or being grown old and bringing a change upon the country." This law charged that no person of African descent was to be set free unless the person so doing paid the charges for transporting the manumitted person of African descent beyond the limits of the colony.

A Virginia law prescribed that "any [European] woman in Virginia marrying a [person of African descent], bond or free," was to be banished.

AFRICA

- Morocco recaptured Arzila.

1692

THE (FUTURE) UNITED STATES

- Maryland law required seven years service by any European man who married or had a child by a woman of African descent. There were penalties for European women who allowed themselves to be with child by a man of African descent and for free or enslaved men of African descent who were found guilty of sexual intercourse with European women.

The "Witch" of Salem: In 1692, a clash of African and European cultures occurred in Massachusetts which resulted in a tragic period of American history. Between March and October of 1692, 20 men and women of Salem, Massachusetts, were executed for witchcraft; 19 were hanged and one man, obstinately silent about his actions, was pressed to death by a stone. Most of these "witches" were once respected parents and grandparents. A deputy constable was among the number, as was a minister. All those who were killed professed to be innocent, while all those who confessed were spared.

The period of collective insanity in Salem began in December of 1691 in the home of the Reverend Samuel Parris. In the Parris home, Betty Parris, age 9 and her cousin 11 year old, Abigail Adams, relieved the tedium of their housebound tasks by talking with the family slave, Tituba, a woman of uncertain years raised in the West Indies (Barbados). In January of

1692, the girls and some of their friends, ranging in ages from 12 to 20, began to be taken with fits, writhing on the floor, contorting themselves and screaming when the Lord's name was spoken. Doctors examined them but found no illness in them.

"Who torments you?" members of the families pled to know. "Tituba," the girls replied.

In March, preliminary hearings were held. While Tituba never invoked Satan's name, she did confess to be Satan's servant, muttering of rats, cats and a book of black magic signed by nine in Salem. The girls shrieked the names of two of the signers, and the witch hunt began. *See 1697 and 1700.*

• In Virginia, an act declared that escaped slaves could be lawfully killed and that the owner would be compensated by the colony with 4,000 pounds of tobacco for his loss.

• In Pennsylvania, an ordinance was enacted which allowed anyone to seize an African whom they found "gadding abroad . . . without a ticket" from their owners. Once seized the African was subject to being jailed without meat or drink and could be publicly whipped with 39 lashes "well laid on, on their bare backs."

AFRICA

• Membo Changamire, Dombo (King) of Urozwi, evicted the Portuguese and made his capital the Great Zimbabwe. The Portuguese would never again dominate Zimbabwe.

• The Faqariyyah hegemony was restored in Cairo.

• Abuna Synnada replaced Abuna Marcos as head of the Ethiopian Church. A synod was subsequently held to resolve certain ecclesiastical disputes.

"Abuna" is the title conferred upon the bishops of the Ethiopian Church. "Abuna" means "our father."

• The English captured Saint Louis (Senegal) and Goree.

1693

THE (FUTURE) UNITED STATES

• George Keith wrote a paper against slavery for presentation at a Quaker meeting in Philadelphia. The paper urged the Quakers to free their slaves. The paper was entitled *An Exhortation and Caution to Friends Concerning Buying or Keeping Negroes.*

• Cotton Mather (1663–1728), a European

American clergyman in Boston, drafted the "Rules for the Society of Negroes" for a group of persons of African descent who were seeking to hold their own prayer meetings on Sunday evenings. These rules were the first known example of an African religious association.

THE AMERICAS

• Gold was discovered in Minas Gerais, Brazil. A rush to Brazil began, a flood of slaves would follow.

AFRICA

• Changamire conquered much of Monomotapa.

• A French diplomatic mission was sent to Morocco.

• The French expelled the English from Saint Louis and Goree.

1694

THE AMERICAS

• The first discovery of gold in Taubate, Brazil increased the demand for African slaves. African slaves were customarily used to work the gold mines.

AFRICA

• There was an exceptionally low Nile flood in 1694 resulting in famine and pestilence in Egypt.

1695

THE (FUTURE) UNITED STATES

• At Goose Creek Parish (in what is today South Carolina), the Reverend Samuel Thomas conducted a school for Africans.

THE AMERICAS

• In Brazil, the Republic of Palmares was overthrown. *See 1630.*

Slave insurrections were often attempted in South America, especially among the Muslim slaves of Bahia, Brazil. About this time, a group revolted and held out for a long period of time. In 1719, a widespread conspiracy failed but many of the leaders fled to the forest. In 1828, a thousand Afro-Brazilians rose in revolt at Bahia. This occurred again in 1830.

From 1831 to 1837, slave revolts were constantly being threatened. In 1835, there was a major revolt of the Muslims, who attempted to enthrone their own queen. The Muslims fought with extreme bravery, but were finally defeated.

AFRICA

• The Cachu (Cacheu) Company (a French-Portuguese interest) contracted with the government of Spain to transport 4,000 slaves annually to America.

• Changamire defeated the Portuguese (in Zimbabwe) and evicted them from his kingdom. Not long after this victory, Changamire died.

1 6 9 6

THE (FUTURE) UNITED STATES

• A yearly meeting of American Quakers admonished all members against importing persons of African descent for slavery and proposed expulsion from membership as the penalty for violators.

The Quakers and Slavery: To their credit, the Society of Friends (the Quakers), after 1696, consistently sought to regulate slavery and to prevent its undue growth. In 1696, the Quakers sought to regulate slavery because slave traders had "flocked in amongst us and . . . increased and multiplied negroes amongst us." At the 1696 meeting, the Quakers decided that members ought not to encourage the further importation of slaves, as there were enough already for all purposes.

In 1711, a more active discouragement of the slave trade was suggested, and, in 1716, the Yearly Meeting warned that even the buying of imported slaves might not be the best policy, although the meeting hastened to call this warning a "caution," not a "censure."

By 1719, the meeting was more adamant that Quakers should not engage in the slave trade, and, in 1730, the Quakers declared that the buying of slaves imported by others to be "disagreeable."

For the next thirteen years, little progress was made by the Quakers on the issue of slavery. The lack of progress was probably due to the alienation felt by some of the more "conservative" members of the Society with regard to the "liberal—liberating" stance taken by so many of the Quaker faithful.

However, in 1743, the question of importing slaves was made into a disciplinary matter, and, in 1754, due to the evangelism of such leading Quakers as Benjamin Lay, John Woolman, and Anthony Benezet, Quakers who did import slaves were actually disciplined.

In 1758, the Quakers finally heeded the admonition given by the Mennonites in 1688 — the Quakers categorically condemned the institution of slavery.

Finally, in 1775, the Quakers took the final step and expelled all slave holders from membership in the Society.

AFRICA

• The Omanis (an Arab people from what today is Oman) besieged Mombasa (Kenya) and took it from the Portuguese after two years. The Omani commander was a Mazrui, the first of his family to appear on the East African coast.

• Deepening chaos in the Mwanamutapa (Monomotapa) Empire was brought on by Portuguese interference and imperialist aggression.

• The first Captain-General of Bissau was appointed.

• The Portuguese gained access to the silver mine in Chicoa.

ASIA

• In 1696, it was reported that there were 20,000 Africans in Pondicherry, India.

1 6 9 7

THE (FUTURE) UNITED STATES

In 1697, the citizens of Massachusetts spent a day of fasting and repentance, recalling the 1692 witch trials and their tacit roles in them. Judge Samuel Sewall, who presided over many of the sad proceedings, attended church services and offered a bill of confession, admitting "the blame and shame." Some former jurors signed a document that read in part, "We fear we have been instrumental with others, though ignorantly and unwillingly, to bring upon ourselves the guilt of innocent blood." The community begged forgiveness of the families of the 20 who died. But there were few apologies for those who escaped the noose, many of whom had fled the colony. As for Tituba, the African slave who initiated the web of fear by telling children tales of black magic, she remained alive somewhere in slavery (January 15). *See 1692 and 1700.*

AFRICA

• Osai Tutu (Osei Tutu) came to the throne of the Ashanti and founded Kumasi.

• Andre de Brue explored Senegal.

• In January, the remaining Portuguese in Fort Jesus, Mombasa, were reduced to twenty by the plague. A small relieving force arrived in September. However, the Portuguese frigate, *Sao Antonio de Tanna*, sank in front of Fort Jesus.

• In 1697, the Turkish governor of Egypt was deposed by the Janissaries.

RELATED HISTORICAL EVENTS

In 1697, the Treaty of Ryswick was signed which turned over the western third of the island of Hispaniola—a land which we now call "Haiti"—to France.

1698

THE (FUTURE) UNITED STATES

• The British Parliament ended the monopoly of the Royal African Company and allowed private traders to operate after payment of a ten percent (10%) duty to the company for the maintenance of its African forts. Parliament believed the slave trade to be "highly beneficial and advantageous to this kingdom and to the Plantations and Colonies." This legally opened the trade to the New England mariners.

By 1700, Boston slave traders had come to dominate the slave trade and Boston was the chief port for slave ships. However, while Bostonians were the principal benefactors of the slave trade, there were actually relatively few slaves in the Boston area. Indeed, it is estimated that during 1700, there were less than a thousand persons of African descent in the entire New England area. The paucity of African slaves in New England was primarily due to the fact that the slave trade was triangular. New England exported food to the West Indies in exchange for rum; the rum was bartered for slaves who were taken to the West Indies and exchanged or sold for more rum, sugar, molasses and cocoa. The making of rum from molasses was the largest industry in New England at the outbreak of the Revolutionary War; shipbuilding and seafaring, important economic enterprises in New England, were also dependent on the slave trade.

• New York had a total population of 18,067 of whom 2,170 were persons of African descent.

• William Southeby, a Pennsylvania Quaker, addressed a letter to Quakers in Barbados calling for the end of shipments of persons of African descent into the state. Southeby was eventually expelled from the Quaker community for his continued attacks on slavery. *See 1696.*

THE AMERICAS

• Between 1698 and 1708, 104,668 slaves were delivered to the West Indies.

AFRICA

• Fort Jesus, Mombasa, surrendered to the Omani after a two year siege (December).

• The Janissaries caused disturbances in Cairo.

• A treaty was effected between France and Algiers whereby Algiers renounced its Holy War.

• The Yoruba conquered Great Ardra.

1699

THE (FUTURE) UNITED STATES

• Virginia put a tax of 20 shillings on each slave imported into the colony.

AFRICA

• In 1699, Wilhelm Adriaan van der Stel became governor of the Cape colony in South Africa.

• The Omani seized Zanzibar.

• Slaves exported from Guinea were required to be previously baptized.

• The Ashanti were at war with the Denkyera.

• The Galla raids reached the environs of Malindi.

RELATED HISTORICAL EVENTS

• One and a half tons of gold—the first large consignment of gold from the mines of Brazil—arrived in Lisbon.

1700–1799

In the 1700s, the Lunda copper trade of Zaire and Angola expanded; the great cities of Khami and Dhlo-Dhlo were built in Zimbabwe; the Bemba and Lozi polities arose, and the Yoruba kingdom entered a period of decay.

On the east coast of Africa, the Omani people asserted their dominance over the region as evidenced by the installation of an Omani governor in Zanzibar.

Meanwhile, the 1700s also marked the ascendancy of the English and their dominance of the world's seas. Along with this dominance, came the English expansion of the slave trade. In the 1700s, the slave trade would reach horrific proportions resulting in the death of millions and the destabilization (devastation) of countless African communities. Spurred on by the demands of the plantations of the American and West Indian colonies; the silver mines of Mexico and Peru; and the gold and diamond mines of Brazil, slavery would reach monumental proportions.

It was the unfolding horror of the slave trade which finally began to take its toll upon the sensibilities of the more enlightened members of European society. Soon many Europeans began advocating the concept of a "noble savage" – for the first time ennobling and humanizing those peoples who had previously only been considered a commodity.

The romantic view of the "noble savage" aroused the European interest in Africans, especially when certain specific Africans were thought to have had high status in their own societies. This humanizing and ennobling of Africans would prompt many Europeans to call for the end of the slave trade. And indeed, in the late 1700s and early 1800s, the romantic interest in Africa would lead to the humanitarian concern which served as the basis for the antislavery movement. Thus, while the 1700s saw the slave trade reach its apex, it also saw the planting of the seeds which would lead to its demise.

1700

THE (FUTURE) UNITED STATES

• Judge Samuel Sewall of Massachusetts published *The Selling of Joseph* in which he advocated the end of the slave trade. Sewall questioned the biblical interpretations used to condone slavery and the legality of the means by which persons of African descent were enslaved. However, Sewall's book gave little hope for the amalgamation of the races if persons of African descent were emancipated. *The Selling of Joseph* provided antislavery arguments well into the 19th century (June 24).

It is perhaps more than coincidence that the Judge Samuel Sewall who authored *The Selling of Joseph* was also one of the principal jurists responsible for the Salem witchcraft misjustice which began with the storytelling of the slave Tituba. Sewall was the only judge involved who subsequently publicly renounced his participation in the witchcraft trials. Sewall's awakening of conscience continued throughout his life and *The Selling of Joseph* was simply another milestone in his enlightened career.

The Selling of Joseph was a three page tract and was the first outright appeal for the abolition of slavery to appear in the British colonies. The pamphlet made a religious argument that drew a strong parallel between the enforced servitude of Africans and the Old Testament story of Joseph, whose brothers sold him into slavery for 20 pieces of silver.

Sewall wrote that "There is no proportion between Twenty Pieces of Silver and LIBERTY." He added, "Joseph was rightfully, no more a Slave to his brethren, than they were to him, and they had not more Authority to Sell him than they had to Slay him." Likewise, contended Sewall, the colonists had no right to enslave their fellow human beings of dark complexion. Sewall was very committed. He personally handed out this tract to those he met on the streets of Boston. *See 1692 and 1697.*

• Pennsylvania gave statutory recognition to slavery.

In 1700, there were 27,817 slaves in the English colonies in North America. Of these 27,817, 5,206 were in the North and 22,611 were in the South. The estimated population of the colonies was 275,000.

• Samuel Sewall and the Boston Committee of 1700, an antislavery group, tried to institute a heavy duty (tax) on the importation of slaves in the hope that the taxation would end the Massachusetts slave trade.
• The first commercial distillery was opened in Boston for the purpose of making rum.

By 1700, Boston slave traders were supplying all the New England colonies, as well as Virginia, with slaves. The American slave trade was almost exclusively a Massachusetts enter-

prise with Boston the chief slave port. However, there were less than 1,000 persons of African descent in all the New England colonies as most of the trade was triangular.

The triangular slave trade began when New England exported staple food commodities (beans, corn, fish, horses, and dairy products) to the West Indies for rum. The rum was then taken to Africa and bartered for slaves, who were then taken to the West Indies for either sale or exchange for more rum, sugar, molasses, and cocoa.

The manufacture of rum from molasses was the largest manufacturing enterprise in New England at the outbreak of the Revolutionary War. Shipbuilding and seafaring, both substantial economic undertakings in New England, were largely dependent on the slave trade.

The part of the triangular trade that brought African slaves to the West Indies was called the Middle Passage. Typically, space of only three feet ten inches for each slave was allowed on a ship between decks. The area was later reduced to three feet three inches. The slaves were packed like sardines and were not able to stand upright while confined within the ship.

Judge Samuel Sewall of Massachusetts attempted to stem the slave trade by imposing a heavy tax on it, but his efforts were not successful.

• Quakers began making conscientious efforts to improve conditions among the slaves. George Fox urged holders of slaves to give religious instruction to them and William Penn established a monthly meeting for persons of African descent.

In 1700, four bills were introduced in Pennsylvania. One bill designed to regulate marriage between slaves was defeated. Another—the Act for the Trial of Negroes—was a draconian measure calling for death, castration, and whipping as appropriate punishments for African Americans. The Act for the Trial of Negroes was passed, but was later rescinded as being too harsh. The other two bills became law and provided for a small duty on imported slaves and the regulation of trade with slaves and servants.

THE AMERICAS

• In Jamaica, Francis Williams, the son of free Afro-Jamaican parents was chosen to be the subject of an experiment. The purpose of the experiment was to see whether a person of African descent might be found as capable of producing literature as an

Englishman. At the instigation of the Duke of Montagu, Williams was sent to Great Britain to study in British grammar schools and at Cambridge University. Out of this experiment, Williams authored a Latin ode, *Integerrimo et fortissimo viro, Georgia Holdane* (To that most upright and valiant man, George Haldane). This ode was produced in honor of Haldane's becoming the governor of Jamaica. The ode would later be included in Edward Long's *History of Jamaica*.

AFRICA

• The Franciscans of Guinea (Guinea-Bissau) protested against the slave trade.
• A royal bodyguard was established in Buganda.
• An Omani governor was installed in Zanzibar.
• The Kasbah Mosque in Rabat (Morocco) was reconstructed by the English renegade Ahmad-al-Inglisi.

1701

THE (FUTURE) UNITED STATES

• In England, the Reverend Thomas Bray, a former representative of the Bishop of London in Maryland, founded the Anglican Society for Promoting Christian Knowledge, better known as the Society for the Propagation of the Gospel. The purposes of the Society were the care and instruction of the English colonists and the conversion of Indigenous Americans and persons of African descent. The society was later incorporated into Dr. Bray's Associates, the precursor to the Abolition Society.
• In Boston, a town meeting was convened at which the abolition of slavery was favorably discussed.

THE AMERICAS

• Catechism was made compulsory for all slaves in Guinea (Guyana).

AFRICA

• War erupted between Morocco and the Ottoman Empire.
• The Ashanti defeated the Denkyira and, thereby, secured the trade with the Dutch at Elmina.

RELATED HISTORICAL EVENTS

The War of the Spanish Succession erupted pitting France, Spain and Bavaria against England, Holland, Portugal, Austria (the Holy Roman Empire) and Denmark. The cause of the war was Louis XIV's acceptance of the Spanish throne on behalf of his grandson, Philip V of Spain, in defiance of the Partition Treaty of 1700, under which the crown would have been passed on to the Archduke Charles of Austria.

Peace was made by the Treaties of Utrecht (1713) and Rastatt (1714). Philip V was recognized as king of Spain, thereby establishing the Bourbon dynasty while England received Gibraltar, Minorca, and Nova Scotia.

The conclusion of the War of the Spanish Succession would also lead to the recognized participation (and dominance) of England with regard to the slave trade.

1702

THE (FUTURE) UNITED STATES

• New Jersey gave statutory recognition to slavery.

THE AMERICAS

• The French Guinea Company (the French Royal Senegal Company) contracted with Spain for the asiento. The company was to deliver 38,000 African slaves per year for 10 to 12 years to the Spanish colonies, or 48,000 if the French-English war (The War of the Spanish Succession) came to an end in that period.

Due to its many wars with England, the French never became great slave traders and their West Indian possessions were supplied mainly by the Dutch and the Portuguese. However, on the island of San Domingo (Haiti), the French did introduce a system of slavery which would have a great influence on Africans throughout the Americas.

AFRICA

• In what is today South Africa, the Xhosa crossed the Kei River and came in contact with the Dutch. The Dutch raided the Xhosa herds and these raids led to an armed conflict between the Dutch and Xhosa.

RELATED HISTORICAL EVENTS

• Governor James Moore of Carolina invaded mid–Florida, forcing Christianized Indigenous (Native) Americans and Spaniards to abandon the Apalachee missions.

The military incursions of the English colonists into Spanish Florida was a recurring enterprise in the 18th century. Spanish Florida was a constant thorn in the side of the English because from Spanish Florida both Spanish and Indigenous Americans could launch raids. Additionally, the Spanish colony was a very attractive haven for escaped African slaves who found freedom among the Indigenous Americans of Florida or in their own Maroon societies *see 1813*. Throughout the 18th century the friction between the Spanish colony and the English colonies would persist.

1 7 0 3

THE (FUTURE) UNITED STATES

• The literary genre known as slave narratives began with the publication of *John Saffin's Tryall*. *John Saffin's Tryall* was a companion to Samuel Sewall's antislavery tract, *The Selling of Joseph see 1700*.
• South Carolina put duty on the importation of slaves.
• Rhode Island gave statutory recognition to slavery.

AFRICA

• Iyasu (Joshua) I, the emperor of Ethiopia, led an expedition against the Galla.

1 7 0 4

THE (FUTURE) UNITED STATES

• Elias Neau, a Frenchman, opened the first school (the Catechism School) for persons of African descent at Trinity Church in New York City. Instruction at the school was halted briefly in 1712 when a slave uprising made some New York slave holders suspicious of Neau's efforts.

The school established by Elias Neau met nightly and had as many as 200 students. The school met until the death of Elias Neau in 1722.
In 1712, Neau's school was implicated in the slave uprising which occurred in New York. Two of Neau's students were charged with planning the uprising. One of the students was eventually cleared, but the other was convicted.

• *The Boston Newsletter*, the first newspaper in the English colonies, was founded, and from the very inception advertisements for the sale of slaves were a prominent part of its advertising (April 24).

The Boston Newsletter was founded by John Campbell, an astute Scot who was also postmaster of Boston. Campbell developed a thriv-

ing business as a bookseller and printer of casual and occasional news on a "half sheet" called *Letters of Intelligence* that was popular with his Boston clientele. The format and content of the newspaper was similar to that of the *London Gazette*, and the new publication was two-thirds filled with items that had been gleaned from the English paper. The other third was made up of brief articles about deaths, sermons, ship arrivals and departures, storms and activities in the courts.

THE AMERICAS

• In France, it was declared that colonies existed solely to serve the mother country and should not compete for industry, commerce, or population. This edict caused French Canada to revert to the fur trade as its primary enterprise and, as a consequence, resulted in an economy which was antithetical to the notion of a mass trade in slaves.

AFRICA

• Many buildings were destroyed by an earthquake in Gondar.
• The French burned Benguela.

1 7 0 5

THE (FUTURE) UNITED STATES

• Virginia enacted a series of laws permitting slave owners to list people as property; prohibiting nonenslaved persons of African descent from holding office; forbidding persons of African descent from acting as witnesses in any case; imposing lifelong servitude upon all imported servants unless said servants had been Christians in their native country or had been nonenslaved in a Christian country (October 23).

The Slave Codes: In the 1700s, slave codes were common in the British colonies. Slave codes were formal recognition that persons of African descent (blacks) were not governed by the laws of other (European) men.
It must be understood that in the 1700s, slaves were considered to be a special kind of property. Slaves were not quite like houses or beasts of burden, and yet they were not quite like "people" either, at least not in the eyes of Europeans or European law.
Because slaves were considered to be a special kind of property, a special kind of law was developed to address the problems associated with this unique form of property. This special set of laws—the slave codes—was

designed to protect the owners of such property and to shield the owners of such property (generally Europeans) against the dangers associated with keeping men in bondage, especially when said men outnumbered the slave holders.

The slave codes began to take shape during the 1600s and continued to be expanded and refined during the 1700s. While each colony had its own particular set of slave codes, the general intent of the codes was the same—the total subordination of the slaves to the will of the slave owners.

Under the slave codes, a slave had no standing in the courts. A slave could not be a party to a suit at law and a slave could not offer legal testimony except against another slave or a freedman.

Under the slave codes, a slave was deemed to have no legal responsibility, and, since a slave had no legal responsibility, the oath of a slave was not binding. Thus, under the reasoning of the slave code authors, a slave could not enter into a contract and his marriage vows were of no legal effect.

Since a slave's marriage was not legally valid, any child born to a slave was inherently illegitimate. In other words, the concept of an African family became a legal impossibility.

Under the slave codes, the ownership of property by slaves was generally forbidden and while some states did permit slaves to possess certain types of holdings, there was no legal basis upon which such possession could be maintained.

Under the slave codes, a slave could not strike a European, even in self-defense. On the other hand, the killing of a slave by a European, however malicious, was rarely regarded as murder.

Under the slave codes, the rape of a female slave was a misdemeanor but only when it involved "trespassing on the property of another."

Under the slave codes, slaves could not leave the plantation without the permission of the plantation owner and any European person encountering a slave could seize the slave and turn him over to the authorities.

Slaves could not possess firearms. Slaves could not purchase or sell goods or visit the homes of Europeans or freedmen. Slaves could not assemble in groups unless a European was present to supervise the assemblage.

Under the slave codes, both slaves and freedmen were prohibited from receiving "incendiary" literature. Indeed, under the slave codes, the mere teaching of a slave to read or write was deemed to be a crime.

While the slave codes were onerous, it is well to keep in mind that enforcement of the codes often depended upon the times, the locale, and the people. When the times were quiet, the laws were generally disregarded. However, when there were rumors of revolts among the slaves, the European community became apprehensive and began to "crack down" on the slave code violators. Additionally, many slave owners considered themselves to be their own sovereign and not necessarily subject to the slave code in the treatment of their own slaves. These slave owners would treat their slaves as they believed to be best, irrespective of the provisions of the slave codes.

• A New York law was enacted which prescribed execution of recaptured slaves who had attempted to escape to Canada.
• Massachusetts placed a duty of 4 pounds (English currency) on imported persons of African descent.
• Intermarriage between Europeans and persons of African descent was declared illegal in Massachusetts. A minister performing such a marriage was fined 50 pounds (English currency). This prohibition remained in effect until 1843, when the law was repealed.

AFRICA

• The Husainids came to power in Tunis. The Husainid Beys originated in Crete. Their Tunisian dynasty would last until 1922.

1706

THE (FUTURE) UNITED STATES

• Statutes enacted in New York and Virginia established that baptism did not alter the condition of slaves.
• In Pennsylvania, another act was passed concerning the trial of persons of African descent. The act provided that persons of African descent should be tried for crimes by two justices of the peace and a jury of six freeholders; robbery and rape were punished by branding and exportation; homicide by death; and stealing by whipping. *See 1700.*

AFRICA

• Iyasu I, the emperor of Ethiopia, was assassinated. He was succeeded by Takla Haimanot I. The assassination of Iyasu would lead to a period of instability on the

Ethiopian throne which would not be rectified until the 1800s.
• The Janissaries caused unrest and disturbances in Cairo, Egypt.

EUROPE

In the early 1700s, a young Abysinnian (Ethiopian) prince was abducted and taken to Constantinople by the Turks. In 1706, while in Constantinople, the young prince was purchased and brought to Russia by Czar Peter the Great. Under the patronage of Peter the Great, and because of his own special talents, the young prince was able to achieve a relatively high position at the Russian court and in the Russian army. In Russia, the young prince went by the name of Abram Petrovich Hannibal and, in addition to his own accomplishments, we know him today for one of his offspring. As fate would have it, Abram Petrovich Hannibal was the great-grandfather of Alexander Sergeevich Pushkin — Russia's greatest poet. *See 1799.*

RELATED HISTORICAL EVENTS

• Benjamin Franklin, one of the founders of the American antislavery movement, was born.

Benjamin Franklin (1706–1790) was born in Boston, but moved to Philadelphia in his youth. Once in Philadelphia, Franklin became a successful printer and publisher. Franklin wrote and published *Poor Richard's Almanac* (1733–1758), one of the most popular publications of its day.

Franklin served in the Pennsylvania Assembly from 1751 to 1764. While he was in the Assembly, he was sent to Great Britain to lobby Parliament about tax grievances and achieved the repeal of the Stamp Act.

After his return to the then British American colonies, Franklin became involved in the debate leading to the Declaration of Independence — a document which Franklin edited.

During the Revolutionary War, Franklin served as the American Ambassador to France, and negotiated the end of the war with Britain in 1783.

As a delegate to the Continental Congress from Pennsylvania, Franklin helped to draft the Constitution for the United States. As one of the most well-traveled of the colonial leaders, Franklin brought an internationalist perspective to the Constitutional Convention.

In addition to his accomplishments as a printer, publisher, author, and statesman, Franklin was a noted scientist. He proved that lightning is a form of electricity, differentiated between positive and negative electricity, and invented the lightning conductor.

Franklin was also responsible for organizing an effective postal system. Scholastically, Franklin taught himself Spanish, French, Italian, and Latin and formed a discussion group in 1743 which evolved into the American Philosophical Society.

In the annals of African American history, Benjamin Franklin was known as a prominent antislavery advocate who throughout his adult life argued against the perpetuation of the institution of slavery. Franklin founded a number of abolitionist organizations, published a number of abolitionist tracts, and, in correspondence and spoken word, argued that the institution of slavery was an evil which was a blight not only upon the Americas but upon Great Britain as well. Of all the so-called "Founding Fathers," Franklin was the founding father who can truly be termed an advocate for, and hero of, Afro-America.

1707

THE (FUTURE) UNITED STATES

• Massachusetts allowed selected free persons of African descent to enter military service.
• In Massachusetts, free persons of African descent could be fined 5 shillings for harboring escaped slaves.
• Mechanics formed a guild in Philadelphia, Pennsylvania, to protest the "unfair" competition from African slaves.

RELATED HISTORICAL EVENTS

• On January 16, the Treaty of the Union of Great Britain was ratified by the Scottish Parliament. On May 1, the Parliament of Great Britain would meet for the first time.

1708

THE (FUTURE) UNITED STATES

• In Pennsylvania, European mechanics protested against the hiring of African mechanics and were successful in getting acts passed which restricted the further importation of slaves.

Generally, laws in the English colonies of the early 1700s did not hinder slaves from learning trades. However, laws against teaching slaves severely hindered them from attaining skill and efficiency in the more sophisticated trades. Most slave tradesmen usually had to work by rule of thumb. However, there were some exceptions and, in the building trades in particular, persons of African descent, to a relative degree, thrived.

The protest waged by the Pennsylvania building mechanics in 1708 led to laws being passed which restricted the importation of additional slaves. However, these laws were invalidated by the English government. Thus, in 1722, the Pennsylvania mechanics were once again led to protest the competition from the slave mechanics. In response to this protest, the Pennsylvania Legislative Assembly declared that the hiring of slave mechanics was "dangerous and injurious to the republic and not to be sanctioned."

The initial Pennsylvania restrictions imposed upon slave participation in the building trades would soon spread to other colonies and be expanded to cover the participation of free African Americans as well. After the Revolutionary War, these restrictions would be codified into state law. Thus, in Maryland, in 1837, the Legislature was urged to prohibit free African Americans from being artisans. In 1840, a bill was reported to keep African American labor out of tobacco warehouses. In 1844, petitions were brought to the legislature urging a prohibition against free African American carpenters and the heavy taxing of free African American mechanics. In 1860, European American mechanics advocated the passing of a law barring free African Americans "from pursuing any mechanical branch of trade." Obviously, this opposition to the participation of African Americans in the building trades, when coupled with restrictions on education, effectively crippled the development of a strong African American middle class.

• Virginia recorded 12,000 persons of African descent with about 1,000 persons of African descent being imported annually.
• In South Carolina, 5,280 European settlers fearfully watched over the enslavement of 2,900 Africans and 1,400 Indigenous Americans.
• In Rhode Island, slavery for life was recognized.
• In 1708, there was a slave uprising in New York. One African woman and three African men were executed in retaliation for the killing of seven Europeans. The African men were hanged and the African woman was burned alive. Some of the other slave participants, including a pregnant woman, were captured. A few of the other slaves, including another woman, committed suicide rather than surrender.

THE AMERICAS

AFRICA

• Spain relinquished control of Oran (Algeria) and Mers el-Kebir.
• Takla Haimanot I, the emperor of Ethiopia, was assassinated. He was succeeded by Theophilus. The assassinations of Iyasu I and Takla Haimanot I ushered in an era of palace intrigue and instability in Ethiopia.
• Agaja ascended to the leadership of the Fon state (Dahomey).

1709

THE (FUTURE) UNITED STATES

• In 1709, Liverpool, England, sent out only one slave ship with a capacity of thirty tons. However, encouraged by Parliamentary subsidies and the colonial consumptive demand for slaves, the shipping from Liverpool dramatically increased during the 1700s. By 1751, 53 ships from Liverpool were involved in the slave trade; by 1765, 86; and by the beginning of the 1800s, there were 185 ships. By the 1800s, the 185 ships from Liverpool carried about 49,000 slaves per year.

THE AMERICAS

• Slavery was made legal in French Canada (April 13).

Slavery in French Canada (New France) was vastly different from the slavery practiced in the British colonies. The institution of slavery was bred by the collective farming associated with sugar and cotton production. These commodities were confined to the warmer climates and were not suitable to Canada. Accordingly, most slaves in Canada tended to be domestic servants rather than field laborers.

Additionally, during the 1600s and 1700s, the French were restricted from participation in the slave trade by the dominance of the Dutch and British naval forces. So the maritime component of the slave trade which profited the New England colonies was not available for New France.

In addition to the foregoing, unlike Protestantism, French Catholicism ameliorated the effects of slavery by integrating slaves into the religious community. Furthermore, in contrast to the British crown, the French crown was a rather reluctant participant in the little slave trade that there was. Finally, the French in Canada tended to prefer enslaving the Indigenous Canadians rather than Africans because the cost of doing so was far less than that associated with the importation of Africans.

All of these factors led to slavery being a rather minimal enterprise under the French in Canada. In 1759, it is estimated that there were only 3,604 slaves in all of New France, of which 1,132 were of African descent.

1710

THE (FUTURE) UNITED STATES

• There were 44,866 slaves in the English colonies in North America: 8,303 in the North, and 36,563 in the South.
• The first use was made in Virginia of the legislative power to reward a slave for cooperation with slave holders. A slave named Will had been of great assistance in uncovering a slave conspiracy against the colonists. In recognition of his "service," a legislative act was passed conferring "freedom" upon him. This act, which ended the physical enslavement of the "Negro Will," was not an indication of a growth of enlightenment among Virginia slave holders. Rather the act was used to discourage slave conspiracies by rewarding slave informants and slave spies.
• Governor Spotswood "took measures to discourage" the importation of slaves into the colony of Virginia because of the colonists alarm at the rapid increase in the number of slaves.

THE AMERICAS

In Barbados, Colonel Christopher Codrington willed two plantations to the Society for the Propagation of the Gospel *see 1701* on the condition that a college be built for the religious instruction and conversion of the slaves to prove that slavery could coexist with Christianity. The Society, however, wanted to retain the profits from the estate and more or less ignored the provisions of the will.

In 1745, the college was finally opened, but for Europeans only. By 1761, 450 new slaves bought from slave traders had been added to Codrington's plantations. However, despite the provisions of the will, by 1793, only three of the Codrington slaves were reported as being literate and all the slaves were worked on Sunday.

• In 1710, there was a widespread slave conspiracy in Brazil which was instigated by the Muslim slaves. Between 1828 and 1837, Muslim slaves in Brazil would repeatedly stage slave revolts.

AFRICA

• The Dutch abandoned the island of Mauritius.
• A treaty was formulated between the French and the Tunisians.

In 1710, the bey of Tunis was recognized as being entitled to hereditary succession. This entitlement reflected the declining power of the Ottoman Turks.

• Construction on an Arab fort was begun at Zanzibar.
• An Arab garrison was installed at Kilwa.

1711

THE (FUTURE) UNITED STATES

• Through the efforts of the Mennonite Quakers, the Pennsylvania Yearly Meeting finally took action, prevailing upon the Pennsylvania colonial legislature to ban the slave trade. The law was enacted but immediately nullified by royal edict of the English crown. *See 1688.*
• A group of Maroons under the leadership of Sebastian led a campaign of armed resistance and slave revolution in South Carolina.

In 1711, the Tuscarora nation became enraged over the incursion of English settlers on Tuscarora land in the Carolina territory. The Tuscarorans launched a series of attacks upon the colonists who had settled along the Roanoke and Chowan Rivers, thereby launching the Tuscarora Wars. This and other conflicts with the Indigenous Americans enabled a great many persons of African descent to escape to freedom (September 22).

• Jupiter Hammon, the first African American poet, was born (October 17).

Jupiter Hammon (1711 [or 1720?]–circa 1800) was born a slave in the Henry Lloyd family of Lloyd's Neck, Long Island, New York. Hammon's first poems predate by several years those of Phillis Wheatley, the person generally regarded as the first African American poet.

Hammon's writings were largely exclamations of Methodist piety in the diction and the rhythm of Wesley and Watts. Such works as

Salvation by Christ with Penitential Cries (1760) and *An Evening's Improvement* advocated the passive resignation of the 18th century faiths. However, Hammon personally abhorred the system of slavery, and was probably instrumental in having his last owner, John Lloyd, Jr., include a clause in his will which provided for the liberation of all Lloyd's slaves upon their 28th birthdays.

Little or nothing is known of Hammon after 1790. Hammon's other works include a poetical address to Phillis Wheatley dated August 4 and published in Hartford, Connecticut, in 1778; *A Winter Piece* which was published in Hartford in 1782; and *An Address to the Negroes of the State of New York* which was presented to the members of the African Society in New York City on September 24, 1786 and was later printed in 1787.

THE AMERICAS

• In Venezuela, a mulatto named Audrestoe led a slave rebellion.
• In Brazil, Africans fought for the Portuguese against the French at Rio de Janeiro.
• Also in Brazil, with the aid of Africans, the Portuguese penetrated the valley of the Amazon from the Parana to Guiana. Africans also helped the Portuguese subdue the Indigenous Brazilians and, eventually, the Portuguese with their African forces conquered the land.

The role of Africans in the development of Brazil cannot be overemphasized. When gold came to dominate the economic life of Brazil, it was the African who washed the pans full of earth in search for the precious metal. When diamonds became important, it was Africans who mined the ore from which the diamonds were produced. It was upon the backs of the African slaves that the Portuguese Empire in both Brazil and Africa survived and prospered.

• In 1711, La Compania Francesa de las Indias (the French Company of the Indies) obtained an asiento for transporting slaves to Spanish America for an unspecified number of years.

AFRICA

• On June 18, the Janissaries were massacred in a battle outside of Cairo, Egypt.
• Yostos I of Ethiopia, the only Ethiopian emperor not of Solomonic blood, came to power.
• The Karamanli dynasty of Tripoli (Libya) came to power. While in the Ottoman sphere of influence, they remained independent of the Turks.

1712

THE (FUTURE) UNITED STATES

• A slave revolt began in New York City (April 7). The revolt arose because the slaves were taking revenge for the abuse they had suffered under their owners. In its aftermath, 12 slaves were executed while six other slaves refused to surrender and took their own lives (July 4). Nine Europeans lost their lives during the uprising. As a consequence of the slave action, Elias Neau's school for persons of African descent was temporarily closed. *See 1704.*
• The Pennsylvania Assembly barred the future importation of slaves into the colony (June 7).

In 1712, William Sotheby petitioned the Pennsylvania Assembly to abolish slavery. The Assembly refused to abolish slavery but it did pass an act which prohibited the importation of slaves (both African and Indigenous American) into the colony. This act was the first act barring the importation of slaves in the English colonies.

• South Carolina's Fugitive Slave Act mentioned mestizos (persons of African and Indigenous American heritage) along with mulattoes, Africans, and Indigenous Americans and implied that there were mestizos who were free as well as mestizos who were slaves.
• South Carolina law permitted manumission (liberation) of slaves and permitted an appeal to the governor by any individuals claiming that their enslavement was illegal.
• By 1712, one-fifth of the population of the Maryland colony was African slaves.
• In 1712, both New York and Massachusetts enacted laws which pertained to the prevention, suppression, and punishment of slave conspiracies and insurrections.

THE AMERICAS

• In 1712, it was reported that the population of Jamaica consisted of 3,500 Europeans and 42,000 Africans.

AFRICA

• The Bambara Kingdom of Segu was founded. *See 1652.*

RELATED HISTORICAL EVENTS

• On January 29, the Congress of Utrecht convened. *See 1701 and 1713.*

In 1713, Great Britain obtained from Spain, by way of the Treaty of Utrecht, a thirty-year monopoly for the transportation of slaves to the Spanish American colonies. The initial number of slaves to be transported on an annual basis was 4,800 per year.

The British counted this franchise for the transport of slaves as a valued prize resulting from the Treaty of Utrecht — the treaty which effectively ended the hostilities with France.

The British would hold this monopoly for thirty-five years until the Treaty of Aix-la-Chapelle. However, the treaty was often broken by "enterprising" sea captains working on their own or for other countries (including France).

1713

THE (FUTURE) UNITED STATES

• Anthony Benezet, a teacher of persons of African descent and a leading abolitionist in Pennsylvania, was born.
• On March 26, by the Treaty of Utrecht, England was granted asiento (a monopoly on the slave trade) with the Spanish colonial possessions. Under the treaty, the South Sea Company, formed in 1711, was allowed to import 4,800 Africans a year for 30 years into the Spanish colonies. The asiento was part of the settlement of Queen Anne's War (also known as the War of the Spanish Succession).

Queen Anne's War (the War of the Spanish Succession) was a war between the Grand Alliance of England and the Netherlands against France and Spain to prevent the union of France and Spain. The war began in 1701 and it ended in 1713 with the Peace of Utrecht (April 11). The treaty with France confirmed Britain's control and possession of many colonies including Acadia (Nova Scotia), Newfoundland, and the Hudson Bay Territory. The Peace also included a treaty with Spain which opened Spanish America to British trade (the Asiento Treaty) and confirmed British ownership of Gibraltar and Minorca. *See 1701.*

The extortion of the Asiento Treaty from the Spaniards at the Peace of Utrecht was feted as a triumph of English statecraft. Now, the British did not have to "smuggle" slaves via the West Indies. Under the treaty, the English acquired the right of supplying the Spanish col-

onies as well as their own. This new "business opportunity" resulted in a boom in English maritime activities. From the port of Liverpool alone, the number of ships employed in the slave trade increased from 15 ships in 1730 to 53 in 1751; 74 in 1760; 96 in 1770; and 132 in 1792. *See 1709.*

THE AMERICAS

• France made manumission (the liberation) of slaves in the Leeward Islands contingent upon permission of the governor-general. A similar ordinance existed for Guadeloupe.

1714

THE (FUTURE) UNITED STATES

• New Hampshire gave statutory recognition to slavery.

THE AMERICAS

• Gold was discovered in Brazil at the settlement of Villa Nova do Principe, a community which had been founded by escaped slaves from plantations in the Brazilian inland regions.

AFRICA

• The French Senegal Company established factories in Guinea (Guinea-Bissau and Senegal). *See 1673.*

1715

THE (FUTURE) UNITED STATES

• The Yamassee nation, encouraged by Spanish agitators, killed hundreds of English settlers and freed a large number of African slaves in South Carolina (April 15).
• The Quaker, John Hepburn, in his pamphlet *The American Defence of the Christian Golden Rule*, argued that slavery was wrong as it robbed men of freedom of choice, the only means by which an individual might pursue moral perfection. Another pamphlet, Elihu Coleman's *A Testimony Against that Anti-Christian Practice of Making Slaves of Men*, propounded the same thesis and was officially accepted at Coleman's Quaker meeting. Both pamphlets presented numerous arguments against slavery, including that of the spiritual damage done to Quakers themselves by accepting slavery.
• In 1715, the North Carolina colony enacted a number of laws affecting the rights of persons of African descent. First, a law

was enacted which prohibited intermarriage between Europeans and persons of African descent. Second, another North Carolina law gave statutory recognition to slavery. Thirdly, still another North Carolina law provided for fines for slave owners who allowed slaves to build a house of worship on the slave owner's land.

In 1715, the total reported population of the British colonies in North America was 434,600. However, this number did not include the population of Indigenous Americans nor the thousands of slaves who had liberated themselves to live with the Indigenous Americans or in their own maroon communities. Of the 434,600 recorded inhabitants, 375,750 were Europeans and 58,850 were persons of African descent. The totals were broken down in the following manner:

Colony	Total Population	Persons of African Descent	Percentage of Persons of African Descent in Population
N.H.	9,650	150	1.4
Mass.	96,000	2,000	2.1
R.I.	9,000	500	5.6
Conn.	47,500	1,500	3.2
N.Y.	31,000	4,000	12.7
N.J.	22,500	1,500	6.6
Pa.	45,800	2,500	5.5
Md.	50,200	9,500	18.6
Va.	95,000	23,000	24.2
N.C.	11,200	3,700	33.4
S.C.	16,750	10,500	60.0

Between 1715 and 1750, an average 2,500 Africans were imported to the English North American colonies each year.

• In South Carolina, where Jews and free persons of African descent had been voting, they were expressly forbidden from doing so.

THE AMERICAS

• Francisco Xavier de Luna Victoria became the first person of African descent to be made a bishop in America (Panama).
• By a royal (Spanish) decree, slaves were introduced into Puerto Rico.
• In Havana, Cuba, Ricardo O'Farrill established a market for the entrance and sale of slaves.
• In Guiana (today's Surinam), fighting continued between the Dutch and maroons.
• In Hispaniola, a militia composed of persons of African descent was formed in the French portion of the island (what is today Haiti).

AFRICA

• By 1715, Sieur Andre de Brue, who went to Saint Louis, Senegal, in 1697, as the governor of the French Senegal Company, had successfully established the French colony of Senegal. *See 1697.*
• In 1715, France took possession of the island of Mauritius and renamed it Ile de France. French colonists from the neighboring island of Bourbon (now Reunion) moved to Mauritius in 1722. The French imported slaves to Mauritius, built a fort, and planted coffee, fruit, spices, sugar, and vegetables. During the Anglo-French conflicts of the 1700s, Mauritius would serve as a French base of operations for French attacks on British shipping in the Indian Ocean and against British settlements in India.
• The first Boer (Dutch heritage) commandos were organized to fight against the Bushmen of South Africa.
• The first tax on wine was imposed on the wine of the Cape colony (South Africa).
• Around 1715, the Zamfara became independent of the Kebbi (Kebbawa). The infiltration of the Zamfara by the Gobir began.

The Zamfara, Kebbawa and Gobir are all ethnic subgroups of Hausa people, the largest ethnic group in today's Nigeria.

EUROPE

• In Portugal, Portuguese law declared that all slaves who set foot on the soil of Portugal were to be considered free.

1716

THE (FUTURE) UNITED STATES

• The first slaves of African descent were introduced into French Louisiana. The slaves came on board two slave ships of the Company of the West (June 6).
• A tract published in Massachusetts claimed that African slavery impeded European immigration to the colonies by limiting the occupations open to new settlers.

AFRICA

• A treaty was reached between Great Britain and Tunis.
• David III ascended to the throne of Ethiopia.

EUROPE

• In 1716, Abram Petrovich Hannibal, the African great-grandfather of the great Russian poet Pushkin, was sent to France by Czar Peter the Great. During his stay in

France, Hannibal would serve in the French Army. Upon his return to Russia, he would relate what he had learned to the Czar.

In the early 1700s, a young Abysinnian (Ethiopian) prince was abducted and taken to Constantinople by the Turks. In 1706, while in Constantinople, the young prince was purchased and brought to Russia by Czar Peter the Great. Under the patronage of Peter the Great, and because of his own special talents, the young prince was able to achieve a relatively high position at the Russian court and in the Russian army. In Russia, the young prince went by the name of Abram Petrovich Hannibal and, in addition to his own accomplishments, we know him today for one of his offspring. As fate would have it, Abram Petrovich Hannibal was the great-grandfather of Alexander Sergeevich Pushkin—Russia's greatest poet. *See 1799.*

RELATED HISTORICAL EVENTS

• Russia's Peter the Great visited Europe.

1717

THE (FUTURE) UNITED STATES

• Cotton Mather began an evening school for Indigenous Americans and persons of African descent in Boston.
• In Maryland, the intermarriage of a liberated person of African descent and a European automatically made the spouse of African descent the slave of the European spouse.
• A South Carolina colonial law forbade marriage between males of African descent and European women.
• In 1717, colonial ships, which were allowed to trade in the West Indies by the Peace of Utrecht, began bringing back cheap French molasses, used to distill rum in New England.

AFRICA

• Prussia sold its African possessions to Holland.

1718

RELATED HISTORICAL EVENTS

• William Penn, Quaker founder of Pennsylvania, died (July 30). Penn was one of the more enlightened founding fathers whose efforts led to Pennsylvania becoming a bastion for African American liberation (abolitionist) efforts.

William Penn (1644–1718) was a famous English Quaker who founded Pennsylvania. The Quakers, or the Society of Friends, were often treated harshly in England. They wanted the right to follow their religious beliefs without scorn or fear of violence. Penn was one of the Quakers' leaders and he was able to persuade King Charles II to let the Quakers set up a colony in America. The colony is today known as the state of Pennsylvania.

Penn was born on October 14, 1644, in London. He was the son of a naval officer later knighted as Admiral Sir William Penn. Penn went to school in Essex. He entered Christ Church, Oxford University, in 1660—the same year that the Stuart family returned to the throne of England. Penn opposed the university rule that required everyone to attend the Church of England. Penn believed in religious freedom and the right of individuals to worship as they pleased. Penn met with other rebellious students, outside the university, and was expelled from school. His father then sent Penn to France and Italy, hoping that the fashionable life there would make the young William forget his religious beliefs, or at least change them.

Penn returned to England after two years of travel and study a much mellower youth. The signs of his religious zeal were gone. Admiral Sir William was pleased and sent the reformed William to study law in London.

In 1667, Penn went to Ireland to manage his father's estates. While in Ireland, he became acquainted with Thomas Loe, a Quaker preacher. Loe convinced Penn of the "truth" of the Quaker faith. Penn was 22 years old at the time. He had a brilliant future ahead of him, but he put it aside to become a Quaker at a time when Quakers were scorned, ridiculed, imprisoned, and sometimes banished. Penn's father was simply heartbroken by his son's decision.

Penn was imprisoned several times for writing and preaching about Quakerism. He was first imprisoned in the Tower of London. After eight months, his father managed to have him released. During his imprisonment, Penn wrote *No Cross, No Crown* (1668), a piece explaining Quaker beliefs and practices.

In 1670, Penn was arrested at a Quaker meeting and accused of planning with another Quaker to start a riot. A jury found Penn not guilty of any crime. But the judge threatened to fine or imprison the jurors unless they changed their verdict. When the jurors refused to do so, the jurors were in fact imprisoned. But on appeal,

England's highest judges prohibited the penalizing of jurors. This action helped establish the independence of juries.

In 1677, Penn went to the Netherlands and Germany with George Fox and other Quaker leaders. In these countries, Penn met other Quakers who were eager to settle in a free, new land. Some people in England also wanted to settle where they could worship in their own way without fear. Penn realized that the only hope for the Quakers was in America.

Charles II owed Penn's father an unpaid debt of about $80,000. In 1680, Penn asked the king to repay the debt with wilderness land in America. On March 4, 1681, a charter was granted, giving Penn the territory west of the Delaware River between New York and Maryland. The charter also gave Penn almost unlimited governing power over the territory. The King's council added *Penn* to the suggested name of Sylvania, making the name Pennsylvania, which means Penn's Woods. Penn attracted settlers to his colony, including many Quakers, with promises of religious liberty and cheap land. Several thousand people came from England, Germany, the Netherlands, and Wales. Penn drafted a frame of government for his colony which greatly influenced later charters. Penn's charter authorized an elected assembly and is credited with having served as a model for the Constitution of the United States.

In October 1682, Penn sailed up the Delaware River and saw his colony for the first time. Also in 1682, Penn made his first treaty with the Indigenous Americans. His dealings with the Indigenous Americans were fair and honest and, unlike the affairs in other American colonies, the Indigenous Americans never felt compelled to attack Penn's colony. After seeing his colony off to a good start, Penn returned to England in 1684.

In his drive for religious tolerance, Penn had become a close ally of King James II of England, a Roman Catholic. King James granted pardons to Quakers and other religious prisoners. However, the Glorious Revolution of 1688 brought William and Mary to the English throne, and James fled abroad. Unfortunately, Penn was suspected of plotting the return of James and was arrested several times.

In 1692, Penn's colony was placed under royal control. It was during this time of trouble that Penn wrote two of his greatest works. In 1693, Penn wrote *An Essay Towards the Present and Future Peace of Europe,* a plan for a league of nations in Europe based on international justice. Also in 1693, Penn authored *Some Fruits of Solitude,* a short book that set forth Penn's philosophy for proper living.

In 1694, Penn's colony was restored to him. That same year, his first wife, Gulielma Maria Springett Penn, died. They had married in 1672 and had eight children. In 1696, Penn married Hannah Callowhill, who was to bear him seven more children.

Penn returned to Pennsylvania in 1699. During his absence, the colony had become beset by problems. Piracy, illegal trade and poor government had arisen. Penn's presence helped to restore some order to the colony. In 1701, Penn drafted a new charter for the colony—the Charter of Privileges. The Charter of Privileges created a unicameral (one-house) elected assembly with greater power. The provincial council was reduced from a legislative body to a small group of advisers to the governor. Efforts by the English government to place all proprietary colonies under royal control caused Penn to return to England in 1701. Penn would never see America again.

The government attempt to gain control failed. However, Penn was arranging to sell Pennsylvania to the English crown in 1712 when he suffered a stroke. The stroke impaired his mental ability and eventually paralyzed him. From 1712 until his death, Penn's affairs in Pennsylvania were handled by his wife (Hannah) and by his colonial secretary, James Logan. Pennsylvania remained a proprietary colony in the Penn family until it gained statehood during the Revolutionary War in America (1775–1783).

From an African American perspective, the role of William Penn was very important because it was through his efforts that the conscience of America (perhaps even the "soul" of America) was created. Penn's advancement of the Quaker faith would have a prolonged and a significant impact on American society and would inevitably lead to the emancipation of African Americans from the shackles of slavery. In a work entitled *Primitive Christianity Revived,* Penn attempted to show that the beliefs and practices of the Society of Friends (the Quakers) were the same as those of the early Christian church, and were, in fact, the correct way to godliness. Penn emphasized the Quaker doctrine of the light of Christ in man, a "divine principle" that, even though it was not inherent in man's nature, was bestowed by God on all men. Accordingly, Quakers held in high regard humanitarian and equalitarian principles, since each individual carried within him a spark of Divine Spirit. The doctrine, which ascribed the Inner Light to all men, regardless of race or creed, marked the rise of a new religious liberalism and a spirit of toleration, especially in Pennsylvania.

For his works and for his life, William Penn must be considered not only one of the great men of American history but also as one of the great men of African American history.

• Lady Mary Wortley-Montague publicized a form of vaccination against smallpox. *See 1721.*

1 7 1 9

THE AMERICAS

• In Brazil, the slaves revolted.

1 7 2 0

THE (FUTURE) UNITED STATES

The triangular trade which led to the subjugation and decimation of indigenous populations on two continents took a new twist in 1720. Before 1720, there was an unfavorable balance of trade with England. Under English law, colonists were forbidden from selling their surplus farm goods in English markets. So instead the colonists sold their goods in such markets as Lisbon, Portugal or Cadiz, Spain. In Lisbon and Cadiz, the traders would obtain a cargo of European goods which were then exchanged in the West Indies for sugar, molasses or silver. A variation of this trade game involved taking rum and iron directly to Africa to "purchase" slaves and then transport slaves to the West Indies where they could be exchanged for molasses and sugar.

The triangular trade soared after the British Parliament rescinded the monopoly once held by the Royal African Company. The commodity rum had also become a favorite, replacing French brandy as the alcoholic beverage of choice.

Additionally, between 1720 and 1767 the French slave trade was handled by a British controlled monopoly. The Company of the Indies (or the Company of the West), which was originally organized by John Law, held the monopoly.

• In 1720, there were an estimated 474,000 people in the American colonies. Boston was the largest city at 12,000; Philadelphia had 10,000, and New York had 7,000. There were 68,839 slaves in the American colonies: 14,091 in the North and 54,748 in the South.

• By 1720, the slave trade was a fairly efficient enterprise. At first, slaves brought to the English North American colonies came primarily from the West Indies. Subsequently, most came directly from Africa. The majority of slaves brought to the colonies from Africa came from a large region lying between the Gambia and the Niger Rivers. Others came primarily from West Africa, particularly from the northwest portion of the Congo. Other sources of slaves were Angola, Cameroon, Sierra Leone, the Gold and Ivory Coasts, and Senegal.

• A slave insurrection occurred in South Carolina. European Americans were attacked on the streets and in their houses in Charleston. Twenty-three slaves were arrested, six were convicted and three were executed.

THE AMERICAS

• In 1720, coffee was introduced into Martinique by the French and soon became another plantation crop.

• In 1720, the Portuguese government prohibited its colonial administrators from engaging in any aspect of the slave trade.

AFRICA

• Beginning in 1720, the Dutch East India Company maintained a depot at Delogoa Bay for slaves from Madagascar and East African slaving centers.

• A treaty was executed between Spain and Tunis.

• Opoku Ware began his reign over the Ashanti.

During his reign, Opoku Ware concentrated on fostering a spirit of national unity among the Ashanti. As part of the effort to develop national unity, Opoku Ware required all the officials of his kingdom to take the "Great Oath" in a solemn, formal ceremony which stressed the allegiance of the official to the state.

Ruling over a kingdom which was rich in gold, ivory and slaves, Opoku Ware maintained a strong trading relationship with the Dutch. However, he also recognized the need to maintain his country's independence from the European traders and to that end supported the development of distilling (rum-making) and weaving industries in his own land.

1 7 2 1

THE (FUTURE) UNITED STATES

• Delaware colonial law forbade marriages between European women and men of African descent. The law also provided that the child of a European woman and a slave would be bound to the county court until the child was 31 years of age.

• The first smallpox inoculations in America were given by Zabdiel Boylston in Boston, Massachusetts. Boylston inoculated his son, Thomas, and two slaves of African descent on the recommendation of Cotton Mather. Mather's slave, Onesimus, had previously told Mather of similar inoculations administered by African tribesmen, and Mather urged Boylston to try the practice. Angry mobs stoned both Mather's and Boylston's homes when they learned of the experiment (May 21).

The smallpox epidemic of 1721 in Boston (population 12,000) had produced 5,889 known cases of the contagious disease and at least 844 deaths. The populace was desperate for some relief from the epidemic and desperation was the mother of experimentation. Boylston ultimately inoculated 240 people. All but six of those who underwent the treatment survived. In this instance, African experience and African medicine proved superior to European practices.

AFRICA

• France annexed Mauritius and renamed it "Ile de France."

• Asma Giorgis "Bacaffa" (Bakaffa) of Ethiopia, the great warrior, traveler, and builder came to power. Bacaffa was legendary for traveling incognito during his inspection forays. On one such incognito inspection, he encountered an enchanting maiden by the name of Menetewab—the woman who was destined to become his wife and who was destined to rule Ethiopia as regent after her husband's untimely death.

EUROPE

• It is believed that Angelo Solliman, a personal acquaintance of royalty, was born in this year.

Angelo Solliman (1721–1776) was friend, favorite and tutor of European royalty. He was a personal attendant of Prince Lobkowitz and later of the Prince de Lichtenstein. Still later, with the express approval of the Empress Maria Theresa who believed that Angelo would be a good influence upon her son, Angelo became the companion of Joseph II of Austria. Francis I, Emperor of the Holy Roman Empire, was so fond of Angelo that he invited him to enter his personal service.

Angelo's notoriety led to his being mentioned in Abbe Gregoire's *An Enquiry Concerning the Intellectual and Moral Faculties and Literature of Negroes.*

RELATED HISTORICAL EVENTS

• In Russia, the sale of slaves was prohibited except as complete families.

1 7 2 2

THE (FUTURE) UNITED STATES

• The Pennsylvania Assembly condemned the "wicked and scandalous practice" of persons of African descent cohabiting with Europeans.

In 1722, in South Carolina, English justices were authorized to search slaves for guns, swords, and other offensive weapons and to confiscate them unless the slave could produce a permit to carry such a weapon less than one month old. Patrols could search slaves and whip those considered dangerous to peace and good order.

After uprisings and numerous attempted uprisings, South Carolina enacted one of the most stringent slave codes in the English colonies. Between Saturday evening and Monday morning, no more than seven slaves were permitted to be together without having an Englishman present; no slaves were permitted to possess firearms or carry them; and, under no circumstances, were Africans to be taught to read or write.

• There was a slave plot in Virginia.

1 7 2 3

THE (FUTURE) UNITED STATES

• Free persons of African descent (along with Indigenous Americans) in Virginia were denied the right to vote and were discriminated against in the levying of taxes. This was a departure from the practice, in effect since 1670, of only restricting voting pursuant to property qualifications.

• Virginia colonial law forbade a free person of African descent from "meeting or visiting slaves."

• In Virginia, free persons of African descent and Indigenous Americans were forbidden to "keep or carry any gun, powder or shot, or any club or other weapon whatsoever, offensive or defensive."

• In this year, as in 1691, laws were enacted in Virginia which limited the increase of the free persons of African descent to natural means and to manumission by special legislative acts. These laws remained in force until 1782, when there were 2,800 free persons of African descent in Virginia.

• The Virginia Legislature delegated to the governor and the council the power to pass upon slaves' claims to freedom and to make judgments based upon meritorious service performed by the slaves.

• Rumors and certain evidence aroused the people of Boston, Massachusetts, concerning a purported plan by persons of African descent to burn the city.

• Philadelphians petitioned the colonial Assembly to take legislative action against the intermarriage of Europeans and persons of African descent.

• Crispus Attucks (1723–1770) was born.

Crispus Attucks was a person of African and Indigenous American (Natick) heritage. Contemporary accounts described Attucks as having been "owned" by a Deacon William Browne of Framingham, Massachusetts. Attucks was the leader of a group which precipitated the so-called Boston Massacre. On March 5, 1770, Attucks led a group of 50 to 60 men, mostly sailors, from Dock Square to State Street in Boston to harass British soldiers. In the fray which followed, an event now known as the "Boston Massacre," three people were killed, including Attucks. It is reported that Attucks was the first to be killed.

Nineteenth century historians transformed Attucks into a full-blooded Indigenous American from the Natick nation but 20th century research, along with 18th century documentation, has brought the true African and Indigenous American heritage of Attucks to light.

In 1888, Boston erected a monument to honor those who died in the incident.

THE AMERICAS

• In 1723, coffee emerged as a major export and a major plantation crop of Brazil.

According to legend, coffee was discovered in Ethiopia when goatherds noticed that their flocks stayed awake all night after feeding on coffee leaves and berries. Coffee reached Arabia in the 1200s.

The word "coffee" comes from the Arabic word "qahwah." Before coffee beans were used to make the beverage we know today, coffee was first used as a food, then a wine, and then a medicine.

Coffee moved from Arabia to Turkey during the 1500s and to Italy in the 1600s. Coffee houses sprang up throughout Europe in the 1600s, and people met there for discussions and to socialize.

Coffee probably came to the Americas in the 1660s and was introduced in Brazil as a cash crop in the 1700s.

AFRICA

• Sultan Ibrahim of Kilwa requested Portuguese aid in expelling the Omani Arabs from the East African coast.

• Agadja (Agaja), the king of Abomey (Dahomey), invaded the kingdom of Allada.

During his reign, Agadja succeeded in expanding the borders of Dahomey and reestablishing it as a military force. However, continued warfare with neighboring states eventually weakened Dahomey and Agadja was forced to ask for peace. Part of the peace effected by Agadja called for the payment of a tribute to the neighboring state of Oyo. In order to make these payments, Agadja was compelled to become involved in and dependent upon the slave trade.

Agadja tried to establish a royal monopoly of the slave trade. This effort led to internal strife within Dahomey which weakened the state and persuaded the European slave traders to seek a more stable trading partner. The abandonment of Dahomey impoverished the kingdom and disabled Dahomey from paying its tribute to Oyo. In 1737, Oyo invaded Dahomey and Agadja was forced to flee. His reign was effectively over.

1724

THE (FUTURE) UNITED STATES

• Louisiana passed its "Black Code." The Black Code contained some fifty-five articles which regulated the government of slaves. Among the punishments authorized by the Black Code were the cutting off of recaptured slaves' ears, the hamstringing of recaptured escaped slaves, and branding recaptured slaves.

• A Virginia religious tract was published which advocated baptism and educational opportunities for African Americans, Indigenous Americans, and mulattoes. The tract also argued that slave owners should be exempt from the payment of taxes on their baptized slaves who were under the age of 18.

AFRICA

• Dahomey conquered the two neighboring states established by three sons of an African monarch in the 1600s. Partly relying upon the recently formed Corps of Amazons, Dahomey captured the Great Ardra. The combined kingdom would, for a brief time, dominate the area.

1725

THE (FUTURE) UNITED STATES

• A South Carolina colonial law imposed a 200 pound (English currency) fine on slave holders who brought their slaves close to the frontier. The law was designed to prevent the encouragement of slave escapes and to curtail interactions between African and Indigenous American peoples.

By 1725, the number of slaves of African descent in the British North American colonies reached 75,000.

• In response to repeated petitions and complaints, the Pennsylvania colony enacted legislation which forbade the mixture of the races.
• The first Church of Colored Baptists was established in Williamsburg, Virginia.

AFRICA

• A treaty was reached between Austria and Tunis.
• 1725 marked the beginning of the decline of the Algerian fleet and the Algerian economy.
• The Kilindi dynasty of Vuga was founded in the Usambara Mountains (Tanzania) by Mbega.

It is said that Mbega entered Usambara as a great hunter. His hunting prowess and generosity moved the Kilindi clans to ask Mbega to establish a kingdom. Mbega did so, and from Vuga the Kilindi clan dominated the Shambaa people.

• A *jihad* was initiated in Futa Toro. The Karamoko Alfa Ba assumed the title of "al-mamy" (alimamy).
• The Imamate of Futa Djallon (Guinea) was established.

1726

THE (FUTURE) UNITED STATES

• The colonial governor of New York asked the chiefs of the Six Nations of the Iroquois Confederacy to return all self-liberated slaves. The chiefs agreed but no slave was ever returned.
• Peter Vantrump, a free person of African descent, agreed to go to Europe with a Captain Mackie. Instead he was taken to North Carolina where he was sold into slavery. Vantrump petitioned the courts for his release. The Honorable Christopher Gale, Chief Justice of the General Court of North Carolina, denied the petition.

THE AMERICAS

• In Surinam, the first of a series of slave rebellions occurred.

AFRICA

• Mahe on the Seychelles Islands was founded by Bertrand Mahe de la Bourdonnais.

EUROPE

• Terence Afer (Terence the African) was an ex-slave living in Rome. He was the author of six plays and was considered to be a great Latin stylist. He is most famous for coining the phrase "Homo sum; humani nihil a me alienum puto"—"I am a man and nothing human is alien to me."

1727

THE (FUTURE) UNITED STATES

• The Junto, an early benevolent association in America established by Benjamin Franklin, pledged its members to oppose slavery and other forms of inhumanity to men.

THE AMERICAS

• The French and the Spanish colonists supported education for persons of African descent insofar as it was needed to convert them to Christianity. In 1727, the Catholics in New Orleans, under the leadership of Ursuline nuns, attempted to educate persons of African descent and Indigenous Americans.

AFRICA

• The first Mazrui governor was appointed to govern Mombasa.
• Agaja, the ruler of the Fon state (Dahomey) embarked on a campaign to conquer the small West African seaboard states

(Ardrah, Ouidah, Jakin) which monopolized the trade with Europeans. Agaja would build a strong, centralized monarchy and would maintain Ouidah as a port for trade with Europeans.
• The Sultan of Pate requested Portuguese aid to expel the Omani Arabs.

RELATED HISTORICAL EVENTS

• The yearly meeting of the Quakers in London censured the slave trade.

1728

THE (FUTURE) UNITED STATES

In 1728, the long simmering rivalry between the English and Spanish settlements on the American continent flared up again when a party of Carolinians attacked a Yamassee village near St. Augustine, Florida. The Yamassees were once friendly to the English colonists but had begun siding with the Spanish *See 1715* as more and more Yamassee land came under the control of the English. The attack occurred for many reasons — as an extension of recent hostilities between Spain and England, as retribution for Yamassee military actions of years gone by, as a means of preventing Spanish Florida from serving as a safe haven for self-liberated slaves, and as an exercise in imperial colonialism. However, the attack on the Yamassee was really just another in a long line of attacks upon the city of St. Augustine by the British. Sir Francis Drake attacked the city in 1586; Captain John Davis in 1665; and other Carolinians in 1702. The attack in 1728 was not to be the last (March 9).

THE AMERICAS

• In 1728, there were approximately 50,000 slaves of African descent in Santo Domingo (Hispaniola).
• Gregorio, the slave of Don Jorge Burgues, served as the town crier in Montevideo (Uruguay). In the creation of the *Cabildo* of Montevideo by order of Zabala, 20 December 1729, persons of color were mentioned in an official order of the Banda Oriental. Africans of mixed ancestry were excluded from serving as aldermen or councilmen. By 1731, records indicated the presence of African slaves owned by a Francisco de Acosta of Montevideo.
• Diamonds were discovered at Minas Gerais, Brazil.

AFRICA

• By 1728, the Ashanti kingdom had become a powerful state in the area of Africa that is today known as Ghana.
• In 1728, the earliest known text written in Swahili was published. The text was titled *Utendi wa Tambuka*.
• A treaty was agreed to by Britain and Morocco under which the British slaves in Morocco were liberated.
• Tunis entered into treaties with France and Holland.
• The Portuguese reoccupied Pate and Mombasa.

1729

THE (FUTURE) UNITED STATES

• Benjamin Franklin printed a book by Ralph Sandyford (Sandiford), a Philadelphia Quaker, against slavery. The book was entitled A *Brief Examination of the Practice of the Times, By the Foregoing and the Present Dispensation.*
• The Society for the Propagation of the Gospel was reorganized as Dr. Bray's Associates. The Reverend Thomas Bray had advocated the religious education of persons of African descent since 1701.

THE AMERICAS

• The discovery of diamonds in Brazil increased the demand for African slaves. *See 1728.* In 1729 and 1730, the Portuguese transported large numbers of Africans to Minas de Geraes, Brazil, to work in the diamond mines.
• The Cabildo of Montevideo excluded mulattoes from serving as aldermen or councilmen.

AFRICA

• The Portuguese were once again expelled from Pate and Mombasa.
• Dahomey was made a tributary of Oyo. *See 1652.*
• Jesus II became king of Ethiopia. With his ascension, a period of feudal wars began. The wars served as a prelude to a political reorganization which would occur in the 1800s.

EUROPE

• In 1729, the York and Talbot Decision held that slaves, alone or accompanied, reaching Great Britain or Ireland were not automatically free.
• It was reported that Ignatius Sancho was

born, in 1729, on board a slave ship bound for South America. Sancho would eventually come to write about his experiences. His *Letters* (edited by a Joseph Jekyll) were published in London in 1782 in a two volume edition. His *Letters* would be highly praised.

1730

THE (FUTURE) UNITED STATES

In 1730, there were 91,021 slaves in the British North American colonies: 17,323 in the North and 73,698 in the South. The total estimated population of the British North American colonies was 654,950.

• A rebellion by persons of African descent in Williamsburg, Virginia, was precipitated by the rumor that Governor Spotswood of Virginia had arrived with instructions to free all persons who had been baptized.
• When a slave conspiracy was discovered in the Norfolk and Princess Anne counties in Virginia, the government ordered European men to carry firearms with them to church.
• The Ursuline nuns of New Orleans, Louisiana, began to instruct the African converts to Catholicism.
• A plot by 200 persons of African descent in South Carolina was discovered. The plot included a raid upon a church at the mouth of the Rappahannock River in Virginia.

THE AMERICAS

• Aleijadinho, a person of African and European descent, was born in this year. Aleijadinho became one of Brazil's greatest 18th century architects.

Antonio Francisco Lisboa (1730–1812) was better known as Aleijadinho ("The Little Cripple"). Aleijadinho was the son of an African slave and a Portuguese architect. Aleijadinho was shunned by both his parents and the world. Aleijadinho suffered from leprosy. His affliction caused him to retreat from the society of men into a world of stone.

Aleijadinho wrought what many consider to be the culmination of Latin American baroque architecture and sculpture. He is noted for his twelve statues of the prophets which he carved in the staircase leading to the Church of the Good Child Jesus in Congonhas do Campo. These statues reject the symmetry of classical sculptures. The statues are three-dimensional, moving statues, rushing down toward the spectator; they are rebellious statutes, twisted in anguish and anger.

Aleijadinho's other major work is the Church of Our Lady of the Pillar in Ouro Preto. The exterior of the church is a perfect rectangle. However, inside everything is curved.

Because of the reaction he received from the eyes of men, Aleijadinho worked at night. It is said that he was surrounded by the dreams of the Brazilian people and that these dreams became his inspiration.

AFRICA

• Ground nut cultivation was first described in Gambia.
• The Empress Mentaub (Menetewab) came to power in Ethiopia.

Mentaub was one of the more intriguing figures in Ethiopian history. Of Portuguese and Ethiopian descent, she became the empress when she married Bakaffa. After Bakaffa died she ruled Ethiopia as regent because her son was uninterested in politics. Mentaub's reign as regent would span the life of both her son and her grandson. After her retirement from public life, Mentaub met the Scottish traveler, James Bruce. It would be Bruce who would record the life story of the great Mentaub.

• The Yao made their first contacts with Arab traders on the coast of Africa.

The Yao live in Mozambique, Malawi, and Tanzania. The Yao were one of the African people for whom slavery was an important supporting aspect of their lives. Domestic slavery was essential to the Yao social system and slaves were obtained through purchase, capture or compensation. The abolition of slavery had a deleterious impact on Yao society.

Over the centuries of serving as middlemen for Arab traders, the Yao have today adopted Arab customs and dress as well as the Muslim religion.

• The trekking of the Boers into the interior of the Cape Colony became more prevalent.

RELATED HISTORICAL EVENTS

• Samuel Sewall died.

In 1730, Samuel Sewall (1652–1730) died. Samuel Sewall was a judge at the famous Salem witchcraft trials in the Massachusetts Bay Colony in 1692. As a result of those trials, nineteen people were convicted of witchcraft and hanged. Judge Sewall was the only judge to ever publicly recant his participation in the trials. In 1697, Sewall made a public confession of error and guilt for his part in the trials.

Sewall was born in Bishopstoke in Hampshire County, England. His family moved to New England when he was nine years old (in 1661). Sewall attended Harvard College and received a bachelor's degree in 1671 and a master's degree in 1674. He became a minister and later a merchant. Sewall also served in the colony's legislature and as a justice in the courts. *See 1697 and 1700.*

Sewall was one of the more enlightened men of his day. He was concerned with the fate of the Indigenous Americans and often wrote of such practical problems as fixing fair boundaries for Indigenous American lands as well as a plan for recruiting missionaries from among the Indigenous Americans themselves for the purpose of spreading the gospel.

Sewall is remembered for a diary he kept for fifty-seven years. In the diary Sewall noted the events of his own and other lives in Boston. The diary was a candid journal which revealed Sewall's vanities as well as his courage — a courage which led Sewall to publicly repent for having participated in the Salem witchcraft trials and a courage which led Sewall to champion social concerns which were not popular in his day.

Sewall's chief notoriety for the purposes of African American history lies in his publication of the "The Selling of Joseph," an antislavery tract which was first printed in 1700. "The Selling of Joseph" would be used throughout the 1700s and 1800s to bolster the arguments against the institution of slavery. Sewall personally handed out this tract to those he met on the streets of Boston, one of the chief slave trading ports of the day. "Forasmuch as liberty is in real value next unto life, none ought to part with it themselves, or deprive others of it, but upon most mature consideration."

——————— 1731 ———————

THE (FUTURE) UNITED STATES

• Benjamin Banneker, a colonial mathematician and astronomer of African descent, was born.

Benjamin Banneker (1731–1806) was born near Baltimore, Maryland (November 9). Banneker was taught to read by his maternal grandmother, Molly Welsh, who was originally an indentured servant from England. Banneker's father, Robert Banneker, an industrious and prosperous farmer with 120 acres outside Baltimore, sent his son to school. Banneker showed himself to be adept at anything mechanical. At the age of 22, Banneker made a clock which struck the hours. From 27 through his middle age years, Banneker was occupied with running his father's farm.

In 1772, Banneker was given some astronomical books by a wealthy Quaker neighbor, George Ellicot. Banneker then read voluminously on geology, astronomy, and physics, and observed the heavens with a makeshift telescope. In 1789, through the influence of Ellicot, Banneker was selected as part of a scientific team to survey and assess the Federal territory designated to become the District of Columbia.

Banneker began publishing his annual almanacs in 1791; these, in addition to factual material, contained commentaries by Banneker on social problems. In the almanac, Banneker wrote a learned dissertation on bees. Banneker was the first man to calculate the locust plague as recurrent in 17-year cycles. On August 19, 1791, Banneker sent a copy of the almanac to Secretary of State Thomas Jefferson. Included in the prefatory note was an appeal to Jefferson on behalf of Banneker's fellow African Americans who were held in bondage (slavery).

In his almanac of 1793, Banneker included an important paper entitled "A *Plan of Peace Office for the U.S.*" Greatly influenced by the optimism of the French Revolution, William Goodwin, Thomas Paine and Richard Price, Banneker included proposals for the formation of a Department of the Interior and a League of Nations. Banneker also opposed capital punishment.

Despite all his accomplishments, in 1802, Banneker lost his right to vote when the Maryland Legislature enacted legislation which disenfranchised persons of African descent. Banneker died in 1806 and, suspiciously, much of his manuscript work was burned two days later.

THE AMERICAS

• There was a slave rebellion in Santiago del Prado, Cuba.
• A royal decree ordered the destruction of the slave "quilombo" of Cumbe. A "quilombo" was a cooperative community of escaped slaves.
• In Guiana (today's Guyana), there were

slave revolts in the Berbice and Essequibo (Esseqibo) regions.

AFRICA

• War erupted between Bornu and Kano.

---

1 7 3 2

THE (FUTURE) UNITED STATES

• Virginia put a five percent (5%) duty on imported slaves for four years. Virginia continued to impose duties on slaves and, in 1759, a duty of 20% was put on all slaves imported into Virginia from other British colonies.
• There was a slave rebellion in Louisiana. An African woman and four African men were executed and their heads were publicly displayed on poles.

THE AMERICAS

• European Moravians established the first missionary settlement in Jamaica. By 1787, the Moravians had outposts in Antigua, St. Christopher and Barbados to convert persons of African descent to Christianity.

AFRICA

• The Spanish fleet recaptured Oran (Algeria).

RELATED HISTORICAL EVENTS

• George Washington, the first President of the United States, was born.

---

1 7 3 3

THE (FUTURE) UNITED STATES

• On February 12, James Oglethorpe, the founder of Georgia, founded Savannah, Georgia. During 1733, the trustees of this experimental colony prohibited the importation or use of slaves. Gradually, these restrictions were relaxed. The prohibition on slavery in Georgia was rescinded in 1749.

James Oglethorpe was a slave holder who kept slaves on his plantations in the Carolinas. Oglethorpe also served as Deputy Governor of the Royal African Company.

The new colony of Georgia prohibited African slavery as being fatal to the interests of the poor British settlers for whose special benefit the colony had been established.

• South Carolina's governor offered a 20 pound (English currency) reward for the capture of Maroons.

• In Boston, a number of slaves petitioned for their freedom.
• Spain confirmed earlier royal decrees that a slave who escaped from a Protestant colony would be considered free in Spanish lands. This policy proved to be a great irritation to the slave holders in the English colonies particularly those on the border of Spanish Florida. *See 1739.*

RELATED HISTORICAL EVENTS

• The British Molasses Act attempted to suppress trade between the West Indies and the British North America colonies.

---

1 7 3 4

THE AMERICAS

• In Jamaica, a state of war existed between Europeans (the British) and Maroons.

The principal leader of the Maroons of Jamaica was Captain Cudjoe. Captain Cudjoe was an inexhaustible leader who used clever guerrilla tactics to subdue the British at every turn. The only way that the British could defeat Cudjoe was by making peace with him — which they did. Cudjoe and his men were given land, were freed from taxation and were granted permission to hunt anywhere on the island *except* for the areas within three miles of a British settlement.

The racial make up of today's Jamaica is largely due to the presence and legacy of Cudjoe. Because the British could not defeat Cudjoe, they came to fear him and did not feel safe on the island. This insecurity prompted many to leave and discouraged many from settling in Jamaica. As a result, the African people of Jamaica came to dominate the island.

AFRICA

• The sultan of Bornu became the overlord of Kano.
• Bertrand Mahe de la Bourdonnais became the governor of Ile de France (Mauritius). The sugar industry was subsequently established on the island.

EUROPE

In 1734, Ayuba Suleiman Diallo of Bondu was known to the Europeans as Job en Solomon. He was captured by enemies during a commercial venture to the Gambia in 1731 and sold as a slave to Maryland where he was put to work growing tobacco.

After an attempted escape, Ayuba was

rescued from slavery by Thomas Bluett. Bluett saw the intelligence of Ayuba and soon learned of his education. With the assistance of other Englishmen, Ayuba was emancipated, taken to England, presented to the British court, and finally helped to return home. Bluett later wrote the memoirs of Ayuba.

While in England, in 1734, Ayuba was elected to the scholarly Spalding Society whose membership had included Newton and Pope. He was also received at Court where the Queen presented him with a gold watch.

• Anthony William Amo, an African born in Guinea, became the first known person of African descent to obtain a European medical doctorate. Amo attended the University of Wittenberg. Eventually, Amo returned to Africa after a thirty-year stay in Europe. *See 1738.*

───────── **1 7 3 5** ─────────

THE (FUTURE) UNITED STATES

• John van Zandt, a Dutch burgher of New York, horsewhipped his African slave to death for having been picked up at night after curfew. A coroner's jury judged that the death of the slave was more attributable to the "visitation of God" than to the beating meted out by van Zandt and no penalty was assessed.

The relations between Europeans and persons of African descent were often tense in New York. In 1735, approximately one fifth of the total population of the colony was of African heritage.

• Prince Hall, an abolitionist and the founder of African American freemasonry, was born.

Prince Hall (1735–1807) was born in Barbados of the British West Indies. Hall was the son of an Englishman and a free woman of African descent. He was apprenticed as a leather worker but abandoned that training to emigrate to Boston.

During the Revolutionary War, Hall and twelve other persons of African descent were inducted into a Masonic Lodge by a group of British soldiers stationed in Boston. After the British evacuated the area, Hall organized a Masonic Lodge for African Americans. This lodge was chartered in England in 1787 as African Lodge No. 459. Hall, the first master of the Boston lodge, subsequently established

additional African American lodges in Pennsylvania and Rhode Island.

Hall, a self-educated clergyman, also championed the establishment of schools for African American children in Boston, urged Massachusetts to legislatively oppose slavery, and proposed measures to protect free African Americans from kidnaping and enslavement.

Upon his death in 1807, the African Grand Lodge became Prince Hall Grand Lodge.

AFRICA

• Ethiopia went to war against the Funj.
• Yorina Bussa founded the Amirate of Borgu.

───────── **1 7 3 6** ─────────

THE (FUTURE) UNITED STATES

• Colonel Byrd II of Virginia remarked that the "saints of New England" brought so many Africans into Virginia that "the colony will sometime or other be confirmed by the name of New Guinea." Byrd's remarks reflected the resentment in the South toward the moral preachment of New England Puritans regarding slavery.
• Benjamin Franklin printed an anti-slavery book by a Quaker, Benjamin Lay.

Benjamin Lay was one of the earliest Quakers to condemn slavery and the slave trade. Lay used both non-violent resistance and a biting pen. His tracts were printed by Benjamin Franklin.

AFRICA

• Between 1736 and 1743, Egypt was ruled by a triumvirate.

───────── **1 7 3 7** ─────────

AFRICA

• The first Moravian mission was established on the Gold Coast.

───────── **1 7 3 8** ─────────

THE (FUTURE) UNITED STATES

• Residents of Nantucket, Massachusetts, uncovered an Indigenous American plot to attack Nantucket at night, sparing only the Africans.
• In Bethlehem, Pennsylvania, Moravians organized a mission to minister to African Americans.

The Moravians are a Protestant denomination which broke away from the Catholic Church in 1467 by ordaining their own ministers. In the 1700s, the Moravians were the most aggressive and controversial religious movement in European Protestantism. The Moravians built large centers in Germany, the Netherlands, Great Britain and in North America. These centers were noted for great creativity in church music, with extensive hymn-composing and high proficiency in performance.

In the mid-1700s, the Moravians established a far-flung missionary endeavor which sent volunteers to the West Indies, Africa, and among the North American Indigenous Americans.

THE AMERICAS

• In 1738, a treaty was signed between the British and the maroons of Jamaica which essentially gave the maroons their autonomy (their freedom).

• Ignoring Britain's monopoly of the trade in Africans with the Spanish territories, the *Cabildo* petitioned in 1738 with the support of the military governor, Don Domingo Santos de Uriarte, that Montevideo (Uruguay) be permitted to use three boats for acquiring slaves in Brazil in exchange for tallow, dried beef, and wheat.

EUROPE

• Anton Wilhelm von Amo published *Tractatus de arte sobrie et accurate philosophandi.*

Anton Wilhelm von Amo was born in Guinea. He came to Europe in 1707 at the age of four. Educated under the supervision of the prince of Brunswick, von Amo's education was completely European. He was fluent in Hebrew, French, Dutch, and German. Von Amo lectured publicly, was a doctor at the University of Wittenberg, and was made a councillor of state by the Court of Berlin.

In 1734, von Amo wrote a dissertation entitled "On Sensations considered as absent from Mind, present in Body." The body of von Amo's published work consisted of Latin treatises on logic, psychology, and history. Von Amo's metaphysical essay (written in Latin) *Tractatus de arte sobrie et accurate philosophandi* was published in 1738.

During his career, von Amo defended African culture against European prejudice and eventually returned to the Gold Coast (Ghana).

1739

THE (FUTURE) UNITED STATES

Three slave revolts broke out in South Carolina. The source of the incidents was attributed to the preaching of Spanish missionaries who allegedly created in the persons of African descent a false expectation of deliverance. On September 9, 1739, a band of escaped slaves from Charleston set out for St. Augustine which was located in Spanish Florida in search of freedom. Along the way, the slaves met resistance and were compelled to fight for their freedom. A massacre followed which resulted in the deaths of 44 persons of African descent and 21 Europeans.

A second insurrection at Stono, South Carolina, (about 20 miles west of Charleston) was led by a slave named Cato. After killing two warehouse guards and securing arms and ammunition, the slaves headed south hoping to reach Florida. An untold number of slaves were killed during this insurrection along with some 30 Europeans. A third insurrection occurred at St. John's Parish in Berkeley County, South Carolina. "A 1715 census showed that, out of all the American colonies, South Carolina had the second largest number of slaves, after Virginia, and the largest percentage of persons of African descent (up to 60 percent) of the total population. South Carolina had serious problems with so-called maroons (escaped slaves) and offered large rewards for their capture. Many slaves sought to reach Spanish lands (Florida) because of a 1733 Spanish decree which freed escaped slaves from the English colonies. *See 1733.*"

• Although the Georgia trustees had been petitioned to allow slavery, another group of settlers opposed it. They claimed in their petition that slaves would endanger the colony, cause deaths and necessitate guard duty by the English colonists.

• Escaped slaves living in St. Augustine, Florida, built a fort to protect their families and to stem British incursions into Spanish territory.

AFRICA

• Muhammed Uthman al-Mazrui became governor of Mombasa.
• Abu al-Qasim became the sultan of Darfur. He would be known for waging an unsuccessful war against Wadai.

EUROPE

• Joseph Boulogne Saint-Georges, a famous Afro-French violinist and composer, was born.

Joseph Boulogne (the Chevalier de) Saint-Georges (circa 1739–1799) was the son of a former councillor in the Parlement at Metz and a woman of African descent from Guadeloupe. Moving first from Guadeloupe to Saint Domingue (Haiti), the family settled in Paris in 1749.

At the age of 13, Saint-Georges became a pupil of La Boessiere, a master of arms. He also studied riding with Dugast at the Tuileries. Over the years, Saint-Georges became very proficient at both arms and riding.

On September 8, 1766, Saint-Georges participated in his first public fencing match in Paris with the renowned Giuseppe Gianfaldoni. Gianfaldoni won but predicted that Saint-Georges would one day become the finest swordsman in Europe. Gianfaldoni was right.

Besides his expertise in fencing and riding, he excelled in dancing, swimming and skating as well as the violin.

Little is known of Saint-Georges' musical training either as a violinist or composer. It is said that he received some instruction with his father's plantation manager while the family was in Haiti. It is also believed that he studied the violin with Leclair and composition with Gossec. But whatever the source of his instruction, Saint-Georges excelled at both.

Saint-Georges made his public debut as a violinist with the Amateurs in 1772, performing violin concertos which he had written for himself. These concertos, like all his others, seem to have been written to demonstrate Saint-Georges' prowess with the violin. The concertos contain violin solos which reveal much about Saint-Georges capabilities. The solos make extensive use of the highest positions and require phenomenal dexterity in crossing the strings and in multiple stopping, often in the quickest of tempos. However, his virtuoso playing was not the only part of his performance. As his friend Louise Fusil wrote: "The expressivity of his performance was his principal merit."

When Gossec became a director of the Concert Spirituel in 1773, Saint-Georges became the musical director and leader of the Amateurs. Under Saint-Georges' leadership, the Amateurs became one of the best orchestras in France.

Between 1772 and 1779, Saint-Georges published most of his instrumental music. He composed quartets for strings and continuo, violin concertos, *symphonies concertantes* and a pair of symphonies. It is upon this body of work that Saint-Georges' reputation as a composer rests.

In 1781, the Amateurs were disbanded. Soon thereafter, Saint-Georges founded the orchestra known as the Concert de la Loge Olympique. As its fame increased, the Concert de la Loge Olympique moved to the presitigious Salle des Gardes in the Tuileries. It was for this ensemble that the Count of Ogny commissioned Haydn's Paris symphonies with Saint-Georges as intermediary.

In 1785, Saint-Georges moved to London, where he gave exhibition fencing matches at Angelo's Academy before the Prince of Wales and other dignitaries. Returning to Paris in 1787, Saint-Georges composed and produced a moderately successful comedy entitled *La fille-garcon* and resumed work with the Loge Olympique.

In 1789, the French Revolution began and the Loge Olympique fell upon hard times. The Loge Olympique was dissolved and Saint-Georges once again moved to England. However, this time he was in the company of the Duke of Orleans, Phillippe Egalite. Again there were fencing matches at Angelo's Academy and at the Royal Pavilion in Brighton before the Prince of Wales.

In 1790, Saint-Georges returned to Paris. Depressed by the turmoil caused by the Revolution and the loss of his orchestra, Saint-Georges decided to leave the city and tour northern France. In 1791, Saint-Georges took up official residence in Lille where he became captain of the National Guard.

Desiring to take a more active role in the ongoing Revolution, Saint-Georges organized a corps of light troops in late summer 1792. The light troops was planned to be comprised of 1000 Afro-French and African troops, including the mulatto Alexandre Dumas. See 1762. Known as the Legion National du Midi, the corps had little military success. Saint-Georges was relieved of his command and subsequently jailed for eighteen months in a house at Houdainville. Upon his release, Saint-Georges was forbidden to live in the vicinity of his former comrades.

Without any means to his former livelihood, Saint-Georges was reduced to living a vagabond life. For a time he returned to Haiti. However, in 1797, he returned to Paris, where he served briefly as director of a new musical organization, the Cercle de l'Harmonie, in the former residence of the Orleans family.

RELATED HISTORICAL EVENTS

• The English courts reversed the opinion of law officers of the Crown that slaves became free by being in England or by being baptized.

―――――― **1 7 4 0** ――――――

THE (FUTURE) UNITED STATES

In 1740, there were 150,024 slaves in the British colonies: 23,958 in the North and 126,066 in the South.

• Georgia colonial governor James Oglethorpe, taking advantage of protection from friendly Indigenous Americans (Creeks), invaded the Spanish colony of Florida. Oglethorpe was momentarily successful and was able to capture Forts Picolata and San Francisco de Pupo. However, his troops were ultimately repelled by Spanish forces which included a contingent of troops composed of Indigenous Americans (Seminoles) and 200 persons of African descent.

In 1740, South Carolina continued to shake from the series of slave insurrections which had begun in 1739.

In Charleston, some fifty slaves were hanged after exposure of insurrection plans (January).

Also in Charleston, an African woman was condemned to death for arson.

In response to the growing fears of the colonists, the South Carolina authorities began to take measures which were designed to keep the slave population in check.

The South Carolina Assembly banned the teaching of slaves to write or the hiring of slaves as scribes. However the South Carolina ban on teaching slaves to write would be enforced inconsistently for the next hundred years. In times of relative quiet, there was little enforcement of this ban. However, as in 1740, after the Prosser incident of 1800 and the Nat Turner insurrection of 1831, South Carolina would reiterate the ban on the teaching of slaves to read or write.

Contrastingly, even in 1740, it was reported that Dr. Bray's Associates, the English philanthropic organization, organized a free school in Charleston, South Carolina, which had about 60 pupils.

South Carolina's consolidated Slave Act included harsh penalties for false appeals to the governor on the part of slaves who felt they had been illegally kept enslaved. The Act also forbade slaves from raising cattle, sheep, horses and other animals. Any animals owned by a slave were to be forfeited.

• In 1740, slaves in New York City were accused of conspiring to kill their masters by poisoning the water supply.
• The first report of an African American dentist practicing in the American colonies appeared in a Pennsylvania newspaper. The article stated that an African American named Simon was able to "bleed and draw teeth."

By 1740, Newport, Rhode Island, had become the hub of the triangular (slave) trade.

AFRICA

• The Lunda kingdom of Kazembe was established.

―――――― **1 7 4 1** ――――――

THE (FUTURE) UNITED STATES

The paranoid climate created by slavery was highlighted in New York City where public suspicion resulted in the hanging of eighteen persons of African descent, the burning at the stake of eleven others of African descent, the deportation of eighty others, and the hanging of four European sympathizers. (A man accused of providing the slaves with weapons, his family and a Catholic priest were the Europeans who were hanged.)

The actions were precipitated by a series of incendiary fires. Public suspicion centered upon persons of African descent for no other reason than that they were present in the area (March–April).

Subsequently, a prosecutor in the case, Daniel Horsemanden, revealed that there was, in fact, no conspiracy. The paranoia stemmed from the fact that, in 1741, twenty percent of the population of New York was composed of persons of African descent (December 31).

THE AMERICAS

• In Guiana (today's Guyana), there was a slave revolt in the Essequibo (Esseqibo) region.
• Tomas Navarro was granted an asiento to supply slaves to Buenos Aires (Argentina) and Montevideo (Uruguay).

AFRICA

• Philip Quaque (Kweku), an African missionary, was born.

Philip Quaque (Kweku) was born on the Gold Coast (in Ghana). He was connected with the slave trade through the merchants who carried it on—not as one of the human cargo.

In 1754, at the age of thirteen, Kweku was sent to England for education, sponsored by the Society for the Propagation of the Gospel in Foreign Parts. He was ordained as a priest of the Church of England, the first African to attain this distinction.

In 1766, Kweku returned to the Gold Coast as a missionary. Over the next fifty years, Kweku wrote a series of letters to the Society for the Propagation of the Gospel in Foreign Parts in London.

RELATED HISTORICAL EVENTS

• Pope Benedict XIV condemned slavery as practiced in Brazil.

1742

THE (FUTURE) UNITED STATES

• Spanish colonial forces attacked Georgia in retaliation for the invasion of 1740. The Spanish colonial forces included a regiment composed of persons of African descent with officers of African lineage.
• David George (1742–1810), the pastor of the first African American Baptist church, the first Afro-Canadian church, and the first African American/Afro-Canadian church in Sierra Leone, was born. *See 1783.*

EUROPE

• In 1742, James Eliza John Capitein published in Amsterdam a volume of sermons and a Latin treatise which was said to have defended slavery as a social institution. Capitein was kidnapped from Africa when he was seven or eight years of age and was educated in Holland at the expense of a philanthropic Dutch merchant. Later Capitein would also publish an essay in Leyden which defended the thesis that slavery per se is not contrary to Christian doctrine.

1743

THE (FUTURE) UNITED STATES

General James Oglethorpe, commander of the armed forces in Georgia and South Caro-

lina, returned from another sortie against the Spanish in Florida. With a force of Highland troops, Oglethorpe ventured to the gates of St. Augustine but the Spanish refused to fight.

The response contrasted sharply with their behavior nine months ago when more than 2,000 Spanish soldiers (including a contingent of African troops) descended upon St. Simons Island. An English force no larger than a fourth their size thrashed the Spanish soundly at the Battle of Bloody Marsh. Oglethorpe's men killed or captured more than 200 Spaniards as they made their way down a narrow road linking Fort St. Simons and Fort Frederica. The battle, one small skirmish in three years of war between England and Spain, capped ten years of tension between England's southernmost colony and the Spanish in Florida. In 1739, the Spaniards killed two Highlanders at Amelia Island and in 1740 Oglethorpe retaliated by harassing the Spanish at St. John's River and seizing Forts Picolata and St. Francisco de Pupa.

• John Woolman began preaching on the evils of slavery to Quaker meetings throughout the colonies.
• A school (Mr. Garden's School) to educate and train African American youth was opened in Charleston, South Carolina, with the support from both African American and European American citizens of the city.
• Quassey, a person of African descent, became a member of a Newton, Rhode Island, Baptist church.
• In 1743, the Society for the Propagation of the Gospel in Foreign Parts established a school in Charleston, South Carolina, to train African American missionaries.

In 1743, Virginia had approximately 42,000 persons of African descent.

THE AMERICAS

• Tomas Navarro exchanged a shipment of Africans for hides in the Port of Montevideo (Uruguay).
• Toussaint L'Ouverture, the revolutionary liberator of Haiti, was born (May 20). *See 1803.*

EUROPE

• In 1743, Benedict the Black, the patron saint of African Americans and the protector of Palermo, was beatified by Pope Benedict XIV and, in 1807, he was canonized by Pope Pius VII. *See 1526.*

RELATED HISTORICAL EVENTS

• Thomas Jefferson, the author of the Declaration of Independence, was born.

Thomas Jefferson (1743-1826) was the third President of the United States and was the founder of the Democratic Republican Party. Jefferson was born in Virginia into a wealthy family. In 1772, he married Martha Wayles Skelton. The couple had one son and five daughters in their ten years of marriage. Martha Jefferson died in 1782, and although he was only 39 years old, Jefferson never remarried.

During the early 1770s, Jefferson served in the Virginia House of Burgesses (the Virginia colonial legislature) where he achieved a measure of notoriety for his ability to draft laws and resolutions in clear and simple English.

In 1774, Jefferson published *A Summary View of the Rights of British America*, a pamphlet which expressed Jefferson's view that the British Parliament had no authority over the American colonies.

As a member of the Continental Congress, Jefferson was the principal author of the Declaration of Independence, including the phrase "We hold these truths to be self-evident, that all men are created equal, ..."

During his political career, Jefferson served as governor of Virginia (1779-1781), ambassador to France (1785-1789), secretary of state in the Washington administration (1789-1793), vice president of the States during the John Adams administration (1797-1801), and president of the United States (1801-1809).

While serving as ambassador to France, Jefferson was supportive of the French Revolution. Also while in France, Jefferson dispatched messages to his ally James Madison with regard to the drafting of the Constitution, especially the need for a Bill of Rights.

During Jefferson's Presidency, there were a number of events which impacted upon both African history and African American history. With regard to African history, in 1801, Tripoli, one of the Barbary states declared war on American shipping because it wanted more tribute money. The smallish navy of the United States blockaded Tripoli's ports, bombarded its fortresses, and ultimately forced Tripoli to honor the American flag.

As for African American history, Jefferson was responsible for buying the Louisiana Territory which would ultimately lead to a battle over the extension of slavery into the Territory—a battle which came to be known as the Civil War. Additionally, in 1808, an act prohibiting the importation of African slavery became law. This act allowed the American abolitionists to shift the focus from the horrific evils of the slave trade to the evils of slavery itself.

To his great credit, Thomas Jefferson was the author of the phrase "We hold these truths to be self-evident, that all men are created equal, ..." It was this phrase which formed a key cornerstone of the most persuasive abolition arguments against the institution of slavery. However, to his discredit it must be stated that Jefferson himself owned slaves. The schism between what Jefferson wrote and what he in practice did is difficult to reconcile.

Another issue of importance to African American history centers around Jefferson's relationship with one of his slaves—a woman by the name of Sally Hemings. The African American descendants of Sally Hemings claim that Sally Hemings was the mistress of Thomas Jefferson. It is often noted that although Jefferson was a sexually active male during his brief married life, and although his wife died when Jefferson was only 39, he never remarried. Some point to Sally Hemings as being part of the reason why Jefferson never needed to remarry.

Of course, there is presently no indisputable proof that Sally Hemings was the mistress of Jefferson—none that is but the belief and conviction held by the African American descendants of Sally Hemings which compels them to assert that they are the contemporary vessels of Thomas Jefferson's blood.

1744

THE (FUTURE) UNITED STATES

• A special school for persons of African descent was established in South Carolina by Samuel Thomas, an Anglican missionary. The school would last for ten years. The teacher at the school was a free person of African descent and the school was intended for free persons of African descent. However, some slaves who hired their time were able to send their children to the school.

• A Virginia colonial law was amended so that any nonenslaved person of African descent or Indigenous American who professed the Christian faith could be admitted as a witness in both civil and criminal suits against any other person of African descent or any Indigenous American (but not against a European).

THE AMERICAS

• In Guiana (today's Guyana), there was a slave revolt in the Essequibo (Esseqibo) region.

AFRICA

• Ethiopia went to war against Sennar (Sannar). The Ethiopians were defeated by the Funj (Fung) with assistance from the Fur.

The Fung are an ethnic group of northern Sudan who inhabit the land on either side of the Blue Nile River, upstream of Sannar.

The Fur are mainly found in the central Darfur province in the northern part of Sudan. The history of the Fur people is one of influence and power. A ruling dynasty of partly Arab origin arose during the seventeenth century and established a Fur sultanate that lasted until 1916.

• Mombasa proclaimed its independence from Oman.

• Ibrahim, a Janissary commander, became ruler of Egypt.

The Janissaries were members of an elite corps of Turkish troops organized in the 1300s and abolished in 1826.

RELATED HISTORICAL EVENTS

• By 1744, half of Liverpool's maritime trade was the trade in slaves.

───────── **1 7 4 5** ─────────

THE (FUTURE) UNITED STATES

• Thomas Ashley, in *A New General Collection of Voyages and Travels,* answered those who argued that slavery was beneficial to persons of African descent by saying that if slavery was so beneficial to persons of African descent then they should be allowed to choose it for themselves.

In 1745, New Jersey had a total population of 61,383: 56,777 Europeans and 4,606 persons of African descent.

• Jean Baptiste Pointe du Sable, the founder of the City of Chicago, was born.

Jean Baptiste Pointe du Sable (1745–1818), a person of African descent who established a trading post which later became the city of Chicago, was born in Haiti of a French mariner

and an African slave girl. Du Sable was sent, by his father, to a Paris boarding school after the death of his mother.

As a young man, Du Sable worked as a seaman for his father's prosperous export-import business until he was shipwrecked in 1765 off the coast of New Orleans. Rescued, du Sable, fearful of being enslaved, was hidden by friendly Jesuits in New Orleans. Du Sable and a few companions (including Jacques Clemorgan of Martinique) traveled upriver to the trading post of St. Louis. Du Sable was adopted and married into the Potawatomi nation. Du Sable traveled throughout, and explored, the entire Midwest in his capacity as a trader. Du Sable kept detailed accounts of his business transactions and the new territories he traversed.

In 1772, du Sable opened a trading post at the southern end of Lake Michigan. The post was lucrative due to its strategic location. Soon a settlement grew around du Sable's trading post. The settlement became the city of Chicago. Du Sable remained a highly respected figure of the early American frontier, and both Chief Pontiac and Daniel Boone were his personal friends.

Du Sable and his Potawatomi wife, Catherine, lived in Chicago for the the better part of two decades. Du Sable and Catherine were devout Catholics and, in 1798, they were formally married in an official church ceremony. Towards the end of the century, du Sable and his wife left Chicago to live with their daughter in St. Charles, Missouri. In 1800, Catherine died and in 1818, when du Sable died, he was interred in St. Charles Borromeo Roman Catholic Cemetery.

AFRICA

• Oman reasserted its suzerainty over Mombasa.

───────── **1 7 4 6** ─────────

THE (FUTURE) UNITED STATES

In 1746, Lucy Terry, sixteen years old and African born, witnessed a battle between Indigenous Americans and her European neighbors in Deerfield, Massachusetts. She subsequently wrote a rhymed account of what she saw. "The Bar's Fight" described Europeans as valiant, brave, and bold and called Indigenous Americans heartless murderers. This poem became the first published by an African American in the New World and made Terry a local celebrity. [Some historians have reported that the poem "The Bar's Fight" may actually have been based on an historical incident which occurred in 1704 known as the Deerfield Massacre. However, this is unlikely given Lucy Terry's age at the time of composition of the poem and the probable unfamiliarity she would have had with the 1704 incident.]

Despite the notoriety Lucy Terry gained from her praise of Europeans, she did not derive a long lasting peace from her service. Terry married an ex-slave named Elijah Prince and two of their sons eventually served in Washington's Revolutionary War army. But after the war, the Princes were beset by a number of mishaps caused by their European American neighbors. The Princes' farm was repeatedly set afire prompting them to plead before the governor for a cease and desist order.

When Mrs. Prince attempted to enroll her youngest son in Williams College, she was told that persons of African descent were not welcomed. Although she eloquently argued for three hours with the trustees, pointing to her family's military record, citing the Bible and the Declaration of Independence, she could not persuade them.

When she died at the age of ninety-one, in 1821, the Massachusetts Legislature was considering legislation which would expel any African American who entered the state.

• The General Assembly of the Province of New Jersey met at Perth Amboy and authorized the president of the General Council and commander-in-chief of the militia, John Hamilton, to raise a force of 500 liberated persons of African descent and Indigenous Americans to serve in Canada against the French.
• In 1746, slaves that cost the equivalent of four to five pounds (English currency) in rum in Africa were sold in the West Indies at prices ranging from 30 to 86 pounds and in the Southern colonies at approximately 100 pounds per head. The obvious profitability of the slave trade was the key factor in its being maintained despite the moral arguments against it.
• Newport Gardner, perhaps the first African American composer, was born.

Newport Gardner (also known as Occramer Marycoo) (1746–1826) was born in Africa and sold into slavery at Newport, Rhode Island, when he was 14. Gardner began to write music in 1764 and it is believed that Gardner became one of the first African American music teachers.

In 1791, Gardner purchased freedom for himself and his family. He then established a singing school in Newport. "Crooked Shanks," one of Gardner's compositions, was the first known composition by an African American to be published (1803).

The text of *Promise Anthem*, one of Gardner's choral pieces which was performed in Newport and Boston still exists.

Gardner was also a founder of the Newport Colored Union Church and Society and became a missionary to Africa in 1826.

AFRICA

• A plague of locusts befell the colonists at the Cape Colony.

1747

THE (FUTURE) UNITED STATES

In 1747, the General Assembly of South Carolina acknowledged that the slaves of African descent had "behaved themselves with great faithfulness and courage in repelling attacks of His Majesty's enemies."

The General Assembly went on to provide that slaves could be enlisted in the militia up to a number equivalent to one-third of the European men in the militia company, as long as not more than one-half of all able-bodied slaves between 16 and 60 were enlisted.

In "time of general alarm and actual invasion of this province, not otherwise, [the slaves were] to be armed with: (a) one sufficient gun, (b) one hatchet, (c) a powder horn and shot pouch with ammunition of powder and bullets for 20 rounds and 6 spare flints." Manumission was to be granted to a slave who captured or killed an enemy.

In 1747, the principal enemies of "His Majesty" were the Spanish in Florida, the neighboring Indigenous Americans, and escaped slaves who lived amongst the Spanish or the Indigenous Americans.

• Absalom Jones, the first African American minister ordained in America, was born a slave in Sussex, Delaware.

Absalom Jones (1747–1818) was born a slave in Sussex, Delaware. However, as a youth, his owner took him to Philadelphia to work as a handyman in a store. While working in the store, Jones was taught how to read and write by a store clerk. He later attended a night school.

Saving the little money he earned on the side, Absalom Jones purchased his freedom and the freedom of his wife. He became a member of the St. George's Methodist Church in Philadelphia. It was there that a momentous event occurred which would shape the course of African American religious life.

While attending services at the St. George's Methodist Church in 1787, Jones along with Richard Allen and other African American worshippers, were ordered to move to the reserved (segregated) seating area for African American worshippers in the church's balcony. The African American worshippers objected to this segregation and, as a result of this discrimination, formed the Free African Society.

The Free African Society was basically a quasi-religious organization. The Free African Society served to provide funding for mutual aid, burial assistance and relief for widows and orphans.

Jones was a close associate of Richard Allen *see 1760* but the two developed separate (albeit parallel paths) when Jones, who as a devout Anglican, became rector of the first Protestant Episcopal (St. Thomas Episcopal Church) congregation composed of African Americans in 1791.

• A Presbyterian church began a program of education for African Americans in Virginia.

AFRICA

• The Funj (Fung) initiated a war against Musabaat.
• Dahomey succumbed to the Yoruba.
• The Mazrui (the Omani) seized Pemba.

1748

AFRICA

• The Virginia Militia Act prohibited freed slaves and Indigenous Americans from bearing arms. However, this provision was dropped during the Revolutionary War to permit free persons of African descent to become soldiers.

THE AMERICAS

Between 1748 and 1782, 127,133 out of 146,799 slaves survived to be sold by the French in the Americas and the West Indies. During this time period, the French made some 541 voyages to Africa as part of their slave enterprises. While the loss of life as part of a despicable business such as the slave trade is never

excusable or laudable, it is of some historical interest to note that the French version of the slave trade was far more humane than the version practiced by the British under which a loss of up to a third of the slave "cargo" was deemed to be a reasonable loss.

1749

THE (FUTURE) UNITED STATES

• The Georgia Trustees' prohibition on the importation of slaves was repealed as a result of pressure from Carolinians settling in the province and the continual flaunting of the regulation by many colonists who wanted slaves for field and house hands. Slaves were supposed to receive religious education; were, theoretically, protected from cruel treatment; were forbidden marriage with Europeans; and could not be hired out. Slave holders were to have one European worker for every four African slaves.

AFRICA

• Dan Juma, the founder of the Amirate of Gumel, came to power.

1750

THE (FUTURE) UNITED STATES

In 1750, there were 236,420 slaves in the British colonies of North America: 30,222 in the North and 206,198 in the South. In Maryland, there were 40,000 persons of African descent and 100,000 Europeans.

• Crispus Attucks, the first martyr of the American Revolution, escaped from slavery and left Framingham, Massachusetts (September 30). *See 1723 and 1770.*
• The British Parliament decreed that for every four Africans in the colony of Georgia there was to be at least one European male servant of militia age. Additionally, Africans were not to be employed in any trade except agriculture nor were they to be apprenticed to artisans with the exception of carpenters.
• In 1750, Father Vivier estimated that there were 1,100 Europeans, 300 slaves of African descent, and 60 Indigenous American slaves in five French villages in the French territory which is today known as Illinois.
• Anthony Benezet, in association with Philadelphia Quakers, opened a free school for persons of African descent. The school

was an evening school taught by Moses Patterson.

• In 1750, a British act for extending and improving the African slave trade was enacted. The act allowed individual merchants (as opposed to syndicates) to engage in the slave trade for small duties. This change opened up the trade and expanded it.

• *Notable Births:* James Varick, the founder of the African Methodist Episcopal (AME) Zion Church, was born.

James Varick (1750–1828), the founder of the African Methodist Episcopal (AME) Zion Church and its first bishop, was born near Newburgh, New York. Varick came to prominence in 1796 when certain African American members of the Methodist Episcopal Church living in New York secured permission to hold meetings by themselves. The church members rented a house on Cross Street, between Mulberry and Orange Streets, and three years later organized a church under the laws of the State of New York.

In 1820, the church declared its independence. Efforts to secure ordination from the Methodist Episcopal bishops having failed, in 1822 Varick and two others were ordained elders by three former ministers of the Methodist Church. Also in 1822, Varick was elected the first bishop of the AME Zion Church and served in that capacity until his death.

THE AMERICAS

• In Brazil, the Jesuit Music Conservatory was established near Rio de Janeiro to instruct African slaves in music.

• By 1750, the system of contratacion by which a slave could purchase his or her freedom at a prearranged agreed upon price was common in Cuba.

AFRICA

• By 1750, the coastal cities of East Africa had partially recovered from the ravages wrought by Portuguese occupation. However, the traditional trade with the other nations bordering the Indian Ocean had not recovered to the volume of pre–Portuguese days.

• In Zambia, the Bemba and Lozi became firmly established.

• In Sudan, a Muslim revival in western Sudan coincided with the rise of a number Muslim states.

• Beginning in 1750, the Wallo Galla began to be converted to Islam. *See 1563.*

• Kwasi Obodun (Kusi Obodum) ascended to the leadership of the Ashanti.

• Around 1750, the Baoule kingship of the South Ivory Coast was founded by Akan immigrants.

RELATED HISTORICAL EVENTS

• The Company of Merchants Trading to Africa was established by Parliament to facilitate the participation of individual merchants in the slave trade.

1751

THE (FUTURE) UNITED STATES

• In a pamphlet entitled "Observations Concerning the Increase of Mankind and the Peopling of Countries," Benjamin Franklin argued that the use of slaves for production was not economically efficient.

• Sugar cane was introduced in Louisiana by the Jesuits. The introduction of sugar cane would increase the demand for slaves in Louisiana.

In the 1750s, about 3,500 Africans were imported annually to the English colonies in North America. However, perhaps as many as one-third as many annually died while in transit.

• *Miscellaneous Legislation:* South Carolina enacted a law authorizing the death penalty, without benefit of clergy, for slaves convicted of attempting to poison a European.

THE AMERICAS

• In 1751, Mackandal, a leader of the Maroons of Haiti, conceived a plot to poison the European slave holders. Mackandal was reported to be a great orator and regarded himself as a prophet. For the next six years, until he was betrayed and captured, Mackandal waged a war of liberation against the European plantations.

AFRICA

• Ryk Tulbagh began a 20-year tenure as the governor of the Cape colony (South Africa).

1752

THE (FUTURE) UNITED STATES

• George Washington, the "Father" of the United States, acquired Mount Vernon, including eighteen slaves upon the death of his half brother Lawrence. With increased prosperity, Washington eventually brought the total number of slaves to approximately 200 (July).

AFRICA

• The first missionaries from the Society for the Propagation of the Gospel in Foreign Parts *see 1701* arrived at the Cape Coast Castle.

• The Portuguese administration of Mozambique was made separate from its administration of Goa (India).

1753

THE (FUTURE) UNITED STATES

Between 1753 and 1773, some 2,800 slaves were annually imported into South Carolina.

• *Notable Births:* Lemuel Haynes, the first African American to serve as a pastor to a European American congregation in the United States, was born (July 18). *See 1775, 1776, and 1785.*

Lemuel Haynes (1753–1833) was born in Connecticut, the son of a father of African heritage and a European woman. Haynes never knew his father and was rejected and abandoned by his mother.

Haynes was educated by the man to whom he was bound as a servant. He served in the Revolutionary Army with some distinction.

In 1785, Haynes was ordained and became a pastor of a European American congregation in Torrington, Connecticut.

Haynes became the first African American to receive an honorary degree when, in 1804, Middlebury College, Vermont, awarded him an honorary master of arts degree.

In 1818, Haynes became the pastor in Manchester, New Hampshire.

• Scipio Morehead, the earliest known African American artist, was born.

• James Robinson, the recipient of a medal for bravery at the Battle of Yorktown, was born. Robinson, after winning his medal, would be promised his freedom. But the promise would prove to be an empty one. Robinson was returned to slavery after the Revolutionary War.

• It is believed that Phillis Wheatley was born in this year.

Phillis Wheatley (circa 1753–1784), the noted African American poet, was born in Africa and brought to America at the age of 8. She was "purchased" by John Wheatley of Boston, a prosperous tailor, as a personal servant for his wife. It was Wheatley's wife who encouraged Phillis to read and write. Phillis was exceptionally bright. She learned English in 16 months and soon gained a considerable reputation in Boston's intellectual circles.

In 1767, at age 14, Phillis published her first poem, "The University of Cambridge in New England," an ode showing the influence of her favorite poets, Gray and Pope. Over the next few years, Ms. Wheatley wrote panegyrics (an essay full of praise) to King George and eulogies for Boston notables, Dr. Sewall and the Reverend George Whitefield. Ms. Wheatley also published a translation from Ovid. Her ideas were poetic commonplaces of the period.

In her poem *Liberty and Peace*, Ms. Wheatley praised, as her New England preceptors would have done, freedom from "Albion's tyrants," but there was no mention of the enslavement of her own people. Indeed, very little autobiographical or personal life entered into her work, perhaps because she did not want to make her audience uncomfortable with the subject or perhaps because she herself could not deal with the contradiction inherent in her writing laudatory pieces praising a people who had enslaved her own. In any event, Ms. Wheatley's poetry lacked a certain depth, a certain "soul" which accordingly limited her and led others to define her work as being competent but not extraordinary.

In 1773, suffering from ill health, Ms. Wheatley traveled to Britain with her owner's son. She was received by several prominent English noblemen and promptly charmed the court circles. Her book, *Poems on Various Subjects, Religious and Moral*, was published and was successful.

By some quirk of fate, the Wheatley family went bankrupt in 1778 which resulted in the emancipation of Phillis. Now "free," Phillis was left to shift for herself. She eventually married John Peters, an emancipated African American. The hardships that befell the couple caused Phillis' health, which had often been fragile, to fail. She died in 1784, at the tender age of 31.

THE AMERICAS

• In 1753, the Cunliffes of Liverpool, England, transported 1,210 slaves to the West Indies. The Cunliffe family amassed a sizable fortune with as many as 12 slave ships making two to three trips a year.

AFRICA

• The laws of the Cape colony concerning slavery were codified.

1754

AFRICA

In 1754, the estimated population of the English colonies, according to a report of the Board of Trade to the king of England, was 1,485,634 of which 1,192,896 were Europeans and 292,738 were persons of African descent. A breakdown for some of the colonies follows:

Colony	Europeans	Persons of African Descent	Percentage of Persons of African Descent in Total Population
Ga.	5,000	2,000	28.5
Md.	104,000	44,000	29.8
N.Y.	85,000	11,000	11.4
N.C.	70,000	20,000	22.2
Pa.	195,000	11,000	5.3
Va.	168,000	116,000	40.9

• In Charleston, South Carolina, a slave-holder named C. Croft had two of his female slaves burned alive because they set fire to his buildings.

• *The Abolition Movement:* John Woolman wrote *Some Considerations on the Keeping of Negroes*, an exhortation to convince Quakers to give up their slaves.

• *The Arts and Sciences:* The first clock made entirely in America was constructed by Benjamin Banneker, age 23. Banneker had never seen a clock before but, ingeniously, constructed one based upon diagrams. Banneker's clock continued to run accurately, striking all hours regularly, for the next 20 years (December). *See 1731.*

THE AMERICAS

• The population of Santo Domingo [Haiti also known as Hispaniola] was estimated at 190,000. The composition was 14,000 Europeans; 4,000 mulattoes; and 172,000 persons of African descent.

AFRICA

• In 1754, a French captain was reported to have bought slaves in the Kilwa region both for use in the Mascarene Islands, Mauritius, Bourbon (today's Reunion), and for transport to St. Domingue (Haiti).

1755

THE (FUTURE) UNITED STATES

In 1755, a macabre story shook Massachusetts.

Mark and Phillis, slaves of John Codman of Charlestown, Massachusetts, learned that Codman had made them free by his will. To expedite their release, Mark and Phillis poisoned Codman. Mark was subsequently hanged and gibleted (disemboweled), and Phillis was burned to death.

• A Maryland census described eight percent (8%) of the persons of African descent as being mulattoes. At this time Maryland had about a seventh of the total population of persons of African descent in the British colonies. It is noteworthy that since sexual relations between males of African descent and European women was legally forbidden (and physically prevented) and interracial marriage was prohibited, the primary way mulattoes could be "produced" in 1755 was through illicit sexual liaisons between European men and their African female slaves.

• Beginning in 1755, slavery became legalized in Georgia. However, in 1793, Georgia would stop the entry of free persons of African descent and, in 1798, under heavy penalties, prohibited the importation of slaves. The provision prohibiting the importation of slaves was placed in the State Constitution, but this provision was poorly enforced albeit never repealed.

THE AMERICAS

• In Brazil, all of the Indigenous Brazilians that had been held in slavery were declared free. This emancipation of the Indigenous Brazilians stimulated the demand for African slaves.

AFRICA

• Ioas of Ethiopia came to the throne. Empress Mentaub served as regent during Ioas' reign. The Ethiopian court was dominated by the Galla. The Ethiopian monarchy was in a state of near collapse. *See 1563.*

1756

AFRICA

• In 1756, there were 120,156 persons of African descent in Virginia, up from the 23,000 estimated in 1715 and, at that time, comprising 40 percent of the total population.

THE AMERICAS

• Black Jasmin Thomassam, a Santo Domingo (Haitian) liberated slave, established a home for poor persons of African descent in Haiti. Thomassam would operate the home for the next forty years.

1 7 5 7

THE (FUTURE) UNITED STATES

Beginning in this year, Quakers in England and America took action against slave-owning members. In Philadelphia, Quakers who dealt in persons of African descent were barred from the business sessions of meetings and could not make contributions. In 1760, it became an offense among New England Quakers to import slaves. In 1761, at the London Yearly Meeting a proposal was forwarded calling for the disownment of all slave dealers.

• Edmund Burke expressd his ideas on slavery in his *An Account of the European Settlements in America* in which Burke advocated that the slaves' situation be improved to minimize the danger of slave rebellions and to increase colonial production.

1 7 5 8

THE (FUTURE) UNITED STATES

• The annual meeting of the Society of Friends (Quakers) in Philadelphia recommended that Quakers refrain from becoming involved in the slave trade in any form.
• The "Bluestone" African Baptist Church was established on the William Byrd plantation in Mecklenberg, Virginia. The congregation's nickname came from its location near the Bluestone River.

THE AMERICAS

• Frances Williams, first college graduate of African descent in the Western Hemisphere, published Latin poems (April 17).
• A book published in Lisbon, Portugal, *The Ethiopian Ransomed, Indentured, Sustained, Corrected, Educated and Liberated* by Manuel Riberro de Rocha, advocated the replacement of African slavery in Brazil with a system of indentured labor.

1 7 5 9

THE (FUTURE) UNITED STATES

• *Notable Births:* Paul Cuffee (Cuffe), an African American business leader and philanthropist, was born in Cuttyhunk, Massachusetts (January 17).

Paul Cuffee (1759–1817) was the son of African and Wampanoag nation parents. At 16, Cuffee joined a whaling ship. On his return to Westport, Connecticut, Cuffee engaged in agriculture and later became a shipowner. Cuffee's lifelong interest was in protecting fellow African Americans from discrimination in the United States.

In 1780, Cuffee, along with his brother, challenged in a Massachusetts court the denial of suffrage to taxpayers, including African American taxpayers. It was this claim which led to the Act of 1783 being passed which secured the legal rights and privileges of emancipated persons of African descent in Massachusetts. Cuffee married Alice Pequit of his mother's Wampanoag nation.

In 1808, he joined the Society of Friends (Quakers) of Westport and began advocating an African American exodus to Africa. Today, Cuffee is generally credited as being the father of the African American back-to-Africa movement.

In 1811, Cuffee sailed in the *Traveller* from Westport to Sierra Leone, at a personal expense of $4,000. Cuffee made another personally financed trip in 1815 with nine African American families (38 settlers) thus becoming the first African American to sponsor a migration of African Americans to Africa.

Cuffee planned to make a yearly voyage to Africa, but his health deteriorated. At his death, he left an estimated estate of $20,000.

• *Scholastic Achievements:* Dr. Bray's Associates established a school for persons of African descent in Philadelphia.

THE AMERICAS

• Between 1759 and 1803, Brazil imported 642,000 slaves from Angola.

RELATED HISTORICAL EVENTS

• William Wilberforce, the noted English advocate of the abolition of slavery, was born.

William Wilberforce (1759–1833) was a leader in the fight to abolish the slave trade and slavery in the British Empire. In 1780, he entered Parliament and became a leading Tory. Wilberforce was noted for his eloquence, especially, in his attacks on slavery.

In 1789, Wilberforce led a campaign against the British slave trade. In 1792, Wilberforce sponsored a bill to end the slave trade which he was successful in getting passed by the House of Commons but which was rejected by the House of Lords.

Eventually, due to the efforts of abolitionists such as Wilberforce, the slave trade was abolished in Britain. When the bill outlawing participation in the slave trade became law in 1807, Wilberforce turned his attention to eradicating the foreign slave trade.

Wilberforce retired from Parliament in 1825, but he continued to support the campaign against the foreign slave trade. Additionally, beginning in 1823, Wilberforce supported the emancipation of slaves within in the British dominions.

--------- 1 7 6 0 ---------

AFRICA

An entry in George Washington's diary from this year read: "Found the new [slave], Cupid, ill of pleurisy at Dogue Run Quarter, and had him brought home in a cart for better care..."

Such entries were common and showed Washington's concern for the physical well-being of his slaves. However, there is little evidence that Washington showed an equal concern for the mental and moral well-being of his slaves.

• In 1760, Barzillai Lew, a person of African descent from Chelmsford, Massachusetts, was listed as a member of Captain Thomas Farrington's company. Lew was one of several persons of African descent who served in the British colonial forces during the French and Indian Wars.

• In 1760, it became an offense among New England Quakers to import slaves.

As late as 1760, Rhode Island Quakers were still involved in the slave trade. Quakers of Philadelphia were not involved after 1730. However, leading Friends (Quakers) continued to be shareholders in the Royal African Company. Seven Quakers were reported to be holding slaves in the Carolinas and Virginia.

• While in London, Benjamin Franklin became a member of Dr. Bray's Associates, a society which was opposed to the slave trade.

In 1760, there were 325,806 slaves in the British North American colonies: 40,033 in the North and 285,773 in the South. These 325,000 slaves constituted 30 percent of the total population in the British North American colonies.

After the British revolution of 1688, and the abolition of monopoly in 1697, the slave trade boomed. Private traders sent more than 8,000 slaves a year to the Southern colonies, and the Royal African Company, on its own, delivered slaves at the rate of 2,500 per year. About 33 percent of Georgia's total population was comprised of slaves.

• *Notable Births:* Richard Allen, founder and first bishop of the African Methodist Episcopal Church, was born.

Richard Allen (1760–1831) was born a slave near Philadelphia (February 14). As a youth, Allen was sold to a farmer in Dover, Delaware. Allen became a religious worker and was converted by Methodists. The Methodists permitted Allen to conduct services at his home, where he converted the farmer who purchased him. Allen eventually bought his freedom by hauling salt, wood, and other products and by laboring in a brickyard.

Allen studied privately and preached to European Americans and African Americans alike. He traveled throughout Delaware, New Jersey, Pennsylvania and Maryland. In 1784, at the first general conference of the Methodist Church in Baltimore, Allen was accepted by the hierarchy as a minister of promise.

He returned to Philadelphia in 1786 and was ocasionally asked to preach. Allen began conducting prayer meetings among African Americans and sought to establish a separate place of worship for his African American congregation. Both African Americans and European Americans opposed the establishment of an African American church. However, Allen attracted large numbers of African Americans to his church services and, when he tried to integrate a church service where he was preaching to a predominantly European American congregation, the European Americans objected to the presence of the African Americans by pulling the African Americans from their knees while they prayed and ordering them up to the gallery. Rather than submit to this insult, the African Americans withdrew and, in 1787, established an independent organization, the Free African Society.

Some of Allen's congregation later broke away and formed the Independent Bethel Church.

Allen was ordained a deacon of the African Methodist Episcopal Church in 1799 and an elder in 1816. By 1816, there were some 16 congregations of the church and, later in that same year of 1816, Allen became its first bishop.

• *Miscellaneous Legislation:* In 1760, the colony of South Carolina banned the slave trade. However, the ban was disallowed by the Privy Council and the governor was reprimanded. In lieu of a total ban, a prohibitive duty of 100 pounds was imposed in 1764.

Publications: In 1760, the first slave narrative was published. Entitled *A Narrative of the Uncommon Sufferings and Surprising Deliverance of Briton Hammon*, it told the story of Briton Hammon, a servant to General Winslow of Marshfield, Massachusetts. This account told of Hammon's escape from captivity by Indigenous Americans, and then from his Spanish rescuers.

The slave narrative became the most important body of African American literature for the next 100 years. The slave narratives were often written by or about ex-slaves. The accounts of the ex-slaves concerning what it had meant to be enslaved served as important ammunition for the antislavery movement, especially in the 1840s, a period of widespread abolitionist activity.

The slave narratives were among the very few personal recollections of men who were enslaved and shipped from Africa. The slave narratives give us some notion of the feelings and attitudes of the many millions of enslaved African Americans whose feelings and attitudes went unrecorded. While not always factual, the slave narratives represent the only source from which we can view slavery from the point of view of the slave.

• Jupiter Hammon, a Long Island slave, published *An Evening Thought, Salvation by Christ, with Penitential Cries*, an eighty-eight line poem. Hammon was probably the first African American poet in the United States (December 15). *See 1711.*

THE AMERICAS

• There was a slave rebellion in Jamaica.

AFRICA

• The Oyo kingdom invaded Borgu and was defeated.
• The Jesuits were expelled from Angola and Mozambique.

RELATED HISTORICAL EVENTS

• Bishop Warburton preached against the slave trade.

• Thomas Clarkson (1760–1849), a prominent advocate for the abolition of slavery, was born.

───────── 1 7 6 1 ─────────

THE (FUTURE) UNITED STATES

• In 1761, at the London Yearly Meeting of the Society of Friends (the Quakers), a proposal was forwarded calling for the exclusion from membership of all slave dealers.
• Phillis Wheatley, an African American poetess of the American Revolutionary War period, arrived in Boston harbor on a slave ship. *See 1753.*

THE AMERICAS

• The Saramakan people, a maroon society in Surinam in South America, secured their freedom after nearly eighty years of struggle against European forces. The Europeans were forced to abandon their efforts to destroy the Saramakan community and, subsequently, to sue for peace. *See 1685.*
• Dominica was settled by the British.

───────── 1 7 6 2 ─────────

THE (FUTURE) UNITED STATES

In 1762, in New York City, one of the more intriguing episodes of African American history began.

In 1762, Fraunces Tavern was bought by Samuel "Black Sam" Fraunces, a West Indian of African and French heritage. Originally named Queen's Head Tavern by Black Sam, the tavern was a favorite of George Washington.

During the Revolutionary War, Washington was a frequent visitor of the tavern as were many of his senior officers. Washington's friendship with Black Sam lasted throughout the years. After the great parade that followed the evacuation of the British from New York on November 24, 1783, the reception for the victorious Revolutionary Army was held at the tavern. It was also the place that served as a forum on November 26, 1783 for Washington's farewell address to his officers before he retired to Mount Vernon. "Washington bid farewell at a private gathering of officers at Fraunces Tavern in New York. At the gathering, Washington, with tears in his eyes, embraced each man, then silently strode out of the room. Finally, after nine years of military service, Washington could look forward to spending the remainder of his life on the family plantation at Mount Vernon."

*****

When New York called for troops at the start of the war, Black Sam was one of the first to enlist. By then, he was a wealthy man. He eventually assisted the Revolutionary cause by providing food and money.

The little known incident of intrigue which is part of the illustrious history of Fraunces Tavern occurred in 1776. In 1776, there were those in England who believed that George Washington posed the primary threat to the British control of its American colonies. These men decided to assassinate Washington.

It happened that a frequenter of Black Sam's place was a young Englishman named Hickey. Hickey had deserted from the British army and enlisted as an American volunteer. Because he was a clever man, Hickey soon became one of Washington's body guards.

Hickey was, in reality, the leader in a plot to kill Washington. The first step in the plan called for Hickey to win the help of the general's housekeeper. At the time, the general's housekeeper was none other than the young, attractive West Indian girl by the name of Phoebe Fraunces, Black Sam's daughter.

Hickey proceeded to enlist the aid of Black Sam's daughter by becoming her lover. After assuring himself that he had won Phoebe's heart, Hickey confided in her his plan to kill Washington and the part that he wanted her to play. The plot called for Phoebe to poison Washington with a bowl of peas.

There is no way to record the struggle that went on in Phoebe's mind concerning the internal struggle between her mind and her heart. What is known is that Phoebe threw the peas out the window. When eaten by chickens in the yard, it caused the immediate death of the birds. Phoebe then revealed the plot to Washington. Washington was saved and would go on to lead the Revolutionary forces to victory. Hickey, the grand conspirator and Phoebe's treacherous lover, was hanged.

• *Notable Births:* James Derham, the first recognized African American doctor, was born.

James Derham (1762–?), the first recognized African American doctor in America, was born in bondage in Philadelphia. Derham learned medicine by serving as an assistant to his enslaver who happened to be a doctor. Later Derham was sold to a New Orleans doctor whom

he assisted as well. Three years later, Derham won his freedom and set up his own practice.

• *Publications:* Anthony Benezet's *A Short Account of that Part of Africa Inhabited by the Negroes* described African civilization and culture and included antislavery writings.

THE AMERICAS

• Throughout the late 1700s, Guiana (today's Guyana) was plagued by slave conspiracies and revolts. In 1762, there was a revolt in the Berbice region. *See also 1763.*

• Grenada and St. Vincent Island were acquired by Britain.

EUROPE

• Alexander Dumas, the father of Alexander Dumas, pere (the author of *The Three Musketeers*), and the grandfather of Alexander Dumas, fils, (the author of *Camille*), was born.

Taking nothing away from his more famous heirs, the first Alexander Dumas (1762–1806) was a truly extraordinary man. Alexander Dumas was the son of a French nobleman (the Marquis de la Pailleterie) who had decided to live amongst the African people of Haiti, and a maiden of African descent by the name of Marie Dumas.

Marie Dumas died while Alexander was still quite young. Thus, when the Marquis returned to France (when Alexander was eighteen), he took Alexander with him.

Alexander had become a giant of a man. He stood six feet two inches tall and was possessed of great strength. He was also an excellent swordsman. Indeed, it was the hot-headed Alexander who fought three duels in a day — a feat that would become memorialized in his son's *The Three Musketeers* by the impetus D'Artagnan.

Alexander's tempestuous nature ran afoul his father. When the Marquis de la Pailleterie took a new wife, he and Alexander quarreled. As a result of the quarrel, the Marquis asked that Alexander not use his name. Alexander granted not only this request but totally rejected anything having to do with his father. Alexander went out on his own under his mother's maiden name — Dumas.

In 1786, Dumas joined the French army and his destiny was set. Enlisting as a private, Dumas immediately gained distinction due to his strength and his swordsmanship. He came to the attention of the Chevalier de Saint-Georges who entered into a bidding war for the services of Dumas. Dumas soon became a lieutenant colonel in the regiment formed by Saint-Georges. See 1739.

Over the next few years, Dumas' heroism was displayed in a number of extraordinary military feats. On one occasion, he captured thirteen of the enemy single-handedly. On another, he single-handedly prevented the enemy from capturing a bridge. For this last act of bravery, Dumas was celebrated throughout France and medals were struck in his honor depicting his valiant stand at the Brixen bridge.

Dumas soon joined the army of Napoleon where he served as a general. He served with distinction in the Italian and Egyptian campaigns. However, Dumas was a staunch republican who opposed Napoleon's imperialistic designs. As a result, there was a falling out between the two. Napoleon essentially relegated Dumas to nonactive status.

Dumas died in 1806, at the young age of 44. His statue stands at the Place Malsherbes in Paris near the statue of his son and his grandson. His name is also inscribed on the Arc de Triomphe.

RELATED HISTORICAL EVENTS

• One hundred years before the Emancipation Proclamation, slavery was formally abolished in Russia. However, as with many such abolitions, the edict of the Czar was not immediately promulgated (January 18).

1763

THE (FUTURE) UNITED STATES

• Chimney sweeps in Charleston, South Carolina, formed the first organization of workers of African descent. The sweeps refused to work until the city raised the prices charged for their labor (October 29).

By 1763, there were 5,214 emancipated persons of African descent in Massachusetts out of a total population of 235,810. Most of the persons of African descent worked in menial jobs, in shipyards and as servants.

• *Notable Births:* John Chavis, one the first African American students at an American college, was born.

In his youth, John Chavis (1763–1838) was sent to Princeton to study privately under President Witherspoon as an experiment designed to prove that African Americans had the "ca-

pacity" for a college education. Chavis passed successfully and became connected with the Presbyteries of Lexington and Hanover, Virginia.

In 1801, Chavis rode as a missionary under the direction of the General Assembly. Chavis established a classical school and prepared students for college. A number of prominent European Americans were among his pupils: William P. Mangum, who became a United States Senator; Charles Manly, who became a governor; and the Reverend William Harris.

• William "Bill" Richmond, one of the first African Americans to fight competitively as a professional boxer, was born to free parents on Staten Island, New York (August 5). In addition to his boxing notoriety, Richmond is known for having served as a hangman at the execution of Nathan Hale during the Revolutionary War. See 1776.

THE AMERICAS

• In February, a treaty was signed bringing an official end to the French and Indian War. France, the loser of the war, ceded all of Canada to Great Britain (February 10). An incidental effect of this transfer of ownership was the legal strengthening of slavery in Canada. Between 1763 and 1790, the British government added to the legal superstructure so that a once vaguely defined system of slavery took on a more institutionalized form.

Between 1763 and 1789, 30,875 Africans were imported into Cuba as slaves.

• There was a slave revolt in the Berbice area of what is today Guyana.

Guyana had a long history of slave conspiracies and revolts. In the Berbice area, there was a revolt in 1731; and there was a revolt in Demerara in 1823. Berbice also had revolts in 1762, 1763–1764, and 1767. The Great Rebellion of 1763–1764 under Cuffy may have involved half the slaves in the colony and led to widespread slave executions. Essequibo, another territory of Guyana, remained relatively quiet after the unsuccessful revolts of 1731, 1741, and 1744. In Demerara there were two revolts in 1772, another in 1773; and two others in 1774–1775. Another revolt was staged in 1803 and another in 1823 when the slaves revolted and staged at least one major battle involving thousands from at least thirty-seven plantations. They were motivated by the cruelty of their owners, unsuccessful attempts to negotiate, a desire for a shorter work week, and the belief that they had been freed by the British and were being held illegally by the planters. They imprisoned most of the whites instead of killing them, but this did not lessen the viciousness of their punishment.

AFRICA

• Kabaka Kyabuga (Kyambugu) came to power in Buganda (Uganda). Kyabuga opened trade with the east coast of Africa. Kyabuga would die in 1780.

• By 1763, the Portuguese had reduced western Angola to little more than a slave market. However, the Portuguese were still unable to penetrate the inland country due to the hostility of the indigenous Angolan people.

• In 1763, the Yoruba Empire of Oyo (Nigeria) was at the height of its power and influence.

• By 1763, the slave trade along the eastern seaboard of Africa was well established. On the French-held African islands of Mauritius and Bourbon, plantations were organized which utilized slave labor.

• In 1763, Senegambia became a British Crown colony.

ASIA

• Abbas, called "El Mahdi," a person of African descent, ruled Yemen on the Arabian Peninsula.

RELATED HISTORICAL EVENTS

• On February 10, the Treaty of Paris was signed thereby ending the Seven Years War (in America called the French and Indian War) between Britain, France, Portugal and Spain. England ceded Minorca to Spain. France ceded Senegal and its Canadian, Indian and West Indian possessions to England, and its Louisiana territory to Spain.

• Quakers in England attached criminality to those who aided and abetted the slave trade in any manner.

—————— 1764 ——————

THE (FUTURE) UNITED STATES

• New England merchants objected to the passage of the Sugar Act of 1764. In their pamphlet "A Statement of the Massachusetts Trade and Fisheries," they argued that sugar and molasses were essential to the slave trade which they considered the "vital commerce" of New England. The increased prices, they argued, would bring economic ruin to the area.

The Sugar Act of 1764 was enacted by Parliament as a revenue-raising measure. The British crown had been financially burdened by the costs associated with keeping troops in America and had incurred a vast debt resulting from the war with France. Additionally, the British people were already subjected to heavy taxes. So while the Americans could protest the Act by saying that it was "taxation without representation," from the standpoint of the British crown any other taxing scheme would have been inequitable since the British people derived little benefit from the expensive French and Indian War, while the American colonists did.

• When admirers of Samuel Adams offered to give his wife an African girl as a slave, Adams, though penniless, refused to have the girl enter his house except as an emancipated woman.

Benjamin Franklin related in *A Narrative of the Late Massacres in Lancaster County, etc., etc.* an anecdote of "an instance of . . . honor in a poor, unenlightened African . . ." in which an African named Cudjoe saved a European's life on the coast of Guinea in 1752. Franklin quoted Captain Seagrave, from whom he heard the story: "I related this to show that some of these dark people have a strong sense of justice and honor, and that even the most brutal among them are capable of feeling the force of reason and of being influenced by a fear of God (if the knowledge of the true God could be introduced among them) since even the fear of a false god when their rage subsided was not without its good effect."

• James Otis, in his *The Rights of the British Colonies Asserted and Proved*, stated that slaves had a right to be free. Otis also issued a polemic criticizing the Sugar Act for taxing colonies without representation (July 23).

By 1764, the American colonists had three major reasons for dissatisfaction with the British crown: (1) the ban upon westward expansion into Indigenous American territory; (2) the taxing of sugar and molasses which threatened the highly lucrative slave trade; and (3) the taxes imposed without adequate colonial representation.

• *Black Enterprise*: Abijah Prince, the former slave of the Reverend Benjamin Doolittle of Wallingford, Connecticut, was recorded as owning 100 acres in Guilford, Vermont. Prince was one of the founders of the town of Sunderland, Vermont.

THE AMERICAS

• In 1764, it was reported that there were 140,000 African slaves in Jamaica.
• The Sugar Act placed a tax on West Indian sugar entering British North American colonies and impacted the sugar plantation economy of the West Indies.

AFRICA

• Osei Kwadwo assumed the leadership of the Ashanti.

RELATED HISTORICAL EVENTS

• 900,000 peasants were freed in Russia.
• By 1764, a quarter of the shipping of Liverpool was involved in the African slave trade. Liverpool merchants accounted for fully one-half of England's trade with Africa.
• Brown University was founded in Providence, Rhode Island. The university was named after the Brown brothers, New England shipowners who were active in the slave trade.

—————— 1765 ——————

THE (FUTURE) UNITED STATES

• Colonial officials asked the Delaware (Indigenous American) nation to return all self-liberated slaves. No slave was ever returned.

In 1765, the total population of the English American colonies was 1,750,000. About 400,000 were persons of African descent, slightly over twenty percent (20%) of the total. All but 40,000 of the persons of African descent were located in the Southern colonies south of Pennsylvania.

• Joshua Johnston (1765–1830), the noted African American portrait painter, was born. *See 1798.*

AFRICA

• Philip Quaque (1741–1816), the first Ghanaian Anglican deacon, was ordained. For fifty years, Quaque served as chaplain of the Cape Coast Castle devoting most of his energy to converting local Africans.
• The British gained control of Senegal and Gambia and formed the British Province of Senegambia.

EUROPE

In Diderot's influential *Encyclopedie*, de Jaucort, in the entry "Traite des Negres" said of slaves:
There is not a single one of these hopeless souls … who does not have the right to be declared free, since he has never lost his freedom; … since neither his ruler nor his father nor anyone else had the right to dispose of his freedom; … this [person of African descent] does not divest himself, indeed cannot under any condition divest himself of his natural rights; he carries them everywhere with him, and he has the right to demand that others allow him to enjoy those rights. Therefore, it is a clear case of inhumanity on the part of the judges in those free countries to which the slave is shipped not to free the slave instantly by legal declaration.

RELATED HISTORICAL EVENTS

• On March 23, the British Parliament passed the Stamp Act. The Stamp Act imposed duties on the British North American colonies. The Stamp Act imposed taxes on such items as newspapers, legal and other documents. In the wake of the passage of the Stamp Act, riots erupted in Massachusetts, New York, North Carolina, and Virginia. Out of the turmoil, the Sons of Liberty were formed.
• Eli Whitney, the inventor of the cotton gin, was born.

Eli Whitney (1765–1825) was an American inventor who is famous for his invention of the cotton gin. Whitney's invention of the cotton gin provided a fast, economical way to separate the embedded cotton seeds from the cotton fibers. Whitney's cotton gin made cotton growing profitable and helped to make the United States the world's leading cotton producer.

Whitney was born in Westborough, Massachusetts, and early in his youth showed a mechanical aptitude. At the age of 12, Whitney made a violin and, while still a teenager, he established a nail-making business.

From 1783 to 1789, Whitney taught at a grammar school. In 1789, he entered Yale College and graduated in 1792.

After graduation from Yale, Whitney went to Savannah, Georgia, to teach and study law. However, once in Savannah, Whitney discovered that the teaching position he had expected to get had instead gone to someone else.

Without a job, Whitney began looking for alternative means of employment. He met Catherine Greene, the widow of Revolutionary War hero, General Nathanael Greene. Catherine Greene invited Whitney to be her house guest while he studied law. In exchange for his room and board, Whitney offered to fix things around the house.

Whitney's mechanical skills impressed Mrs. Greene. One night, while entertaining guests, the dinner table conversation focused on the production of green seed cotton and the difficulty involved in cleaning it by hand. Mrs. Greene chimed in, "Mr. Whitney can make a machine to clean it."

Whitney accepted the challenge and, by April, 1793, had built the cotton gin. Whitney's cotton gin could clean as much cotton in a day as 50 slaves could working by hand.

In 1794, Whitney obtained a patent for the cotton gin. With the financial backing of his partner, Phineas Miller, Whitney began to make cotton gins in New Haven, Connecticut. However, the demand exceeded the supply and Whitney soon found that his patented invention was being pirated by others. Cotton gin imitations began to crop up. When Whitney discovered the illegal manufacturers, he sued them.

After years of litigation, Whitney won his suits. However, by the time that he was able to assert his patent rights, his patent rights had come to an end and Congress rejected his petition for a renewal.

During the years that the patent for the cotton gin was tied up in litigation, Whitney also made arms for the United States government. In 1798, the Department of the Treasury gave him a contract to produce muskets. To facilitate the production of these arms, Whitney built a number of machines that manufactured interchangeable parts. Based upon this success, Whitney became a proponent of the "interchangeable parts system."

1766

THE (FUTURE) UNITED STATES

• John Adams reported in his diary on November 5 that Massachusetts slaves brought a court action of trespass against their enslavers to challenge the legality of slavery. The action proved futile.

• George Washington instructed Captain Thompson to sell his (Washington's) "Negro Tom" who had been defiant and had escaped. The instructions ordered that the slave was to be sold in the West Indies for molasses, rum, limes, tamerines and sweetmeats, and "good old spirits." Captain Thompson was instructed to keep the slave "handcuffed till you get to sea."

• James Forten, Sr., a noted African American businessman, was born.

James Forten, Sr., (1766–1842) invented a novel sail handling device. This invention brought Forten considerable wealth and affluence. In 1798, Forten became the owner of a sail loft, and by 1832 was a wealthy businessman employing 40 workers.

Because of his wealth, Forten became one of the more notable leaders of the American Anti-Slavery Society.

Forten's daughters Margaretta, Sarah, and Harriet, along with his granddaughter Charlotte Forten Grimke would continue Forten's civil rights legacy.

THE AMERICAS

• In Haiti, an order was given to throw into the sea a certain kind of flour which was supposed to aid in the dissemination of a specially fatal tertian ague at Port au Prince. Of the sixty barrels thrown into the sea, seven belonged to Lambert, a free Afro-Haitian, who was the only man to come of his own accord and offer his flour to the authorities for public use.

EUROPE

• On September 8, 1766, Joseph Boulogne (the Chevalier de) Saint-Georges, an Afro-French violinist who was also an excellent swordsman, participated in his first public fencing match in Paris with the renowned Giuseppe Gianfaldoni. Gianfaldoni won but predicted that Saint-Georges would one day become the finest swordsman in Europe. Gianfaldoni was right. *See 1739.*

RELATED HISTORICAL EVENTS

• The Stamp Act was repealed. However, the Declaratory Act was passed which asserted the right to tax British North American colonies. Under this Act, duties were imposed on commodities (such as tea, paper, and paint) entering the British North American colonies.

1767

THE (FUTURE) UNITED STATES

• *Notable Births:* Denmark Vesey, the organizer of an unsuccessful slave revolt, was born.

Denmark Vesey (circa 1767–1822), was the slave of Captain Vesey, a slaver of Charleston, South Carolina, who traded from St. Thomas to Santo Domingo. Vesey sailed with Captain Vesey for 20 years. In 1800, Vesey purchased his freedom and set himself up as a carpenter in Charleston, South Carolina. He was admitted to the Second Presbyterian Church in 1817 but, subsequently, joined the African Methodist Episcopal Church.

Resenting slavery, Vesey spoke of liberating slaves on plantations from the Santee to the Guhaws, an area of over 100 miles. At meetings held at his home, Vesey collected contributions for the purchase of arms. Some of the preparations made by Vesey for his uprising included instructing a blacksmith to make daggers, pikes and bayonets, and having a European American barber fashion wigs and whiskers of European hair.

The conspirators were betrayed and advanced the date for the uprising to June 16, 1822, but such effective precautions had been taken against the rebels that the conspiracy collapsed.

Vesey was captured on June 22, 1822. He defended himself well in court, but on the testimony of informers, some of whom saved themselves, he was condemned to be hanged. On July 3, 1822, Vesey and 35 others were executed.

THE AMERICAS

• Father Jose Mauricio, an Afro-Brazilian who is considered to be the founder of a famous Brazilian school of music, was born.

Father Jose Mauricio (1767–1830) was born in Rio de Janeiro. Upon ordination, Father Mauricio was named Choir Master of the Rio de Janeiro Cathedral. As Choir Master, Father Mauricio taught and influenced many students. A number of his students formed the renowned Orchestra of the Royal Chapel.

Father Mauricio was also a composer. As a composer, his compositions were principally confined to sacred music.

Father Mauricio was also an author. His treatise on harmony was completed shortly before his death.

AFRICA

• Throughout the late 1700s, Guiana (today's Guyana) was plagued by slave conspiracies and revolts. In 1767, there was a revolt in the Berbice region. *See also 1763.*
• A treaty was entered into between Morocco and Spain.

RELATED HISTORICAL EVENTS

• The Jesuits were banished from America.
• The British Parliament passed the Townshend Act. The Townshend Act taxed the importation of tea, paper, glass and painters' colors into the American colonies.

1768

THE AMERICAS

• In 1768, coffee was introduced as a plantation crop in Cuba.

AFRICA

• Babba Zaki (Babari?) became king of Kano. Babba Zaki established a royal guard of musketeers.
• By 1768, the Yao of Malawi began trading with Kilwa.

1769

THE (FUTURE) UNITED STATES

• When Thomas Jefferson was elected to the House of Burgesses (the colonial legislature) in Virginia, his first legislative action was to introduce a measure providing for the emancipation of slaves. This proposal was, of course, rejected. Another act was passed, however, that exempted emancipated persons of African descent from "the payment of any public county or parish levies." This came as a result of a petition brought to the Virginia Legislature by emancipated persons of African descent asking that their wives and daughters be exempt from taxation, which they called burdensome and derogatory to the rights of emancipated subjects.

A petition signed by freedmen (former slaves) was sent to the Virginia Legislature. The petition asked that the wives and daughters of the petitioners be exempt from taxation. The petition met with approval and an act was passed which, after declaring that the former tax was burdensome and derogatory to the rights of emancipated subjects, exempted from the payment of any public county or parish levies all emancipated persons of African descent and Indigenous American women, and all wives other than slaves of emancipated persons of African descent and Indigenous Americans.

• *Notable Deaths:* Emanuel Bernoon, a person of African descent, died leaving a house and lot and personal property valued at 539 pounds (British currency). Bernoon earned his money with a catering business that he had established in Providence, Rhode Island, in 1736, and later with an oyster house in Providence.

AFRICA

• Ali Bey, the Turkish viceroy of Egypt, declared Egypt independent of Turkish rule and entered into a treaty with Russia against the Turks.

Ali Bey (1728–1773) was born in the Caucasus Mountain region of southern Russia. In his youth, he was carried off to Egypt as a slave. By 1766, Ali Bey had become one of the Mameluke (Turkish) beys (governors). Gaining followers and influence, during the next five years Ali Bey proceeded to dispatch his enemies and rivals. He slaughtered the other Mameluke beys and seized power for himself. At the time that he declared Egypt independent of Turkish rule, Ali Bey also declared himself Sultan of Egypt.

Ali Bey would go on to conquer Syria and parts of Arabia. However, one of his sons-in-law, Abu al-Dhahab, turned against him and defeated him in battle near Cairo in 1773.

• Venice launched a punitive attack against the Barbary (Tunisian) pirates.
• The Portuguese initiated an unsuccessful military expedition to retake Mombasa.
• James Bruce of Kinnaird (Great Britain) travelled through Ethiopia.
• Takla Haimanot II ascended to the throne of Ethiopia. However, during this time, the role of the masafents—the regional kings—would greatly influence the governance of Ethiopia.

RELATED HISTORICAL EVENTS

• Napoleon Bonaparte (1769–1821) was born (August 13).

--------- **1 7 7 0** ---------

THE (FUTURE) UNITED STATES

• Nine British soldiers guarding the Boston customhouse fired into a crowd of hecklers who were armed with clubs. Five colonists were killed, and news of the "Boston Massacre" spread quickly through the colonies. Crispus Attucks, a person of African and Indigenous American (Natick Nation) descent, was the first of five men to be killed in the incident. The slain men were given heroes' burials (March 5).

A verbal confrontation turned into a historic event when a young barber named Edward Garrick accused a soldier of the 29th Regiment of striking his head with a gun. Captain Thomas Preston mustered a small group of soldiers to assist the sentry, but they were all attacked by a mob led by Crispus Attucks. Sticks, oyster shells and snowballs were thrown as the mob dared the British troops to fire and people shouted: "Come on, you bloodybacks [redcoats], you lobster scoundrels, fire if you dare, God damn you, fire and be damned, we know you dare not." It is not clear whether Preston himself ordered the soldiers to fire, but a short while later Attucks and the other men lay dead in the street.

On December 12, the last of the trials resulting from the so-called March Massacre ended, and the verdicts outraged the citizenry of Boston. Captain Thomas Preston, eight soldiers and four Customs house workers who had been accused of shooting five patriots to death were cleared of murder charges. Two soldiers were found guilty of manslaughter, but were spared prison terms. Their hands were branded as punishment.

The defense of the British was led by John Adams and Josiah Quincy, Jr., both of Massachusetts. Adams, a cousin of Sam Adams, a patriot leader, opposed many of Britain's policies in America, but he distanced himself from his cousin Sam's activities. In taking the case, Adams was said to have argued that even the British soldiery was entitled to the best available defense. Adams was also critical of the politicking that took place outside the courtroom when he said, "The law is deaf, deaf as an adder, to the clamors of the populace." Adams described one of the victims, Crispus Attucks, as a man "whose very look was enough to terrify any person" and he successfully argued that the Preston men acted legally when the firing erupted.

• In Virginia, George Washington signed a resolution of the "Association for the Counteraction of Various Acts of Oppression on the Part of Great Britain," agreeing not to import into the colony or purchase slaves that had not been on the continent of North America for at least a year. This resolution appears to have been inspired by the desire to retaliate against England, not by scruples against slavery or the slave trade.

In 1770, of the 2,312,000 estimated total population of the thirteen colonies, 462,000 were slaves of African descent.

Also, in 1770, the foreign trade emanating from Boston employed some 600 vessels on an annual basis. Many of these vessels were slave ships.

• *Notable Births:* Salih Bilali was born.

Salih Bilali was born in Massina. Bilali was captured, enslaved, and shipped from the Gold Coast in about 1790. Known by his slave name "Tom," in 1816, Bilali became the head driver of Hopeton Plantation in Georgia.

Bilali is notable because in the Muslim Fulbe community on the Gold Coast in which he was raised, all the children were taught to read and write Arabic by the mullahs. Thus, Bilali was a literate man before he came to the United States.

The reminiscences of Salih Bilali were published by William Brown Hodgson in *Notes on Northern Africa, the Sahara, and the Soudan* (1884).

• Morris Brown, a Bishop of the African Methodist Episcopal church, was born.

Morris Brown (1770–1849) was born to free parents of African descent in Charleston, South Carolina. Brown was part of a group of Charleston African Americans that had such close blood relations with the aristocratic Charleston European Americans that they were legally (or in practice) exempt from most of the legal and social restrictions against African Americans.

Brown was ordained a deacon in 1817 and an elder in 1818. He became a traveling minister. His career as a preacher came to a close when the Denmark Vesey insurrection broke out in 1822. Because of the Vesey incident, any African American of influence in the African American community was suspected of being implicated in the plot.

Brown escaped the reprisals and repression that followed the Vesey incident and reached Philadelphia in 1823. He was made a member of the Episcopate of the Philadelphia AME church in 1828, and, in 1831, a bishop. Under Brown, the influence of the African Methodist Episcopal church was extended to states that had not been hitherto affected.

• *Notable Deaths:* Crispus Attucks died. *See 1723 and above.*
• *Miscellaneous Legislation:* A bill was passed to prohibit the introduction of slaves into Rhode Island.
• In Georgia, a bill was passed which prohibited slaves from assembling on the pretense of feasting. Any constable was authorized to disperse such an assemblage and any slave found at such an assemblage was subject to being whipped.

• *Scholastic Achievements:* Anthony Benezet and other Quakers opened a school for African Americans in Philadelphia under Moses Patterson. The school was one of the first such schools in America and was an outgrowth of Quaker concern about the rights of persons of African descent. The school eventually became known as the Benezet House (June 28).

The first school for persons of African descent in America was started by the Reverend Cotton Mather when he arranged for night classes for persons of African descent and Indigenous Americans in 1717. Another school for persons of African descent was opened in South Carolina by Anglican missionary Samuel Thomas in 1744.

Slave holders had long considered it dangerous to educate persons of African descent, fearing that they would gain the knowledge that would enable them to liberate themselves. This attitude was frequently disguised with the claim that it was impossible to educate persons of African descent because they were incapable of learning.

THE AMERICAS

• Abbe Raynal, in his *Histoire des deux Indes* argued that slavery was contrary to nature and had been introduced into America by pirates and adventurers who, because of greed, began the cultivation of sugar and the exploitation of Africa.

AFRICA

• Ali Bey, the governor of Egypt, seized Syria and Hijaz. The forces of Ali Bey would also take Mecca. In tribute, the sharif of Mecca recognized Ali Bey as the sultan of Egypt.
• The Ashanti seized Gomba.
• Bizerta was bombarded by the French fleet.
• By 1770, slavery was a well-established institution in the colony at the Cape of Good Hope (South Africa).
• The Oyo came under the leadership of Alafin Obiudun (Abiodun). Obiudun was the last great ruler of the Yoruba state of Oyo. During his reign, Obiudun counted 600 towns and villages under his control. Trade was brisk, especially in the trade of slaves.

RELATED HISTORICAL EVENTS

• For the first time, the word "race" appeared in the Oxford English Dictionary.

1771

THE (FUTURE) UNITED STATES

Beginning in 1771, the average number of persons of African descent imported into the American colonies fell to 1,700 each year essentially due to the growing opposition to the slave trade. However, the statistics also indicated that an increasing number of slaves were dying en route to America from Africa. The increased mortality was due to overcrowding, a lack of hygiene, and the generally poor care provided by the slave traders. Where slavers once made provisions for the "welfare" of their cargo, by 1771, they would tend to use every inch of space for human bodies.

• Vermont had only 19 persons of African descent in its total population of 4,669, or 0.04% of the total population.
• *Miscellaneous Legislation:* The Connecticut Legislature forbade the slave trade.
• In Massachusetts, a bill to prohibit the introduction of slaves into Massachusetts failed.
• *Publications:* Phillis Wheatley published *To Mrs. Leonard, on the Death of Her Husband. See 1753.*

AFRICA

• The emperor of Ethiopia fought three battles against Ras Michael Sehul at Sarbakuse.
• Jan van Plettenburg became governor of the Cape colony.

EUROPE

• In 1771, the French Minister of Colonies issued an edict against the granting of citizenship to mulattoes and proclaimed that King Louis XV would maintain the principle that persons of African descent would never be permitted the same advantages as Europeans. After 1777, mulattoes were refused the right to come to France.
• Damascus and other Syrian cities were taken by Ali Bey's Egyptian forces which were under the command of Abu al-Dhahab. Abu al-Dhahab subsequently deserted Ali Bey and negotiated with the Porte.

RELATED HISTORICAL EVENTS

• Serfdom was abolished in Savoy.

1772

THE (FUTURE) UNITED STATES

In a letter to his friend, Anthony Benezet,

Benjamin Franklin wrote: "I have made a little extract of yours of April 27 of the number of slaves imported and perishing with some close remarks on the hypocrisy of this country [*England*] which encourages such a detestable commerce by laws for promoting the Guinea [*slave*] trade, while it piqued itself on its virtue, love and liberty, and the equity of its courts, in setting free a single [*slave*]. This was inserted in the "London Chronicle," of the 20th of June last ... I am glad to hear that the disposition against keeping [*slaves*] grows more general in North America. Several pieces have been lately printed here against the practice, and I hope in time it will be taken into consideration and suppressed by the legislative. Your labors have already been attended with great effects. I hope, therefore, you and your friends will be encouraged to proceed."

• A Rhode Island person of African descent named Aaron took part in the burning of the British revenue cutter, *Gaspee*, at Providence, Rhode Island (June 10). A group of American colonists led by Abraham Whipple seized and destroyed the cutter after it ran aground on a sandpit at Namquit Point near Providence. Lieutenant William Dudingston, the *Gaspee* commander, was put ashore with his crew before the ship was burned.
• George Stewart, a mulatto, was convicted of having participated in a riot near Gloucester, Massachusetts. He was sentenced to sit on the gallows for an hour with a rope around his neck and to be given 20 lashes.
• In 1772, New Jersey had 67,710 Europeans and 3,313 persons of African descent.

Figures obtained from slave ships in 1772 indicated that an increasing number of slaves were dying en route to America from Africa. The increased number of deaths was attributed to overcrowding, a lack of hygiene and the generally poor care provided by the slave traders. The figures also indicate that the average number of slaves imported into the colonies each year had dropped to 1700 due in part to the nonimportation agreement among the colonies.

• *Notable Deaths:* At his death, Cuffe Slocum, father of Paul Cuffe, owned 100 acres at Cuttyhunk, Massachusetts.
• *Miscellaneous Legislation:* By 1772, the Virginia Legislature, as a demonstration of defiance against the application of the Townshend Acts, had passed 33 acts to

prohibit the importation of slaves. These acts were uniformly rejected by England.

• *Publications*: In a pamphlet published in Boston, *Oration upon the Beauties of Liberty*, the Reverend Isaac Skillman demanded immediate abolition of slavery and declared that slaves had a right to rebel, conformable to the laws of nature.

• Phillis Wheatley published *To the Rev. Mr. Pitkin on the Death of His Lady*.

THE AMERICAS

• King Carlos III of Spain condemned slavery and declared free any escaped slaves who set foot on Spanish territory while at the same time permitting slavery in Spanish territory.

• In the Demerara region of Guyana, there were two slave revolts in 1772.

AFRICA

• Ali Bey was usurped in Egypt by Abu al-Dhahab. Ali Bey fled from Egypt to Acre. *See 1771*.

EUROPE

In 1772, Lord Mansfield handed down his decision in the *Somersett* case against the existence of slavery on English soil. Somersett, a slave owned by a Mr. Stewart, was brought to England and escaped. When Mr. Stewart put the recaptured slave on a ship for Jamaica, a writ of habeas corpus was instituted on behalf of Somersett. Granville Sharp, an antislavery lawyer, argued the matter before the court of Lord Mansfield.

Mansfield decided that the state of a slave is so odious it could only be maintained by specific authorization of a positive law. Since no positive law existed creating slavery, it could not be practiced in England, and, therefore, there was no legal way of taking a man's liberty by arguing that he was a slave.

Somersett was freed and the Mansfield decision became the foundation of England's attitude and England's law with respect to escaped slaves on English soil. In 1772, there were approximately 15,000 slaves in England. With the Mansfield decision, the slaves held in England were set free.

However, the Mansfield decision had little impact upon the slave trade or upon the institution of slavery as practiced in the American colonies. The main salutary effect of the Mansfield case on the American colonies was that it did stimulate requests for legislative action against slavery in New England (June 22).

Joseph Boulogne (the Chevalier de) Saint-Georges, the noted Afro-French violinist and composer, made his public debut as a violinist with the Amateurs in Paris, performing violin concertos which he had written for himself. These concertos, like all his others, seem to have been written to demonstrate Saint-Georges' prowess with the violin. The concertos contain violin solos which reveal much about Saint-Georges' capabilities. The solos make extensive use of the highest positions and require phenomenal dexterity in crossing the strings and in multiple stopping, often in the quickest of tempos. However, his virtuoso playing was not the only part of his performance. As his friend Louise Fusil wrote: "The expressivity of his performance was his principal merit." *See 1739*.

RELATED HISTORICAL EVENTS

• The Boston Assembly threatened to secede from Britain unless colonists' rights were protected. In response, Lord North removed all taxes except for the tax on tea.

———— 1773 ————

THE (FUTURE) UNITED STATES

In 1773, Benjamin Franklin wrote Dean Woodward from London: "I have since had the satisfaction to learn that a disposition to abolish slavery prevails in North America; that many of the Pennsylvanians have set their slaves at liberty; and that even the Virginia Assembly have petitioned the King for permission to make a law preventing the importation of more into that Colony. This request, however, will probably not be granted, and as the interest of a few merchants here [*London*] has more weight with the government than that of thousands at a distance."

• In the wake of the Mansfield decision *see 1772*, Massachusetts slaves petitioned the colonial legislature for their freedom (January 6). Later in the year, slaves of African descent petitioned the Massachusetts General Court asking for the right to earn money to purchase their emancipation (April). In June, other slaves petitioned the General Court and General Gage for emancipation and land.

In their initial petition, the Massachusetts slaves pleaded that they had no property, no wives, no children, no city, no country, and neither they nor their children to all generations would be able to possess and enjoy anything, not even life itself, unless they had freedom.

- Jean Baptiste Point du Sable, the first permanent settler in Chicago, purchased the house and land of Jean Baptiste Millet at "Old Peoria Fort."
- Cesar Hendricks, a slave in Massachusetts, sued his owner "for detaining him in slavery." The European American jury which heard the case sided with Hendricks. He was freed and was awarded damages.
- Phillis Wheatley, the African American poetess, was freed from slavery.

In 1773, South Carolina had about 110,000 slaves. It is estimated that about 25,000 slaves escaped during the Revolution, and South Carolina's slave population did not reach 110,000 again until 1790, despite the importation of thousands of slaves each year after the Revolutionary War had ended. Many of the slaves that escaped from South Carolina came to reside in maroon communites of their own or amongst the Indigenous American tribes. It was the exodus of so many slaves to places such as Spanish Florida, French Louisiana, and the Indigenous American nations, along with the need to curtail their threat to the institution of slavery, which increased the expansive tendencies of the young American nation.

- *The Abolition Movement:* In 1773, Benjamin Rush published *An Address to the Inhabitants of the British Settlements, on the Slavery of the Negroes in America.* This publication was one of the most important antislavery documents of the 1700s. Rush, a signer of the Declaration of Independence and a pioneer American physician, was also a founder of the first antislavery society in the United States. In his address, Rush provided a basic understanding of the eighteenth century antislavery position.
- In 1773, at their Yearly Meeting, the Quakers of New England banned members from owning slaves. By 1782, the Quakers could note that no Quaker in New England owned slaves.

Despite their antislavery stance, most Quakers still retained a racial bias and displayed as much anti–African American sentiment as other Americans.

Many local meetings of the Quakers barred African Americans from admission. Those that did allow African Americans to attend usually insisted that attendance be on a segregated basis. In all too many Quaker meeting halls, "Negro benches" were set aside for African American attendees.

- *The Colonization Movement:* Ezra Stiles, Yale president, and Congregational clergyman Samuel Hopkins proposed sending emancipated persons of African descent to colonize West Africa.
- In 1773, one of the earliest requests to return to Africa and freedom was made in a petition made by Peter Bestes and other slaves to Boston authorities. This request would be repeated in 1774, 1777, and 1779.
- *Notable Births:* Sally Hemings (1773–1835), the African American slave who was reputed to have been the mistress of Thomas Jefferson, was born in Virginia.

Sally Hemings' place in American and African American history rests on her association with Thomas Jefferson. While there is no "indisputable" proof of the matter, it has long been rumored that Thomas Jefferson was the father of Sally Hemings' children. What is known is that Sally Hemings was the halfsister of Jefferson's wife; that Jefferson took Hemings to Paris in 1787 and that, when the Jefferson family returned, Sally Hemings was pregnant; that the father of all of the Hemings children (six in all) was a man of European descent; and that Jefferson was present at Monticello or in Paris at the time that the children of Sally Hemings were conceived.

Adding to this circumstantial evidence is a statement made by James Callender, one of Jefferson's enemies. In 1802, Callender wrote: "It is well known that the man [Jefferson] ... keeps and for many years has kept, as his concubine, one of his slaves. Her name is Sally. The name of her eldest son is Tom. His features are said to bear a striking, though sable resemblance to those of the President himself... By ... Sally, our president has had several children. There is not an individual in the neighborhood of Charlottesville who does not believe the story, and not a few who know it."

While historians discount the rumors and the circumstantial evidence by noting that the parentage of Hemings' children could just as well have been the responsibility of Jefferson's nephews, the claims of the modern day descendants of Sally Hemings may be equally meritorious. In any event, the possibility of a union between Jefferson and Hemings has had a long life and, if not gracing the pages of American history, at least has inspired a number of books including William Wells Brown's African American classic, *Clotel, or the President's Daughter, A Narrative of Slave Life in the United States.* See 1816.

• *Miscellaneous Legislation:* New York's Common Council in Albany passed a curfew to prevent African and Indigenous American slaves from appearing on the streets after eight at night without a lantern with a lighted candle in it.

• *Publications:* Phillis Wheatley, a 20 year old Boston slave whose poetry was lauded by New England's literati, published *Poems on Various Subjects, Religious and Moral.* The publisher was Archibald Bell, a British printer, who accepted the work after the book was rejected by American houses. Wheatley, who went to London in June of 1772 for a long literary tour, began writing poetry at the age of 12, five years after a slave ship brought her to the Boston household of John and Susannah Wheatley, who eventually served as her agents. Wheatley first tasted fame in 1771, when her elegy for a British evangelist captivated colonial readers (September 1). It is believed that this publication was the first book published by an African American and was the second book published by an American woman. *See 1753.*

• Phillis Wheatley published *To the Hon'ble Thomas Hubbard, Esq; on the Death of Mrs. Thankfull Leonard.*

• Scipio Morehead (circa 1773), the first noted African American painter and a contemporary of Phillis Wheatley, was honored by a poem written by Ms. Wheatley. The poem was entitled *To S.M., a Young African Painter, on Seeing His Works,* in which Ms. Wheatley described two of Morehead's classical allegorical paintings done in the style of Reynolds and Romney. The paintings were entitled *Aurora* and *Damon and Pythias.* It is said that Morehead, a Boston slave, painted Wheatley's portrait and that this rendering of Wheatley was engraved as the frontispiece to her book. *See 1753.*

• *The Black Church:* David George, George Liele and Andrew Bryan organized the first Baptist Church for persons of African descent in Savannah, Georgia. David George served as its first pastor.

By 1773, the Baptists had a number of preachers of African descent for the Africans and mulattoes in their congregations. However, these preachers were generally under the supervision of Europeans and the African American preachers had no voice in church affairs.

• An African American Baptist church was started in Silver Bluff, South Carolina.

• *The Arts: See Scipio Morehead above.*

THE AMERICAS

• In 1773, Jamaica's population included 202,787 slaves of African descent, 12,737 Europeans and 4,093 free persons of African descent.

• In Tucaman, Argentina, all the houses had large numbers of slaves. In Cordoba, a thousand slaves were sold from only two plantations owned by religious orders. Among the slaves of Argentina were musicians and others skilled in all of the various trades.

• In 1773, the Black Caribs of St. Vincent signed a treaty with the British under which the Black Caribs were given control over one-third of the island as their property. The signing of the treaty ended seventy-five years of fighting during which the Black Caribs fought the British and the Indigenous Carib of St. Vincent Island. By 1773, the Black Caribs had exterminated the Indigenous Caribs and the treaty with the British recognized their dominant presence on the island.

• The Marquis of Case Eirle obtained the privilege of selling African slaves in Cuba.

• In the Demerara region of Guyana, there was a slave revolt in 1773.

AFRICA

• Abu al-Dhahab became the viceroy of Egypt *see 1771.* A struggle ensued amongst the Mamluks for power.

• There was a successful uprising in Kilwa against additional taxation.

• Ali Bey, the former viceroy of Egypt, died.

EUROPE

• Abram Petrovich Hannibal, the Ethiopian who was a favorite general in the army of Peter the Great, had several children. One of his children became an admiral and commanded the Russian fleet at the Battle of Navarins in 1773. *See 1781.*

• Joseph Boulogne (the Chevalier de) Saint-Georges, the noted Afro-French composer, became the musical director and leader of the Amateurs. Under Saint-Georges' leadership, the Amateurs became one of the best orchestras in France. *See 1739.*

RELATED HISTORICAL EVENTS

• In 1773, Portugal abolished slavery. It was the Portuguese who began the mass

European enslavement of Africans in 1441. *See 1441.*

• On December 16, the "Boston Tea Party" occurred. Samuel Adams and his followers emptied 343 chests of tea into Boston harbor.

1774

THE (FUTURE) UNITED STATES

In his first printed work, *A Summary View of the Rights of British America,* Thomas Jefferson declared that the abolition of slavery was the great object of desire in the colonies.

Jefferson wrote: "For the most trifling reasons, and sometimes for no conceivable reason at all, His Majesty has rejected laws of the most salutary tendency. The abolition of domestic slavery is the great object of desire in those colonies where it was unhappily introduced in their infant state. But previous to the enfranchisement of the slaves we have, it is necessary to exclude all further importations from Africa. Yet our repeated attempts to effect this by prohibitions, and by imposing duties which might amount to a prohibition, have been hitherto defeated by His Majesty's negative, thus preferring the immediate advantages of a few British corsairs to the lasting interests of the American states, and to the rights of human nature deeply wounded by this infamous practice."

• The Fairfax Resolves, adopted at a meeting in Virginia of which Washington was chairperson, included a resolution (No. 17) stating "that it is the opinion of this meeting that during our present difficulties and distress, no slaves ought to be imported into any of the British colonies on this continent; and we take this opportunity of declaring our most earnest wishes to see an entire stop forever put to such a wicked, cruel and unnatural trade."

George Washington signed the Fairfax Resolves which barred the importation of slaves and threatened to put a halt to all colonial exports to England.The influential landowner George Mason was the author of the document, which pledged the colony's loyalty to Britain. But the resolutions stipulated that exports were to end within the month unless the king faced up to the grievances of the colonists. Washington, although he owned slaves, agreed to the sections that called for an end to the "wicked, cruel and unnatural trade" (December 1).

• The Continental Congress in its "Articles of Association" called for an end to the slave trade and to stop by December of 1775 generally all trade and manufacture with countries which kept on with the slave trade (October 20).

The Articles of Association provided that, "We will neither import nor purchase any slave imported after the 1st day of December next; after which time, we will wholly discontinue the slave trade and will neither be concerned in it ourselves, nor will we hire our vessels, nor sell our commodities or manufactures to those who are concerned in it."

• A convention to form a provincial congress met at New Berne, North Carolina, and decided that all importation of African slaves should cease.

John Adam's wife, Abigail, wrote to her husband on occasion of the discovery of a slave conspiracy in Boston: "I wish most sincerely there was not a slave in the province. It always appeared a most iniquitous scheme to me— fight ourselfs for what we are daily robbing and plundering from those who have as good a right to freedom as we have."

• The Massachusetts General Court and General Gage received another petition by slaves of African descent asking for their emancipation as a natural right.

As tensions began to mount between the American colonies and the British crown, a number of slaves in Boston began to enlist the support of the British against their American owners in an attempt to gain their freedom.

• In Massachusetts, the Committees of Safety organized the Minutemen companies. In enlisting volunteers for the companies, both European Americans and African Americans were allowed to enlist.

• The Society of Friends decreed the expulsion of any member who engaged in the slave trade.

• In 1774, the Massachusetts Committee of Safety organized Minutemen companies which enlisted both European Americans and African Americans. Lemuel Haynes enlisted as one of the first Minutemen. Haynes was a person of African descent from Connecticut. He served at Lexington and with the Ticonderoga Expedition. Haynes would later become a theologian.

• A slave revolt in St. Andrews Parish, Georgia, in December resulted in the deaths of four Europeans and the wounding of three others before the rebellion was suppressed. The slave leaders were burned to death as a punishment.

In 1774, the estimated total population of the British American colonies was 2,600,000, of whom 2,100,000 were Europeans and 500,000 were persons of African descent. There were between 160,000 and 200,000 persons of African descent in Virginia. In Georgia, the population was almost equally divided between Europeans and persons of African descent. There were 17,000 Europeans and 15,000 persons of African descent.

By 1774, nearly all the American slave markets were overstocked with slaves. Many of the strongest partisans of the system were bullish on the market, and desired to raise the value of slaves by a temporary stoppage of the slave trade.

   • *Miscellaneous Legislation:* A Rhode Island law freed any slave thereafter brought into the colony. However, the law did not emancipate the slaves that were already there.
   • The importation of slaves into Connecticut was prohibited because the increase in the slave population was injurious to the poor in that slaves took away economic opportunites (jobs) from the poor.
   • The British Parliament passed the Quebec Act which enlarged the boundaries of Quebec to include French speaking settlements in Michigan, Ohio, and Illinois. The Act also restored French civil law to the area while retaining the British criminal code. This act was significant because it affected the slaves which were held in Detroit and brought them under a more lenient law.
   • *Scholastic Achievements:* The free African Americans of Charleston, South Carolina, established a school to teach free African Americans.
   • Benjamin Franklin and other Philadelphians opened a school for African Americans for the purpose of educating slaves in anticipation of their eventual freedom.

THE AMERICAS

   • In 1774, the population of Cuba consisted of 96,340 Europeans; 30,847 emancipated persons of African descent; and 44,333 slaves. In other words, there were some 75,180 persons of African descent in Cuba in 1774.
   • In the Demerara region of Guyana, there were two slave revolts in 1774–1775.

AFRICA

   • All Christian slaves were liberated in Morocco.

RELATED HISTORICAL EVENTS

   • The English Methodist, John Wesley, in his *Thoughts Upon Slavery* contrasted the moral and gentle relationships among Africans recently enslaved with the insensibility and cruelty of the slavers. He called for repentance from the slave holders and said that they (the slave holders) would continue in sin unless they emancipated their slaves.
   • The "Continental Congress" was convened in Philadelphia. It was the first assembly of colonists from the various colonies in British North America. At this convention, Samuel Adams of Boston demanded that the colonies seek their independence.

———— 1775 ————

THE (FUTURE) UNITED STATES

In 1775, the tense relationship between Great Britain and its American colonies erupted into armed hostilities. While never enjoying the full fruits of colonial citizenship, persons of African descent throughout the American colonies, nevertheless, came to the defense of the American cause.

Peter Salem of Framingham, Massachusetts, and Samuel Craft of Newton, Massachusetts, were among the many persons of African descent to serve as Minutemen and engage the British at Concord Bridge (April 19). Caesar Ferrit and his son, John, both of Natick, Massachusetts; Pomp Blackman; and Lemuel Haynes of West Hartford, Connecticut, were also present.

Lemuel Haynes, Primas Black and Epheram Blackman, African American members of Ethan Allen's Green Mountain Boys of Vermont, took part in the capture of Fort Ticonderoga (May 10).

The Battle of Bunker Hill (actually Breed's Hill) was fought in Charlestown, outside Boston. The rebels, including a number of African Americans, fought well during the battle and the British losses were heavy. Of particular note was the British loss of Major John Pitcairn, who was shot just after shouting, "The day is ours." Peter Salem, one of the African American rebels who had recently been freed from slavery, was credited with shooting down Major Pitcairn and became one of the heroes of the day. Salem would go on to fight at Saratoga and

Stony Point. Other African Americans at Bunker Hill included Titus Coburn, Seymour Burr, Grant Cooper, Cato Howe, Charlestown Eads, Barzillai Lew, Sampson Talbert, Caesar Basom, Alexander Eames, Caesar Jahar, Cuff Blanchard, Caesar Post, Salem Poor, Prince Hall and Caesar Brown. Caesar Brown was killed during the battle while Salem Poor was commended for wounding a British officer. Several Revolutionary Army members petitioned the Continental Congress on the behalf of Salem Poor to have him formally recognized as "a brave and gallant soldier" (June 17).

"Soon after George Washington took command of the Continental Army, he insisted that slaves not be allowed to serve because he feared that arming the slaves would lead to conspiracies and insurrections. Abiding by Washington's wishes (and acting upon the recommendation of a committee headed by Benjamin Franklin), the Continental Congress passed a resolution barring persons of African descent from serving in the army (October 13 or 23). However, Lord Dunmore, royal governor of Virginia, issued a proclamation offering emancipation to all male slaves who joined the British forces (November 7). The response to Dunmore's proclamation was overwhelming. Dunmore was able to actually form an "Ethiopian Regiment" composed of former slaves who had been promised their freedom in exchange for fighting against the Americans. Washington, alarmed by the response, hastily ordered recruiting officers to begin accepting free emancipated persons of African descent into the army (December 31).

Various estimates as to the number of slaves who escaped during the Revolution exist. Several hundred obtained their freedom by serving in British armies under Lord Dunmore in Virginia, Prevost in Georgia, and Leslie in South Carolina. In Georgia, large numbers of slaves fled to British lines, to Florida or into the wilderness during the Revolution. On the British side, Delancey's Rangers, a marauding band made up of Tories and persons of African descent, plagued New York throughout the war.

The presence of so many unknowables was of great concern to the colonial legislatures and caused many of them to overreact. In Virginia, a law was passed which allowed for the sale, banishment or execution of slaves caught attempting to escape. The law was enforced in 1776, when four escaped slaves were hanged and 25 others were sold to the West Indies.

In South Carolina, the General Assembly provided for the use of slaves in the army for one year as pioneers, laborers, and for other manual tasks, but later the Assembly forbade the use of slaves in the war in any capacity.

In North and South Carolina slave uprising conspiracies evolved. In North Carolina, severe penalties were meted out to the suspected conspirators, including the infliction of 80 lashes to many of the conspirators. It was a generally uneasy time for slave holders in the Southern colonies.

However, while many persons of African descent did take advantage of the war to obtain their freedom, a surprising number of persons of African descent did respond to the call of the Continental Army. Generally, they fought in integrated units. In the period covered by the Revolutionary War (1775–1783) between 8,000 and 10,000 persons of African descent served in the Continental Army in various capacities with approximately 5,000 serving as regular soldiers. Massachusetts forces had 572 persons of African descent while Virginia had 250 and Rhode Island had 100 in a single battalion and hundreds of others scattered throughout other regiments. Connecticut's Second Company of the Third Regiment had 19 persons of African descent. Several hundred were in other regiments, and volunteers came from at least 47 towns in the Connecticut colony. Almost every person of African descent of military age in New Hampshire enlisted. Persons of African descent fought in mixed companies in Pennsylvania, New York and New Jersey. In 1780, New York alone had two battalions composed of persons of African descent while Maryland had a regiment of 780 persons of African descent as well as some integrated ranks. Even a group of slaves from Georgia were known to have fought against the British. For their service they received pensions and land and citations for "bravery and fortitude which would have honored a free man."

Persons of African descent were particulary useful as spies, guerilla fighters, and navy pilots. In 1775, there were twenty persons of African descent on the *Royal Lewis* under Captain Stephen Decatur and the colonists' victory on December 8 under Colonel Woodford against the British under Captain Fordyce at Edenton, North Carolina, was largely the result of the success of an African American spy in persuading the British to attack hastily by convincing them that the colonial forces were weak, when in fact the opposite was true.

The approximate slave population in the colonies at the beginning of the Revolutionary War was more than half a million (in addition to a considerable population of emancipated persons of African descent and an unknown number of Maroons). A breakdown by colony follows:

New Hampshire	629
Massachusetts	3,500
Rhode Island	4,373
Connecticut	5,000
New York	15,000
New Jersey	7,600
Delaware	9,000
Pennsylvania	10,000
Maryland	80,000
Virginia	165,000
North Carolina	75,000
South Carolina	110,000
Georgia	16,000

The presence of so many persons of African descent (one out of every five inhabitants of the colonies was an African American) was a concern for the colonists because the colonists were never certain as to which side the slaves' loyalties would lie.

• The first lodge of African American Free Masons was founded by Prince Hall.

Prince Hall (1735–1807) and fourteen other African Americans joined a Masonic lodge sponsored by the British Army officers stationed at Castle William near Boston on March 6. On September 29, 1784, the British Grand Lodge approved the formation of African Lodge No. 459, but the notification did not arrive until 1787.

The African Grand Lodge was established on June 24, 1791, with Prince Hall as the grandmaster. A second African American Lodge was formed in Philadelphia in 1797.

In 1808, the existing African American lodges formed the Prince Hall Masons, an organization which declared itself independent from all other Masonic lodges.

• An African slave guided Daniel Boone's party from Virginia into Kentucky.
• Five slaves in Maryland were convicted of conspiring to poison whites.
• African Americans of Bristol and Worcester counties in Massachusetts petitioned the Worcester County Committee of Correspondence to aid them in obtaining freedom. As a result, a convention of European Americans resolved to work for the emancipation of enslaved African Americans.

• *The Abolition Movement:* Benjamin Franklin was elected president of the first abolition society organized in America by the Quakers in Philadelphia. Benjamin Franklin and Benjamin Rush were the primary organizers of the society which was named the Society for the Relief of Free Negroes Unlawfully Held in Bondage (later known as the Pennyslvania Society for the Abolition of Slavery) (April 14).

• Thomas Paine wrote his first published essay in the cause of abolition in a Pennsylvania newspaper, *The Pennsylvania Journal.* The essay was signed "Humanus" and was entitled *African Slavery in America.* In the essay, Paine denounced slavery, demanded its abolition and urged that African Americans be given land and economic opportunity.

• John Woolman published *Some Considerations on the Keeping of Negroes.* Woolman was one of the most influential antislavery activists of the 1700s. *Some Considerations on the Keeping of Negroes* was one his most important antislavery works.

• *Notable Births:* Gabriel Prosser, leader of a historic slave uprising in Virginia, was born a slave. *See 1800.*

• *Miscellaneous Legislation:* North Carolina colonial law forbade manumission of slaves except for meritorious service approved by a county court.

The purpose behind this North Carolina law was to make the freeing of slaves difficult and thereby prevent the growth of the free African American population within the state. Limiting the growth of the free African American population was deemed to be desirable because free African Americans were viewed by European Americans as competition for jobs and as potential sources of slave unrest.

• A bill to prohibit the importation of slaves into Delaware was vetoed by the governor.

The Sciences: In 1775, a young German scientist named Johann Friedrich Blumenbach presented his dissertation *De Generis Humani Varietate Nativa* ("On the Natural Variety of Mankind") wherein he collected experimental physiological proofs showing the nonsense and fallacy of the race theories at a time when the scientists like Linne and enlightened philosophers like Hume and Voltaire considered the African as something less than human.

Blumenbach was the first to demonstrate that the skull of the African is essentially the same as the skull of a European with a capacity equal to European skulls. Blumenbach also showed that the brains of Africans and Europeans are completely alike. Blumenbach's findings were known and discussed at the early meetings of the American Philosophical Society when Franklin and Jefferson were the respective presidents of the society.

AFRICA

• The Xhosa crossed the Fish River, which was an informal line of separation between the Africans and Dutch in South Africa.

The Xhosa are a people who live along the coastal areas of South Africa. They are known for their great hospitality and their strict adherence to the rule of law. It is the Xhosa who would come to dominate the organization which is known as the African National Congress — the political party of Nelson Mandela.

• The Ovaherero (Herero) and the Damaras came into Southeast Africa. South of the empire of the Congo and along the ocean arose the state of Mataman, composed of the Herero, Damaras, and the Hottentots.

The Herero are an ethnic group living in the northern part of modern day Namibia. The Damara live in western Namibia and the Hottentots (Khoikhoi) were the inhabitants of coastal South Africa when the Dutch arrived.

• Slaves in Algiers were declared to be free unless held by the state.
• The Spanish army was sent to relieve the garrisons at Ceuta and Melilla (Morocco).
• The Masai expanded reaching the Ngong Hills. *See 1675.*
• The Imamate of Futa Toro (Senegal) was established thereby ending the Denianke dynasty.

———— 1776 ————

THE UNITED STATES

The most significant event of 1776 in African American history was the signing of the Declaration of Independence. The Declaration of Independence is important in African American history because it contains a provision upon which all the arguments for African American

freedom and equality have been based. The Declaration of Independence — the foundation upon which this nation was formed — states: "We hold these truths to be self-evident, that all men are created equal, that they are endowed by their Creator with certain unalienable Rights, that among these are Life, Liberty and the pursuit of Happiness."

Only the Bible, the Emancipation Proclamation, and the United States Supreme Court decision in *Brown v. Board of Education* have had such a profound liberating effect for African American people. Due to its importance, the entire text of the Declaration follows:

The Declaration of Independence
In Congress, July 4, 1776
The unanimous Declaration of the thirteen united States of America
When in the Course of human events, it becomes necessary for one people to dissolve the political bands which have connected them with another, and to assume among the powers of the earth, the separate and equal station to which the Laws of Nature and of Nature's God entitle them, a decent respect to the opinions of mankind requires that they should declare the causes which impel them to the separation. —We hold these truths to be self-evident, that all men are created equal, that they are endowed by their Creator with certain unalienable Rights, that among these are Life, Liberty and the pursuit of Happiness. —That to secure these rights, Governments are instituted among Men, deriving their just powers from the consent of the governed. —That whenever any Form of Government becomes destructive of these ends, it is the Right of the People to alter or to abolish it, and to institute new Government, laying its foundation on such principles and organizing its powers in such form, as to them shall seem most likely to effect their Safety and Happiness. Prudence, indeed, will dictate that Governments long established should not be changed for light and transient causes; and accordingly all experience hath shewn, that mankind are more disposed to suffer, while evils are sufferable, than to right themselves by abolishing the forms to which they are accustomed. But when a long train of abuses and usurpations, pursuing invariably the same Object evinces a design to reduce them under absolute Despotism, it is their right, it is their duty, to throw off such Government, and to provide new Guards for their

future security. —Such has been the patient sufferance of these Colonies; and such is now the necessity which constrains them to alter their former Systems of Government. The history of the present King of Great Britain is a history of repeated injuries and usurpation, all having in direct object the establishment of an absolute Tyranny over these States. To prove this, let Facts be submitted to a candid world. —He has refused his Assent to Laws, the most wholesome and necessary for the public good. —He has forbidden his Governors to pass Laws of immediate and pressing importance, unless suspended in their operation till his Assent should be obtained; and when so suspended, he has utterly neglected to attend to them. —He has refused to pass other Laws for the accommodation of large districts of people, unless those people would relinquish the right of Representation in the Legislature, a right inestimable to them and formidable to tyrants only. —He has called together legislative bodies at places unusual, uncomfortable, and distant from the depository of their public Records, for the sole purpose of fatiguing them into compliance with his measures. —He has dissolved Representative Houses repeatedly, for opposing with manly firmness his invasions on the rights of the people. —He has refused for a long time, after such dissolutions, to cause others to be elected; whereby the Legislative powers, incapable of Annihilation, have returned to the People at large for their exercise; the State remaining in the mean time exposed to all the dangers of invasion from without and convulsions within. —He has endeavored to prevent the population of these States; for that purpose obstructing the Laws for Naturalization of Foreigners; refusing to pass others to encourage their migrations hither, and raising the conditions of new Appropriations of Lands. —He has obstructed the Administration of Justice, by refusing his Assent to Laws for establishing Judiciary powers. —He has made Judges dependent on his Will alone, for the tenure of their office, and the amount and payment of their salaries. —He has erected a multitude of New Offices, and sent hither swarms of Officers to harrass our people, and eat out their substance. —He has kept among us, in times of peace, Standing Armies without the Consent of our legislatures. — He has affected to render the Military independent of and superior to the Civil power. —He has combined with others to subject us to a jurisdiction foreign to our constitu-

tion, and unacknowledged by our laws; giving his Assent to their Acts of pretended Legislation: —For quartering large bodies of armed troops among us: —For protecting them, by a mock Trial, from punishment for any Murders which they should commit on the inhabitants of these States: —For cutting off our Trade with all parts of the world: —For imposing Taxes on us without our Consent: —For depriving us in many cases, of the benefits of Trial by jury: —For transporting us beyond Seas to be tried for pretended offences: —For abolishing the free System of English Laws in a neighbouring Province, establishing therein an Arbitrary government, and enlarging its Boundaries so as to render it at once an example and fit instrument for introducing the same absolute rule into these Colonies: —For taking away our Charters, abolishing our most valuable laws, and altering fundamentally the Forms of our Governments: —For suspending our own Legislatures, and declaring themselves invested with power to legislate for us in all cases whatsoever. —He has abdicated Government here, by declaring us out of his Protection and waging War against us. —He has plundered our seas, ravaged our Coasts, burnt our towns, and destroyed the lives of our people. —He is at this time transporting large Armies of foreign Mercenaries to compleat the works of death, desolation and tyranny, already begun with circumstances of Cruelty & perfidy scarcely paralleled in the most barbarous ages, and totally unworthy the Head of a civilized nation. —He has constrained our fellow Citizens taken Captive on the high Seas to bear Arms against their Country, to become the executioners of their friends and Brethren, or to fall themselves by their Hands. —He has excited domestic insurrections amongst us, and has endeavoured to bring on the inhabitants of our frontiers, the merciless Indian Savages, whose known rule of warfare, is an undistinguished destruction of all ages, sexes and conditions. In every stage of these Oppressions We have Petitioned for Redress in the most humble terms: Our repeated Petitions have been answered only by repeated injury. A Prince, whose character is thus marked by every act which may define a Tyrant, is unfit to be the ruler of a free people. Nor have We been wanting in attentions to our British brethren. We have warned them from time to time of attempts by their legislature to extend an unwarrantable jurisdiction over us. We have reminded them of the circumstances of our emigration and settlement here. We have appealed to their native justice and magnanimity, and we have conjured them by the ties of our common kindred to disavow these usurpations, which, would inevitably interrupt our connections and correspondence. They too have been deaf to the voice of justice and of consanquinity. We must, therefore, acquiesce in the necessity, which denounces our Separation, and hold them, as we hold the rest of mankind, Enemies in War, in Peace Friends.

We, therefore, the Representatives of the united States of America, in General Congress, Assembled, appealing to the Supreme Judge of the world for the rectitude of our intentions, do, in the Name, and by Authority of the good People of these Colonies, solemnly publish and declare, That these United Colonies are, and of Right ought to be Free and Independent States; that they are Absolved from all Allegiance to the British Crown, and that all political connection between them and the State of Great Britain, is and ought to be totally dissolved; and that as Free and Independent States, they have full Power to levy War, conclude Peace, contract Alliances, establish Commerce, and to do all other Acts and Things which Independent States may of right do.—And for the support of this Declaration, with a firm reliance on the protection of divine Providence, we mutually pledge to each other our Lives, our Fortunes and our sacred Honor.

*****

Thomas Jefferson was the principal author of the Declaration of Independence. In Thomas Jefferson's original draft of the Declaration of Independence, the following accusation against George III was made: "He has waged cruel war against human nature itself, violating its most sacred rights of life and liberty in the persons of a distant people who never offended him, captivating them and carrying them into slavery in another hemisphere, or to incur miserable death in their transportation thither. This piratical warfare, the opprobrium of *infidel* powers, is the warfare of the *Christian* King of Great Britain. Determined to keep open a market where MEN should be bought and sold, he has prostituted his negative for suppressing every legislative attempt to prohibit or to restrain this execrable commerce; and that this assemblage of horrors might want no fact of distinguished die, he is now exciting these very people to rise in arms among us, and to purchase that liberty of which *he* deprived them, by murdering the

people on whom *he* also obtruded them; thus paying off the former crimes committed against the *liberties* of one people, with crimes he urges them to commit against the *lives* of another."

At the request of delegates from South Carolina and Georgia, and some slave-trading New England states, the accusation was deleted. After all, while the King may have sponsored and sanctioned the slave trade, it was the colonists who profited from its existence and perpetuation. *See 1774.*

*****

For all too many African Americans, the Declaration of Independence is simply a document evidencing America's hypocrisy. After all, how could the founding fathers truly profess such profound beliefs in liberty and equality while at the same time denying those same inalienable rights to their African American brethren?

However, a condemnation on the basis of hypocrisy, while perhaps accurate from the perspective of an individual lifespan, fails to account for the long arc of history. The long arc of history indicates that the principles of equality and liberty enunciated by Jefferson were not an accomplished fact but were rather an ideal—an ideal which this nation should be dedicated to achieving and protecting for its citizenry. As Lincoln would put it some eighty-seven years later in a speech honoring those who had lost their lives at Gettysburg: "Four score and seven years ago our fathers brought forth on this continent, a new nation, conceived in Liberty, and dedicated to the proposition that all men are created equal.

Now we are engaged in a great civil war, testing whether that nation, or any nation so conceived and so dedicated, can long endure. We are met on a great battlefield of that war. We have come to dedicate a portion of that field, as a final resting place for those who here gave their lives that that nation might live. It is altogether fitting and proper that we should do this.

But, in a larger sense, we cannot dedicate—we cannot consecrate—we cannot hallow—this ground. The brave men, living and dead, who struggled here, have consecrated it, far above our poor power to add or detract. The world will little note, nor long remember what we say here, but it can never forget what they did here. It is for us the living, rather, to be dedicated here to the unfinished work which they who fought here have thus far so nobly advanced. It is rather for us to be here dedicated to the great task remaining before us—that from these honored dead we take increased devotion to that cause for which they gave the last full measure of devotion—that we here highly resolve that these dead shall not have died in vain—that this nation, under God, shall have a new birth of freedom—and that government of the people, by the people, for the people, shall not perish from the earth."

The arc of history indicates that each generation must dedicate itself anew to the principles upon which this nation was based and that the greatness of this nation and its people will be dependent on the dedication shown in the quest to achieve and preserve the Jeffersonian—the American—principles of liberty and equality.

*****

In reading the Declaration of Independence one cannot escape the inconsistency between the reality of the world of 1776 and the lofty ideals set forth in the Declaration. From the inception of the Declaration of Independence, the document's inherent inconsistencies with the social practices of contemporary society disturbed the consciences of many Americans. Indeed, these same inconsistencies are what continue to trouble so many Americans to this very day.

Perhaps one of the more cogent expressions of the disturbance caused by the principles declared in the Declaration of Independence was made in 1776 by Samuel Hopkins a Congregational minister in Newport, Rhode Island. In 1776, Samuel Hopkins published A *Dialogue Concerning the Slavery of the Africans* which he sent to the Continental Congress, urging it to abolish the institution of slavery. Hopkins' *Dialogue* required a great deal of courage on his part because, at the time, Newport, Rhode Island, was one of the centers of the slaveholding interest. Many of the most prominent members of Hopkins' own congregation were either slave holders or at least financially involved in the slave trade. Hopkins' statement, therefore, was one of those rare instances in American history where a person speaks with clarity and courage on an issue of conscience. The following are a few of Hopkins' enlightening remarks:

Excerpts from
A *Dialogue Concerning
the Slavery of the Africans*
by Samuel Hopkins

"The present situation of our public affairs and our struggle for liberty, and the abundant conversation this occasions in all companies—while the poor [Africans] look on and hear what an aversion we have to slavery and how much liberty is prized, they often hearing it declared publicly and in private, as the voice of all, that slavery is more to be dreaded than death, and we are resolved to live free or die, etc.—this, I say, necessarily leads them to attend to their wretched situation more than otherwise they could. They see themselves deprived of all liberty and property, and their children after them, to the latest posterity, subject to the will of those who appear to have no feeling for their misery, and are guilty of many instances of hardheartedness and cruelty toward them, . . .; and often if they have a comparatively good master now, with constant dread they see a young one growing up, who bids fair to rule over them, or their children, with rigor. . .

"No wonder there are many and great difficulties in reforming an evil practice of this kind, which has got such deep root by length of time and is become so common. But it does not yet appear that [it] cannot be removed by the united wisdom and strength of the American colonies, without any injury to the slaves or disadvantage to the public. Yea, the contrary is most certain, as the slaves cannot be put into a more wretched situation, ourselves being judges, and the community cannot take a more likely step to escape ruin and obtain the smiles and protection of Heaven. This matter ought, doubtless, to be attended to by the general assemblies, and continental and provincial congresses; and if they were as much united and engaged in devising ways and means to set at liberty these injured slaves as they are to defend themselves from tyranny, it would soon be effected. . . . Surely we have no reason to conclude it cannot be done till we see a suitable zeal and resolution among all orders of men, and answerable attempts are thoroughly made.

"Let this iniquity be viewed in its true magnitude and in the shocking light in which it has been set in this conversation; let the wretched case of the poor blacks be considered with proper pity and benevolence, together with the probably dreadful consequence to this land of retaining them in bondage, and all objections against liberating them would vanish. . . .

"If parents have a son pressed on board a king's ship, how greatly are they affected with it! They are filled with grief and distress, and will cheerfully be at almost any cost and pains to procure his liberty; and we wonder not at it, but think their exercises and engagedness for his deliverance very just, and stand ready to condemn him who has no feeling for them and their son, and is not ready to afford all the assistance in his power in order to recover him. At the same time, we behold vast numbers of blacks among us, torn from their native country and all their relations, not to serve on board a man-of-war for a few years but to be abject, despised slaves for life, and their children after them, and yet [we] have not the least feelings for them or desire [for] their freedom. These very parents [of conscripted sailors], perhaps, have a number of [African] slaves on whom they have not the least pity, and stand ready highly to resent it if anyone espouses their cause so much as to propose they should be set at liberty. What reason for this partiality? Ought this so to be? An impartial person, who is not under the prejudices of interest, education, and custom, is shocked with it beyond all expression. The poor [Africans] have sense enough to see and feel it, but have no friend to speak a word for them, none to whom they may complain. . . .

"The slaves who are become unprofitable to their masters by the present calamitous state of our country will be with the less reluctance set at liberty, it is hoped; and if no public provision be made for them that they may be transported to Africa, where they might probably live better than in any other country, or be removed into those places in this land where they may have profitable business and are wanted,   ; I say, . . . the masters, by freeing them, would lose nothing by it, even though they continue to support them, till some way shall be open for them to help themselves. I must here again desire every owner of slaves to make their case his own, and consider, if he or his children were unjustly in a state of slavery, whether he should think such an objection against their being set at liberty of any weight.

"Would he not rather think it reasonable that the masters who had held them in bondage against all right and reason would consider their being, by an extraordinary Providence, rendered unprofitable to them, as an admonition to break off their sins by righteousness and their iniquity by showing mercy to these poor; and that it ought to be a greater satisfaction to them thus to do justice without delay and relieve

these oppressed poor than to possess all the riches, honors, and pleasures of this world? And if these masters should disregard such an admonition and neglect this opportunity to set them at liberty, putting it off to a more convenient season, would it not be very grievous to him and overwhelm him in despair of their ever doing it? Is it not very certain that they who make this objection against freeing their slaves without delay would not free them if the times should change and they again become profitable? If they must maintain them, can they not do it as well when they are free as while they are slaves, and ought they not to do it with much more satisfaction? . . .

"But if we obstinately refuse to reform what we have implicitly declared to be wrong, and engaged to put away . . . holding the Africans in slavery, which is so particularly pointed out by the evil with which we are threatened and is such a glaring contradiction to our professed aversion to slavery and struggle for civil liberty, and improve the favor God is showing us as an argument in favor of this iniquity and encouragement to persist in it . . . have we not the greatest reason to fear, yea, may we not with great certainty conclude, God will yet withdraw His kind protection and punish us yet seven times more? This has been God's usual way of dealing with His professing people; and who can say it is not most reasonable and wise?

"He, then, acts the most friendly part to these colonies and to the masters of slaves, as well as to the slaves themselves, who does his utmost to effect a general emancipation of the Africans among us. And, in this view, I could wish the conversation we have now had on this subject, if nothing better is like to be done, were published and spread through all the colonies, and had the attentive perusal of every American."

• The Continental Congress approved Washington's action of permitting free African Americans to enlist in the Revolutionary Army (January 16).

• The Mason-Dixon line was named for two English surveyors, Charles Mason and Jeremiah Dixon. Mason and Dixon were hired in 1763 to settle a dispute between the colonies of Pennsylvania and Maryland stemming from a dispute over boundaries that can be traced to the grant and charter obtained by William Penn in 1681 which included many indefinite and some impossible clauses (February 18).

• Phillis Wheatley was invited by General Washington to visit him at his headquarters in Cambridge, Massachusetts, so that he might express his appreciation for her poem in his honor. George Washington's letter to Phillis Wheatley spoke of her "elegant lines" and "poetical talents." Washington also said, "If you ever come to Cambridge, or near headquarters, I shall be happy to see a person favored by the Muses, and to whom nature has been so liberal and beneficent in her dispensations." In his letter, Washington addressed Wheatley as "Miss Phillis," not Miss Wheatley, a common practice among European Americans when addressing slaves (February 28).

• The Continental Congress passed a resolution in April calling for an end to the importation of slaves (April 9).

• The Declaration of Independence was adopted without the provision denouncing the slave trade, one of the original grievances against King George III (July 4). *See above.*

In a debate in the Continental Congress on July 30, the delegate Thomas Lynch of South Carolina said "If it is debated, whether their slaves are their property, there is an end to confederation. Our slaves being our property, why should they be taxed more than the land, sheep, cattle, horses, etc.? Freemen cannot go to work in our Colonies; it is not the ability or inclination of freemen to do the work that the *slaves* do."

To which Benjamin Franklin answered: "Slaves rather weaken than strengthen the State, and there is therefore some difference between them and sheep; sheep will never make any insurrection."

The threat of slave insurrections and slave alliances with the British was more than an idle one. In July of 1776, the British Army on Staten Island included 800 former American slaves who had joined the British on the promise of freedom.

Later in the year, the Virginia Committee of Safety ordered the removal inland away from British forces of all slaves over 13 years of age from the eastern counties of Norfolk and Princess Anne to guard against their escape to British lines. The Congress of North Carolina ordered all male adult slaves south of the rather appropriately named Cape Fear River to be moved inland. In November, an appeal was printed in a Williamsburg, Virginia, newspaper urging slaves not to be misled by Lord Dunmore's offer of freedom, arguing that the British would sell them in the West Indies after the war was over. The flow of slaves to British lines decreased somewhat thereafter. Apparently, some slaves actually were being sold in the West Indies instead of being freed and used as soldiers.

• Thomas Kench called for a separate detachment of African American soldiers (European American commissioned officers would be the detachment commanders), saying, "We have divers of them (African Americans) in our service, mixed with (European American) men, but I think it would be more proper to raise a body by themselves than to have them intermixed with (European American) men." One of two such companies was formed in Massachusetts under the command of Samuel Lawrence, a European American.

• In the Battle of Long Island, 140 African American soldiers were among those who covered Washington's retreat, for which Lafayette praised them.

• It is said that Bill Richmond, the first known African American prizefighter, served as a hangman at the execution of Nathan Hale. Hale had been accused by the British of being an American spy. Before he was executed, presumably by Richmond, Hale said "I only regret that I have but one life to lose for my country."

• Two African Americans, Prince Whipple and Oliver Cromwell, were with General Washington when he crossed the Delaware River to attack the Hessians at Trenton on Christmas Day (December 25). Cromwell served 6 years and 9 months in all, and later fought in the battles of Brandywine and Monmouth. African American troops also fought under Sullivan in successful rear guard actions at Trenton and Princeton to cover the withdrawal of Washington's troops.

In 1776, the total population of the New England colonies was 659,446, of whom 10,034 (or 2.4%) were persons of African descent. Massachusetts had a total population of 338,667, of whom 5,249 were persons of African descent.

In 1776, New York had 21,993 persons of African descent out of a population of 191,741.

• *The Abolition Movement:* The Society of Friends (the Quakers) made the manumission of any slaves owned by its members obligatory for continued membership.

• *Notable Births:* John Gloucester, the first African American to serve as a minister of the Presbyterian Church, was born in Kentucky.

• *Notable Deaths*: A slave woman was executed in Maryland for setting fire to her owner's house, outhouses, and tobacco house.

• *Legislation*: A Virginia colonial law organizing the militia provided that emancipated mulattoes in the companies would be employed as drummers, fifers or pioneers.

In 1776, when Virginia adopted a frame of government, it was charged that the king had perverted his position and that his position had devolved into a "detestable and insupportable tyranny, by ... prompting our negroes to rise in arms among us, those very negroes whom, by an inhuman use of his negative, he hath refused to us permission to exclude by law."

• In the Delaware Constitution, the importation or exportation of slaves was prohibited.

• *Publications*: Adam Smith published the *Wealth of Nations* which became the standard work of economic theory. In the work, Smith offered the following opinion concerning slavery as practiced in the British colonies: "*The* work done by slaves, though it appears to cost only their maintenance, is in the end the dearest of any. The work done by freemen comes cheaper in the end than that performed by slaves. It is found to be so at Boston, New York, and Philadelphia, where the wages of common labor are so very high."

Adam Smith was a retired professor of philosophy at Oxford and Glasgow Universities when he published the *Wealth of Nations* (or the *Inquiry into the Nature and Causes of the Wealth of Nations* as it was officially known). The *Wealth of Nations* was an exhaustive treatise on political economy. The work advocated an economic system that allowed the individual to pursue his own self-interest, free of excessive governmental restraint. Smith also proposed that the American colonies be represented in Parliament and he predicted that the American colonies were destined to become "one of the foremost nations of the world" (March 9).

• Phillis Wheatley published "Letter ... to His Excellency General Washington.

• *The Black Church*: An African Baptist church was organized in Williamsburg, Virginia.

AFRICA

• The French made contact with Kilwa for purposes of overseas slave trade; they concluded a treaty with the sultan of Kilwa. This treaty granted to the French an exclusive franchise to purchase slaves from Kilwa as well as to build a fort there if they wished. Under the treaty the French slave trader J. V. Morice was to contract with the sultan of Kilwa to receive 1,000 slaves annually for 100 years. The fort was never built because the entire East African seaboard soon came under the control of the British navy after the Napoleonic Wars; however, the agreement did result in a number of slaves being provided.

• Abd al-Qadir (Abdul Kader) and Terobe Fulani, overthrew the Denianke dynasty of Futa Toro (Senegal). A jihad against their Wolof neighbors followed.

• In 1776, an annual caravan crossed from Kilwa to Angola.

• Around 1776, the first direct contacts were made between the Dutch and Xhosa on the Zeekee River.

• Islam was introduced into Dahomey by the Yoruba.

EUROPE

• Angelo Solliman, friend, favorite and tutor of European royalty, died. *See 1721.*

RELATED HISTORICAL EVENTS

• In England, the first attempt to prohibit the slave trade was introduced in Parliament.

• A resolution was introduced in the House of Commons which stated that slavery was contrary to the law of God. The resolution was defeated.

———— 1777 ————

THE UNITED STATES

During 1777 and 1778, the role of African Americans in the Continental Army became more prominent. Connecticut raised a company of 56 African American slaves. This was on the passage of a Connecticut law offering freedom and equal pay with European American soldiers to slaves who enlisted.

There were thirty-three African Americans in the Second Regiment of Pennsylvania under Washington at the Battle of Monmouth.

A regiment of African American troops from Rhode Island was sent to aid Washington at Valley Forge, and also fought at Monmouth and Red Bank, New Jersey. At Monmouth, 700 African Americans fought alongside European

Americans to achieve a victory on June 28, 1778. "It is notable that during the winter at Valley Forge, Washington's men deserted in large numbers, but the African Americans deserted at a lower rate than the European American soldiers did. Quite possibly because they had fewer options as to places to desert to."

An African American slave, Pompey Lamb, served as a spy for the American forces before the Battle of Stony Point. Lamb spied on the British while selling vegetables to the British garrison. He also aided General Wayne and the Americans in their entrance into the fort and the capture of it.

An African American named Prince Whipple (also known as Jack Sisson) was among 41 soldiers chosen by Lieutenant Colonel William Barton for a raid on British headquarters at Newport, Rhode Island. Whipple helped to capture General Prescott and Major Barrington so that the Americans might bargain for the release of a captured American, General Lee.

Edward Hector, an African American in the artillery regiment at the Battle of Brandywine, refused to abandon his ammunition wagon at the order of retreat and heroically collected other abandoned weapons as he brought his wagon, team, and munitions to safety.

In general, African American troops were sprinkled throughout the Continental Army. A Hessian officer, Shloezer, wrote in a letter that there was no regiment among the Americans "in which there are not *persons of African descent* in abundance, and among them are able-bodied, strong and brave fellows." After the winter at Valley Forge where Washington saw his army melt away, Washington felt compelled to ask the Continental Congress to approve the reenlistment of African Americans. The Congress consented.

• George Washington authorized the inoculation of his troops against smallpox. The use of inoculation was a practice which was first used in the American colonies in 1721 in Boston, Massachusetts. The practice was based upon an African practice as related by the slave Onesimus to Dr. Zabdiel Boylston (January). *See 1721.*

The Civil Rights Movement: In a petition to the Massachusetts Legislature, Boston slaves called attention to the fact that African Americans were aware that they were in a Christian country; that, in common with all other men, African Americans had a natural and inalien-able right to freedom; that African Americans had been unjustly brought to this country; and that African Americans had presented petition after petition to the legislature of Massachusetts that had never received due consideration despite the fact that European Americans were at the time voicing similar complaints (and experiencing similar difficulties) with Great Britain.

In presenting their petition, the Massachusetts African Americans expressed "astonishment that it has never been considered that every principle from which America has acted in the course of their unhappy difficulties with Great Britain pleads stronger than a thousand arguments in favor of *the abolition of slavery.*"

• *Legislation:* The Constitution for the Colony Vermont prohibited slavery. Vermont was the first colony—the first state—to abolish slavery (July 2–8).

• North Carolina law made manumission more difficult in order to discourage "the evil and pernicious practice of freeing slaves."

• The Council of Virginia gave the governor power to move slaves wherever and whenever he thought necessary.

• *Scholastic Achievements:* New Jersey began a program for the education of African American children.

THE AMERICAS

• Mulattoes from Haiti were forbidden to come to France.

• In Chile, a paramilitary organization was established for persons of color.

AFRICA

• Spain acquired Fernando Po for the purpose of establishing a slave factory.

• An uprising of al-Azhar students against the misappropriation of Waqf funds by the Beys occurred.

• Osei Kwame came to power in the kingdom of the Ashanti.

RELATED HISTORICAL EVENTS

• On November 15, the Articles of Confederation were drafted by the Continental Congress.

1778

THE UNITED STATES

As the war moved into its fourth year, the manpower needs of the Continental Army increased and the utilization of African American troops became more desirable.

The Georgia Assembly authorized the governor to use 200 slaves from confiscated Loyalist estates as pioneers for the Continental Army in an expedition against East Florida and authorized 100 more to serve in the state militia.

The Second Maryland Brigade was reported to have 60 African Americans.

Massachusetts enacted a law which permitted the enlistment of slaves as soldiers in the colonial forces. Any slaves which did so were deemed emancipated.

On August 24, the adjutant general of the Continental Army reported a total of 755 African Americans in the army in New Jersey. These men represented soldiers from several colonies. It was also reported that there were 58 African Americans in the North Carolina Brigade under General Washington.

Washington, impressed with the utility of his African American soldiers, endeavored to obtain more. He forwarded to the governor of Rhode Island a letter from General Varnum of Rhode Island saying that a battalion of African Americans could easily be raised. Washington later on sent a letter to the Continental Congress recommending the utilization of African Americans in the Carolinas, Virginia and Georgia to serve as wagoners.

However, while thousands of African Americans were serving with European Americans in the war of liberation from the British, other African Americans took the opportunity created by the war to liberate themselves. Thomas Jefferson estimated that in 1778 alone over 30,000 slaves escaped from Virginia (presumably to the British, to form their own maroon communities, or to live with the neighboring Indigenous Americans).

So great was the number of escaped slaves that in the treaties negotiated between 1778 and 1786 with the Indigenous Americans, the United States included provisions for the return of escaped slaves.

Meanwhile as the war progressed, all too often reports were received like the one noted by Lafayette. Lafayette, in writing to Henry Laurens, mentioned a report of a slave plot to set fire to Albany, New York.

• African Americans were instrumental in forcing the British withdrawal from the field at Monmouth, New Jersey (June 28). *See* 1777.

• An African American battalion of 400 was formed in Rhode Island with former slaves receiving the same compensation given the European American soldiers and being promised emancipation after the war. Named the First Rhode Island Regiment, the battalion fought in the Battle of Rhode Island (August 28) and drove back the Hessians three times, killing 1,300 Hessians while losing 211. Part of this battalion fought again under Colonel Greene at Ponts Bridge in New York.

• *Legislation:* On the motion of Thomas Jefferson, the importation of slaves into Virginia was prohibited.

In 1778, the states of Connecticut, Delaware, Pennsylvania, Rhode Island and Virginia would all prohibit the importation of slaves.

• *Scholastic Achievements:* The Quakers recommended education for the children of freed slaves.

THE AMERICAS

• In a census taken by order of Vertiz y Salcedo, the population of Buenos Aires (Argentina) was reported to be more than 24,000. Out of the 24,000, 15,719 were Euro-Argentinians, 7,269 were Afro-Argentinians, and 1,218 were Indigenous Argentinians or mestizos.

• In 1778, the Buenos Aires militia included eight cavalry companies composed of freed mulattoes and three companies of infantry composed of freed slaves.

• In 1778, there were 300 persons of African descent in the Jesuit *Colegio* in Buenos Aires.

AFRICA

• The island of Fernando Po was ceded to Spain by the Portuguese.

• The Dutch and Xhosa demarcated their respective territories along the Fish River.

EUROPE

• An Afro-Jamaican named Joseph Knight was taken to Scotland by his Scottish owner. Knight claimed his freedom and the matter went to court. In his initial trial, Knight failed to secure his freedom. However, on appeal to the Edinburgh Court of Session, Knight was able to prevail. The Court noted the precedent of the 1772 Somersett decision as being a major factor in its decision. *See* 1772.

─────── 1 7 7 9 ───────

THE UNITED STATES

In 1779, Henry Laurens, of South Carolina, wrote to General Washington, requesting approval and arms for the raising of 3,000 slave soldiers. The Continental Congress approved and agreed to pay full compensation to the slave owners. However, the South Carolina Legislature refused to approve the plan.

Alexander Hamilton wrote to the president of the Continental Congress concerning Laurens' plan to use slaves as soldiers in the South, "I have not the least doubt that the [slaves] will make very excellent soldiers, ... I hear it frequently objected to the scheme of embodying [slaves], that they are too stupid to make soldiers. This is so far from appearing to me a valid objection, ... for their natural faculties are as good as ours...."

Hamilton continued in his letter, "The contempt we have been taught to entertain for the blacks, makes us fancy many things that are founded neither in reason nor experience; and an unwillingness to part with property of so valuable a kind, will furnish a thousand arguments to show the impracticability, or pernicious tendency of a scheme which requires such sacrifices. But it should be considered, that if we do not make use of them in this way, the enemy probably will, and that the best way to counteract the temptations they will hold out, will be to offer them ourselves. An essential part of the plan is to give them freedom with their swords. This will secure their fidelity, animate their courage, and, I believe will have a good influence upon those that remain, by opening a door to their emancipation. This circumstance, I confess, has no small weight in inducing me to wish the success of the project; for the dictates of humanity and true policy, equally interests me in favor of this unfortunate class of men."

However, not everyone agreed with Hamilton. On this subject Washington, in a letter to Henry Laurens, questioned the arming of slaves on the grounds that a "discrimination" might "render slavery more irksome to those who remained in it. Most of the good and evil things in this life are judged of by comparison; and I fear a comparison in this case will be productive of much discontent in those who are held in servitude."

• Anthony Wayne's victory at Stony Point was made possible by the espionage efforts of Pompey Lamb (July 15). *See 1777.*
• Twenty slaves petitioned the New Hampshire Legislature to abolish slavery. In the petition, which was presented to the Legislature sitting in Portsmouth, New Hampshire, the slaves argued that "the God of nature gave them life and freedom upon the terms of most perfect equality with other men; that freedom is an inherent right of the human species, not to be surrendered but by consent" (November 12).

The arguments utilized by these African Americans showed the influence Jefferson's Declaration of Independence was beginning to have on the arguments to be used in the African American quest for freedom.

• *Legislation:* In Vermont, the slaves were emancipated.
• In Rhode Island, the slave trade was restricted.

THE AMERICAS

• In 1779, in Buenos Aires, Argentina, out of a total population of 24,000, approximately one-third were slaves of African descent. The slaves were employed in every sort of service and occupation.

During the Revolutionary War, the French undertook to assist the American cause in many ways. One of the ways was to utilize Haitian troops. The Comte d'Estaing raised a force of some 800 volunteers from among the Afro-Haitians. Among this contingent were Rigaud and the famed Christophe. At the siege of Savannah, it was Christophe who saved the American army from annihilation by the British.

AFRICA

• The Cape colonists demanded a written constitution from Holland.
• Takla Giorgis I came to power in Ethiopia.

EUROPE

After emancipation following the Somersett decision of 1772, many Africans in Britain learned to play musical instruments both for pleasure and also as a means of earning a living. Many of these Afro-Anglos came to be employed throughout the country as bandsmen.

• George Polgreen Bridgetower, a famed violinist, was born.

George (Augustus) Polgreen Bridgetower (1779–1860) was born in Biala, Poland. His father was an African and his mother was either Polish or German. Bridgetower was a violin prodigy who made his debut at the age of nine at the Concert Spirituel in Paris (April 13, 1789). Bridgetower's musician father brought him to London at the age of ten. In London, the young Bridgetower soon gained fame as a violin virtuoso. His solo interpolations between the parts of *Messiah* at Drury Lane Theatre attracted the attention of the Prince of Wales (the future King George IV). The Prince of Wales became Bridgewater's patron and had him taught the violin (by Barthelemon and Jarnowick) and composition (by Attwood).

During his career, Bridgetower would play in concerts in the company of Haydn. His name is found among the performers at the Salomon concerts of 1791 and those of Barthelemon in 1792 and 1794. For a time, Bridgetower was the the Prince of Wales's leading violinist at the Brighton Pavilion.

In 1802, Bridgetower received permission to visit his mother in Dresden (Germany). In Dresden, he gave two concerts (July 24, 1802 and March 18, 1803) that were enthusiastically received. In tribute to Bridgetower's talent, Bridgetower was given letters of introduction to the highest aristocratic circles in Vienna.

While in Vienna, a certain Prince Lichnowsky introduced Bridgetower to a composer by the name of Beethoven and offered to finance a concert combining their talents. At the time, Beethoven was already working on two movements for violin and piano. When the financing for the concert with Bridgetower was finalized, he quickly finished the violin and piano movements and added a previously composed finale to make up a three movement sonata.

There was not enough time to have the violin part of the second movement copied before the performance in the Augarten on May 24. Bridgetower was compelled to read it from Beethoven's own manuscript. Nevertheless, Bridgetower's performance was a smashing success. At the conclusion of the piece, the audience unanimously called for an encore of the second movement.

The sonata first played by Bridgetower in the Augarten has come to be known as the *Kreutzer* sonata. It is named for the eminent French violinist Rodolphe Kreutzer—a man who ironically never played it.

There is no question that Beethoven, who spoke highly of Bridgetower both as a soloist and as a quartet player, intended to dedicate the *"Kreutzer"* sonata to Bridgetower. On a rough composing score of the work, Beethoven scribbled the humorous inscription: "Sonata mulattica composta per il mulatto Brischdauer, gran pazzo e compositore mulattico." However,

Bridgetower and Beethoven soon became estranged. The source of the estrangement was reputedly a quarrel over a woman. Thus, the sonata which marked the height of their collaboration was named for someone else.

Bridgetower soon returned to England. In 1811, he earned a degree in music from Cambridge University. Bridgetower played with the Philharmonic Society during its first season.

Bridgetower would leave England and spend almost thirty years abroad. Towards the end of his life, he returned to England.

Bridgetower died on February 29, 1860, in Peckham, London, England.

1780

THE UNITED STATES

In 1780, there were 575,420 slaves in the United States. 56,796 in the Northern states and 518,624 in the South.

The relations between slaves and slave holders with respect to the war remained in a schizophrenic state.

In Maryland, a law was passed which made emancipated African Americans liable to be drafted. The law also permitted the recruitment of slaves on the consent of both the slave and the slave holder.

In South Carolina, a law was passed which granted a "prime" slave to European American volunteers in the Continental Army as part of their bounty for enlisting.

In April, a slave named Jack of Botecourt County, Virginia, was sentenced to hang for attempting to lead slaves to Cornwallis' (the British) army.

In Albany, New York, six African Americans were jailed for attempting to flee to Canada. Later in the same town of Albany, New York, several slaves and two European Americans were arrested for plotting rebellion and for burning the Half-Moon Settlement outside the city.

• One of the earliest efforts to organize a mutual benefit society took place in Newport, Rhode Island. In Newport, a certain Newport Gardner and his friend met to establish the African Union Society. The purpose of the African Union Society was to promote the welfare of the African American community by providing a record of births, deaths, and marriages; by assisting African Americans to secure apprenticeships in trades; and by aiding African Americans in times of distress. The African Union Society was absorbed in 1803 by the African Benevolent Society which provided a school that continued in operation until the city of Newport opened a school for African American children in 1842.

• *The Civil Rights Movement*: Emancipated African Americans in Dartmouth, Massachusetts, petitioned the Massachusetts General Court for relief from taxation because they were denied the privileges of citizenship. The signers were Paul Cuffee, Adventur Childe, Paul Cuve, Samuel Gray, Pero Howland, Pero Russell and Pero Coggeshall. *See 1759.*

Paul Cuffee was a noted civil rights activist of his day. In the events leading up to the petition of 1780, Paul and his brother John petitioned the Massachusetts Legislature seeking the right to vote. At that time, Americans linked the right to citizenship with the possession of property and the right to vote and to hold public office depended upon an individual's property holdings. However, despite their affluence and position as property owners, the Cuffees were denied their right of citizenship and their right to vote.

Being denied the right to vote, the Cuffees next petitioned the Commonwealth of Massachusetts and the authorities in Bristol County and the Town of Dartmouth requesting exemption from the payment of property taxes and poll taxes. The Cuffees argued that since African Americans and Indigenous Americans were denied the rights of citizenship, they should, therefore, not be required to pay property or poll taxes. The Cuffees pointed out that African Americans were not allowed to vote in the town meetings nor to vote for a public official. Thus, in a very real sense, Africans Americans were being subjected to taxation without representation.

The Commonwealth of Massachusetts rejected the Cuffees' petition.

The Cuffee brothers persisted in their struggle for equal rights. They refused to pay their county property taxes and poll taxes during the years 1778, 1779, and 1780.

On December 15, 1780, the Massachusetts authorities issued a warrant for the arrest of John and Paul Cuffee. The Cuffees were arrested on December 19 and placed in the common jail in Taunton. A writ of habeas corpus was served and the Cuffees were released within a few hours.

Delays and postponements prevented the trial of the Cuffees from occurring until March 1781. Upon reflection, the Cuffees acknowledged defeat and paid their fine on June 11, 1781. On June 12, 1781, the proceedings were dismissed.

• *Notable Births*: Lott Carey, an early African American Baptist missionary, was born.

Lott Carey (1780–1828), an early African American Baptist missionary, was born a slave in Charles City County, Virginia.

Carey purchased his emancipation in 1813. He became a preacher in the First Baptist Church of Richmond, Virginia.

On May 1, 1819, he was received for service by the Baptist Board of Foreign Missions and prepared to embark for Liberia. Before leaving, he organized the First Baptist Church of Liberia with himself as pastor. Carey sailed in the *Nautilus* from Norfolk with 28 colonists and children, sponsored by the American Colonization Society. In 1822, the group founded Liberia. Carey was the second agent in 1826.

In 1828, while defending the colony from attack, he died.

• York, the slave companion of William Clark, who accompanied William Clark on the famous Lewis and Clark expedition, was born to house slaves in Virginia.

York was born to house slaves of the Clark family in Virginia and grew up as a special friend of William, who was York's age. In 1799, William inherited the family estate and the estate included his childhood companion, York.

In 1803, the United States purchased the Louisiana Territory from France. President Jefferson asked his secretary Meriwether Lewis to lead an exploratory expedition into the new territory. Lewis accepted and promptly chose his friend, William Clark, to accompany him on this adventure, and Clark, in turn, decided to bring along York.

At age 23, York was an imposing man. He stood over six feet tall and weigh over two hundred pounds in an era when the average man was only five foot six inches tall. During the course of the expedition, York proved to be one of the explorer's best hunters, fishermen and scouts. York also proved to be adept at trading with the Indigenous Americans that were encountered along the way and often served as the chief trader for the party.

For the Plains Indigenous Americans of 1803 and 1804, the sight of an African American was a curious phenomenon. York's size and agility won him many friends among the Indigenous

Americans and many admirers among the Indigenous American women that he encountered. Fascinated by this son of Africa, some Mandan villagers decided to rub York's skin with a wet finger to see if the color would come off. This incident was reported in Lewis and Clark's notes of the expedition and later became the subject of a noted painting by the Western painter Charles Russell.

By the end of 1805, York, along with the Shoshone woman Sacagawea, had become an influential voice in the expedition and was accorded certain privileges which belied his status as a slave.

Upon the expedition's return to St. Louis, York returned to his status as simply a slave and companion to William Clark. When Clark was appointed Governor of the Missouri Territory and Director of Indian Affairs, York went with him. Later York hired himself out near Louisville so that he could be near his wife.

Clark eventually emancipated York and gave him a wagon and six horses as a recognition of his service. With these, York ran a transportation business between Nashville and Richmond. However, the venture failed and York eventually died of cholera.

• *Legislation:* After a campaign by an alliance of Philadelphians of African descent and Philadelphia European American shopkeepers and artisans, Pennsylvania passed a law providing for the gradual abolition of slavery (March 1).

The Act of the Gradual Abolition of Slavery was passed by the Pennsylvania Legislature. The Act, which began with a strong condemnation of slavery, provided that no child thereafter born in Pennsylvania would be a slaver. The children of slaves born after 1780 were to be bond servants until twenty-one years of age.

THE AMERICAS

• In 1780, after eight years of warfare with the French and Spanish, the maroons of San Domingo (Hispaniola) completed a treaty of peace with the French. The Hispaniola maroons historically were organized under chieftains. Among the notable chieftains were Pere Jean (1679), Michel (1713), Colas (1720), Polydor (1730), Macandel (1758), Conga (1777), and Santiague (1782).

Between 1780 and 1789, the French West Indies imported 30,000 slaves a year.

AFRICA

• The Treaty of Aranjuez was arranged formalizing the friendship and the commerce between Morocco and Spain.
• The Awallini dynasty of Haggaro was established.
• Between 1780 and 1800, some 10,000 slaves would be exported from Mozambique to South America.

RELATED HISTORICAL EVENTS

• As a result of the Revolutionary War, over 60,000 American colonists who remained loyal to the British crown became refugees. After the War, these refugees would leave the American colonies for Canada, the West Indies, and England. As they did so, many of the loyalists would take their slaves with them.
• Another consequence of the Revolutionary War was the war between Holland and Great Britain. Holland sided with the American colonists in their struggle against the British. As a result of this alliance, the British engaged in hostilities against the Dutch—hostilities which led to sporadic outbursts between the Dutch and British in West Africa. These hostilities would eventually lead to Britain declaring war on Holland on November 20.

1781

THE UNITED STATES

In 1781, the City of Los Angeles was founded by forty-four people, of whom two were Europeans. The other forty-two were African, Indigenous American or a mixture of the three peoples. Francisco Reyes, one of the founders of Los Angeles with African ancestry, would come to own the San Fernando Valley. In 1790, Reyes would sell the property and become mayor of Los Angeles.

• The New York Legislature provided for the raising of two regiments composed of African American troops.

Earlier in the year, African Americans formed the bulk of the American force which took part in an abortive march from Saratoga toward the British forces at Oswego in February. Many froze to death and the whole party was led off course.

• African American soldiers were among those present at the surrender of Cornwallis at Yorktown, Virginia. A Rhode Island

African American, Bristol Rhodes, lost a leg and an arm in the siege.

James Armistead, a Virginia slave, infiltrated General Cornwallis' headquarters as a servant and was hired by the British to spy on the Americans. However, Armistead served as a double agent. He passed key information about the size and movements of the British troops to Lafayette. The information provided by Armistead would prove to be essential in contributing to the defeat of Cornwallis at Yorktown.

• Richard Henry Lee wrote to his brother that neighbors, Colonel Taliaferro and Colonel Travis, had lost all their slaves to the British while another neighbor, a Mr. Paradise, lost all but one.
• A slave of Prince William County, Virginia, was hanged for leading attacks by maroons on plantations.
• Slaves in Williamsburg, Virginia, set fire to several buildings, including the capitol building. One European American man was killed.
• "Black" Harry Hosier (1750–1806) delivered his sermon "Barren Fig Tree" at Adams Chapel in Fairfax County, Virginia.

AFRICA

• Uthman dan Fodio became tutor to the royal family of Gobir. One of his students was Yunfa, the future ruler of Gobir.

From humble beginnings, Uthman dan Fodio (1754–1817) became the charismatic leader of an Islamic revolution in the Hausa states of Nigeria. As a young man Uthman dan Fodio gained a reputation as a scholar noted for his intellectual abilities. Uthman dan Fodio devoted a great amount of his time and energy to studying and writing, especially poetry. The son of an imam, Uthman dan Fodio aspired to make a pilgrimage to Mecca. However, this aspiration went unfulfilled.

For a while, Uthman dan Fodio was an itinerant missionary. However, after more than a decade of such work, he added another profession and became employed as a tutor.

Beginning in 1789, Uthman dan Fodio experienced a series of visions. He began to preach a doctrine which called for a renewal of faith among Muslims and which called for a holy war—a jihad—if necessary. Influenced by Sufism (a form of mystical Islam), Uthman dan Fodio's call found a receptive audience, including his pupil, Yunfa.

When Yunfa became ruler of Gobir in 1801, Yunfa began to heed Uthman's call. However,

as Uthman's influence grew, Yunfa became fearful and attempted to assassinate Uthman. The assassination was unsuccessful and Uthman's reputation only grew. Uthman retired from the capital and settled in Gudu.

In 1804, war broke out between the followers of Uthman and Gobir. After a bitter four year struggle, Uthman emerged victorious. Meanwhile he persuaded Fula leaders in the surrounding states to take up the jihad and they swore their allegiance to formal affiliation. By 1812, the conquest of northern Nigeria was largely completed.

• The kingdom of Oyo went to war against Dahomey.

EUROPE

• Abram Petrovich Hannibal, former commander of Peter the Great's army and the great-grandfather of Alexander Pushkin, Russia's greatest poet, died.

Abram Petrovich Hannibal (1696–1781) was an Ethiopian slave who was brought to Constantinople and then stolen by the Russian envoy. Peter the Great became the godfather of Hannibal and gave him an education. Under Peter's patronage, Hannibal studied military science and fortifications in France and took part in the War of the Spanish Succession.

After a brilliant career, Hannibal died in 1781. At the peak of his career, Hannibal was a lieutenant general in the Engineering Corps and commander-in-chief of Peter the Great's army.

Hannibal had several children. One of his children became an admiral and commanded the fleet at the Battle of Navarins in 1773.

Hannibal was married twice. His second wife was a Livonian gentlewoman. Out of this union, a granddaughter would come by the name of Nadezhda. Nadezhda married Sergei, the son of Leo Alezandrovich Pushkin. To Nadezhda and Sergei would be born Alexander Sergeyevich Pushkin, Russia's greatest poet.

RELATED HISTORICAL EVENTS

• The defeat of the British forces under Lord Cornwallis at Yorktown effectively ended the Revolutionary War and made possible the establishment of the United States (October 19).

1 7 8 2

THE UNITED STATES

Thomas Jefferson, writing in his *Notes on Virginia*, said, "the whole commerce between [slave holder] and slave is a perpetual exercise of the most boisterous passions, the most unremitting despotism on the other. Our children see this, and learn to imitate it; for a man is an imitative animal ... the child ... puts on the same airs in the circle of smaller slaves ... and thus nursed, educated, and daily exercised in tyranny, cannot but be stamped by it with odious peculiarities. The man must be a prodigy who can retain his manners and morals undepraved by such circumstances."

Jefferson also stated his belief that African Americans should not remain among European Americans after emancipation because of "deep-rooted prejudices entertained" by European Americans and "ten thousand recollections" by African Americans of "the injuries they have sustained." Jefferson also noted the "distinctions which nature has made; and many other circumstances, *which* will divide us into parties, and produce convulsions, which will probably never end but in the extermination of our or of the other race."

- In Virginia, a notorious integrated marauding band, led by a European American man, was active.
- Deborah Gannett, an African American woman, served under the name of Robert Shurtliff in the Fourth Massachusetts Regiment of the Continental Army for 17 months, from May, 1782, to October, 1783. In 1792, she was cited by the Massachusetts Legislature for "an extraordinary instance of female heroism."
- The state of Rhode Island freed a slave, Quaco Honeyman, as a tribute to his services as a spy during the Revolution.
- British ships leaving Savannah, Georgia, carried about 5,000 persons of African descent.
- In Massachusetts, a "Petition of an African" was presented to the Senate and the House of Representatives by Belinda, a slave who was reportedly seventy years old. In the petition, Belinda demanded protection for herself and her daughter from their owner. Belinda's petition may have been the first recorded indictment of slavery by a person of African descent living in the new United States.

Beginning in 1782, Louisiana was the site of numerous maroon attacks. When twenty-five members of a maroon community were taken prisoner, the men and the women were both severely punished.

- *Miscellaneous State Laws:* Virginia law removed restrictions on voluntary manumissions. This law was repealed five years later.

THE AMERICAS

- Vincente Guerrero, a person of Indigenous American, African, and European descent who was destined to become president of Mexico, was born in Ixtla.

Vincente Guerrero (1782–1831) was a hero of the Mexican war of independence from Spain. Guerrero began his military career in 1810. Soon thereafter, Guerrero was commissioned by the Mexican independence leader Jose Maria Morelos to promote the revolutionary movement in the highlands of southwestern Mexico (in the provincial region which now bears his name).

After Morelos' execution 1815, Guerrero continued to lead his guerrilla forces against the Spanish. In 1821, he combined his forces with Augustin de Iturbide. Guerrero and Iturbide jointly issued the "Plan of Iguala" which became the political platform for the Mexican independence movement.

Guerrero's and Iturbide's forces ultimately prevailed over the Spaniards and achieved independence for Mexico in August of 1821.

In 1829, Guerrero became president of Mexico. During his tenure, he abolished slavery within Mexico, including the Mexican territory known today as Texas. This act along with other issues led to the Texans own war of independence in 1836. *See 1836.*

Guerrero, a relatively uneducated man, was more a soldier than a politician. Later in 1829, he was deposed by the more politically sophisticated and charismatic General Antonio Lopez de Santa Anna.

In 1831, as was an all too frequent occurrence in early Mexican history, Guerrero, a national hero, was tried and executed.

AFRICA

- Spain abandoned the island of Fernando Po.

RELATED HISTORICAL EVENTS

In 1782, Gregon, a Liverpool shipping firm, sued the insurers of the slaver *Zong* for nonpayment of a claim. The *Zong* made the passage from Africa to Jamaica. However, when the *Zong* failed to make its intended landfall, its captain, fearing that the supply of water would run out, ordered the "cargo" of one hundred thirty-three slaves to be thrown overboard.

The owners of the *Zong* claimed that they were entitled to the value of the drowned slaves. In the trial of the matter (held in 1783), the magistrates found for the owners.

The insurers appealed to Lord Mansfield's court where their counsel argued that the drowning of the slaves was murder.

Mansfield, the author of the landmark Somersett decision, held that a charge of murder could not be sustained. From the bench, he commented, "Though it shocks me very much to say so, the case of the slaves was the same as if horses had been thrown overboard."

However, Mansfield did order that a new trial be held on the issue of compensating the owners for their "loss." The owners subsequently abandoned their suit.

The macabre nature of this case outraged a number of abolitionists in England. Granville Sharp, a noted abolitionist, pursued the matter at the behest of a freed slave Olaudah Equiano, whose own slave narrative had brought him a measure of notoriety.

Sharp appealed to the Prime Minister and the Duke of Portland asking that the Royal Navy prevent the recurrence of such atrocities on British ships.

1 7 8 3

THE UNITED STATES

In 1783, Lafayette wrote to George Washington, proposing that the two join in buying an estate to experiment with emancipating slaves and using them as tenants to demonstrate the practicability of emancipation, Washington replied: "The scheme . . . which you propose . . . is a striking evidence of the benevolence of your heart. I shall be happy to join you in so laudable a work, but will deter going into a detail of the business till I have the pleasure of seeing you." Lafayette later undertook this project alone.

• A group of Revolutionary War African American soldiers known as "The Black Regiment" was disbanded at Saratoga, New York (June 13).
• Samuel "Black Sam" Fraunces hosted George Washington as Washington bade farewell to his troops. *See 1762.*
• Oliver Cromwell, an African American soldier who crossed the Delaware with

Washington and fought at Brandywine, Monmouth, and Yorktown, received from Washington a badge of merit for his six years of service.
• The treaty which ended the Revolutionary War, the Treaty of Paris, was written with a provision which promised the return of all slaves to their American owners (The Treaty of Paris, Article VII).

Although slaves were to be returned pursuant to the Treaty of Paris, the British ships that left New York harbor after the Treaty of Paris was signed contained well over 3,000 persons of African descent (including the famous African American fighter Bill Richmond). The British ships which left Charleston, South Carolina, carried about 6,500 persons of African descent (including the African American clergyman David George). *See also 1814 — The Treaty of Ghent.*

• The Philadelphia Yearly Meeting of Quakers voted to admit an African American to the Society of Friends.
• Peter Williams, Sr., a slave, was purchased by the John Street Methodist Church of New York. The church immediately liberated him. Williams remained with the church as the church sexton until his death in 1823.
• *Legislation:* Virginia law emancipated slaves who served in the Continental Army with the consent of their owners.
• Maryland prohibited the slave trade.
• Slavery was prohibited in New Hampshire.
• *Notable Cases:* Slavery was abolished by judicial decision in Massachusetts. The case involved a slave, Quork Walker, who had sued for freedom on the basis of his master's verbal promise. Chief Justice William Cushing declared that slavery was altogether inconsistent with the newly adopted Massachusetts Declaration of Rights.
• By court decision in a case initiated by Paul Cuffee and his brother John, Massachusetts African Americans who were subject to taxation were declared entitled to suffrage. *See 1780.*
• *Publications:* In 1783, Anthony Benezet published *A Serious Address to the Rulers of America.* In this publication, Benezet noted the hypocrisy of Americans on the issue of slavery. Benezet contrasted the American protests against British encroachment on the American right to liberty with the Americans' entrenched injustice in tolerating and perpetuating the institution of slavery.

• *The Arts:* Newport Gardner started teaching music in Newport, Rhode Island.

THE AMERICAS

• In 1783, more than 30,000 American British loyalists migrated to Nova Scotia. Many of these loyalists were slave holders who took their slaves with them. Once in Nova Scotia, the labor of the slaves was not in great demand. As a result, a serious effort was made to relocate these excess slaves to their homeland of Africa.

• David George, a relocated African American clergyman from South Carolina, established the first Afro-Canadian church in Nova Scotia, Canada.

David George (1742–1810) was born a slave in Virginia. As a young man, he escaped and for a time lived among the Creek Indians. Recaptured and sold to George Gaufin, David George was eventually enslaved on a plantation near Silver Bluff, South Carolina.

While in Silver Bluff, George became pastor of the first African American Baptist church *see 1773.* During the British occupation of Charleston, South Carolina, Gaufin, George's owner, moved to the Charleston and took George with him. When the British evacuated the city, George and his family accompanied the evacuating Loyalists.

George was relocated to Nova Scotia, Canada, where he once again established a church. However, the climate (both natural and man-influenced) was not amenable to the relocated African Americans, including David George. In 1792, George and almost his entire Charleston (Nova Scotia) congregation emigrated to Sierra Leone, becoming the first African Americans to be resettled in Africa.

At the time of his death in 1810, George had a congregation of nearly two hundred members.

AFRICA

• The United States went to war against the Barbary pirates. As a result of this war, the United States was compelled to pay a tribute to the pirates.

• Spain bombarded Algiers.

EUROPE

• In 1783, *Letters of the Late Ignatius Sancho, An African* were published in two volumes in London, England. Ignatius Sancho made a name for himself as a writer after having been brought to England from the West Indies as a child.

RELATED HISTORICAL EVENTS

• The captain of the Liverpool slave ship, *Zong,* ordered 133 slaves to be thrown overboard and drowned. He defended the action by explaining that the slaves were weak and likely to die on board ship. If they died at sea, the loss would be borne by the underwriters of the voyage and not the owners. The owners brought suit in Kings Bench and were awarded the verdict. *See 1782.*

Between 1783 and 1793, the Liverpool slave trade employed 878 ships and transported 303,737 Africans. The price paid for the Africans was some 15,186,850 pounds (British currency). The gross return for the merchants was 1,700,000 pounds per year.

• As an outgrowth of the Somersett and Zong decisions, in 1783, the Quakers of England established a society for the abolition of the slave trade. In this year, the Quakers would also petition the British Parliament for the abolition of the slave trade.

• On September 3, the Treaty of Versailles was signed. Under this treaty, Great Britain recognized the independence of the United States. However, under this agreement, France recovered its Indian and West Indian possessions along with the African possessions of Goree and Senegal. Also, Spain recovered the island of Minorca.

• Simon Bolivar, the great liberator of South America, was born.

1784

THE UNITED STATES

During 1784, a number of states adopted legislation affecting the status of African Americans.

In Rhode Island, a law was passed authorizing the gradual abolition of slavery. All persons born after March 1784 were declared free and participation in the slave trade was forbidden.

In Connecticut, a gradual emancipation law was passed (while at the same time another Connecticut law forbade African Americans from serving in the militia despite the fact that they had served the new nation so well during the Revolutionary War).

In New Jersey, a law was passed which freed all African Americans who had taken part in the Revolution.

• North Carolina answered the petition of Edward Griffin, an African American

Revolutionary War soldier, by commending his meritorious service and freeing him from slavery (May 4).

• *The Abolition Movement*: Thomas Jefferson was chairperson of a congressional committee that recommended a plan for governing the land that was to become Kentucky, Tennessee, Mississippi, and Alabama. The committee report suggested that after 1800 there should be no slavery in the area. This clause failed adoption by one vote.

• The Methodist Church declared slavery contrary to the law of God, and gave members 12 months to free their slaves. This directive was later suspended at the demand of Virginia and other Southern states.

• *The Labor Movement*: In Virginia, a protest by unemployed European American seamen led to the adoptiong of a law which limited the number of slaves who could work on ships harbored in Virginia's ports.

• *Notable Births*: Tom Molineaux (1784–1818), a noted African American fighter of the early 1800s was born a slave in Washington, D. C.

• *Notable Deaths*: Phillis Wheatley Peters, the noted African American poet, died in Boston (December 5). *See 1753*.

• *Publications*: Phillis Wheatley Peters published *An elegy, sacred to the memory of that great divine, the reverend and learned Dr. Samuel Cooper. See 1753.*

• Phillis Wheatley Peters published "Liberty and Peace," a poem. *See 1753*.

• *The Black Church*: "Black" Harry Hosier preached a sermon at Thomas Chapel, Chapeltown, Delaware, before a European American congregation.

• *Black Enterprise*: Paul Cuffee became the owner and captain of his own ship.

THE AMERICAS

• In 1784, there were 304 slaves in the District of Montreal in Canada.

• In 1784, George Liele, an African American born in Virginia, went to Jamaica as a missionary. By 1791, he had baptized over 400 persons there.

• In Argentina, the branding of slaves was prohibited.

AFRICA

• In 1784, new conflicts arose between the Swahili cities of East Africa and the resurgent forces of Oman. In this year, there was an abortive attempt by Saif Ahmad al-Busaidi, a pretender to be sultan of Oman and Muscat, to stir up a rebellion along the East African coast.

• Iyasu III of Ethiopia came to power.

RELATED HISTORICAL EVENTS

• The "Meeting for Sufferings" published *The Case of our fellow creatures, the oppressed Africans.*

1785

THE UNITED STATES

• The United States Congress passed an ordinance which prohibited the expansion of slavery into the Northwest Territories.

• *The Abolition Movement*: The New York Manumission Society was founded with John Jay (the future Chief Justice of the United States Supreme Court) as president.

• *Notable Births*: David Walker, the first African American to attack slavery in published writings, was born.

David Walker (1785–1830) was born in Wilmington, North Carolina (September 28) of emancipated parents. He traveled widely in the South, and at an early age acquired a deep sympathy for the enslaved members of his race.

In 1827, Walker went to Boston and established a second-hand clothing business on Brattle Street.

While in Boston, in 1829, Walker published *Walker's Appeal in 4 articles, together with a Preamble to the Colored Citizens of the World, but in Particular and very expressly to those of the U.S.A.* The pamphlet called on African Americans to rise against their oppressors. A second edition in 1830 penetrated the South, spreading consternation among slave holders. In a single day, after a copy was discovered in Georgia, the legislature rushed through a law that made "the circulation of pamphlets of evil tendency among our domestics," a capital offense.

• *Miscellaneous State Laws*: New York issued a partial prohibition of the slave trade.

• *Publications*: John Marrant published *A Narrative of the Lord's Wonderful Dealings with J. Marrant, a Black . . . Taken Down from His Own Relation.* This narrative was one of the first autobiographies written in English by a person of African descent.

• *The Black Church*: An African American Baptist church was organized at Williamsburg, Virginia.

• In addition to the church in Williamsburg, Virginia, there was also an African American church reported in Savannah, Georgia.

• The Colored Methodist Society was organized in Baltimore, Maryland.

• Lemuel Haynes, an African American, became pastor of a European American congregation in Torrington, Connecticut. He was the first African American Congregational pastor. *See 1753, 1774, 1775 and 1776.*

THE AMERICAS

• In 1785, the slave code for Santo Domingo insisted on the provision of adequate food and clothing for slaves but prohibited slaves from ownership of property and from obtaining education and religious instruction. Whipping was allowed for contradicting a European and persons of African descent were barred from artisan trades.

AFRICA

• The United States vessels *Maria* and *Dauphin* were seized by Algerian (Barbary) pirates near Gibraltar.
• Bizerta was again bombarded by the French fleet.

1 7 8 6

THE UNITED STATES

In 1786, Washington wrote in a letter to Lafayette: "To set the slaves afloat at once would, I believe, be productive of much inconvenience and mischief; but, by degrees it certainly might, and assuredly ought to be, effected, and that too, by legislative authority." In 1786, Washington owned 216 slaves.

• The state of Virginia emancipated James, a slave held by William Armstead. James was emancipated because of his espionage activities on behalf of Lafayette in 1781. *See 1781.*
• *Miscellaneous State Laws:* New Jersey forbade the importation of slaves.
• North Carolina prohibited the importation of slaves.
• Participation in the slave trade was prohibited in Vermont.
• *Publications:* In 1786, *The Life and Confession of Johnson Green, who is to be Executed this Day, August 17th 1786 for the Atrocious Crime of Burglary together with his Last and Dying Words* was written.

AFRICA

• The Ottoman (Turkish) fleet was dispatched to restore Turkish authority in Egypt.
• A treaty was executed between Morocco and the United States.

EUROPE

• In 1786, a proposal was forwarded by Dr. Henry Smeatham to found a settlement for slaves who had found asylum in England from the West Indies and the United States.
• Geoffrey L'Islet (also referred to as "Jean-Baptiste L'Islet-Geoffrey) was an officer of artillery and guardian of the depot of maps and plans of the Isle of France (Mauritius). In 1786, L'Islet was named a correspondent of the French Academy of Sciences to which he regularly transmitted meteorological observations and hydrographical journals. In the almanac of the Isle of France, several contributions of L'Islet's were inserted. A collection of his manuscript memoirs is deposited in the archives of the Academy of Sciences. L'Islet was well versed in botany, natural philosophy, geology, and astronomy. L'Islet established a scientific society on the Isle of France of which some Frenchmen refused to become members merely because the society's founder was a person of African descent.

RELATED HISTORICAL EVENTS

• A treaty was executed between Spain and the Ottoman Empire which was designed to end acts of piracy in the West Mediterranean.

1 7 8 7

THE UNITED STATES

The Constitution of the United States was approved containing provisions making slaves count as three-fifths of a person for purposes of representation (Article I, Section 2); placing a twenty-year moratorium on antislavery legislation (Article I, Section 9); taxing slave traders ten dollars per imported slave (Article I, Section 9); and requiring the return of escaped slaves upon demand of their owners (Article IV, Section 2) (September 17).

Of the 55 delegates to the Constitutional Convention, 16 held "productive" slaves, and 9 more had at least "a few slaves around the house." Charles Cotesworth Pinckney of South Carolina declared that South Carolina and Georgia could not do without slaves. Cotesworth Pinckney defended slavery as justified by the examples of Greece, Rome, and modern states such as France, Holland, and England. He declared that South Carolina would not agree to any government which abolished the slave trade, but that South Carolina would probably abolish it herself gradually if left to herself.

Cotesworth Pinckney's fellow South Carolinian, John Rutledge, argued that it was in the interest of the Northern states not to oppose slavery because they would benefit by transporting the products of slave labor.

Roger Sherman, of Connecticut, said that the slave trade was "iniquitous" but he did not feel bound to oppose it.

George Mason, of Virginia, who owned 200 slaves, declared that the slave trade was brought about by the "avarice of British merchants" and that the British government had "constantly checked the attempts of Virginia to put a stop to it." He said slavery encouraged slave holders to be petty tyrants and discouraged arts and manufacturing. Mason wanted the federal government to have the power to prevent the increase or spread of slavery. However, Mason eventually refused to sign the Constitution because he objected to the powers that the Constitution gave to the federal government.

James Madison, another Virginian and the person called the "Father of the Constitution" because he was a leading member of the convention and wrote a record of the delegates' debate, wrote in his notebook during the Constitutional Convention: "Where slavery exists, the republican theory becomes still more fallacious." Madison opposed slavery and fought during the convention against the postponement of the prohibition of the slave trade until 1808. He said rather prophetically during the debate: "Twenty years will produce all the mischief that can be apprehended from the liberty to import slaves. So long a term will be more dishonorable to the American character than to say nothing about it in the constitution."

Gouverneur Morris, a delegate from Pennsylvania and the person who actually wrote the Constitution, called slavery "a nefarious institution, the curse of heaven on the states where it prevailed." Morris worried about the possibility of the North having to send militias to defend the South against slave insurrections.

The Constitutional Convention's final compromise on slavery provided that an import tax on slaves would not exceed $10 per head (Article I, Section 9); that the importation of slaves could not be abolished before 1808 (Article I, Section 9); and that slaves would be counted for taxation and representation purposes for various states in the federal government, with 5 slaves considered equivalent to three European Americans (Article I, Section 2).

A delegate, Pierce Butler of South Carolina, proposed a fugitive (escaped) slave clause which drew little debate and was adopted as Article IV, Section 2.

Delaware became the first state to ratify the Constitution (December 7.)

*****

The Secret Iniquity of the Constitution

History records that, in the interest of creating a union, the Constitutional Convention adopted a provision which made every slave considered the equivalent of three-fifths of a European American for the purposes of taxation and representation. This provision has often been viewed with some bitterness by African Americans because it implies that the founders seemingly viewed slaves as being something less than a human being.

However, what is rarely discussed is that this same provision also served to make Northern European Americans something less than their Southern counterparts in the exercise of the rights set forth in the Constitution. The expression of this secret iniquity became clear some sixty-seven years later during the debate over the Kansas-Nebraska Act. During that debate, a former congressman from Illinois, by the name of Abraham Lincoln, shed light on the inequalities between Northerners and Southerners as set forth in the Constitution. Lincoln said: "[T]here are constitutional relations between the slave and free States, which are degrading to the latter. We are under legal obligations to catch and return their runaway slaves to them — a sort of dirty, disagreeable job, which I believe, as a general rule the slaveholders will not perform for one another. Then again, in the control of the government — the management of the partnership affairs — they have greatly the advantage of us. By the constitution, each State has two Senators — each has a number of Representatives; in proportion to the number of its people — each has a number of presidential electors, equal to the whole number of its Senators and Representatives together. But in ascertaining the number of the people, for this purpose, five slaves are counted as being equal to three whites. The slaves do not vote; they are only counted and so used, as to swell the influence of the white people's votes. The practical effect of this is more aptly shown by a comparison of the States of South Carolina and Maine. South

Carolina has six representatives, and so has Maine; South Carolina has eight presidential electors, and so has Maine. This is precise equality so far; and, of course, they are equal in Senators, each having two. Thus in the control of the government, the two States are equals precisely. But how are they in the number of their white people? Maine has 581,813 — while South Carolina has 274,567. Maine has twice as many as South Carolina, and 32,679 over. Thus each white man in South Carolina is more than the double of any man in Maine. This is all because South Carolina, besides her free people, has 384,984 slaves. The South Carolinian has precisely the same advantage over the white man in every other free state, as well as in Maine. He is more than the double of any one of us in this crowd. The same advantage, but not to the same extent, is held by all the citizens of the slave States, over those of the free; and it is an absolute truth, without an exception, that there is no voter in any slave State, but who has more legal power in the government, than any voter in any free State. There is no instance of exact equality; and the disadvantage is against us the whole chapter through."

• Congress added a provision to the Northwest Ordinance forbidding slavery in the territory covered by the Ordinance (Section 14, Article VI) (July 13). The sixth clause of the Northwest Ordinance provided that there should be no slavery or involuntary servitude, except as punishment for a crime, in the Northwest Territory (an area which would come to comprise the states of Ohio, Indiana, Illinois, Michigan, and Wisconsin). The Ordinance also included a provision for returning slaves who escaped into the territory.

• Prince Hall, an African American originally from Barbados and a veteran of the Revolutionary War, succeeded in obtaining a charter for an African American Masonic lodge in Boston, Massachusetts. The charter came from the Grand Lodge in England (September 12). *See 1748, 1775, 1787 and 1788.*

In 1787, Samuel Hopkins wrote: "The inhabitants of Rhode Island, especially those of Newport, have had by far the grand share in this traffic, of all these United States. This trade in human species has been the first wheel of commerce in Newport, on which every other movement in business has chiefly depended. That town has been built up, and flourished in times past, at the expense of the blood, the liberty, and happiness of the poor Africans; and the inhabitants have lived on this, and by it have gotten most of their wealth and riches."

• *The Abolition Movement:* Quakers and others organized the Pennsylvania Society for Promoting the Abolition of Slavery. It replaced the Abolition Society of 1775. Benjamin Franklin was elected president.

• Isaac T. Hopper, of Philadelphia, developed a plan to aid slaves escaping from the South.

• *The Civil Rights Movement:* African Americans in Boston, led by Prince Hall, petitioned the Massachusetts government for equal school facilities for African American students.

• *Notable Births:* Abraham, chief counselor of the Seminoles, was born.

Abraham, or Abram, (1787–?) was born of slave parents in Pensacola, Florida. As a young man, while serving as a slave to a Dr. Sierra, Abraham escaped from slavery to live among the Seminoles.

Among the Seminoles, Abraham was still enslaved. However, among the Seminoles, slaves were considered the dependents, or even the proteges, of their owners.

While with the Seminoles, Abraham served as an interpreter. As an interpreter, he played a key role for the Seminole delegation that traveled to Washington, D.C. in 1826.

On his return from Washington, Abraham was freed as a reward for his meritorious service. Abraham married a Seminole woman who was the widow of the former chief of the Seminole nation. Abraham was also appointed to a position amongst the Seminoles which combined the duties of private secretary, chief counsellor, and spokesman.

• *Miscellaneous State Laws:* In Delaware, the exportation of slaves was prohibited.

• In South Carolina, the importation of slaves was prohibited.

• The importation of slaves was prohibited in Rhode Island.

• *Publications:* Jupiter Hammon published *An Address to the Negroes in the State of New York.* Hammon's works reflected his resignation to his status as a slave. In his address, Hammon wrote: "Now whether it is right, and lawful, in the sight of God, for them to make slaves of us or not, I am certain that while we are slaves, it is our duty to obey our masters, in all their lawful commands, and mind them unless we are bid to do that which we know to be sin, or forbidden in God's word." *See 1711.*

• *Poems on comic, serious and moral subjects* by Phillis Wheatley Peters was published posthumously.

• *Scholastic Achievements:* In October, Prince Hall and other Boston African Americans petitioned the Massachusetts Legislature for equal school facilities for African Americans.

• The first free school for African Americans in New York City opened. The New York Manumission Society organized the African Free School in New York City. It began as a one-room school with 40 pupils (November 1).

• *The Black Church:* Richard Allen and Absalom Jones, African Americans, organized other Philadelphia African Americans in the Free African Society which eventually became an "African Church," affiliated with the Protestant Episcopal Church. (April 12) *See 1760.*

In Philadelphia, African American Methodists organized the Free African Society for benevolent and religious purposes. The Society was organized as a result of the discriminatory practices (the segregated seating) encountered as they worshipped with European Americans at St. George's Methodist Episcopal Church. Under the leadership of Richard Allen and Absalom Jones, the society later developed into St. Thomas Protestant Episcopal Church. Absalom Jones served as the first rector of this church. The society was also responsible for the Bethel Church, a Methodist church which was organized by Richard Allen.

Over time, the Free African Society would gain a national reputation. The Free African Society would add a strong chorus to the calls for the abolition of slavery and would provide medical assistance and other forms of relief for the poor. The African Free Society would also serve to facilitate the creation of an information "grapevine" for African Americans in the South.

THE AMERICAS

• In Montevideo, Uruguay, *Caserio* for Africans of the Royal Company of the Philippines was established.

AFRICA

In 1787, the concept of repatriating freed slaves to Africa was finally acted upon. The first African settlers sailed from Portsmouth, England, under the charge of Captain B. Thomson. These settlers arrived in Sierra Leone and settled on land purchased from "King Tom"—at a site known as Granville Town.

Over the next few years, some 400 Africans would be repatriated in Sierra Leone by the British. Interestingly, accompanying these Africans were some 60 Englishwomen who were deemed to be prostitutes and, ultimately, became wives for some of the repatriated Africans.

• The plague killed 17,000 people in Algiers.

• Andrianampoinimerina, the king of the Merina, came to power in Madagascar. During his reign, the Merina kingdom would be expanded in Madagascar.

EUROPE

• In 1787, *Thoughts and Sentiments on the Evil and Wicked Traffic of Slavery and Commerce of the Human Species, Humbly Submitted to the Inhabitants of Great Britain* was published. This publication was attributed to Attabah Cugoano, who had been freed from slavery in Grenada and placed as a servant in homes in England.

• Returning to Paris in 1787, Joseph Boulogne (the Chevalier de) Saint-Georges composed and produced a moderately successful comedy entitled *La fille-garcon* and resumed work with the Loge Olympique. *See 1739.*

RELATED HISTORICAL EVENTS

• Peter Peckard published *Am I not a Man? And a brother?* which was addressed to the British Parliament.

• A committee on the abolition of slavery was organized in Great Britain. Granville Sharp was made president of the committee.

• The Association for the Abolition of Slavery was founded in England.

1788

THE UNITED STATES

Jefferson wrote from Paris to a friend, Dr. Gordon, of his anger at Cornwallis' plundering in 1781 of his estate and the seizure of thirty slaves: "Had this been to give them freedom, he would have done right; but it was to consign them to inevitable death from the small pox and putrid fever, then raging in his [Cornwallis'] camp."

• New Hampshire was the ninth state to ratify the Constitution thereby putting it into effect (June 21). Virginia ratified the document on June 25 and New York followed on July 26. *See 1787.*

• James Derham, a former slave who had purchased his freedom, was recognized as a leading doctor in New Orleans. *See 1762.*

• *The Civil Rights Movement:* African Americans in Boston, under the leadership of Prince Hall, protested the kidnaping and sale into slavery of free African Americans.

• *The Colonization Movement:* The African Union of Newport, Rhode Island called for an exodus of free African Americans to Africa. The Philadelphia Free African Society vetoed the suggestion.

The African Union of Newport, Rhode Island, proposed a general exodus to Africa, but the Free African Society of Philadelphia responded: "With regard to the emigration to Africa you mention, we have at present but little to communicate on that head, apprehending every pious man is a good citizen of the world."

• *Miscellaneous State Laws:* An incident in which free persons of African descent were abducted and transported to Martinique led to a protest in Boston. Led by Revolutionary War veteran Prince Hall, founder of the first African American Masonic lodge, the free African Americans of Massachusetts brought their grievances to the state assembly which, with the backing of Governor John Hancock, obtained the return of the African Americans and subsequently passed a law which declared slave trading illegal and offered monetary damages to kidnaping victims (February 27).

• In New York, the slave trade was prohibited.

• North Carolina law provided for the apprehension and sale (with twenty percent of the sale price going to the informer) of all illegally manumitted African Americans. In response to this legislation, many of the free African Americans of North Carolina fled the state.

• In New Jersey, a law was enacted which mandated that slave owners teach their slaves to read. The penalty for failure to abide by the law was set at five pounds (British currency).

• In Pennsylvania, the slave trade was prohibited by amending the Act of 1780. The amendment sought to prevent internal and foreign trade and to correct kidnaping and other abuses.

• In South Carolina, the slave trade was prohibited for a period of five years.

• *Publications:* "An Essay on Negro Slav-ery" appeared in the November and December issues of the *American Museum.* The article was signed by a person using the pen name "Othello" of Maryland.

• *The Black Church:* Andrew Bryan, a slave, was ordained as the first pastor of the First African Baptist Church (a.k.a. Bryan Baptist Church) which was organized in Savannah, Georgia (January 19–20). By 1791, the church had 200 members.

THE AMERICAS

• In 1788, there were 15,000 slaves out of a total population of 120,000 in the Spanish portion of Santo Domingo.

During 1788, there were brought to San Domingo 29,500 slaves in some 98 vessels. Over a ten-year period from 1782 to 1792, the number of slaves employed on the plantations of San Domingo doubled.

• The Cabildo of Buenos Aires warned of the inherent danger in the gathering of multitudes of free slaves within the city.

AFRICA

• The Galla state of Begember was formed.

RELATED HISTORICAL EVENTS

• On January 9, the Association for Promoting the Discovery of the Interior Parts of Africa was founded in London, England.

• William Pitt, William Wyndham Grenville, and William Wilberforce appeared before Parliament and demanded the abolition of the slave trade.

• Thomas Clarkson published *An Essay on the Impolicy of the African Slave Trade.*

• James Ramsey published *Objections to the Abolition of the Slave Trade with Answers.*

• *Societe des Amis des Noirs* (Society of the Friends of Blacks) was established in France for the abolition of the slave trade and slavery.

——— 1789 ———

THE UNITED STATES

In January, all of the states that had ratified the Constitution (except New York) selected presidential electors in their legislatures or by a direct vote of the people. On February 4, the electors named George Washington as the first president of the United States. The first Congress under the Constitution met in New York City on March 4. Washington was inaugurated on April 30. However, North Carolina and Rhode Island refused to approve the Constitution or take part in the new government until Congress agreed to add a bill of rights.

• The Virginia Legislature emancipated two African Americans, Jack Knight and William Boush, for having "faithfully served on board the armed vessels" of Virginia. The legislature purchased the freedom of Caesar, the slave of Mary Tarrant of Elizabeth for entering "very early into the service of his country and continuing to pilot the armed vessels of this state during the late war."

• In 1789, through the influence of George Ellicot, Benjamin Banneker, the African American mathematician, was selected as part of a scientific team to survey and assess the federal territory designated to become the District of Columbia. *See 1731.*

• *The Abolition Movement:* Benjamin Franklin, noted scientist, scholar, businessman and the president of a Pennsylvania abolition society, sent a message to Congress on behalf of the society urging the abolition of slavery (November 9).

In 1789, the ever thoughtful Franklin wrote: "Slavery is such an atrocious debasement of human nature, that its very extirpation, if not performed with solicitous care, may sometimes open a source of serious evils. . . . The unhappy man, who has long been treated as a brute animal, too frequently sinks beneath the common standard of the human species. The galling chains that bind his body do also fetter his intellectual faculties, and impair the social affectations of the heart. Accustomed to move like a mere machine, . . . reflection is suspended; he has not the power of choice; and reason and conscience have but little influence over his conduct, because he is chiefly governed by the passion of fear. He is poor and friendless, perhaps worn out by extreme labor, age and disease. Under such circumstances freedom may often prove a misfortune to himself and prejudicial to society."

• The Baptist Church declared slavery a violation of the rights of nature.

• A Spanish royal decree, making special reference to Florida, granted land and freedom to fugitive slaves.

• *Notable Births:* Josiah Henson, the model for Harriet Beecher Stowe's "Uncle Tom" of *Uncle Tom's Cabin,* was born.

Josiah Henson (1789–1883) was born on June 15 in Charles County, Maryland, on the farm of Francis Newman. As a youth, Henson saw his parents brutally assaulted by Newman.

In 1828, Henson became a preacher. When Henson tried to purchase his freedom, the Newmans sent him to New Orleans to be sold. He then decided to escape. On October 28, 1830, Henson crossed over into Canada.

Henson helped other slaves to escape and tried to start a community. He traveled to England, where he was honored by Lord John Russell, the prime minister, and invited by Lord Grey to go to India to supervise cotton raising.

During his travels, while passing through Andover, Massachusetts, Henson happened to tell his story to Harriet Beecher Stowe. She referred to him in *A Key to Uncle Tom's Cabin,* published in 1853.

In 1849, Henson published *The Life of Josiah Henson, Formerly a Slave, Now an Inhabitant of Canada as Narrated by himself,* and in 1858 an enlarged edition appeared with an introduction by Harriet Beecher Stowe, under the title *Truth Stranger than Fiction, an Autobiography of the Rev. Josiah Henson* was published.

• *Miscellaneous State Laws:* North Carolina put a high duty on imported slaves.

• The slave trade was prohibited in Delaware.

• *Publications:* John Marrant's *A Sermon; Preached on the 24th Day of June, 1789, Being the Festival of St. John the Baptist, at the Request of the Right Worshipful the Grand Master, Prince Hall, and the Rest of the Brethren of the African Lodge of the Honourable Society of Free and Accepted Masons in Boston* was published.

• "A Letter on Slavery" by a "Free Negro" was published in the *American Museum.*

• *Scholastic Achievements:* The Society for the Free Instruction of Orderly Blacks and People of Color was organized in Philadelphia. As early as 1760, two schools for the education of people of African descent had existed in Philadelphia.

THE AMERICAS

• Charles III of Spain issued the Real Cedula which insisted on records of slave births, deaths, etc., and adequate food and religious instruction. It provided for punishing cruel slave holders and forbade branding but said slaves could be used only for agriculture. These restrictions were largely ignored by Spanish slaveholders.

In 1789, Julian Raymond and Vincent Oge went to Paris as members of a delegation representing San Domingo (Haiti). Raymond and Oge presented a petition to the National Assembly requesting citizenship rights for the free Afro-Haitians.

In 1790, the Constituent Assembly of France voted, by a large majority, not to interfere with the interior government of the colonies, nor to subject them to laws "incompatible with their local establishments." The Assembly also buttressed the slave trade by declaring that the National Assembly would not make any innovation directly or indirectly "in any system of commerce in which the colonies were already concerned."

Disappointed by the failure to obtain full citizenship rights for free Afro-Haitians, Oge returned by way of the United States in order to collect arms and escape observation.

Landing secretly in the north of San Domingo, Oge collected a force of 300 men. These three hundred men were immediately attacked by a much larger force from Cap Francois and compelled to take refuge in the Spanish part of the island (today's Dominican Republic).

The Spanish governor subsequently surrendered Oge and his followers to the French authorities. On March 12, 1791, Oge and Chavannes, the two leaders of the rebellion, were sentenced to death. The sentence for the two leaders required: "[Whilst] alive to have their arms, legs, thighs and spines broken; and afterward to be placed on a wheel, their faces toward Heaven, and there to stay as long as it would please God to preserve their lives; and when dead, their heads were to be cut off and exposed on poles."

AFRICA

• A smallpox epidemic broke out at the Cape coast.
• The Xhosa crossed the Fish River and were allowed to remain "without prejudice to the ownership of Europeans."
• Saint Louis, Senegal, sent a cahier of grievances to the French Estates General.
• Hezekias of Ethiopia came to the throne.

EUROPE

In 1789, the memoirs of Olaudah Equiano were published. The memoirs of Olaudah Equiano relate the story of one man's many travels during, and eventual release from, slavery.

Olaudah Equiano was kidnaped as a boy from his home in what is now Benin. After several changes of owners, Equiano was sold to British slavers in 1756 and brought by them to Barbados.

From Barbados, Equiano was taken to Virginia, where a British naval officer bought him and took him to England as a servant, giving him the name of Gustavus Vassa.

After serving with his owner in the British navy during the Seven Years War, Equiano hoped that he might acquire his freedom. Instead his owner returned him to the West Indies for resale.

In 1766, Equiano bought his freedom.

In 1786, Equiano was involved in the preparations of the expedition of the "Black Poor" which resulted in the establishment of Freetown, Sierra Leone. *See 1787.*

• George Bridgetower made his debut as a violinist at the Concert Spirituel in Paris at the age of nine (April 13). *See 1779.*

RELATED HISTORICAL EVENTS

• Benjamin Lundy (1789–1839), the publisher of the antislavery newspaper *The Genius of Universal Emancipation*, was born (January 4).
• The French Revolution began.

1790

THE UNITED STATES

In 1790, Congress authorized the first national census. When completed in August, it showed a total population of 3,929,625 with an African American population at 757,181 — 697,624 being slaves and 59,557 being emancipated. Massachusetts and Maine were the only states to report no slaves (March 1).

An alternative tally placed the number of African Americans at 757,363 in the United States, representing 19.3% of the population. Of these, 59,466 were emancipated, and 697,897 were slaves. The number of African Americans, slave and free, and percentages of state populations were:

State Percentage of Total Population	African Americans		
	Slave	Free	
Maine	none	538	.56
N.H	158	630	.55
Vt.	17	255	.32
Mass.	none	5,463	1.44
R.I.	952	3,469	6.40
Conn.	2,759	2,801	2.33

	African Americans		Percentage of Total
State	Slave	Free	Population
N.Y.	21,324	4,654	7.64
N.J.	11,423	2,762	7.70
Pa.	3,737	6,537	2.37
Del.	8,887	3,899	21.64
Md.	103,036	8,043	34.74
Va.	293,427	12,766	40.92
N.C.	100,572	4,975	26.80
S.C.	107,094	1,801	43.72
Ga.	29,264	398	35.93
Ky.	11,830	114	16.34
Tenn.	3,417	361	10.56

Between this year and 1800, the European American population of Virginia grew by 16.2%, the slave population by 17.8%, and the emancipated (free) African American population by 56.4%. In North Carolina, the African American population in these same years increased by 32% (41.6% among emancipated African Americans) while the population as a whole showed a growth of 17%. The bulk of this disproportion centered in the eastern portion of the state. Of the 174,017 European American families in New England, only one percent owned slaves. In New England, the only instance of African Americans owning slaves between 1638 and 1790 was in Connecticut where six African American families owned slaves.

In 1790, New York City had 3,252 African Americans, of whom 2,184 were slaves and 1,078 emancipated. Philadelphia, on the other hand, had 1,630 African Americans of whom 210 were slaves. Baltimore had 1,578 African Americans, of whom 323 were emancipated. Boston had 791 African Americans, all of whom were free.

• Congress passed a law which limited naturalization to European Americans.
• Henry Evans, an African American, organized a European American Methodist church in Fayetteville, North Carolina.
• In Charleston, South Carolina, emancipated mulattoes organized the Brown Fellowship Society which admitted "brown" men of good character and had an admission fee of $50. This society provided for the education of emancipated African Americans, assisted widows and orphans, and maintained a clubhouse and a society cemetery.
• Fernando Reyes became mayor of Los Angeles, the first person of African descent to hold such a position. *See 1781.*

A 1790 Spanish census of California found 18 percent of the population of San Francisco, 24 percent of San Jose, 20 percent of Santa Barbara, and 18 percent of Monterey had African ancestors.

• *The Abolition Movement:* The Pennsylvania Abolition Society petitioned Congress to abolish slavery (February 3).

Benjamin Franklin's last public act before his death was to sign the memorial to Congress of the Pennsylvania Abolition Society, opposing slavery and urging Congress to remove "this inconsistency (slavery) from the character of the American people" and to "promote mercy and justice toward this distressed race" and to discourage "every species of traffic in the persons of our fellow-men." Franklin's memorial was rebuffed by the House of Representatives, and Franklin replied in an article in the Federal Gazette with a parody of the proslavery view presented as a Muslim argument in favor of enslaving Christians.

George Washington writing to David Stuart concerning the proposal forwarded by the Quakers and the Pennsylvania Abolition Society noted that "The memorial of the Quakers (and a very malapropos one it was) has at length been put to sleep, and will scarcely awaken before the year 1808."

• The Pennsylvania Abolition Society appointed a committee to supervise the education of emancipated African Americans and to encourage school attendance.
• *Notable Births:* Samuel Cornish, one of the founders of *Freedom's Journal*, was born in Delaware.
• *Miscellaneous State Laws:* The Pennsylvania state constitution was adopted with provisions which failed to explicitly deny African Americans the right to vote.

Between 1790 and 1810, legislators in Maryland, Kentucky and Tennessee made serious attempts to pass laws permitting manumission. In 1790, in Maryland and Kentucky, efforts were made to enact laws for gradual emancipation. However, during this same period, there was a constant fear of slave rebellions. This paranoia prompted the passage of numerous regulations restricting or prohibiting the slave trade: the Federal acts of 1794 and 1800 as well as legislation in South Carolina (1792, 1796, 1800 and 1801); Georgia (1793); North Carolina (1794); and Maryland (1796).

• *Miscellaneous Publications:* A "Negro's Prayer" by a Virginia slave was appended to an abridged edition of *The Life and Adventures* of *Olaudah Equiano, or Gustavus Vassa, the African.*

• *An Essay on the African Slave Trade* by "Historicus" (Benjamin Franklin) was published.

• *Black Enterprise:* Jean Baptiste Pointe du Sable established a trading post at "Eschikagou" on the southern shore of Lake Michigan. Du Sable's trading post would evolve into the city known as Chicago. *See 1745.*

THE AMERICAS

• In 1790, there were 455,000 persons of African descent in the British West Indies. Persons of African descent represented 86 percent of the population. The 260,000 persons of African descent in Jamaica equaled 95 percent of the population. Of the persons of African descent in Jamaica, 97.5 percent were slaves.

• Abu Bakr al-Siddiq was born.

In 1790, Abu Bakr al-Siddiq was born in Timbuktu. Abu claimed descent from the Prophet Mohammed. His family belonged to the class of learned men who were scholars at the great university at Timbuktu for generations.

Abu received his early education at Jenne where he was instructed in reading and comprehending the Koran. In Buona, Abu continued his education with more advanced work on the Koran although he was not old enough to proceed to the studies of logic and rhetoric.

Abu was taken as a prisoner to the port of Lagos, where in about 1805, he was sold and transported on an English ship to the West Indies.

In 1834, Abu was set free. The inhabitants of Kingston, Jamaica, donated twenty pounds to Abu Bakr by public subscription.

Abu Bakr Al-Siddiq left two autobiographical fragments written in Arabic.

• Between 1790 and 1820 Cuba imported 225,574 slaves. By 1853, over 644,000 African Americans had been imported into Cuba.

• In Haiti, a society was formed to free slaves and demand political rights for mulattoes. The society was called Amis des Noirs ("Friends of the Blacks").

The *Amis des Noirs* in France was organized by Gregoire, Robespierre, Mirabeau, Condorcet.

In 1790, the Constituent Assembly of France voted, by a large majority, not to interfere with the interior government of the colonies, nor to subject them to laws "incompatible with their local establishments." The assembly also buttressed the slave trade by declaring that the National Assembly would not make any innovation directly or indirectly "in any system of commerce in which the colonies were already concerned."

The *Amis des Noirs* was instrumental in getting the decree of March 8, 1790, supplemented on March 28 with an amendment which recognized the right to vote in parishes of all free persons twenty-five years of age. However, the colonial governments of Martinique, Guadeloupe, and Saint Domingue all decreed that this amendment only applied to Euro-Caribbeans.

Among the notable American members of *Amis des Noirs* were Benjamin Franklin and Thomas Paine. Thomas Jefferson was a corresponding member.

*****

In 1790, there were about a half million slaves in the French portion of Santo Domingo (Haiti). It was estimated, however, that mulattoes owned at least ten percent of the productive land and over 50,000 slaves. Out of the 7,000 mulatto women in Santo Domingo, 5,000 were reported to be prostitutes or the "kept" mistresses of European men.

AFRICA

• Yazid Muhammed, the sharif of Morocco, came to power. Yazid Muhammed would be known for his persecution of Christians, Jews and even of Muslims.

• Buganda greatly expanded its frontiers, incorporating Buddu.

• By 1790, the Lunda Empire was at its apogee as a trading power.

• Beginning in 1790, the Tijaniyyah order began to rapidly grow in Mauritania.

EUROPE

• George Bridgetower gave an inspired violin solo during the performance of *Messiah* at Drury Lane Theatre in London. This performance attracted the attention of the Prince of Wales (the future King George IV) who became the patron of George Bridgetower. *See 1779.*

• Gustavus Vassa (Olaudah Equiano) presented a petition for the suppression of the slave trade to the queen and the British Parliament.

RELATED HISTORICAL EVENTS

• Benjamin Franklin (1706–1790) died (April 17). He was eighty-four. *See 1706.*

• The Casa de Contratacion was abolished in Spain.

——— 1 7 9 1 ———

THE UNITED STATES

The Haitian Revolution began and its rever-
berations were felt throughout the Southern
United States.

   • Inspired by the Haitian revolution, slaves
in Louisiana attempted a similar revolt. It
was poorly coordinated and failed. Twenty-
three slaves were hanged as suspected participants and three European men involved
in the plot were expelled from the colony.
   • Benjamin Banneker was appointed, at
the suggestion of Thomas Jefferson, to serve
as a member of the commission headed by
L'Enfant to lay out plans for the city of
Washington, D.C. (November 9). After L'Enfant left the commission, Banneker repro-
duced L'Enfant's plans for the city. Banneker was also the principal assistant to Andrew
Elliot, geographer general of the United
States, in the official survey of the site
chosen for the new nation's capital.

In 1791, Benjamin Banneker sent Thomas
Jefferson, then the secretary of state, a manuscript copy of his first almanac together with a
letter concerning the emancipation of African
Americans. Banneker stated that he hoped
Jefferson would "...embrace every opportunity to eradicate that train of absurd and false
ideas and opinions which so generally prevails
with respect to us; and that your sentiments are
concurrent with mine...."

   • When some of Washington's slaves were
taken to Pennsylvania, Pennsylvania officials
claimed that they could not be returned to
Virginia. Washington instructed Tobias Lear
to bring the slaves back to Virginia in a manner that would "deceive both the slaves and
the public."
   • When Robert Pleasants wrote to James
Madison asking him to present an anti-
slavery petition to Congress, Madison refused so as not to give "a public wound ...
to an interest on which [his constituents] set
so great a value."
   • *The Abolition Movement:* There were approximately twelve abolition societies in the
United States from Massachusetts to Virginia.
   • *The Civil Rights Movement:* Emancipated African Americans in Charleston,
South Carolina, petitioned the state legislature concerning the legal inequities to
which they were subject. The protestors
specifically mentioned the prohibitions
against African Americans testifying in court

and against African Americans instituting
suits in court. The petition was rejected.
   • *Publications:* Benjamin Banneker began
publishing his annual almanacs in 1791;
these, in addition to factual material, contained commentaries by Banneker on social
problems. In the almanac, Banneker wrote a
learned dissertation on bees. Banneker was
the first man to calculate the locust plague
as recurrent in 17-year cycles. On August 19,
1791, Banneker sent a copy of the almanac
to Secretary of State Thomas Jefferson. Included in the prefatory note was an appeal
to Jefferson on behalf of Banneker's fellow
African Americans who were held in bondage (slavery). *See 1731.*
   • *The Black Church:* St. Thomas Episcopal
Church was organized in Philadelphia by
African Americans, led by Absalom Jones.
Jones was ordained and became the first African American rector in the United States.
   • The African Baptist Church of Petersburg, Virginia, with 500 members, was
officially recognized by the Dover Association. The originator of the church was a
slave named Moses who persisted in preaching and holding meetings in spite of the
whippings he received in an effort to dis-
suade him from doing so.

THE AMERICAS

   • The Haitian Revolution began (August
22).

The Haitian revolution, masterminded by
Haitian slaves, was successful in overthrowing
French rule of Haiti.

The history of Haiti is long and colorful.
Christopher Columbus landed on the island of
Hispaniola in 1492. One of his ships, the Santa
Maria, ran aground on the reefs near the
present-day city of Cap-Haitien on Christmas
Day, 1492. Columbus' crew used the ship's
timber to build a fort which Columbus named
Fort Navidad. Some of the crew stayed to hold
the fort when Columbus sailed back to Spain.

Upon his return, Columbus discovered gold
on the eastern portion of the island in what is
today the Dominican Republic. Upon this discovery, other Spanish adventurers rushed to
Hispaniola. The Spaniards instituted a reign of
terror on Hispaniola which became an era of
genocide for the indigenous people (the
Arawaks) of Hispaniola. Of the estimated
250,000 Arawaks who inhabited Hispaniola in
1492, only a few hundred remained in 1530.
The decimation of the local indigenous popula-

tion compelled the Spaniards to introduce African slavery into the island.

As the gold fields of Hispaniola gradually became depleted, more and more Spaniards left for more prosperous settlements in Peru and Mexico. By 1606, there were so few Spaniards on the island that the king of Spain deemed it necessary to order all of them to move closer to the city of Santo Domingo (in what is now the Dominican Republic).

During the 1600s, French, English and Dutch pirates terrorized Hispaniola and eventually took over the abandoned northern and western coasts. The pirates used the small island of Tortuga as a base and attacked ships carrying gold and silver to Spain. The Spanish tried to drive out the pirates, but failed. In 1697, the Spanish relinquished control of the western third of the island (modern day Haiti) to the French.

The French renamed the western portion of the island, Saint Domingue. French colonists brought in additional African slaves and developed big coffee and spice plantations. By 1788, there were eight times as many slaves (almost 500,000 in total) as there were French colonists. The colony of Saint Domingue prospered and during the 1700s was more important to France than France's colony in Canada.

In 1791, during the French Revolution, the slaves in Saint Domingue (Haiti) rebelled against French domination. The slaves destroyed plantations and towns. Toussaint L'Ouverture, a former slave, took control of the government and restored a modicum of order to the island. *See also 1789.*

The success of the Haitian slave revolution alarmed slave holders in the United States and the legal and psychological constraints of the American institution of slavery became more tightly wound.

Nevertheless, by word of mouth, American slaves became aware of the success of their Haitian brethren and the threat of massive slave revolts became a preoccupation for both slave and slave owner for the next seventy years.

- The European population of Cuba was 153,559; the non–European population (persons of African descent) was 118,741, of whom 54,151 were emancipated and 64,590 were slaves.
- The French National Assembly granted mulattoes the right of representation in colonial assemblies. They also gave the right to vote to every mulatto in Haiti born of free parents (May 15).

Abbe Gregoire, a protagonist of the Afro-Haitians, wrote a famous letter to the Afro-Haitians in which he said: "You were men, you are now citizens."

- A slave insurrection in Dominica, under Farcel, caused great concern in England and served to delay the abolition of the slave trade.
- By royal decree, Montevideo (Uruguay) was decreed to be the sole port of entry for slaves in the southern part of South America.
- By 1791, Jamaica had 767 sugar plantations with 140,000 Afro-Jamaican slaves; 607 coffee plantations with 21,000 Afro-Jamaican slaves; 1,047 grazing and breeding farms with 31,000 Afro-Jamaicans; and a number of small establishments for cotton, ginger, and pimento which employed 58,000 Afro-Jamaicans.

AFRICA

- A charter was granted to the Sierra Leone Company for trade and aid to the colonists.
- Freetown, Sierra Leone, was founded.

EUROPE

- George Bridgetower, the famed violinist, performed at the Salomon concert. *See 1779.*
- Joe Lashley, a person of African descent, fought a boxing match in England.

RELATED HISTORICAL EVENTS

- The first ten amendments to the United States Constitution were approved.
- France abolished slavery. However, it was later reintroduced and would not be finally eradicated until 1848.

—————— **1792** ——————

THE UNITED STATES

In the wake of the Haitian Revolution, signs of slave unrest and conspiracies resulted in appeals on the part of the Southern militias for more arms.

Reports of slave uprisings in various counties of Virginia and neighboring North Carolina resulted in slaves being arrested and tried. Some of the slaves were whipped, some were banished (sold) to the West Indies and at least three were executed.

• A law of Congress restricted enrollment in the peacetime militia to able-bodied European American male citizens.

• Antoine Blanc founded the first African American Catholic sisterhood in the United States (October 11).

• Virginia freed Saul, a slave of George Kelly, for "very essential services rendered to the Commonwealth during the late War."

• Deborah Gannett, an African American woman, who served under the name of Robert Shurtliff in the Fourth Massachusetts Regiment of the Continental Army for 17 months was cited by the Massachusetts Legislature for "an extraordinary instance of female heroism."

• *Notable Births:* Frank Johnson, one of the first African American bandleaders, was born.

By 1820, Frank Johnson (1792–1844) had established himself as a versatile musician while playing with European American bands in Philadelphia. When Johnson organized his own band, principally a woodwind ensemble, it won national acclaim for its excellent performances at parades and dances. Frank Johnson's Colored Band, as it was called, even performed on plantations as far south as Virginia. Johnson became noted for his ability to "distort a song into a reel, jig, or country dance." Johnson also composed music, including the "Recognition March on the Independence of Hayti" in 1825. In 1838, Frank Johnson would receive a singular recognition when he gave a command performance before Queen Victoria at Buckingham Palace. For his performance, Johnson was awarded a silver bugle.

• *Miscellaneous State Laws:* The Rhode Island legislature appointed a commission of three men to investigate conditions of ex-slaves who had fought in the Revolutionary War and were now unable to support themselves.

• Kentucky was admitted to the United States as a slave state. However, the Kentucky Constitution did not specifically deny suffrage to emancipated African Americans.

• In South Carolina, the importation of slaves was prohibited until 1795.

• *Miscellaneous Publications:* From this year to 1802, Benjamin Banneker annually published an almanac for Maryland and neighboring states.

• *The Black Church:* Construction began on the first African Baptist church in Savannah, Georgia. Under the leadership of Andrew Bryan, the church would be completed in 1794 and become the first structure erected for the sole purpose of facilitating African American worship. Andrew Bryan (1737–1812) was another example of a slave who refused to give up his mission in spite of whippings and imprisonment.

• Joshua Bishop, a slave, became pastor of the First Baptist Church in Portsmouth, Virginia. The First Baptist Church was a church with a European American and African American congregation. Bishop's congregation is notable because it purchased Bishop's freedom and that of his family.

• *The Arts:* The play *Yorker's Strategem* concerning the story of a comic Yankee who marries a West Indian mulatto woman and the problems created by the union was published.

THE AMERICAS

• Jamaican law required owners to care for disabled slaves. Regulations regarding minimal allotments of food and clothing had already been passed.

• In Haiti, the French authorities, in an effort to entice slaves to fight for them, issued a decree which granted freedom to all slaves who joined the French army.

• On April 4, 1792, the Legislative Assembly of France authorized all free persons of African descent the right to vote in electoral assemblies and to hold public office.

• Fifteen vessels sailed with about 1200 persons of African descent from Nova Scotia (Canada). An African American, Thomas Peters, who had served as a sergeant under Sir Henry Clinton in the British army during the Revolutionary War, went to England seeking an allotment of land for his fellow African American British sympathizers. The Sierra Leone Company welcomed Peters and offered free passage and land in Sierra Leone to the African people of Nova Scotia.

AFRICA

• A company of 1,190 freed slaves (including the preacher David George) brought from Nova Scotia (Canada) by Lieutenant John Clarkson arrived in Sierra Leone. In Sierra Leone, they helped to establish Freetown. *See 1783.*

• The Oyo Empire reached its apex.

• "Patriots" took control of Bourbon and Ile de France (Reunion and Mauritius).

EUROPE

• In England, two notable publications appeared in 1792. In *Trial of Captain John Kimber, for the murder of a Negro girl, on board the ship Recovery,* the trial record of the murder of a slave girl by suspending her by the legs and arms, and flogging her in a most cruel and barbarous manner was published. In *No Rum! No Sugar! or, The Voice of Blood*: a conversation between an African and Englishman was related in which the horrible nature of the slave trade was described and a method of terminating the practice was discussed.

• George Bridgetower, the famed violinist, performed in a concert organized by Barthelemon. *See 1779.*

• Desiring to take a more active role in the ongoing Revolution, Joseph Boulogne (the Chevalier de) Saint-Georges, the noted Afro-French violinist and composer, organized a corps of light troops in late summer 1792. The light troops was comprised of 1000 Afro-French and African troops, including the mulatto Alexandre Dumas. Known as the Legion National du Midi, the corps had little military success. Saint-Georges was relieved of his command and subsequently jailed for eighteen months in a house at Houdainville. Upon his release, Saint-Georges was forbidden to live in the vicinity of his former comrades. *See 1739.*

RELATED HISTORICAL EVENTS

• In 1792, some 499 petitions were presented to the British Parliament protesting against slavery.

• Denmark abolished slavery and the slave trade in her dominions after 1802.

• The French royalty was abolished and the first French Republic was formed.

—————— 1 7 9 3 ——————

THE UNITED STATES

The first fugitive slave law (The Fugitive Slave Act) was enacted by Congress, making it a criminal offense to protect an escaped slave. The Federal Fugitive Law, which was designed to provide for the extradition of criminals, became known as the Fugitive Slave Law because it also allowed a slave holder to seize an escaped slave in another state, take the slave before a magistrate and acquire the authority to take the escaped slave back into captivity in the slave holders home state. The act made it a crime to harbor an escaped slave or to prevent his or her capture (February 12).

• Militia appeals for arms to avert rumored and actual slave uprisings reached the governor of Virginia in August, September, and November. Officials of Richmond,

Elizabeth City, and Powhatan sent such requests and prepared themselves for uprisings.

• In a presidential ordinance of April 7, John Adams approved organizing the Mississippi Territory, then belonging to Georgia but which now makes up the states of Alabama and Mississippi. The ordinance exempted the Mississippi Territory from the antislavery clause of the Northwestern Territories by using the following words: "Exempting and Excluding the last article of the Ordinance of 1787."

• Dr. Benjamin Rush of Philadelphia sought the aid of the African American residents of the city to administer medicines and care for the sick during the yellow fever epidemic. At the time, it was believed that African Americans were immune from the disease.

• In November, slaves set several fires in Albany, New York, that caused damages totaling a quarter of a million dollars. For this act of rebellion, three men and two women were executed early in 1794.

• Eli Whitney sought a patent for the cotton gin (March 14).

In 1793, Eli Whitney invented the cotton gin. The invention of the cotton gin increased the productivity of cotton plantations and increased the demand for slave labor on those plantations, thereby strengthening slavery as an institution. The cotton gin enabled the Southern plantation owner to mechanically separate the cotton fiber from the seed and export a great deal more than he had previously been able to do. The invention helped to economically bolster the Southern economy, and thereby perpetuated the institution of slavery in the South

• *Miscellaneous State Laws:* In Virginia, a law was passed which forbade emancipated African Americans from entering the state.

• Emancipated African Americans in South Carolina protested against the state poll tax. The December, 1793, a petition was signed by 23 emancipated African American men and women from Camden. This petition was accompanied by supportive signatures of European American neighbors.

• In Georgia, the importation of free African Americans was prohibited.

• *Publications:* "A Plan for a Peace Office" was placed prominently in the 1793 Almanac published by Benjamin Banneker. The "Plan" proposed the establishment of a Department of Peace in the national administration to offset the existing Department of War. *See 1731.*

THE AMERICAS

• The legislature of Upper Canada authorized the gradual emancipation of African slaves within Canada.

• In 1793, there were 6,000 Africans and nearly a half million Afro-mestizos reported in Mexico.

• In Haiti, the slaves in the northern provinces were proclaimed free.

While the emancipation of the slaves of Haiti was proclaimed and confirmed in 1793, nevertheless, in 1801, Napoleon Bonaparte would reestablish slavery in Haiti.

AFRICA

• The practice of slavery was suppressed in Senegal.

• Additional American ships were seized by Algiers.

• James Watt and Matthew Winterbottom began exploring West Africa.

RELATED HISTORICAL EVENTS

• Louis XVI, the former king of France, was guillotined (January 21). Marie Antoinette would soon follow (October 16).

1794

THE UNITED STATES

Congress passed a law forbidding the slave trade to foreign ports and forbidding the outfitting of foreign slave-trade vessels in United States ports. The purpose was to avoid spreading the Haitian Revolution to African American slaves (March 22).

• New Englander Eli Whitney received a patent for the cotton gin, a cyclinder with circular saws and bristles that stripped the seeds from the cotton (March 14). This invention would lead to the increased production of cotton in the South and contribute to the perpetuation of slavery for another seventy years.

• The mayor of Philadelphia, Matthew Clarkson, praised African Americans Absalom Jones and Richard Allen, who had organized African Americans in the city during the previous year (1793) in an effort to fight the yellow fever epidemic. The African Americans of Philadelphia had been used primarily to take care of the sick and to bury the dead.

In 1794, George Washington wrote in a letter to Alexander Spotswood: "Were it not then, that I am principled against selling *African*

Americans, as you would cattle at a market, I would not in twelve months from this date, be possessed of one as a slave. I shall be happily mistaken if they are not found to be a very troublesome species of property ere many years pass over our heads."

• *The Abolition Movement:* The American Convention of Abolition Societies was formed in Philadelphia by delegates from nine societies. Delegates came from Rhode Island, Connecticut, New York, New Jersey, Pennsylvania, Delaware, Maryland, and Virginia.

In a petition to state legislatures, the American Convention of Abolition Societies condemned not only slavery and the slave trade, but also the legal restrictions on emancipated African Americans: "Of what use is his hard-earned property, if the law does not spread its defence around him? ... how is his liberty secured, if he loses little more than the name of a slave? Donations so ineffectual, and benevolence so incomplete, can only excite dissatisfaction, and suppress industry. To acquire an useful member of the community, we should hold up to his view a participation in its privileges. We promote industry by rewarding it, and encourage knowledge, by rendering it the means of perceiving happiness."

• *Miscellaneous State Laws:* North Carolina passed a law forbidding the further importation of slaves.

• In Kentucky, the importation of slaves, except for personal use, was prohibited.

• *Publications:* In 1794, *A Narrative of the Proceedings of the Black People during the Late Awful Calamity in Philadelphia; and a Refutation of Some Censures Thrown upon them in Some Late Publications* was published by Richard Allen and Absalom Jones. The calamity referred to in the publication was yellow fever which had been epidemic in Philadelphia. *See above.*

• *The Black Church:* Richard Allen organized Bethel Church, an African Methodist Episcopal Church, in Philadelphia (June 10).

• St. Thomas Church, in Philadelphia, the first African American Episcopal congregation, was dedicated on July 17. Absalom Jones was ordained as the first deacon and, subsequently, became the pastor of St. Thomas.

• The African Zoar Church was organized as a mission church in Philadelphia. This church was comprised of African Americans who decided to remain affiliated with the European American Methodist Episcopal Church.

THE UNITED STATES

Between 1795 and 1804, 1099 ships left Liverpool with a total of 323,770 slaves; 155 ships left London with 46,505 slaves, and 29 left Bristol with 10,718 slaves. All these British ships were bound for the United States and the West Indies. The merchants of Liverpool made large profits from these voyages. The *Lottery* made 11,039 pounds (British currency) from 305 slaves sold in Jamaica; the *Enterprise* made 6,428 pounds on 392 slaves sold in Cuba; and the *Fortune* made 1,847 pounds on 343 slaves.

• Slaves in Point Coupee Parish, Louisiana, planned a rebellion. The conspirators' lack of cooperation and inability to decide when to actually start the rebellion led to its disclosure. Militia units of the parish government were immediately pressed into service to apprehend the insurgents. Some of the slaves resisted capture, and in the ensuing struggle about 25 slaves were killed. Another 25 were executed and the bodies of several of the slaves were left hanging in various parts of the parish. A number of Europeans, probably three, were implicated in this effort and were banished from the colony. Another conspiracy was reported in the same year in St. Landry Parish, Louisiana.

• Jeremy Belknap, one of the founders of the Massachusetts Historical Society and an abolitionist, wrote to Judge Tucker in Virginia: "The winter here was always unfavorable to the African constitution. For this reason European laborers were preferred to blacks." Belknap also wrote in 1795 that the European working man's opposition to slavery had much to do with abolishing slavery in the New England States.

• When one of George Washington's slaves ran away, Washington advertised for his return, but did not allow his name to appear in the advertisement north of Virginia.

• In November, fires that swept through Charleston, South Carolina, were suspected of being set by slaves.

In 1795, John Adams wrote: "I have through my whole life, held the practice of slavery in such abhorrence, that I have never owned [*an African*] or any other slave, though I have lived for many years in times when the practice was not disgraceful; when the best men in my vicinity thought it not inconsistent with their character, and when it has cost me thousands of dollars for the labor and sustenance of free men, which I might have saved by the purchase

• Sunday catechism classes were conducted for African Americans in Baltimore, Maryland. Maryland and Louisiana are historically the two areas of the United States with a substantial population of African American Catholics.

THE AMERICAS

• Jose de Bolonha, a Capuchin friar, was expelled from Bahia, Brazil, for questioning the legality of African slavery.
• There were slave revolts in Cuba and Dominica.
• The French National Assembly abolished slavery in the French colonies.
• In 1794, the approximate population of Haiti was 40,000 Europeans, 28,000 emancipated persons of African descent and 500,000 slaves of African descent.

Toussaint l'Ouverture, a leader of the Haitian Revolution against the French, attained a high rank in the Spanish army. L'Ouverture commanded 4,000 troops. L'Ouverture deserted the Spanish in April of 1794, and his defection led to the surrender of the Spanish garrisons in Santo Domingo.

L'Ouverture along with Jean-Jacques Dessalines and Henri Christophe were the principal leaders of both the revolt and the subsequent government of Haiti. The government established by L'Ouverture was the first independent government of African peoples outside of Africa. During his tenure, Toussaint l'Ouverture issued a constitution which abolished slavery.

AFRICA

• The French residents of Ile de France (Mauritius) ignored the decree of the French National Assembly.

EUROPE

• George Bridgetower, the famed violinist, performed in a concert organized by Barthelemon in London. *See 1779.*

RELATED HISTORICAL EVENTS

• The French National Assembly proclaimed all slaves to be free and ordered the immediate abolition of slavery in the French colonies without compensation to the slave owners.
• In 1794, the English wrested the Caribbean islands of Martinique, St. Lucia, and Guadaloupe from French control.

of [*Africans*] at times when they were very cheap.

• *The Abolition Movement:* The Education Committee of the Pennsylvania Abolition Society asked the Pennsylvania Legislature to provide free schools without discrimination of color and to establish in large towns special schools for African Americans.

The American Convention of Abolition Societies in its *Memorial to Free Africans and other free people of color* instructed them "to act worthily of the rank you have acquired," "to do credit to yourselves, and to justify the friends and advocates of your color in the eyes of the world." The convention suggested: "a regular attention to the important duty of public worship;" learning to read, write and do arithmetic; "useful trades" for the children; frugality and simplicity of dress and manner; temperance and avoidance of "frolicking, and amusements which lead to expense and idleness;" "civil and respectful" behavior "to prevent contention and remove every just occasion of complaint."

• *The Colonization Movement:* In 1795, the Free African Society of Newport, Rhode Island, sent out a party of African Americans to the west coast of Africa to explore the possibilities of establishing a colony for free African Americans.

• *Scholastic Achievements:* Amos Fortune founded the Jaffrey Social Library. Fortune was brought to the United States from Africa as a slave. In 1770, Fortune purchased his emancipation when he was 60 years old. Fortune lived in Woburn, Massachusetts, and then in Jaffrey, New Hampshire, where he set himself up in the tanning business and became one of the town's leading citizens.

• *The Black Church:* The Episcopal Convention voted that St. Thomas African Episcopal Church could not participate in the sect's annual meeting and, therefore, could not send a clergyman or deputies to the Annual Meeting of the Pennsylvania Diocese. *See 1794.*

• *The Arts:* In James Murdock's *The Triumph of Love*, an African American played a role which was refreshingly not a stereotypical comic servant. In the play the role was a secondary romantic character.

THE AMERICAS

• Jose Saldanha, an Afro-Brazilian poet, was born.

Jose Saldanha (1795–1830), a Brazilian romantic poet, was born in Recife, the son of a priest and an African woman. Saldanha's verse was, for the most part, free of references to persons of African descent. One of the few exceptions was his *Ode to Henrique Dias,* a poem in honor of the great Afro-Brazilian captain who defeated the Dutch. *See 1605.* In *Ode to Henrique Dias,* the stereotype of the noble African or the equivalent of Chateaubriand's "Noble Savage," was created for subsequent Brazilian writers.

In a few of his short poems, Saldanha did make reference to the discrimination he suffered while in the United States and Venezuela.

• In 1795, a census of the Spanish colonies in the Americas revealed that out of Venezuela's population of 1,000,000, 72,000 were slaves of African descent. In Paraguay, approximately 2% of the population was of African origin. In Chile's population of 500,000, 30,000 were persons of African descent. Peru had 100,000 persons of African descent; Ecuador had 50,000 and Colombia 210,000.

• In Buenos Aires (Argentina), a conspiracy of Frenchmen and Africans to free all the slaves and Indigenous Argentinians, and then to redistribute the land, was conceived. The Frenchmen and Africans essentially went on strike in an attempt to secure their demands.

• In Haiti, Toussaint L'Ouverture won his first battle.

• There was a slave revolt in Jamaica.

In Jamaica, maroons rebelled and tried to incite a general slave insurrection. For a time, the maroons successfully outfought the British forces, essentially using guerrilla tactics. However, the British soon brought in bloodhounds to track the maroons down.

The maroons eventually offered to surrender but only under the express condition that none of the maroons would be deported from the island, as the legislature of Jamaica had decreed. General Walpole, the commander of the British forces on Jamaica, at first resisted the conditional surrender. But after an assessment of the military situation, Walpole concluded that peace could be obtained on no other terms and agreed to the conditional surrender tendered by the maroons.

The maroons surrendered and handed in their guns to the British. Immediately after the surrender had been effected and the guns turned in, the British forcibly seized 600 of the maroon leaders and shipped them to Nova Scotia, Canada.

The colonial legislature subsequently voted to award a sword worth 1000 pounds to General Walpole. However, Walpole was an honorable man who was appalled at the dishonor associated with the treatment of the Jamaican rebels. Walpole indignantly refused to accept the award.

Eventually, the maroons of Jamaica who had been taken to Nova Scotia would be taken to Sierra Leone.

AFRICA

• Great Britain took possession of the Cape of Good Hope, ending the reign of the Dutch in South Africa.

In 1795, there were 16,000 persons of European descent at the Cape colony. There were also 17,000 slaves of various nationalities and an unknown number of Khoikhoi and other Indigenous South Africans.

By 1795, the Napoleonic Wars were just beginning in Europe and the European powers were endeavoring to consolidate spheres of influence and trading routes. The British fleet which seized the Cape colony was composed of nine British warships.

In 1795, the Khoikhoi were essentially considered to be freemen. Much like the Indigenous Americans, the Khoikhoi were poorly suited to serve as slaves because of their susceptibility to European diseases. Also, like their Indigenous American counterparts, the Khoikhoi tribal system had been disrupted by the European presence and most of the Khoikhoi lands had been usurped by the Europeans.

• Mungo Park explored Segu and the river Niger.

Mungo Park (1771-1806) was a British explorer, born in Foulshiels, Selkirk, Scotland. In 1795, Park went to Africa to explore the Niger River. Upon arriving in what today is known as Gambia, Park traveled some 300 kilometers (200 miles) up the Gambia to the trading station of Pisania (today known as Karantaba). From there he traveled east into what was then unexplored territory. While exploring the land, Park was captured by a local chief but managed to escape.

In 1796, Park reached the Niger River at the town of Segu (Segou). From there, he traveled downstream as far as Silla before his supplies became exhausted. After his return to Great Britain in 1797, Park published an account of his trip in *Travels in the Interior of Africa*.

In 1805, Park returned to Africa to explore the Niger, from Segu to the mouth of the river, by canoe. During this expedition, Park was attacked at Bussa and drowned. An account of Park's second journey (taken from his journals) was published posthumously in London in 1815.

RELATED HISTORICAL EVENTS

• France acquired the eastern portion of Hispaniola from Spain.

——— 1 7 9 6 ———

THE UNITED STATES

In this year, a Charlotte, North Carolina, grand jury blamed the Quakers for slave unrest and cited as proof the frequency of arson in North Carolina. They also cited the same conditions in Charleston; New York City; Elizabeth, New Jersey; Savannah, Georgia; and Baltimore, Maryland.

• Tennessee was admitted into the Union as a slave state. However, the Tennessee Constitution did not explicitly deny suffrage to emancipated African Americans.
• The Boston African Society was organized in Boston with 44 members. The purpose of the society was to care for sick and impoverished members—particularly women and children.
• *The Civil Rights Movement:* The Philadelphia Yearly Meeting of Quakers resolved that prospective members should be admitted without regard to color.
• *Miscellaneous State Laws:* In Maryland, the importation of slaves was prohibited.
• In South Carolina, the importation of slaves was prohibited until the year 1799.
• *The Black Church:* James Varick and other African American Methodists secured permission to hold separate meetings. Out of these separate meetings, the Zion Methodist Church of New York City was born.
• Peter Williams, Sr., a former slave and sexton of the John Street Methodist Church, organized the African Chapel for Methodists in a cabinetmaker's shop owned by William Miller, a fellow member of John Street Methodist Church. Services were held in the cabinetmaker's shop until 1800 when the church known as the African Methodist Episcopal Zion Church was completed.

THE AMERICAS

• Jamaicans of African descent were allowed to testify against Europeans.
• In St. Lucia, there was a slave revolt

against the British. The revolt was ended when the British convinced the slaves that if they laid down their arms, they would be set free.

AFRICA

• Mungo Park, sailing under the patronage of the English African Society, explored the river Niger at Segu.
• The United States entered into treaties with Tunis and Tripoli.

From the 1500s through the 1800s, the north coast of Africa was occupied by several independent Muslim states and polities under the sovereignty of the Ottoman Turks. Beginning in the 1500s, these states—the Barbary states—were centers for pirates who preyed upon the commerce of European nations in the Mediterranean Sea and the Atlantic Ocean.

After the American Revolutionary War, the Barbary pirates began to disrupt the shipping of the United States. Following the example set by the European nations, the United States at first entered into treaties with the Barbary pirates which paid tribute to the pirates in exchange for immunity from their attacks.

However, these treaties were not long lasting. Tripoli and Algiers broke the treaties and war ensued. American naval action against Tripoli (1801–1805) and Algiers (1815) led by the American naval officer Stephen Decatur was instrumental in ending the piracy.

RELATED HISTORICAL EVENTS

• Napoleon Bonaparte was nominated to command the French army in Italy.
• The Dutch established a settlement in Guiana.

1797

THE UNITED STATES

In 1797, George Washington wrote to his nephew Laurence Washington: "I wish from my soul that the legislature of this state could see the policy of gradual abolition of slavery. It might prevent much future mischief."

In a letter to another nephew Robert Lewis, Washington said, "It is demonstrably clear that on this estate I have more working [*African Americans*] by a full moiety, than can be employed to any advantage in the farming system, and I shall never turn planter thereon. To sell the surplus I cannot, because I am principled against this kind of traffic in the human species.

To hire them out is almost as bad because they could not be disposed of in families to any advantage, and to disperse the families I have an aversion. What then is to be done? Something must, or I shall be ruined; for all the money (in addition to what I raise by crops and rents) that have been received for lands sold within the last four years to the amount of $50,000 has scarcely been able to keep me afloat."

Perhaps in response to his inability to find an economic solution to his peculiar slave problem, in his will, George Washington wrote: "Upon the decease of my wife, it is my will and desire that all slaves whom I hold in my own right shall receive their freedom."

Washington provided for the care of the freed slaves too old to work, and the binding out and education of freed children. He also forbade the sale or transportation out of Virginia of any of his slaves. Washington gave immediate freedom to "my mulatto man, William, calling himself William Lee" and a life annuity of 30 dollars.

Washington's humanitarian gesture at the end of his life, while not compensating for his relative ambivalence on the slavery issue, nevertheless, was of great symbolic usefulness for the growing abolition movement.

• At the meeting of the American Philosophical Society, Benjamin Rush argued that the Moss case provided proof that black skin color was a disease akin to leprosy. Previously, Samuel Stanhope Smith had argued that dark skin color was a phenomenon similar to freckles, and that European people would develop dark skin coloration with sufficient exposure to the sun. Smith illustrated the reverse process with the celebrated case of Henry Moss, a Virginia slave who appeared to have suffered a loss of pigmentation after having moved to the North.
• The Constitution of the Friendly Society of St. Thomas Protestant Episcopal Church in Philadelphia, a church with African American members, made provisions for loans to its members, when funds were available, to purchase land.
• *The Abolition Movement:* Henry Clay, as a young lawyer, urged legislation for the gradual emancipation of slaves upon the Kentucky Legislature, and frequently volunteered as a lawyer for slaves suing for their freedom.
• *The Civil Rights Movement:* The first petition signed by African Americans was submitted to Congress protesting a North

Carolina law requiring African Americans who had been freed by their Quaker owners to be returned to the state and to their slavery status. The petition was signed by four "illegally" manumitted North Carolina African Americans who had fled North to avoid reenslavement. The petition asked for freedom not only for the four petitioners but also asked for "our relief as a people." Congress rejected the petition (January 30).

• *Notable Births:* Sojourner Truth, one of the leading abolitionist figures in American history, was born.

Sojourner Truth (1797–1883), was born a slave in Hurley, New York. Sojourner Truth was born Isabella Baumfree (Bomefree). She lived in New York City after having been freed in 1827 by the New York State Emancipation Act. After receiving a divine revelation in 1843, Isabella Baumfree changed her name to Sojourner Truth and began traveling and speaking for emancipation and women's rights.

During the Civil War, Sojourner Truth helped emancipated slaves who had emigrated to the North and made visits to army camps. After the Civil War, Sojourner Truth lectured and toured, advocating better educational opportunities for African Americans.

• George Moses Horton, an African American poet, was born.

George Moses Horton (1797–1883) was born a slave and lived at Chapel Hill, North Carolina. He worked as a janitor at the University of North Carolina where the college president was his owner. Horton made money writing love poems for the male students; the prices for his poems ranging from 25 cents to 50 cents a lyric, depending upon the warmth desired. His first book of poems, published in 1829, was to raise funds for his manumission. Unfortunately, it was a financial failure.

Horton was well into his 60's when Union soldiers finally freed him. During his literary career prior to liberation, there were only a few general statements against slavery in Horton's poetry, but these were too vague and mild to cause any controversy. However, in his second volume of poems, *Naked Genius*, published after the Civil War, Horton was more outspoken. He lampooned Jefferson Davis' attempt at escape (dressed as a woman), and in one poem, "The Slave," he expressed his true feelings on being a slave.

• *Publications:* An address by Abraham Johnstone was handed out on the morning of his execution and later published in Philadelphia. The address was a protest against slavery and injustice against African Americans.

• *Scholastic Achievements:* After initially failing, Paul Cuffe finally succeeded in building a school house in Massachusetts. The school house was built at his own expense on his own property. However, the school allowed anyone who desired to attend.

THE AMERICAS

• In Montreal, Canada, the last slave was publicly sold.
• In Cuba, Juan Francisco Manzano, the great Cuban poet was born.

Juan Francisco Manzano (1797–1854) was the son of a mestizo slave (Toribio Castro) and Maria del Pilar Manzano, the favorite slave of the Marquesa Justiz de Santa Ana.

At the death of the Marquesa de Santa Ana, Maria and her son Juan became the property of the Marquesa de Prado Amemo. This happened when Juan was twelve years of age. For the next nine years, he would suffer at the hands of the Marquesa de Prado Amemo who treated him badly.

In 1818, Nicolas de Cardenas y Manzano brought Juan to Havana where he began educating himself by using the books in the library of his protector.

Juan soon began to write poetry. His first poems, *Poesias Liricas*, were published with special permission because slaves were not permitted to publish books.

In 1835, Juan married the mestizo pianist Delia. Delia was the inspiration for his classic poem *La Musica* which was published in 1837.

In 1836, Juan was able to secure his freedom. Appearing before a literary group, Juan read "Mis Treinta Anos." The members of the group were so touched by the poem that they decided to purchase Juan's freedom. They collected 850 pesos and gave it to the ever-demanding Marquesa de Prado Amemo.

AFRICA

• In what is today known as South Africa, war broke out between the British colonists and the Xhosa. The British won the engagement and drove the Xhosa back across the Fish River.
• The United States signed a treaty with Algiers. *See* 1796.
• Semakokiro became the kabaka of

Uganda. Under his reign, regular trade with the east coast of Africa was emphasized.

RELATED HISTORICAL EVENTS

• Trinidad was taken by the British from Spain.

---

1 7 9 8

THE UNITED STATES

Fifteen years after the Revolutionary War came to an end, certain military authorities came to the conclusion that the presence of African Americans in the armed forces of the nation was not an advisable policy, especially in light of the revolt in Haiti and the presence of so many enslaved and oppressed African Americans.

On March 16, Secretary of War James Mc-Henry wrote to a marine lieutenant on the frigate *Constellation*, "No [*African American*] or [*Indigenous American was*] to be enlisted, nor any description of men except [*European Americans*] of fair conduct, or foreigners of unequivocal character for sobriety and fidelity."

On August 8, Secretary of the Navy Stoddert prohibited the enlistment of African Americans on men-of-war. Before this edict, men had been recruited without reference to race or color. This order of the Secretary of the Navy appears to have been the first navy restriction against the enlistment of African Americans.

Despite the order of Secretary Stoddert, some African Americans did serve on American ships during engagements with French ships. Among them was William Brown, a "powder monkey" on the *Constellation*. Brown was wounded in an engagement with the French frigate *L'Insurgente*. He was later granted 160 acres of land for his service. Another African American, George Diggs, was a quartermaster on the schooner *Experiment*.

The secretaries of war and navy also prohibited African American enlistments in the Marine Corps.

• Just after cotton became profitable, $200 was a good price for a field hand. By 1822, the average value of a slave was reported to be $300, and in 1830, $600. In 1840, superior cotton pickers were worth $1,000 or more, and in 1859, at Savannah, Georgia, a female slave sold for $1,100 and a male slave sold for as high as $1,300.

• Thaddeus Kosciusko, a Revolutionary War hero from Poland, left a will providing for the education of African Americans (May 5).

• *Notable Births*: James P. Beckwourth, a famous African American scout and explorer, was born.

James P. Beckwourth (1798–1867), a scout for General John Fremont and noted explorer of the West, was born in Virginia to a slave woman of African descent and a European American slave holder. Beckwourth's father was an officer in the Revolutionary Army. In the early years of the 19th century, the Beckwourths (who had 13 children) relocated to a settlement near what is the present-day city of St. Louis, Missouri. In 1816, James Beckwourth, who had been apprenticed to a blacksmith, ran away to New Orleans. Once in New Orleans, Beckwourth soon found that there was no work so in desperation Beckwourth signed up as a scout for General Henry Ashley's Rocky Mountain expedition.

Beckwourth discovered that he liked the nomadic life of a expeditionary scout. As a scout, Beckwourth was independent—he was his own man. Like a number of his fellow African Americans, one of the prime motives for Beckwourth's nomadic existence was an unwillingness to accept the role assigned to African American males in Euro-centric American society.

During the 1820s and 1830s, the heyday of the mountain men and the fur trade, Beckwourth became a legendary figure. Like his friends Jim Bridger and Kit Carson, Beckwourth was one of the great scouts, hunters and "Indian fighters" of his time. During the Second Seminole War of 1835, Beckwourth served as a scout for the United States Army in its struggle against the Seminoles. Later when Beckwourth moved to the West, he endeared himself with the Indigenous Americans of the region. The Indigenous Americans respected him so highly that he was accepted into their tribes, first by the Blackfeet and later the Crows. Among the Crows, Beckwourth was an honorary chief.

In 1848, Beckwourth became the chief scout for John C. Fremont's exploring expedition in the Rockies.

In 1851, Beckwourth discovered a pass between the Feather and Truckee Rivers in California which provided a gateway through the Sierra Nevadas. The pass was named the Beckwourth Pass in his honor.

Beckwourth Pass over the Sierra Nevadas

was discovered in 1851 by James Beckwourth, trapper, scout, and honorary chief of the Crow Indians. Beckwourth discovered the pass while on a prospecting expedition as he and his party crossed the mountains from the American River valley to the Pit River valley. The Beckwourth Pass, at 5,212 feet, is the lowest pass over the summit of the Sierras. The Beckwourth Pass is about two miles east of Chilcoot, California. Fifteen miles to the west of the pass is the town of Beckwourth, a town named in honor of James Beckwourth.

After discovering the pass, Beckwourth proposed to the residents of Bidwell Bar and Marysville that a wagon road be made through this pass, across the Sierra Valley to the Middle Fork of the Feather River, and down the ridge east of the river past Bidwell Bar to Marysville. The citizens of Bidwell Bar and Marysville eventually adopted Beckwourth's plan and a trail was constructed.

Soon after completion of the trail, Beckwourth, while at Truckee in the Sierra Nevada, persuaded a passing emigrant train to try the new pass. The party liked the pass and spread the word of the relatively easy crossing. Others soon followed in their footsteps. Beckwourth Pass soon became a well-beaten trail.

The popularity of Beckwourth Pass, led Beckwourth to build a cabin (the first house in the Sierra Valley) on the pass route. This cabin served as a trading post and a hotel for the passersby. The cabin stood on a hillside two and a half miles west of what is today the town of Beckwourth. Beckwourth soon built a second cabin near to the first. Both of these cabins were eventually burned down by the local Indigenous Americans. However, undaunted, Beckwourth built a third cabin—a cabin which is today maintained as a historical landmark by the State of California.

A year after the discovery of Beckwourth Pass, an emigrant train of ox-drawn schooners from St. Louis, Missouri, came through the pass carrying an eleven year old child named Ina Coolbrith. Coolbrith was destined to become California's first poet laureate and her passage through Beckwourth Pass was an event which she was never to forget.

At a luncheon given in her honor in San Francisco, California, on April 24, 1927—some seventy-five years after going through the pass—Coolbrith recalled: "Ours was the first of the covered wagon trains to break the trail through Beckwourth Pass into California. We were guided by the famous scout, Jim Beckwourth, who was a historical figure, and to my mind one of the most beautiful creatures that ever lived. He was rather dark and wore his hair in two long braids, twisted with colored cord that gave him a picturesque appearance. He wore a leather coat and moccasins and rode a horse without a saddle.

"When we made that long journey toward the West over the deserts and mountains, our wagon train was driven over ground without a single mark of a wagon wheel until it was broken by ours. And when Jim Beckwourth said he would like to have my mother's little girls ride into California on his horse in front of him, I was the happiest little girl in the world.

"After two or three days of heavy riding we came at last in sight of California and there on the boundary line he stopped, and pointing forward, said: 'Here is California, little girls, here is your kingdom.'"

• *Miscellaneous State Laws:* Georgia's Constitution made the penalty for killing or maiming a slave the same as for killing or maiming a European American. However, in practice the penalty was seldom equally applied.
• The importation of slaves from Africa or any foreign place into the State of Georgia was prohibited.
• The slave trade was prohibited in New Jersey.
• The importation of slaves into Mississippi was prohibited.
• *Publications: A Narrative of the Life and Adventures of Venture, a Native of Africa, but Resident About Sixty Years in the United States of America* was published by Venture (Broteer Smith?).

In his narrative, Venture (1729–1805) recalled his royal descent in Africa; his slavery in Connecticut and Long Island, New York; and his relative prosperity after he was able to purchase his freedom at the age of 46.

• *Scholastic Achievements:* The New York delegates reported to the American Convention of Abolition Societies that in Queen's County, Long Island, "the education of children of color in the same school with [*Euro-American*] children . . . has produced great benefit to the community."
Prince (Primus?) Hall, an African American, ran a school for African Americans in his Boston home. A European American teacher taught the African American pupils

in the Boston school which was funded by African Americans.

• *The Arts:* The first advertisement by Joshua Johnston, a portrait artist of African descent, appeared in the *Baltimore Intelligencer* (December 19).

Joshua Johnston (1765–1830) achieved recognition as a portrait painter. Born a slave, Johnston lived and worked in the Baltimore, Maryland, area. Very adept at painting portraits, Johnston soon established a reputation for such in and about Baltimore.

• *Black Enterprise:* John C. Stanley was freed by a legislative act. He became a prosperous barber who invested heavily in plantations and bought and freed many African Americans. He was one of the wealthiest men in Craven County, North Carolina, and was reported at one time to be worth over $40,000.

• James Forten, Sr., established a sail making shop in Philadelphia and invented a sail handling device. *See 1766.*

THE AMERICAS

• In 1798, half of the population of Brazil was composed of persons of African descent, with 400,000 emancipated and 1,350,000 as slaves.

There was a rebellion of Afro-Brazilians in Bahia.

• On Santo Domingo (Haiti), while the slave population was estimated in 1798 at 450,000 people, the number of slaves that had been imported in the previous 100 years amounted to an estimated 1,000,000 people. The death rate was abnormally high in Santo Domingo (Haiti).

On October 1, 1798, Toussaint L'Ouverture entered Mole St. Nicholas as the conqueror. The European troops saluted him. Toussaint was feted in the public square and dined in the square using silverware which was afterward presented to him in the name of the king of England. A treaty was signed by which England agreed to give up its claims to the island, to recognize Haiti as independent, and to become a trading partner with the new government of Haiti. The English also tried to entice Toussaint into declaring himself the "King of Haiti." Toussaint refused.

AFRICA

• Sayyid Said of Oman signed a treaty of trade and friendship with the British East India Company by which Said made the British his ally.

• The French forces under Napoleon Bonaparte captured Alexandria, Egypt (July 1–3). After the Battle of the Pyramids, Bonaparte seized Cairo (July 21). However, the French Egyptian foray would be curtailed by the destruction of the French fleet by the British under Admiral Nelson at Aboukir Bay (August 1).

Napoleon's Egyptian foray was an attempt to strike at British trade with the East. He succeeded in conquering Egypt, but the defeat of his navy left him stranded.

While in Egypt, Napoleon reformed the Egyptian government and law, abolished serfdom and feudalism, and guaranteed basic civil rights. The French scholars who accompanied him began a scientific study of ancient Egyptian history—a study which would eventually lead to the deciphering of the Rosetta stone, the key text to the written language of Ancient Egypt.

In 1799, Napoleon would abandon Egypt because of a need to save France.

• Francisco Lacerda's expedition across Africa began.

EUROPE

• Osifekunde of Ijebu was born.

Osifekunde was born in Warri. In 1820, he was enslaved and shipped to Brazil. He would spend the next twenty years in Brazil.

Around 1840, Osifekunde went to France with his owner. Osifekunde subsequently lived in Paris employed as a servant.

In Paris, Osifekunde met Marie Armand Pascal d'Avezac-Macaya, who was, at that time, the vice-president of the Société Ethnologique of Paris and a member of numerous geographical societies and associations with interests in Africa and the Orient. D'Avezac realized that Joaquin (as Osifekunde was known in France) came from a kingdom which had been identified on maps of the seventeenth and eighteenth centuries but which Europeans knew very little about. D'Avezac interrogated Osifekunde for weeks concerning aspects of his homeland and his native language.

D'Avezac eventually arranged for Osifekunde to return to Africa. However, Osifekunde refused the offer. Osifekunde preferred to remain in servitude under his former owner in Brazil where he could be with his son. Upon his return to Brazil, Osifekunde retreated from the light of history.

RELATED HISTORICAL EVENTS

• Levi Coffin, organizer of the underground railroad, was born (October 28).

1799

THE UNITED STATES

George Washington died leaving a will which freed his slaves upon the death of his wife Martha. Washington's will provided that "Upon the decease of my wife, it is my will and desire that all slaves whom I hold in my own right shall receive their freedom."

Washington's will also provided for the care of the freed slaves too old to work, and the binding out and education of freed children. Washington also prohibited the sale or transportation out of Virginia of any of his slaves. Additionally, Washington gave immediate freedom to "my mulatto man, William, calling himself William Lee" and a life annuity of $30 to Lee.

• African Americans started fires in Fredericksburg and Richmond, Virginia.

• A group of African American slaves in Southampton County, Virginia, slew two European Americans who were transporting them. As an act of reprisal four to ten slaves were executed in retribution.

• *The Abolition Movement:* Absalom Jones led seventy-three others to address a petition to the legislature of Pennsylvania requesting the immediate abolition of slavery. Jones' group also petitioned Congress to repeal the fugitive slave law and emancipate all African Americans. This latter petition created an uproar in the House of Representatives. It was charged that the petition was instigated by the Haitian revolutionaries and Jones' contingent were censured for the more inflammatory (liberating) portions of the petition.

• Gradual emancipation began in New York and New Jersey.

• *Notable Births:* John Brown Russwurm, the first superintendent of schools in Liberia and governor of the African colony of Maryland, was born.

John Brown Russwurm (1799–1851) was born in Port Antonio, Jamaica, of a European American father and a mother with African lineage. Russwurm attended school in Canada and was graduated from Bowdoin College in Maine in 1826.

After graduation from college, Russwurm settled in New York City and established a newspaper, *Freedom's Journal*. In 1829, Russwurm emigrated to Liberia, and from 1830 to 1834 he was colonial secretary and edited and published the *Liberian Herald*. In 1836, he was appointed Governor of Maryland Colony. Russwurm was instrumental in uniting the Maryland colony and Liberia.

• *Miscellaneous State Laws:* New York passed a gradual emancipation law.

• *The Black Church:* James Varick's independent African American Methodist congregation organized as a church in New York.

• Richard Allen was ordained a deacon of the African Methodist Episcopal Church. *See 1760.*

• *The Arts and Sciences:* A young German musician, Gottlieb Graupner, who arrived in South Carolina in 1795, blackened his face and sang African American songs he had heard in Charleston. He billed himself as "The Gay Negro Boy" in the Federal Street Theatre in Boston. This was the first minstrel performance on record. Graupner later organized the Boston Philharmonic Society.

THE AMERICAS

• By 1799, 141,391 persons of African descent had come to Cuba as slaves.

AFRICA

• Napoleon Bonaparte defeated the Turks at Aboukir (Egypt) (July 24). However, on August 22, Bonaparte secretly abandoned Egypt for France, leaving Kleber in command. *See 1798.*

• A commercial treaty was executed between Morocco and Spain.

• The United States defaulted on its tribute payments to the Barbary states of Algiers, Tripoli, and Tunis. *See 1796.*

EUROPE

• Alexander Pushkin, a Russian poet of African descent, was born in Moscow.

Alexander Pushkin (1799–1837) is considered by most authorities to be Russia's greatest poet. Pushkin is best known for his long narrative poems. However, he is also known for the many beautiful short lyric poems, plays in verse, and prose short stories that he wrote. Several of his works inspired ballets and operas by some of Russia's greatest composers.

Alexander Sergeyevich Pushkin was born in Moscow on June 6, 1799. One of his great-grandfathers was an Abyssinian (an Ethiopian) courtier to the Russian czar Peter the Great. Pushkin took great pride in his African ancestry and noble heritage. Pushkin was the son of Sergei Lvovich Pushkin, a retired army officer and his wife, Nadezhda Osipovna (nee Hannibal). On his father's side the family lineage can be traced to the fifteenth century when the Pushkins were among the noblest families in Russia. However, gradually the family lost its wealth and its influence to the point where by the time Pushkin was born the family had been relegated to the position of minor nobility of decidedly lesser importance.

On his mother's side, Pushkin's great-grandfather was Abram Petrovich Hannibal. Abram Petrovich Hannibal was the son of an Abysinnian (Ethiopian) prince. Abram was seized, held as a hostage, and taken to Constantinople by the Turks. While in Constantinople, Abram was later purchased and brought to Russia by Czar Peter the Great. *See 1706.*

Because of his unusual talents, Abram achieved a relatively high position at the Court and in the army. Some biographers of Pushkin profess to see evidence of the Pushkin's African blood in his facial features, in his restless temperament, in his imagination and in his "sense of rhythm."

Pushkin took great pride in his African heritage. His unfinished historical novel *Arap Petra Velikogo* (The Negro of Peter the Great) was to be the story of his great-grandfather.

Pushkin began writing poetry at the age of 12, about the same time that he started his formal education. After completing his studies in 1817, Pushkin took a job in the civil service. However, most of his time was spent participating in the social life of St. Petersburg.

As a child growing up in the Pushkin household, Pushkin encountered domestic turmoil. His happy-go-lucky but egotistical father and his domineering mother often left the moody Alexander to himself. At home French was spoken in the family circle and it was only from servants, his nurse, and occasionally, from his maternal grandmother that Pushkin learned Russian. In 1811, Alexander was accepted at the Lyceum in Tsarskoe Selo, an exclusive government school for young noblemen who were to be educated for civil service and diplomacy.

At the Lyceum, Alexander found in the school a substitute for the domestic turmoil at home and formed a strong attachment to the school and his school friends. The education offered by the Lyceum was remarkably liberal for its time, offering considerable contact with European thought, cultural trends, and tastes. At the Lyceum, Pushkin's poetic talent was almost immediately recognized by his school mates and his teachers. Alexander was only fifteen when his first poem was published in the most influential Russian literary magazine, *Vestnik Europy* (The Messenger of Europe).

In 1817, Pushkin graduated from the Lyceum and received a nominal appointment to the foreign office with the rather insubstantial salary of 700 rubles a year. Pushkin spent the next three years in St. Petersburg, then the capital of Russia. In St. Petersburg, Pushkin led a life of debauchery—a life of little restraint filled with drinking bouts and parties, gambling and duel challenges, and frequent visits to actresses and ladies of the night.

And yet, despite all the distractions, Pushkin was still able to write and to maintain his literary connections and friendships.

Pushkin wrote a number of poems which were critical of the Russian government. These poems caused the czar's secret police to begin monitoring Pushkin's activities. In 1820, he was exiled to southern Russia because of his political poetry.

Pushkin had a tendency to ridicule certain factions in verse. Among his sharp epigrams which circulated in St. Petersburg in manuscript copies were some which unmercifully mocked persons close to the Court. These epigrams along with Pushkin's *Vol'nost* (Ode to Freedom), written in 1817, made for powerful expressions of Pushkin's political liberalism and of his association with suspect groups. These expressions ultimately got Pushkin into serious political difficulty. Only his influential friends were able to save him from exile in Siberia.

In lieu of the Siberian exile, Pushkin was sent to serve in the army corps in southern Russia. Pushkin left St. Petersburg in May of 1820. A short time after his departure, his first major poetic success, *Ruslan i Ludmila* (Ruslan and Ludmila), was published. *Ruslan i Ludmila* was an ironic romance which skillfully and with wit used the forms and conventions of the fairy tale, and which was enthusiastically hailed as a work of considerable maturity of poetic expression.

Pushkin spent most of his exile in the provincial Bessarabian city of Kishinev. He hated

Kishinev. Fortunately, he was able to visit the picturesque Caucasus region—an area of Russia which was at that time inhabited by non–Russian ethnic groups which were largely unaffected by European civilization.

Pushkin's stay in the Caucasus made a deep impression on him and inspired a great deal of his poetry during this time. During this time period, the poet Lord Byron was also influential and traces of Byron can be found in Pushkin's poetry.

Kavkazskii Plennik (The Prisoner of the Caucasus, 1821); *Brat'ia Razboiniki* (The Robber Brothers, 1822); *Bakhchisaraiskii Fontan* (The Fountain of Bakhchisarai, 1823); and *Cygany* (The Gypsies, 1824) are all poems in which the influence of Byron can be found in Pushkin's poetry.

In the particularly poignant tale of *Cygany*, Pushkin tells the story of a young Russian in search of freedom which, when he finds it among the gypsies, he is unwilling to grant to others. This ironic twist occurs because the young Russian is simply unable to overcome the corruptive influence of his civilization.

In 1823, Pushkin's exile became more enjoyable when he was transferred to Odessa, a large city with a strong European influence. Also, by 1823, Pushkin began receiving a modest income from his poetry.

While in Odessa, Pushkin developed a romantic relationship with a married woman. He had an affair with the Countess Elizaveta Vorontsova, the wife of the viceroy.

In 1826, the new czar, Nicholas I, summoned Pushkin to Moscow and gave him a personal pardon. By this time, Pushkin's reputation had been established—he was Russia's leading poet.

After his pardon and for the rest of his all too brief life, Pushkin combined writing with historical research. In 1836, he founded a literary journal called *The Contemporary*.

In 1831, Pushkin married Natalya Goncharo-vea, a famous beauty. His wife had a number of male admirers. His wife's admirers made Pushkin jealous. Pushkin was especially jealous of a certain Baron Georges d'Anthes, a Frenchman living in Russia. In 1837, Pushkin challenged the baron to a duel. Pushkin was wounded in the duel and died two days later.

Pushkin's literary career while short, was prolific and profound. His most famous poem is *Eugene Onegin*. *Eugene Onegin* is a novel in verse form which was written between the years 1825 and 1832. The title character is intelligent, good-hearted, and liberal, but he lacks moral discipline and a serious occupation or purpose in life. As a result, Onegin destroys himself and those around him. Much of *Eugene Onegin* deals with Onegin's romantic relationship with a beautiful country girl named Tatyana. These two characters, the weak Eugene and the sincere, devoted Tatyana, served as models for many characters throughout Russian literature.

Pushkin's drama *Boris Godunov* was written in blank verse in 1825. *Boris Godunov* introduced Shakespearean historical tragedy to the Russian stage. The play tells the story of a czar who is haunted by the guilt over a murder he committed in order to secure the throne.

Pushkin wrote many lyric poems about love, the fear of madness, and the obligation of the poet to lead society to the truth. The most popular of Pushkin's prose stories is "The Queen of Spades" which was written in 1834.

• Joseph Boulogne Saint-Georges, a famous Afro-French violinist and composer, died. *See 1739.*

RELATED HISTORICAL EVENTS

• Napoleon Bonaparte was given command of all the armies of France (November 9) and by the end of the year had become the de facto ruler of France.

1800–1865

In both Africa and the Americas, the 1800s were marked by the push towards the abolition of the African slave trade and slavery itself.

As European nation after European nation came to view slavery as an evil practice, official sanctioning of the slave trade and slavery itself began to vanish. By the middle of the 1800s, Europeans had come to accept that slavery was barbarous and should not be condoned by "civilized" "Christian" nations.

Leading the charge against the slave trade was none other than Great Britain. Having been one of the major benefactors of slavery and the slave trade in the 1700s, it was as though Great Britain went through a great conversion. Not only was slavery abolished within Great Britain itself but in all of its dominions — dominions which at the time were the greatest in the world.

However, Great Britain did not stop there. Britain also took the lead in a vain attempt to curtail the Arab-controlled slave trade of East Africa. Treaty after treaty was negotiated by the British with the Arab chieftains. And when it became evident that the Arab practice could not be negotiated away, the British missionaries descended upon the African continent in an effort to dry up the source by Christianizing the African chiefs who provided the bulk of the slaves.

In many respects, the activities of the British were acts of redemption which, while not totally eliminating the blemish of previous centuries, were certainly of great significance in the march toward the abolition of slavery.

Meanwhile in the Americas, as the Latin American nations strove for independence, the enslavement of the Africans within those nations became a point of contention which could not be ignored. Led by such sympathetic leaders as Simon Bolivar (of Venezuela) and Vincente Guerrero (of Mexico), slavery would be abolished not long after the Latin American nations were themselves made free.

As for the United States, the most painful time in American history would occur as brother fought brother at such places as Antietam, Vicksburg, Gettysburg, and Petersburg. Ostensibly the issue which these brothers fought over was the issue of union versus state's rights. But underlying it all was the issue of slavery and the undeniable corollary issue of whether a nation conceived on the principle *that "all men are created equal" could ignore that principle without suffering a weakening of its own foundations.*

From 1800 to 1865, the great debate on these issues would be waged, first with heated words in the parlor and ultimately with the warm blood that was shed on the battle field.

1 8 0 0

THE UNITED STATES

In 1800, the United States Census reported that there were 1,002,037 African Americans in the United States. This number represented 18.9 percent of the total population (5.3 million). Of the 1,002,037 African Americans, 893,602 were listed as slaves while 108,435 (10.8 percent) were designated as free. Of the 893,602 African Americans designated as slaves, 36,505 were located in the northern states, principally New York and New Jersey. By the year 1800, most northern states had abolished slavery or provided for the gradual emancipation of African American slaves located within their borders.

• The free African Americans of Philadelphia, lead by Reverend Absalom Jones, presented a petition to Congress opposing the slave trade, the Fugitive Slave Act of 1793, and the institution of slavery itself. Representative John Rutledge, Jr., of South Carolina denounced the petition as a result of "this new-fangled French philosophy of liberty and equality." Congress, by a vote of 85 to 1, rejected the petition and issued a statement that such petitions were to receive "no encouragement or countenance" (January 2).

• Gabriel Prosser, age 24, a Virginia slave, was betrayed in his plot to lead thousands of slaves in an attack on the state capitol of Richmond, Virginia. Dozens of slaves, including Gabriel, were hanged while many others were imprisoned (August 30).

Gabriel Prosser (1775?–1800) planned a slave revolt with his wife and two brothers. They organized the slaves outside Richmond, Virginia, and armed them with crude weapons (swords, bayonets and some rifles). Estimates of the number of slaves involved in the preparations vary. The governor of Virginia, James Monroe, wrote that the plans for the revolt "...embraced most of the slaves in this city [Richmond] and the neighborhood." Monroe ventured that there was good cause to believe "that knowledge of such a project pervaded other parts, if not the whole, of the state."

Prosser's objective was to end slavery by seizing Richmond arsenals and executing all the whites in the city except for Frenchmen, Methodists, and Quakers. Prosser planned also to attack other towns and to possibly become the "King of Virginia."

On Saturday, August 30, over one thousand slaves (some armed with scythes, bayonets and a few with some guns) met outside of Richmond, Virginia. The group disbanded, however, when they discovered that a storm the night before had made an essential bridge impassable.

Governor (and future President) James Monroe had heard rumors of a revolt and when two slaves (belonging to Mosby Sheppard) disclosed Prosser's plans, Monroe called on the state militia. Numerous arrests were made. Prosser himself fled, but was captured in Norfolk on September 25.

Gabriel Prosser and between 24 and 35 others were tried and hanged (with compensation paid to their owners for their loss). Governor Monroe, who personally interviewed Prosser, reported: "From what he said to me, he seemed to have made up his mind to die, and to have resolved to say but little of the subject of the conspiracy."

After Prosser's aborted revolt, rumors continued to be circulated (especially in North and South Carolina) concerning slaves plotting uprisings. In November, renewed slave unrest in Virginia resulted in the arrest of dozens of suspected rebels.

Increased agitation among the slave populations increased doubts among slave owners (and Southerners in general) concerning the wisdom of slavery. A resident of Louisiana expressed his opposition to the projected recommencement of the slave trade. He wrote: "The proposed reopening of the slave trade was a project conceived of by foreigners for their own profit; and that, if the planters themselves were consulted, they would raise a terrible clamor against the measure, and would paint a fearful picture of the disorders to which the colony is prey because of insubordination of the slaves."

• James Derham, the first recognized African American doctor, began practicing medicine in New Orleans.

• In 1800, Americans were forbidden to trade in slaves from one country to another or to serve on board any vessel so employed.

• Secretary of State Charles Lee wrote to the governor of Puerto Rico, seeking honorable treatment for an African American, Moses Armstead. Armstead was being held for murder on the high seas after leading a revolt against the crew of a French ship on which he had been held captive as a prisoner of war.

• Denmark Vesey won a lottery and purchased his freedom. Between 1800 and 1822, he worked as a successful carpenter in Charleston, South Carolina.

In 1800, the United States reported exports of cotton exceeded 17 million pounds.

• *Notable Births:* Nat Turner, destined to lead a major slave rebellion, was born a slave in Southhampton County, Virginia (October 2).

Nat Turner (1800–1831), the son of Nancy, a slave, and a native of Africa, was born on the plantation of his mother's owner, Benjamin Turner, in Southampton, Virginia. Turner himself was successively owned by Samuel Turner, Thomas Moore, and Putnam Moore. Turner had been a precocious child and had been given the rudiments of an education by one of his previous owner's sons. He learned not only how to read but he also learned how to make paper, gunpowder, and pottery. As an adult, Turner became an eloquent preacher and he soon was recognized as a leader among the African Americans on the Travis plantation.

In 1830, Nat Turner was hired out to Joseph Travis. Upon arrival on the Travis plantation, Turner became an eloquent preacher and he soon was recognized as a leader among the African Americans on the plantation. At this time, Turner also began to believe that he was chosen to lead his people out of bondage. Turner spent a great deal of time fasting and praying and came to believe that divine voices spoke to him. It was these divine communications which inspired him to plot his rebellion.

With four other slaves, Turner plotted an uprising for July 4, 1831, but abandoned his plans at the last moment. However, on August 21, 1831, Turner, along with seven others, attacked the Travis family and executed them all.

Securing arms and horses and enlisting other slaves, Turner and his band ravaged the surrounding communities. In one day and night, Turner's rebels killed 51 whites.

Turner's revolt collapsed on August 25. Turner went into hiding and eluded the authorities for six weeks. He was eventually discovered, tried and hanged at Jerusalem, the county seat. *See 1831.*

• *Notable Deaths:* Gabriel Prosser *See above.*

• *Miscellaneous State Laws:* A South Carolina law prohibited the importation of persons of African descent from beyond the shores of the United States. The law also prohibited anyone from bringing in over ten slaves from any part of the nation.

• A South Carolina Slave Code provided that all meetings at which slaves were present were to be open—never closed or barred. Slaves were also prohibited from meeting together or assembling for the purpose of mental instruction or religious worship "either before the rising of the sun or after the going down of the same."

• Boston authorities ordered the deportation of 240 African Americans (natives of Rhode Island, New York, Philadelphia and the West Indies) on the basis of a law expelling all African Americans who were not citizens of the state.

• *Scholastic Achievements:* The African American residents of Boston petitioned the city to establish a school for African Americans. When the request was denied, they established the school on their own utilizing the services of two Harvard men as instructors.

• *The Black Church:* African Americans attended camp meetings at Gaspar River and Cane Ridge, Kentucky. These camp meetings were part of the Great Western Revival and was significant because of the inclusion of African Americans with European American worshipers. Such camp meetings led to the conversion of a great many African Americans to the Christian faith.

• Henry Evans, an African American, established the first Methodist Church in Fayetteville, North Carolina. The church included European American members. As the years passed, the number of European Americans increased until the African Americans were ultimately displaced. Even Henry Evans was replaced as minister of the church.

THE AMERICAS

• Between 1800 and 1900, approximately four million African slaves were brought to Latin America. Indeed, between 1800 and 1850, the export of slaves from Mozambique to South America rose over 15,000 to reach 25,000 annually.

• The *Cabildo* of Montevideo (Uruguay) planned to set up a pillory for punishment of those audacious Africans who walked about armed with knives and clubs. The pillory was not erected and Africans continued to plot insurrections. In 1800, slaves were known to kill their owners, and Europeans lived in fear. On one slave a note was found with the inscription "Long live freedom." The possession of this note was sufficient evidence, in the minds of the European authorities, to warrant questioning and torture.

Between 1800 and 1865, Cuba imported 386,437 African slaves.

• In 1800, it is estimated that there were over 776,000 Africans in Spanish America and there were 300,000 persons of African descent on the island of Jamaica alone.

• In 1800, it is estimated that half of the population of Brazil was of African descent.

Between 1800 and 1850, it is estimated that some two million Africans were imported to Brazil as slaves.

AFRICA

• In 1800, the Portuguese slave exports from Mozambique were about 15,000 a year.

• In Freetown (Sierra Leone), 550 maroons from Jamaica arrived. These maroons were former slaves who had been deported to Nova Scotia from their Jamaican homeland in 1796 following a slave rebellion *see 1795*. After staying in the cold of Nova Scotia for a few years, the Jamaicans volunteered to go to Sierra Leone.

• Father Hornemann died after visiting Bilma, Kuka, Katsina, and the Nupe.

• In Egypt, the treaty of El Arish was agreed to between Bonaparte's Kleber and the English under Sir Sidney Smith (January 24). On March 20, following the formal denunciation of the treaty by the British government, fresh hostilities erupted in Egypt. Kleber was able to suppress the rebellion, but after doing so was assassinated (June 14).

RELATED HISTORICAL EVENTS

As the British slave trade declined, those who had participated in the trade experienced consequential economic losses. In Great Britain, Parliament had to loan the West Indian merchants of Liverpool over a million pounds (British currency) because the profit in American slavery and the slave trade was decreasing.

• France purchased the Louisiana Territory from Spain.

• John Brown, the noted abolitionist, was born in Torrington, Connecticut (May 9).

While John Brown (1800–1859) was born in Torrington, Connecticut, he spent his childhood in Ohio. Brown was employed in a number of jobs and initiated several businesses. However, he was not very successful at his work or with his businesses. Brown had two marriages and some 20 children. This prolificacy, coupled with his unsuccessful business ventures, made for an insecure existence for the John Brown family.

As a youth, Brown developed a hatred of slavery. Early on, Brown worked on the Underground Railroad helping slaves escape to Canada.

Brown lived in Springfield, Massachusetts, from 1846 to 1849. In 1849, he moved to North Elba, New York, an area that was settled by African Americans. While in North Elba, Brown organized a mutual protection society among the African Americans to aid in their struggle against the slave catchers. It was in North Elba that Brown's body would be laid to rest.

In 1855, John Brown followed five of his sons to Kansas. The Brown clan settled in Osawatomie and worked to keep Kansas from becoming a slave state. In May 1856, proslavery men attacked and burned the nearby town of Lawrence. Two days later, Brown led an expedition to Pottawotomie Creek, where his men massacred the five proslavery settlers.

A number of small but bloody battles broke out between Free State men and those who wanted slavery. Brown became famous as "Old Osawatomie Brown" after he defended Osawatomie from attack by proslavery men in 1856.

After his "success" in Kansas, Brown began to plan an "invasion" of the South. In 1857, he began to recruit men and to collect arms for the purpose of invading the South. Although he was considered an outlaw by the authorities, Brown received aid and sympathy from many of the antislavery residents of Kansas. Brown's plan called for a raid on the United States arsenal at Harpers Ferry, Virginia (now West Virginia). After taking the arsenal, Brown planned on retreating to the mountains, encouraging slaves to rebel.

On October 17, 1859, Brown and 18 of his followers captured the arsenal at Harpers Ferry, but they failed to escape. The local militia bottled Brown up inside the arsenal. A then Colonel Robert E. Lee forced the fort open on October 18 and captured Brown.

Brown was tried for his crimes. At his trial, Brown conducted himself bravely and intelligently. Northern efforts were made to have him declared insane, but he was convicted on charges of treason. On December 2, 1859, John Brown was hanged.

John Brown's actions may have ended in failure, but his gallantry in the face of death served to inspire other abolitionists and to aggravate the grievances between the North and the South which would lead to Civil War.

Of John Brown, Ralph Waldo Emerson would say that his death would made the gallows "as glorious as a cross" and, during the Civil War, Union soldiers would sing:

John Brown's body lies a-mouldering
  in the grave,
His soul goes marching on.

1801

THE UNITED STATES

In the aftermath of the Prosser incident of 1800, the American Convention of Abolition Societies wrote in its address to the Citizens of the United States that "an amelioration of the present situation of the slaves, and the adoption of a system of gradual emancipation ... would ... be an effectual security against revolt."

In January, Governor James Monroe of Virginia, received more warnings of slave unrest. In anticipation of trouble, on January 7, Monroe ordered 50 pounds of grapeshot and 75 pounds of powder sent to Petersburg, Virginia. On that same day, two slaves of Nottoway County were convicted of conspiring to rebel. They had planned to annihilate whites for, as they saw it, "if the white people were destroyed, they would be free." Both slaves were hanged.

• The Louisiana slave trade was recommenced and flourished.
• *Miscellaneous State Laws:* A South Carolina law was enacted which prohibited anyone from importing more than two slaves from within the United States. The law also

required that all imported slaves were to be used for personal services only.
• In 1801, the slave trade was prohibited in New York.
• *Scholastic Achievements:* A school was held one day a week for African American children in Wilmington, Delaware, by a member of the Abolition Society.
• *The Black Church:* Two African Americans, Peter Williams and Francis Jacobs, obtained a charter for the African Methodist Zion Church in New York.
• James Varick and others incorporated the Zion Church as the African Methodist Episcopal Church in New York.
• Richard Allen compiled a hymnal composed of songs frequently used in African American services. The hymnal was entitled *Collection of Spiritual Songs and Hymns, Selected from Various Authors.*
• In Wilmington, Delaware, African Americans withdrew from Asbury Methodist Church. Under the leadership of Peter Spencer and William Anderson, the African Americans established Ezion Church.
• John Chavis (1763–1838), an African American, was commissioned by the General Assembly of Presbyterians as a missionary to African Americans.

THE AMERICAS

• Toussaint l'Ouverture captured Santo Domingo and became the ruler of the entire island of Hispaniola. In the aftermath of this victory, slavery was abolished on the island.

In the late 1790s, the African slaves led by Toussaint L'Ouverture rebelled against the French slave owners. By 1801, the forces of Toussaint L'Ouverture had conquered both the French and Spanish portions of the island of Hispaniola.

In 1802, France and Spain combined forces to recover their colonies. They succeeded, but only temporarily. In 1803, the Haitians defeated the European powers.

After a series of internecine struggles which divided the island, in 1822 the Haitians once again gained control of the entire island.

In 1844, Juan Pablo Duarte, Francisco del Rosario Sanchez, and Ramon Mella led a successful revolt against the Haitians and established the Dominican Republic.

At the Dominican's request, from 1861 to 1865, Spain governed the country to protect it from the Haitians.

AFRICA

• On March 21, the French were defeated by the British and Turks at Alexandria, Egypt. By September 3, the French would evacuate from Egypt.

• After the French evacuation, the Turkish emissary, Muhammed Ali, arrived in Eygpt with local levies from Kavalla.

Kavalla is a city and port of Macedonia, Greece, which during the early 1800s was part of the Ottoman Empire. Nearby is Philippi, the site of the battle where Mark Antony and Octavian defeated Brutus and Cassius in 42 b.c. and where Saint Paul first preached on the European continent. Philippi is also where Saint Paul wrote his epistle to the Philippians.

• Pursuant to the Treaty of Paris of 1801, Egypt was given back to Turkey as a condition of restoring the diplomatic relations between France and the Ottoman Empire.

• The bey (governor) of Tripoli insisted on the payment of the tributary debt owed by the United States. The United States declined and the Four Years War ensued. *See 1796.*

RELATED HISTORICAL EVENTS

• Upon hearing of the developments in Haiti (Santo Domingo), Napoleon Bonaparte decreed that slavery be reestablished in the French colonies.

On December 14, 1801, General Charles Victor Emmanuel Le Clerc, with a fleet of five squadrons, departed from France to Haiti. His mission was to reconquer the island.

Napoleon could not tolerate "colored" people. In commissioning Le Clerc, Napoleon admonished him: "Remember that blacks are not human beings."

• Thomas Jefferson became president of the United States.

• The Treaty of Saint Ildefonso was executed between France and Spain. Under the terms of the treaty, Spain ceded the lands that came to be known as the Louisiana Territory to France.

---

1 8 0 2

THE UNITED STATES

By 1802, all states north of the Mason-Dixon line had passed antislavery laws or measures for gradual emancipation, except New Jersey. New Jersey passed an antislavery act in 1804.

• In Congress, a bill was introduced to make the Fugitive Slave Law of 1793 more stringent. However, the bill was defeated by a vote of 43 ayes to 46 noes.

• Slave conspiracies were reported in six counties in North Carolina. In May, an outlawed African American, Tom Cooper, was credited with a plot to lead a slave uprising in Elizabeth County, North Carolina. As many as fifteen slaves were executed.

Throughout the year of 1802, suspicions of slave insurrections plagued Virginia. Letters were intercepted and slaves were arrested, flogged, banished or hanged for alleged conspiracies in Williamsburg, Brunswick, Halifax, Princess Anne, Norfolk, Hanover County, Richmond, King and Queen County, and Madison. It was reported that some European American (white) men participated in a slave conspiracy in Halifax, Virginia.

• *Miscellaneous State Laws:* In Ohio, the Ohio Constitution prohibited slavery and permitted suffrage (voting) by African American males.

• In South Carolina, fears of a massive slave rebellion began to subside. Accordingly, the legislature relaxed its restrictions of 1800 and 1801 on the number of slaves permitted to be imported for personal use in the state.

• In Mississippi, a bill to forbid the importation, for any purpose, of male slaves was introduced but was eventually defeated.

THE AMERICAS

• Napoleon sent an expeditionary force of French and Spanish forces to reconquer Haiti. Resistance was fierce. The French asked for a truce. During the truce talks, Toussaint l'Ouverture was seized and deported to France where he was incarcerated. L'Ouverture died in prison in 1803. *See 1801.*

When Napoleon restored the institution of slavery on the islands of Haiti, Martinique and Guadeloupe, he effectively undermined any semblance of legitimate French rule of the island of Hispaniola because the island was predominantly populated by former African slaves.

AFRICA

• John Trutor and William Somerville explored Bechuanaland.

Bechuanaland is the name by which the country of Botswana was known until 1966.

EUROPE

• Alexandre Dumas, the author of the *Three Musketeers* and the *Count of Monte Cristo*, was born in France.

Alexandre Dumas (1802–1870) was a famous French author and playwright. Dumas was born at Villers-Cotterets in France. Dumas' father was General Alexandre Dumas, a mulatto who was born in Haiti, the son of a French marquis and an African woman.

Dumas grew up in poverty. He was educated by a local priest who befriended him.

In 1827, Dumas went to Paris. In Paris, he began writing vaudeville sketches and plays. The Duke of Orleans became a patron of Dumas and Dumas' career began to blossom. Dumas became a prolific playwright. *Antony*, *Richard Darlington*, and *Mademoiselle de Belle Isle* were among his most well-received plays.

Dumas soon turned his attention to the writing of historical novels. His novels were revisionist in nature, but were extremely popular. In 1844, he wrote the immortal *Three Musketeers* and *Count of Monte Cristo*. It was these two works by which Dumas is best known and best remembered.

• George Bridgetower, the famous violinist, gave a concert in Dresden (July 24). *See 1779.*

RELATED HISTORICAL EVENTS

• In 1802, *The Romance of Antar*, a cycle of poems published in Cairo in thirty-two volumes, was introduced to European readers. A Bedouin romance translated from the Arabic by Tarrick Hamilton, *The Romance of Antar* was a companion piece to the *Arabian Nights*, and a classic work of Arabia. The storyline of *The Romance of Antar* centered on the career of the son of Sheik Shedad and an African woman. One of the poems from this classic was hung in the temple at Mecca and was considered to be among the greatest poems ever written.

• The Treaty of Amiens was executed between France and England. The treaty would bring peace to Europe for the first time in ten years. One of the conditions of the treaty was the return of the British-held Cape colony to the Batavian Republic (the Dutch).

• Napoleon Bonaparte was proclaimed First Consul for life by the French National Assembly.

1803

THE UNITED STATES

In 1803, a most significant event in American history and African American history occurred in of all places the island nation we now know as Haiti.

In Haiti, Jean Jacques Dessalines, the successor to the martyred Toussaint l'Ouverture, defeated the French army. Dessalines and his troops captured Port-au-Prince and essentially controlled the island. Facing utter defeat, the French agreed to leave. Dessalines then proclaimed the independence of Haiti.

The defeat of the French forces in Haiti was a sharp blow to the pride of Napoleon Bonaparte. He was severely disturbed by the fact that people he considered to be less than human had defeated his forces—forces which, theoretically, all of Europe feared. This stunning defeat caused Napoleon to reassess his plans for an American Empire.

Upon the departure of Rochambeau and the end of the official French presence on Haiti, Napoleon decided to abandoned any grandiose plans for the Americas. The abandonment of Napoleon's plans for an American Empire directly led to his decision to sell a wilderness area on the North American mainland. This wilderness area became the subject of a deal with the fledgling American government. An agreement was reached and what became known as the Louisiana Purchase became a reality. "Praise, if you will, the work of a Robert Livingstone or a Jefferson, but today let us not forget our debt to Toussaint L'Ouverture, who was indirectly the means of America's expansion by the Louisiana Purchase of 1803" (DeWitt Talmadge in *Christian Herald*, November 28, 1906).

• In 1803, the House of Representatives passed a resolution "to inquire into the expediency of granting protection to such American seamen, citizens of the United States, as are free persons of color."

• African Americans in New York City plotted to burn the city, and actually set fire to a number of houses, 11 of which were destroyed. Some of the conspirators were arrested, but others remained at large conducting a reign of terror in the city which lasted for several days. Eventually, 20 African Americans were convicted of arson.

• The conviction of an African American woman, Margaret Bradley, of attempting to poison two whites precipitated racial unrest in the town of York, Pennsylvania. The African American residents of the community rioted in an attempt to destroy the town by fire. Over a period of three weeks, 11 buildings were burned. Town-sponsored patrols were established, strong guards were set up, the militia was dispatched to the scene of the unrest at Governor McKean's orders, and a reward of $300 was offered for the capture of any insurrectionists.

• Congress admitted Ohio to the Union as the seventeenth state. With a large population of migrants from New England, Ohio was the first state in which slavery was outlawed from the start, and in time, Ohio would serve as the major thoroughfare for the Underground Railroad (February 19).

• *Notable Births*: Lunsford Lane, a noted lecturer for the Anti-Slavery Society, was born a slave in Raleigh, North Carolina.

• *Notable Deaths*: Toussaint L'Ouverture died while being held in a French prison (April 27). *See below.*

• *Miscellaneous State Laws*: South Carolina's Legislature opened the slave trade to allow for the importation of slaves from South America and the West Indies.

• *Scholastic Achievements*: The African Union Society of Newport, Rhode Island, one of the first African American mutual benefit societies, was absorbed in 1803 by the African Benevolent Society which operated a school that continued in operation until the city of Newport opened a school for African American children in 1842.

• *The Arts*: Newport Gardner composed "Crooked Shanks," a musical composition believed to be the first composed by an African American.

THE AMERICAS

• In Montevideo (Uruguay), the plan of a group of slaves to escape and fortify themselves in the forest was uncovered.

• Toussaint l'Ouverture, slave leader of the Haitian Revolution, died while being held in a French prison (April 27). He was 56 years old. His death made him a martyr to the natives of Haiti and his life was an inspiration to persons of African descent throughout the Caribbean.

Toussaint l'Ouverture: Pierre Dominique Toussaint-Breda (1743–1803) was an Afro-Haitian revolutionary general who became the ruler of Haiti. Toussaint was born a slave to slave parents. He worked as a slave for almost the first 50 years of his life.

After the news of the revolution in France reached the French colony of Haiti, slave uprisings took place. The slave uprising of 1791 was eventually led by Toussaint. During this uprising, Toussaint got his surname "L'Ouverture"—The Opening. This surname was taken from a remark made by the French governor of Haiti who, with some admiration of Toussaint's ability to consistently break through enemy lines, said "this man finds an opening everywhere."

Toussaint's army initially fought against the French. However, in 1793, the National Convention in France proclaimed freedom for all slaves in France and its possessions. Upon hearing this declaration, Toussaint came to the aid of the French who were engaged in armed conflict with the British and the Spanish on the island.

In 1799, a civil war broke out between the Africans and the mulattoes of Haiti. By 1801, Toussaint, as leader of the Africans, was able to gain control of the country. Haiti prospered under Toussaint's rule.

In 1802, Napoleon Bonaparte signed the Peace of Amiens. The Peace of Amiens allowed Napoleon to concentrate on the French possessions in the West Indies. He decided to reconquer Haiti and to reintroduce slavery.

Toussaint refused to accept French domination and a return to slavery. Napoleon sent an expeditionary force against the Haitians. During a truce between the French and Haitian forces, the French captured Toussaint and deported him to France. Toussaint would die in a French prison. He died a martyr for Haitian independence and for freedom-loving Africans throughout the Americas and the world.

AFRICA

• In 1803, the Batavian Republic ruled the Cape. The Xhosa claimed territory between the Fish River and the Sunday River. Dutch commando raids were initiated against the Khoikhoi. *See 1802.*

• American naval operations continued against the Barbary pirates of Tripoli.

• In 1803, the first Ashanti war under King Osai Tutu Kwamina (Osei Kwame) began with the theft of gold and valuables from a grave—a blasphemy of death and eternal life. The king of the Ashanti demanded redress, but his messengers to the accused Fanti were killed. A war between the Ashanti and the Fanti erupted and in this war, the British decided to side with the Fanti.

Between 1803 and 1874, there would be six wars between the British and the Ashanti. Ostensibly, these wars were aimed at curtailing the custom of human sacrifice practiced by the Ashanti along with the Ashanti's aggression against the Fanti, a people subjugated by the Ashanti, but who had become the ally of the British. However, in reality, the wars between the British and the Ashanti were all aimed at the purpose of creating a trade monopoly and at developing an economic and physical empire for the British.

EUROPE

• George Bridgetower, the famous violinist, gave a concert in Dresden (March 18). This concert was enthusiastically received and led to Bridgetower being given letters of introduction to the aristocratic society of Vienna.

While in Vienna, a certain Prince Lichnowsky introduced Bridgetower to a composer by the name of Beethoven and offered to finance a concert combining their talents. At the time, Beethoven was already working on two movements for violin and piano. When the financing for the concert with Bridgetower was finalized, he quickly finished the violin and piano movements and added a previously composed finale to make up a three-movement sonata.

There was not enough time to have the violin part of the second movement copied before the performance in the Augarten on May 24. Bridgetower was, thus, compelled to read it from Beethoven's own manuscript. Nevertheless, Bridgetower's performance was a smashing success. At the conclusion of the piece, the audience unanimously called for an encore of the second movement.

The sonata first played by Bridgetower in the Augarten has come to be known as the *Kreutzer* sonata. It is named for the eminent French violinist Rodolphe Kreutzer—a man who ironically never played it.

There is no question that Beethoven, who spoke highly of Bridgetower both as a soloist and as a quartet player, intended to dedicate the "*Kreutzer*" sonata to Bridgetower. On a rough composing score of the work, Beethoven scribbled the humorous inscription: "Sonata mulattica composta per il mulatto Brischdauer, gran pazzo e compositore mulattico." However, Bridgetower and Beethoven soon became estranged. The source of the estrangement was reputedly a quarrel over a woman. Thus, the sonata which marked the height of their collaboration came to be named for someone else. *See 1779.*

RELATED HISTORICAL EVENTS

• On April 30, France sold the Louisiana Territory to the United States for $15 million dollars.
• Meriwether Lewis and William Clark began their trek across the newly purchased Louisiana Territory.
• British Guiana was ceded to Britain while Tobago and St. Lucia were acquired by Great Britain.
• The United States Supreme Court rendered its decision in the case of *Marbury v. Madison* and thereby established its right to review the laws passed by Congress and by state legislatures.

——— 1804 ———

THE UNITED STATES

General Thomas Boude, a Revolutionary War officer in the Continental Army, purchased a slave, Stephen Smith, and took him to Columbia, Pennsylvania. Smith's mother escaped and followed her son. The Boudes took her in and refused to give her up to her mistress. Some historians cite this incident as the beginning of the Underground Railroad.

The Underground Railroad was a network of escape routes used by slaves during the 1800s to escape from slavery in the slave states to freedom in the free states and Canada. In actuality, the network of escape routes consisted of an informal system of safe houses and abolition sympathizers which were organized to assist slaves to freedom.

The Underground Railroad was neither underground nor a railroad. The network was called the "Underground Railroad" because of the swift way in which slaves were transported to freedom and because railroad terminology was used describe various aspects of the network. For instance, hiding places or safe houses were called "stations," and the people who assisted the slaves to freedom were called "conductors."

The Underground Railroad had no formal organization. Generally, the slaves traveled by whatever means they could. However, most travel was done under the cover of night.

The travelers on the Underground Railroad were aided by free African Americans and sympathetic European Americans in both the North and the South. These "conductors" provided the slaves with food, clothing, directions, and places to hide. Indeed, even some Southern slaves risked their lives and their own safety to help their brethren escape. In the North, the Quakers were particularly notable in their efforts to conduct the escaped slaves to safety.

The term "Underground Railroad" was first used about 1830. From 1830 until 1860, the Underground Railroad transported thousands of slaves to freedom. Some of these liberated slaves settled in the Northern states. However, if they did so they were legally subject to being recaptured and re-enslaved. Therefore, once free, many slaves went to Canada where they were beyond the reach of American law.

The major lines of the Underground Railroad ran through Ohio, Indiana, and western Pennsylvania. Large numbers of slaves followed these routes and reached Canada by way of Detroit or Niagara Falls, New York. Others sailed across Lake Erie to Ontario from such ports as Erie, Pennsylvania, and Sandusky, Ohio. In the East, the chief center of the Underground Railroad was southeastern Pennsylvania.

A few people became famous for the work they did on the Underground Railroad. It is said that Levi Coffin, a Quaker who was called the "president of the Underground Railroad" assisted more than 3,000 slaves to freedom. Harriet Tubman, the most famous African American conductor, returned to the South some 19 times and rescued over 300 of her fellow slaves.

The existence of the Underground Railroad was important not solely for its ability to lead slaves to freedom. The existence of the Underground Railroad also served to undermine the discourse and compromises of the day. *See 1854.* The Underground Railroad showed the determination of African Americans and sympathetic European Americans to end slavery in the United States. Its continued viability despite the enactment of federal laws angered many Southerners and contributed to the increasing hostility between the North and the South—a hostility which would lead to an armed conflict known as the Civil War. *See 1850.*

• In Georgia, South Carolina, and Virginia, there were arrests and imprisonments of slaves for attempted arson, and patrols against an alleged insurrection. About 20 slaves were executed for poisoning European American (white) citizens.

An Englishman reported the speech of a condemned slave: "I have nothing more to offer [in my defense] than what General Washington would have had to offer had he been taken by the British and put to trial by them. I have adventured my life in endeavoring to obtain the liberty of my countrymen, and am a willing sacrifice to their cause; and I beg, as a favor, that I may be immediately led to execution. I know that you have predetermined to shed my blood, why then all this mockery of a trial?"

• York, an African American who accompanied the Lewis and Clark expedition, reached the mouth of the Columbia River. York, the slave of William Clark, accompanied Clark on the famous Lewis and Clark exploration of the Louisiana Territory. *See 1780.*
• *The Abolition Movement:* 1804 marked the genesis of the Underground Railroad. *See the above.*
• *Miscellaneous State Laws:* The Ohio Legislature enacted the first of the "Black Laws" which restricted the rights and freedom of movement of African Americans in the North. Other Northern states soon passed similar legislation (January 5).
• By passing a law requiring gradual emancipation, New Jersey became the last Northern state to abolish slavery (February 15).
• In Virginia, the Act of 1804 prohibited all evening meetings of slaves. This act was modified in 1805 in order to permit a slave, in the company of a European American, to listen to a European American minister in the evening hours.

By 1804, all of the Northern states had passed antislavery laws or measures to allow for the gradual emancipation of the slaves.

• *Publications:* Thomas Branagan published *A Preliminary Essay on the Oppression of the Exiled Sons of Africa.* Branagan, a Dublin man who became a slave trader during the late 1700s, wrote this scathing denunciation of the African slave trade.
• *Scholastic Achievements:* Lemuel Haynes received an honorary degree (master of arts) from Middlebury College, Vermont. *See 1753.*

THE AMERICAS

• On January 1, 1804, Haiti declared its independence. Jean Jacques Dessalines was made governor for life. He later made himself Emperor Jacques I. The white (European) inhabitants of Haiti were either killed or forced to flee. Dessalines abolished slavery but instituted forced labor.

Jean Jacques Dessalines (1758–1806) was born a slave in Grande Rivière du Nord. As a youth, Dessalines adopted the name of his owner as his own.

In 1790, Dessalines joined the revolutionary forces against the French. Beginning in 1797, Dessalines served under the Haitian liberator Toussaint L'Ouverture, eventually becoming Toussaint's lieutenant general.

In 1802, Dessalines surrendered to the French General Charles Victor Emmanuel Leclerc. However, unlike Toussaint L'Ouverture, Dessalines was not taken to France for imprisonment. Thus, when the opportunity arose in 1803 to drive the French out of Haiti, Dessalines was there.

After driving out the French, Dessalines helped to establish the Haitian Republic but had himself appointed the governor-general for life. In October of 1804, Dessalines went one step farther by proclaiming himself to be the Emperor Jean Jacques I.

The self-aggrandisement exhibited by Dessalines (along with his cruel massacre of the Europeans and those mulattoes and African Haitians who opposed him) made Dessalines many enemies among his own followers. Two of these followers, Henri Christophe and Alexandre Sabes Petion, assassinated Dessalines in 1806 in an ambush near Port-au-Prince.

AFRICA

• Muhammed Ali expelled the Mameluks from Cairo, Egypt.

• A *jihad* occurred in the northern Nigeria area. Uthman dan Fodio became ruler of Sokoto, the chief town of the Fulani people.

In 1804, Uthman dan Fodio, a Fulani reformer, began a jihad. The jihad of Uthman dan Fodio would lead to a Fulani hegemony (domination) over most of northern Nigeria under the first Fulani Amir al Mumenin, Muhammed Bello, (Uthman dan Fodio's son) whose capital would be at Sokoto.

• The Battle of Tsuntua took place. Two hundred scholars were killed as a result of the battle.

• By 1804, the Nyamwezi had achieved supremacy as inland traders in central Tanzania.

With the advent of the 1800s, the trade in ivory with the inland countries of Africa blossomed. However, along with ivory, a trade in inland African slaves and guns also began to develop. All three areas of trade, would eventually serve to undermine and impoverish many of the inland peoples of Africa.

RELATED HISTORICAL EVENTS

• Napoleon Bonaparte was proclaimed Emperor by the French National Assembly (May 18). On December 2, the coronation of Napoleon and Josephine in Notre Dame cathedral was held.

• The British Foreign Bible Society was founded.

——— 1805 ———

THE UNITED STATES

• The General Assembly of Virginia sent a resolution to the United States government asking that African Americans be settled in some of the new lands opened up by the Louisiana Purchase.

• There were reports of slave plots or insurrections in North Carolina, Virginia, South Carolina, Maryland, and New Orleans.

• The slave trade to the Orleans Territory was authorized.

• *Notable Births:* Ira Frederick Aldridge, a noted African American thespian, was born (July 24).

Ira Frederick Aldridge (1805 [1807 or 1810]–1867), a great African American thespian (actor), was born in New York City. Aldridge was educated as a freeman in the African School in New York. While in his teens, Aldridge made his acting debut with an all African American cast in New York in Sheridan's *Pizzaro*.

The young Aldridge went to Scotland to study and, in 1826, he made his London debut at the Royalty Theater, playing Othello. Aldridge played at Covent Garden and toured the English and Irish provinces.

Aldridge's reputation as an actor grew. He traveled throughout the European continent. A star of the first magnitude, Aldridge was decorated by the king of Prussia and the czar of Russia, and he was knighted by the king of Sweden.

In Sweden, Aldridge married a Swedish baroness by whom he had three children. By 1857, Aldridge was commonly regarded as one of the two or three greatest actors in the world.

• *Miscellaneous State Laws:* A Maryland law prohibited freed African Americans from selling corn, wheat or tobacco without first obtaining a license to do so.

• The Black Laws of Ohio were passed. These laws prohibited African Americans from giving evidence in any court and restricted the exercise of civil rights by African Americans.

• *Miscellaneous Cases:* A case arose involving an African American who had been taken from Maryland to Kentucky to serve a limited time of servitude. Upon the expiration of the period of servitude, the African American was enslaved. The African American sued for his freedom. In the case of *Thompson v. Wilmot,* the court agreed with Thompson, the African American; set Thompson free; and awarded Thompson $691.25 in damages. The decision was affirmed on appeal in 1809.

• *The Black Church:* Joseph Willis, a free African American, established a Baptist church with an interracial congregation in Mississippi.

• *Sports:* In England, Bill Richmond, an African American, defeated Youssep in 6 rounds (May 11) and Jack Holmes in 26 rounds (July 8) but lost to the British champion Tom Cribb in a battle which lasted an hour and thirty minutes (October 8). *See 1763.*

AFRICA

• The British sent sixty-one ships and seized the Cape colony. At the time, there were 25,000 Boers (Dutch settlers), 25,000 Khoikhoi (Hottentots), and 25,000 slaves of various origin inhabiting the colony (July).

• On May 12, Muhammed Ali was installed as viceroy of Egypt. Egypt would be ruled by Muhammed Ali under a loose Ottoman suzerainty.

RELATED HISTORICAL EVENTS

• Alexander I of Russia decreed that land owners could liberate their slaves. However, few landowners decided to do so.

• The English fleet defeated the combined French and Spanish fleet at Trafalgar. The British Admiral Nelson was killed.

• William Lloyd Garrison was born.

William Lloyd Garrison (1805–1879) was an American journalist and reformer who became famous in the 1830s for his denunciations of slavery. Before his time, abolitionists had made moderate appeals to slaveholders and legislators on behalf of slaves. This method was employed in the hope of achieving the gradual abolition of slavery.

Garrison changed this attitude. Garrison said that slavery was evil and that it should be ended "immediately." Garrison also took umbrage with all who did not entirely agree with him.

Garrison was raised in Newburyport, Massa-chusetts. As an impoverished youth, Garrison was apprenticed to a printer at the age of 13. By 1827, Garrison had become a veteran journalist. He soon became the editor of the *National Philanthropist,* America's first temperance newspaper.

In 1828, Garrison met Benjamin Lundy, a Quaker and a pioneer antislavery propagandist and organizer. Not long afterwards, Garrison became an ardent abolitionist.

Writing for Lundy's newspaper, Garrison wrote scathing attacks on the institution of slavery. His attacks on slave dealers caused Garrison to be jailed for seven months.

In 1831, Garrison began publishing *The Liberator* in Boston. *The Liberator* had a small circulation, but it was influential and at times aroused violent public reaction.

In 1832, Garrison was instrumental in organizing the first society for the immediate abolition of slavery. Garrison was able to attract associates such as Wendell Phillips and influenced such individuals as Theodore Parker and Henry David Thoreau.

Garrison was also an advocate of women's rights. His fight to give women equal rights within the American Anti-Slavery Society split the abolitionist movement.

Garrison was a non-Unionist. He believed that the Northern states ought to separate from the South. Garrison refused to vote, and opposed the United States government because it permitted slavery. Eventually, however, Garrison did come to support Abraham Lincoln and Lincoln's efforts during the Civil War.

1806

THE UNITED STATES

• Free African Americans built the African Meeting House in Boston.

• *Notable Births:* Maria Weston Chapman, a noted abolitionist, was born (July 25).

• Norbert Rillieux, inventor and scientist, was born in New Orleans.

Norbert Rillieux, (1806–1894), an African American inventor and scientist, was the son of a wealthy white engineer and a mulatto woman. Rillieux's father, Vincent Rillieux, sent Norbert to Paris to study engineering. In 1830, Norbert Rillieux became an instructor in Paris at the L'École Centrale. Norbert Rillieux taught applied mechanics at L'École Centrale. Also, in 1830, Norbert Rillieux published a series of articles on steam engine mechanics and steam economy. Finally, in 1830, Rillieux is credited with inventing the triple-effect evaporator used in sugar refining.

In 1846, Rillieux patented a vacuum cup which "revolutionized sugar refining methods in that day." By 1855, the Rillieux system of steam evaporation was installed in all the sugar refineries in the southern United States, Cuba, and Mexico.

In 1881, Rillieux devised a system for the production of beet sugar. This invention was highly successful and became a common sight on sugar beet plantations.

Despite his achievements, Rillieux remained unappreciated in his native Louisiana. Two of his suggestions for improvement of the state (a method of draining the bayous of Louisiana and a sewage system for the city of New Orleans) were rejected primarily because of Rillieux's race. Rillieux died in his adopted country. Rillieux died in Paris.

• *Notable Deaths:* Benjamin Banneker, the famed African American mathematician and astronomer, died on October 9. *See 1731.*

• *Miscellaneous State Laws:* A Virginia law was enacted which required all slaves freed after May 1 to leave the state unless permission to remain in the state was granted by the state legislature.

• *Scholastic Achievements:* Boston granted $200 a year to an African American school. The African American students who attended the school paid 12 cents a week as tuition.

• *The Black Church:* The Africa Meeting House (the Joy Street Baptist Church) was constructed in Boston, Massachusetts.

THE AMERICAS

• In Argentina, one out of every five battalions formed to defend Buenos Aires from a British invasion was composed of persons of African descent.

One of the leaders of the mulattoes of Argentina, and one of the heroes in the defeat of the British, was Bernardino Rivadavia (1780–1845). Bernardino Rivadavia, a mulatto, would later distinguish himself in Argentina's quest for independence and, in 1826, was elected the first president of the Republic of Argentina.

• On October 17, Jean Jacques Dessalines was assassinated in Haiti. Henri Christophe and Alexander Petion seized control of the country with Christophe controlling the north and Petion controlling the south.

After the expulsion of the French, peace continued to elude the Haitian people. The country was plagued by dissension between the mulattoes and those of relatively direct African heritage.

The leaders that came to the fore after the assassination of Dessalines represented this dissension. Henri Christophe was an African Haitian who had been born a slave, while Alexander Petion was a mulatto, the son of a Frenchman and a free African woman. As history records, after the French were gone, the African Haitians and the mulattoes began to fight each other. As a tenuous resolution of the disputes, the leaders of the two groups, Christophe and Petion, eventually divided the country. Christophe came to rule the northern part of the country while Petion came to rule the southern portion.

AFRICA

• Mungo Park died. *See 1795.*

• The Ashanti-Fante war began.

• British occupation of the Cape settlement was consolidated after a brief threat from the French.

• Sayyid Said bin Sultan became ruler of Oman, Muscat and Zanzibar. When Sayyid Said (Seyyid Said ibn Sultan) became ruler of Oman, he embarked on a new policy of expansion along the East African coast. Said established a main base on Zanzibar where clove planting was introduced in 1818.

—————— 1807 ——————

THE UNITED STATES

In 1807, the United States Congress passed a law prohibiting the importation of slaves from Africa after the end of the year. Fines of $800 were to be imposed on those who knowingly bought illegally imported Africans and fines of $20,000 were imposed on those found guilty of equipping a slave ship. The individual states were allowed to dispose of the illegally imported Africans as they saw fit. This law of the land would be widely violated with illegal cargoes of slaves continuing to arrive up to the time of the Civil War.

• Two boatloads of newly arrived African slaves starved themselves to death at the port of Charleston, South Carolina.

• One of the four men the British took by force from the American frigate *Chesapeake* was David Martin, an African American from Massachusetts. The four men were seized because the British believed them to be deserters from the British navy.

• *The Abolition Movement:* An antislavery society called Friends of Humanity was formed in Kentucky.

• *Notable Births:* Charles Bennett Ray, minister, editor, lecturer, organizer, and abolitionist, was born in Massachusetts (December 25).

Charles Bennett Ray (1807–1886) was born in Falmouth, Massachusetts. Ray attended school in Falmouth and worked for five years on his grandfather's farm in Westerly, Rhode Island. Ray studied at Wesleyan Seminary and Wesleyan University in Middletown, Connecticut. In 1832, Ray went to New York and opened a boot and shoe store. While in New York, Ray joined the Anti-Slavery Society and helped runaway slaves. In 1837, Ray became an ordained minister in the Methodist church. In 1846, he became pastor of the Bethesda Congregational Church in New York City.

In 1837, Ray became an appointed agent of the African American publication, *Colored American* and, between 1839 and 1842, Ray served as the sole editor of said publication. By 1843, Ray had also become the corresponding secretary of the Committee of Vigilance—an organization created to protect and assist slaves fleeing from bondage. In 1850, Charles Ray was made a member of the executive committee of the New York State Vigilance Committee.

• *Notable Deaths:* Prince Hall died in Boston (December 4).

• *Miscellaneous State Laws:* In the Indiana Territory, an indenture law was passed which essentially created a form of slavery. This law was repealed in 1810.

• New Jersey law limited suffrage (the right to vote) to free white male citizens. The 1776 Constitution of New Jersey had placed no restrictions on suffrage except for age and a requirement that the voter possess 50 pounds in money or property.

• *Scholastic Achievements:* In Washington, D.C., the first schoolhouse (in the nation's capital) for African Americans was built by three African Americans—George Bell, Nicholas Franklin, and Moses Liverpool.

• *The Black Church:* The first African Presbyterian church was established in Philadelphia by John Gloucester, an African American originally from Tennessee.

THE AMERICAS

• Between 1807 and 1835, Muslim slaves in Bahia, Brazil, staged numerous insurrec-

tions, often led by the alufa, the Muslim priest.

• In Haiti, two governments were formed. One of the governments was headed by Henri Christophe under a dictatorship while the other government was a republic with Alexander Petion (a mulatto) serving as president.

AFRICA

• In March, the British occupied Alexandria, Egypt.

• Mombasa (Kenya) installed a puppet sultanate in Pate.

• The slave trade was stopped at the Cape colony and the Earl of Caledon became the first English civil governor of the colony.

• Abd al-Qadir (1807–1883), an Algerian resistance leader, was born.

RELATED HISTORICAL EVENTS

• The British Parliament abolished the slave trade (March 25). The effective date of the act was to be March 1, 1808.

While England may have abolished the slave trade in 1807, it was not until 1833 that the British Parliament passed an act eliminating slavery from the British colonies and it was not until 1838 that the slave prohibition was actually enforced.

• In London, the African Institution was founded. The mission of the African Institution was the abolition of slavery.

• Thomas Clarkson published *Three Letters to the Planters and Slave Merchants.*

• In November, the French army marched through Spain and attacked Portugal. On November 13, the Portuguese royal family withdrew, in exile, to Brazil with an exile court of 2,000 persons.

• Robert E. Lee (1807–1870), the commander of the Confederate forces during the Civil War, was born.

• John Greenleaf Whittier, a European American poet noted for his antislavery poetry, was born.

John Greenleaf Whittier (1807–1892) was born in Haverhill, Massachusetts. His parents were Quaker farmers. Whittier's poetry showed the influence of his Quaker religion and rural New England background. Whittier is often called the "Quaker poet."

The Scottish poet Robert Burns also influenced Whittier. Like Burns, Whittier wrote many ballads on rural themes. However, unlike Burns, Whittier's poems lacked a certain witticism.

From 1833 to 1863, Whittier was active in politics and the antislavery movement. Whittier called for the abolition of slavery in newspaper articles and while serving in the Massachusetts Legislature in 1835. The abolitionist cause also dominated his poetry. In "Moral Warfare" (1838) and "Massachusetts to Virginia" (1843), Whittier attacked the injustices of slavery. Whittier also condemned what he considered to be the hypocrisy of the United States—a nation founded on the ideals of freedom but which perpetuated the evil institution of slavery.

Whittier's most noted poem was "Ichabod" (1850). In "Ichabod," Whittier criticized Senator Daniel Webster of Massachusetts for his pivotal role in the passage of the Compromise of 1850. Whittier objected to the compromise because it required that runaway slaves be returned to their owners. However, instead of being a hyperbolic polemic, Whittier's "Ichabod" uses a dignified, restrained tone that makes the poem seem more like an expression of sympathy for Senator Webster rather than an attack upon him.

1808

THE UNITED STATES

In 1808, it was estimated that the slave population in the United States surpassed the one million mark.

The federal law (Act to Prohibit the Importation of Slaves) barring the African slave trade went into effect (January 1).

The law stipulated that persons convicted of violating its provisions would be fined anywhere from $800 to $20,000. Illegally imported slaves were to come under the jurisdiction of state legislatures which were to decide their fate.

Despite the law, it has been reported that approximately 250,000 slaves were imported into the United States between 1808 and 1860. Additionally, the disruption of the slave trade spawned a new practice—the kidnapping of free African Americans.

As early as 1808, slave traders began to engage in the practice of kidnapping free African Americans especially in states bordering on the Mason-Dixon line. The traders defended their actions by citing the Fugitive Slave Law of 1793 which permitted a slave owner to seize an escaped slave in another state, take the slave before a magistrate and acquire authority to take the slave home. However, the slave traders frequently ignored the provision regarding the need to go before a magistrate and simply sold their kidnapped victims back into slavery.

• *The Abolition Movement:* The Society of Friends (the Quakers) of North Carolina began to receive slaves from slave owners who desired to free their slaves but found it difficult to do so under the provisions of North Carolina's slave laws. The Quakers essentially freed the slaves under their care and often sent them to live in states which had abolished slavery. In 1814 alone, the Quakers were able to assist 350 slaves to obtain their freedom.

• *The Civil Rights Movement:* Peter Williams, Jr., who would later become rector of St. Philip's Church in New York City, organized a group to improve the conditions of the African American. The group petitioned the legislature for a Charter of Incorporation.

• *The Colonization Movement:* In 1808, Paul Cuffee, an African American shipowner, joined the Society of Friends (Quakers) of Westport and began advocating an African American exodus to Africa. Today, Cuffee is generally credited as being the father of the African American back-to-Africa movement. *See 1759.*

• *Miscellaneous State Laws:* In Mississippi, the importation of slaves was regulated by placing a tax of $5 on each African brought into the state.

• In Maryland, a law was enacted which allowed testimony from slaves or free African Americans to be utilized in criminal cases which involved slaves or free African Americans.

• In New York, the slave trade was abolished.

• *Miscellaneous Cases:* In the case of *United States v. Mullany* which originated in Washington, D.C., free-born African Americans were declared competent to testify as witnesses in court cases.

• A case originating out of Virginia—the case of *Sarah v. Henry*—decided that a slave owner was responsible for the court costs of the plaintiff in a suit for freedom, even if the suit was eventually decided in favor of the owner.

• *Publications: An Oration on The Abolition of the Slave Trade; delivered in The African Church in the City of New York 1 January 1808 by Peter Williams, Jun., a Descendant of Africa* was published.

• *Thanksgiving Sermon, preached 1 January 1808 in St. Thomas's or the African Episcopal Church, Philadelphia: on account of The Abo-*

lition of the Slave Trade, on that Day, By the Congress of the United States, was published by Absalom Jones, rector of the African Episcopal Church for use by the church's congregation.

• *The Black Church*: The Reverend Thomas Paul of Boston, helped to organize the New York City congregation of what became known as the Abyssinian Baptist Church.

THE AMERICAS

• Alexander Petion governed the southern portion of Haiti, while Henri Christophe ruled the northern portion.

AFRICA

• Sierra Leone became a British colony.
• Uthman dan Fodio captured Bornu.
• Gambia became a British colony.

RELATED HISTORICAL EVENTS

• Thomas Clarkson published *History of the Rise, Progress and Accomplishment of the Abolition of the African Slave-Trade.* The history was compiled by Thomas Thompson (1776–1861), a pharmaceutical and manufacturing chemist who lived in Liverpool and who was a lifelong member of the Society of Friends (the Quakers).

• Dom Joao, the regent of Portugal, went into exile in Brazil with 2,000 followers. He established a court in exile in Rio de Janeiro.

Some historians have written that Dom Joao (John VI) (1767–1826) was of African descent. The main evidence for Dom Joao's heritage lies in the written descriptions provided by contemporaries; portraits which portray him as a dark complexioned man with features which were described as African; and the fact that after nearly four hundred years of intermingling it had become virtually impossible to distinguish which Portuguese had been the slave owners and which Portuguese had been the slaves.

• In March, 100,000 French troops seized north Spain. The Spanish royal family was forced to flee to America. Charles IV of Spain abdicated in favour of his son, Ferdinand. Ferdinand was forced by Napoleon to abdicate in favor of his father. Charles IV then abdicated in favor of Napoleon.

———— 1809 ————

THE UNITED STATES

On February 25, Thomas Jefferson wrote a letter to Henri Gregoire concerning his views on African Americans. Jefferson wrote: "I have received the favor of your letter of August 17th, and with it the volume you were so kind as to send me on the 'Literature of Negroes.' Be assured that no person living wishes more sincerely than I do, to see a complete refutation of the doubts I have myself entertained and expressed on the grade of understanding allotted to them by nature, and to find that in this respect they are on a par with ourselves. My doubts were the result of personal observation on the limited sphere of my own State, where the opportunities for the development of their genius were not favorable, and those of exercising it still less so. I expressed them therefore with great hesitation; but whatever be their degree of talent it is no measure of their rights. Because Sir Isaac Newton was superior to others in understanding, he was not therefore lord of the person or property of others. On this subject they are gaining daily in the opinions of nations, and hopeful advances are making towards their re-establishment on an equal footing with the other colors of the human family. I pray you therefore to accept my thanks for the many instances you have enabled me to observe of respectable intelligence in that race of men, which cannot fail to have effect in hastening the day of their relief; and to be assured of the sentiments of high and just esteem and consideration which I tender to yourself with all sincerity." *See 1743, 1776 and 1782.*

• In 1809, New Orleans had a slave population of over 9,000.

• The South Carolina Conference of Methodists organized the first Methodist mission among African Americans. By 1857, there would be 8,114 African Americans who were listed on the membership rolls of the Methodist churches.

• *Notable Births*: Elizabeth Taylor Greenfield, an African American singer known as the "Black Swan," was born.

Elizabeth Taylor Greenfield was born in Natchez, Mississippi. As an infant, she was taken to Philadelphia and adopted by a Quaker woman named Greenfield who arranged for her to study music and to sing at private parties.

In 1851, Greenfield made her debut at a concert sponsored by the Buffalo Music Association. After her debut in Buffalo, Greenfield toured the Northern states between 1851 and 1853.

In 1854, Greenfield toured England and gave a command performance before Queen Victoria in Buckingham Palace. A critic of the day described Greenfield's voice as one of "amazing power," "flexibility," and "ease of execution."

Greenfield was, quite simply, the best known African American concert artist of the 1800s.

• James W. C. Pennington, a leader in the Free Negro Convention Movement which outlined an ideology and tactics for the African American protest movement of the 19th century, was born a slave in Washington County, Maryland.

James W. C. Pennington (1809–1870), was a teacher, preacher, and author who was born into slavery on the eastern shore of Maryland. At the age of 21, Pennington escaped from his enslavement, but he was soon recaptured. However, with the help of a Pennsylvania Quaker, Pennington persisted and eventually won his freedom. Pennington left Maryland. After leaving Maryland, he spent a brief time in Pennsylvania, and then moved to western Long Island in New York where he worked during the day and attended night school. At the age of 26, Pennington was certified to teach in the schools which had been established to teach African American children. Pennington first taught in Newton on Long Island, New York. He later taught in New Haven, Connecticut.

While in New Haven, Pennington studied theology. His eloquence attracted favorable attention, and Pennington served twice as president of the Hartford Central Association of Congregational Ministers, of which he was the only African American member. Pennington was five times elected a member of the General Convention for the Improvement of Free People of Color, and in 1843 represented Connecticut at the World Anti-Slavery Convention in London. Pennington's published works were *The Fugitive Blacksmith* (London 1849) and *Textbook of the Origin and History of the Colored People* (1841).

• Joseph Jenkins Roberts, the first president of Liberia, was born in Petersburg, Virginia.

The parents of Joseph Jenkins Roberts (1809–1876) were free African Americans who resided in Petersburg, Virginia. In 1829, Roberts migrated to Liberia with his widowed mother and younger brothers, and became a merchant. In 1842, he became the first president of the colony of Liberia—a colony created by the American Colonization Society to accept freed African slaves from the United States.

The colony of Liberia experienced some difficulty with the native inhabitants of the area, and in an attempt to raise money, they decided to lay import duties on goods brought into Liberia. This caused international problems, because Liberia was not a sovereign nation nor was it actually an official colony of the United States.

In 1844, Roberts returned to the United States on a diplomatic mission. He hoped to resolve the dispute concerning Liberia's import tax but the American government avoided taking a stand in defense of Liberia ostensibly because the annexation of Texas had compelled the issue of slavery to the forefront of political debate. Eventually, the American Colonization Society gave up all claims on the Liberian colony and left the African American colonists on their own.

Roberts returned to Liberia and resumed purchasing land for the colony. In 1847, he convened a conference at which the new Republic of Liberia was proclaimed and he was elected its first president. Roberts was reelected in 1849, 1851, and 1853.

In 1849, under Roberts' leadership, the Republic of Liberia agreed to a commercial treaty with Great Britain. Subsequent visits by Roberts to France and Belgium were instrumental in achieving recognition for Liberia as a sovereign country. In 1856, Roberts was elected the first president of the new College of Liberia. On another subsequent visit to the United States, in 1869, Roberts addressed the annual meeting of the African Colonization Society at Washington. In 1871, Roberts was once again elected president of Liberia and he served in that capacity until his death in 1876.

• *Miscellaneous State Laws:* In Maryland, a law was enacted which facilitated manumission. It provided, however, that children of a freed slave remained slaves unless they too were specifically emancipated by their owner.
• *Miscellaneous Cases:* In the Louisiana case of *Girod v. Lewis,* the court held that while the marriage of slaves had no civil effect while they were slaves, from the moment of their emancipation, the marriage between two freed slaves was as legally valid as a marriage between whites.
• *Publications: An Oration Commemorative of the Abolition of The Slave Trade in the United States delivered before the Wilberforce Philanthropic Association, in the City of New York, on the Second of January, 1809* was published by Joseph Sidney.

• *Oration on the Abolition of the Slave Trade* delivered in The African Church in the City of New York, 2 January 1809, by Henry Sipkins was published.
• *The Black Church*: In Philadelphia, the first African Baptist church was established by 13 African Americans.
• In Boston, African Americans established an independent Baptist church under the leadership of the Reverend Thomas Paul.
• The Abyssinian Baptist Church was formally organized in New York City (July 5).
• *Sports*: In England, Bill Richmond fought a series of bouts in which he defeated Isaac Wood in 23 rounds (April 11), Jack Carter in 25 minutes (April 14), and George Maddox in 52 minutes (August 9). *See 1763.*

THE AMERICAS

• The French were evicted from Dominica. The first republic of Dominica was proclaimed.
• Paul Brito, a noted personality in Brazilian literary circles, was born.

Paul Brito (1809–1861), a person of African descent, played an important role in Brazilian literature, not as a writer, but as a publisher whose Rio de Janeiro bookshop became a meeting place for the leading Brazilian writers.

• The town square in Buenos Aires was named *Plaza Fidelidad* in commemoration of the loyalty of the Africans and Indigenous Argentinians who were volunteers against the British in 1806.
• Placido, the Afro-Cuban poet, was born.

Placido (Gabriel de la Concepcion Valdes) (1809–1844) was born in Mantanzas, Cuba, the son of an Afro-Cuban barber and a Spanish dancer.
Placido was known for his protest in verse against Spanish oppression on the island, and is considered to be one of Cuba's greatest poets.
In 1844, Placido was charged with conspiring against the government and executed without any proof of guilt. The Spanish govenor had accused Placido of participating in a "racial conspiracy" composed of Afro-Cubans and mestizos.

AFRICA

• The Fante attacked Accra and Elmina.
• Henry Salt began his expedition to Ethiopia.
• In the Cape colony, the Khoikhoi were placed under British colonial law.
• Samuel Ajayi Crowther (1809 [1808?]–1891), the first Yoruban to become an Anglican bishop, was born.

RELATED HISTORICAL EVENTS

• Charles Darwin (1809–1882), explorer, naturalist, scientist and one of the originators of the theory of natural selection, was born.
• Abraham Lincoln, the great emancipator, was born in Harden County, Kentucky (February 12).

Abraham Lincoln (1809–1865) was born in a log cabin on a farm located about 5 miles south of Elizabethtown, Kentucky. Raised on the Indiana frontier, as a young man Lincoln settled in Illinois. Self-educated, Lincoln began his practice of law in 1837, in Springfield, Illinois.
In 1846, Lincoln was elected to the House of Representatives as a member of the Whig Party. However, Lincoln joined the new Republican Party in 1856 when the Whig Party split over the issue of slavery.
Although Lincoln's public antislavery views were limited to a stated desire to keep the institution of slavery from spreading to the new territories, he was seen by Southerners a dangerous enemy. Lincoln's refusal to concede to Confederate demands for the evacuation of the federal garrison at Fort Sumter, South Carolina, led to the eruption of hostilities which became the Civil War.
At the inception of the Civil War, Lincoln's chief concern was the preservation of the Union as opposed to the abolition of slavery. However, as the war dragged on, the abolition of slavery became more and more a political necessity. Thus, Lincoln's issuance of the Emancipation Proclamation was more a political document than a grand statement of moral principle.
Despite common misconceptions, the Emancipation Proclamation did not end slavery. The Emancipation Proclamation merely set free those slaves who were located in states still engaged in rebellion against the federal government. The slaves who were located in the border states that remained loyal to the Union remained enslaved. However, with the Emancipation Proclamation, the Union cause became a moral cause and the Proclamation served to end European sympathies for the Confederacy.
Lincoln was reelected with a large majority in 1864 on a National Union platform. With a Union victory in sight, in his second inaugural address, Lincoln advocated a policy of reconciliation with the South stressing a need to reconcile "with malice toward none, with charity for all."

The Confederate forces of Robert E. Lee surrendered to Ulysses S. Grant on April 9, 1865. Five days later, Abraham Lincoln was shot in a Washington, D. C. theater by an actor and Confederate sympathizer, John Wilkes Booth.

In the intervening years since Lincoln's death, much has been written concerning Lincoln's preoccupation with the preservation of the Union over the eradication of slavery—concerning Lincoln's desire to maximize the opportunities of European Americans as a reason for his opposition to the expansion of slavery—concerning Lincoln's reticence at issuing the Emancipation Proclamation. However, despite the criticisms, in reading Lincoln's words and reviewing his career, one cannot help but be persuaded by his overriding humanity.

In African American history, one finds Lincoln to be a compelling person. Lincoln was a man who was a product of his time but whose life legacy transcends time.

Lincoln, better than any other person, enunciated the arguments against slavery in a manner which made them comprehensible to the common person—to the average American. His words often communicated not just to the mind but to the soul of European America.

In the long run, history will record that the greatness of Lincoln rests with his emancipation of his people. To the extent that Lincoln's words (and deeds) led to the spiritual emancipation—the uplifting—of the European American,—and to the extent that the spiritual emancipation of the European American, in turn, led to the physical emancipation of African Americans—it is to this extent that the greatness of Abraham Lincoln cannot be denied.

> Four score and seven years ago our fathers brought forth, upon this continent, a new nation, conceived in Liberty, and dedicated to the proposition that all men are created equal.
>
> Now we are engaged in a great civil war, testing whether that nation, or any nation, so conceived, and so dedicated, can long endure. We are met here on a great battlefield of that war. We have come to dedicate a portion of it as a final resting place for those who here gave their lives that that nation might live. It is altogether fitting and proper that we should do this.
>
> But in a larger sense we cannot dedicate—we cannot consecrate—we cannot hallow this ground. The brave men, living and dead, who struggled here, have consecrated it far above our poor power to add or detract. The world will little note, nor long remember, what we say here, but can never forget what they did here. It is for us, the living, rather to be dedicated here to the unfinished work which they have, thus far, so nobly carried on. It is rather for us to be here dedicated to the great task remaining before us—that from these honored dead we take increased devotion to that cause for which they here gave the last full measure of devotion—*that we here highly resolve that these dead shall not have died in vain; that this nation shall have a new birth of freedom; and this government of the people, by the people, for the people, shall not perish from the earth.* (Lincoln's Gettysburg Address)

• On May 1, Napoleon annexed the Papal States and took Pope Pius VII prisoner. On June 12, Napoleon Bonaparte was excommunicated. On December 16, Napoleon divorced Josephine de Beauharnais.

• James Madison became President of the United States.

— 1 8 1 0 —

THE UNITED STATES

In 1810, the United States census reported that there were 1,377,808 African Americans in the United States representing 19% of the population. Of the 1,377,808 African Americans, 1,191,362 were listed as slaves while 186,466 (about 13.5% of all African Americans) were listed as free.

• In a message to Congress, President James Madison made note of the widespread violation of the antislave trade act of 1807 and requested that Congress take measures to curtail the violations. Madison's remarks, to a large extent, would go unheeded and violations would continue to occur. In 1816, some six years later, Madison would repeat his request for Congressional action to abate the illegal slave trade.

Madison said: "It appears that American citizens are instrumental in carrying on a traffic in enslaved Africans, equally in violation of the laws of humanity, and in defiance of those of their own country. The same just and benevolent motives which produced the interdiction in force against this criminal conduct will doubtless be felt by Congress, in devising further means of suppressing the evil."

• A federal law was enacted which prohibited African Americans from carrying mail. *See 1828.*

Beginning in 1810 and lasting until 1816, the South experienced an economic depression. The depression was caused by a number of factors not the least of which were the exhaustion of the soil, a British embargo, the nonintercourse acts, and the War of 1812. Of particular note, the War of 1812 caused considerable devastation in eastern Maryland and Virginia. These events served to destabilize the labor force in the South and limited the exportation of Southern goods while increasing the costs associated with purchasing imported goods.

The turmoil that existed in the decade led to unrest among the slave population. In economic hard times, it was the slaves which suffered the most and with the societal disruption caused by the war, opportunities arose for slave unrest to escalate to slave revolts.

In March of 1810, correspondence between slaves in North Carolina, Georgia, Tennessee and Virginia revealed plans for slave insurrections. Rumors arose in North Carolina which asserted that North Carolina slaves would mass together and stage a raid on Virginia. These rumors were taken seriously and were duly reported to the governor of Virginia, John Tyler.

In November of 1810, in Lexington, Kentucky, a slave conspiracy was uncovered. The conspirators were subsequently arrested.

• *Notable Births:* Thomy Lafon (1810–1893), an African American philanthropist who supported the American Anti-Slavery Society and the Underground Railroad, was born in New Orleans.

• William Leidesdorff (1810–1848), a prominent African American businessman in California, was born in the Virgin Islands, the son of a Danish man and a mulatto woman.

• Charles Lenox Remond, a leader of the American Anti-Slavery Society, was born in Massachusetts (February 1).

Charles Lenox Remond (1810–1873) was born a free African American in Salem, Massachusetts. In 1838, Remond was appointed an agent of the Massachusetts Anti-Slavery Society. As an agent of the Society, Remond canvassed Massachusetts, Rhode Island, and Maine.

Remond became a delegate to the American Anti-Slavery Society and attended the World Anti-Slavery Convention in London in 1840. Afterwards, Remond lectured in England and Ireland on the subject of slavery. In 1841, he returned to the United States and continued his work. During the Civil War, Remond recruited African American men to serve as soldiers in the 54th Massachusetts Infantry, the first African American regiment to be sent into action during the war (and later the subject of a popular 1989 theatrical release entitled *Glory*).

• David Ruggles (1810–1849), founder of the *Mirror of Liberty*—the first African American periodical—was born.

• *Notable Deaths:* David George (1742–1810), the pastor of the first African American Baptist church, the first Afro-Canadian church, and the first African American/Afro-Canadian church in Sierra Leone, died. *See 1783.*

• *Miscellaneous State Laws:* In New York, a law was enacted which prohibited New York residents from importing slaves. Another New York law required all slave owners to teach their slave children to read the Bible.

• Indiana repealed its severe indenture law. *See 1807.*

• In Maryland, free African Americans lost the right to vote.

• In Georgia, free African Americans were required to register and give full details concerning themselves and their reasons for entering the state.

• *Miscellaneous Cases:* In the Louisiana case of *Adelle v. Beauregard,* the court held that "a person of color" was presumed to be free unless proved otherwise. A similar ruling was pronounced in the subsequent Louisiana case of *State v. Cecil* which would be decided in 1812.

• In a New York case involving an African American named "the Negro Tom," Tom was able to secure his emancipation on the basis of a deed of a former owner that freed him upon the owner's death even though the owner subsequently sold Tom to another person.

• *Publications:* In Charleston, South Carolina, Lewis Dupre published a pamphlet entitled *An Admonitory Picture and a Solemn Warning Principally Addressed to Professing Christians in the Southern States.* In this pamphlet, Dupre argued for the progressive emancipation of the slaves and attempted to prove the immorality associated with the institution of slavery.

• *Scholastic Achievements:* In South Carolina, African Americans organized the Minor Society for the purpose of educating orphans and freed African Americans.

• *Black Enterprise:* The African Insurance Company of Philadelphia was organized. The company was not incorporated, but did have assets valued at $5,000. John Randolph was the president; Carey Porter, the treasurer; and William Coleman, the secretary.

• *Sports:* In England, Bill Richmond defeated Young Powers in a fight lasting 15 minutes (May 1). *See 1763.*

• Thomas Molineaux, the African American protege of Bill Richmond, defeated Tom Blake in 8 rounds (July 14) but lost to the British champion Tom Cribb in a grueling (and controversial) 33-round bout staged in London (December 10).

THE AMERICAS

• New Granada had 210,000 persons of African descent out of a total population of 1,400,000.

• David George (1742–1810), the pastor of the first African American Baptist church, the first Afro-Canadian church, and the first African American/Afro-Canadian church in Sierra Leone, died. *See 1783.*

• In Venezuela, there were 493,000 Africans and mulattoes out of a total population of about 900,000.

Although the Congress of the United States passed a law in 1807 forbidding American participation in the slave trade, in 1810, Americans were reported by eyewitnesses to have been seen transporting slaves to the Rio de la Plata (Argentina) on the eve of the revolution of 1810.

AFRICA

• The legendary military career of Shaka, the infamous king of the Zulus, began.

Shaka, King of the Zulus

As the legend goes, Shaka (circa 1785–1828) was the product of a casual sexual encounter between Senzangakona, heir to the throne of the insignificant Zulu chiefdom, and Nandi, a member of the even smaller and more insignificant Langeni clan.

One day in 1785, Senzangakona observed Nandi bathing in a stream and, overcome with lust, proposed "ukuhlobonga," a custom which allowed the young to engage in sexual foreplay but which did not allow for actual intercourse. However, once he began, Senzangakona was unable to limit himself. He had intercourse with Nandi and impregnated her.

Three months later, a Langeni messenger arrived at the Zulu camp with the news that Nandi was with child and that Senzangakona was the father. The Zulu elders scoffed at the message and suggested that Nandi had caught "ushaka," a bug which supposedly delayed menstruation. However, after Nandi gave birth to a son whom she affectionately named Shaka,

Senzangakona grudgingly admitted that he was the father.

To the embarrassment of the Zulu, Nandi of the insignificant Langeni, had become the wife of the chief of the Zulu people. However, the marriage was never a happy one, and although the union produced a second child (a daughter), it remained tenuous.

One day the young Shaka was accused of causing the death of a sheep and, on this pretext, Shaka, Nandi and Nandi's daughter were all made outcasts.

Cast adrift, Nandi and her children wandered about the countryside. They first returned to the Langeni, but were not welcomed. They then went to the Qwabe and finally, in 1809, found themselves among the Mthethwa. With the Mthethwa, Nandi and her now adult children found a home.

The leader of the Mthethwa was a former outcast himself. His name was Dingiswayo and he soon found a young protégé in Shaka. Impressed by Shaka, Dingiswayo soon made Shaka a regimental commander. Shaka, in turn, showed his gratitude by playing a leading role in reorganizing the fighting methods of the Mthethwa army.

From the very beginning of his military career, Shaka criticized the method of fighting. He believed that it was inefficient for two armies to line up some 50 paces apart and to throw spears and abuse at each other until one of them lost heart. Shaka believed that there was a better way.

In 1810, Shaka was given the opportunity to demonstrate his better way. A dispute erupted with the Buthelezi chiefdom. As was the custom, the two sides lined up against each other and proceeded to hurl insults. However, this time the champion warrior of the Buthelezi stepped forward and challenged someone from the Mthethwa to fight. The time for Shaka had come.

Armed only with a shield and a short, cut-off spear, Shaka advanced on the Buthelezi championed who was armed with three long spears. As Shaka came closer, the startled Buthelezi hurled one of the spears, and then another. Using his shield, Shaka easily deflected these spears.

The Buthelezi champion then prepared to throw his final spear. However, before he could do so, Shaka sprinted up to him, hooked his shield around the man and plunged his cut-off spear deep into the Buthelezi with such force that it went right through him. The Buthelezi champion was dead and the legend of Shaka came to life.

Like most innovations in warfare, the employment of Shaka's stabbing spear proved to be a sad development not only for Natal but for all of southern Africa. The stabbing spear led to bloodier, more decisive wars. And with Shaka employing it, it enabled him to conquer an area as large as the country of Portugal.

Shaka's reward for defeating the Buthelezi was the post of supreme commander of the Mthethwa army. As the army commander, Shaka was given the opportunity to introduce other military innovations. One such innovation was the discarding of footwear and a physical conditioning regimen which included long distance running. Shaka himself accompanied his troops on these exercise runs, and it was said that Shaka was the best runner in the country. Those years wandering around the countryside were beginning to pay off.

Shaka also instituted the regimental system based on age groups, quartered at separate kraals (villages) and distinguished by uniform markings on shields and by various combinations of headdress and ornaments.

Shaka developed a standardized set of tactics which the Zulu used in every battle. The available regiments (known collectively as the "impi") were divided into four groups. The strongest, termed the "chest" closed with the enemy to pin him down while two flanking arms—the "horns"—raced out to encircle and attack the opposing forces from behind. A reserve force known as the "loins" was positioned nearby with its back to the battle so as not to become unduly excited or discouraged. These reserve forces could be sent to reinforce any part of Zulu ring if the enemy threatened to break out. During the battle, the Zulu forces were commanded by "indunas" who used hand signals to direct the regiments.

An "impi" in Shaka's army consistently covered 50 miles a day, living off grain and cattle requisitioned from the kraals it passed and, accompanied by boys who carried the warriors' sleeping mats and cooking utensils.

When Shaka fought, it was to the death. His campaigns were campaigns of extermination which decimated the warriors of the opposing clans and then incorporated the clan remnants into the Zulu nation.

The first targets of Shaka's wrath were the clans which resided in the near vicinity of the Zulu, especially those tribes which caused Shaka and his mother grief when he was young.

Starting with the Langeni, Shaka sought out the men who had made his childhood a nightmare and impaled them on the sharpened stakes of their own kraal fences. Employing Shaka's discipline and tactics, within a year, the Zulu had quadrupled in number.

In 1817, Dingiswayo, Shaka's mentor and chief, died. With Dingiswayo's death, Shaka was truly unleashed. With an unprecedented fury, Shaka began to conquer everything in his sight. Within two years, he eliminated all the clans that could pose a threat to him. By 1823, Natal was a depopulated land dotted with the burned-out kraals of the now deposed clans.

Although Shaka's devastations were limited to Natal, they impacted other areas throughout southern Africa. The terrified survivors of Shaka's war began to wander through the land and as they wandered, they too began to displace other people. In what has come to be known as the "Mfecane"—the Crushing—marauding clans, fleeing Shaka's wrath and searching for new land of their own, began a genocidal game of musical chairs that undermined clan structure within the interior of southern Africa and resulted in a holocaust that left 2,000,000 dead.

The "Mfecane" is an important event in African history because this internecine holocaust made possible the Great Trek which would be so important to the creation of South Africa. When the Boer trekkers first ventured into the lands devastated by Shaka, they were able to do so with success because there were so few of the indigenous South Africans left to oppose them.

In 1824, the first Europeans arrived in Port Natal. A dozen settlers of the Farewell Trading Company established a post on the landlocked bay and soon made contact with Shaka. Intrigued by the ways of the Europeans, but convinced of the superiority of his Zulu civilization, Shaka permitted the Europeans to stay. Two of the early settlers were the adventurers and profiteers, Henry Francis Fynn and Nathaniel Isaacs. Fynn and Isaacs, motivated by a greed for ivory, were able to learn the Zulu language and eventually became fluent in it. Despite their self-interested bias, it is from these two that much of the story of Shaka is known.

In 1827, Nandi, Shaka's mother, died. Wracked by grief, Shaka became psychotic. In a twisted tribute in mourning, Shaka ordered 7,000 Zulus killed and decreed that no crops were to be planted nor milk to be consumed. All women found pregnant were slain with their husbands, as were thousands of milch cows, so that even the calves might know what it was to lose a mother.

Early in 1828, Shaka sent his army south on a military maneuver that carried the warriors clear to the borders of the Cape colony. Upon their return, and before they could be rested, Shaka immediately dispatched them off on another maneuver far in the north. The insanity that had engulfed Shaka had become too much.

On September 22, 1828, two of Shaka's half-brothers, Dingane and Mhlangana, along with an induna named Mbopa, assassinated Shaka.

In the annals of African history, Shaka's name continues to elicit awe. However, despite his military genius, one cannot overlook the destruction and death that Shaka caused and the fact that his mad grasp on power enabled Europeans to more easily impose their will and their presence on the land that is today known as South Africa.

- The English seized Bourbon Island (July 7-8) and Ile de France (Mauritius) (December 3).
- Shaikh Ahmad Loba conquered Massina.
- Radama I, the Merina ruler, opened Madagascar to European influences.
- David George (1742–1810), the pastor of the first African American Baptist church, the first Afro-Canadian church, and the first African American/Afro-Canadian church in Sierra Leone, died. *See 1783.*
- Abiodun, the Alafin of Oyo, died. Upon his death, the Yoruba Kingdom began to disintegrate.

EUROPE

In 1810, an oddity of history occurred in Europe. In 1810, a Khoikhoi (an Indigenous South African) by the name of Venus was brought from South Africa with promises that she would make a fortune by putting her body, with her prominent buttocks, on display to the public. Once on display, Venus was monstrously exploited.

The exploitation of Venus raised the ire of the abolitionist organizations. The abolitionists sought to have Venus released from bondage by seeking a writ of habeas corpus. However, Venus declared that she did not wish to be freed nor to go home. She stated that she liked England and the money that was given her by her keeper. Thus, the exploitation of Venus continued.

In 1815, Venus died in Paris. She had acquired an addiction to alcohol which led to her demise.

After her death, her skeleton and a plaster cast of her body were placed in the Musée de l'Homme.

RELATED HISTORICAL EVENTS

- Theodore Parker, liberal minister, was born (August 24).
- Cassius M. Clay, Kentucky emancipationist, was born (October 19).
- In April, a *junta* was set up to govern Venezuela in Caracas. A delegation which included Simon Bolivar was sent to London and Paris to request recognition. Upon his return to Venezuela, Francisco de Miranda proclaimed himself commander-in-chief and dictator.

1811

THE UNITED STATES

On the afternoon of January 9, 1811, whites fled in terror from the parishes of St. Charles and St. John the Baptist to New Orleans. The whites fled the 35 miles to safety after an uprising of over 400 African slaves had occurred on the night of January 8. Armed with cane knives, axes, and clubs, and later with a few guns, the slaves began their revolt on the plantation of Major Andry where they killed the major's son. The slaves then went on to other plantations. Some of the plantations were destroyed and at least one other white person was killed.

Charles Deslondes, reputedly a free mulatto from Santo Domingo, was among the leaders of the rebellious slaves. Major Andry and a group of other planters pursued some of the slaves into the woods and indiscriminately executed them.

Governor Claiborne called out the militia and prohibited male African Americans to go at large in New Orleans. Brigadier General Hampton and Major Milton's federal and state troops surrounded the main body of rebellious slaves on January 10. In the massacre which followed, 66 slaves were killed or executed, 16 captured and 17 were reported missing, although they too were assumed dead.

The captured slaves were taken back to New Orleans where they were tried, found guilty of high crimes, and executed. After their execution, the heads of the slaves were severed from their bodies and mounted on posts. These heads were then posted at intervals from New Orleans to Major Andry's plantation.

• A rebel slave community in Cabarrus County, North Carolina, was attacked by a force sent to recover or annihilate the self-emancipated slaves. It was reported that two African American men were killed, one was wounded, and two African American women were captured.

Just before the outbreak of the War of 1812 in December of 1811, a Virginia slaveholder and Congressman, John Randolph, wrote that he would

> touch this subject, the danger arising from the black population, as tenderly as possible; it was with reluctance that he touched it at all. . . . While talking of taking Canada, some of us are shuddering for our safety at home. I speak from facts when I say that the night bell never tolls for fire in Richmond, that the mother does not hug the infant more closely to her bosom. I have been a witness of some of the alarms in the capital of Virginia.

• *The Colonization Movement:* In 1811, Paul Cuffee, an African American shipowner, traveled from Westport to Sierra Leone at a personal expense of $4,000. Cuffee explored Sierra Leone for the purposes of colonization and trade. Cuffee firmly believed that African Americans should return to Africa as colonists. On his 1811 sojourn to Africa, Cuffee helped relocate thirty-eight African Americans on the West African coast at his own expense.

As was reported in the British press, "On the first of the present month of August, 1811, a vessel arrived at Liverpool, with a cargo from Sierra Leone, the owner, master, mate, and whole crew of which are free Negroes. The master, who is also owner, is the son of an American slave, and is said to be very well skilled both in trade and navigation, as well as to be of a very pious and moral character. It must have been a strange and animating spectacle to see this free and enlighted African entering as an independent trader, with his black crew, into that port which was so lately the (center) of the Slave Trade."

• *Notable Births:* The Reverend Daniel A. Payne, an African Methodist Episcopalian who helped to establish Wilberforce University in Ohio, was born (February 24).

Daniel Alexander Payne (1811–1893) was a bishop of the African Methodist Episcopal Church. Payne was born in Charleston, South Carolina to parents who were free African Americans. As a student, Payne attended the Minor's Moralist Society School—a school established by free African Americans. Under the tutelage of Thomas Bonneau, Payne excelled at mathematics, English, Latin, Greek and French. In 1826, Payne joined the Methodist Episcopal Church and, in 1829, he opened a school for African American children which became the most successful institution of its kind in Charleston. The school flourished until the South Carolina Legislature passed a law in 1834 against teaching African Americans to read or write.

Payne soon left South Carolina. He went to Pennsylvania and attended the Lutheran Theological Seminary at Gettysburg. In 1839, Payne was ordained as a minister. In 1840, Payne opened a school in Philadelphia and, in 1842, he joined the African Methodist Episcopal Church. Chosen as historiographer of the African Methodist Episcopal Church in 1848, Payne traveled extensively throughout the United States. Payne was elected bishop in 1852.

In 1863, Payne purchased Wilberforce University and served as president of the university for thirteen years. Among his publications were *Pleasures and Other Miscellaneous Poems* (1850), *The Semi-Centenary of the African Methodist Episcopal Church in the U.S.A.* (1866), *A Treatise on Domestic Education* (1885), *Recollections of Seventy Years* (1888), and *The History of the AME Church from 1816 to 1856* (1891).

• *Miscellaneous State Laws:* In Kentucky, a law was enacted which made conspiracy among slaves or poisoning by slaves crimes punishable by death.

• In Delaware, the legislature prohibited the immigration of free African Americans into the state. Upon entering Delaware, African Americans were given ten days notice to leave, after which they were to be fined $10 a week. Any free African American who was a native of the state and who happened to leave the state was considered a nonresident after an absence of six months and subject to expulsion upon his or her return.

• In Georgia, a law provided that ordinary trials of slaves were to be before a justice of the peace, but for cases involving capital punishment there should be a jury trial in a county court.

• In New York, the law required that free African Americans present certificates documenting their free status. The certificates were issued by a county clerk and were required to be presented before the African Americans would be allowed to vote.

Miscellaneous Cases: In the Maryland case of *Commonwealth v. Dolly Chapple*, it was held that African Americans could be witnesses against a European American in cases where the European American committed an act of mayhem on an African American.

- *Sports:* Thomas Molineaux fought and defeated Jim Rimmer in 21 rounds (May 21) but once again lost to the British champion, Tom Cribb, in 11 rounds (September 28).

THE AMERICAS

- In Brazil, Prince Regent Joao issued a proclamation which stated that: "All soldiers shall be drawn from the class of whites which shall consist of those whose great-grandparents were not black and whose parents were born free."
- In Chile, the children born of slaves were declared free.
- In Haiti, Henri Christophe was crowned King Henry I of Haiti.

AFRICA

Between 1811 and 1877, there were six Kafir-English Wars in South Africa. The one in 1818 grew out of the interference of the English with the Kafir family system. A war between 1834 and 1835 was followed by the annexation of all the country as far as the Kei River. Intratribal fighting among the Xhosa concerning the chieftainship further weakened the Xhosa and permitted the British to strengthen their hold over the land.

- On March 1, Muhammed Ali massacred the Mameluks in Cairo, Egypt.
- Muhammed Ali of Egypt made war on the Wahhabi at the request of the Porte.
- Further war between the Ashanti and the Fante erupted.
- The Sokoto Caliphate began.
- The Fulani overran the Oyo Kingdom.

ASIA

- The Abolition Act of 1811 was passed. This act prohibited the importation of African slaves into British India.

The British and the Abolition of Slavery

By the early 1800s, the British had begun to take a lead role in the abolition of African slavery. More specifically, concentrating on the East African slave trade, the British took measures designed to eliminate the Asian demand for African slaves.

At first, the British attempted to eliminate the Asian and Arab slave destinations. The Abolition Act of 1811 was but one of the actions

taken by the British. Others included the negotiation of agreements with the Persian Gulf sheiks in 1820, 1838, and 1856; with the shah of Persia in 1851, and the king of Mukalla in 1863. Additionally, in 1855 and 1856, the British negotiated restrictive agreements with a number of Somali kings.

However, despite the agreements negotiated by the British, the slave trade continued to flourish. Having had little success in shutting off the slave trade destinations, the British began to concentrate on the slave trade originations.

In the mid-1800s, the activities of such missionaries as David Livingstone would emphasize that Christianity provided an alternative path to prosperity and the foundation for community for the people of the African interior. It was Livingstone who spearheaded the effort to persuade the African communities which were the source of the slaves to convert to other "trading commodities."

The efforts of the Christian missionary Livingstone would eventually prove to be more successful than the early diplomatic efforts of the British government. Bolstered by the Livingstone legend and legacy, African slavery was gradually brought to end, — but not until some one hundred years had passed following Livingstone's death in 1873. Sometimes a great evil can live for a very long time.

EUROPE

- George Bridgetower, the famed violinist, received a degree in music from Cambridge University. *See 1779.*

RELATED HISTORICAL EVENTS

- Venezuela declared itself independent of Spain. A civil war ensued in which Simon Bolivar emerged as the commander-in-chief of the rebel forces.

The "Mother" of Simon Bolivar

Simon Bolivar (1783–1830) is known as the Great Liberator. He was a soldier and statesman who was the principal leader in the struggle for South American independence from Spain.

Bolivar was born into a wealthy creole family in Caracas, Venezuela, on July 24, 1783. He was educated by private tutors in Caracas as well as in Spain. Bolivar was greatly influenced by the French political philosopher Jean Jacques Rousseau. Bolivar fought under the command of Francisco Miranda, who led the revolt against the Spanish in Venezuela in 1810. The rebels were defeated by the Spanish royalists, and Bolivar was forced to flee the country.

In 1812, Bolivar led another expedition to Venezuela. He captured Caracas in 1813 and became the dictator of the country. Royalist forces defeated him again in 1814, and Bolivar was forced into exile in Jamaica and later in Haiti.

Uniting his forces with those of Jose Antonio Paez and European volunteers, Bolivar again invaded Venezuela in 1817. He established a revolutionary government at Angostura (now Ciudad Bolivar), and was elected president of Venezuela.

In 1819, Bolivar's army crossed the Andes Mountains into New Granada (now Colombia), defeating the Spanish at Boyaca, thus ending royalist rule there. Several months later, on December 17, 1819, the republic of Colombia, consisting of Venezuela and New Granada, was proclaimed, with Bolivar as president.

Bolivar countered a resurgence of royalist activity by leading his army on June 24, 1821, to an overwhelming victory near Carabobo. This victory helped to ensure the independence of Venezuela.

Bolivar, with a vision of a united Spanish America, secured independence for Quito (now known as Ecuador) in 1822, which then became part of the republic of Colombia. In 1824, he led the revolutionary military forces of Peru, which had enlisted his services in its fight for independence. Victorious, Bolivar was also elected president of Peru in February of 1825. The following May, Bolivar organized a new republic in southern Peru—a republic which was named in his honor and which is today known as Bolivia.

From September 1826, when he departed from Peru, to 1830, Bolivar sought in vain to maintain the political unity of the republic of Colombia. Although he resigned the presidency of the republic in August 1828, Bolivar assumed dictatorial control of the republic in September 1828.

Unable to pacify the various factions within the republic, Bolivar relinquished power on April 27, 1830. He died on December 17 of the same year, a defeated, disillusioned and despised man.

Despite his ignoble end, today Bolivar is revered throughout South America, and in Venezuela and Bolivia his birthday is a national holiday.

The racial heritage of Simon Bolivar, the Great Liberator of South America, is the subject of much discussion. The Bolivars arrived in Venezuela—a country populated by Indigenous Venezuelans and African slaves—in the sixteenth century. After two centuries of residing among the Indigenous Venezuelan and African daughters of Aprhodite, many Spanish families, became, or included, mestizos and mulattoes. It is believed that Bolivar's family may have also had a similar heritage.

However, what is known for a fact about Bolivar's heritage is that the Great Liberator owed much of his character and desire to an African woman—a woman named Hipolita.

Bolivar, who was the scion of a rich family of landowners and army officers, came to know sorrow early in his life. His father died when he was three, and his mother died when he was nine. From then on Bolivar considered his African nursemaid, Hipolita, his true father and mother. It was Hipolita who helped mold the youth into the man known as the Great Liberator and to the extent that parents are greatly responsible for their children's success so too must Hipolita be partly credited with the success that was Bolivar's.

• Harriet Beecher Stowe, the European American author of *Uncle Tom's Cabin*, was born (June 14).

Today Harriet Beecher Stowe (1811–1896) is best remembered for her antislavery novel, *Uncle Tom's Cabin*.

Stowe was born on June 14, 1811, in Litchfield, Connecticut. Her father, Lyman Beecher, was a Presbyterian minister and her siblings included the famous clergyman, Henry Ward Beecher, and the reformer and educator, Catherine Beecher.

Stowe was educated at the academy in Litchfield and at Hartford Female Seminary. From 1832 to 1850, Stowe lived in Cincinnati, Ohio, where her father served as president of Lane Theological Seminary.

In 1836, Harriet married Calvin Stowe, a member of the Lane Theological Seminary faculty. Harriet's years in Cincinnati would form the basis for many of the characters and incidents in *Uncle Tom's Cabin*, which was written while Harriet was staying in Brunswick, Maine.

After the publication of the *Uncle Tom's Cabin*, Stowe became famous overnight. On a visit to England, she was welcomed by the English abolitionists and soon became a favorite of the abolitionists on both sides of the ocean.

Uncle Tom's Cabin is often described as melodramatic and sentimental, but it is more than a melodrama. *Uncle Tom's Cabin* recreates characters, scenes, and incidents with humor and realism. It analyzes the issue of slavery in the Midwest, New England, and the South during the days of the Fugitive Slave Law.

Uncle Tom's Cabin was published on the heels of the Compromise of 1850. The book served to intensify the disagreement between the North and the South which led to the Civil War. Stowe's name was anathema in the South, and many historians believe that the bitter feelings aroused by Stowe's book helped cause the Civil War.

It is important to understand that the images that most people have of the characters in *Uncle Tom's Cabin* are not the way the characters are actually portrayed in the book. After the Civil War, *Uncle Tom's Cabin* became known chiefly through abridgements of the novel and by plays (particularly George L. Aiken's play) based on the book. However, these versions distorted the original story and characters. By the late 1800s, most people believed that *Uncle Tom's Cabin* dealt primarily with the death of Tom and Little Eva, Topsy's antics, and Eliza's escape. The term "Uncle Tom" as derived from the plays and distortions came to stand for an African American man who, for selfish reasons or through fear, adopted a humble, often self-degrading, manner to gain the favor of European Americans. However, in Stowe's novel, Uncle Tom is portrayed as a brave man who dies rather than betray two fellow slaves.

Stowe's other works dealt with New England in the late 1700s and early 1800s. These works include *The Minister's Wooing* (1859); *The Pearl of Orr's Island* (1862); *Oldtown Folks* (1869); and *Sam Lawson's Oldtown Fireside Stories* (1872). Another novel *Dred, A Tale of the Great Dismal Swamp* (1856) dealt with slavery in the South.

• Charles Sumner, the great European American advocate of African American rights, was born (January 6).

Charles Sumner (1811–1874) was a statesman and antislavery leader. Sumner was born in Boston, Massachusetts.

After a career as a lawyer who championed antislavery causes, in 1851, Charles Sumner was elected to the United States Senate. In 1856, Sumner made a Senate speech which included several sneering references to Senator Andrew P. Butler of South Carolina. Three days later, Representative Preston S. Brooks,

Butler's nephew, attacked Sumner in the Senate, beating Sumner senseless.

Sumner was one of the founders of the Republican Party. Sumner favored freeing the slaves and giving them the right to vote.

As the Civil War neared its end, Sumner advocated treating the South harshly. He opposed President Lincoln's moderate plans for the reconstruction of the South. Later Sumner also opposed President Andrew Johnson's reconstruction plans.

During Ulysses S. Grant's presidency, in 1869, the president of the Dominican Republic offered to sell his country to the United States. Grant's secretary, General Orville Babcock, signed a treaty of annexation with the black republic. Charles Sumner, who was then chairman of the Senate Foreign Relations Committee, attacked the treaty and denounced Grant. Sumner, always the staunch supporter of political rights for persons of African descent, was angered at the thought of an African-dominated republic losing its independence. Based on Sumner's opposition, the Senate rejected the treaty and the Dominican Republic remained seemingly independent.

1812

THE UNITED STATES

In 1812, the United States and Great Britain engaged in armed hostilities which came to be known as the War of 1812. During the War of 1812, African Americans comprised almost one out of every six seamen in the United States Navy. These African Americans often served with distinction and valor.

• In 1812, Louisiana was admitted into the Union as a slave state. However, even Louisiana, despite the slave uprising of only a year ago, recognized the perils of the times and the needs of the country for able-bodied men, and allowed free African Americans to enlist in the state militia.

• In various parts of the South, rumored slave uprisings and rebellions caused a paranoid repression of any slave groups or meetings. In July, several African Americans suspected of planning an insurrection were summarily arrested in the Mississippi Territory.

• *The Abolition Movement:* In New York, the General Conference of the Methodist Church met and adopted a resolution that no slave owner (if he lived in an area where he could legally free his slaves) was eligible to be an elder in any Methodist church.

• *Notable Births:* Martin R. Delany, newspaper editor, author and Union Army major, was born (May 6).

Martin Robinson Delany (1812–1885) was the first African American major in the United States Army, a medical doctor, an African American nationalist and a writer. He was born in Charlestown, Virginia. His parents were Samuel Delany, a slave, and Pati (Peace) Delany, a free African American. Martin's paternal grandfather was a prince of a Mandingo tribe who had been captured in the Niger Valley, sold into slavery, and subsequently brought to America.

Delany was educated in the African Free School of New York City, the Canaan Academy in New Hampshire, and the Oneida Institute in New York. Delany also studied under the Reverend Louis Woodson, who was employed by a society of African Americans interested in education. Dr. Andrew McDowell taught him medicine. In 1843, Delany began publishing *The Mystery* in Pittsburgh. Between 1847 and 1849, Delany was associated with Frederick Douglass and assisted in the publication of *The North Star*.

In 1849, Delany studied medicine at Harvard University. Upon completion of his medical studies, in 1852, Delany was cited for doing outstanding work in battling a cholera epidemic in Pittsburgh.

Delany was an ardent black nationalist. His compatriot, Frederick Douglass, once remarked: "I thank God for making me a man simply; but Delany always thanks Him for making him a black man."

In 1854, Delany issued a call for a National Emigration Convention, which met in Cleveland in August. The second convention was also held in Cleveland in 1856.

Delany moved to Chatham, Ontario, Canada and practiced medicine. The third National Emigration Convention was held in Chatham in 1858. At this convention, Delany was chosen as the chief commissioner and was designated to explore the valley of the Niger as a possible relocation site. According to his commission, Delany was to make inquiries "for the purpose of science and for general information and without reference to, and with the board being entirely opposed to any emigration there as such."

Delany sailed to the Niger in 1859. He departed from New York aboard the *Mendi*, a vessel owned by three African merchants. While in Nigeria, Delany negotiated treaties with a number of African chiefs who granted lands for prospective African American immigrants. In 1861, Delany published the official report of the Niger Valley exploration.

During the Civil War, Delany helped recruit soldiers for the Union Army. On February 8, 1865, Delany received a commission as a major in the Union Army and was ordered to Charleston, South Carolina, where he would serve as an army physician.

After the Civil War, Delany served with the Freedmen's Bureau for three years for which he worked as trial judge in Charleston, South Carolina. Delany was a leader of the Honest Government League and a severe critic of the corruption of the Reconstruction period in South Carolina. Delany was nominated for lieutenant governor of South Carolina on the Independent Republican ticket in 1874, but was defeated.

In 1879, Delany published *Principia of Ethnology: The Origin of Races and Color, etc.* This publication espoused Delany's views on race.

• John Horse (Juan Caballo) (c. 1812–1882), a leader of the Black Seminoles was born in Florida, the son of a Seminole man and an African woman. *See 1837 and 1850.*

• Armand Lanusse (1812–1867), the originator of *Les Cenelles*, an anthology of poetry by African American poets in New Orleans, was born

Les Cenelles was published in French and English and contained 82 poems which were the work of 17 New Orleans poets. Reviewed in *La Chronique* on January 30, 1848, *Les Cenelles* was the brainchild of Armand Lanusse, a free African American born in New Orleans in 1812. Lanusse himself contributed 16 poems to the anthology.

• *Miscellaneous State Laws:* In Georgia and North Carolina, the laws were relaxed to permit free African Americans to serve in the state militia.

• In Tennessee, a law was enacted which prohibited the importation of slaves into the state.

• The legislature of the Illinois Territory prohibited the immigration of free African Americans and required the registration of free African Americans within the territory.

• In Georgia, the inciting, or the attempted inciting, of slave rebellions was declared to be a capital offense.

• *Publications:* While in Sierra Leone, Paul Cuffee, an African American shipowner and philanthropist, wrote A *Brief Account of the Settlement and Present Situation of the Colony of Sierra Leone.*

• *Scholastic Achievements:* In Boston, financial assistance was provided by the city for the maintenance of an African American school.

• *The Black Church:* African American clergymen, including Bishop Richard Allen and the Reverend Absalom Jones, were requested to help organize defenses for Philadelphia against the British who had recently attacked Washington, D.C.

• Joseph Willis (1762–1854) established a Baptist church in the Bayou Chicot District of Louisiana.

THE AMERICAS

• The South American Catholic Church admitted mulattoes to holy orders for the first time.

• In Cuba, a conspiracy was led by Aponte with slave support. This caused the intendant Don Alejandro Ramirez to seek increased Spanish colonization of the island.

• Teixeira E. Sousa, a noted Afro-Brazilian novelist, was born.

Teixeira E. Sousa (1812–1881) published the first Brazilian novel, *Filha do Pescador,* in 1843. Sousa's masterpiece, the epic A *Independencia do Brasil,* dealt with the nation on the eve of its break with Portugal. Sousa emphasized the multiracial nature of the populace and showed his desire that the races mix so that the true Brazilian, a mulatto, would ultimately emerge.

In 1852, Sousa published *Maria ou a Menina Rouhada* in Paul Brito's magazine, *Marmota Fluminense. Maria* was the first novel in Brazilian literature in which Afro-Brazilians were the leading characters. The novel dealt with Afro-Brazilian customs, religion and sorcery. *See 1809.*

• Aleijadinho, the great Afro-Brazilian architect, died. *See 1730.*

AFRICA

• Muhammed Ali dispatched a diplomatic mission to the Fuaj.

• The Xhosa were driven back behind the Fish River.

• Radama I of Madagascar increased his control over the island.

• Sahela Selassie became king of Shoa.

RELATED HISTORICAL EVENTS

• Napoleon conducted a disastrous Russian campaign. Despite taking Moscow, he was forced to retreat and in doing so, lost 400,000 of his 500,000 man army.

• On July 31, Caracas was retaken by Spanish royalists. Francisco de Miranda was taken prisoner and deported to Spain. Bolivar was allowed to exile in Colombia.

————— 1813 —————

THE UNITED STATES

In 1813, the war between the United States and Great Britain dominated the American scene, and as would be shown over and over again in American history, the perils of war provided golden opportunities for African Americans to demonstrate that they possessed qualities of courage, integrity and honor which transcended their oppressed condition.

When Oliver Hazard Perry won the Battle of Lake Erie, somewhere between ten and twenty-five percent of Perry's 432 men were African Americans. One of Perry's commanders, a Commodore Chauncey, wrote to then Captain Perry concerning Perry's complaint at being sent African American sailors as reinforcements: "I have yet to learn that the color of the skin . . . can affect a man's qualifications or usefulness. I have nearly 50 blacks on board this ship, and many of them are among my best men."

A large proportion of the crew of the United States ship, *Chesapeake,* were African American. The *Chesapeake* engaged the British ship *Shannon* off the coast of Massachusetts near Boston.

Nathaniel Shaler, commander of the United States ship, the *Governor Tompkins,* posthumously praised the bravery of two African Americans in his crew, John Johnson and John Davis. John Johnson and John Davis, two of the many Afro-Americans who served in the Navy on the Great Lakes during the War of 1812, were praised by their commander after their deaths during battle with these words: "When America has such tars, she has little to fear from tyrants of the ocean."

An African American named Jeffrey leaped on to a horse and rallied the American forces to fight off a British charge in the Battle of Fort Boyer near Mobile, Alabama. The rally was successful and Andrew Jackson gave Jeffrey the honorific title of "major" for his bravery.

These are but a few of the many instances of bravery and initiative shown by African Americans during the War of 1812.

• Rumors of minor slave insurrections reached the governor of Virginia in March, April, July and September.
• Lieutenant Colonel Thomas Smith wrote of destroying an African fort in Florida.

The Black Seminoles of Florida

The history of Africans in the Americas can not be adequately told without mentioning the interaction between Africans and the indigenous populations of this New World. Slavery, as practiced in the Americas, could not bind all slaves. Some were able to escape. Many of those who did, found refuge among the native peoples. Among these native peoples, the Africans lived and, after a time, became one with them. Such was the case with the black Seminoles of Florida.

During the 1700s, Florida was a Spanish colony bordering the English colonies. The relationship between the two countries was never cordial and, as a result, Florida was perceived as a haven for those slaves who were fortunate enough to escape from the plantations in Georgia and the Carolinas.

In Florida, the escaped slaves encountered a branch of the Creek (Indigenous American) nation. These Creeks incorporated (accepted) the escaped slaves into their communities and, after time, the two peoples became one. The presence of Africans among the Creeks was so prevalent that the Spaniards began calling both groups "cimarrones." This Spanish word was transformed by the English into the word "seminole" and it is by this name that we know the Seminoles today.

• *The Civil Rights Movement:* In 1813, James Forten, a Philadelphia African American, sent an appeal called "Letters from a Man of Color on a Late Bill" to the Senate of Pennsylvania. The letter was sent in response to a bill introduced in the Pennsylvania Legislature which would have prohibited free African Americans from immigrating to the state. In his appeal, Forten condemned slavery, claimed equality with whites (European Americans) and asserted that African Americans also had certain "inalienable rights." His arguments were persuasive. The bill was never passed and was never considered again.
• *Notable Births:* James McCune Smith, a physician and writer, was born of slaves in New York City.

James McCune Smith (1813–1865) was born in New York City. Smith was the son of a slave

who owed his freedom to the Emancipation Act of the New York state and a self-emancipated bondswoman. Smith was educated in the African Free School, and entered the University of Glasgow in Scotland in 1832. In 1835, Smith received a Bachelor of Arts degree; in 1836, a Master of Arts; and, in 1837, a Doctorate of Medicine.

Smith soon returned to New York to practice medicine. He opened a pharmacy in New York and served for twenty-three years on the medical staff of the Free Negro Orphan Asylum. An opponent of the American Colonization Society, Smith became active in the New York Underground Railroad and a contributor to *The Emancipator.* In 1839, Smith was made the editor of the *Colored American,* to which he contributed "Abolition of Slavery and the Slave Trade in the French and British Colonies."

Smith was a prolific writer. Two of his more influential writings included a pamphlet entitled *A Lecture on the Haytien Revolutions: with a Sketch of the Character of Toussaint l'Ouverture* (1841); an article entitled "Freedom and Slavery for Africans," published in 1844 in the *New York Tribune,* and reprinted in the *Liberator* in 1844. Some of Smith's other works were: "Civilization: Its Dependence on Physical Circumstances," "The German Invasion," "Citizenship, a Discussion of the Dred Scott Decision," "On the 14th Query of Thomas Jefferson's Notes on Virginia" (*see 1782*), and "The Influence of Climate upon Longevity."

Henry Highland Garnet, an abolitionist contemporary of Smith's (*see 1815*), considered Smith to be the most scholarly African American of the era. Smith eventually accepted an appointment as professor of anthropology at Wilberforce University in 1863.

• *Miscellaneous State Laws:* Free African Americans in Virginia were required to pay a poll tax of $1.50 in order to vote.
• *Miscellaneous Cases:* In the case of the *United States v. Douglass,* a case heard in the United States Circuit Court for the District of Columbia, the court held that a free-born African American was competent to bear witness against a white person (European American).
• *Publications: Letters from a Man of Color on a Late Bill* was published *see above.*
• George Lawrence published *Oration on the Abolition of the Slave Trade, delivered on the First Day of January 1813 in the African Methodist Church.*
• *Scholastic Achievements:* The Pennsyl-

vania Abolition Society completed the building of a school for African Americans in Philadelphia at a cost of over $3,000.

• *The Black Church:* African Americans in Wilmington, Delaware, incorporated the Union Church of Africans, the first formal, separate African American Methodist denomination.

The African Americans of Ezion Church in Wilmington, Delaware, withdrew from the Methodist Church when they were unable to retain control of the building *see 1801.*

These African Americans formed the Union Church of Africans, an independent, all–African American, Methodist church.

• Lott Carey organized the African Mission Society.

• *Sports:* Thomas Molineaux defeated Jack Carter in 25 rounds (April 2).

AFRICA

• Mazrui attempted to seize Lamu.

• J. L. Burckhardt explored Upper Egypt and Nubia.

• Muhammed Ali initiated a policy of sending Egyptians to study in Europe.

RELATED HISTORICAL EVENTS

• Sweden abolished its slave trade.

• Henry Ward Beecher, a European American clergyman and promoter of equal rights, was born (June 24).

Henry Ward Beecher (1813–1887) was born in Litchfield, Connecticut. He was the son of Lyman Beecher, a prominent Presbyterian clergyman.

Beecher was educated at Amherst College and at the Lane Theological Seminary. In 1847, after serving as pastor to Presbyterian congregations in Lawrenceburg, Indiana, and Indianapolis, Indiana, Beecher became the pastor of the Plymouth Church of the Pilgrims in Brooklyn, New York. Beecher would hold this post for the rest of his life.

As his career progressed, Beecher became one of the most famous pulpit orators and lecturers in American history. Beecher's theological views were fairly orthodox, but nevertheless, he attracted and held huge audiences in the United States and England with his brilliant speeches and leadership at services and revival meetings and by his espousal of such controversial causes as the biological theory of evolution and scientific historical study of biblical texts.

One of the earliest and best-known sup-

porters of the abolitionists, Beecher was also an effective proponent of women's rights, particularly woman suffrage.

From 1861 to 1863, Beecher was the editor in chief of the *Independent,* a religious and political periodical largely devoted to the abolition of slavery and the advancement of women's rights. From 1870 to 1881, Beecher edited *The Christian Observer,* another publication devoted to the advancement of civil rights.

In 1874, Beecher's former friend and successor as editor of the *Independent,* the American journalist and writer Theodore Tilton (1835–1907) sued Beecher and charged Beecher with having committed adultery with Tilton's wife. A trial held in that year ended in a hung jury, leaving Beecher's reputation besmirched. The cloud of adultery would hang over Beecher for the rest of his life.

• Dr. David Livingstone, a Scottish explorer, traveler and writer, was born.

David Livingstone (1813–1873) was a Scottish doctor and missionary who is considered to be one of the most important explorers of Africa.

Livingstone was born on March 19, 1813, in Blantyre, Scotland. In 1823, Livingstone began to work in a cotton-textile factory. Later, during his medical studies in Glasgow, Livingstone also began attending theology courses. In 1838, Livingstone offered his services to the London Missionary Society. Upon the completion of his medical course in 1840, Livingstone was ordained and was sent as a medical missionary to South Africa.

In 1841, Livingstone reached Kuruman, a settlement founded in Bechuanaland (Botswana) by the Scottish missionary Robert Moffat (1795–1883).

Livingstone began his missionary work among the Africans of Bechuanaland and began to make his way northward despite opposition from the Boer settlers of the region. In 1845, he married his mentor's daughter, Mary Moffat, and together they traveled into regions where no Europeans had ever been before.

In 1849, Livingstone crossed the Kalahari Desert and became the first European to see Lake Ngami. In 1851, accompanied by his wife and children, Livingstone became the first European to encounter the Zambezi River.

On another expedition (1852–1856), while looking for a route to the interior from the east or west coast, Livingstone traveled north from Cape Town to the Zambezi River, and then west to Luanda on the Atlantic coast. Living-stone then retraced his journey to the Zambezi.

On the return trip, Livingstone followed the Zambezi River to the point where it emptied into the Indian Ocean. In the process, Livingstone was the first European to cast his eyes upon the glory of the great Victoria Falls.

Livingstone's explorations resulted in a revision of the European's understanding of the African continent and enabled cartographers to give definition to what was then largely unknown territory. Upon his return to Great Britain in 1856, Livingstone was welcomed as a great explorer and his book *Missionary Travels and Researches in South Africa* (1857) made him famous. Livingstone soon thereafter resigned from the missionary society.

In 1858, the British government appointed Livingstone Consul to Quelimane (Mozambique) and made him the commander of an expedition to explore East and Central Africa. Upon his return to Africa, Livingstone led an expedition up the Shire River, a tributary of the Zambezi. On this expedition, Livingstone became the first European to see Lake Nyasa. Then, in 1859, Livingstone explored the Rovuma River and "discovered" Lake Chilwa.

During these later explorations, Livingstone became concerned with the plight of the Indigenous Africans who were being exploited by Arab and Portuguese slave traders. In 1865, while on a visit to England, Livingstone wrote *Narrative of an Expedition to the Zambezi and Its Tributaries*. In this book, Livingstone issued a condemnation of the still thriving slave trade and offered an expository on the commercial possibilities of the East African coast.

In 1866, financed mostly by friends and admirers, Livingstone led an expedition to discover the sources of the Nile. Traveling along the Rovuma River, the explorer made his way toward Lake Tanganyika, reaching its shores in 1869.

During this Nile expedition, little was heard from Livingstone and his welfare became a matter of international concern. In 1870, Livingstone journeyed to Ujiji, on Lake Tanganyika, into the region lying west of the lake, thereby becoming the first European to visit the Lualaba River (in present-day Zaire).

After enduring great privations, Livingstone made his return to Ujiji. Upon his arrival, he was met by a "rescue party" led by Henry Morton Stanley, a European American journalist. The story goes that at this meeting Stanley reportedly greeted Livingstone with the famous question, "Dr. Livingstone, I presume?"

Stanley and Livingstone went on to explore the country north of Lake Tanganyika together. Later Livingstone set out on his own again to continue his search for the source of the Nile.

Livingstone died in Chitambo's village (in Zambia) sometime around April 30, 1873. His body was found on May 1. Livingstone's followers cut out his heart and buried it at the foot of the tree where his body was found and then transported his body to Zanzibar.

In 1874, Livingstone's remains were buried in Westminster Abbey.

Livingstone's name reverberates through history as a great explorer of the continent of Africa. But his name reverberates through African and African American history because of his poignant opposition to the East African slave trade.

- In August, Simon Bolivar, with republican forces, recaptured Caracas, Venezuela. In October, Bolivar was acclaimed liberator of Venezuela.

----- **1 8 1 4** -----

THE UNITED STATES

In 1814, the war dominated the minds and bodies of many African Americans. Among the American troops gathered under General Winder for the defense of Washington, D.C. against the British were African Americans such as John B. Vashon of Leesburg, Virginia (who volunteered in response to a plea for African Americans to defend "their country") and Louis Boulah. Boulah also later served in the navy. At a skirmish with the British at Bladensburg near Washington, African Americans served under Commodore Barney in constructing earthworks and as teamsters and soldiers.

After the burning of Washington, D.C., the Vigilance Committee of Philadelphia asked James Forten, Bishop Allen and Absalom Jones to enlist African Americans in the task of building defenses for the city. Over two thousand African Americans worked for two days on the project. A battalion of African Americans was also organized in Philadelphia, but saw no action because peace soon ensued.

In Baltimore, free African Americans and slaves, along with whites (European Americans) who had been exempted from military service, erected breastworks in August to defend the city against British attack.

In New York, a law was enacted which provided for the raising of two regiments of African Americans of approximately one thousand each. The regiments were to receive the same pay as white (European American) soldiers. Slaves were allowed to enlist with the permission of their owners and were to be freed at the end of the war. The commissioned officers of the African American regiments were to be European Americans. As a result of this legislation, some 2000 African Americans enlisted and were sent to serve with the army at Sacketts Harbor. (*October 24*).

A group of African Americans, including Robert Van Vranken of Albany, was attached to the victorious American forces at Plattsburg, New York. At Plattsburg, the American forces forced British troops numbering about 14,000 to retreat.

At the Battle of Lake Champlain, many of the victorious American gunners were African American, including John Day, a marine on board the ship *Viper*. Day later went to the Mediterranean with Commander Bainbridge and served in the navy until March, 1816. Another African American who fought with distinction at Lake Champlain was Charles Black. He had earlier been forced into the service of England and had been imprisoned in England along with 400 other African Americans and many whites (European Americans) when he refused to serve. Black's father had fought at Bunker Hill during the Revolutionary War, and his grandfather had fought in the French and Indian Wars.

African Americans were with the American forces at the Battle of Thames in Canada.

In the South, Andrew Jackson issued a proclamation in Mobile, Alabama, calling upon the African Americans to aid in the fight against the British (*September 21*). A few months later, while in New Orleans, Jackson would issue another proclamation praising the African American troops.

Ironically, despite the heroism and unselfish service demonstrated by so many African Americans, the end of the war did not alleviate the oppression of slavery. The Treaty of Ghent which ended the War of 1812 included a provision for the restoration of slaves who had taken sanctuary with the British. In 1826, the United States Minister to the Court of Saint James (Albert Gallatin of Pennsylvania) obtained $1,204,960 from the British for slaves not returned in spite of the treaty.

• James Forten, Absalom Jones, Richard Allen, and other African American leaders were asked, in the midst of the alarm felt at the approach of the British, to raise "colored troops." A meeting was called and 2,500 African American volunteers were secured—a number representing three-fourths of the African American adult male population of Philadelphia. The African American contingent marched to Gray's Ferry and built its fortifications. A battalion for service in the field was also formed but was never utilized.

• *The Abolition Movement:* The Manumission Society of Tennessee was founded by Charles Osborn and others.

• In 1814, the Quakers of North Carolina were able to assist 350 slaves in obtaining their freedom.

• *Miscellaneous State Laws:* In Illinois, the Territorial Legislature passed a bill which permitted the hiring of slaves from outside the territory.

• In 1814, Louisiana law prohibited free African Americans from immigrating into the state. Louisiana law also provided for the death penalty for any slave who wilfully harmed any white (European American). The law required that at least one white (European American) adult male be present for every thirty slaves on a plantation, and that the parish judges make biannual inspections of the plantations to make sure that this ratio was maintained.

• *Miscellaneous Cases:* In the Louisiana case of *Davenport v. the Commonwealth*, a man who had arrested and sold a free African American woman was fined, imprisoned and required to pay damages. But this judicial enlightenment was not reflected elsewhere in the state. In the same year, Louisiana law prohibited free African Americans from immigrating into the state. Louisiana law also provided for the death penalty for any slave who wilfully harmed any white (European American). The law required that at least one white (European American) adult male be present for every thirty slaves on a plantation, and that the parish judges make biannual inspections of the plantations to make sure that this ratio was maintained.

• *Publications:* Russell Parrott published *Oration of the Abolition of the Slave Trade*, an oration which was delivered at the African Church of St. Thomas in Philadelphia.

• *Sports:* In England, Bill Richmond defeated Jack Davis in 13 rounds (April 7). *See 1763.*

• Thomas Molineaux, the one-time protégé of Bill Richmond, defeated Bill Fuller in 2 rounds (May 27).

AFRICA

• The Cape colony (South Africa) was ceded by Holland (the Dutch) to Great Britain (August 13). Lord Charles Somerset was made governor of the colony.

• Abdallah bin Ahman al-Mazrui declared Mombasa (Kenya) independent.

EUROPE

• Alexander Pushkin, the great Afro-Russian poet, was only fifteen when his first poem was published in the most influential Russian literary magazine, *Vestnik Europy* (The Messenger of Europe) in 1814. *See 1799.*

• The *Narrative of the Most Remarkable Particulars in the Life of James Albert Ukawsaw Gronniosaw, an African Prince* was published in England. Gronniosaw was a former slave from New York who lived in England in 1814 under the guardianship of the Countess Huntingdon's Calvinistic Methodist Circle.

RELATED HISTORICAL EVENTS

• In January, Bolivar was made dictator of Venezuela. But in September, Spain reconquered Venezuela and Bolivar was sent into exile in Haiti.

When Bolivar had been defeated and had been refused asylum by other countries, Alexander Petion of southern Haiti welcomed him. Petion restored Bolivar's spirit. He also supplied Bolivar with money, arms, food, and a printing press. Afterwards Bolivar would credit Petion with being "the author" of the liberation of Venezuela and the grateful populace of Venezuela honored this great Haitian by erecting a statue to him in their capital.

• On April 6, Napoleon abdicated as emperor of the French Empire. Pursuant to the Treaty of Paris, Napoleon was made king of (sent in exile to) Elba.

• The Congress of Vienna declared that the slave trade was contrary to human and humane principles.

• Holland (the Dutch) abolished its slave trade.

• France abolished its slave trade.

• Daniel Reaves Goodloe, a European American emancipationist from North Carolina, was born (May 28).

• Spain temporarily regained control of Santo Domingo (the Dominican Republic).

• On December 24, the United States and Great Britain executed the Treaty of Ghent, ending the War of 1812.

1815

THE UNITED STATES

With the winding down of the war known as the War of 1812, a general dislocation of the populace began as people began to flock in earnest to the Northwest Territory—an area of the country which was essentially the Great Lakes region west of Pittsburgh and north of the Ohio River, and is now referred to by historians as the Old Northwest. Among the pioneers were a number of African Americans. These African American pioneers, in addition to encountering a hostile environment, often had to contend with a hostile citizenry. The general trend was toleration from 1800 to 1826; persecution from 1826 to 1841; and, in a relativistic sense, amelioration from 1841 to 1861.

As for the war itself, in the Battle of New Orleans—a battle which perhaps need not have been fought—a battalion of about 280 New Orleans African Americans under the command of Major Lacoste and a battalion of about 150 Africans from Santo Domingo (Haiti) under the command of Major Daquin, assisted in erecting the fortifications for Andrew Jackson and fought successfully against the British. A total of over 600 African Americans, some with African American line officers, fought under Jackson at the Battle of New Orleans.

As a consequence of the British defeat, when the British abandoned Fort Blount, on the Apalachicola Bay in Florida, about 300 escaped slaves from Georgia and some 30 Creeks drove the Seminole remnant from the fort and occupied it. The escaped slaves created a nearby "maroon" community and used the fort as a haven for other escaped slaves as well as a base of operations for occasional expeditions into Georgia and Alabama against slave holders.

• The General Assembly of the Presbyterian Church stated that it was not strong enough to take action on the issue of slavery.

• *The Abolition Movement:* In 1815, George Boxley, a European American, decided to attempt to emancipate the slaves. Boxley led a group of fellow conspirators in Spotsylvania and Orange County, Virginia. A few of the conspirators obtained guns while others had swords and clubs. The rebels planned on meeting during the harvest time at Boxley's house from where they would stage an attack on Fredericksburg. The conspiracy came to be known as Boxley's Conspiracy.

Early in 1816, an African American woman, belonging to a Spotsylvania, Virginia, slaveholder, betrayed George Boxley's plan to free the slaves of Virginia. Military and police measures were at once instituted and about thirty slaves were immediately arrested.

Boxley, after vainly trying to organize a rescue party, fled. He finally surrendered and was imprisoned. However, with the aid of his wife, Boxley somehow managed to escape. Although a reward of $1,000 was offered for his capture, he never was.

Eventually six slaves were executed for this conspiracy. However, six others that had been condemned to hang were reprieved and banished from the state.

• *The Colonization Movement:* Paul Cuffee, an African American shipowner, made another personally financed trip to Sierra Leone with nine African American families (38 settlers) thus becoming the first African American to sponsor a migration of African Americans to Africa. *See 1759.*

• *Notable Births:* Henry Highland Garnet, minister, abolitionist, and diplomat, was born a slave in Kent County, Maryland (December 23).

Henry Highland Garnet (1815–1882) was an educator and a clergyman. He was born a slave at New Market in Kent County, Maryland. Garnet's grandfather was said to have been a ruler of a tribe in the Mandingo Empire of West Africa.

In 1824, Garnet, with his father, escaped and went to New York. In New York, Garnet sought and obtained an education. After finishing his studies, he divided his time between preaching the Gospel in church and advocating the abolition of slavery with the American Anti-Slavery Society.

Garnet continued with his dual avocations until 1843 when he made an address at the National Convention of the Free People of Color at Buffalo, New York, in which he called upon slaves to rise up and slay their masters. The National Convention refused to endorse these sentiments, and he was especially criticized by Frederick Douglass. Garnet's popularity fell and his influence waned.

Garnet returned to the pulpit and concentrated more upon preaching the Gospel. He served as pastor of the Liberty Street Presbyterian Church in Troy, New York, from 1843 to 1848. In 1848, Garnet published *The Past and Present Condition, and the Destiny of the Colored Race.* Garnet also published *The National Watchman* with William G. Allen.

In 1852, he was sent as a missionary to Jamaica. On February 12, 1865, Garnet preached a sermon in the House of Representatives commemorating the passage of the 13th Amendment. In 1881, Garnet was appointed minister to Liberia.

• Myrtilla Miner, founder of Miner's Teachers College, was born (March 4).
• Edward James Roye, the fifth president of Liberia, was born.

Edward James Roye (1815–1872) was born in Newark, Ohio. He arrived in Liberia in 1846 and became a leading merchant. He entered politics and became the Speaker of the House of Representatives in 1849.

From 1865 to 1868, Roye served as chief justice of the Liberian Supreme Court. He was elected president in January 1871.

As president, Roye undertook the complete financial reconstruction of Liberia. He also introduced measures for improving the schools and the system of roads in Liberia. However, despite this initial promise, Roye's presidency was destined to be brought down by scandal and tragedy.

The cause of Roye's demise lay in his dealings before assuming the presidency. In 1870, Roye had gone to England to negotiate a loan. He was successful in securing a $500,000 loan. However, the very severe terms for the repayment of the loan caused great resentment in Liberia. Roye was accused of embezzlement. Roye became defensive and autocratic. He issued an edict which extended his term in office, but the people of Liberia would not obey it. An insurrection ensued and Roye was deposed from office.

Summoned to a trial for his crimes, Roye fled. He attempted to find a safe haven with an English ship that was in the nearby harbor. However, as Roye paddled out to the ship in a native canoe, the canoe was overturned by the waves. Roye was drowned.

• *Miscellaneous State Laws:* In 1815, Louisiana enacted a law which permitted the organization of a police corps comprised of free African Americans. In Kentucky, a law was adopted which prohibited the introduction of slaves for sale. While in Virginia, free African Americans were required to pay a poll tax of $2.50.

• *Publications: An Oration on the Abolition of the Slave Trade* was delivered at the Episcopal Asbury African Church, New York on January 2, 1815.

• *Sports:* Thomas Molineaux, a one-time protégé of Bill Richmond, lost a fight to George Cooper in 14 rounds (March 10).

• In England, Bill Richmond defeated Tom Shelton in 23 rounds (August 11). *See 1763.*

AFRICA

By 1815, five hundred thousand square miles of the African continent (an area almost equal in size to all of Europe), was under European control and domination.

• Edward James Roye, the fifth president of Liberia, was born. *See 1815: Notable Births, above.*

• Napoleon arrived on the island of Saint Helena and his final exile began (October 13).

• The United States signed peace treaties with Algiers and Tripoli.

• The French reoccupied Bourbon.

• Namiembali became the first king of the Mangbetu dynasty and greatly expanded the Mangbetu kingdom.

The Mangbetu are an ethnic group living in Zaire between the Ituri and Vele rivers.

• Joseph Wright was born.

Joseph Wright, was of the Egba subgroup of the Yoruba people. He was born in what is today Nigeria.

Wright was enslaved and shipped from Lagos (Nigeria) in 1826 or 1827. His life was later chronicled in "The Life of Joseph Wright: A Native of Ackoo," a segment of John Beecham's *Ashantee and the Gold Coast* (1841).

EUROPE

• John Baptist Philip, a person of African descent from Trinidad, was awarded a Doctor of Medicine degree from Edinburgh University.

RELATED HISTORICAL EVENTS

• On February 26, Napoleon left his exile on Elba and returned to France. On March 1, he disembarked near Cannes, and thus began the Hundred Days. On March 20, Napoleon reentered Paris. On June 7, Napoleon opened the legislature in Paris, and on June 18, Napoleon led his army in the monumental battle of Waterloo where he was defeated. On June 21, Napoleon returned to Paris and, on June 22, he abdicated once again. On August 8, Napoleon was exiled to St. Helena where he would stay until his death in 1821.

• On December 16, the exiled Dom Joao (Prince John) proclaimed Brazil to be an independent empire equal to Portugal.

Between 1815 and 1830, Spain and Portugal gradually abolished their participation in the slave trade.

1816

THE UNITED STATES

In June of 1816, a slave held by Colonel Chestnut betrayed a plot involving slaves in and around Camden, South Carolina, about a month after the escape of George Boxley (*see 1815*). According to the plan, July 4 was to be the day for the revolt. The revolt was to start by setting fire to several houses in Camden.

The informer was rewarded for his betrayal. His freedom was purchased by the South Carolina Legislature and he was given a lifetime pension of $50.

Meanwhile the slave conspirators were sentenced to death. Six of the leaders were hanged, one was pardoned, and one was sentenced to a year in irons followed by banishment.

• The Seminole Wars with General Andrew Jackson in charge of United States forces began with an attack on a fort in western Florida which contained hundreds of escaped slaves living among the Creek and Seminole Indians who occupied it.

The First Seminole War

In 1816, Florida was a Spanish possession eyed by the United States as prime lands for expansion. Additionally, there was ever mounting hostility between the Seminoles and the European Americans along the Florida-Georgia border over the issue of the Seminoles harboring escaped slaves.

Negotiations for the purchase of Florida between the United States and Spain had been going on for a number of years with little immediated prospects of closure. However, even though Florida remained the sovereign territory of Spain, incidents involving the Seminoles provided the United States with a golden opportunity to establish a military presence near and in Florida. Under the orders of President James Monroe and Secretary of War John Calhoun, the President's favorite general, the hero of New Orleans, Andrew Jackson, was sent to Florida to stabilize the situation. *See 1815.*

In 1816, a detachment of United States troops crossed the Florida border in pursuit of escaped slaves and destroyed Negro Fort—maroon fortifications along the Apalachicola River which would later become the site of Fort Gadsden. Of the 300 maroon inhabitants of Negro Fort, only 40 remained alive after the ten day siege of the United States Army.

In 1817, troops from Fort Scott attacked the Seminole village of Fowltown in northwest Florida when Chief Neamathla insisted that the soldiers stop trespassing on Seminole hunting grounds. Both black and red Seminoles, along with a number of European American soldiers, were killed in the battle. Thus began the First Seminole War.

In March of 1818, General Jackson, having had recent success in the Creek War of 1813, gathered an armed force at Fort Scott. It consisted of 800 regular army personnel, 900 Georgia militiamen, as well as a force of Creeks under the command of William MacIntosh, an individual of mixed European and Indigenous American heritage. Jackson took his forces across the border and marched on St. Marks, a settlement on the Apalachee Bay south of Tallahassee which was reputedly held by the Seminoles.

However, the Seminoles were clever fighters and knew that a direct confrontation with such a large force was not advisable. The Seminoles learned of Jackson's plans and abandoned the fort at St. Marks. When Jackson's forces arrived at St. Marks, they were met by an old Scottish trader, Alexander Arbuthnot, and two Creek chiefs who had been active in the Creek War. Jackson executed the Creeks at once and held Arbuthnot for trial.

Jackson then directed his forces in a southeasterly direction to the village of a Chief Boleck on the Suwanee River. However, once again the Seminoles eluded Jackson by simply vanishing into the Florida jungle. This time Jackson captured only two Englishmen who had been living among the Seminoles, Lieutenant Robert Ambrister of the Royal Marines and Peter Cook. The troops burned the village and then returned to St. Marks. At St. Marks, a "trial" was convened under which Arbuthnot and Ambrister were sentenced to death. They were hanged for ostensibly aiding and abetting the Seminoles.

Frustrated by the Seminoles' unwillingness to fight, Jackson turned his attention on the hapless Spanish. He marched his forces westward to the Spanish fort at Pensacola. After a three-day siege, the Spanish surrendered and Jackson boldly claimed all of west Florida for the United States.

Of course, Jackson's actions were illegal under international law. Both Spain and England protested his incursion. However, the new administration of President John Quincy Adams backed Jackson and sent an ultimatum to Spain to either control the Seminoles or to cede the territory. In 1819, a treaty between the United States and Spain was signed which provided for the sale of the remainder of Florida to the United States. Official occupation took place in 1821 and Florida was organized as a territory in 1822.

As soon as Florida became a possession of the United States, European Americans began flooding into the land. The European Americans laid claim to and took over the lands which had been the Seminoles'. In 1823, some of the Seminole chieftains were pressured into signing the Treaty of Tampa, in which they assented to move to a reservation inland from Tampa Bay. It was no coincidence that the pressure was being asserted by the then governor of the Florida Territory—none other than the man known as "Sharp Knife," Andrew Jackson, the soon to be President of the United States.

- Bob, an English speaking person of African descent who would later be baptized as Juan Crisobal, arrived in California.
- *The Abolition Movement:* Quakers in North Carolina formed the Manumission Society.
- Russell Parrott, an African American from Philadelphia, addressed a celebration of the abolition of the slave trade by expressing the empathy that free African Americans had for their enslaved brethren.
- John Randolph of Virginia proposed that Congress end the "infamous traffic" in slaves in the District of Columbia.
- *The Colonization Movement:* The Virginia Assembly passed a resolution asking that the United States government find a place on the northern Pacific Coast where free African Americans from Virginia could be settled.

In 1816, the American Colonization Society was founded in Washington, with Bushrod Washington as president, and Henry Clay, Francis Scott Key, John C. Calhoun and John Randolph among its sponsors. At the first meeting of the society, Clay praised the society's aim of ridding the "country of a useless and pernicious, if not dangerous, portion of its population"—the freed African Americans (December 28).

• *Notable Births:* William Wells Brown, an African American historian, was born.

William Wells Brown (1816 [1814?]–1884) was a noted African American reformer and historian. He was born in Lexington, Kentucky. His mother was an attractive mulatto slave and his father was said to be a European American slaveholder by the name of George Higgins.

William Wells Brown was taken to St. Louis and, once he became old enough to hire out for work, he was hired out on a steamboat. For a time he also worked for Elijah P. Lovejoy, the editor of the *St. Louis Times.* However, his stay there was brief and he was once again hired out on a steamboat.

In 1834, Brown escaped to Ohio. His original purpose was to go to Canada. He was sheltered by a Quaker who inspired him to assist other slaves to escape.

Between 1843 and 1849, Brown worked as a lecturer for the western New York Anti-Slavery Society and the Massachusetts Anti-Slavery Society.

William Wells Brown was also interested in temperance, women's suffrage, and prison reform. In 1849, he visited England and represented the American Peace Society at the Peace Congress in Paris. Brown stayed abroad until 1854.

Although Brown also studied medicine, his fame rests largely on his reputation as a historian. His works include *Narrative of William Wells Brown, a Fugitive Slave* (1847); *Three Years in Europe* (1852) (also known as *The American Fugitive in Europe: Sketches of Places and People Abroad*); and *Clotel, or the President's Daughter, A Narrative of Slave Life in the United States,* a novel published in 1853.

Brown also wrote plays. His plays include *The Dough Face* and *The Escape, or a Leap for Freedom.* His historical works include: *The Black Man, His Antecedents, His Genius and His Achievements* (1863); *The Negro in the American Rebellion, His Heroism and His Fidelity* (1867); and *The Rising Son, or the Antecedents and the Advancements of the Colored Race* (1874).

• John Jones (1816–1879), "the most prominent citizen of Chicago" during his lifetime, was born in Greene County, North Carolina.

Jones was born free in North Carolina. Jones was a civil rights advocate and the first African American elected Cook County commissioner.

• William Cooper Nell, an African American writer, was born in Boston.

William Cooper Nell (1816–1874) was born in Boston, Massachusetts, the son of William G. Nell and Louisa Nell. He attended a primary school for African American children and, ultimately, read law in the office of William I. Bowditch. Nell became affiliated with the antislavery movement, but concentrated his efforts on opening public schools for the education of African American children.

In 1851, Nell assisted Frederick Douglass in the publication of the *North Star.* His pamphlet *Services of Colored Americans in the Wars of 1776 and 1812* was published in May of 1851.

In 1855, *Colored Patriots of the American Revolution,* with an introduction by Harriet Beecher Stowe, was published.

Nell became the first African American to hold a civil service post under the federal government when he was made a postal clerk by John G. Palfrey, the postmaster of Boston.

• *Notable Deaths:* Peter Salem, hero of Bunker Hill, died (August 16). See 1775.

• *Miscellaneous State Laws:* In 1816, a Louisiana law provided that no slave could serve as a witness against European Americans nor could a slave serve as a witness against a free African American, unless the free African American happened to be engaged in a slave plot or revolt. Another Louisiana law provided that any slave who shot or stabbed a European American was to be executed, and any slave found guilty of arson or of administering poison was to be imprisoned in chains and subjected to hard labor for the remainder of the slave's life.

• In 1816, a Georgia law declared that inciting or attempting to incite a slave rebellion was a capital offense. Another Georgia law provided that the killing or maiming of slaves or free African Americans by European Americans would carry the same punishment as the commission of the same offense by European Americans against fellow European Americans. A third Georgia law granted a stipend for old or infirm slaves who had been abandoned by their owners and assessed the slave's owners for reimbursement. A fourth Georgia law prohibited any further importation of slaves. However, this law was repealed in 1824 only to be revived again in 1829.

• In South Carolina, the legislature prohibited the importation of slaves but, as in Georgia, this edict was repealed.

• In Indiana, the Indiana Constitution outlawed slavery.

• *Miscellaneous Cases:* In 1816, in the Louisiana case of *Forsyth, et. al. v. Nash*, the court held that an African American could not be proved to be a slave on the basis of a bill of sale executed in Detroit, Michigan, because slavery was prohibited in the state of Michigan.

• In South Carolina, the case of *Pepeon v. Clarke* was decided. The case of *Pepeon* involved a person who moved to South Carolina from Maryland, bringing a slave girl with him. The court held that the owner's admission that the girl's mother had been a free African American was sufficient to offset the presumption of color. The girl was set free and awarded damages.

• *Publications:* In 1816, *The Book and Slavery Irreconcilable* was published. Written by George Bourne, *The Book and Slavery Irreconcilable* was one of the most famous of all abolitionist works. Bourne was a Presbyterian minister in Virginia. After the publication of *The Book and Slavery Irreconcilable*, Bourne lost his position and was charged with heresy. Bourne later became a founder of the American Anti-Slavery Society. Bourne was an outspoken and militant abolitionist, and was perhaps the first European American to demand the immediate emancipation of the slaves.

• *Scholastic Achievements:* In Baltimore, the Bethel Charity School was founded by Daniel Coker for the education of African Americans. Meanwhile, in Wilmington, Delaware, a school and library were established for the sole purpose of educating African Americans and an African American teacher was employed.

• The Black Church: The African Methodist Episcopal Church became independent of jurisdictional control by non–African American bodies (April 9).

The Philadelphia gathering of African American Methodists organized the National African Methodist Episcopal Church. The conference delegates elected Daniel Coker as the first bishop, but Coker deferred in favor of Richard Allen. *See 1760.*

• John Stewart (1786–1823), an African American Methodist, became a missionary to the Wyandottes (Indigenous Americans). Stewart was accompanied by Jonathan Poyn-

ter, an African American who was raised by the Wyandottes.

THE AMERICAS

• In Argentina, the exportation of slaves from the country was prohibited.

• In Barbados, a great deal of property was destroyed as the result of a slave insurrection led by Washington Franklin.

• Prince Saunders published the Haytian Papers. These papers were translated excerpts from the *Code Henri* and other Haytian Laws.

AFRICA

• An Anglo-Dutch fleet under Lord Exmouth destroyed the port and fleet of Algiers.

• Bathurst was founded.

Bathurst is the the former name given for the city of Banjul, the capital of Gambia.

• Egyptians under Ibrahim Pasha began operations against the Wahhabis.

• A school of engineering was founded in Cairo.

EUROPE

• In Great Britain, a slave registry was instituted for the purpose of checking the importation of new slaves or the enslavement of free Africans.

• In London, *Remarks on the Insurrection in Barbadoes* was published.

RELATED HISTORICAL EVENTS

• In March, Bolivar returned to Venezuela from his exile in Haiti. Upon his return, he was declared the "Supreme Chief of the Republic." In December, using the army which had been equipped in Haiti, Bolivar seized the Orinoco estuary. Again the independence of Venezuela was proclaimed with Angostura as capital.

——— 1817 ———

THE UNITED STATES

In 1817, free African Americans in the large cities held protest meetings against the American Colonization Society's efforts to "exile us from the land of our nativity" (January). In Philadelphia, African Americans met at Bethel Church to protest. About 300 African Americans were involved in the protest. The protestors were led by Richard Allen and James Forten. James Forten, an African American abolitionist, was elected chairperson of this delegation of protestors. Forten and Russell

Parrott charged that the American Colonization Society had issued false and damaging propaganda against free African Americans. The protestors declared that African Americans would never leave the United States. (January 23).

• In 1817, troops from Fort Scott attacked the Seminole village of Fowltown in northwest Florida when Chief Neamathla insisted that the soldiers stop trespassing on Seminole hunting grounds. Both black and red Seminoles, along with a number of European American soldiers, were killed in the battle. Thus began the first formal engagement of the First Seminole War. *See 1816.*

• On April 7, a slave riot erupted in St. Mary's County, Maryland. Approximately 200 slaves were involved. A number of European Americans were injured by sticks and brickbats, and two houses were ransacked before the police and citizen patrols restored order.

• *The Abolition Movement:* The American Conventions of Abolition Societies resolved "that the gradual and total emancipation of all persons of colour, and their literary and moral education, should precede their colonization" in Africa. This resolution was a concession to the prevailing sentiment in the United States. However, in principle, abolitionists were strongly opposed to colonization.

• *The Colonization Movement: See above.*

• *Notable Births:* John Mifflin Brown, a bishop in the African Methodist Episcopal Church, was born.

John Mifflin Brown (1817–1893), an American of African American and European American parentage, was born in Cantwell's Bridge (now called Odessa), Delaware. In 1836, Brown joined the Bethel African Methodist Episcopal Church. He prepared for the ministry and attended Wesleyan Academy and Oberlin College.

Between 1844 and 1847, Brown served as principal of the Union Seminary, which is now known as Wilberforce University. Union Seminary was the first higher educational effort of the African Methodist Episcopal Church.

In 1864, Brown was chosen editor of the *Christian Recorder,* the oldest African American newspaper in the United States.

In 1868, Brown was ordained a bishop in the African Methodist Episcopal Church. During his twenty-five years of service as a bishop, Brown is credited with establishing the Payne Institute (now known as Allen University) at Columbia, South Carolina, and Paul Quinn College at Waco, Texas.

• According to many African American historians, Frederick Douglass, orator, editor and statesman, was born a slave in Talbot County, Maryland on February 14 of this year. However, the validity of this date is uncertain. As Douglass himself said, "I have no accurate knowledge of my age, never having seen any authentic record containing it. By far the larger part of the slaves know as little of their age as horses know of theirs, and it is the wish of most masters within my knowledge to keep their slaves thus ignorant."

Frederick Douglass (1817 [1818?]–1895) was born Frederick Augustus Washington Bailey. However, Douglass assumed the name Frederick Douglass shortly after his escape to freedom. Douglass' father was an unknown European American, his mother, Harriet Bailey, an African American slave.

In his youth, Douglass was sent to Baltimore to serve as a house servant. It was while serving as a house servant that he learned how to read and write. Upon the death of the slaveholder who owned Douglass, Douglass was sent back to the country to work as a field hand.

Douglass despised the work he was consigned to do and decided to escape. Along with a dozen other slaves, he prepared an escape plan. But before the plan could be put into effect, Douglass and his fellow conspirators were betrayed. Douglass was jailed.

Upon his release from jail, Douglass was returned to Baltimore. However, despite the jail stay, Douglass was determined to be free. He disguised himself as a sailor and attempted his second escape on September 3, 1838. On this second attempt, Douglass was successful.

Douglass fled to New York City. He soon became involved in abolitionist causes. In 1841, he attended a convention of the Massachusetts Anti-Slavery Society in Nantucket. He later was employed as an agent by the society and took an active part in the society's Rhode Island campaign against a new state constitution which would have disenfranchised African Americans. Douglass became a central figure in the famous 100 Conventions of the New England Anti-Slavery Society.

In 1845, Frederick Douglass published the classic *Narrative of the Life of Frederick Douglass.* This book added to Douglass' growing fame and stature. The next two years after the publication of this book, Douglass spent lecturing in Britain and Ireland on slavery and women's rights issues. The money he received from his book and his lectures enabled Douglass to actually purchase his freedom from his former owner.

Douglass established a newspaper, the *North Star*, in Rochester, New York, which helped him to espouse his abolitionist views. Douglass also joined forces with Harriet Beecher Stowe to establish an industrial school for young African Americans.

Douglass was an ardent abolitionist and this passion brought him in contact with some of the more noted abolitionist personalities of the era. One such personality was John Brown. For a time, Douglass consulted with and counseled John Brown. This association was to create some problems for Douglass. After John Brown's failed insurrection and capture, Douglass was outlawed in the State of Virginia. Fearing for his general safety, Douglass fled to Canada.

Douglass returned to the United States upon the outbreak of initial hostilities of the Civil War. During the Civil War, Douglass helped to recruit the 54th and 55th Massachusetts Negro Regiments, the first African American units to serve in the Civil War.

After the War, Douglass held a number of posts. He was a member of the Territorial Legislature of Washington, D.C.; the secretary of the Santo Domingo Commission; police commissioner, marshal, and recorder of deeds of the District of Columbia; United States Minister to Haiti; and chargé d'affaires for Santo Domingo.

While in Haiti, Douglass noted with disgust the exploitation of the people and the land which was being perpetrated by American business interests. In protest to this exploitation, Douglass resigned his position as chargé d'affaires in 1891.

Douglass published a number of works. Among his most noteworthy works are *Narrative of the Life of Frederick Douglass* (1845); *Lectures on American Slavery* (1851); *My Bondage and My Freedom* (1855); and *U.S. Grant and the Colored People* (1872).

By any measure, Frederick Douglass stands as not only a giant in African American history but also a giant in American history.

[Despite the fact that Frederick Douglass believed that he was born in 1817, documentation discovered after his death indicates that his actual date of birth was 1818. In a very tragic sense, this learned man remained throughout his life ignorant of the essential truth of the date of his birth.]

• Victor Séjour, a Creole poet and dramatist, was born the son of Louis Victor Séjour Marou, a free person of African descent from Haiti, and Heloise Philippe Ferrand, a quadroon of New Orleans (June 2).

Victor Séjour (1817–1874) was born in New Orleans. In 1834, Victor was listed on the membership role of an organization of free African American mechanics. The organization was called "Les Artisans." But Victor's destiny lay in another "artistic" arena.

Victor's parents sent him to Paris to study in an attempt to avoid Victor being handicapped by the social disadvantage of his race. In Paris, Victor became enchanted with the theatre. He frequented drama circles and was often in the company of successful dramatists such as Dumas (*see 1802*) and Emile Augier. In 1844, Le Théatre-Français produced Séjour's first play. The play was entitled *Diegareas* and it launched Séjour on to a successful career. Séjour became one of the most commercially successful dramatists in Paris during the 1800s and on this basis lies his claim to fame.

• Samuel Ringgold Ward (1817–1866), the "Black Daniel Webster," was born in Maryland the son of slaves, William and Anne Ward. He was one of the most noted abolitionists (October 17).

In 1839, Samuel Ringgold Ward, an escaped slave, became a professional antislavery agent for the American Anti-Slavery Society. Ward had been educated in New York and became a Presbyterian minister there. Ward pastored a European American church in South Butler, New York. Ward was also one of the first African Americans to join the Liberty Party. Ward later lived abroad, first, in England and, lastly, in Jamaica. He would die in poverty in Jamaica.

• George Washington, pioneer, humanitarian and founder of Centralia, Washington, was born a slave (August 15).

George Washington (1817–1905) was born in Virginia. His European American mother gave him up for adoption to a European American family which moved to the American frontier.

In 1850, Washington moved to the Oregon Territory and, eventually, homesteaded in present-day Washington.

In 1872, Washington established Centralia when the Northern Pacific Railroad crossed his land. Today in Centralia, Washington, a city park bears his name.

• *Notable Deaths:* Paul Cuffee, an African American shipbuilder, philanthropist and African colonizer, died. *See 1759.*
• *Miscellaneous State Laws:* In 1817, Mississippi was admitted into the Union as a slave state. The Constitution for Mississippi required that an owner care for his slaves and refrain from injuring them under penalty of having the slaves sold by the state. The Constitution also provided for jury trials for slaves involved in capital cases.
• In New York, the legislature passed the Abolition Act. The Act provided that on July 4, 1827, every African American born in New York before July 4, 1799, would be set free, and all African American males born after July 4, 1799 would be set free when they reached the age of 28. As for African American women, all African American women born after July 4, 1799 were to be set free when they reached the age of 25. On July 4, 1827, this law did take effect and on that day 10,000 slaves were freed *without* compensation to their owners.
• Kidnappers of African Americans in New York were sentenced to three years in the penitentiary while kidnappers of African Americans in Maryland were sentenced to five years in the penitentiary.
• In Tennessee, a law was enacted which forbade the selling of a slave who had brought a suit for his or her freedom.
• In North Carolina, a law was passed which declared that the killing of a slave was homicide and should be punished as homicide.
• *Miscellaneous Cases:* In the Maryland case of *Burrows Admiralty v. Negro Anna*, the court held that gifts of property by a slave owner to his slave entitled the slave to "freedom by implication," since the law forbade slaves from inheriting or holding property.
• *Publications:* Charles Osborn, a European American, began publishing *The Philanthropist*, an antislavery newspaper in Mt. Pleasant, Ohio (August 29).
• *Scholastic Achievements:* Morris Brown, a free African American of Charleston, South Carolina, was ordained a deacon in the African Methodist Episcopal Church.
• *The Black Church:* In 1817, Jarena Lee (1783–?), an African American woman, rose in Bethel Church in Philadelphia, to give a spontaneous talk. Thus, began her career as a preacher.

THE AMERICAS

• Between 1817 and 1850 an estimated 3 to 5 million slaves were imported to Brazil.
• In 1817, the Afro-Cuban population in Cuba was 339,959. This number represented 54 percent of the total population. Out of the 339,959 Afro-Cubans, 115,691 were listed as free and 225,268 were listed as slaves.

AFRICA

• Privateering was forbidden by the sultan of Morocco.
• Uthman dan Fodio died.
• Muhammed Bello succeeded Uthman dan Fodio as the sultan of Sokoto.
• The British relinquished control of their Senegal possessions to France.
• The British executed a treaty with the Ashanti.
• The British executed a treaty with Radama I of Madagascar.

EUROPE

• Alexander Pushkin, the great Afro-Russian poet, published *Vol'nost* (Ode to Freedom), a powerful expression of Pushkin's political liberalism. *See 1799.*
• Auguste Lacaussade, one of France's most gifted poets, and a person of African descent, was born in Ile de la Réunion. Lacaussade repeatedly protested against the enslavement of his fellow Africans.

RELATED HISTORICAL EVENTS

• In January, the army of the Andes, led by Jose de San Martin, crossed the Andes from Argentina into Chile. On February 12, San Martin routed the Spanish army at Chacabuco. On February 15, San Martin was elected governor of Chile but he declined the honor in favor of Bernardo O'Higgins, a Chilean hero.

It is important to note that out of his 5,000-man force, San Martin's army of the Andes included some 1,500 persons of African descent. These Africans were instrumental in the success of the army of the Andes and in securing the independence of not only Chile but also the other Latin American republics as well.

• Ferdinand VII of Spain bought Russian warships to mount an expedition against rebels in South America. In response, Bolivar solicited volunteer reinforcements from England.
• In 1817, Spain abolished its participation in the slave trade north of the equator. This abolition was prompted by the payment of 400,000 pounds (English currency) from the British government to the Spanish Crown.

1 8 1 8

THE UNITED STATES

In 1818, maroon activities disturbed the tranquility in South Carolina, Virginia, and North Carolina. *See 1816: The First Seminole War.* Disturbances in North Carolina became serious enough in November to evoke considerable notice from the local press. Later on, an attack upon a store by maroons led by Andy (alias Billy James, and even better known by the name Abaellino) was repulsed by armed residents. *See also 1816: The First Seminole War for an account of the attack upon the maroon (black Seminoles) of Florida.*

• In Manchester, New Hampshire, Lemuel Haynes, an African American, became the pastor of a European American (white) Congregational church.

• *The Abolition Movement:* The General Assembly of the Presbyterian Church declared slavery to be "a gross violation of the most precious and sacred rights of human nature."

• *Notable Births:* Charles Lewis Reason (1818–1893), an African American writer, was born in New York City, the son of Michael and Elizabeth Reason, immigrants from the West Indies (July 21).

• *Notable Deaths:* Absalom Jones, the first African American minister ordained in America, died in Philadelphia (February 13).

• Thomas Molineaux, an African American boxer, died in Galway, Ireland (August 4).

• Jean Baptiste Pointe du Sable, a person of African descent who was the founder of the city of Chicago, died. *See 1745.*

• *Miscellaneous State Laws:* In Illinois, the Illinois Constitution forbade slavery.

• In the Missouri Territory, a law was enacted which provided for the death penalty, without benefit of clergy, for stealing or selling a free African American into slavery when the person had knowledge that the African American was free.

• In New Jersey, a law provided severe penalties for the exportation of slaves from the state.

• In Connecticut, African Americans were disenfranchised (denied the right to vote).

• In Georgia, a law forbade free African Americans from owning real estate or slaves. (This law would be repealed in 1819 except for in Savannah, Augusta, and Darien.) Another Georgia slave code required incoming free African Americans to register and give full details concerning themselves and

reasons for entering the state. Additionally, the manumission of slaves was prohibited.

• *Miscellaneous Cases:* In Mississippi, in the case of *Harvy and Others v. Decker*, the court held that slaves taken from Virginia to Indiana in 1784 and then taken to Mississippi in 1816 had been freed by the Northwest Ordinance of 1787 and could no longer be enslaved.

• In Delaware, in the case of *Meunier v. Duperrow*, two African American women were found guilty of kidnapping African Americans who were later sold into slavery.

• In South Carolina, in the case of *Arthur v. Wells*, the court held that it was unlawful to kill an escaped slave unless the pursuer was in danger due to the slave's resistance to recapture. Another South Carolina case held that falsely calling a person a mulatto was actionable as libel.

• In a decision rendered by the United States Circuit Court in Washington, D.C. in the case of *Sarah v. Taylor*, the court held that children born between the date of promise to manumit and the date of actual manumission were entitled to freedom at the same time as their mother.

• *Publications:* Prince Saunders published *A Memoir presented to The American Convention for Promoting the Abolition of Slavery and Improving the Condition of the African Race 11 December 1818.*

• *Scholastic Achievements:* In Philadelphia, free African Americans established the Pennsylvania Augustine Society, "for the education of people of colour."

• In Philadelphia and Columbia, Pennsylvania, public funding was provided to African American schools.

• *The Black Church:* George Erskine, a slave, was licensed by the Presbyterians to preach in Tennessee. After buying his freedom, and that of his wife and seven children, Erskine made his way to Africa where he served as a missionary.

• *The Arts:* Frank (Francis) Johnson (1792–1844), an African American composer and band leader, published sheet music for his band.

• *Black Enterprise:* Thomas Day, an African American, became a recognized furniture maker in the South. Day's shop (the Yellow Tavern) was located in Milton, North Carolina.

THE AMERICAS

• Jean Pierre Boyer succeeded Alexandre Petion as ruler of the southern part of Haiti.

Under Jean Pierre Boyer (1775–1850) the entire island of Hispaniola would be reunited under his rule. Boyer, a sound administrator, was able to overcome the bitter divisiveness that existed between the mulattoes and the blacks of Haiti. Boyer carried out the reforms begun by his predecessor, Alexandre Petion. Today his quarter-century administration of Haiti is known as "The Golden Age of Haiti."

• In 1818, Brazil's population was estimated at 3,800,000. Out of these 3,800,000, 1,043,000 were European, 1,930,000 were African, and 526,000 were mulatto.

AFRICA

• Shaka, the king of the Zulus, defeated the Ndwandwe. The defeat of the Ndwandwe set off the Wars of Wandering (the Mfecane)—wars which were so named because of the mass migrations that they caused.
• Muhammad Ali of Egypt was made the wali of Ethiopia.
• The French expanded their sphere of influence in Senegal.
• Cloves were introduced into Zanzibar.
• The sultan of Fezzan raised taxes on the 4,000 slaves which passed through his territory on annual basis.

RELATED HISTORICAL EVENTS

• France declared that the slave trade was illegal.
• Chile was proclaimed independent by San Martin (February 12). In March, San Martin was defeated by the Spanish at Cancha Rayada, but on April 5, Spanish royalist forces were defeated by San Martin at Maipu, Chile.
• Karl Marx (1818–1883), the father of Communism, was born.

————— 1819 —————

THE UNITED STATES

In 1819, James Madison wrote that the proposition that the emancipation of African Americans "ought, like remedies for other deep rooted and widespread evils, to be gradual, is so obvious, that there seems to be no difference of opinion on that point. To be equitable and satisfactory, the consent of both the master and the slave should be obtained" and that compensation should be paid to the owners.

Madison continued by saying, "To be consistent with existing and probably unalterable prejudices in the United States, the free blacks ought to be permanently removed beyond the region occupied by, or allotted to, a white population." In other words, the African Americans should be removed to areas such as the then relatively uninhabited American West.

Madison concluded that "The objections to a thorough incorporation of the two people are insuperable."

Madison's opinions expressed the sentiment of the day but ignored the fact that the very color of the skin of all too many African Americans indisputably indicated that "a thorough incorporation of the two people" had already occurred and was irreversible.

• In 1819, Roger B. Taney, who would later become chief justice of the United States Supreme Court and who, in 1857, would hand down the Dred Scott decision, defended the Reverend Jacob Gruber in Gruber's trial for inciting insurrection among the slaves. Taney denounced slavery as an evil that must be gradually wiped out.
• In the spring of 1819, slaves in Augusta, Georgia, conspired to burn the city. The plot was exposed and the leader of the conspiracy, a slave named Coot or Coco, was caught and executed.
• In Philadelphia, three European American women stoned an African American woman to death.
• In 1819, President Madison authorized the return to Africa of any Africans who had been illegally imported and seized within the United States and offered a reward of $50 to anyone who informed on illegal slave traders.
• *The Colonization Movement: See above.*
• The Act of 1819 provided for the establishment of an American depot in Africa for the repatriation of slaves seized as contraband. An agent of the American Colonization Society was sent to Africa to form a settlement. This settlement eventually became Liberia. *See 1820.*
• *Notable Births:* Alexander Crummell (1819–1898), an African American and an ordained Episcopal minister who later had a parish in New York, was born in New York, the son of Boston Crummell, an African from Sierra Leone, and a free African American woman.
• *Miscellaneous State Laws:* In 1819, Alabama entered the United States as a slave state. Its Constitution gave the legislature the power to abolish slavery with compensation, with or without the consent of the owners. The Constitution also provided for a jury trial for slaves when the slaves were accused of crimes above petty larceny, and that the malicious killing or maiming of a slave was to receive the same punishment as

such action would receive against a European American utilizing the same evidentiary standard except in cases of insurrection.

• In Missouri, a law was enacted which prohibited slaves or free African Americans from assembling and which outlawed teaching slaves to read. In Illinois, a statute provided that all African Americans in the state without certificates would be considered to be escaped slaves and, as such, the African Americans would be subject to arrest, being hired out and advertised. If the African Americans were not claimed by slave owners within a year, they would be given certificates and released.

• In Virginia, a law was enacted which prohibited "all meetings or assemblages of slaves or free Negroes or mulattoes, mixing and associating with such slaves, . . . at any school or schools for teaching them reading and writing, either in the day or night." Nevertheless, free African Americans continued to educate themselves and maintain some small schools in Virginia up until the Nat Turner insurrection of 1831.

• *Publications:* Charles Osborn initiated the publication of the antislavery paper, *The Manumission Intelligencer,* in Tennessee.

• *Scholastic Achievements:* Julian Froumontaine, a native of Haiti, openly conducted a school for free African Americans in Savannah, Georgia, from 1819 to 1829 and continued to operate the school after the repression of 1829.

• *The Black Church:* St. Philip's Episcopal Church was opened for African Americans in New York City (July 3).

THE AMERICAS

• In 1819, the attorney general of Upper Canada stated that "since freedom of the person was the most important civil right protected by the law of England . . . , [persons of African descent] were entitled to personal freedom through residence in the country, and any attempt to infringe their rights would be resisted by the Courts."

AFRICA

• The Cape colony troops campaigned against the Ndhlambi.

• Muhammed Ali of Egypt toured Nubia.

• The first British consul was appointed to Kumasi.

Kumasi is a town in central southern Ghana and the capital of the Ashanti people.

RELATED HISTORICAL EVENTS

• Bolivar captured Bogota (August 7) with an army which included some 5,000 English, Irish and Scots. On December 17, the Republic of Gran Colombia (Venezuela, Ecuador, and New Granada) was proclaimed with Bolivar as president.

• Spain formally ceded Florida to the United States.

• France officially ended its participation in the slave trade.

—— 1820 ——

THE UNITED STATES

In 1820, the United States census reported that the African American population was 1,771,656. This number represented 18.4% of the total population of the United States. Out of the 1,771,656 African Americans listed, 233,634 (13.2%) were listed as free.

The city of New York reported having 10,886 African Americans. The State of Pennsylvania reported 30,202 African Americans with 7,582 of those counted being found to reside in the city of Philadelphia. Ohio had 4,723 African Americans, and in Boston, Massachusetts, there were 1,690 African Americans representing 3.9% of the total population.

• After a furious debate and passage in the House of Representatives, the Missouri Compromise was enacted with the hope that the compromise would resolve the conflict between opponents and advocates of slavery. The act prohibited slavery north of the state of Missouri, but did allow slavery to creep over the previous boundary known as the Mason-Dixon line (March 3).

The seminal event of 1820 for African Americans and, indeed, for the country was the drafting of the Missouri Compromise. The Missouri Compromise admitted Maine as a free state and Missouri as a slave state, but prohibited slavery in future states north of 36 degrees, 30 minutes latitude. The compromise included a fugitive (escaped) slave clause. The compromise provided trial by jury for slaves, the same punishment for slaves and European Americans for the same offense and court-assigned counsel for the defense of African Americans.

The Missouri Compromise would serve as the basis upon which the Union could be maintained until 1857 when the Dred Scott decision essentially nullified the compromise that had been reached.

• In February, a Presidential Order was issued which forbade the acceptance of African Americans into the United States Army.

• In 1820, Congress declared that participation in the slave trade was an act of piracy.

• In 1820, the South was considered a high risk area for fire insurance purposes because of the fires which were constantly being set by rebellious slaves. An official of the American Fire Insurance Company of Philadelphia wrote to a man in Savannah, Georgia: "I have received your letter . . . respecting the insurance of your house and furniture in Savannah. In answer thereto, I am to inform you that this company, for the present, decline (sic) making insurance in any of the slave states."

• In Raleigh, North Carolina, a European American (a white man) was executed for murdering an African American. This execution was pursuant to the state law which called for the death penalty for the "wilful and malicious" killing of a slave.

• In Philadelphia, the homes of African Americans were burned by angry European Americans.

• The New York African Society for Mutual Relief was formed. This benevolent organization would serve as the model for the Union Society, the Clarkson Association, the Wilberforce Benevolent Society, and the Woolman Society of Brooklyn.

• Congress authorized citizens of Washington, D.C. to elect European American ("white") city officials and to adopt a code governing free African Americans.

• *The Colonization Movement:* Eighty-six free persons of African descent sailed out of New York harbor aboard the *Mayflower of Liberia* (also known as the brig *Elizabeth*). Their destination was Sierra Leone, a British colony that welcomed free persons of African descent and freed slaves. In the 1700s, British abolitionists established a settlement in Sierra Leone for the purpose of resettling liberated slaves (February 6). After arriving in Sierra Leone, the colonists proceeded to the Sherbro Islands. Upon arrival at the Sherbro Islands, the colonists discovered that the promises which had been made to them had not been kept. Accordingly, they returned to Sierra Leone.

• The American Colonization Society founded Liberia, an African American republic in West Africa.

The Lesson of Liberia

In the late 1700s and early 1800s, many Euro-pean Americans became concerned about the existence of freed slaves in the United States. Some slaveholders believed that the existence of freed slaves increased discontent among those still in slavery, while even nonslaveholders objected to the integration of the freed African Americans into "their" society.

In 1816, a group of European Americans established the American Colonization Society. The goal of the American Colonization Society was to return free African Americans to Africa. To accomplish this goal, the American Colonization Society bought land along the Grain Coast from inhabitants of the region and started a settlement. The society named the settlement Monrovia, after then President James Monroe.

In 1822, the first group of free African Americans arrived at the settlement by ship. These settlers were soon joined by a number of African slaves who had been seized from ships illegally involved in the slave trade.

The settlers faced many difficulties. They had trouble finding sufficient food, and many died from disease. Additionally, the indigenous Liberians, who feared losing their land to the Americo-Liberians, often attacked the settlers.

In 1838, the Monrovia settlement joined with other neighboring settlements that had been established in the region to form the Commonwealth of Liberia. The commonwealth handled some of its own affairs, but it was still essentially controlled by the American Colonization Society. Joseph Jenkins Roberts (*see 1809*), an Americo-Liberian from Virginia, became governor. Roberts tried to increase trade income by establishing taxes (customs duties) on imports and exports. However, European and American traders refused to recognize the right of the commonwealth to do so.

Disputes also soon arose between the settlers and the American Colonization Society. Many Americo-Liberians sought independence, and members of the American Colonization Society resented the expense of supporting Liberia. Liberia became an independent nation on July 26, 1847. Roberts became its first president. The birth of the new nation was frought with hardship and economic turmoil. The taxes (customs duties) on imports and exports imposed by Liberia increased the cost of trading with the country. Liberia's trade declined and its economy suffered. In the late 1800s and the early 1900s, Liberia's government was forced to take large loans in foreign countries to pay its bills. *See Edward James Roye in 1815.* Liberia soon found that it could only obtain funds to repay its debts by continuing the upward spiral of ever increasing customs duties.

In 1926, Liberia entered into a lease of large amounts of land to the American Firestone Company for rubber plantations. The rent paid by the company provided important income to the country. The plantations also created jobs for many Liberians. However, it also created a certain dependency which required that the Liberian government assiduously maintain a business relationship with a large American corporation in order to secure economic viability.

In 1944, William V. S. Tubman became president of Liberia. Tubman was determined to develop the economy and to integrate the Americo-Liberians with the indigenous Liberians, who up to that time had continued to largely live apart. During Tubman's rule, foreign trade expanded and the mining of iron ore experienced considerable growth. Tubman's social policies were aimed at providing more political and economic opportunities for the indigenous Africans. Unfortunately, Tubman still wanted the real power to remain with a small group of Americo-Liberian families that had dominated Liberia for most its history.

In 1971, Tubman died. He was succeeded by another Americo-Liberian, William R. Tolbert, Jr. Tolbert tried to carry out Tubman's policies, but he met with little success. A worldwide recession in the 1970s caused the prices for iron ore and rubber prices to drop and Liberia's economy faltered. In 1979, a rise in the cost of rice caused food riots and looting to occur as people demonstrated against the price rise. Under Tolbert's increasingly decrepit rule, the rich (generally the Americo-Liberians) prospered while the poor (generally the indigenous Liberians) became poorer.

In 1980, a small group of military men from the indigenous Liberian population killed Tolbert and took control of the government. The junta installed Samuel K. Doe (an army sergeant) as president of Liberia.

In 1984, a new Liberian constitution was approved and, in 1985, elections were held to choose a president and a legislature. Doe was declared winner of the presidency, and his party—the National Democratic Party of Liberia—was awarded a majority of seats in the legislature. Doe's new government took office in 1986.

Unfortunately, Doe's new government did not bring peace to Liberia. In December of 1989, a civil war erupted when about 150 guerrillas of the National Patriotic Front of Liberia (NPFL) crossed over the border from the Ivory Coast. The rebels were members of the Gio and Mano ethnic groups, which had suffered atrocities at the hands of Doe and had opposed the monopoly on power held by Doe and his Krahn kinsfolk. The leader of the NPFL was Charles Taylor, a former official in the Doe regime.

The NPFL's ranks expanded as Taylor recruited new members from other ethnic groups who also opposed Doe's oppressive rule. During a six-month advance toward the capital city of Monrovia, the NPFL ravaged several Krahn villages and brutally persecuted those it accused of aiding Doe. Doe's forces were equally brutal in punishing suspected rebel sympathizers.

By June of 1990, the NPFL occupied most of the country. Doe found himself isolated in the fortified executive mansion in Monrovia with 5,600 security guards surrounding him. But despite this rather hopeless position, Doe refused to resign.

As the rebel force closed in on Monrovia in July 1990, it split into two competing groups. The leaders of the factions were Charles Taylor and Prince Y. Johnson. Johnson had split from Taylor because he believed that Taylor wanted to set up a dictatorship once he had seized power.

It was Johnson's faction which dominated the siege of Doe's Monrovia. They captured Doe when he ventured outside his mansion under a flag of truce to visit the headquarters of a peacekeeping force that had been sent to Monrovia by the Liberia's neighboring nations.

On September 10, 1990, Samuel K. Doe was executed.

The execution of Doe did not end the war. The Taylor and Johnson factions continued to fight each other. By the end of 1993, peace had still not been achieved although over 100,000 had been killed and hundreds of thousands were left homeless and destitute.

Sometimes the road to hell really is paved with good intentions. The tragedy that has marked the recent history of Liberia has its roots in an ill conceived "Back to Africa" plan of some 170 years ago. The African Americans who returned to Africa were no longer simply Africans. They were a hybrid—a new people—and the integration of the new with the old was, and still is, a very problematic proposition.

The lesson of Liberia is that the solution to

the problems of African Americans in America does not lie in African Americans assuming that a return to Africa would be a welcome return home. The lesson of Liberia is that the solution to the problems of African Americans must be found within the confines of America and not in some perceived dream land that lies on some distant shore.

The Labor Movement: Between 1820 and 1830, there was considerable discord between European American craftsmen and their African American counterparts.

In Ohio, the European American Mechanics' societies combined against African Americans. One master mechanic (the president of the Mechanical Association of Cincinnati) was publicly tried by the society for assisting a young African American to learn a trade.

One African American cabinet maker who had purchased his freedom in Kentucky came to Cincinnati and, for a long time, could get no work. When one Englishman employed him, the European Americans refused to work with him and went on strike. Eventually, this African American craftsman was compelled to become an unskilled laborer until, by saving his meager funds, he could begin to take small contracts and hire African American mechanics of his own.

In Philadelphia, Washington, D.C., New York and other Northern cities, riots would erupt because European American mechanics became upset over the employment of African Americans. These riots would occur throughout the decade with often tragic results.

• *Notable Births:* Robert Duncanson, famed African American artist, was born.

Robert Duncanson (1820 [1817?]–1872) was born in Cincinnati. His father was a Scotsman and his mother was a mulatto. Duncanson studied in Canada, Great Britain and Scotland and first became prominent in Canada with his painting *Lotus Eaters*. In 1857, Duncanson returned to Cincinnati and painted commission portraits. During the Civil War, Duncanson stayed in England. While in England, he became very successful and included Tennyson and the duchesses of Sutherland and Essex among his patrons. The *London Art Journal* of 1866 selected Duncanson as one of the outstanding landscapists of his day.

Duncanson also painted murals and historical subjects. Among his surviving historical paintings are *Shylock and Jessica, Ruins of Carthage, Lotus Eaters, Trial of Shakespeare,* and *Battleground of the Raison River.*

• George Vashon, an African American lawyer and poet, was born in Carlisle, Pennsylvania (July 25).

George Vashon (1820 [1824?]–1878) emphasized Haitian history as the subject matter of his poetry. Vashon visited Haiti during the early 1850s and immersed himself in Haitian culture. At the time, Haiti was an ideal for African Americans because it was a country which proved that people of African descent could govern themselves.

Based upon his Haitian experiences, Vashon wrote his most famous poem *Vincent Oge (Victor Oge)*. *Vincent Oge* was a romantic narrative about a real life mulatto hero of the Haitian Revolution. The significance of *Vincent Oge* is essentially twofold: First, it was the first narrative, nonlyrical poem ever written by a prominent African American writer and, secondly, the poem was the first poetic tribute written by an African American concerning a revolutionary of African descent.

Vincent Oge was published in 1856 as part of Vashon's *Autographs of Freedom*. The poem remains one of the best examples of antislavery poetry.

On January 11, 1848, George Vashon became the first African American licensed to practice law in the state of New York.

• *Miscellaneous State Laws:* In Maine, the Maine Constitution gave the right to vote and granted school attendance privileges to all citizens regardless of race and color.

By 1820, the northward stream of escaping slaves and free African Americans had significantly increased. This migration occasioned bitterness between the North and South. In response, the Southern states successfully sponsored the Fugitive Slave Act of 1820, and in retaliation many Northern states enacted abolitionist-leaning legislation.

By 1820, the laws of many of the Northern states reflected a growing abolitionist sentiment. In Pennsylvania, the law provided for fines from $500 to $2,000 and imprisonment for anywhere from seven to twenty-one years for the kidnapping of free African Americans for the purpose of enslaving them. In New Jersey, a law was passed which provided for the emancipation of slaves. However, compliance with the law was voluntary and slaves remained in New Jersey as late as 1860. In Delaware, the legislature passed a resolution which advocated the Congressional prohibition of slavery in new states.

• The New Jersey Legislature reaffirmed the disenfranchisement of African Americans.

• *Miscellaneous Cases:* In Mississippi, in the case of *State v. Isaac Jones,* the court held that the killing of a slave might be murder and that a slaveholder's rights over his or her slaves were limited to those rights conferred by law.

• In Kentucky, in the case of *Rankin v. Lydia,* the court upheld the principle of the freedom granted to a slave by removal of the slave to a free state. A similar holding was made in the Virginia case of *Griffith v. Fanny.*

• *Publications:* Elihu Embree, a Quaker, began publishing the *Emancipator,* a monthly antislavery periodical, in Jonesboro, Tennessee. This publication was discontinued a year later due to Embree's death.

• *Scholastic Achievements:* A primary school for African American children was founded in Boston.

The thirst of African Americans for knowledge took many forms and twists in 1820.

In the Georgetown area of Washington, D.C., a fifteen year old African American girl by the name of Maria Becraft started a school for African American girls on Dumbarton Street.

In Pennsylvania, the Pennsylvania Abolition Society made an unsuccessful attempt to have public school money applied to the education of African Americans.

In New York, a second building was completed for the African Free School. The new school building housed some 500 pupils. It was located on Mulberry Street. The first school building was built in 1815 on William Street and accommodated 200 students.

In Cincinnati, Ohio, African Americans established their own schools.

In Baltimore, Maryland, Adam Hodgson, an English traveler, reported that there was an adult African American school in Baltimore with 180 pupils. Additionally, in this same year in Baltimore, there were some 600 African Americans in Sunday school. These African Americans formed the Bible Association, an affiliate of the Baltimore Bible Society.

• In Maine, the Maine Constitution gave the right to vote and granted school attendance privileges to all citizens regardless of race and color.

• *The Black Church:* The African Methodist Episcopal Zion Church declared its independence from the Methodist Episcopal organization in New York. James Varick and Abraham Thompson were elected elders of the church. *See 1750.*

• Saint Phillips Church was incorporated by African Americans as an Episcopal congregation in New York. The Reverend Peter Williams, the first African American ordained as an Episcopalian priest, held the position as rector until his death in 1840.

• Daniel Coker (1780–1846), the man who declined the offer to become the first bishop of the African Methodist Episcopal Church, was sent to Liberia by the Maryland Colonization Society. However, Coker's group was detained in Sierra Leone and, in Sierra Leone, Coker would remain for the rest of his life.

• African Americans organized the Dixwell Congregational Church in New Haven, Connecticut.

The number of African American Congregationalists has never been great but the influence of African American Congregationalists certainly has been.

Through its American Missionary Association, the Congregationalists founded, or financially supported, over 500 schools in the South after the Civil War. These included such prominent black colleges as Fisk University in Tennessee, Atlanta Christian College in Georgia, Hampton Institute in Virginia, Tougaloo College in Missouri, and Dillard College in Louisiana.

THE AMERICAS

• The private physician of San Martin, the great South American liberator, was a Dr. Zapata, a person of African descent. Dr. Zapata was from Lima, Peru.

• In the north of Haiti, a revolt against the King Henry I (Christophe) broke out. Christophe, paralyzed from the waist down, committed suicide. In the aftermath of Christophe's demise, Jean Pierre Boyer reunited all of the island of Hispaniola under Haitian rule.

Between 1820 and 1830, slave insurrections would erupt in Martinique, Puerto Rico, Cuba, Antigua, Demarara and Jamaica.

AFRICA

• The American Colonization Society founded Liberia, an African American republic in West Africa. *See above.*

Between 1820 and 1833, approximately 1500 African Americans were sent to Africa by the

American Colonization Society. Colonization became more popular in 1832 in the wake of the Nat Turner insurrection.

• A semi-autonomous Turco-Egyptian regime governed Egypt.

• Muhammed Ali, the Ottoman Turk viceroy of Egypt, sent an armed force of Turks and Arabs to conquer Nubia. Leading the army was Muhammed Ali's son. The expeditionary force defeated the Mameluk Beys at Dongola and then marched through Ethiopia. However, in 1822, Muhammed Ali's son was killed not long after he had founded the city of Khartoum.

• In 1820, Daniel Coker wrote the *Journal of Daniel Coker, a Descendant of Africa, from the Time of Leaving New York in the Ship Elizabeth, Capt. Sebor, for ... Africa, in Company with Three Agents and about Ninety Persons of Color.*

• By 1820, Great Britain had become the predominant naval power in the world. Increasingly, Britain showed interest in the east coast of Africa, largely for imperialistic reasons but also because it desired to end the Indian Ocean slave trade.

The Arab Slave Trade

Because of the paucity of records, it is impossible to give a precise number for the Africans that were transported by Arabs to Asian destinations as part of the Arab slave trade. However, what can be said is that the Arab trade in African slaves lasted for over a millenia and touched millions of African lives.

The Arab slave trade was particularly noticeable during the 1800s because it became the focal point of British abolition efforts. Using slaves to transport ivory, the Arab slave traders were able to supply two markets with commodities in great demand — ivory and slaves. Some of the East African ports controlled by the Arabs would deport up to 20,000 Africans on an annual basis.

In many respects, the Arab slave trade was just as horrific as the Atlantic slave trade. Millions were enslaved, and hundreds of thousands of Africans — men, women, and children — died in transit. These deaths, and the Africans' existence in Arab slavery, could be just as brutal as anything witnessed during the Atlantic slave trade era. After all, inhumanity has the same face all over the world.

However, in some respects the Arab slave trade did have some redeeming aspects to it. With the Arabs, there was an actual creative marriage of cultures that created a new people — the Swahili. There was an exchange of ideas and to a certain extent a sharing of wealth and achievement which served to enhance the African continent as opposed to diminishing it. In this regard, there were certain benefits that must be attributed to the Arab slave trade.

Nevertheless, by the 1800s, the existence of the Arab slave trade had come to be perceived as a barbaric anachronism. And as with most anachronisms, the time had come for it to go.

• 1820 saw an expansion of the power of the Bemba under Chitimukulu and other chieftains. The Bemba formed a confederacy but did not unite into a single government under one ruler. *See 1652.*

• War erupted between the Sakalava and the Merina of Madagascar.

• Zulu "impis" were organized by Dingiswayo, the king of the Abetetwa.

• Approximately 5,000 British colonists were allotted 100 acre farms in the Cape colony.

EUROPE

• In May of 1820, Alexander Pushkin, the great Afro-Russian poet left St. Petersburg. A short time after his departure, his first major poetic success, *Ruslan i Ludmila* (Ruslan and Ludmila) was published. *Ruslan i Ludmila* was an ironic romance which skillfully, and with wit, used the forms and conventions of the fairy tale, and which was enthusiastically hailed as a work of considerable maturity of poetic expression. *See 1799.*

• In *The History of Prince Lee Boo*, an account of the life of Paul Cuffee was included. *See 1759.*

RELATED HISTORICAL EVENTS

• Bolivar and the Spanish royalists of Venezuela reached an armistice (November).

• In 1820, Spain abolished the slave trade south of the equator.

• In Great Britain, the registration of slaves in the British colonies was advocated as a way of preventing the illegal importation of slaves.

• The British attempted to curtail the Arab-controlled East African slave trade by negotiating an agreement with the Persian Gulf sheiks.

• Joseph Smith received his visions which led to the foundation of the Mormon Church.

1821

THE UNITED STATES

In 1821, two of America's greatest men, Thomas Jefferson, the author of Declaration of

Independence, and James Madison, the architect of the Constitution, wrote pieces concerning the slave problem.

In Thomas Jefferson's *Autobiography*, Jefferson wrote:

Nothing is more certainly written in the book of fate than that these people (African American slaves) are to be free. Nor is it less certain that the two races, equally free, cannot live in the same government. Nature, habit, opinion has drawn indelible lines of distinction between them. It is still in our power to direct the process of emancipation and deportation peaceably and in such slow degree as that the evil will wear off insensibly, and their place be ... filled up by white (European American) laborers. If on the contrary it is left to force itself on, human nature must shudder at the prospect held up. *Parenthetical phrases added.*

In a letter to the Marquis de Lafayette, James Madison wrote:

If an asylum could be found in Africa, that would be the appropriate destination for the unhappy race (the African Americans) among us. Some are sanguine that the efforts of an existing colonization society (the American Colonization Society) will accomplish such a provision; but a very partial success seems the most that can be expected. Some other region must, therefore, be found for them as they become free and willing to emigrate. The repugnance of the whites (European Americans) to their (the African Americans) continuance among them (European Americans) is founded on prejudices, themselves founded upon physical distinctions, which are not likely soon, if ever, to be eradicated. *Parenthetical phrases added.*

• In 1821, the United States Attorney General William Wirt advised a Norfolk, Virginia, port official that African Americans could not legally qualify to command naval vessels because the maritime laws required that the command of vessels be by citizens and African Americans were not deemed to be citizens of the country. *See 1831.*

• The First Negro Benevolent Society was founded in Baltimore.

• James Forten, an African American veteran of the Revolutionary War, who became a wealthy Philadelphia businessman (sail manufacturer), was awarded a certificate of merit for rescuing a number of Philadelphia citizens who were in danger of drowning.

In 1821, in Pennsylvania, a number of items were reported which affected and reflected upon the condition of African Americans.

The Pennsylvania Legislature enacted a statute which gave a more formal trial to African Americans who were claimed to be escaped slaves and prohibited justices of the peace and aldermen from officiating in such cases.

In the small town of Kennett Square, when an escaped slave was discovered in the town, the townspeople fought to prevent an attempt by the slave's owner and overseer to recapture him. In the melee, the slave owner and the overseer lost their lives.

A report of the Pennsylvania Abolition Society noted that a smaller proportion of African Americans in Pennsylvania were likely to be paupers as compared to European Americans. It was also reported that African Americans in Philadelphia owned $281,162 worth of real property, exclusive of church property.

• *The Abolition Movement:* In Tennessee, a petition supporting the gradual emancipation of slaves resulted in the formation of a legislative committee which recommended a law allowing manumissions and gradual emancipation, but the proposals met with little success.

• *The Colonization Movement:* Lott Carey, an African American minister and pioneer leader in Liberia, departed from Norfolk, Virginia, and sailed for Liberia (January 23). Lott Carey and his fellow missionary, Collin Teague, established the First Baptist Church of Monrovia. They were sent to Liberia as missionaries by the Baptist Triennial Convention. *See 1780.*

It is estimated that only 20,000 African Americans ever emigrated to Liberia.

• *Notable Births:* William Still, author of *Underground Railroad*, and a leading underground railroad spokesperson, was born near Medford in New Jersey (October 7).

William Still (1821–1902) was the son of Levin Steel, a former Maryland slave who had purchased his freedom and changed his name from "Steel" to "Still" to protect his wife, Sidney, who had escaped from slavery. William Still moved to Philadelphia in 1844, and in 1847 he became a clerk in the office of the Pennsylvania Society for the Abolition of Slavery.

Between 1851 and 1861, Still served as chairperson and corresponding secretary of the Philadelphia branch of the Underground Railroad. His account of the activities of the Underground Railroad was published in 1872 under the highly appropriate title of *Underground Railroad*.

In 1864, Still was appointed post sutler (camp supply provisioner) at Camp William Penn, a military post for African American soldiers which was located near Philadelphia. Later in his life, Still was involved in the campaign against the regulation of Philadelphia streetcar lines compelling all persons of color to ride in the front of platforms.

Still's literary works included *A Brief Narrative of the Struggle for the Rights of the Colored People of Philadelphia in the City Railway Cars* (1867), and *An Address on Voting and Laboring* (1874). In 1880, Still helped to establish the first African American YMCA.

• Harriet Tubman was born a slave in Dorchester County, Maryland.

Harriet Tubman (c.1821–1913) was a legendary conductor on the Underground Railroad. For the first twenty-eight years of her life she was a slave. In 1844, while she was working as a field hand, she was forced by her mother to marry John Tubman, a free African American. In 1849, fearing the prospect of being sold to the Deep South, Tubman escaped.

Tubman became associated with the Underground Railroad. The Underground Railroad ferreted slaves from slavery in the Southern states to freedom in the northern United States or in Canada. Sometimes Harriet was compelled to encourage her timid charges forward by using a loaded revolver as an added incentive for continuing on the Railroad.

Harriet Tubman worked, for a time, with John Brown and other abolitionists. During the Civil War, she assisted the Union cause by serving as a cook, guide, spy and nurse.

After the Civil War, Tubman became active in establishing schools for the newly freed slaves of North Carolina.

In 1869, Sarah Hopkins Bradford published *Scenes in the Life of Harriet Tubman*. This book was later revised in 1886 and retitled *Harriet, the Moses of her People*.

• *Miscellaneous State Laws*: The Pennsylvania Legislature enacted a statute which gave a more formal trial to African Americans who were claimed to be escaped slaves and prohibited justices of the peace and aldermen from officiating in such cases.

• In Massachusetts, the Legislature appointed a committee to study the drafting of a law which would expel African Americans who entered the state.

• In New York, the New York State Constitutional Convention, with regard to the right of African Americans to vote, passed higher property requirements for African Americans than for European Americans; imposed higher residency requirements; and enacted a provision that required African Americans who had evidence of military service to still pay taxes for a continuation of voting privileges. These new requirements were in stark contrast to the language of the 1777 New York Constitution which had guaranteed the right to vote "to every adult male."

• In South Carolina, the legislature repealed its law of 1740 which provided a fine of 700 pounds for the willful murder of a slave, 350 pounds for murder committed in a sudden heat and passion and 100 pounds for cutting out the tongue, putting out the eye, castrating or scalding a slave.

• In Maine, a state law nullified marriages between European Americans and African Americans, Indigenous (Native) Americans, or mulattos.

• *Miscellaneous Cases*: In a decision rendered by the United States Circuit Court in Washington, D.C., in the case of *United States v. Neale*, the court held that an African American who was reputed to be free was competent to testify against a free African American.

• In the Maryland case of *Hall v. Mullin*, the court decided that a bequest of property by an owner of a slave entitled the slave to "freedom by implication" since by state law no slave could inherit or hold property.

• In Ohio, various court decisions stated that persons with only one-quarter African blood were entitled to all the rights, privileges and duties of European Americans.

• *Publications*: Benjamin Lundy, a Quaker born in New Jersey, established in Ohio *The Genius of Universal Emancipation*, the most successful antislavery paper of the 1820s. The paper subsequently relocated to Greenville, Tennessee; Baltimore, Maryland; Washington, D.C.; and, finally, to Philadelphia in 1834. For a short while William Lloyd Garrison assisted in publishing the newspaper, but Garrison's views proved to be too extreme for Lundy. Lundy was primarily interested in aiding the emigration of African Americans who wished to leave the United States. *The Genius of Universal Emancipation* ceased publication in 1835.

• *Scholastic Achievements*: In Providence, Rhode Island, an African Union meeting and schoolhouse was completed.

• In Boston, a school commission was established for the administration of a school for African Americans. The school was located on the lower floor of the Colored Baptist Church on Belknap Street and was a continuation of an African American school founded by Primus Hall in 1798.

• In Washington, D.C., Mrs. Mary Billing, an Englishwoman, opened a school for African Americans on "H" Street in the house of Daniel Jones, an African American resident of the city.

• *The Black Church:* Lott Carey, African American minister and pioneer leader in Liberia, departed from Norfolk, Virginia, and sailed for Liberia (January 23). Lott Carey and his fellow missionary, Collin Teague, established the First Baptist Church of Monrovia. They were sent to Liberia as missionaries by the Baptist Triennial Convention. *See 1780.*

• African Methodist Episcopal Zion Church was founded in New York City (June 21). James Varick was named district chairperson of the church and became the first bishop of the church in the following year. The African Methodist Episcopal Zion Church formed a confederation of several affiliate churches including congregations in Philadelphia, New Haven, Long Island, and New York City. *See 1750.*

• Samuel Cornish (1795–1858) established an African American Presbyterian church in New York City. It was named the First Colored Presbyterian Church and it was located on New Demeter Street.

• *The Arts:* The first all–African American acting troupe, the African Company (the African Grove), started performing in a theater at Mercer Street (Greenwich Village) in New York, playing Shakespearean drama, the classics and lighter popular melodrama. James Hewlett played *Othello* and *Richard the Third.* The company was founded by Henry Brown and would perform until 1823. Ira Aldridge, the famed African American thespian (*see 1805*), was an extra in this theater while he was a student at the African Free School.

• *Black Enterprise:* The earliest known patent given to an African American inventor was given to Thomas L. Jennings (1791–1859) for his invention of a dry cleaning process (March 3).

THE AMERICAS

• Dominican patriots again proclaimed their independence from Haiti.

• Peru declared that all children born of slaves after July 28, 1821, were to be free.

AFRICA

• On May 5, Napoleon Bonaparte died on Saint Helena island.

• Muhammed Ali introduced cotton into Egypt.

• The explorers Oudney, Denham and Clapperton explored Nigeria.

• The Sudan came under British administration.

• Sierra Leone, Gambia and the Gold Coast (Ghana) were united as British West Africa.

EUROPE

• Alexander Pushkin, the great Afro-Russian poet, published *Kavkazskii Plennik* (The Prisoner of the Caucasus, 1821). *See 1799.*

RELATED HISTORICAL EVENTS

• The Anti-Slavery Society, with Wilberforce as president, was organized in Great Britain.

• The African Company, a principal participant in the slave trade, was terminated by an act of the British Parliament and all its assets were transferred to the Crown.

• Bolivar's army defeated the Spanish forces at Carabobo (June 24).

• Jose de San Martin led his army of liberation into Lima (July 9). On July 28, Peru was proclaimed independent in San Martin's absence.

• Dom Joao (Prince John) departed from Brazil for Portugal. Dom Pedro was named regent of Brazil.

• Sir Richard Francis Burton (1821–1890), a British explorer of Africa, writer and anthropologist, was born.

1822

THE UNITED STATES

In 1822, Denmark Vesey planned one of the most extensive slave uprisings ever recorded in United States history.

Denmark Vesey (*see 1767*) was an African American ship's carpenter who purchased his freedom with money he won in a lottery. Vesey plotted a slave insurrection in Charleston, South Carolina.

Vesey had been owned by a slave trader and had traveled widely throughout the South. He also spoke many languages. Working as a skilled carpenter, Vesey acquired money and property. For several years he urged the African Americans of Charleston to take up arms to fight the evils of slavery. With Peter Poyas as his lieutenant, Vesey built an organization based upon cells, each with its own leader who recruited additional cell members and made assignments. Pursuant to Vesey's direction, only the cell leaders were made privy to the details of the rebel's plan.

Vesey's insurrection plan was a half year in the making and may have anticipated involving as many as 5,000 slaves. The date set for the uprising was July 16, 1822. According to the plan, military arsenals, guardhouses, powder magazines, and naval stores were to be taken and all European Americans (whites) were to be killed.

In spite of the careful planning, Vesey's conspiracy was betrayed at the last moment and Vesey and 130 African Americans were arrested (June 22). Among the conspirators, Vesey and 34 others were executed (July 3).

The Vesey conspiracy deeply disturbed the authorities. What concerned them most was the fact that the primary conspirators were some of the most respectable free African Americans in South Carolina at that time. These were the "privileged" African Americans who enjoyed the highest confidence of the European American community. Nevertheless, these trusted African Americans were quite willing to betray that confidence and were quite willing to kill all of the European Americans in the city.

As a result of the Denmark Vesey insurrection plot, South Carolina enacted laws limiting the movements and occupations of free African Americans. South Carolina also passed a law forbidding the return of free African Americans who left the state. Additionally, the state required free African Americans to have a guardian. "Negro Seamen Acts" were passed requiring African American seamen to remain in jail for the time their ship stayed in a South Carolina port. When a British ship with a large contingent of African seamen happened to visit the port, almost the entire crew was locked up.

South Carolina's draconian race laws were protested by many. However, in spite of the protests of the British and the declaration of the United States Attorney General that the "Negro Seamen Acts" were unconstitutional, South Carolina refused to repeal the laws and they remained in effect until the Civil War. *See 1831.*

• *The Abolition Movement:* The Kentucky Abolition Society reported having 250 members and five or six branch associations.

• The Tennessee Manumission Society sent a petition to Congress for the abolition of slavery in Washington, D.C.

• *The Colonization Movement:* The American Colonization Society purchased a site, Cape Mesurado on the West African coast (in Liberia). The society sent Jehudi Ashmun, a Congregationalist minister, to Liberia to organize the survival of the newly founded colony of Monrovia. When the African American colonists first arrived, they were beset by fever and attacks by the native Liberians. *See 1820.*

• *Notable Births:* Hiram R. Revels, the first African American United States Senator, was born free in Fayetteville, North Carolina (September 27).

Possibly of Croatan Indigenous American and African American descent, Hiram Rhoades Revels (1822–1901) attended Quaker seminaries in Indiana and Ohio, and Knox College in Illinois. Revels was ordained a minister of the African Methodist Episcopal Church in 1845 and for the next fifteen years, he taught and preached in the Northwestern states. During the Civil War, Revels helped to organize African American regiments. He was made a chaplain for African American troops stationed in Mississippi.

In 1866, Revels settled in Natchez, Mississippi. In Natchez, he was elected an alderman (1868) and later became a senator in the state legislature (1870). In 1870, Revels became the United States senator for the state of Mississippi when he was elected by the legislature to fill an unexpired term.

After 1871, Revels devoted his time to religious and educational activities. Revels was president of Alcorn College, and in 1876 he became the editor of the *Southwestern Christian Advocate.*

• James Whitfield (1822–1871), an African American poet and abolitionist, was born in New Hampshire (April 10).

• *Notable Deaths:* The Reverend John Gloucester, the first African American minister of a Presbyterian church, died. Gloucester was born in Kentucky around 1776.

• Denmark Vesey, an African American who conspired to lead a slave revolt in South Carolina (July 2). *See above. See 1767.*

• *Miscellaneous State Laws:* The Rhode Island Constitution disenfranchised (took away the vote from) free African Americans.

• Tennessee passed a law prohibiting marriage between European Americans and African Americans.

• A law passed in Florida declared that in cases involving capital crimes slaves should be tried and punished like European Americans.

• *Miscellaneous Cases:* In the Washington, D.C. case of *Matilda v. Mason, et. al.*, the court held that it was not necessary to dismiss all jurors who did not favor slavery from a jury panel. This apparently had been a common practice in cases involving slave owners and their slaves or involving African Americans.

• In the South Carolina case of *State v. William H. Taylor*, a man was fined heavily for killing a slave.

• In the New York case of *Overseers of Marbletown v. Overseers of Kingston*, Judge Platt decided that in a marriage between a slave and a free African American neither party's status changed as a result of the marriage and the children of such marriage were free *if* the mother was free.

• A slave taken from Washington, D.C., to reside in Pennsylvania was set free by the court decision set forth in *Commission v. Robinson*. In this case, the court held that the slave must be set free because the removal of a slave to a free state automatically set the slave free.

• *Publications: The Genius of Universal Emancipation* reported that in Virginia a man was given a nominal fine for killing a slave.

• In Illinois, the *Illinois Intelligencer*, an antislavery journal, began publication.

• John Finely Crowe began to publish the *Abolition Intelligencer* in Shelby, Kentucky.

• *Negro Plot*, an account of the Vesey insurrection in Charleston, South Carolina, was published.

• *Scholastic Achievements:* Henry Smothers built the Smothers School-House for African Americans on the corner of 14th and H streets in Washington, D. C. The school had an enrollment of between 100 and 150 students.

• The Bird School, later known as the James Forten, was opened on 6th Street in Philadelphia. This was the first school for African Americans located within the city.

• *The Black Church:* James Varick was elected bishop of the African Methodist Episcopal Zion Church (July 30). *See 1750.*

• By 1822, two Baptist churches belonging to African Americans and an African missionary society composed of African Americans had been established Petersburg, Virginia.

• Nathan Paul became pastor of the African Baptist Church in Albany, New York.

• The American Methodist Episcopal Church in Charleston, South Carolina, under the stewardship of the Reverend Morris Brown, numbered 3,000 members.

• *Black Enterprise:* The land holdings of African Americans in Providence, Rhode Island, approximated $10,000.

THE AMERICAS

• After a series of internecine struggles which divided the island, in 1822, the Haitians once again gained control of the entire island of Hispaniola. Jean Pierre Boyer of Haiti marched on Santo Domingo (the Dominican Republic) and reunited the island of Hispaniola. *See 1801.*

AFRICA

• The American Colonization Society purchased a site, Cape Mesurado on the West African coast (in Liberia). The society sent Jehudi Ashmun, a Congregationalist minister, to Liberia to organize the survival of the newly founded colony of Monrovia. When the African American colonists first arrived, they were beset by fever and attacks by the native Liberians. *See 1820.*

• There was an uprising in Sudan. Ismail Pasha and his retinue were massacred.

• The Bulaq Press was established in Cairo.

• There was a revolt in Luanda.

• The Omani suzerainty was forcefully asserted in East Africa.

• English was made the official language of the Cape colony.

• The construction of Khartoum (Sudan) began.

EUROPE

• Alexander Pushkin, the great Afro-Russian poet, published *Brat'ia Razboiniki* (The Robber Brothers, 1822). *See 1799.*

RELATED HISTORICAL EVENTS

• On May 24, General Sucre captured Quito, Ecuador, using an army provided by Bolivar.

• Bolivar and San Martin, the two great liberators of South America, held a summit meeting at Guayaquil, Ecuador.

• On September 7, Brazil became independent from Portugal. Dom Pedro was crowned emperor of Brazil.

• Russian landowners were permitted to deport their slaves to Siberia.

1823

THE UNITED STATES

In 1823, negotiations began between the United States and Great Britain to declare a legislative prohibition of the slave trade under the penalty of piracy. The negotiations led to a treaty proposal between the two nations. This treaty proposal was later joined by other nations. The treaty proposal authorized the seizure of slavers on the "coast of Africa, America, and the West Indies."

The British Parliament gave its approval of the treaty proposal. However, the United States Senate, after a long debate, ratified the treaty after striking out the word "America" from the key treaty phrase. This modification was rejected by the British and, as a result, no treaty was concluded.

In 1824, a similar treaty between Colombia and the United States also failed to be ratified by the United States Senate even though the phrase "coast of America" was deleted. Apparently, the members of the United States Senate were not willing to risk penalizing those who would be most likely involved in the American slave trade.

• *The Abolition Movement:* The Tennessee Manumission Society, which reported 20 branches with a membership of over 600, sent memorials to Congress calling for the prohibition of slavery in new states.

• *Notable Births:* Mary Ann Shadd Cary (1823–1893), a noted abolitionist lecturer and journalist, was born (October 9) in Wilmington, Delaware. Cary would come to publish and edit the *Provincial Freeman*, a Canadian newspaper published for those African Americans who had fled the United States for Canada after the passage of the Fugitive Slave Law of 1850.

• Mifflin Winstar Gibbs (1823–1918), a lawyer, judge, United States consul to Madagascar, and civil rights advocate, was born.

• *Notable Deaths:* In 1783, Peter Williams, Sr., a slave, was purchased by the John Street Methodist Church of New York. The church immediately liberated him. Williams remained with the church for forty years and served as the church sexton until his death in 1823. *See 1783.*

• *Miscellaneous State Laws:* A Mississippi law prohibited meetings of more than five slaves or free African Americans. The same law also forbade any meeting of African Americans at public houses at night, along with the teaching of reading and writing to African Americans. The penalty for violation of the law was 39 lashes.

• *Miscellaneous Cases:* In a case originating out of the United States Circuit Court in Pennsylvania, the court held that the removal of a slave from a slave state to a free state rendered the slave free. This holding would later be overturned by the United

States Supreme Court ruling in the Dred Scott decision. *Ex Parte Simmons.*

• In the case of *United States v. Brockett,* which was heard by the United States Circuit Court in Washington, D.C., the court held that "to cruelly, inhumanely, and maliciously cut, slash, beat and ill treat one's own slave is an indictable offence at common law."

• *Publications:* John Rankin published a series of letters on slavery in *The Castigator. The Castigator* was edited by David Amen and published in Ripley, Ohio. Rankin was a Garrisonian abolitionist who had advocated the emancipation of all slaves as early as 1817. The letters published by Rankin expressed his extreme hatred of the institution of slavery. The letters were later published in book form and enjoyed a wide circulation, particularly in Kentucky and Tennessee.

• In answering a query from a Dr. Morse of Liverpool, James Madison wrote that free African Americans were "generally idle and depraved; appearing to retain the bad qualities of the slaves, with whom they continue to associate, without acquiring any of the good ones of the whites, from whom they continue to be separated by prejudices against their color, and other peculiarities."

• *Scholastic Achievements:* Alexander Lucious Twilight (1795–1857) graduated from Middlebury College (Vermont) with a Bachelor of Arts degree. Twilight is considered to be the first-known African American graduate of an American college.

• Louise Parke Costin, a 19-year-old African American girl, established a school for free African Americans in her father's house in Washington, D.C., on A Street South. Costin operated the school until her death in 1831. The school was later reopened by her younger sister, Martha, and stayed in operation until 1839.

• *The Black Church:* African Americans in Richmond, Virginia, petitioned the State Legislature for a permit to build a Baptist church because there was not enough room in the "white" church for them to attend. The petition was denied.

• *The Arts: The Tailor in Distress,* a comedy, utilized an African American, Edwin Forest, in the role of an African American washerwoman. Forest was the first African American actor to become popular with European American audiences.

• Henry Brown, a Caribbean-born playwright, presented *The Drama of King Shotaway* at the African Grove Theater in New York. Produced by the African Company, the play dealt with the insurrection of the

Caribs on Saint Vincent Island and featured James Hewlett.

THE AMERICAS

• In Brazil, Jose Bonifacio noted that despite importing 40,000 slaves annually, the total Afro-Brazilian population did not increase. Bonifacio also noted that the absence of any increase was due to the ill treatment of Brazilian slaves which resulted in many untimely deaths. Bonifacio argued that the slave trade should be abolished in order to force slave owners to take better care of their property.

• Antonio Goncalves Dias, the well-known pantheistic Afro-Brazilian poet, was born.

Antonio Goncalves Dias (1823–1864) was born in Maranhao. In his work, there is an exquisite expression of Dias' feeling for nature, the landscape, the rivers, forests, vegetation, and birds of his native land. His poetry was noted for its attainment of an extraordinary lyrical intensity. Dias included references to all of the Brazilian people—European, African, and Indigenous—in his poetry. He taught Latin and Brazilian history at the Colegio Dom Pedro II.

• In Chile, the enslavement of Africans was abolished.

• A proclamation was issued by Parliament. The proclamation was designed to facilitate the admission of slaves in the British colonies to the Christian Church. It allowed their marriage by Christian rites, validated the oath of a Christian slave in a court of law, ensured proper food and clothing, limited working hours, restricted the severity and frequency of punishment, and protected the slave from maltreatment and the master from unfounded or frivolous complaint.

AFRICA

• Shaka attacked the Natal.
• The first caravan from Zanzibar, led by Musa Mzuri, an Indian, reached Lake Tanganyika.
• The Ashanti went to war against the British.
• The Makololo migrated to Lake Ngami (Botswana).

The Makololo are an ethnic group living in southwest Zambia. They were historically involved in the slave trade. Their culture and social and political organization are similar to that of the Lozi, whom they subdued in 1836 after being forced to flee South Africa due to Zulu invasions in the early nineteenth century.

In 1864, the Lozi defeated the Makololo and reestablished their kingdom.

EUROPE

• Alexander Pushkin, the great Afro-Russian poet published *Bakhchisaraiskii Fontan* (The Fountain of Bakhchisarai, 1823). *See 1799.*

RELATED HISTORICAL EVENTS

• Thomas Wentworth Higginson, European American commander of African American soldiers, was born.
• On December 2, President James Monroe enunciated the "Monroe Doctrine."

The Monroe Doctrine was set forth by President Monroe in a message he delivered to the United States Congress on December 2, 1823. The Monroe Doctrine essentially stated that the United States would guarantee that the independent nations of the Western Hemisphere would be free from European interference and the United States would oppose any attempt by a European power to influence a Western Hemisphere nation "for the purpose of oppressing them, or controlling in any other manner their destiny."

The Monroe Doctrine also stated that the Western Hemisphere nations were "henceforth not to be considered as subjects for future colonization by any European powers." This meant that the United States would not allow new colonies to be created in the Americas, nor would it permit existing colonies to extend their boundaries.

• William Wilberforce organized the British and Foreign Anti-Slavery Society.

————— 1 8 2 4 —————

THE UNITED STATES

In October, a melee erupted between African Americans and European Americans in Providence, Rhode Island. A mob of between 400 and 500 European Americans gathered to protest the employment of African Americans and destroyed the "Hard Scrabble" district in which African Americans had begun to reside. Four European American men were tried for their part in the riot. Two were found guilty, but were later freed on a legal technicality.

• *The Abolition Movement:* The New Jersey Legislature adopted a resolution favoring the gradual emancipation of all slaves within the United States.

• The Methodist Episcopal Church abandoned its advancement of the abolition of slavery and instead proposed rules to govern the treatment of slaves by church members.

• *The Colonization Movement:* The General Assembly of Ohio urged the colonization of slaves after their emancipation.

• *Miscellaneous State Laws:* A Missouri law enabled slaves to file a lawsuit to obtain their freedom.

• The Indiana Fugitive Act allowed claimants to bring escaped slaves before any justice of the peace for a decision. Either party had the right to appeal, and the appeal trial was to be a jury trial. This act would be declared unconstitutional in 1850.

• *Miscellaneous Cases:* A Louisiana court ruled that a slave taken from Kentucky to Ohio and eventually brought to Louisiana was free. Emancipation was based upon the fact that local Ohio laws granted freedom to slaves and that once set free an African American could not subsequently be again enslaved.

• A Virginia court decided that freeing a slave woman by will at a specified future date did not free any children born to the woman in the interim.

• *Scholastic Achievements:* The African Free School in New York City recorded an attendance of about 600 pupils and began to receive support from the New York Common Council.

• The trustees of Dartmouth College reversed a decision to deny admission to an African American applicant after a protest by the student body. Dartmouth soon adopted a permanent policy of admitting African Americans.

• *The Black Church:* By 1824, the African Episcopal Church had a membership of 9,888 with 14 elders and 26 deacons.

• African Americans in Newport, Rhode Island, purchased a lot on Church and Division Streets and constructed the first African American church in the state. The church was named the Colored Union Church, and its pastor was the Reverend Jacon C. Perry.

• The Sisters of Loretto in Loretto, Kentucky, attempted to build a community composed of three African American nuns.

THE AMERICAS

• Spain emancipated the slaves held in the United Provinces of Central America.

• The abolition of slavery in Central America was proclaimed by the Central American Congress.

• In 1824, *An Appeal and a Caution to the British Nation* was published. The *Appeal* forwarded proposals for the immediate and the gradual emancipation of the slaves. The *Appeal* advocated that compensation to slave owners precede emancipation. The *Appeal* was authored by a member of the Dominica Legislature.

Between 1824 and 1831, 25,000 African slaves were imported into Brazil on an annual basis.

AFRICA

• Conscription was introduced in Egypt.

• The Ashanti army surrounded the British. Sir C. McCarthy committed suicide.

• Sokoto went to war against Bornu.

• The first fort was built at Khartoum.

• A British Protectorate was established over Mombasa.

• In February, Muhammed Ali of Egypt was sent by the Porte (Turkey) to suppress the Greek rebellion. At the Battle of Missolonghi between Greek and Turkish forces, Britain's famous poet, Lord Byron, participated in the battle. After the battle, Lord Byron would die of fever.

The "Porte" is the name for the Turkish government before 1923.

• The Muhammed Ali Mosque was begun in Cairo, Egypt.

EUROPE

• Alexander Pushkin, the great Afro-Russian poet published *Cygany* (The Gypsies, 1824). *See 1799.*

• Alexander Dumas, fils, the son of the author of *The Three Musketeers* and a noted Afro-French writer in his own right, was born.

Alexandre Dumas (1824–1895) was born in Paris, France, the illegitimate son of the famous Afro-French writer Alexandre Dumas, the author of *The Three Musketeers.* Alexandre Dumas the younger is known as Alexandre Dumas *fils.* "Fils" is the French word for "son." The senior Alexandre Dumas is known as Alexandre Dumas *pere.* "Pere" is the French word for father.

The stigma of illegitimacy clouded the childhood of the young Dumas. He suffered and his suffering made him empathetic to the suffering of fellow victims of society. Additionally, the lack of a stable family relationship became an ideal which was often reflected in his written works.

Dumas wrote both novels and plays. However, his principal claim to fame rests chiefly with his plays. His first play, *The Lady of the*

Camellias (often called *Camille*), was an overnight success when performed in 1852. The tragic love story is set in the fashionable Parisian society of Dumas's era. The author based the play on his novel of the same name which had been published in 1848. This popular play would inspire the great composer Giuseppe Verdi and formed the basis for his opera *La Traviata*.

Dumas came to believe that plays should teach social and moral values. He defended the ideal of a stable family life in *The Wife of Claude* (1873), *Denise* (1885), and *Francillon* (1887). Although he often attacked the sinful acts of men, he also stressed forgiveness for those who repented. His *The Ideas of Madame Aubray* (1867) is a prime example of the repentance and forgiveness which Dumas advocated.

RELATED HISTORICAL EVENTS

• In August, an army of liberation commanded by Bolivar entered the Peruvian highlands. On December 9, Bolivar's army under General Sucre defeated the Spanish royalists at Ayacucho, Peru.

• In 1824, Great Britain declared that participation in the slave trade was an act of piracy.

• Elizabeth (Coltman) Heyrick of Leicester, England, published *Immediate, not gradual abolition, or, An Inquiry into the shortest, safest, and most effectual means of getting rid of West Indian slavery.*

• J. F. Champollion published *Precis du systeme hieroglyphique.* This work deciphered the ancient puzzle concerning the meaning of the Rosetta Stone and provided the key to understanding the hieroglyphics of ancient Egypt.

• Anglican bishoprics of Barbados and Jamaica were established.

———— 1 8 2 5 ————

THE UNITED STATES

In 1825, Josiah Henson (*see* 1789), a slave, led a party of his fellow slaves from Maryland across the free territory of Ohio to Kentucky. Henson later became the leader of a community of escaped African Americans at Dresden in Ontario, Canada. It is believed that Henson was the model for Harriet Beecher Stowe's "Uncle Tom" in *Uncle Tom's Cabin.*

• An advertisement appeared in *The Genius of Universal Emancipation* for eight or ten slaves and their families to be educated for freedom under the auspices of the Emancipating Labor Society of Kentucky. Frances Wright established a similar institution in west Tennessee. Both seem to have failed.

• In 1825, there were 1,414 free African Americans and four African American slaves in Providence, Rhode Island.

• *The Abolition Movement:* The Maryland Anti-Slavery Society was founded with several hundred members in four branches. Daniel Raymond was its president and Edward Needles its secretary. For several years, the society supported Raymond and his anti-slavery platform in his bids for a seat in the Maryland General Assembly.

• The Manumission Society of North Carolina surveyed the opinion of people in the state on the issue of emancipation. The survey revealed that only one in 20 was opposed to emancipation but that only one in 30 was in support of immediate emancipation.

• *The Colonization Movement:* John Mosely, a wealthy African American, willed $1000 to the American Colonization Society.

• *Notable Births:* Alexander Thomas Augusta (1825–1890), the first African American surgeon in the United States Army, was born in Norfolk, Virginia (March 8).

• Richard Harvey Cain, an African American and a member of Congress, was born in Virginia.

Richard Harvey Cain (1825–1887) was born the son of a Cherokee mother and a free African American father in Greenbriar County, Virginia. Cain was ordained a deacon of the African Methodist Episcopal Church in 1859 and transferred to Brooklyn, New York in 1862. In Brooklyn, he became an elder of the church and also published a newspaper called *The Missionary Record.*

In 1865, Cain was sent to the South Carolina Conference and, in 1868, he was a member of the Constitutional Convention. In 1868, Cain became a state senator representing the Charleston District of South Carolina. From 1873 to 1875 and from 1877 to 1879, Cain served in the House of Representatives as a representative of South Carolina.

Cain helped organize the Honest Government League. In 1880, he was appointed Bishop of the African Methodist Episcopal diocese of Louisiana and Texas.

• Frances Ellen Watkins Harper, poet and orator, was born in Baltimore, Maryland (September 24).

Frances Ellen Watkins Harper (1825–1911) was an African American activist in the abolitionist movement. In her day, Harper's lectures and poems were very popular. Her literary models were Longfellow, Whittier and Mrs. Hemans. In addition to antislavery poems such as *The Slave Mother* and *Bury Me in a Free Land,* poems noted for their simplicity and directness, Harper also wrote propaganda for the feminist movement. Her biblical narratives, such as *Truth* and *Moses,* were not well received. One of her more successful works was *Sketches of a Southern Life* (1873), a series of verse portraits of African Americans in the South.

• Peter Randolph, a Baptist minister, a justice of the peace, and the author of *From Slave Cabin to the Pulpit: The Autobiography of Reverend Peter Randolph: The Southern Question Illustrated and Sketches of Slave Life* (1893), was born.

Peter Randolph (1825–1897) was born into slavery in Virginia. Freed in 1847, he moved to Boston where he would eventually become a Baptist minister with a ministry in Massachusetts, Connecticut, New York, Rhode Island, and Richmond, Virginia. Later in his life, Randolph took up the study of law and became a justice of the peace in Boston.

• Benjamin S. Turner, an African American member of Congress, was born a slave in Halifax, North Carolina.

Benjamin S. Turner (1825–1894) was born a slave in Halifax, North Carolina, but was taken to Alabama, freed and given a basic education. Before becoming a prosperous small businessman in Selma, Alabama, Turner served as a tax collector and city councilman. In 1870, Turner was elected as a Republican to the House of Representatives. Defeated in 1872, Turner retired from politics.

• *Notable Deaths:* John Mosely, a wealthy African American, willed $1000 to the American Colonization Society.
• *Miscellaneous State Laws:* The new constitution of Missouri provided the same penalty for killing or maiming a slave as for when the same offense was committed against a European American.
• Pennsylvania passed "personal liberty" statutes to protect free African Americans living in the state.
• A re-enacted Maryland law provided for the banishment of free African Americans who could not give "security for proper behavior." Any free African American in

Maryland or traveling through the state without a job had to provide security for good behavior or leave the state within 15 days. The law carried a punishment of $50 fine or being sold into slavery for up to six months.
• In Maryland, the state law required that any free African American who engaged in selling tobacco needed a certificate from a justice of the peace which was supported by the testimony of two European Americans.
• *Miscellaneous Cases:* In the Kentucky case of *Busch's Representative v. White and Wife,* the court upheld the principle that removal of a slave to a free state automatically made the slave free.
• *Scholastic Achievements:* A day and night school for African Americans was founded in Baltimore. The subjects taught included English, French and Latin.
• To promote the education and protection of African Americans, an antislavery society was formed in New Haven, Connecticut, by Leonard Bacon, Luther Wright, Alexander Twining, Edward Beecher (Harriet Beecher Stowe's brother) and Theodore D. Woolsey (all European Americans).
• *The Arts:* Ira Aldridge made his first appearance on a London stage, appearing at the Coburg Theater (October).

THE AMERICAS

• In 1825, a group of Venezuelans who were caught practicing the slave trade were declared to be pirates.
• By 1825, slavery was abolished in Argentina, Peru, Chile, Bolivia, and Paraguay.
• The United States and Great Britain recognized the independence of Haiti.

AFRICA

• In February, the Egyptian army arrived in Morea to assist with the Turkish effort to suppress the Greek rebellion. The Egyptians captured Pylos. In July, the Greeks formally requested assistance from the British.
• 1825 marked the beginning of the formation of Basutoland by Mosheshwe (Moshoeshoe).

Moshoeshoe (also Mshweshwe or Moshesh) (1786–1870) was born near the upper Caledon River in what is today Lesotho. His original name was "Lepoqo." Lepoqo was the son of a lesser chieftain who won a reputation for leadership by conducting cattle raids upon the neighboring tribes. According to tradition, in 1806, Lepoqo visited the chief and a wise man named Mohlomi and asked them how he could become a great chief. Mohlomi advised Lepoqo to be gentle and benevolent and, most importantly, to extend his influence by marrying many wives. It was this advice that would guide Lepoqo (Moshoeshoe) throughout his life.

In 1809, Lepoqo took the name Moshoeshoe, an imitation of the sounds made by a knife when shaving and under this new name the legend would grow. A series of cattle raids and conquests brought Moshoeshoe great prestige. Moshoeshoe eventually united the various small groups to form the Sotho nation—the nation known as Basutoland. Ruling from his mountain citadel, Thaba Bosiu ("Mountain of the Night"), Moshoeshoe ruled his kingdom with a policy which pursued peace and prosperity.

Moshoeshoe never drank or smoked but did follow Mohlomi's advice and had between 30 and 40 wives.

As evidence of his sagacity, when Moshoeshoe's kingdom was threatened by a powerful neighboring chieftain named Ngwane, Moshoeshoe concentrated on developing good relations with the all powerful Shaka (*see 1810*) by sending Shaka gifts. When the gifts stopped arriving, Shaka sent a messenger to inquire as to why. Moshoeshoe then told Shaka that Ngwane was preventing him from sending the gifts. Naturally, this angered Shaka. Shaka attacked Ngwane and eliminated him as a threat to Moshoeshoe. Moshoeshoe had defeated his enemy without shedding the blood of his people.

Aware of the growing presence of the English and Boers in South Africa, in 1833, Moshoeshoe welcomed French missionaries into his land. Although he encouraged the French in their evangelizing activities, Moshoeshoe continued to support the old customs and religion. His principal interest in the French was in the advice they could provide with regard to how to deal with the encroaching British and Boers.

With characteristic diplomacy, Moshoeshoe maintained his power by playing the British and the Boers against each other until 1843 when he aligned himself with the British to prevent increased encroachment by the trekking Boers.

The tenuous alliance between Moshoeshoe and the British ended five years later when a dispute led to hostilities between Moshoeshoe and British. However, to the surprise of the over-confident (arrogant) British, Moshoeshoe had taken the precaution of arming his warriors with some modern weapons. Moshoeshoe defeated the British.

Moshoeshoe continued to fight against the encroaching British and Boers. However, the creation of the Orange Free State in 1854 led to a series of debilitating wars which began to weaken Moshoeshoe. When the conflict began to go against him, Moshoeshoe persuaded the British to annex his lands.

In 1868, the British did finally annex the Sotho lands. Thereafter the region was officially known by the name the British gave it Basutoland.

Though Moshoeshoe's power was diminished, he continued to be revered by his people. When he died in 1870, Moshoeshoe was 84 years old and had managed to keep his people and his nation together for over forty years.

• The assembly of notables was inaugurated in Khartoum.

• A mutiny was recorded in Bissau.

• An advisory council for the government of the Cape colony was established.

EUROPE

• *A Narrative of Some Remarkable Incidents in the Life of Solomon Bayley, formerly A Slave in the State of Delaware, North America written by himself and published for his Benefit to which are prefixed a few remarks by Robert Hurnard* was published in London.

• Alexander Pushkin, the Afro-Russian poet, published *Boris Godunov.*

RELATED HISTORICAL EVENTS

• Bolivia (the highlands of upper Peru) was declared an independent republic and was called the "Republic of Bolivar" after the great liberator.

• Portugal recognized the independence of Brazil.

• France recognized the independence of Haiti.

• Thomas Fisher, an abolitionist, published *The Negro's Memorial, or, Abolitionist's Catechism.*

• Eli Whitney, the inventor of the cotton gin, died. *See 1765.*

——— 1826 ———

THE UNITED STATES

1826 was notable for the debate between the proponents of gradual emancipation and the proponents of immediate emancipation which was being waged within the abolition movement. The advocates for gradual emancipation believed that gradual emancipation was the best course because it made accommodations for protecting the property interests of slaveholders; facilitated the possibility of colonizing the freed slaves; and would present the least disruption to the economy of the South.

The advocates of immediate emancipation noted that slavery was an evil which should not be allowed to continue; that the slaveholder's interest in maintaining their "property" dimmed the prospects for gradual emancipation; and that the sheer numbers of slaves precluded their recolonization.

Such was the debate which was waged throughout the country, in community after community, and often at the dinner tables of concerned citizens.

At Williams College in western Massachusetts, an abolition society was formed. The society called for the abolition of slavery but preferred gradual emancipation to immediate emancipation.

At the American Convention for Promoting the Abolition of Slavery, only the society from Sunsbury, Monroe County, Ohio, called for the complete and immediate abolition of slavery and the immediate granting of citizenship privileges to free African Americans.

Pennsylvania adopted a resolution favoring the gradual emancipation of slaves throughout the nation.

A memorial from Baltimore County, favoring the gradual and total abolition of slavery, was presented to the Maryland Legislature.

The Monthly Meeting of Friends (Quakers) in Delaware demanded that the Delaware Legislature immediately abolish slavery.

• A free African American from Westchester County, New York, Gilbert Horton, swam ashore in Washington, D.C., while the ship on which he served was in port. Horton was seized and imprisoned as a runaway slave. A month later, the marshal of Washington advertised for Horton's owner to claim him. If no one claimed him, Horton was to be sold into slavery as reimbursement for jail fees and court expenses. Horton was rescued by a letter from Governor DeWitt Clinton of New York. Later in the same year, Horton was arrested again. This time the local sheriff paid the court costs and fees.
• In 1826, the United States minister to the Court of Saint James (Albert Gallatin of Pennsylvania) obtained $1,204,960 from the British for slaves not returned in spite of the Treaty of Ghent which ended the War of 1812.
• In Virginia, the brother-in-law of Edward Cole, a reputed antislavery candidate, was elected to the Virginia Legislature.
• In South Carolina, a confrontation between maroons and a South Carolina militia led to the deaths of an African American woman and child.
• Among the Seminoles, a former African slave named Abraham served as an interpreter. As an interpreter, Abraham played a key role for the Seminole delegation that traveled to Washington, D.C. in 1826. *See* 1787.
• Peter Ranne (Ranee), an African American, arrived in California via an overland means of conveyance.
• In 1826, Cincinnati, Ohio, registered 690 African Americans as residents. In this same year, a European American mob tried to drive these African Americans out of Cincinnati.

A study published in this year revealed that African Americans were disproportionately represented in the criminal justice system. In Massachusetts, the ratio of African Americans to European Americans was 1:74 but the ratio of African American prisoners to European Americans was 1:6. In New York, African Americans were 1/35 of the general population but were 1/4 of the prisoners while in Pennsylvania they were 1/34 of the general population but were 1/3 of the prison population.

Ostensibly, the overrepresentation of African Americans in the penal system was attributed to the fact that African Americans were frequently arrested for minor offenses such as vagrancy which were overlooked by authorities when the same offenses were committed by European Americans. Additionally, African Americans suffered disproportionately because they were unable to obtain good legal counsel. Finally, African Americans were often sentenced for longer terms than European Americans convicted for the same offenses; African Americans usually had to pay stiffer fines; and African Americans encountered a more difficult time in securing pardons.

The overrepresentation of African Americans in the American penal system has changed little in the intervening years.

• *The Abolition Movement:* Daniel Raymond estimated that nearly 3,000 citizens of North Carolina had joined North Carolina antislavery societies during a two-year period of time.
• In 1826, the Manumission Society of North Carolina reported over 40 branches statewide and 2,000 members. A member of

the Manumission Society was elected to the state Senate.

• In Boston, African Americans founded the General Colored Association of Massachusetts to promote the welfare of African Americans and to work against slavery. Members of the association included Hosea and Joshua Easton, Johnny E. Scarlett, Thomas Cole, James G. Barbadoes, William C. Nell, Thomas Dalton, John T. Hilton, Fred Brimley, Coffin Pitts and Walter Lewis.

• *The Colonization Movement:* The North Carolina Yearly Meeting of Quakers received almost $5,000 to pay for the emigration of African Americans.

• *Notable Births:* James Madison Bell, poet and abolitionist, was born free at Gallipolis, Ohio (April 3).

James Madison Bell (1826–1902) was a noted African American poet. In 1842, Bell moved to Cincinnati and, in 1854, he moved to Chatham, Canada. Bell was a personal friend of the abolitionist John Brown. In 1859, Bell assisted Brown in raising funds and recruiting followers for his tragic raid.

In 1860, Bell moved to California and, while in California, his career as a poet began to be noticed. Bell's most successful poems were *The Day and the War* and *The Progress of Liberty.* In 1865, Bell left California for his native Ohio. Upon his return, he was elected a delegate to the Ohio State Convention for Lucas County. Bell later became a delegate-at-large from Ohio to the National Republican Convention.

• Sarah Remond (1826–1894), an African American civil rights activist, was born in Salem, Massachusetts (June 6).

• *Miscellaneous State Laws:* In Pennsylvania, the Society for the Abolition of Slavery was successful in sponsoring a statute which prohibited taking an African American from the state for the purpose of enslaving him or her.

• In North Carolina, a law was enacted which forbade the entry of free African Americans into the state. A fine was imposed upon any free African American who illegally entered the state. The fine was $500. North Carolina law also restricted free African Americans from trading in certain articles, and required a license for them to peddle outside their county of residence.

• In South Carolina, African Americans were prohibited from gathering for religious purposes even if European Americans were present.

• In Maryland, by law, a free African American, upon release from prison, was given $30 and banished from the state. If a specific free African American had not left the state within 60 days, that African American could be sold into slavery for the term of the original conviction.

• In Delaware, the legislature enacted a statute which made it a crime for an escaped slave to enter the state and prohibited African Americans from leaving the state without a legal pass. The law also imposed penalties for the kidnapping of slaves. The penalties for kidnapping were a fine of $1,000 or more, one hour on the pillory, 60 lashes on the bare back, imprisonment for three years or more, and servitude for seven years after imprisonment.

• A Pennsylvania law required that a slave owner obtain a warrant for the arrest of an African American suspected of being an escaped slave and that the examination of the African American was to be held before a judge. However, officials were required to aid the owner in recovering an escaped slave and permitted officials to detain suspected escaped slaves in jail while the owner gathered evidence against the slave.

• *Miscellaneous Cases:* A reputation for freedom and the submission of proof that an African American had enjoyed freedom for more than 20 years was considered evidence of actual freedom in the New Jersey case of *Fox v. Lambson.*

• In the South Carolina case of *Real Estate of Mrs. Hardcastle, Ads Porcher, etc.,* free African Americans were held capable of holding real estate.

• *Publications: The African Observer,* an antislavery journal, began publication in Philadelphia.

• *The National Philanthropist,* an antislavery journal, was founded by Collier in Boston.

• Samuel E. Cornish, a free African American in New York, wrote *A Remonstrance Against the Abuse of the Blacks,* which was printed in newspapers. In this publication, Cornish protested against the stereotyping of African Americans as uneducated and of poor conduct.

• *Scholastic Achievements:* Edward A. Jones, an African American from Charleston, South Carolina, became the first documented person of African descent to graduate from an American college when he graduated from Amherst College in Amherst, Massachusetts (August 23). Jones graduated fourteen days before John Russworm (*see 1799*) graduated from Bowdoin College in Maine (September 6). Jones would later become an Episcopal priest. He would emigrate to Sierra Leone and helped establish Fourah Bay College there, the first institution of higher education on the West African coast.

While Edward A. Jones and John Russworm have historically been recognized as the first African Americans to graduate from American colleges, history, as always, depends upon the writer and upon the publicity surrounding the event. It is quite possible that other African Americans may have attended and graduated from American colleges before either Jones or Russworm. For years, it was and has been a common practice for light-skinned African Americans to pass for "white." Given the sexual interaction between European Americans and African Americans, it is more than conceivable that in the 1700s and 1800s, fair-skinned African Americans may have graduated from American institutions of higher learning as respected, unassuming European Americans. No one knew, no one has known, perhaps, no one will ever know.

However, with regard to that which we do know, recent research indicates that a certain Alexander Lucius Twilight, an African American born in Corinth, Vermont, may have graduated from Middlebury College as early as 1823. Twilight became an educator and a clergyman. He also was the first African American elected to the Vermont State Legislature in 1836.

- By 1826, 15 schools for African American children had been established in the District of the Synod of Kentucky of the Presbyterian Church.
- *The Black Church:* Peter Williams, Jr., was ordained as a minister in the Episcopal Church and became the rector of St. Phillip's Church in New York City.
- *The Arts and Sciences:* Ira F. Aldridge made his London debut at the Royalty playing the title role in *Othello.* Aldridge never returned to America but became the most famous Shakespearean actor of his time.

THE AMERICAS

- In 1826, a convention was held between Great Britain and Brazil. At this convention, it was agreed that Brazil would end its participation in the slave trade by 1830.
- The Canadian government refused to agree to surrender American slaves who managed to escape to Canada.
- Slavery was ended in Chile.
- In Brazil, the slave trade was abolished in the parts of the country which were north of the equator and it was agreed that the slave trade would be abolished within three years.
- There was a slave insurrection in La Guayra.

AFRICA

From 1826 to 1834, there was a great deal of negotiation as to the methods of emancipation to be employed in Britain's Cape colony (South Africa). Some of the Dutch farmers threatened rebellion at the notion of general emancipation. It was arranged that the former slaves were to be apprenticed to their former owners for four years after 1834. For their labors, the former slaves were to be paid a modest compensation.

- The Burgher Senate of the Cape colony (South Africa) refused to publish the British Slave Ordinance of 1826. The Burgher Senate finally relented under threat of British action being taken against it.
- J. Ashmun published *History of the American Colony in Liberia, from Dec. 1821 to 1823.*
- The first Sudanese officers were commissioned in the Egyptian army.
- Shilluk was raided for slaves.
- The British routed the Ashanti at Dodawa.
- Three Criqua states were established in South Africa.
- The construction of the Beylical Palace of Constantine, Algeria, was begun.
- Major Alexander Gordon Laing (1793–1826) reached Timbuktu and was killed in the Sahara while attempting to return home.

RELATED HISTORICAL EVENTS

In 1826, a packet of documents was presented to the British Parliament concerning the slave trade. The packet of documents consisted of correspondence between British commissioners and certain "foreign" powers. The correspondence provided detailed information on various aspects of the slave trade and British efforts to abolish it in Sierra Leone, Cuba, Brazil, and Surinam. Topics covered in the correspondence included the number of slave vessels captured, legal developments connected with the slave trade, reports from mixed commission courts, treaty negotiations, contraventions of treaties, and the extent of the slave trade in particular areas of the world. These documents reveal the gradual alignment of British policies with those of other colonial powers—an alignment which would enable British diplomacy and pressure to curtail the slave trade.

• Simon Bolivar convened a congress of the newly formed South American republics. At this convention, Bolivar proposed a precursor of the League of Nations.

• In 1826, a convention was held between Great Britain and the United States regarding indemnity (compensation) for freed slaves under the Treaty of 1822.

1827

THE UNITED STATES

Slavery was officially abolished in the state of New York (July 4).

Upon its abolition of slavery, New York freed 10,000 slaves. The New York Abolition Society made arrangements after abolition: (1) for house-to-house visitation of African Americans in New York; (2) for the Dorcas Society of Colored Women to sew for the needy; and (3) for a refuge for the children of destitute African American parents. The New York Abolition Society also joined with the Washington (D.C.) Society and petitioned Congress for the general (national) abolition of slavery.

Among the slaves freed in New York in this year was Sojourner Truth, a future advocate for the emancipation of not only slaves but also of women. *See 1797.*

• Of the 130 abolition societies in the United States, 106 were in western Virginia, Tennessee, Kentucky and the southern part of the Northwest Territory. These 106 societies had 5,125 of the total 6,625 members of all the abolitionist societies in the nation.

• The American Colonization Society sought a Congressional appropriation for the colonization of African Americans in Liberia. Georgia and South Carolina were opposed and denied the right of Congress to use public money for such a purpose. Maryland, Kentucky, Ohio and Vermont gave their support.

• An attempt was made to form an abolition society at Smithfield, Virginia. The local magistrates broke up the meeting on the ground that since there was no law authorizing such a meeting, it must be illegal.

• In the Mexican territory of Texas, the Mexican government prohibited the introduction of slaves into the Texas territory. *See 1829 and 1836.*

• The Presbyterian Synod of Ohio declared slaveholding a sufficient sin to exclude a man from communion.

African Americans and the Mormon Church

Between 1827 and 1835, the attitude of the Mormon Church toward African Americans changed. Initially, the Mormons, many of them from New England, New York and Ohio, had abolitionist leanings and believed in racial equality, as evidenced by the text located at Chapter 26, 2 Nephi, of the *Book of Mormon*, which indicates that all men, black and white, are alike with God.

"Hath he commanded any that they should not partake of his salvation? Behold I say unto you, Nay; but he hath given it free for all men; and he hath commanded his people that they should persuade all men to repentance." 2 Nephi 26:27

"Behold, hath the Lord commanded any that they should not partake of his goodness? Behold I say unto you, Nay; but all men are privileged the one like unto the other, and none are forbidden." 2 Nephi 26:28

"...the Lord God hath commanded that men should not murder; that they should not steal; that they should not have malice; that they should not contend one with another; that they should not commit whoredoms; and that they should do none of these things; for whoso doeth them shall perish." 2 Nephi 26:32

"For none of these iniquities come of the Lord; for he doeth that which is good among the children of men; and he doeth nothing save it be plain unto the children of men; and he inviteth them all to come unto him and partake of his goodness; *and he denieth none that come unto him, black and white, bond and free, male and female; and he remembereth the heathen; and all are alike unto God, both Jew and Gentile.*" 2 Nephi 26:33

Despite these inclusionary provisions from the Second Book of Nephi, in 1835, Joseph Smith in the Book of Abraham part of the *Pearls of Great Price* stated that the descendants of Ham were cursed by Noah and could, therefore, not enter the priesthood. The curse of Ham was considered to be black skin. The Mormons also believed that Ham married an African who had the mark of Cain upon her.

The Mormons believed that Smith's writings were divinely inspired and for almost 150 years persons of African descent were excluded from the priesthood of the church. But as the church expanded its ministry throughout the world and continually encountered people whose skin color was various shades of brown, and as the racial climate within the United States changed to frown upon racial discrimination, the long-standing doctrine of the Mormon Church which excluded African people from participation in the priesthood of the church began to be reconsidered.

In 1978, the Twelfth President, "Prophet, Seer and Revelator" of the Church of Jesus Christ of Latter Day Saints (the Mormon Church), Spencer W. Kimball, declared, pursuant to "a *new* divine revelation," that the Melchizedek priesthood, the priesthood of the Mormon Church, was to be open to all "worthy" male members of the church, irrespective of race or skin color.

• Father Vanlomen, a Catholic priest of Holy Trinity Church, established a seminary for African American girls in Georgetown, D.C. The seminary was run by Maria Becraft, an African American woman, and the seminary had an enrollment of between 30 and 35 students.

• *Miscellaneous State Laws:* Most new states, especially in the old Northwest Territory, either barred African Americans or required certified proof of freedom and the posting of a bond of $500 to $1,000 guaranteeing good behavior. This was done in Illinois in 1829, in Indiana in 1831, in the Michigan Territory in 1827, and in the Iowa Territory in 1839.

• A Florida law restricted voting to European Americans.

• An Illinois law passed in February declared all African Americans, mulattoes and Indigenous Americans incompetent to be witnesses in any court case against a European American. Under this law, a mulatto was defined as anyone with one-quarter African blood or more. This law was re-enacted in 1845.

• Alabama law stated that a slave found guilty of manslaughter might be punished by whipping and branding, if the victim was another slave.

• *Miscellaneous Cases:* In the Kentucky case of *Hart v. Fanny Ann*, the court upheld the principle that children born to a slave who had been promised freedom were free.

• In the case of *Trustees of the Quaker Society of Contentnea v. Dickenson*, the highest court in North Carolina decided that Quakers could not hold slaves on the ground that a Quaker's owning a slave was tantamount to emancipation. At the time, North Carolina state law only permitted emancipation for slaves who provided meritorious service. Quakers, because of their religious beliefs were likely to emancipate a slave irrespective of the service the slave had provided. Therefore, the court reasoned that, as a whole, Quaker ownership of slaves was contrary to state law and was invalid.

• In South Carolina, a free African American woman and her three children were enslaved because the woman helped two slave children, ages six and nine, to escape.

• *Publications: Freedom's Journal,* the first African American newspaper, was published in New York City by John Russworm and Samuel Cornish (March 16).

Freedom's Journal was a weekly newspaper edited by Samuel E. Cornish and John B. Russwurm. Cornish left the paper in September 1827. Russwurm continued the paper until February 1829 when he gave up the editorship of the paper. At that point, Cornish resumed his interest in the publication. Cornish assumed control of the paper and renamed it *Rights For All.*

In its inaugural year, *Freedom's Journal* published two notable letters. On August 10, *Freedom's Journal* published a letter written by an African American woman—a certain Matilda—concerning women's rights. On November 2, *Freedom's Journal* published Richard Allen's "Letter on Colonization," a letter expressing Allen's opposition to colonization in Africa.

The purpose of *Freedom's Journal* was "to arrest the progress of prejudice, and to shield ourselves against its consequent evils."

The significance of *Freedom's Journal* was not in its longevity but rather in its existence. This publication, for the first time, offered a vehicle for African Americans to express themselves on a regular basis on the issues that directly impacted their lives.

• *The Investigator* was founded by William Goodell in Providence, Rhode Island. Among the reforms this publication advocated was the abolition of slavery. In 1829, the publication was merged with the *National Philanthropist*, and, in 1830, the operations of the combined publication was moved to New York City with a new banner—*The Genius of Temperance.*

• The editor of the *Delaware Weekly Advertiser* of Wilmington refused to publish an advertisement offering a reward for the return of an escaped slave.

• On July 4, William Hamilton delivered a sermon in the African Zion Church of New York. The sermon was entitled "In Commemoration of the Abolition of Domestic Slavery in this State of New York."

• In 1827, *The Missionary Pioneer; or, A Brief Memoir of the Life, Labours, and Death of John Stewart, (Man of Colour), Founder under God of the Mission among the Wyandotts at Upper Sandusky, Ohio* was published.

• *The Black Church:* The Negro Baptist Church of St. Louis, Missouri, was founded.

• The African Methodist Episcopal Church ordained the Reverend Scipio Bean to do missionary work in Haiti.

THE AMERICAS

• In 1827, Afro-Cubans comprised 55.9% of the total population of Cuba. Of the 393,436 Afro-Cubans on the island, 106,494 were registered as free while 286,942 were listed as slaves.

AFRICA

• In 1827, Rena Caillie (1799–1838), a French explorer, left Senegal on the west coast of Africa in search of the fabled city of Timbuktu. Caillie would find the city in 1828 and upon his return became the first known European to have visited Timbuktu and live to tell about it.

• On October 4, the French renewed hostilities against the dey of Algiers.

• Britain seized Fernando Po.

• A school of medicine was founded in Cairo.

• Sayyid Said of Oman received the submission of Mazrui in Mombasa.

• The administration of justice was reformed in the Cape colony.

1828

THE UNITED STATES

In 1828, "Jim Crow," a song and dance routine, was performed for the first time by Thomas D. Rice. Rice was a European American comedian from New York who gave the first solo performance in black face at a Louisville, Kentucky, show. Rice became known as "the father of American minstrelsy" and his character "Jim Crow" became a trade mark character in most minstrel shows. Rice is said to have based "Jim Crow" on an African American stable boy who lived behind Rice's theater.

• The Postmaster General for the United States, John McLean, issued an order which allowed African Americans to be utilized in carrying mail bags from stage coaches to post offices, provided that a "responsible" white person (European American) supervised the exchange. *See 1810.*

• *The Abolition Movement:* The New York Manumission Society wrote to the American Convention of Abolition Societies: "We believe it is not the color, abstractly considered, which causes . . . prejudice; but the condition in which we have been accustomed to view the unfortunate (*African American*). And hence, by a natural association, the mind connects with the color of the skin the idea of that debasement of character which is inseparable from their condition."

It is an unfortunate fact of history that the European/European American perception of Africans/African Americans has in no small measure been influenced by the oppression which the European/European Americans themselves inflicted upon the African/African Americans.

• A three-day antislavery convention was held in Winchester, Virginia. Its meetings were public, were widely advertised and were held in the town hall. Despite the publicity and its convening in a slave state, the convention aroused no opposition.

• In Washington, D.C., the citizens of the nation's capital presented a memorial with 1,060 signatures to the House of Representatives proposing gradual emancipation.

• The Presbyterian Synod of Indiana sent a memorial to the General Assembly expressing the belief in the immorality of slaveholding.

• *Notable Births:* Edward Mitchell Bannister, an African American artist, was born.

Edward Mitchell Bannister (1828–1901) was born in New Brunswick, Canada. His parents were Edward Bannister of Barbados and Hannah Alexander Bannister, a native of St. Andrews, in New Brunswick, Canada.

Bannister studied in Boston, but later moved to Providence, Rhode Island. While in Providence, Bannister helped to start the Providence Art Club and became the first African American to achieve recognition as a landscape artist. Specializing in marine landscapes, Bannister was awarded a medal at the Philadelphia Centennial Exposition in 1876 for a landscape painting entitled *Under the Oaks. Narragansett Bay* and *After the Storm* are two of Bannister's other most noted paintings.

• *Notable Deaths:* Lott Carey, first missionary to Liberia, died at the age of 48 (April 1). Carey died defending Liberia from attack. *See 1780.*

• James Varick, the founder of the African Methodist Episcopal (AME) Zion Church, died. *See 1750.*

Miscellaneous Cases: In Missouri, two cases, *La Grange v. Chouteau* and *Milly v. Stephen Smith*, upheld the principle that whenever a slave was moved to a free state, the slave would be set free.

• In the Virginia case of *Isaac v. West's Ex*, the court held that children born to a slave mother after she had been promised her freedom became free when she did.

• *Publications:* In 1828, the great abolitionist, William Lloyd Garrison, who was then the editor of the *Journal of the Times* in Bennington, Vermont, began his antislavery career. The beginning occurred with an article Garrison submitted to *The Nationalist Philanthropist* in which Garrison denounced slavery and a South Carolina bill which prohibited the schooling of slaves.

• The *Free Press*, an abolitionist journal, began publication in Bennington, Vermont.

• *The Liberalist*, an antislavery journal, began publication in New Orleans.

• *The New England Weekly Review*, an antislavery periodical began publication.

• *Essay, 1828* by Isaiah G. DeGrass (age 15) of the New York African Free School appeared in the *Minutes of the Adjourned Session of the Twentieth Biennial American Convention for Promoting the Abolition of Slavery and Improving the Conditions of the African Race, Held in Baltimore* (November).

• In 1828, *Essay to the American Convention for Promoting the Abolition of Slavery and Improving the Condition of the African Race* by George R. Allen; *Poem on Slavery* by George R. Allen; and *Poem on Freedom* by Thomas S. Sidney were published as part of the minutes and proceedings papers from the American Convention for Promoting the Abolition of Slavery and Improving the Condition of the African Race which was held in Baltimore.

• *Scholastic Achievements:* William Whipper, a Philadelphia African American, helped to found a Reading Room Society in Philadelphia for educating African Americans and for the development of antislavery sentiment. The society was supported by monthly dues and an initiation fee and was under the care of a librarian who circulated books once a week. The society's library eventually included works of ancient and modern history, the *Laws of Pennsylvania*, *The Freedom's Journal* and *The Genius of Universal Emancipation*.

• Twenty-one African American women proposed the African Dorcas Society which was officially organized in February. The purpose of the African Dorcas Society was to assist young African Americans in attending school by supplying them with clothing, hats, and shoes.

• Theodore Sedgwick Wright (1797–1847), an African American, was graduated from Princeton Theological Seminary. Wright became a pastor of a Presbyterian church in New York, where he worked for antislavery causes.

In New Haven, Connecticut, there were two schools for the 800 African Americans listed as residents. In Boston, Massachusetts, there were three schools for the city's 2,000 African Americans. Portland, Maryland, had a single school for its 900 African American residents. Philadelphia had 20,000 African Americans and three schools. New York City had 15,000 African Americans and two schools.

Some of the African American schools were supported by bequests. One of the schools in New Haven was supported by public school money for six months out of the year and supported by parent funds for the rest of the year. In Pennsylvania, the education of African Americans was at public expense but was confined to strictures governing the education of the poor.

• The free African Americans of Providence, Rhode Island, petitioned for a separate school.

• *The Black Church:* The Negro Baptist Church in Boston was organized with the Reverend Samuel Snowdon as pastor.

• Saint Thomas' Episcopal Church in Philadelphia became the first African American church to own an organ. St. Thomas would also introduce the concept of a trained choir into services.

• Christopher Rush became bishop of the African Methodist Episcopal Zion Church upon the death of James Varick.

• Morris Brown became bishop of the African Methodist Episcopal Church in Philadelphia. Brown had helped numerous slaves to purchase their freedom. Due to his activism concerning the plight of his brethren, Brown was forced to flee his native South Carolina and seek a new life in Philadelphia. *See 1770.*

• The Alabama Baptist Association purchased a slave named Caesar for $625. The association sent Caesar to preach the gospel among his fellow slaves. Caesar was to be the companion of James McLemore, a European American evangelist.

THE AMERICAS

• A census taken in Havana, Cuba, reported that 50% of the Cuban population was Euro-Cuban, 10% was mulatto, and 40% was Afro-Cuban. The census also reported that 89% of the island's mulattoes and 40% of the Afro-Cubans were emancipated.

• In 1828, 47,450 African slaves were disembarked in Rio de Janeiro, Brazil.

Between 1828 and 1837, Muslim Afro-Brazilian slaves staged a series of revolts.

AFRICA

• In the Cape colony (South Africa), as a precursor to freeing the slaves, the native Khoikhoi, Bushmen, and other "colored" people were given the right to own land.

• Freedom of the press was guaranteed in the Cape colony.

• Shaka was assassinated. He was succeeded by Dingane.

Dingane (also Dingaan) (c. 1795–1843) was the Zulu king of Natal who assumed power after taking part in the assassination of his half brother—Shaka—in 1828.

Dingane's reign was noted by two major events in South African history. In February 1838, Dingane ambushed the Voortrekker (Boer) leader Piet Retief, seized him and had Retief and his negotiating party stoned to death. Within a few days, Dingane's warriors also descended on a group of unsuspecting trekkers at a place now called Weenen ("weeping") and killed them.

The massacres of Retief and the Weenen trekkers were soon avenged at the second major event of Dingane's reign. At dawn on December 16, 1838, 10,000 of Dingane's Zulu warriors swept towards a Voortrekker laager (an encircled wagon train). The Voortrekker's responded with musket and cannon fire. When the sustained gunfire began to weaken the Zulu lines, mounted trekkers charged from the laager and routed the remaining Zulu warriors. The final tally was more than 3,000 Zulu killed while of the 468 trekkers who fought them only three were injured, none fatally. A nearby stream which became flooded with the blood of the Zulus provided the name for this battle—the Battle of Blood River.

The Battle of Blood River would long be remembered as a glorious moment in Boer history. As for the Zulus, the debacle of Blood River led to a Zulu civil war which, in turn, led to the overthrow of Dingane by his own half brother, Mpande, in January 1840.

Dingane fled to Swaziland but he could not remain safe for long. In 1843, Dingane was assassinated.

• In 1828, the British Gold Coast settlements were governed by the Committee of Merchants.

• *Al-Waqai al-Misriyah*, the first Egyptian newspaper, was founded.

• Ranavalona I became the queen of the Merina in Madagascar.

RELATED HISTORICAL EVENTS

• Alexander Barclay published *A Practical View of the Present State of Slavery in the West Indies: Or, an Examination of Mr. Stephen's "Slavery in the British West Indies Colonies"*.

1829

THE UNITED STATES

In 1829, slavery was abolished in Mexico by Vincente Guerrero, the Afro-mestizo president of Mexico. However, pressure from American interests in Texas forced the Mexican government to reinstitute the practice in Texas. The differences over slavery between the Texans and the Mexicans would be a continuing issue which helped to widen the rift between the Texans and the government of Mexico. The resolution of this difference was achieved when the Texans fought for and obtained their independence from the Mexican nation (*see 1836*). It is ironic that one of the primary reasons for the Texans to seek their independence was so that they could continue to deny independence to those whose skin color was a darker shade of brown.

• A riot in Cincinnati, Ohio, prompted 1,200 African Americans to leave the city to reside in Canada.

Members of the Negro Methodist Episcopal Church in Cincinnati, Ohio, in reaction to the race riots that occurred during the year, refused to join in an appeal to the legislature which called for the repeal of the "black laws," the state laws which curtailed the activities of African Americans. The congregation of the church in an attempt to curry the favor of the city's European Americans, refused to join the appeal by asking for "a continuation of the smiles of the white people as we have hitherto enjoyed them."

• An anti–African American riot erupted in Philadelphia. It was set off by a personal quarrel and the abolitionist speeches by a Scottish woman, Fanny Wright Darusmont.

• African Americans attended the inaugural

reception for President Andrew Jackson at the White House.

• Charles C. Pinckney of South Carolina defended slavery as no greater an evil than poverty, while South Carolina Governor Stephen D. Miller called slavery "not a national evil" but a "national benefit."

• John B. Vashon, an African American veteran of the War of 1812, moved his family to Pittsburgh where he helped establish the first public baths in the city.

• Charles Miner of Pennsylvania introduced resolutions in Congress which called for the investigation of slavery as it existed in Washington, D.C. Miner's resolutions also called for the gradual abolition of slavery in the District of Columbia. The resolutions were passed but were not enacted into law.

• In Augusta, Georgia, an African American woman was convicted for having caused a devastating fire in the community. As her punishment, the woman was executed, dissected and publicly exposed.

In 1829, a group of slaves, who were being led from Maryland to be sold in the South, plotted to kill the traders and make their way to freedom. One of the traders was killed but the others escaped. A posse was formed and tracked down the escaped slaves. Of the six slave leaders sentenced to death, one was a woman who happened to be pregnant. As an act of "mercy," the woman was permitted to carry the child to term. After the birth of her baby, the woman was publicly hanged and her child carried on her legacy in slavery.

• *The Abolition Movement:* The New York African Clarkson Society was established by African Americans to foster antislavery opinions.

• *The Colonization Movement:* The Massachusetts Legislature stated that the removal of African Americans would be beneficial to the country and endorsed the American Colonization Society.

• *Notable Births:* James Theodore Holly, an African American bishop of the Episcopal Church, was born.

James Theodore Holly (1829–1911) was born in Washington, D.C., of free African American parents. In 1844, Holly moved to New York and attended school there.

In 1851, Holly and his bride Charlotte moved to Canada. In this same year, Holly organized the Amherstburg Convention. Between 1851 and 1853, Holly served as associate editor of the *Voice of the Fugitive*, an antislavery publication which was published in Windsor, Canada.

In 1854, Holly was appointed to the post of public school principal in Buffalo, New York. He was instrumental in arranging the National Emigration Convention of Colored Men at Cleveland, Ohio, and, in 1854, he led a group of African Americans who wanted to go to Haiti.

Upon returning from Haiti, Holly made a report to the Immigration Convention. In 1857, Holly published A *Vindication of the Capacity of the Negro Race for Self-Government and Civilized Progress,* a lecture based on the history of Haiti.

In 1861, Holly returned to Haiti with another shipload of emigrants. Embarking from Philadelphia, the emigrant contingent numbered 2,000. By the time their ship arrived in Port-au-Prince, only a third of the original 2,000 survived.

In 1861, Holly was consecrated Bishop of Haiti by the Episcopal Church.

• John Mercer Langston, distinguished soldier, educator, diplomat, and Congressman, was born (December 14).

John Mercer Langston (1829–1897) was born a slave in Louisa County, Virginia. Langston's father was Captain Ralph Quarles, the European American plantation owner and Lucy Langston, a woman of African and Indigenous American heritage. Freed on the death of his father, Langston was sent to Ohio and educated in private schools. He graduated from Oberlin College and went on to study theology and law. In 1854, Langston was admitted to the Ohio bar.

In 1855, Langston was elected the town clerk of Brownhelm, Ohio, perhaps becoming the first African American to hold such a position.

During the Civil War, Langston left his practice of the law in Brownhelm, Ohio, to recruit African Americans into the Union cause. After the war, he served as an inspector general of the Freedmen's Bureau and, from 1869 to 1876, he was the dean of Howard University.

From 1877 to 1885, Langston served in the diplomatic corps as minister resident to Haiti and chargé d'affaires to Santo Domingo. Upon returning to the United States, Langston was named president of the Virginia Normal and Collegiate Institute.

In 1888, Langston was elected to the House of Representatives — the first African American to serve in that capacity for the Commonwealth of Virginia.

Langston's works include *Freedom and Citizenship* (1883), a collection of his speeches, and

From the Virginia Plantation to the National Capitol (1894), an autobiography.

• *Notable Deaths:* Thomas B. Dalton, an African American bootblack in Boston who later became proprietor of a clothing shop on Brattle Street, left an estate of over $50,000 upon his death. *See 1826.*
• Bill Richmond, the African American pugilist, died in London, England (December 28). *See 1763.*
• *Miscellaneous State Laws:* Georgia law provided for a fine of up to $500 and imprisonment for any European American (white person) found guilty of teaching African Americans to read or write. If an African American was found guilty of this "crime," the African American could also be whipped. An 1833 amendment to this law also penalized the use of slaves in printing offices to set type.
• Another Georgia law made any ship carrying free persons of color (free African Americans) subject to a 40-day quarantine.
• Ohio law excluded African Americans from public schools, but reimbursed African Americans for the school taxes paid by them.
• In Illinois, marriages between African Americans and European Americans were prohibited.
• Mississippi law provided for the care of children of poor free African Americans and mulattoes in the same way as for poor European American children.
• *Miscellaneous Cases:* In the Tennessee case of *Field v. The State of Tennessee*, the court held that a slave owner had an unlimited power over the life of his or her slaves. The court also held that the slave owner retained all rights over the slaves' lives except those expressly taken away by municipal or state law.
• In Louisiana, the case of *Pilie v. Lalande, et. al.* confirmed the principle that presumption of slavery and the burden of proof rested upon those of clearly African descent as opposed to mulattoes. The court also noted that actual enjoyment of freedom was considered prima facie evidence of freedom.
• In 1829, two Virginia cases were decided which impacted the lives of African Americans. In *Hunter v. Fulcher*, a slave who was taken to Maryland for a number of years and then returned to Virginia was declared free on the ground that Maryland law forbade the importation of slaves from other states. In *Davenport v. The Commonwealth of Virginia*, the court held that stealing a free African American youth to sell him into slavery was punishable as kidnapping, even if the offender did not know that the youth was free or even if the youth consented to be sold.
• *Publications: Walker's Appeal*, a militant antislavery pamphlet published by David Walker, was distributed throughout the country and aroused African Americans while provoking slaveholders. The pamphlet called upon slaves to revolt against their oppressors—the slave owners. Walker, a free African American in Boston, was born in North Carolina to a free African American woman and a slave. In 1827, Walker opened a second-hand clothing store in Boston and, in 1829, the first *Walker's Appeal* was published. Walker died, under mysterious circumstances, in 1830 after the third edition of *Walker's Appeal* was published. *See 1785.*

Walker's Appeal was actually entitled *David Walker's Appeal, in Four Articles; together with a Preamble, to the Coloured Citizens of the World, but in Particular and very Expressly to Those of the United States of America, written in Boston, State of Massachusetts, September 28, 1829, third and last edition with additional notes, corrections.* This appeal was considered radical and revolutionary, even by liberal abolitionists. The governors of North Carolina and Virginia protested the appeal to the Massachusetts Legislature and the governor of Georgia asked the mayor of Boston to suppress the publication of the appeal.

• Robert Alexander Young, an African American, published a pamphlet called *An Ethiopian Manifesto*. The pamphlet condemned slavery in biblical language, and prophesied the coming of a black Messiah who would forcibly liberate the African American people.
• After its first editor, John Russworm, left for Liberia, the antislavery publication *Freedom's Journal* changed its name to *Rights of All*. Samuel Cornish assumed the role of editor.
• William Lloyd Garrison, in *The Genius of Universal Emancipation*, declared himself for immediate emancipation.
• George Moses Horton published *The Hope of Liberty*, his first book of poems. The book was published to raise funds to purchase his freedom. The book was unsuccessful. *See 1797.*
• *Scholastic Achievements:* Daniel A. Payne, an African American, opened a school for African American children which soon became "the most successful institution of its kind in Charleston, South Carolina." The school was discontinued in 1834 when South

Carolina law prohibited free African Americans from teaching slaves or other free African Americans to read or write. *See 1811.*

• Saint Francis Academy for Colored Girls was founded in Baltimore, in affiliation with the Oblate Sisters of Providence Convent, and with the support of the archbishop of Baltimore, the Most Reverend James Whitfield. The school was established partly for black Catholic refugees from Santo Domingo who had come to Baltimore in considerable numbers in the 1790's. The Oblate Sisters of Providence was an order of African American women dedicated to the Christian education of African American girls. The initial enrollment was twenty-four students.

• The African Free School for boys was established in Baltimore and taught between 150 and 175 students every Sunday.

• Edward Mitchell, an African American, graduated from Dartmouth College.

• *The Black Church:* Members of the Negro Methodist Episcopal Church in Cincinnati, Ohio, in reaction to the race riots that occurred during the year, refused to join in an appeal to the legislature which called for the repeal of the "black laws," the state laws which curtailed the activities of African Americans. The congregation of the church in an attempt to curry the favor of the city's European Americans, refused to join the appeal by asking for "a continuation of the smiles of the white people as we have hitherto enjoyed them."

• The Oblate Sisters of Providence, a permanent order of African American nuns, was founded in Baltimore, Maryland (July ?). The order was founded through the efforts of a French priest, James Joubert, and four women of African descent from the Caribbean: Elizabeth Lange, Rosine Boegues, Mary Frances Balas, and Mary Theresa Duchemin.

• William Levingston, an African American priest, began missionary work in the South. Levingston would later establish Saint James's Church in Baltimore, Maryland.

• The African Improvement Society in New Haven, Connecticut, supported a church, a Sunday school with average attendance of 80, Bible classes and an evening school.

• *The Arts and Sciences:* James Hemmenway, an African American composer, wrote a song, "That Rest So Sweet Like Bliss Above," which was published in *Casket-Flowers of Literature, Wit and Sentiment,* a journal.

THE AMERICAS

• The Executive Council of Lower Canada pronounced that "The state of slavery is not recognized by the law of Canada, nor does the law admit that any man can be the proprietor of another. Every slave therefore who comes into the province is immediately free whether he has been brought in by violence or entered it of his own accord."

• In 1829, 57,100 African slaves were imported into Brazil.

AFRICA

• An advisory council was set up in Cairo, Egypt.

• An abortive French expedition was launched against Madagascar.

1830

THE UNITED STATES

In 1830, the United States census reported that the African American population was 2,328,642 which comprised 18.1% of the total population. 319,599 African Americans (13.7% of the African American population) were listed as free and 52% of all free African Americans were reported to be living in the Southern states and Washington, D.C. The free African American population was distributed as follows:

States

Maine	1,190
New Hampshire	604
Massachusetts	7,048
Rhode Island	3,561
Connecticut	8,047
Vermont	881
New York	44,870
New Jersey	18,303
Pennsylvania	37,930
Delaware	15,855
Maryland	52,938
Virginia	47,348
North Carolina	19,543
South Carolina	7,921
Georgia	2,486
Alabama	1,572
Mississippi	519
Louisiana	16,710
Tennessee	4,555
Kentucky	4,917
Ohio	9,568
Indiana	3,628
Illinois	1,637
Missouri	569
Michigan	261
Arkansas	141
Florida	844

Cities

Washington, D.C.	6,152
Boston	1,875
New York City	14,083
Philadelphia	9,796
Baltimore	14,790

| Charleston | 2,106 |
| New Orleans | 11,906 |

Of the free African Americans in North Carolina, most lived in coastal counties. The census reported that only about 4% lived in the nine largest towns of the state. The free African Americans amounted to 2.6% of the total state population, and African American slaves numbered 245,601, or 33.1% of the total state population.

The Census Bureau also reported that 3,777 African Americans were heads of families who owned slaves, mostly in Louisiana, Maryland, Virginia, North Carolina, and South Carolina.

What the 1830 census could not, and did not report was the number of African Americans living in separate maroon communities in such places as Florida, Oklahoma, and Texas, or living with the Indigenous Americans throughout the country. These uncounted, "invisible" African Americans were several thousand in number and they would serve as a very real thorn in side of the United States for many years to come.

• In 1830, the Quakers of North Carolina owned 402 slaves, the majority of whom had been received from slave owners who wanted to emancipate them but could not because of the conditions placed on manumission by state law. To circumvent the law, the Quakers gave the slaves virtual freedom and sent them to free states when possible, often at considerable expense. In North Carolina, the process of emancipation was complicated and required a freedman to leave the state within 90 days unless he was freed for "meritorious service."

• Virginia exported 8,500 slaves annually at this time. The slave trade became a profitable business between 1830 and 1860. Virginia alone exported close to 300,000 slaves and South Carolina 179,000.

• The president of a "mechanical association" in Cincinnati was publicly tried by the association for assisting an African American youth to learn a trade.

• In January of 1830, 80 out of 200 African Americans in Portsmouth, Ohio, were driven out of town.

• In Philadelphia, a group of citizens urged the expulsion of African Americans from both the city and the state.

• Mr. Shay, an Englishman, who ran a school for African Americans in Georgetown and later in Washington, D.C., was sent to prison for helping a slave to gain his freedom.

• Josiah Henson, the model for Harriet Beecher Stowe's "Uncle Tom" in *Uncle Tom's Cabin,* crossed over to Canada in his quest for freedom from slavery (October 28). *See 1789.*

• In 1830, Louisiana protested to the federal government that slaves were escaping to Mexico.

The Abolition Movement: In 1830, James Forten helped to assemble a national convention of free African Americans, "to consider the plight of the free [African American], to plan his social redemption, and . . . to strike again at the colonization idea." Forten was attempting to shift African American opinion from emigration to abolition.

The convention convened by Forten, the first national African American convention of its kind, was held in September at the Bethel African Methodist Episcopal Church in Philadelphia. Bishop Richard Allen was chosen president; Belfast Burton of Philadelphia and Austin Seward of Rochester, New York, were named vice-presidents. Junius C. Morell of Pennsylvania was named secretary.

At the convention, each state was represented by seven delegates. Delegates from Delaware, Maryland, New York, Pennsylvania and Virginia attended. The convention adopted resolutions calling for improvements in the social status of African Americans. The delegates also considered projects to establish an African American college and to encourage African Americans to emigrate to Canada. However, these proposals were not approved.

The convention did forward a resolution calling for the creation of a Free Produce Society to encourage free labor by pledging not to use slave-produced goods. 230 of the convention attendees signed the resolution.

The convention became known as the "First National Negro Convention." However, its full title reveals more of its purpose. The full title for the convention was "The American Society of Free Persons of Colour, for Improving their Condition in the United States; for Purchasing Lands; and for the Establishment of a Settlement in Upper Canada" (September 20-24).

• Citizens of Maine petitioned the United States Senate to abolish slavery in Washington, D.C.

• There were 50 African American antislavery societies in the United States. After this year, the number of manumissions declined because of legislation restricting manumission and because of a change in slave-owner attitudes concerning the role manumitted slaves could play in society.

• In Kentucky, a resolution was introduced which called for the convening of a convention to amend the United States Constitution to allow for the abolition of slavery. The resolution failed.

By 1830, slavery in the North had been virtually abolished by legislative edict or judicial action. However, in New Jersey, 3,568 enslaved African Americans still remained.

• *The Civil Rights Movement:* The Free Produce Society was formed in Philadelphia during the First National Negro Convention. The Free Produce Society was composed of 230 persons who pledged not to use slave-produced products. *See above.*

• *The Colonization Movement:* In 1830, Peter Williams, Jr., published *Discourse Delivered in St. Phillips Church for the Benefit of the Coloured Community of Wilberforce, In Upper Canada.* This publication protested the abuses of racial prejudice and presented plans for a Canadian colony for persons of African descent. *See above.*

• *Notable Births:* James Augustine Healy, the first African American Roman Catholic bishop in America, was born to an Irish planter and a slave of African descent on a plantation near Macon, Georgia (April 6).

James Augustine Healy (1830–1900) was the first African American Roman Catholic priest and the first African American Roman Catholic bishop in the United States.

James Augustine Healy was born on a plantation near Macon, Georgia. His father (Michael Morris Healy) was an Irish immigrant and his mother (Mary Eliza Smith) was a mulatto slave.

In 1837, Healy's Irish planter father sent Healy to a Quaker school on Long Island, New York. In 1849, Healy graduated from Holy Cross College.

In 1852, Healy entered the Sulpician Seminary in Paris. On June 10, 1854, he was ordained a priest in Notre Dame Cathedral in Paris. Healy's first assignment as a priest was in a European American parish in Boston.

Healy later became secretary to the bishop of Boston. When his superior died, Healy became pastor of the New Saint James Church.

Healy's prominence in the New England Catholic hierarchy continued to rise. In 1874, he was appointed bishop of Maine and was consecrated in the cathedral at Portland, Maine, on June 2, 1875.

Although Healy served a predominately European American parish, the parishioners held him in high regard and the bishop was only rarely subjected to racial abuse.

Healy was one of three brothers to attain distinction in African American history. His brother, Patrick Francis Healy, served as president of Georgetown University from 1873 to 1882. Another brother, Michael Healy, became a ship captain who sailed the waters of Alaska and is believed to have been the model for Jack London's *Sea Wolf. See also James Michener's Alaska.*

• James Whitfield, an African American poet, was born in New Hampshire.

Although born in New Hampshire, James Whitfield (1830 [1822?]–1870) came to live in Buffalo, a city which, at the time, was a center of the abolitionist movement. With his friend and co-worker, Martin Delany (*see 1812*), Whitfield engaged in a dialogue with Frederick Douglass concerning African American nationalism. Whitfield and Delany were strong nationalists while Douglass was not.

In his book, *America and Other Poems,* Whitfield's most successful poems were those which were blatantly nationalistic and propagandist. In the title poem, Whitfield wrote of American hypocrisy. It is said that in some respects Whitfield's poetry bore great resemblance to the verse of Lord Byron.

• *Notable Deaths:* David Walker, the author of *Walker's Appeal,* died.

Walker's Appeal, a militant antislavery pamphlet published by David Walker, was distributed throughout the country and aroused African Americans while provoking slaveholders (January 18). The pamphlet called upon slaves to revolt against their oppressors—the slave owners. Walker, a free African American in Boston, was born in North Carolina to a free African American woman and a slave. In 1827, Walker opened a second-hand clothing store in Boston and, in 1829, the first *Walker's Appeal* was published. Walker died in 1830 after the third edition of *Walker's Appeal* was published. *See 1785.*

Miscellaneous State Laws: From 1830 to 1832, many state laws were enacted prohibiting the instruction of slaves; limiting African American preachers; and forbidding the assembly of African Americans except when supervised by European Americans (whites). These state laws also limited the hiring of slaves; outlawed drums, whistles and musical instruments; required the prompt deportation of emancipated slaves; and regulated the vocations and movement of African Americans throughout the applicable state.

• Ohio law made African Americans ineligible for service in the state militia.

• Louisiana required all free African Americans (except for those who were there before 1825) to leave the state within 60 days. The same law provided for violators to be imprisoned at hard labor for life or to be subject to the death penalty for the writing, printing, publishing or distributing of anything having a tendency to produce discontent among the free African American population or insubordination among the slaves. The law also provided a penalty of one month to one year imprisonment for teaching, or permitting, or causing to be taught, any slave to read and write.

• Mississippi law prohibited employment of African Americans in printing offices and prohibited African Americans from keeping a house of entertainment.

• A Kentucky law taxed all inhabitants of each school district, according to property, for the support of common schools. However, African Americans were not allowed to vote or to use the schools even though they paid taxes.

• *Miscellaneous Cases:* In the Missouri case of *Vincent v. James Duncan,* the Missouri court affirmed the principle that removal of a slave to a free state resulted in freedom for the slave.

• In the Kentucky case of *Fanny v. Bryant,* the court held that children of a slave mother who had been promised freedom became free if they were born to her after the date of the promise.

• *Publications:* In New Orleans, the antislavery publication, the *Liberalist,* was published by Milo Mower. Mower was later imprisoned for circulating handbills advertising the paper.

• William Swain of North Carolina wrote an address to the people of North Carolina on the evils of slavery. Swain was editor of the *Greensboro Patriot,* a newspaper which advocated the manumission of slaves and published antislavery material. Swain was also manager of the Manumission Society of North Carolina. He assisted Lundy in the publication of *The Genius of Universal Emancipation* for about six months in 1827 and 1828.

• In 1830, Peter Williams, Jr., published *Discourse Delivered in St. Phillips Church for the Benefit of the Coloured Community of Wilberforce, In Upper Canada.* This publication protested the abuses of racial prejudice and presented plans for a Canadian colony for persons of African descent.

• *Scholastic Achievements:* The African Americans of Hartford, Connecticut, requested a separate school because of the "intolerant spirit of the whites" which made it difficult for African American children to attend ordinary schools.

• William Wormley, a wealthy African American who owned a livery stable in Washington, D.C., built a school house for his sister, Mary Wormley, to operate. Miss Wormley, however, soon became ill and died. An Englishman, Mr. Calvert, taught there for a time. In 1834, William Thomas Lee established a school in the building. In the riots of 1835, the building was sacked and partly destroyed by fire. William Wormley and William Thomas Lee were forced to flee. Afterwards, Wormley's health and business deteriorated under continued harassment and persecution.

• New York African Americans founded the New York Philomathean Society, a literary and debating society. The society later became the Odd Fellows Lodge.

• *The Sciences:* In 1830, Norbert Rillieux published a series of articles on steam engine mechanics and steam economy. *See 1806.*

• In 1830, Norbert Rillieux was credited with inventing the triple-effect evaporator used in sugar refining. *See 1806.*

• *Black Enterprise:* In Louisiana, free African Americans owned sugar and cotton plantations with slaves, had prosperous businesses, practiced many professions and trades, educated their children both in private schools and by private teachers. They also sent their children to Northern and French schools. Approximately 750 free African Americans in New Orleans owned slaves. A free African American, named McCarty, owned 32 slaves, the largest number among the African American owners of slaves. Upon his death in 1845, Martin Donato of Plaquemine Brule, a free African American, left an estate consisting of 89 slaves, 4,500 arpents of land, and personal property valued at $46,000.

In 1830, it was reported that some 4,500 African Americans were slave owners. Sometimes African Americans owned slaves for philanthropic purposes. Sometimes African Americans owned slaves because the slaves were their relatives. But sometimes, sadly, African Americans owned other African Americans purely for economic reasons.

THE AMERICAS

In 1830, Portugal and Brazil abolished the slave trade south of the equator and, in Brazil, participation in the slave trade was deemed an act of piracy.

• In the decade ending in 1830, more than 400,000 African slaves were brought to Brazil to work on the coffee plantations. Coffee production was growing so fast that 600,000 slaves were imported into Brazil in 1848 alone.

• Luis Gonzaga de Pinto Gama, a famed Brazilian poet and abolitionist, was born.

Luis Gonzaga de Pinto Gama (1830–1882) was born free in Bahia, Brazil. Luis was the son of a Portuguese aristocrat and a free Afro-Brazilian woman, Luiza Mahin, who participated in the Hausa uprising in Bahia.

In 1840, Gama was sold into slavery by his father and sent to Sao Paulo. While in Sao Paulo, Gama was taught how who to read by his owner's friend and, by the age of 17, had secured his freedom.

Gama became a lawyer and became prominent for defending escaped slaves. During his career, he is credited with retrieving some 500 slaves from forced servitude. He was also noted for advocating slave revolts.

In his poetry, Gama was the first poet to glorify African women and to refer to the beauty of African women as being superior to that of European women. His poems *Junto a Estatua* and *Laura* were prime examples of his pride in the beauty of "black" women.

Gama also wrote satires about Afro-Brazilians who tried to pass for "white." *Pacotilha* and *Bodarrada* are two of the more noted satires.

Luis Gama was the first-known writer of African descent to advocate black pride—to advance the notion of negritude.

• Jose Saldanha, the Afro-Brazilian author of *Ode to Henrique Dias*, died. *See 1795.*

• Father Jose Mauricio, an Afro-Brazilian who is considered to be the founder of the famous Brazilian school of music, the Orchestra of the Royal Chapel, died. *See 1767.*

• In 1830, Peter Williams, Jr., published *Discourse Delivered in St. Phillips Church for the Benefit of the Coloured Community of Wilberforce, In Upper Canada.* This publication protested the abuses of racial prejudice and presented plans for a Canadian colony for persons of African descent.

Wilberforce, a Canadian community about twelve miles from London, Ontario, was founded by African Americans who came from Cincinnati, Ohio.

• In 1830, 32,200 African slaves were imported into Brazil.

• The Four Orders-in-Council was formed to regulate slavery in Trinidad, Saint Lucia, Demerara, and Berbice.

• Codrington College in Barbados was completed.

• The Mico Training School was opened in Kingston, Jamaica.

AFRICA

• The brothers Lander, sent out by the British government, traced the Niger from Busa to the sea and established its outlet in the Gulf of Guinea.

• In 1830, British slave trade commissioners occupied the island of Fernando Po, off the west coast of Africa, in an attempt to curb the slave trade.

• On June 14, French troops disembarked on the Algerian coast. On June 19, the Battle of Staoueli was waged. The French captured Algiers (July 4), Bone, Bougie, and Oran. With these seizures, the French occupation of Algeria began.

• Egba established Abeokuta.

• The kingdom of Oyo was rebuilt while Ibadan was made the Yoruba military headquarters.

• The Luba army was annihilated.

• The French launched a military expedition against Blida.

• Around 1830, Moshesh (Moshoeshoe) united the Basuto confederacy.

• Around 1830, a conical tower and the Great Outer Wall were built at Zimbabwe.

RELATED HISTORICAL EVENTS

• Simon Bolivar, the great liberator, died. *See 1810.*

• The *Book of Mormon* was published and the Mormon Church was organized.

1831

THE UNITED STATES

In 1831, Nat Turner led the largest slave rebellion ever to occur in the United States. In the wake of this rebellion, the whole South was thrown into a panic and more than two hundred European Americans and African Americans were killed before the revolt ended (August 21–23). *See 1800.*

The slave rebellion broke out under the leadership of Nat Turner, a slave who could read. Turner's chief deputies were Henry Porter,

Hark Travis, Nelson Williams and Samuel Francis. A group of 20 to 30 slaves killed some 60 European Americans in Southampton County, Virginia. Approximately 3,000 armed European American men responded to the slave uprising and a wholesale slaughter of African Americans ensued. In less than two days, 120 African Americans were killed, most of them were slain by men who shot them as if they were pursuing game. One individual rejoiced that he had been instrumental in killing between ten to fifteen African Americans by himself.

After the slaughter, fifty-three African Americans were arraigned. Seventeen were convicted and executed, twelve were convicted and transported, and ten were acquitted. (The fate of the other fourteen is not clear.)

As for Nat Turner, he was captured on October 30, tried and convicted on November 5, and hanged on November 11, 1831, in Jerusalem, Virginia. *See 1800.*

After the rebellion, *The Confession of Nat Turner,* was published. This book was edited by Thomas R. Gray and was published in Baltimore. In its text, the book evokes a confessional and autobiographical style which made it a prototype for a whole genre of African American literature.

In the aftermath of the Turner rebellion, the oppression of slaves increased. Slaves were subjected to the stringent enforcement of slave codes, denied any educational opportunities, and were no longer set free by manumission. In Virginia, it was decreed that slaves and free African Americans could not preach, attend religious services at night without permission, nor be taught to read or write.

The general oppression that occurred in the wake of the Turner rebellion also led to the "repatriation" efforts of the American Colonization Society falling into disrepute amongst its Southern constituency.

 • In debates in the Virginia Legislature of 1831 and 1832, Thomas Dew said with pride that "Virginia is in fact a Negro-raising state for other states" and that raising slaves for sale was "one of [Virginia's] greatest sources of profit."
 • The United States Attorney General John Berrien declared that the South Carolina Negro Seamen Act of 1822 was a constitutional exercise of a state's police power to "regulate persons of color within its own limits." The next attorney general, Roger Taney, also upheld the act in the face of British protests and affirmed the legal inferiority of all African Americans in the United States. Foreshadowing his 1857 decision in the *Dred Scott* case as chief justice of the Supreme Court, Taney found that African Americans possessed no constitutional rights because the framers of the Constitution did not regard African Americans as citizens.
 • A white (European American) mob descended on an African American area of Providence, Rhode Island. In the riot that followed, a European American sailor was killed by a shot fired by an African American who was defending himself against the mob. More violence erupted on the following day. The militia was called in but was repulsed by stones thrown by the mob. On the fourth day of violence, two companies of militia were called in and finally stopped the mob by firing into the crowd, killing four rioters and wounding fourteen others. 18 houses were destroyed. It was alleged that the riot was caused by the reaction of European American workers against the employment of African American workers.

The first Annual Convention of the People of Color was convened in Philadelphia, Pennsylvania, from June 6 through June 11. The convention was located at Wesleyan Church on Lombard Street. John Bowers of Philadelphia was elected president, and Abraham D. Shadd of Delaware and William Duncan of Virginia were elected vice-presidents. William Whipper of Philadelphia was named secretary and Thomas Jennings of New York was named assistant secretary.

Delegates from five states attended the proceedings. The delegates resolved to (1) study conditions of free African Americans; (2) study settlement in Canada; (3) recommend an annual convention of free African Americans; (4) oppose the American Colonization Society; and (5) approve the raising of money for a proposed industrial college in New Haven, Connecticut *provided that* African Americans were guaranteed that they would comprise a majority of the board of trustees for the college.

 • *The Abolition Movement:* The New England Anti-Slavery Society was established by William Lloyd Garrison and eleven other European Americans who convened at the African Baptist Church in Boston.
 • *The Colonization Movement:* By 1831, The American Colonization Society had sent 1,420 African Americans to Africa.
 • *The Labor Movement:* In South Carolina,

a petition was filed by European American artisans which claimed unfair competition from free African Americans. The petition claimed that the state did not benefit from the presence of free African Americans and that their behavior was not beneficial to slaves because they encouraged insubordination by precept and example. The European American artisans feared that eventually only African Americans would be carpenters, painters, blacksmiths, and other skilled artisans.

• *Notable Births:* James Walker Hood, a bishop of the African Methodist Episcopal Zion Church, was born.

James Walker Hood (1831–1918) was granted a license to preach in 1856. In 1860, he was ordained a deacon in the African Methodist Episcopal Church located in Boston, Massachusetts. Upon his elevation, Hood sailed for Halifax, Nova Scotia, Canada.

Hood returned to the United States in 1863 and became a member of the Reconstruction Constitutional Convention. He was ordained a bishop in 1872. His published works were: *The Negro in the Christian Pulpit* (1884), *One Hundred Years of the Methodist Episcopal Zion Church* (1895), and *The Plan of the Apocalypse* (1900).

• Bishop John Walden, advocate of African American education, was born (February 11).

• *Notable Deaths:* Richard Allen, founder and first bishop of the African Methodist Episcopal Church, died. *See 1760.*

• Nat Turner was executed (November 11). *See 1800.*

• *Miscellaneous State Laws:* In Alabama, the law of 1832 prohibited the assembling of more than five male slaves at any place off the plantation to which they belonged, but nothing in the act was to be considered as forbidding attendance at places of public worship held by European Americans.

• The municipal corporation of Georgetown in Washington, D.C. passed an ordinance which prohibited free African Americans from taking copies of the *Liberator*, an antislavery publication, from the local post office. The penalty for taking the publication was 25 lashes and imprisonment with the possibility of being sold into slavery.

• Ohio law prevented African Americans from serving on juries.

• North Carolina law required all African American traders and peddlers to be licensed. Another North Carolina law prohibited slaves and free African Americans from preaching, exhorting or teaching "in any prayer meeting or other association for worship where slaves of different families are collected together" on penalty of not more than 39 lashes. Maryland, Georgia, and other states had similar laws.

• South Carolina law prohibited the manufacture or sale of liquor by African Americans.

• Indiana law required African Americans entering the state to post a bond. Those African Americans unable to do so would be hired out and, possibly, expelled from the state. The law also provided for a penalty for harboring African Americans who had not posted a bond and guaranteed the right of a slave owner to transport his slaves throughout the state.

• Mississippi law prohibited free African Americans from remaining in the state. Mississippi law also prohibited any slave or free African American from preaching the gospel except to African Americans in their own neighborhood with written permission of the slave owner and with six respectable European American slave owners present. The penalty for violating the law was 39 lashes.

• *Miscellaneous Cases:* In the Ohio case of *Polly Gray v. Ohio*, the Ohio State Supreme Court ruled that a person having more "white" blood than "black" blood was white and thus not subject to the "black laws." The case involved the eligibility of an African American to testify as a witness in the trial of a quadroon—a person with one black grandparent. This decision would be re-affirmed in 1834 in the case of *Williams v. Directors of School District.*

• *Publications:* The first issue of the *Liberator* was published by William Lloyd Garrison (January 1).

The *Liberator*, edited by William Lloyd Garrison and financially supported by such prominent African Americans as James Forten, began publication on New Year's day in Boston. The avowed purposes of the *Liberator* were the abolition of slavery and the moral and intellectual elevation of the African American.

William Lloyd Garrison's *Liberator* advocated the immediate and unconditional emancipation of the slaves. Garrison would later write that he struggled through the first year of the existence of the *Liberator* with about 50 European American and 400 African American subscribers. Garrison's *Liberator* survived to see the day when the guns were fired to signal the War of Liberation—the Civil War. Then, and only then, did it cease publication.

The municipal corporation of Georgetown

in Washington, D.C. passed an ordinance which prohibited free African Americans from taking copies of the *Liberator* from the local post office. The penalty for taking the publication was 25 lashes and imprisonment with the possibility of being sold into slavery.

In June of 1831, Garrison published his *Address Delivered Before the Free People of Color in Philadelphia, New York and Other Cities* in which he urged African Americans to sell and buy from each other in preference to engaging in commerce with European Americans. He also urged African Americans to vote whenever possible and, if possible, to vote for fellow African Americans.

In 1831, Garrison, along with fellow abolitionists, founded the New England Anti-Slavery Society.

• For a little over a year, the African American newspaper, *The African Sentinel and Journal of Liberty*, was published in Albany, New York, by John E. Stewart.

• In 1831, *Religion and the Pure Principles of Morality—The Sure Foundation on which we must Build. Productions from the Pen of Mrs. Maria W. Steward* was published. Maria W. Steward was one of the earliest, if not the first, African American woman lecturers. Maria Steward's speeches stressed the necessity for self-improvement, education, and moral resistance to the oppressor.

• John B. Russwurm published a "Letter to the *United States Gazette*" in the April 30 edition of the *Liberator*. By 1831, Russwurm was considered a traitor by many African Americans and by the antislavery press because of his work with the American Colonization Society.

• *Scholastic Achievements:* In New Haven, Connecticut, a town meeting voted 700 to 4 to deny a proposal calling for the construction of an African American college in the city. The proposed college, for instructing African Americans in agriculture, mechanical arts, science, etc., was to be under the leadership of Simon Jocelyn and Arthur Tappan.

In nearly every one of the dozen or more Negro conventions held between 1831 to 1860, there was strong advocacy of trade schools for black youths. Arthur Tappan, the philanthropist, bought several acres in the southern part of New Haven, Connecticut, and completed arrangements for erecting a building, fully equipped for the purpose. But the people of New Haven, and of Connecticut, were bitterly opposed to the location of the institution. The commonwealth subsequently passed a law prohibiting the establishment of any institution of learning "for the instruction of persons of color of other states."

• An African American grammar school was established by the city of Boston in the North End area of the city. However, it was discontinued in 1835 because of the low attendance caused by the movement of African Americans from the North End to the western part of the city.

• A high school was established by African American men in New York for the purpose of instruction in the classics. One of the first pupils of this school was Henry Highland Garnet. *See 1815.*

• African American women in Philadelphia formed the Female Literary Society. By 1832, this society had twenty members. The members wrote literary pieces which the group criticized.

• *The Black Church:* The Oblate Sisters of Providence, a teaching order composed of African American nuns which was located in Baltimore, Maryland, was formally recognized by the Catholic Church (October 2).

• *Black Enterprise:* James Forten, a veteran of the Revolutionary War, manufactured sails in Philadelphia and amassed a fortune estimated at $100,000—a very substantial sum in the early 1800s. James Forten also was a substantial contributor to the *Liberator*.

• John Mashow, an African American, began a shipbuilding operation centered in South Dartmouth, Massachusetts.

THE AMERICAS

• Slavery was prohibited in the Bolivian Constitution.

• Brazil passed a law providing for the abolition of the African slave trade.

• A slave rebellion in Jamaica destroyed nearly $3.5 million worth of property and brought widespread ruin to the planters.

• Among the famous "Treinta y Tres" (the Thirty-Three) who accompanied Captain Lavalleya in the campaign for Uruguayan independence were two African slaves: Joaquin Artigas and Dionisio Oribe.

AFRICA

• A large number of Boer (Dutch heritage) farmers settled in the interior of South Africa thereby creating the foundations for the Orange Free State, the Transvaal, and the Natal.

• Between 1831 and 1841, Egyptian forces occupied Syria and Lebanon. Ibrahim Pasha served as governor.

• The slave trade was prohibited in Senegal.

• A treaty was negotiated between the Ashanti and Great Britain.

• Matabele was at war with Griqua and Korana.

• The Egyptians launched an unsuccessful expedition against the Hadendowa.

The Hadendowa are a subgroup of the Beja. The Beja live in northeast Sudan.

EUROPE

• In London, Mary Prince published *The History of Mary Prince, A West Indian Slave, Related by Herself, With a Supplement by the Editor, to Which is Added the Narrative of Asa-Asa, a Captured African.*

RELATED HISTORICAL EVENTS

• Great Britain and France entered into a treaty for the suppression of the slave trade.

• On December 27, the voyage of the *Beagle* began with Charles Darwin aboard as a geologist. The mission of the *Beagle* would last for five years and the observations made by Darwin during this voyage would lead to his writing the monumental *On the Origin of Species.*

1832

THE UNITED STATES

In 1832, slave prices dramatically increased. The sharp rise in prices was due to the increase in demand for slaves throughout the Southwest, improved methods of agriculture, and the need for slave labor in factories. The price for slaves rose 25% over the previous three years and reflected the increased value and dependence the South placed on slave labor. Along with the increased value of slaves came an increased hostility to abolition and those who espoused it.

In 1832, the average price for a prime field hand between the ages of 18 and 25 was $500.

• In a debate in the Virginia Legislature, the state's small farmers argued that the plantation system based on slavery was a threat to their way of life (January 20).

• In Philadelphia, the Second Convention of People of Color met in Benezet Hall on June 4 and the next day in the First African Presbyterian Church. The attendees resolved to establish a society or agent to purchase land in Canada for African Americans "who may be, by oppressive enactments, obliged to flee from these United States," and to raise money to aid the project. Eight states were represented at this convention

by 30 delegates. The convention opposed national aid to the American Colonization Society and urged the abolition of slavery in Washington, D.C.

• In his commencement address to the graduating class of the University of North Carolina, Judge William Gaston referred to slavery as "the worst evil that affects the southern part of our Confederacy" and urged its "extirpation."

• Thomas Dew, as the editor of a pro-slavery paper, used historical, theological, and anthropological arguments in defense of slavery. These views were readily accepted in the deep South. Dew denied the possibility or advisability of solving the slavery problem by colonization.

• In Savannah, Georgia, European Americans founded the Georgia Infirmary. The Georgia Infirmary was a hospital and asylum established for the relief and protection of elderly and afflicted African Americans.

• The Brotherly Union Society was organized in Philadelphia "for relieving the wants and distress of each other." The members of the society agreed that any funds remaining after relief had been provided were to be distributed to the members to be invested in real estate, bonds and mortgages.

• *The Abolition Movement:* When the New England Anti-Slavery Society was founded in Boston, approximately one out of every four of its members was African American.

• In Salem, Massachusetts, a number of "females of color" formed an antislavery society (February 22).

• *The Civil Rights Movement:* A contingent of Philadelphia African Americans met to protest legislative efforts to curtail the liberties enjoyed by African Americans. This African American contingent informed the city's legislative body that, while African Americans comprised 8% of the city's population, African Americans were only 4% of the city's paupers. The contingent also noted that 400 to 500 African Americans were mechanics despite the prejudices and obstacles encountered in learning trades.

• *The Colonization Movement:* Two hundred African Americans emigrated from New York to Trinidad.

• In 1832, there were American Colonization Society chapters in every state except Rhode Island and South Carolina.

• In the January 2, 1832 edition of the *Liberator*, an African American woman from Philadelphia expressed her support of African American emigration to Mexico where "all men are born free and equal," where "the climate is healthy and warm," where the "soil is rich and fertile," and where the country "would afford us a large field of speculation, were we to remove thither."

• *Notable Births*: Dr. Edward W. Blyden, distinguished scholar and diplomat and president of Liberia College, was born (August 3).

• Joseph H. Rainey, African American Congressperson from South Carolina, was born (June 21).

Joseph Hayne Rainey (1832–1887) was a barber at the outbreak of the Civil War. In 1862, Confederate authorities drafted him to work on the fortifications of Charleston. He escaped and went to the West Indies. In 1867, after returning to the United States, Rainey became a member of the executive committee of the newly formed Republican Party of South Carolina. The following year, Rainey was elected a delegate from Georgetown to the State Constitutional Convention. He was subsequently elected to the State Senate. In 1870, Rainey was elected to the United States House of Representatives where he took the place of B. F. Whittemore, a person whose credentials the House of Representatives refused to accept. Rainey continued to serve in the House until 1879 when he was replaced by a Democrat.

• *Miscellaneous State Laws*: Alabama law established a fine of $250 to $500 for teaching a free African American or a slave to read, write or spell and set punishment by flogging for any free African American who associated with slaves without written permission from the owners or overseer of the slaves. It prohibited the assembling of more than five male slaves at any place off the plantation to which they belonged except in places of public worship in the presence of European Americans. No slave or free African American could "preach, exhort, or harangue" any slave or free African American except in the presence of five "respectable slaveholders," unless the person preaching was licensed by a Christian body of the neighborhood and the listeners were members of that body.

A special exception would be made to Alabama's law to accommodate the education of Creoles. In 1833, the Creoles of Mobile, Alabama, were permitted to be educated pursuant to the treaty signed in 1803.

• Virginia law labeled all meetings of free African Americans for teaching, reading, or writing as an "unlawful assembly" and authorized magistrates to break up such meetings and inflict up to 20 lashes on offenders. The same law provided fines of $10 to $100 for any European American (white person) caught teaching slaves to read. In the new post–Nat Turner climate of the South, the law was strictly enforced whereas a similar law, passed in 1819, had not been.

• The Connecticut Legislature passed a law forbidding a school for African Americans who were not residents of the state without first obtaining the written permission of the town selectmen.

• *Publications*: John Chavis published a sermon in North Carolina called *The Extent of the Atonement*, which became quite popular. Chavis was an African American who had studied privately with President Witherspoon at the College of New Jersey (Princeton University). Chavis became a minister and often preached to both African American and European American audiences.

• William Lloyd Garrison published *Thoughts on African Colonization ... Part I and Part II*.

• *Scholastic Achievements*: The New York African Free School had an enrollment of 862 students.

• African Americans in Pittsburgh, Pennsylvania, established the Pittsburgh African Education Society.

When Charles B. Ray, an African American, entered Wesleyan University in Middletown, Connecticut, the students protested until he agreed to leave. Ray went to New York where he opened a boot and shoe store.

• African Americans formed a Sunday school in Washington, D.C., in the Smothers School-House, after African American children were expelled from Sabbath schools and European American churches.

In 1832, Prudence Crandall admitted an African American girl named Sarah Harris to her school in Canterbury, Connecticut. The townspeople of Canterbury protested and the European American students were withdrawn. In response, Miss Crandall admitted more African American students. The Connecticut Legislature passed a law prohibiting the admission of African Americans into schools unless the town selectmen approved of the admission. Miss Crandall was subsequently imprisoned and ostracized. The school was vandalized and demolished.

• The establishment of literary societies by African Americans in Philadelphia continued.

One such society was the Library Company while another was the Banneker Society.

• African American women in Boston formed the Afric-American Female Intelligence Society. In 1832, the society was addressed by Maria Steward who is considered to be the first African American woman lecturer and writer.

• *The Black Church:* William Paul Quinn began his work as a circuit preacher and missionary of the African Methodist Episcopal Church in western Pennsylvania, Ohio, Indiana, and Illinois. By 1844, Quinn had established 47 churches with a membership of two thousand.

• African Americans in Providence, Rhode Island, organized the Providence Temperance Society. At its height, this society had approximately 200 members.

• John Chavis published a sermon in North Carolina called *The Extent of the Atonement,* which became quite popular. Chavis was an African American who had studied privately with President Witherspoon at the College of New Jersey (Princeton University). Chavis became a minister and often preached to both African American and European American audiences.

• *Black Enterprise:* In 1832, it was reported that African Americans in Philadelphia owned $350,000 worth of taxable property.

THE AMERICAS

• In 1832, a report was issued by the Select Committee on the Extinction of Slavery throughout the British Dominions at the earliest period compatible with the safety of all classes in the colonies.

AFRICA

• The African colonies of Portugal were reorganized.

• The French expanded their trading stations in West Africa.

• A diplomatic mission was sent from Zanzibar to Madagascar.

• R. Lander began his exploration of the River Niger.

• Between 1832 and 1836, a series of frontier wars flared up between Egypt and Kwara, Ethiopia.

• Between 1832 and 1843, Abd-el-Kader waged a war of resistance against the French in Algeria.

• Between 1832 and 1835, the Karagwe became a prominent African power under King Ndagara.

The Karagwe comprise one of the early states of the Haya. The Haya are, today, one of the largest Tanzanian ethnic groups.

The Karagwe kingdom was a dominant force in the area of modern-day Tanzania in the late 1700s and 1800s.

1833

THE UNITED STATES

The American Anti-Slavery Society was formed in Philadelphia by African Americans and European Americans (December 4). Among the African Americans who helped organize the society were Robert Purvis, a wealthy young African American who lived in a suburb of Philadelphia; James McCrummell, a Philadelphia dentist; and James G. Barbadoes, a Boston reformer. There were three African Americans on the first executive committee. They were: Samuel E. Cornish, minister and editor; Theodore S. Wright, a minister in New York; and Peter S. Williams, an Episcopal priest.

The American Anti-Slavery Society advocated the immediate and total abolition of slavery in the United States. During its existence, the American Anti-Slavery Society served as a clearinghouse for a successful propaganda campaign mounted by agents and agitators who looked to moral persuasion for their power. The society's program initially called for moral agitation directed at individual citizens in both sections of the country to make them see and feel the sinfulness of slavery. The mission of the society was to change people's hearts and their habits were soon to follow.

The years immediately following the formation of the American Anti-Slavery Society saw a great growth in the abolitionist movement. Thousands of petitions with hundreds of thousands of signatures were forwarded to Congress. Hundreds of antislavery agents swept over New England, New York and the Ohio Valley lecturing and distributing incendiary abolitionist literature. A dozen state auxiliaries and two score abolitionist newspapers were established.

Additionally, abolitionist radicals associated with the society were often involved in the Underground Railroad. These brave souls succeeded in developing a network which served to lead many hundreds of slaves to freedom.

By 1836, the crusade against slavery conducted by the American Anti-Slavery Society had succeeded in turning the tide against slavery and the course of American politics.

• An English visitor to New York City noted that most of the African Americans in the city favored the Whig Party and were opposed to the policies of President Andrew Jackson.

• In Savannah, Georgia, an organizational meeting of the Georgia Infirmary was held at the Exchange, a mercantile building (January 15). The Georgia Infirmary was a hospital founded by European Americans for the relief and protection of elderly and afflicted African Americans.

• One of the reasons why the Mormons were driven out of Independence, Missouri, was because the local residents believed the Mormons were trying to free the slaves. *See* 1827.

• The Charleston, South Carolina *Courier* called slavery a blessing and necessary for agriculture.

• An attack on African Americans in Detroit was set off by the rescue of Thornton Blackburn and his wife from arrest as fugitive slaves.

• The Presbyterian Synod of South Carolina and Georgia reported that throughout the South, there were "not twelve men exclusively devoted to the religious instruction" of African Americans. The synod also noted that there were only five African American churches in the South and that not enough room existed in the "white" churches to accommodate the African Americans. Finally, the synod stated that there were no Bibles available for the African Americans.

In 1833, the Reverend Nathaniel Paul went to England to raise money for the Wilberforce Settlement (located in Upper Canada). While in England, Paul delivered a speech at the Anti-Colonization Meeting held in Exeter Hall in London. In this speech, Paul launched a scathing two-pronged attack against the Colonization Society, deeming it cruel because it sought to expel an innocent and patriotic element "who contributed blood, sweat and tears to the development of the United States" primarily because they were of a "different complexion."

• *The Abolition Movement:* John B. Vashon, an African American veteran of the War of 1812, organized the "first Anti-Slavery Society west of the mountains" in Pittsburgh. He also promoted the foundation of an educational institution and was its first president.

• *The Civil Rights Movement:* Prudence Crandall was arrested and imprisoned for admitting an African American girl, Sarah Harris, to her academy for girls in Canterbury, Connecticut. After Crandall's legal difficul-

ties, her school was vandalized and subsequently demolished.

• Maria W. Stewart (1803–1879) gave a lecture in defense of women's rights in Boston.

• Theodore S. Wright, an early civil rights advocate, introduced a resolution to the American Anti-Slavery Society on May 10 which recommended that the society provide equal opportunities for African Americans to learn trades.

• *The Colonization Movement:* James Madison, former President of the United States and long an advocate of the colonization of free African Americans, became president of the American Colonization Society.

• *Miscellaneous State Laws:* Virginia law established a colonization board to be supported by a poll tax on free African Americans. The board's purpose was to deport African Americans to Liberia.

• A Savannah, Georgia, ordinance provided for fines of up to $100 or a whipping of up to 39 lashes for a slave or free African American who taught a slave or free African American to read or write.

• Another Georgia law prohibited the employment of African Americans in printing offices in any capacity that required knowledge of reading or writing.

• Delaware law imposed a tax of $5 for every slave sold to a person in another state and for every slave brought into the state. The money provided for the education of European American children. No provision was made for the education of African American children.

• Connecticut law prohibited the establishment of a school for African Americans who were not inhabitants of Connecticut, and prohibited the boarding of any free African American for instruction purposes unless the African American was an inhabitant of the town in which the school was located *and* the African American had obtained the written consent of a majority of the magistrates and selectmen of the town. This law would be repealed in 1838.

• The Alabama Legislature authorized the mayor and aldermen of Mobile, Alabama, to grant licenses to individuals for the purpose of instructing the children of "free colored Creoles." The children instructed had to have a certificate from the mayor and aldermen in order to be eligible for instruction. This licensing procedure was an exception to Alabama's general prohibition against the instruction of African Americans. The rationale for this exception was based on the treaty of 1803 with France under which the rights of citizenship (and, therefore, the right to an education) had been guaranteed to Creoles. *See 1832.*

• *Miscellaneous Cases:* In the North Carolina case of *State v. Edmund,* Judge Daniel upheld the right of a free African American to own slaves when he stated: "By the laws of this State, a free man of color may own land and hold lands and personal property including slaves."

• *Publications: Letters on Slavery* by James D. Paxton, a Presbyterian minister in Virginia, was published. The letters were intended to prove the "moral evil of slavery" and "the duty of Christians" to free slaves.

• In 1833, John Rankin published *Letters on American Slavery.* Rankin was a Tennessee abolitionist who was forced to flee because of his antislavery preaching. A Presbyterian minister, Rankin had a profound influence on the antislavery wing of his sect. His book, *Letters on American Slavery,* became a manual for antislavery speakers.

• David L. Child published *The Despotism of Freedom — Or The Tyranny and Cruelty of American Republican Slavemasters.*

• William Innes compiled and published *Liberia: Or, The Early History and Signal Preservation of the American Colony of Free Negroes on the Coast of Africa.*

• *Scholastic Achievements:* Oberlin College opened and admitted African Americans from the outset. When Professor Asa Mahan of Lane Seminary was offered the presidency of Oberlin in 1835, he accepted on the condition that African Americans be accepted on equal terms with European American students. By the outbreak of the Civil War, African Americans comprised one-third of the student body of Oberlin.

Perhaps because of its origins, Oberlin College became a center for clandestine abolitionist activity. Notably, three African American Oberlin students were with John Brown during his ill-fated raid on Harper's Ferry. *See 1859.*

• The Alabama Legislature authorized the mayor and aldermen of Mobile, Alabama, to grant licenses to individuals for the purpose of instructing the children of "free colored Creoles." The children instructed had to have a certificate from the mayor and aldermen in order to be eligible for instruction. This licensing procedure was an exception to Alabama's general prohibition against the instruction of African Americans. The rationale for this exception was based on the treaty of 1803 with France under which the rights of citizenship (and, therefore, the right to an education) had been guaranteed to Creoles.

• James Enoch Ambush, an African American, established a school for African Americans in the basement of the Israel Bethel Church on Capitol Hill in Washington, D.C. In 1843, Ambush established a school known as the Wesleyan Seminary.

• The Philadelphia Negro Library was organized.

In 1833, libraries, reading rooms, and debating societies, intended primarily for African Americans, were reported in Philadelphia.

• Benjamin M. McCoy, an African American, opened a school for African Americans on "L" Street in Washington, D.C. McCoy left in 1836 to run the free public Colored School in Lancaster County, Pennsylvania, but returned to Washington in 1837 and reopened his school in the basement of Asbury Church, remaining there for twelve years.

• Fanny Hampton, an African American, opened a school for African Americans on the corner of "K" and 19th streets.

• A certain Mr. Talbot, a European American, opened a school for African Americans in a private house in the rear of Franklin Row, Washington, D.C.

• In New York, African Americans formed the Phoenix Society, a literary society. The group started ward societies whose function included registering all African Americans in the ward, urging them to join the society and to attend school, maintaining a circulating library in the ward and procuring employment for those African Americans with skills. The society conducted an evening school for adults and also a high school for African Americans.

In response to the Prudence Crandall incident (*see above*), in 1833, Connecticut passed a law pertaining to the education of African Americans. The law stated:

No person shall set up or establish in this state any school, academy or other literary institution for the instruction or education of colored persons who are not inhabitants of this State, or harbor or board, for the purpose of attending or being taught or instructed in any such school, academy or literary institution, any colored person who is not an inhabitant of any town in this State without consent, in writing, first obtained, of a majority of the civil authority, and also of the selectmen of the town in which each school, academy or literary institution is situated.

• *The Arts and Sciences:* Ira Aldridge, the great Shakespearean actor, opened at Covent Garden in London as Othello opposite Ellen Terry, one of England's foremost actresses, playing Desdemona. *See 1805.*

• *Black Enterprise:* Solomon Humphries, a free African American, operated a successful grocery store in Macon, Georgia. Humphries owned property worth about $20,000 and had several slaves.

THE AMERICAS

• Publication began of *O Homem de Cor*, the first Brazilian newspaper devoted to Afro-Brazilians. As its motto, it published a quotation from the Imperial Constitution on the masthead: "Every citizen may be admitted to civil, political and military public offices, with no qualifications except those of his talents and virtues." The periodical lasted only for five issues but its importance endures. Its lasting significance lies in the fact that it was in the forefront of the abolition movement; it was devoted exclusively to the progress of Afro-Brazilians; and its publisher was an Afro-Brazilian.

• The act (the British Act of August 1833) which abolished slavery within the British Empire, included the abolition of slavery within the Dominion of Canada.

• On the British Isle of Antigua, all of the slaves were set free in 1833.

AFRICA

• On May 4, the negotiations for the Turco-Egyptian treaty of Kontaiah were concluded. Under the terms of this treaty, the independence of Egypt was recognized.

• The government of Sudan was centralized.

• A new constitution was adopted for the Cape colony.

EUROPE

• Ira Aldridge, the great Shakespearean actor, opened at Covent Garden in London as Othello opposite Ellen Terry, one of England's foremost actresses, playing Desdemona. *See 1805.*

RELATED HISTORICAL EVENTS

• Slavery was abolished in the British Empire (August 1).

The British Act of August 1833 abolished slavery throughout the British colonies, called for the promotion of industry among the manumitted slaves, and provided for the compensation of slave owners.

Under the act, Parliament awarded West In-dian slaveholders compensation in the amount of 20 million pounds upon the abolition of slavery. All children younger than six years and all newborn Afro-Caribbeans were deemed to be free. All other slaves became free upon the expiration of specified years of servitude. House slaves were to be freed after five years of service, while field slaves were to be freed after seven years of service. At the time of passage of the act, there were an estimated 800,000 (770,280) slaves in the British West Indies.

Although official (legal) slavery "technically" ended in 1833, in actuality, it continued in some of the West Indies until 1870.

In the wake of the abolition of slavery, a great deal of unrest erupted in the West Indies.

• William Wilberforce, the noted English advocate of the abolition of slavery, died. It was perhaps a most fitting tribute that slavery was abolished within the British Empire in the same year that this great English abolitionist died. *See 1759.*

1834

THE UNITED STATES

In the summer of 1834, a group of about 500 European Americans stormed into the Flying Horse, an amusement area in the African American quarter of Philadelphia. The mob attempted to drive the African Americans out of the area. In the ensuing street fight, the European Americans were repulsed.

The following night, a regrouped mob of European Americans rampaged through the African American quarter destroying homes and personal property and beating African Americans.

On the third night of the riot, the mob of European Americans was finally dispersed by the mayor and sheriff, supported by a posse.

One African American, Stephen James, was killed. Thirty-one houses and two churches were destroyed.

The Philadelphia town meeting of September 15 condemned the riots and voted reparations for the damage done by the rioters. However, town elders also condemned the harboring of escaped slaves by the quarter's African American residents and criticized the propensity for African American churches to be "noisy."

In the aftermath of the riot, it was determined that the primary reason for the disturbance was economic. Many European Americans were angered by the employment of African American workers while many European Americans were unemployed. It was recommended that African Americans take care to behave "inoffensively" and not to be "obtrusive" in passing along the streets or in assemblies together.

The Philadelphia riot was followed by similar disturbances in Columbia, Pennsylvania; Trenton, New Jersey; Rochester, New York; and Southwark, Lancaster, and Bloomfield, New Jersey.

In Columbia, Pennsylvania, after a mob of European Americans destroyed the homes of African Americans, a meeting of European American workingmen blamed the riot on abolitionist attempts to integrate the races. The European American workingmen agreed on a boycott of merchants who hired African Americans. Later a group of European American leaders met with African American property owners to urge them to sell their property at "a fair valuation" to local European Americans.

Meanwhile, mob violence against the African American residents of Columbia continued. The disturbances compelled a wealthy African American member of the community to sell his businesses at a loss.

• A Palmyra, New York, citizens meeting in October resolved that owners of houses and tenements occupied by African Americans of poor character be requested to use all rightful means to remove these tenants and not to rent thereafter to any person of color.

• African American youth leaders formed the Garrison Literary and Benevolent Association of New York in order "to begin, in early life, to assist each other to alleviate the afflicted...."

• In New Haven, Connecticut, a petition circulated by a group of citizens complained that the movement of African Americans into previously European American neighborhoods caused real estate values to fall by 20 to 50%.

In 1834, a group of Connecticut citizens petitioned the legislature for entry restrictions against African Americans to prevent a great influx of cheap African American labor that would drive out the "sons of Connecticut."

• In Utica, New York, a mob drove delegates to an antislavery meeting out of town.
• Bishop Onderdonk of the New York Diocese of the Protestant Church strongly urged the Reverend Peter Williams, an African American and a minister at Saint Philips Episcopal Church in New York, to resign from the American Anti-Slavery Society so that the church might avoid controversial issues and maintain itself "on the Christian side of meekness, order and self-sacrifice to common good, and the peace of the community." Williams complied.

• The New York City Zoological Institute issued a pamphlet which stated that "people of color are not permitted to enter except when in attendance upon children and families."

• Among the 396 slaves owned by Franklin and Armfield which had been shipped to New Orleans, there were only two families with both the father and mother left intact. There were 20 husbandless mothers who were the single parents providing parental guidance for 33 children.

• *The Abolition Movement:* The Colored Female Anti-Slavery Society of Middletown, Connecticut, was organized on April 2, 1834, as an antislavery society and for mutual improvement and increased intellectual and moral happiness.

• *The Civil Rights Movement:* A Convention of People of Color met in New York. It set aside July 4th as a day of prayer and speeches addressing the condition of African Americans in the United States.

• African Americans in Philadelphia received passports stating that they were citizens of the United States.

• *The Labor Movement:* "Les Artisans," an organization of free African American mechanics, was incorporated in New Orleans. Among the members of the new organization was seventeen year old Victor Sejour—a youth destined to become a famed poet and dramatist. *See 1817.*

• *Notable Births:* Patrick Francis Healy (1834–1910), the first African American to earn a doctorate and the first African American to become a Jesuit priest, was born in Georgia (February 7). Healy would become the president of Georgetown University. Healy was the brother of James Augustine Healy (*see 1830*) and Michael Augustine Healy (*see 1839*).

• Bishop Isaac Lane, founder of Lane College in Jackson, Tennessee, was born.

• Rufus Lewis Perry, an African American clergyman, was born a slave in Smith County, Tennessee.

Rufus Lewis Perry (1834–1895) was an African American missionary, educator, and journalist. His parents were Lewis and Mary Perry, slaves owned by Archibald Overton. Rufus' father, Lewis, was a Baptist preacher and an able mechanic and carpenter. Lewis Perry was allowed to work in Nashville where Rufus attended school until one day when Rufus' father fled to Canada, leaving his family behind.

The Perry family was forced to return to the Overton plantation and, in 1852, Rufus was sold to a slave dealer who intended to take him to Mississippi. It was then Rufus who decided to flee.

Rufus went to Canada. In Canada, he became a teacher and was ordained a minister in 1861.

Perry served as editor of the *Sunbeam* and of the *People's Journal*. He was coeditor of the *American Baptist* from 1869 until 1871. From 1872 until 1895, Perry was joint editor of *The National Monitor*.

In 1887, Perry was awarded a doctorate in philosophy (a Ph.D.) from the state university at Louisville, Kentucky, and, in 1893, he published *The Cushite; or the Descendants of Ham as seen by Ancient Historians*.

• Alonzo J. Ransier, an African American and a United States Congressperson, was born in Charleston, South Carolina.

Alonzo J. Ransier (1834–1882) was born to free parents in Charleston, South Carolina. Before the Civil War, he worked as a shipping clerk. In 1865, Ransier served as a registrar of elections. In 1866, he attended the first Republican Convention in South Carolina. After the convention, Ransier went to Washington, D.C., to lobby for federal protection of African Americans.

In 1868, Ransier became presidential elector and the chairman of the State Executive Committee. In 1870, he was elected lieutenant governor of the State of South Carolina.

Ransier was elected to the House of Representatives in 1873. While in Congress, he worked for civil rights protection, a national tariff, a six-year presidential term, and funds for the improvement of Charleston harbor.

• Henry McNeal Turner, bishop of the African Methodist Episcopal Church, was born near Abbeville, South Carolina.

Henry McNeal Turner (1834–1915) worked in the cotton fields after his father's death and was apprenticed to a blacksmith. Turner learned to read at 15, and he was later employed by a law firm where he learned to write.

In 1853, after joining the Methodist Episcopal Church, he received a license to preach.

Turner became a successful revivalist among African Americans and was ordained a deacon in 1860 and an elder in 1862.

Installed as pastor of the Israel Church in Washington, D.C., Turner was made an army chaplain by President Lincoln in 1863. In this capacity, Turner was attached to the First Regiment of Colored Troops.

Upon the conclusion of the Civil War, President Andrew Johnson appointed Turner chaplain in the regular army. Turner subsequently resigned in order to build up the African Methodist Episcopal Church in Georgia.

Turner was one of the founders of the Republican Party of Georgia. He was elected a delegate to the Georgia Constitutional Convention of 1867.

In 1869, Turner was appointed postmaster at Macon, Georgia, by President Grant. He eventually relinquished this post because of the opposition voiced by European Americans in the area. Serving as a customs inspector and government detective, Turner then, in 1876, became manager of the African Methodist Episcopal Book Concern in Philadelphia.

From 1880 through 1892 Turner served as bishop of the AME Church in Georgia. After 1892, Turner served as chancellor of Morris Brown College in Atlanta, Georgia.

Turner traveled widely. He visited South and West Africa where he introduced African Methodism. In his later years, Turner became an advocate for the return of African Americans to Africa.

Turner founded several periodicals during his career. In 1889, he founded *The Southern Christian Recorder* and, in 1892, he founded the *Voice of the Missions*. Turner also authored *The Genius and Method of Methodist Policy* which was published in 1885.

• *Miscellaneous State Laws:* The New Jersey Constitution confined suffrage to European Americans.

• South Carolina law prohibited teaching a slave to read or write, aiding him to read or write, or keeping a school for teaching slaves or free African Americans. The penalty imposed for violation of the law was a fine of up to $100 and imprisonment for up to six months for European Americans, up to a $50 fine and 50 lashes for free African Americans and up to 50 lashes for slaves. Any informer involved in catching the violators was declared a competent witness and was given one-half of the fine. This same South Carolina law restricted the employment of African Americans as clerks and salesmen.

• The Tennessee Constitution in 1834 declared free African Americans exempt from military duty in peace time and from paying the poll tax.

• Robert Purvis and his wife, Philadelphia African Americans, received passports to travel abroad. The significance of the passports was that they were official United States documents and that they indisputably declared that Purvis and his wife were United States citizens.

• John B. Vashon, an African American, was elected president of a temperance society and of the Moral Reform Society in Pittsburgh.

• William Wells Brown escaped from slavery by fleeing to Ohio while serving on a steamboat. Brown would thereafter resume his trade on Lake Erie. *See 1816.*

• *Publications:* William Lloyd Garrison reported that three-quarters of the subscribers to the *Liberator* were African Americans.

• The *Memoirs of Phillis Wheatley*, edited by Margaretta Matilda Odell and B. B. Thatcher, was published.

• *The "Extinguisher" Extinguished* by David Ruggles was published. Ruggles, an African American abolitionist, was secretary of the Committee of Vigilance and an ardent promoter of the Underground Railroad. Among the slaves Ruggles was credited with helping to freedom was none other than Frederick Douglass. *The "Extinguisher" Extinguished was a reply to two proslavery publications: A Brief Review of the First Annual Report of the American Anti-Slavery Society* by David Reese and *An Address on Slavery and against Immediate Emancipation* by Heran Howlett. In his reply to Reese's claims that the abolitionists approved of the intermarriage between African Americans and European Americans, Ruggles said "What of it? It is certainly not repugnant to nature." Ruggles then asked "Where are the pious Indians that can refer to the Puritans as their spiritual fathers in Christ Jesus? The Soil that was once peaceably pressed with their footsteps, has been drenched with their blood: they are hunted down and driven from mount to mount like the wild beasts of the forest."

• *Scholastic Achievements:* The first school for African Americans in Cincinnati, paid for by themselves, was opened.

• An academy which admitted African Americans was opened at Canaan, New Hampshire. The academy had an enrollment of 28 European Americans and 14 African Americans.

• The New York African Free School was transferred from the Manumission Society to the New York Public School Society. At the time, the New York African Free School property was appraised at $12,130.22. The enrollment was 1,400 students (although the actual attendance was about half that number). After the transfer, the school attendance of African Americans fell. The enrollment decline was partly attibutable to the climate of intolerance created by the 1834 riots. However, the decline was also attributable to the fact that the Public School Society was less well known than the Manumission Society and the fact that the Public School Society discontinued some of the practices of the Manumission Society and dismissed a number of teachers.

• *The Black Church:* In 1834, a conference of the African Methodist Episcopal Church was held in Washington, D.C. It was the first meeting of African Americans to be held in the nation's capital. Hundreds of European Americans as well as African Americans attended the conference. The city officials promised protection to the attendees "should any evil designed persons attempt" to interrupt the proceedings and the President of the United States wished the conference success.

• The Providence Association of Ohio an association of African American Baptist churches was formed.

• Beginning in 1834, African American preachers were gradually outlawed in many Southern states and slaves were required to attend the church of their owners.

• *Black Enterprise:* David Ruggles (1810–1849), an African American, opened a bookshop in New York City. This bookshop would be burned down by an angry European American mob in September of 1835.

• Henry Blair (c. 1804–1860) of Glenross, Maryland, received a patent for his invention of a corn harvester (October 14).

• Theodore Weld reported that approximately 75% of the 3,000 African Americans in Cincinnati had "worked out their own freedom."

THE AMERICAS

• Slavery was outlawed in Jamaica.

AFRICA

• 1834 marked the beginning of the "Trek" movement in South Africa. The trekking of the Boers (Dutch heritage South Africans) away from the British-held Cape colony to

the Orange Free State was prompted by a perception that the Cape colony had grown too small and did not provide opportunities for the new generation of Boers to acquire new land.
- The French military government of Algeria was reorganized.
- The British restored Fernando Po to Spain.
- The colony of Angola ignored the Portuguese abolition of the slave trade.
- 12,000 Xhosa attacked the Cape colony.
- Kassala was founded by the Egyptians.

Kassala is a market town in the center of a cotton-growing region of Sudan. Kassala is about 400 kilometers (250 miles) east of Khartoum.

RELATED HISTORICAL EVENTS

- The *Anti-Slavery Reporter*, a periodical containing extracts from Clarkson's thoughts on the practicability, the safety, and the advantage to all concerned of the emancipation of the slaves began publication. (There was also the *Anti-Slavery Reporter* under the sanction of the British and Foreign Anti-Slavery Society.)
- Gottlieb Daimler (1834–1900), the inventor of the motorized vehicle, was born.

1835

THE UNITED STATES

1835 was a year in which acts of intolerance (and acts of violence) towards African Americans were all too common throughout the country.

In Washington, D.C., a Georgetown mob tried to lynch Reuben Crandall. Crandall was in the local jail on the charge of distributing abolitionist literature. When the mob failed to lynch Crandall, they vented their wrath upon the homes and churches of free African Americans living in the area.

In Tennessee, Amos Dresser, an African American member of the Ohio Abolition Society, was arrested in Nashville, and was accused of circulating insurrectionary pamphlets among the slaves. A committee of vigilance composed of 62 citizens tried him, found him guilty, beat him, and forced him to leave the city.

In Philadelphia, a riot erupted when a "half-witted Negro" attempted to murder a European American. As in 1834, the police did little to bring the riot under control.

In St. Louis, Missouri, an African American, named McIntosh, was burned to death for killing an officer who was trying to arrest him. The newspaper publisher Elijah Lovejoy protested the burning of McIntosh. In retaliation, angry European Americans destroyed Lovejoy's printing office.

In Pittsburgh, a barber shop owned and operated by an African American was mobbed. Afterwards, attempts were made to rid the city of all African Americans.

In Washington, D.C., European American mechanics demolished the restaurant owned by African American Benjamin Snow. Snow was accused of making derogatory remarks concerning European American women including the wives of the mechanics. Snow escaped being lynched and fled to Canada.

Also in Washington, D.C., a riot growing out of a dispute at the Navy Yard developed into a general ransacking of the homes of prominent African Americans, ostensibly for the purpose of searching for antislavery literature. During this riot, most of the city's African American schoolhouses were burned down. John F. Cook, principal of the Smothers School, was forced to flee. Cook went to Columbia, Pennsylvania, and established a school.

In North Carolina, free African Americans were disenfranchised—denied the right to vote.

Finally as indicative of the times, in 1835, the Mormon leader, Joseph Smith, in the Book of Abraham part of the *Pearls of Great Price* stated that the descendants of Ham were cursed by Noah and could therefore not enter the priesthood. The curse of Ham was considered to be black skin. The Mormons also believed that Ham married an African who had the mark of Cain upon her.

- The Fifth National Negro Convention resolved to recommend that African Americans remove the word "African" from the names of their institutions and organizations, and also to abandon the use of the word "colored" when referring to themselves (June 1–5).
- In Charleston, South Carolina, antislavery propaganda pamphlets were taken from the mails and publicly burned.
- New York City African Americans formed a vigilance committee to prevent the kidnapping of African Americans and to assist fugitive slaves.
- In the Virginia Legislature, Representative Wise declared that "attacking the institution of slavery means attacking the safety and welfare of our country."

In 1835, a committee of the Ohio Anti-Slavery Convention assumed that a survey of two districts of Cincinnati was a representative sample of the approximately 2,500 African Americans in the city. Based on this assumption, the convention concluded that the following estimates were valid:

1. 476 slaves purchased their freedom for a total of $215,522.04, averaging $452.77 for each emancipated slave.

2. 346 African American children were still in slavery.

3. A number of African Americans were still working on securing their freedom while their manumission papers were retained as security.

• *The Abolition Movement:* The American Anti-Slavery Society raised money for the distribution of antislavery tracts in the South. By midsummer, 25,000 copies of *Slave's Friend* and 50,000 copies each of *Human Rights, Anti-Slavery Record* and *The Emancipator* had been printed and many sent to the South. The result of this abolitionist propaganda was increased paranoia (bordering on terror and panic) in the South.

To limit the activities of the abolitionists and antislavery societies, President Andrew Jackson sent a message to Congress which contained the following passage:

I must also invite your attention to the painful excitement produced in the South, by attempts to circulate through the mails, inflammatory appeals, addresses to the passion of the slaves, in prints and in various sorts of publications calculated to stimulate them in insurrection, and produce all the horrors of a servile war. There is, doubtless, no respectable portion of our countrymen who can be so far misled as to feel any other sentiment than that of indignant regret, at conduct so destructive of the harmony and peace of the country, and so repugnant to the principles of our national compact, and to the dictate of humanity and religion.

Jackson then urged Congress to enact legislation which would

prohibit, under severe penalties, the circulation in the Southern States, through the mails, of incendiary publications, intended to instigate the slaves to insurrection.

• William Whipper helped to found the American Moral Reform Society, an African American abolitionist group.

The American Moral Reform Society was composed primarily of Philadelphia African Americans. The society was created to replace the African American convention movement. The society urged the abandonment of separate African American conventions, integration into European American society wherever possible, and adherence to principles of brotherly love and nonresistance.

The principles of the American Moral Reform Society were not universally well received. Some African American leaders strongly opposed the passive assimilation concept advocated by the society. Among the African Americans opposed to principles of the society was Samuel Cornish, the editor of the *Colored American.*

• David Ruggles became secretary of the New York Vigilance Committee. In this post, Ruggles' assignment was to raise funds to help slaves escaping to freedom.

• *Notable Births:* Benjamin Tucker Tanner, a bishop of the African Methodist Episcopal Church, was born in Pittsburgh, Pennsylvania.

From 1852 to 1857, Benjamin Tucker Tanner (1835–1923) attended Avery College in Allegheny City, Pennsylvania. In 1856, he became a licensed preacher of the African Methodist Episcopal Church. In 1857, Tanner entered the Western Theological Seminary.

In 1858, Benjamin Tucker Tanner married Sarah Elizabeth Miller (August 19). Together they would produce one of the most prominent and illustrious African American families in African American history.

In 1859, the first child of Benjamin and Sarah was born (June 21). His name was Henry Ossawa Tanner (1859–1937), the foremost African American artist of his time. *See 1859.*

In 1860, Benjamin Tanner was ordained a deacon and then an elder in the African Methodist Episcopal Church. In this year, Bishop Daniel Payne (*see 1811*) assigned him to Washington, D.C. to serve as an interim minister at the Fifteenth Street Colored Presbyterian Church.

In 1861, Benjamin Tanner established a Sabbath School for Freedmen in Washington, D. C., and, in 1862, he became the director of Alexander Mission for Freedmen.

In 1863, Tanner was reassigned to be the pastor of the African Methodist Episcopal Church in Georgetown in the Washington, D.C. area.

In 1864, a daughter, Halle Turner (1864–1901) was born. Halle Turner would become the first licensed African American physician in Alabama. Halle would be followed by Mary Louise

Tanner (1866–1935), the future wife of Aaron Mossell, the first African American to graduate from the University of Pennsylvania Law School; Isabella Tanner (1867–?), an educator and evangelist; Carlton Tanner (1870–1933), the future managing editor of the South African *Christian Recorder*; Sarah Elizabeth Tanner (1873–1900), the future wife of Lewis B. Moore, the first African American to receive a doctorate from the University of Pennsylvania; and Bertha Tanner (1878–1962), a social worker.

In 1864, Tanner was made the principal of the African Methodist Episcopal Conference School in Frederick, Maryland. While at this school he wrote (and later published in 1867) *An Apology for African Methodism. An Apology of African Methodism* was one of the first intellectual and theological accounts of the schisms between African American and European American branches of the Methodist Church. This book was a critical success and launched Tanner on his great clerical career.

In 1868, Tanner became the editor of the *Christian Recorder*, the weekly journal of the African Methodist Episcopal Church. In 1881, Tanner traveled to London to attend the Ecumenical Conference of Methodism. In 1884, Benjamin Tanner launched the *A.M.E. Church Review*, the only national magazine published for African Americans at that time.

In 1888, Benjamin Tanner was elected eighteenth bishop in the African Methodist Episcopal Church and was assigned the Eleventh Episcopal District, an area which included Canada, the West Indies, British Guiana, and South America.

In 1897, Bishop Tanner was reassigned to Kansas City, Kansas, to serve the Fifth Episcopal District, an area covering Missouri, Kansas, and Colorado.

In 1900, Bishop Tanner and his family returned to Philadelphia. In 1901, Bishop Tanner was a delegate to the Third Ecumenical Conference of Methodism which was held in London.

Bishop Tanner retired in 1908 and became the first African Methodist Episcopal bishop to receive a pension. He died on January 15, 1923.

• *Notable Deaths:* Sally Hemings, an African American woman who was believed to be the mistress of Thomas Jefferson, died. See 1773.
• *Miscellaneous State Laws:* In Georgia, a law was enacted which prohibited the employment of slaves or free African Americans in drug stores and required that poisonous drugs be kept under lock and key.
• The Michigan Constitution limited the right to vote to European Americans.
• In North Carolina, a provision in the 1776 Constitution which gave all adult freemen, who owned property, the right to vote irrespective of their race was repealed by a vote of 66 to 61. North Carolina was the last state in the South to deny free African Americans the right to vote.
• Another North Carolina law abolished schools for free African Americans even though the free African Americans themselves had financially supported the schools.
• *Publications:* William Ellery Channing published *Slavery* as a reply to Southern apologists of slavery. Channing attacked the institution of slavery on the grounds that it was irrational and immoral, and a denial of democracy. Channing argued that the Southern planter's concept of a Golden Age of Greece resting on slavery was an absurdity. He also noted that the most essential property right of the individual is the right to the fruits of his own abilities. Since slavery deprived its victims of this right, it was, according to Channing, immoral robbery.
• John Greenleaf Whittier published his poem, "My Countrymen in Chains."
• In 1835, Joseph Smith in the Book of Abraham part of the *Pearls of Great Price* stated that the descendants of Ham were cursed by Noah and could therefore not enter the priesthood. The curse of Ham was considered to be black skin. The Mormons also believed that Ham married an African who had the mark of Cain upon her. *See* 1827.
• *Scholastic Achievements:* By a majority vote of one, the Oberlin College Board of Trustees voted to admit African Americans.
• Noyes Academy in Canaan, New Hampshire, which had an enrollment which consisted of African American and European American students was relocated to nearby swamps after its relocation had been voted on at a town meeting.
• In Charleston, South Carolina, city authorities suppressed schools for free African American children conducted by clergymen. Daniel Payne (*see* 1811), an African American born of free parents in Charleston, South Carolina, was forced by state law to close the school he had operated there for the previous six years. Payne would leave South Carolina for New York and would later teach at the Lutheran Seminary in Gettysburg, Pennsylvania.

• A school for African American children was established in the Baptist church on Western Row in Cincinnati. The teachers' salaries were paid partly by a European American educational society and partly by contributions from African Americans. The teachers and the school encountered great opposition in the city leading occasionally to the closing of the school.

• The Mulberry Street building of the African Free School in New York City became the Colored Grammar School No. 1, with an attendance of 317 pupils and with A. Libolt as principal. There were six primary schools for African Americans in various parts of the city, with a combined attendance of 925. In 1836, John Peterson, an African American, replaced Libolt as principal of Colored Grammar School No. 1.

• The Smith School House was built for the education of African American children in Boston with money left by Abiel Smith. The city of Boston contributed $200 a year to the school and the parents of the students paid about 13 cents per week.

• Nelson Wells, an African American, established the Wells School in Maryland for the instruction of free African American children. Wells left $7,000 to the school on his death.

• The charter for the city of Cleveland, Ohio, stated that schools were to be open to all European American children. However, African American children were regularly admitted along with European American children.

• *The Black Church:* In Baltimore, there were ten African American congregations. Slaves and free African Americans were members of the congregations. Baltimore also had 35 African American benevolent societies.

• *The Arts:* At the annual meeting of the American Anti-Slavery Society in May, African American and European American choirs sang on the same platform. Some abolitionists objected bitterly and later cited this integration as being a spark that helped to provoke anti–African American riots in New York that July.

THE AMERICAS

• In 1835, there were slave insurrections in Jaruco, Havana, and Matanzas in Cuba.

• A force of some 300 slaves came close to seizing Bahia, Brazil.

AFRICA

• In South Africa, the Great Trek began.

• On November 26, a French expedition was initiated against Mascara, Algeria.

• The Egyptians defeated the Ethiopians at Kwara, Ethiopia.

• Coffee growing was introduced into the Gold Coast.

• The Rozwi state (in today's Zimbabwe) was dismantled.

• The practice of Christianity was proscribed in Madagascar.

• The Ngoni began to migrate northward.

The Ngoni are a people who live in southeast Zambia. The Ngoni originated in South Africa where they lived along the coastal areas of Natal, the Cape, and southeastern Transvaal. However, during the early 1800s, southeast Africa experienced a number of social upheavals (called the "mfekane") which displaced whole peoples. One such people were the Ngoni, who traveled northward, absorbing other ethnic groups as they went.

One of the Ngoni groups which fled South Africa was led by Chief Shoshangana. Chief Shoshangana became the founder of the Gaza dynasty which came to dominate southern Mozambique.

At the height of their power (circa 1850), the Ngoni dominated the territory between the Zambezi and the Incomati rivers. Using military techniques that the Ngoni learned from the Zulus, the Ngoni developed a reputation as fierce warriors and were greatly feared.

The Mozambique Ngoni were known for their harassment of the Portuguese and fought a series of battles against these colonial rulers from 1832 to 1895 when they were finally subjugated. The subjugated Ngoni were then used by the Portuguese as mercenaries because of their reputation as fierce warriors.

The main body of Ngoni came to Zambia and Malawi in a mass migration from South Africa led by a Chief Zwangendaba. By the time of Zwangendaba's death in 1848, the Ngoni had reached the area of what is now the Malawi-Tanzanian border.

Internecine conflicts between Zwangendaba's successors led to splinter groups moving away from the main body of the Ngoni. One such group reached the territory of the Nsenga in 1860 and initiated a number of attempts to take over the prosperous Chewa kingdom (of Mozambique). This they did in 1880.

The main body of Ngoni (of Zambia) were relatively independent until 1898 when they were defeated by the British. But even then, a Ngoni chief was appointed administrative head of the region.

• Mark Twain (Samuel Clemens) (1835–1910), the great American novelist, was born.

─────── 1 8 3 6 ───────

THE UNITED STATES

Remember the Alamo

The Alamo was a mission fortress in San Antonio, Texas. In 1836, Texas was a part of Mexico which was heavily populated by Americans. The Americans who lived in Texas tended to have a Southern perspective on life and this perspective included a reliance upon slavery.

In 1829, Mexico emancipated all of its slaves. However, this general emancipation didn't fit into the plans of American Texans. They protested and the government of Mexico, for the time, relented. Nevertheless, the issue of slavery remained an issue of contention between the American Texans and the Mexican government, and slavery was to become one of the key issues which ultimately led to the American Texans declaring their independence from Mexico.

One of the key battles in the Texans' war for independence was the Battle at the Alamo. From February 23 through March 6 of 1836, American Texans holed up in the Alamo were besieged by General Santa Anna and a force of 4,000 Mexicans. The 180 American Texans within the Alamo fought valiantly but the superior numbers of the Mexicans eventually prevailed and almost the entire garrison was killed. Among the dead were such legendary American figures as Davy Crockett and Jim Bowie.

The "heroic" struggle of the American Texans at the Alamo became an inspirational rallying point for the American Texans. Under the leadership of Sam Houston, the American Texans eventually defeated General Santa Anna and won their independence.

The irony about the Texans' War of Independence—and the irony connected with the Battle of the Alamo—was that, to a rather significant degree, the war and the battle were fought so that men would be free to enslave other men.

• A free African American, George Jones, was arrested in New York City on a fabricated charge of assault and battery. Jones surrendered to his captors on his employer's assurance that he would be protected. Less than two hours after his capture, Jones was taken before the city recorder, declared to be a slave solely on the basis of the word of his kidnappers, and summarily shipped to the South.

• Elijah Abel (?–1884), an African American, became an elder (priest) in the Mormon Church while the Mormons were located in Nauvoo, Illinois.

Elijah Abel was an undertaker who was converted to Mormonism in 1832. After becoming an elder, Abel moved with the Mormons to Salt Lake City, Utah. In Salt Lake City, he became a hotel manager. Abel would be active in the Mormon Church throughout his life.

• The Methodist Episcopal Church, which had opposed slavery in 1780, changed its position and announced that the Church had no "intention to interfere in the civil and political relation between master and slave, as it existed in the slaveholding states of the Union."

• *The Abolition Movement:* In 1836, a memorial was presented in the United States Senate which requested the abolition of slavery. This memorial was just one of many antislavery petitions which began to be presented to Congress. In an effort to avoid the acrimonious debates which accompanied any discussion of slavery, Congress introduced a "gag rule" which provided that no antislavery petition should be read, printed, committed or in any way acted upon by the House, but should instead be laid upon the table without debate or discussion. This rule was generally considered a direct violation of the Constitution. In 1845, this "gag rule" was repealed, largely due to the efforts of Congressman (and ex–President) John Quincy Adams.

Adams and other opponents of the gag rule argued that the rule was an effort to deny European American men the right of freedom of speech by way of petition solely for the purpose of attempting to keep African Americans slaves. At one point, more than 200,000 petitions were received by Congress in a single session.

By 1836, the cooperation between the Southern and Northern Whig Party members had deteriorated due to their opposing views on the issue of slavery. Northern Whigs were generally hostile to slavery, while the Whig Party in the South included the owners of 60 to 80 percent of all the slaves in the South. Indeed, in September of the previous year (1835), the *Richmond Whig* advocated cessation of trade with the North until abolitionist activity was ended.

• The New York's Women's Anti-Slavery Society barred African Americans from membership. A similar society in Fall River, Massachusetts, did admit African Americans as members despite protests from some members.

• Lewis Tappan proposed that an African American minister deliver an address before the American Anti-Slavery Society. The other abolitionist leaders objected that the time had not yet come to socialize with African Americans in public.

• *The Civil Rights Movement:* The Reverend Peter Williams, a New York African American, received a United States passport stating that he was a United States citizen.

• *Notable Births:* Jefferson F. Long, an African American and a member of Congress, was born.

Jefferson F. Long (1836–1900) was born a slave near Knoxville, Georgia. He moved to Macon, Georgia, after working for a merchant tailor, and opened a tailoring shop of his own.

From 1865 through 1869, Long was influential in the Georgia Republican Party. In 1869, he was elected to Congress. While in Congress, Long advocated the enforcement of the 15th Amendment and universal suffrage.

Long only served one term, but remained active in the Georgia Republican Party throughout his life.

• Amanda Berry Smith, a prominent missionary, was born into slavery in Maryland (January 23). Because of the African Methodist Episcopal Church's refusal to ordain women, Smith was compelled to pursue her preaching career on three other continents.

• *Miscellaneous State Laws:* North Carolina law required that a $1,000 bond be posted before a slave could be manumitted. This bond was required to insure the good behavior of the freed slave and to insure that the slave departed the state within 90 days.

• *Miscellaneous Cases:* In the Pennsylvania case of *Fogg v. Hobbs*, the court decided that free African Americans were not entitled to vote because they did not qualify as freemen under the state constitution.

• *Publications:* James G. Birney began publication of *The Philanthropist* in Cincinnati. A few weeks later a mob destroyed his press. The mob then began to ravage the African American section of Cincinnati.

• The *Alton Observer,* an antislavery newspaper, was first published in Alton, Illinois.

• Robert Benjamin Lewis published *Light and Truth,* a pseudohistorical book which sought to substantiate an African presence in history and which asserted that the Indigenous Americans were the descendants of the lost tribes of Israel. Robert Lewis happened to have been a person of both African and Indigenous American heritage.

• Lydia Maria Child published *An Appeal in Favor of that Class of Americans Called Africans.* Child was one of the leading abolitionists and this work was an early proponent for African American civil rights.

• R. G. Williams published *The Slave's Friend.*

• *Scholastic Achievements:* Theodore S. Wright became the first African American to receive a degree from a theological seminary (Princeton) in the United States (November 5).

• Isaiah D. DeGrasse, an African American, sought admission to the General Theological Seminary of the Protestant Episcopal Church of New York. DeGrasse was told by Bishop Benjamin T. Onderdonk of the New York Diocese that he might attend classes, but could not live in the dormitory or be a formal member of the school. DeGrasse refused to accept the arrangement and left.

• Dr. John H. Fleet opened a school for African Americans in a schoolhouse on New York Avenue in Washington, D.C. Fleet was an African American who had been educated in schools with European American children, such as the Georgetown Lancasterian School. He studied medicine in Washington in the office of Dr. Thomas Henderson, and attended lectures at the Medical College. His school continued until 1843 when it was burned.

• The Reverend J. W. Lewis, an African American, established the New England Union Academy in Providence, Rhode Island. The school offered African Americans instruction in history, botany, bookkeeping, and natural philosophy. Tuition was $3 a quarter.

• The Society for the Promotion of Education Among Colored Children was organized in New York. The society established two schools for African Americans, one on Thomas Street and one on Center Street.

• Colored Grammar School No. 2 opened in New York City in a new building with 210 pupils and R. F. Wake, an African American, as principal.

• Philadelphia African Americans founded the Rush Library Company and Debating Society.

• *The Black Church:* In 1836, the African Methodist Episcopal Church reported a membership of 7,594 members. The church consisted of 86 churches, 4 conferences, 2 bishops, 27 ministers, and property worth an estimated $125,000. In 1836, the African Methodist Episcopal Church conference set up a quarterly magazine under the editorship of George Hogarth of Brooklyn, New York.

• The first Negro Baptist church in Baltimore was established. The founders were M. C. Clayton and Noah Davis.

• African Americans organized the Providence Baptist Association in Ohio. This was an association of African American Baptist churches and was the first such African American association in the United States.

Black Enterprise: In 1836, Henry Boyd, an African American, built a factory at the corner of 8th Street and Broadway in Cincinnati for the manufacture of bedsteads. When Boyd arrived in Ohio in 1826, he was unable to find work because of prejudice. However, Boyd, because of his craftmanship, was able to initiate a joint venture with a European American and this joint venture became quite successful. At one time, Boyd's enterprise required 4 buildings and 50 workmen, African American and European American. Boyd invented a machine to produce rails for beds. Boyd sought a patent for his invention in the name of a European American partner. During the periods of racial unrest in Cincinnati, Boyd's business was often the target of mobs. His buildings were frequently damaged or destroyed by fire. Ultimately, Boyd was forced to abandon his business because he was unable to obtain insurance to pay for the damage of the last fire in 1859.

• Henry Blair received a second patent for his corn harvester (corn planter) machine (August 31).

THE AMERICAS

• George Paddington, a person of African descent from Dublin, Ireland, was ordained by Bishop John England in Port-au-Prince, Haiti (May 21).

• In 1836, the Afro-Cuban poet, Juan Francisco Manzano read his poem "Mis Treinta Anos" to a literary group. The group was so moved by the reading that they purchased Juan's freedom. *See 1797.*

• *Suspiros Poeticos* was published in Paris. *Suspiros Poeticos* included a poem, "A Saudade." "A Saudade" marked the first appearance of the slave as a figure in Brazilian literature. The poet Domingos Magalhaes' portrayal of the oppressed Afro-Brazilian, longing for freedom and a return to his homeland from the New World exile, was

poignant. "A Saudade" became a stereotype poem for the Brazilian romantic movement. Magalhaes, a Euro-Brazilian, was a crusading abolitionist journalist, as well as a poet.

AFRICA

• The *Bible* was translated into Mandingo.

The Mandingo are a people of western Africa centering around the upper Niger valley. Mandingo is the language of the Mandingo people.

• On January 5, the French launched an expedition against Tlemcen (western Algeria). This would be followed by another expedition against Constantine (eastern Algeria) on November 9.

• The Egyptians initiated another military campaign against Kwara, Ethiopia.

• By 1836, the Great Trek of South Africa had reached the Transvaal and the Orange Free State. In this year, Potgeiter and Maritz would set up their own republic.

• A treaty was negotiated between Britain and the Matabele.

• The plague depopulated Mogadishu (Somalia).

EUROPE

• A *Narrative of Travels, etc. of John Ismael Agustus James, An African of the Mandingo Tribe, who was Captured, sold into Slavery, and subsequently liberated by a Benevolent English Gentlemen* was published in England. The narrative was subsequently criticized as being a "pious hoax" concocted by the antislavery proponents.

RELATED HISTORICAL EVENTS

• On March 2, Texas was proclaimed an independent republic. On March 6, the Battle of the Alamo was fought *see above.* On April 21, the Texas militia defeated the Mexican army and captured Santa Anna.

• Portugal prohibited the exportation of slaves from any Portuguese possession.

• A report from the Select Committee of Parliament reported on the apprenticeship program in the British colonies which was to replace slavery.

———— 1 8 3 7 ————

THE UNITED STATES

The Second Seminole War

In 1830, the United States Congress passed the Indian Removal Act which called for the relocation of eastern Indigenous Americans to the "Indian Territory" west of the Mississippi

River. In 1832, James Gadsden, a representative of Secretary of War Lewis Cass, forced some of the Seminole leaders to agree to the Treaty of Payne's Landing. Under this treaty, the Seminoles were required to evacuate Florida within three years in exchange for lands out west, a sum of money, plus blankets for men and frocks for women. The Treaty of Payne's Landing also established that any Seminoles with African blood were to be treated as escaped slaves subject to a return to slavery. Because of the fairly common intermarriage of Seminoles and Africans, this provision of the treaty meant that many Seminole families would have been disintegrated. Such a disintegration was abhorrent to most of the Seminoles and most of them resolved not to abide by the treaty.

By the end of the three-year period set forth in the Treaty of Payne's Landing, no Seminoles had moved west. In 1835, the Indian agent General Wiley Thompson convened the Seminole leaders at Fort King for the purpose of reaffirming the terms of the Treaty of Payne's Landing. At this meeting, a Creek who had become affiliated with the Seminoles rose and voiced his opposition to the relocation of the Seminoles. The Creek who spoke was named Osceola and he said: "My brothers! . . . The white man says I shall go, and he will send people to make me go; but I have a rifle, and I have some powder and some lead. I say, we must not leave our homes and lands. If any of our people want to go west we won't let them; and I tell them they are our enemies, and we will treat them so, for the great spirit will protect us."

For this demonstration of defiance, General Thompson locked up Osceola and warned Osceola that he would not be released unless he agreed to relocation.

After a night of incarceration, Osceola agreed. However, his agreement was only given by him to effect his escape. Soon after he was released, Osceola killed Charley Emathla, one of the Seminole leaders who supported removal, and, as a symbolic gesture, scattered to the wind the money the European Americans had paid him. With this act of violence, the Second Seminole War began.

The Seminoles sequestered their women and children deep into the Florida swamps and forests. Meanwhile, the Seminole men formed small marauding parties which relied upon guerrilla tactics to achieve military success. Three of the earliest Seminole victories took place during the last week of 1835. Osceola and

a small band of warriors got revenge for the humiliation suffered at the hands of General Thompson by ambushing and killing the general and four other European Americans at Fort King. On the same day, a contingent of 300 Seminoles under the command of Micanopy, Alligator Sam Jones, and Jumper attacked and massacred a column of 100 soldiers under the command of Major Francis Dade. Only three of Dade's soldiers were able to escape (by feigning death). Three days later, on New Year's Eve, several hundred Seminoles under Osceola and Alligator Sam Jones surprised a superior force comprised of 300 regular army troops and 500 militia men. The American forces under the command of General Clinch were routed by the smaller Seminole force.

This war between the United States and the Seminoles would last for the next seven years. A whole contingent of American generals would be frustrated by the guerrilla war in the Florida swamps. The old Indian fighter, President Andrew Jackson, would send Generals Edmund Gaines, Duncan Clinch, Winfield Scott, Robert Call, Thomas Jessup, Alexander McComb, Walker Armistead, and William North (along with Colonel Zachary Taylor) against the Seminoles but to little avail. The Seminole warriors, though small in number, fought skillfully. They would cut up any small groups of soldiers that ventured from the forts while avoiding any direct confrontation with the main body of the army. The inability of the army to subdue the few hundred naked, hungry Seminole warriors soon became a national joke.

One general, Thomas Jessup, attempted to bring a halt to the war by capturing what he perceived to be the Seminoles' leader. In December of 1837, Jessup invited Osceola to a truce parley. Osceola, weary from two years of constant warfare and inadequate food, agreed to the parley. However, when Osceola appeared for the parley, Jessup had him seized. Osceola, weakened by the war, made no effort to resist.

Jessup sent Osceola to St. Augustine with a guard contingent of two columns of troops. Osceola, who was too ill to walk, rode on horseback.

While in captivity, Osceola grew weaker and weaker. Wracked by malaria and a throat disease, Osceola knew that the time for his death was near. On January 30, 1838, Osceola called for his battle dress, and rising from his bed, he pulled on his shirt, leggings, and moccasins, and strapped his war belt around his waist. According to Dr. Frederick Weedon, the post surgeon, Osceola then called for red paint, and his looking-glass, which was held before him. Osceola then deliberately painted one-half of his face, his neck and throat—his wrists—the backs of his hands, and the handle of his knife, red with vermillion; a custom practiced when the irrevocable oath of war and destruction is taken.

"After recovering his strength for a moment, the dying Osceola rose up as before, and with most benignant and pleasing smiles, extended his hand to me and to all the officers . . . and shook hands with us all in dead silence. . . . He made a signal for them to lower him down upon his bed, which was done, and he then slowly drew from his war belt his scalping knife, which he firmly grasped in his right hand, laying it across the other on his breast, and a moment later smiled away his last breath, without a struggle or groan."

Dr. Weedon's touching account of Osceola's death apparently did not quite touch the good doctor's heart. Almost as soon as Osceola breathed his last breath, Dr. Weedon cut off his head. Dr. Weedon would keep this grisly souvenir for years.

The capture and death of Osceola did not end the Second Seminole War. The deception perpetrated by General Jessup and the brave martyrdom of Osceola only served to enrage and inspire the Seminoles.

In May of 1838, the tired and beleaguered General Jessup turned over his command to Colonel Zachary Taylor—an Andrew Jackson protégé. In 1837, Taylor had achieved some success against the Seminoles at the Battle of Lake Okeechobee when Taylor's forces surprised the Seminoles and won the ground.

In December of 1837, a black Seminole named John Horse shared command of the Seminole forces with Alligator Sam Jones and Wild Cat during the Seminole battle against American troops under Colonel Zachary Taylor at the Battle of Lake Okeechobee. Taylor defeated the Seminoles.

However, even this victory was tainted by the fact that the American troops suffered more casualties than the Seminoles.

Taylor devised a new strategy. He divided Florida into a grid of squares twenty miles on a side and assigned a garrison to patrol each square. Using this method, Taylor took scores of Seminole prisoners and sent them west. But despite this success, the war went on.

The American public became outraged by the length of the war and the cost. The public was also embarrassed by the way the war had been conducted. The capture of Osceola under a flag of truce was a shameful affair. Zachary Taylor's subsequent use of bloodhounds to track down Seminoles was also deemed deplorable.

But to a certain extent Taylor's tactics began to work. The tactics forced the Seminoles to go deeper and deeper into the swamps of southern Florida. Eventually, the war of attrition forced most of the Seminoles to surrender and be subjected to relocation. The last notable surrender occurred in 1841, when a Seminole chieftain named Coacoochee (also known as Wild Cat) and two of his lieutenants were captured. The capture of Wild Cat ended the hostilities of the Second Seminole War.

The Second Seminole War was the costliest Indian war ever fought by the United States government. For every two Seminoles relocated to the Indian Territory of Oklahoma, one American soldier died. (From 1835 to 1842, some 3,000 Seminoles were transported to Oklahoma.) The cost of the war in monetary terms is estimated to have been $20 million dollars. And even though the hostilities came to an end, the war was never officially concluded. In 1842, the United States government decided that the task of flushing out the remaining Seminoles from the swamps of the Florida Everglades was too costly and so the United States simply gave up trying. Thus, the Second Seminole War ended, but the Seminoles were never formally conquered.

Today, Seminoles, red, black and mixed, still live in the Florida Everglades. They point with pride and distinction to the fact that they never surrendered, and these Seminoles claim with arrogance that they and their lands are a sovereign nation—independent and free from the United States.

• The First Annual Meeting of the American Moral Reform Society was held in Philadelphia from August 14 through August 19. The American Moral Reform Society had been organized at the Fifth Annual Convention for the Improvement of the Free People of Color. The purpose of the American Moral Reform Society was to extend the principles of universal peace and good will to all mankind, by promoting sound morality, by the influence of education, temperance, economy and all those virtues that alone can render man acceptable in the eyes of God or the civilized world.

• Of the 737 African Americans jailed

pending trial in Philadelphia in the first six months of the year, only 123 were actually brought to trial.

• 235 of 1,673 inmates of the Philadelphia County Almshouse were African Americans. This number represented fourteen percent of the paupers in the Almshouse or roughly twice the proportion of African Americans in the general population of the city.

• Just before the Panic of 1837, the price of a "prime field hand" 18 to 25 years old was $1,300.

• *The Abolition Movement:* In May, the Anti-Slavery Women of America met in convention in New York with Sarah Douglass, an African American, on the Central Committee.

Beginning in 1837 through 1848, many officials in Northern and Western states refused to comply with requests from Southern officials to return fugitive slaves.

• *Notable Births:* Francis L. Cardozo, an African American educator and minister, was born in Charleston, South Carolina (February 1).

• P.B.S. Pinchback, an African American Reconstructionist statesman from Louisiana, was born (May 10).

Pinckney Benton Stewart Pinchback, also known as Percy Bysshe Shelley Pinchback (1837–1921), the son of a European American planter and an African American slave mother, was born free because his mother had been freed.

As a boy, Pinchback was sent to Ohio. Returning to the South (New Orleans) during the Civil War, in 1862, Pinchback created the Corps d'Afrique, a unit composed of African American troops for the Union Army. Pinchback resigned in September of 1862 over racial difficulties but, subsequently, he was commissioned to raise a company of African American cavalry.

After the Civil War, Pinchback organized a local Republican club. In 1868, Pinchback was elected to the Louisiana Constitutional Convention and then the State Senate. In 1871, he was elected president pro tem of the State Senate and subsequently became the lieutenant governor when the incumbent died.

Between December 9, 1872 and January 13, 1873, Pinchback served as governor of Louisiana while Governor Warmoth was being subjected to impeachment proceedings. Later in January 1873, Pinchback was elected to the United States Senate.

Upon his arrival in Washington, D.C. to assume his post, Pinchback was refused his seat. One of the reasons why Pinchback was denied his seat in the Senate was over the resentment caused by his marriage to a European American woman. Pinchback fought for three years to be seated — but he never was.

In later years, Pinchback would serve as a surveyor of customs in New Orleans and to other honorary posts.

• Quiltmaker Harriet Powers was born in Georgia (October 29).

• James T. Rapier, an African American and a member of the House of Representatives, was born.

James T. Rapier (1837–1882) was born of free parents in Florence, Alabama. Rapier's father was a wealthy planter and provided Rapier with a tutor for his primary education. Later on, Rapier was sent to Montreal College in Canada, the University of Glasgow in Scotland, and Franklin College in Tennessee.

As a successful cotton planter, Rapier became involved in reform of the Alabama State Constitution and the founding of the state Republican Party, serving as its vice-president.

Interested in organizing urban and rural workers, Rapier helped to establish, and chaired, the first state African American labor convention. Rapier edited and published the *Montgomery Sentinel* to present his views on African American solidarity and was elected to the House of Representatives in 1872.

Although the power of the Ku Klux Klan and the Democratic Party ended his political career after only one term in Congress, Rapier continued to dabble in politics. He would later serve as a United States revenue officer in Alabama.

• *Notable Deaths:* Elijah P. Lovejoy, a European American, was murdered by a mob in Alton, Illinois, when he refused to stop publishing antislavery material (November 7). Using his publication the *Observer* as a forum, Lovejoy advocated the immediate abolition of slavery. Angry proslavery mobs destroyed three of his presses. Lovejoy was killed while trying to protect one of his last presses.

• *Miscellaneous State Laws:* Indiana law provided that only European American inhabitants in each township should make up the local school corporation.

• In Pennsylvania, African Americans were disenfranchised.

• *Miscellaneous Cases:* The Pennsylvania Supreme Court ruled in July that African

Americans could not legally vote. The court cited a 1795 court decision which barred African American suffrage. There was no written record of the 1795 case, but the Chief Justice of the Pennsylvania Supreme Court asserted that the "memory" of a good friend, a Philadelphia lawyer, was a sufficient enough record.

• Judge John Fox of Bucks County, Pennsylvania, ruled in favor of Democratic candidates for county office who claimed that they had been defeated by the margin of African Americans who had cast votes. Fox ruled that since African Americans did not have the right to vote, their votes could not be counted.

• *Publications:* The sensation of the year was the publication of *A Narrative of Events Since the First of August, 1834.* This narrative was supposed to have been the story of a certain James Williams—a slave. However, the author of the story, the famous John Greenleaf Whittier, who had unwittingly recorded the story as being true, later found out that it was not. However, Williams' story was so poignant and valuable as a propaganda tool that it was published by the Anti-Slavery Society as fact and no mention was made that Whittier was the author.

A copy of the narrative was sent to each member of Congress. But, in October of 1838, the circulation of the *Narrative* was ordered suppressed by the society. The controversy over Williams was the sensation of the year in the antislavery press. In the wake of the furor, Williams was sent to England to calm the situation and to avoid being captured as an escaped slave.

• William Whipper published "An Address on Non-Resistance to Offensive Aggression"—an article written twelve years before Thoreau's famous essay on nonviolence, and more than 125 years before the career of Martin Luther King, Jr.

• Henry B. Stanton published *Remarks of Henry Brewster Stanton in the Representatives Hall, on the 23rd and 24th of February, 1837.* The publication went through at least five editions in one year and for a quarter of a century set the pattern for abolitionist arguments on the issue of abolishing slavery in the District of Columbia.

• *The Weekly Advocate*, a New York newspaper, was founded. The editor was Samuel E. Cornish; the publisher was Philip A. Bell; and the general manager was Charles B. Ray. Later editors included C. P. Bell, James McCune Smith and Charles B. Ray.

• *The Colored American* denounced segregated schools as providing little advantage because they "so shackled the intellect of colored youth." The publication also deplored separate churches and all separate institutions for African Americans as contributors to the persecution and neglect of African Americans.

• The Reverend Hosea Easton published *A Treatise on the Intellectual Character and Civil and Political Condition of the Colored People of the United States, and the Prejudice Exercised Towards Them.* The treatise was a sociological history of the oppression of African Americans as seen from the perspective of an African American scholar.

In his *Treatise* Hosea Easton answered the question often expressed as to why African Americans did not attend European American churches. Easton explained that African Americans did not attend European American churches because European Americans made the African Americans feel different. He concluded that the treatment received by African Americans from European Americans was caused by public sentiment fostered by undemocratic education and not because of the African Americans' color or condition of servitude.

Easton's *Treatise* defended the intellectual capacity of African Americans by referring to the African Americans' cultural past in Egypt and Ethiopia and the part Africans played in ancient cultures. Easton declared:

> From the fourth up to the sixteenth century, they (*Europeans*) were in the deepest state of heathenish barbarity. Their spread over different countries caused almost an entire extinction of all civil and religious governments, and of the liberal arts and sciences. And ever since that period, all Europe and America have been little else than one great universal battlefield. ...It is true that there is a great advance in the arts and sciences from where they once were: but whether they are anywhere near its standard, as they once existed in Africa, is a matter of doubt. ...The Egyptians have done more to cultivate such improvements as comport to the happiness of mankind than of the descendants of Japhet put together."

Easton's *Treatise* is one of the earliest known proponents of what is today described as the "Afro-centric" perspective of history.

• George Moses Horton's *The Hope of Liberty* was reprinted in Philadelphia under the title *Poems of a Slave.*

• *Olaudah Equiano or Gustavus Vassa*, the autobiography of a slave, was published in Boston.

• Leicester A. Sawyer published *A Dissertation on Servitude: Embracing an Examination of the Scripture Doctrines on the Subject, and an Inquiry into the Character and Relations of Slavery*.

• George Bourne published *Slavery Illustrated in Its Effects Upon Women and Domestic Society*.

• *The Life of Jim Crow*, supposedly written by himself was published. Jim Crow was the name of a minstrel dance routine. This "autobiography" was about a Louisville African American who claimed to have been called Jim Crow.

• *Narrative of the Adventures and Escape of Moses Roper, From American Slavery* was published. Roper was born in Caswell County, North Carolina. He claimed that his father was a slave owner who owned his mother. According to Roper, soon after his birth, the slave owner's wife attempted to stab the infant because she was jealous of Roper's mother and wanted to extract her revenge. Roper's father hurriedly sold Roper and his mother to another slave owner who, in turn, sold Roper and his mother again. After the second sale Roper became separated from his mother. Roper made many attempts to escape and, finally, succeeded. He made his way to Savannah, New York, Boston, and, eventually, to Liverpool, England. In England, Roper was sent to school and was trained to serve as a missionary among the Afro-Caribbeans of the British West Indies.

• *Scholastic Achievements*: James McCune Smith received a Doctor of Medicine degree from the University of Glasgow (Scotland).

• Madame Bernard Couvent, a free African American woman in New Orleans who owned several slaves, left her property on Grands Hommes and Union streets for the establishment of a free school for African American orphans. This school was eventually built in 1848.

• The Institute for Colored Youth was established with $10,000 left by Richard Humphreys. The school was run by the Society of Friends (Quakers), and taught mechanical and agricultural arts and trade. In 1839, a farm was purchased in Bristol in Philadelphia County where boys could be taught farming, shoemaking, etc. The school continued until 1846. The school was revived in Philadelphia in 1852 with Charles L. Reason as teacher with branches for boys and girls.

• African Americans of Cincinnati formed the School Fund Institute of Ohio to provide for the education of African Americans.

• *The Black Church*: Philadelphia African Americans had 16 churches with over 4,000 communicants.

• The first National Negro Catholic Congress was convened in Washington, D. C.

• *The Arts and Sciences*: James McCune Smith, an African American, established a medical practice in New York after receiving his M.D. from the University of Glasgow. Smith later gained a reputation for calculating mortality rates for insurance companies. Smith was the author of several scientific papers, and a man of wide interests and reputation. *See 1813.*

• James McCune Smith, a University of Glasgow graduate, conducted pioneer work in the scientific study of race. *See 1813.*

• *Black Enterprise*: New York City African Americans owned $1,400,000 worth of taxable real estate, and had $600,000 deposited in savings banks.

• There were 18,768 African Americans in Philadelphia. 250 of these African Americans had paid a total of $79,612 to secure their freedom. The real and personal property owned by African Americans in Philadelphia was almost $1,500,000. The Philadelphia African Americans owned taxable property of $359,626.

THE AMERICAS

• Afro-Canadians were given the right to vote.

• Juan Francisco Manzano, the great Afro-Cuban poet, published *La Musica*. The poem was inspired by his mestizo pianist wife, Delia.

• In British Guiana, slavery was abolished.

AFRICA

• The administration of Egypt was reformed.

• Regular steam ship services began between London and Alexandria, Egypt, and Suez, Egypt, and Bombay, India.

• The Ethiopians defeated the Egyptians at Wad Kaltabu.

• Piet Retief joined the Great Trek.

• The Xhosa ceded half of Natal to Great Britain.

• The Sanusiyah confraternity was founded by the Algerian Shaykh al-Sanusi. From this beginning, it quickly spread throughout Libya and formed the basis for the Sanusi dynasty.

• The French captured Constantine (Algeria).

RELATED HISTORICAL EVENTS

• Robert Gould Shaw, a colonel in the 54th Massachusetts Union Regiment (the first African American army unit sent from the free states) was born in Boston of a "proper" Bostonian family which was deeply committed to the cause of African American freedom (October 10).

1838

THE UNITED STATES

In 1838, a "formal organization" of workers of the Underground Railroad was set up in Philadelphia under the presidency of Robert Purvis, a wealthy African American of Philadelphia.

• By 1838, there were 100 African American "benefit societies" with 7,448 members in Philadelphia. The initiation fees were between $2.50 and $5.00, and the monthly dues were $.50. The societies provided sick benefits at $1.50 to $5.00 per month; paid funeral expenses; and provided aid for widows. The society also organized social clubs.
• A mob in Philadelphia burned a shelter for African American orphans, stoned an African American church, and attempted to burn another African American church. Soon after the Philadelphia incidents, violence spread to other cities.
• Frederick Douglass escaped from slavery in Baltimore (September 3). *See 1817.*

By 1838, the words "Jim Crow" had become synonymous for "African American."

• *The Abolition Movement:* Charles Lenox Remond became the first African American lecturer employed by an antislavery society. *See 1810.*

In 1838, Charles Remond became a professional abolitionist. At first a follower of William Lloyd Garrison and an advocate of nonviolence, Remond later favored slave revolts. Remond was vice-president of the New England Anti-Slavery Society.

Remond was the first African American lecturer employed by an antislavery society, but he was not the most famous. With the emergence of Frederick Douglass, Remond became overshadowed. As time went by, Remond became resentful towards Douglass and this resentment became evident in his interactions with Douglass. *See 1810.*

• The Abolition Society of Philadelphia reported that 997 out of 17,500 African Americans in Philadelphia County had learned trades, but that only 350 of these African Americans had actually worked at their trades at that time.
• *The Civil Rights Movement:* Massachusetts African Americans demanded an end to segregation on trains, steamboats and stagecoaches. Although no law was passed, the threat of legislative action in the 1840's gradually prompted railroad directors to abandon segregation in Massachusetts.
• *The Labor Movement:* The *Colored American* reported that the arrival of destitute Irishmen was forcing African Americans out of their places of business and labor, especially on the wharves and in domestic service. However, some want-ads specified a preference for African Americans, not Irishmen.
• A railroad corporation bought 140 slaves for $159,000 to work on the construction of a railroad between Jackson and Brandon, Mississippi.
• *Notable Deaths:* John Chavis, one the first African American students at an American college and a noted African American minister and teacher, died (June 13). *See 1763.*
• *Miscellaneous State Laws:* Connecticut law provided for a trial by jury for African Americans who appealed their seizure in fugitive slave cases.
• The new Pennsylvania Constitution, with the right to vote restricted to European Americans, was overwhelmingly approved by the electorate in October, despite protests by Philadelphia African Americans who stated that the Constitution amounted to taxation without representation.

In 1838, African Americans held a meeting in Philadelphia to protest the action taken at the Pennsylvania Reform Convention of 1837 which denied African Americans the right to vote.

At the convention, the attendees argued that the denial of suffrage would make political rights dependent upon the "skin in which a man is born" and would eventually "divide what our fathers bled to unite, to wit, TAXATION AND REPRESENTATION."

The attendees argued that they were citizens as recognized by Article IV of the Articles of Confederation which stated:

The free inhabitants of each of these states, paupers, vagabonds, and fugitives excepted, shall be entitled to all privileges and immunities of free citizens in the several states.

According to the petition the conveners submitted, the constitution of the United States made no changes to their rights of citizenship.

The petition asked the people of Pennsylvania to reject the new Constitution. However, the plea fell on a great many deaf ears. The new state constitution with the clauses disenfranchising African Americans was approved.

• Virginia law prohibited the return to the state of African Americans who had gone North to school.

• Ohio law denied African Americans the right to an education at public expense.

• North Carolina law declared void all marriages between European Americans and African Americans (or people of color with African blood less than three generations removed).

• North Carolina law relieved master workmen of the obligation to teach free African American apprentices to read and write. However, many continued to do so.

• Kentucky law prohibited slaves from traveling within the state.

• *Publications:* The first African American periodical, *Mirror of Freedom*, began publishing in New York City (August 30).

• The *Colored American* reported that the arrival of destitute Irishmen was forcing African Americans out of their places of business and labor, especially on the wharves and in domestic service. However, some want-ads specified a preference for African Americans, not Irishmen.

• A periodical entitled *The National Reformer* was begun by William Whipper and other African Americans. This was the publication of the Moral Reformers.

• *The Mirror of Liberty*, a quarterly magazine, began publication with David Ruggles, an African American, as the editor.

• *Scholastic Achievements:* In 1838, there were nine free schools for African Americans in Philadelphia. The schools had an enrollment of 1,116 pupils and an average attendance of 713. There were also three partly free schools with enrollments of 226 pupils and an average attendance of 125; three pay schools with European American teachers where the African American enrollment was 102 with an average attendance of 89; ten pay schools with African American teachers with an enrollment of 288 pupils and an average attendance of 260. All totalled, there were 25 schools available to African Americans. At these 25 schools, there were 1,732 African American students enrolled and 1,187 attended on a regular basis. At the time, the total school age population for African Americans in Philadelphia was 3,025.

• Free African Americans in Fredericksburg, Virginia, asked the state legislature for permission to send their children out of the state for educational purposes. The Virginia Legislature denied the request.

• Edward A. Jones, an African American, was attacked by students in the College of New Jersey (now Princeton University) when he returned to the campus of the Theological Seminary for his ten-year class reunion. *See 1826.*

• In New Bedford, Massachusetts, African Americans were allowed to attend public schools with European Americans.

• In Providence, Rhode Island, the city leaders voted to support two schools for African Americans.

• Because African Americans were not given free privileges in the libraries of New York, in 1838, David Ruggles, the African American secretary of the Committee of Vigilance of New York, opened a reading room for the exclusive use of African Americans.

• *The Black Church:* Of sixteen African American churches in Philadelphia, there were: one Episcopal church with 100 members and $36,000 worth of property; one Lutheran church with 10 members and $120 worth of property; eight Methodist churches with 2,860 members and $50,800 worth of property; two Presbyterian churches with 325 members and $20,000 worth of property. In total, the combined membership of the churches was 3,995 and the total valuation of the property was $114,000.

• The First Bethel Baptist Church was organized in Jacksonville, Florida, with four European American and two African American members. Later the European Americans and the African Americans separated.

• Twelve African American Baptist churches in Illinois joined together in the Wood River Baptist Association.

• The African Methodist Zion Church in Boston was founded with the Reverend Jehial C. Beman as pastor.

• *The Arts:* Frank Johnson, one of the first African American band leaders, gave a command performance before Queen Victoria at Buckingham Palace. After the performance, Johnson was presented with a silver bugle.

THE AMERICAS

• The Canada Mission was founded to assist in providing food and clothing for African American refugees.

AFRICA

• The Commonwealth of Liberia was formed. *See 1820.*
• Muhammed Ali (of Egypt) visited Sudan.
• Bonet-Willaumez began exploring West Africa.
• The Portuguese governor of Angola was removed for his participation in the slave trade.
• In South Africa, Sir George Napier tried to halt the Great Trek.
• The Boers of the Great Trek established the Republic of Natal.

On December 16, 1838, one of the most famous battles in the history of South Africa occurred. On this day, a battle would take place on the Ncome River which would forever change the name of the river and the future of South Africa.

At dawn on December 16, 1838, 10,000 of Dingane's Zulu warriors swept towards a Voortrekker laager (an encircled wagon train). The Voortrekker's responded with musket and cannon fire. When the sustained gunfire began to weaken the Zulu lines, mounted trekkers charged from the laager and routed the remaining Zulu warriors. The final tally was more than 3,000 Zulus killed while of the 468 trekkers who fought them only three were injured, none fatally. A nearby stream which became flooded with the blood of the Zulus provided the name for this battle—the Battle of Blood River.

• The French became more entrenched in Algeria.
• The Egyptians raided Qalabat causing a panic in Gondar (Gonder).

Gonder is a city approximately 400 kilometers (250 miles) north and slightly west of Addis Adaba, Ethiopia. It was the royal town of the Abyssinian Empire from about 1700 to 1855.

RELATED HISTORICAL EVENTS

• The British attempted to curtail the Arab-controlled East African slave trade by negotiating an agreement with the Persian Gulf sheiks.
• Slavery was abolished in India.

1 8 3 9

THE UNITED STATES

In 1839, the Liberty Party, the first antislavery political party, was organized (November 13).

James G. Birney, an abolitionist, organized the Liberty Party and ran as the Liberty Party candidate for President of the United States in 1840 and 1844. In addition to being the first abolitionist political organization, the Liberty Party favored government action to find markets for western wheat. The Liberty Party felt that the United States government only heeded the commercial needs of the South.

At the London General Anti-Slavery Convention in 1840, Birney urged England to buy western wheat and use India as its source of cotton. Birney received 62,300 votes in the 1840 Presidential election, most of his votes coming from the New England states. The votes Birney took away from Clay in the election of 1844 allowed Polk to win the Presidential election. The Liberty Party received support from several leading African American abolitionists, including Henry Highland Garnet and Samuel R. Ward.

• European Americans burned the African American section of Pittsburgh.
• The United States State Department rejected the application of a Philadelphia African American for a passport on the grounds that the Pennsylvania Constitution limited suffrage to European American males, and thus did not recognize African Americans as citizens.
• *The Abolition Movement:* Lunsford Lane of North Carolina made an abolition speech before a Southern audience (April 30).
• Samuel Ringgold Ward, an escaped slave, became a professional antislavery agent for the American Anti-Slavery Society. Ward had been educated in New York and became a Presbyterian minister there. Ward pastored a European American church in South Butler, New York. Ward was also one of the first African Americans to join the Liberty Party. *See 1817.*
• *The Labor Movement:* In several New York cities, there were riots against the employment of African American workers.
• *Notable Births:* Michael Healy (1839–1904), a noted African American ship captain was born in Georgia (September 22). His life would serve as inspiration for Jack London's *Sea Wolf* and would be highlighted in James Michener's *Alaska.* Healy was the brother of James Augustine Healy (*see 1830*) and Patrick Francis Healy (*see 1834*).

In 1865, Michael Healy enlisted in the United States Revenue Service, the precursor to the United States Coast Guard. In 1886, Healy was assigned to command the famous cutter *Bear* and became the chief federal law enforcement officer in the northern waters off the coast of Alaska.

• Robert Smalls, Civil War hero and Reconstructionist Congressman, was born in Beaufort, South Carolina (April 5).

Robert Smalls (1839–1915) was the son of Robert and Lydia Smalls, slaves of the McKee family. Smalls was allowed to acquire a limited education. Smalls moved with the McKee family to Charleston, where he became a waiter.

In 1861, Confederate authorities pressed Smalls into the service of the Confederate navy. He became a member of the crew of the *Planter*. In 1862, in the absence of Confederate officers, Smalls navigated the *Planter* into the line of the blockading federal squadron outside Charleston harbor. The federal forces, upon receiving the *Planter*, made Smalls a pilot in the United States Navy, commissioned him a captain, and then promoted him to commander.

At a meeting of African Americans and Northeners in 1864 at Port Royal, Smalls was elected to the National Union Convention. Smalls became a delegate in 1868 to the State Constitutional Convention, and served in the State House of Representatives. Between 1870 and 1874, Smalls served as a state senator.

In 1875, Smalls was elected to Congress and served until 1887. While in Congress, Smalls spoke against the election tactics of South Carolina Democrats and supported a bill to provide equal accommodations for the races on interstate conveyances.

From 1865 to 1877, Smalls served in the South Carolina state militia, rising to the rank of major general. While in office, in 1877, he was convicted of accepting a bribe. However, he was pardoned by Governor W. D. Simpson.

In 1895, as one of the African American members of the South Carolina Constitutional Convention, Smalls made an attempt to prevent the disenfranchisement of African Americans within the state. He was not successful.

For the last 20 years of his life, Smalls lived in Beaufort where he was the collector of duties at the local port.

• *Notable Deaths:* Benjamin Lundy, an advocate for a separate African American colony, died at age 46 (August 22).
• *Miscellaneous State Laws:* In response to African American petitions for the repeal of anti-immigration laws, the Ohio Legislature declared that African American residents possessed no constitutional right to petition the legislature for any purpose.

• Ohio passed a strict fugitive (escaped) slave law.
• *Miscellaneous Cases:* The most famous slave revolt aboard a slave ship took place on the Spanish slaver, the *Amistad*. John Quincy Adams, at the age of 73 and out of law practice for more than thirty years, argued the case before the United States Supreme Court. Cinque, the young African leader, and his fellow crewmen were freed by the court.

In July of 1839, a group of Africans led by Cinque staged a slave revolt aboard the Spanish ship, *Amistad*. The slaves killed the captain of the ship and seized control of the ship off the coast of Cuba. The slaves then sailed the ship to Montauk, Long Island, New York.

When tried before the Supreme Court, John Quincy Adams defended them and won their freedom. The 54 Africans gained much public attention and learned to read and write. With the help of Lewis Tappan, public appearances were arranged to raise enough money to pay the Africans' passage home.

Cinque gave several public lectures in his native Mendi language which were translated. The slaves received religious instruction and when one of the group was asked if he would kill the slave ship captain again, he replied that he would rather pray for him than kill him. Cinque when asked if he would pray for the captain replied, "Yes, I would pray for him, and kill him too."

In 1841, accompanied by five missionaries, the Africans returned to their native land.

• *Publications:* The *Colored American* criticized the abolitionists for concentrating too heavily on the elimination of slavery in the South while ignoring the "soul-crushing bondage of the Northern states."
• *Scholastic Achievements:* A school for African American boys was founded in Pennsylvania. This school would one day become Cheyney State College.
• *The Black Church:* The African Baptist Church in Mobile, Alabama, was formed when African Americans and European Americans of the First Baptist Church split. The African American church was admitted that year to the Bethel Association.
• The first African American Baptist church in Washington, D.C., was organized by Sampson White.
• Daniel Payne was ordained by the Franckean Synod of the Lutheran Church, and became a pastor of a Presbyterian church in East Troy, New York. Payne later

joined the African Methodist Episcopal Church and became a bishop of the AME Church in 1852. Payne became the president of Wilberforce University in Ohio during and after the Civil War. *See 1811.*

• *Black Enterprise:* African American real estate holdings in Providence, Rhode Island, were valued at $50,000. Over two-thirds of the African Americans in Providence lived in houses which they themselves owned.

• In Cincinnati, Ohio, African Americans formed the Iron Chest Company, a real estate company which constructed three brick buildings and rented them to European Americans.

THE AMERICAS

• In 1839, Afro-Canadians were admitted to jury service.

• The *Oeuvres des Noirs* was founded by Father F. M. P. Libermann in Haiti.

• Joaquim Machado de Assis, an Afro-Brazilian writer, was born.

Joaquim Machado de Assis (1839–1908) was a mulatto born in Recife who is considered to be one of Brazil's great novelists. His novels centered on the activities of the upper-class Carioca society of Brazil—a society which was almost totally European. Although Machado was sympathetic to the plight of Afro-Brazilians, he did little to help them and rarely involved them in his works. This disassociation was perhaps due to Machado's acceptance into the Carioca society of which he wrote. Machado even married a Portuguese aristocrat.

In 1878, Machado published *Yaya Garcia.* In this novel, a faithful slave, Raymundo, is the only fully drawn Afro-Brazilian character that appears in any of Machado's works.

In 1881, Machado published *Memorias Posthumas de Braz Cubas.* In this work, one of the ancillary themes is the pernicious effects of slavery on both the slave and the slave owner.

• Tobias Barreto, an Afro-Brazilian jurist and poet, was born.

Tobias Barreto (1839–1889) was a successful jurist, lawyer, linguist, and poet. A light-skinned Afro-Brazilian, Barreto did his best to hide his African heritage in order to gain acceptance into upper-class Euro-Brazilian society. As a result, only one of his poems, *A Escraxidao*, dealt with Africans and the subject of slavery.

AFRICA

• Mahmud II of Turkey attacked Muhammed Ali of Egypt. The Turkish forces were defeated at Nezib (Nizzib, Syria) (June 24) and a week later Mahmud II died (July 1).

• On July 1, the Turkish fleet surrendered in Alexandria harbor.

• The French reached Portes-aux-Fer, Algeria (October 28).

• Dingane acknowledged Boer claims in the Natal region.

• By 1839, there were frequent caravans from Zanzibar into the East African interior. Often these caravans were searching for ivory and slaves.

• In 1839, a Methodist mission was established in Kumasi (Ghana).

• Jamal al-Din al-Afghani (1839–1897), an Egyptian religious teacher and the first Islamic modernist, was born.

RELATED HISTORICAL EVENTS

• Pope Gregory XVI issued the papal bull, *In supremo*, in which slavery and the slave trade was condemned.

Pope Gregory XVI in his Bull (papal edict) against the slave trade cited the edict of Pope Pius II in 1462 to support the antislavery attitude of the Catholic Church. The pope also claimed that previous popes [Paul III (in 1537), Urban VIII (in 1639), Benedict XIV (in 1741), and Pius VII)] had opposed the slave trade. However, Pope Gregory XVI ignored the fact that the previous papal edicts were often limited to a papal concern that prisoners of European wars not be reduced to slavery.

—— 1 8 4 0 ——

THE UNITED STATES

In 1840, the United States census reported that there were 2,873,648 African Americans in the United States. This number represented 16.1% of the total United States population. Of the 2,873,648 African Americans, 2,487,355 were listed as slaves while 386,293 (13.4%) were designated as free. In 1840, the free African Americans living in the Northern states lived in states where they were legally excluded from voting. Only Massachusetts, New Hampshire, Vermont, and Maine permitted African Americans to vote on an equal basis with European Americans.

The United States census for 1840 was the first census to report on, and enumerate, the "insane and idiots" in the United States. The census revealed that the incidence of such mentally disturbed persons was 11 times higher among free African Americans than among slaves. In the South, one out of every 1,558 African Americans was deemed to be insane while, in the North, one out of every 144.5 African Americans was deemed to be insane.

Both Southern and Northern advocates of slavery seized upon these statistics to support their positions. Slavery advocates such as John Calhoun argued that the statistics were proof of the benefits of slavery and the evils of freedom for African Americans.

However, Dr. Edward Jarvis, a Massachusetts doctor and specialist in mental disorders and a founder of the American Statistical Association, investigated the census statistics and reported, in January of 1844, that many Northern towns listed more insane African Americans than their total African American population. Additionally, some Northern towns which listed a number of insane African Americans actually had no African Americans at all.

The American Statistical Association in conjunction with a group of New York African Americans petitioned Congress to have the census corrected. But the petition fell on deaf ears.

• The British government paid an indemnity (compensation) for slaves freed when American vessels were forced by inclement weather into British colonial harbors (i.e., the harbors of the West Indies and Bermuda). In 1835, the British government had refused to pay a similar claim by declaring that Britain could not take responsibility for fugitives, since slavery had been abolished in the British colonies.

The census reported that there were 2,427 African Americans in Boston, representing 2.5% of the total population of the city.

The free African American population in North Carolina was 22,732. This number represented 3.01% of the total state population. Slaves numbered 245,817 or 32.6% of the total population.

In Pennsylvania, there were 47,854 free African Americans, and 27% of the African Americans in Philadelphia were servants.

The Abolition Movement: 1840 was a momentous year for American abolitionist societies. At the American Anti-Slavery Convention, a strident contingent led by William Lloyd Garrison seized control of the organization. A dissident group of abolitionists from New York, led by Lewis Tappan, separated from the American Anti-Slavery Society and formed the American and Foreign Anti-Slavery Society. Among Tappan's group were five African Americans who served on the new organization's executive committee. Samuel E. Cornish (*see 1826*), Christopher Rush (*see 1829*), George Whipple, Charles B. Ray (*see 1807*), and James W. C. Pennington (*see 1809*) were the prominent African Americans associated with the new organization.

The new American and Foreign Anti-Slavery Society formed the nucleus for the newly established Liberty Party. The Liberty Party ran James G. Birney as its Presidential candidate in the 1840 election. James G. Birney received 62,300 votes in the 1840 Presidential election, most of his votes coming from the New England states. *See 1839.*

• Henry Highland Garnet delivered a speech attacking slavery at the American Anti-Slavery Convention.
• At the London General Anti-Slavery Convention in 1840, James G. Birney, of the abolitionist Liberty Party, urged England to buy western wheat and use India as its source of cotton rather than the American South. *See 1839.*
• In 1840, Charles Lenox Remond attended the World Anti-Slavery Convention in London. At the World Anti-Slavery Convention, Charles Lenox Remond, an African American delegate, refused to take his seat when women delegates were segregated from the main floor by placement in the gallery. *See 1810.*

By 1840, the American Anti-Slavery Society had 2,000 local chapters with a membership of over 200,000. The organization's activities included the publication of periodicals, pamphlets and books—and barraging Congress with hundreds of thousands of petitions opposing slavery.

• *The Colonization Movement:* In 1840, 160 African Americans emigrated from Philadelphia to Trinidad.
• *Notable Births:* John Wesley Gaines, a leader in the establishment of the African Methodist Episcopal Church in the South, was born.

John Wesley Gaines (1840–1912) was born a slave on the plantation of Gabriel Toombs. He was licensed to preach in 1865. Afterwards, Gaines helped to organize churches for the African Methodist Episcopal (AME) Church. Gaines was the founder, treasurer, and president of the board of trustees of Morris Brown College in Atlanta, Georgia, which opened in 1885. In 1888, he became a bishop of the AME Church.

Gaines published two notable works. *African Methodism in the South* was published in 1890 and, in 1897, *The Negro and the White Man* was published.

• John A. Hyman, a future member of Congress, was born.

John A. Hyman (1840–1891) was born a slave near Warrenton, North Carolina. Hyman was sold and taken to Alabama but still managed to educate himself.

In 1868, Hyman attended the North Carolina Constitutional Convention. He served in the North Carolina Legislature for six years. In 1875, Hyman was elected to the House of Representatives. He served one term.

At the end of his term in office, Hyman stayed in Washington, D.C., where he worked in a minor post in the revenue service.

• James Milton Turner, a Lincoln University founder, was born. (May 16).

James Milton Turner (1840–1915) was born a slave in St. Louis County, Virginia, on the plantation of Charles A. Loring. Turner's father, John Turner (also known as John Colburn) was removed from Virginia by Benjamin Tillman after the 1831 slave insurrection led by Nat Turner. John Turner fell under the tutelage of a Benjamin Tillman who taught John veterinary medicine. With these new skills, John Turner was able to purchase his freedom and, in 1843, he purchased the freedom of his wife and their young son, James Milton Turner.

At age 14, James's parents sent him to Oberlin College in Ohio. During the Civil War, he served as a Union officer's servant. After the War, Turner settled in Missouri and directed his attention to public education for African American children.

In 1866, James Turner was appointed to the Kansas City School Board. He was authorized to conduct a school for African Americans during the winter—the first such school reported to be operating in the state of Missouri. Turner was subsequently reappointed to his school board position in 1868.

Later on, Turner became interested in the Negro Institute which was located in Jefferson City, Missouri. He gave and collected money for the institute and served as trustee for the renamed institute—Lincoln University.

During Reconstruction, Turner became involved in Republican politics. On March 1, 1871, Turner was appointed to be the minister resident and consul general to the Republic of Liberia. Turner would hold this post until 1878.

In 1886, Turner presented to President Cleveland a claim of the African American members of the Cherokee nation. He secured $75,000 of the federal funds allotted to the Cherokee nation for the Afro-Cherokee people.

In 1915, Turner was killed in an explosion in Ardmore, Oklahoma. His body was transported back to St. Louis, Missouri, where a funeral conducted by the African American Masons was the largest ever held for an African American in the city.

• *Miscellaneous State Laws:* A New York law provided that any person accused of being an escaped (fugitive) slave be granted a jury trial to determine his or her status.

• In 1840, Vermont instituted a law which required that escaped slaves be awarded a jury trial before being returned to slavery. This statute was repealed in 1843, but reinstated in 1850.

• In Massachusetts, the legislature repealed a law which prohibited intermarriage between European Americans and African Americans, mulattoes and Indigenous Americans.

• In Indiana, the state law prohibited marriage between European Americans and persons with one-eighth or more African American blood. There were fines of $1,000 to $5,000 and prison terms of 10 to 20 years imposed on violators of the law. Clerks who issued marriage licenses to violators of the law were subject to $500 fines, while the ministers who married such individuals were subject to $1,000 to $10,000 fines. In 1841, the penalties were repealed, although the prohibition remained. In 1842, the penalties were re-enacted and remained in effect until 1852.

• Tennessee law provided that all children between the ages of 6 and 21 were entitled to attend the public schools. Although no law prohibited the education of African Americans, in practice, public schools were attended exclusively by European Americans.

• *Miscellaneous Cases:* Cinque and the other slaves who seized control of the slave ship *Amistad* were ordered to be set free by the United States Supreme Court (March 9).

• Near Cincinnati, Ohio, a certain Mr. Van Zandt was fined $12,000 (his entire estate) for carrying nine escaped slaves from Kentucky to Ohio in his farm wagon.

• *Publications:* The *National Anti-Slavery Standard*, an African American newspaper, carried on a debate with the *Colored Ameri-*

can concerning the Afro-centric (nationalistic) perspective of the *Colored American*. The *National Anti-Slavery Standard* opposed the nationalistic position and stated that "all exclusive action on the part of the colored people except where the clearest necessity demands it," should be avoided because separate actions—separate institutions—merely perpetuated public prejudices.

• The Elyria, Ohio, *Advertiser* reported that residents of Troy, Ohio, destroyed a school for African American children established by a European American man.

• The *Demosthenian Shield*, the first African American newspaper in Philadelphia, made its debut.

• Samuel E. Cornish and Theodore S. Wright published *The Colonization Scheme Considered in Its Rejection by the Colored People*, in Newark, New Jersey.

• *Scholastic Achievements:* In 1840, Daniel Alexander Payne opened a school in Philadelphia. *See 1811.*

• The Delaware Society of Friends (the Quakers) formed the African School Association in Wilmington. The association established a school for girls and another for boys.

• William C. Nell, a Boston African American, was one of the prominent signatories of a petition to the Massachusetts Legislature asking that public schools be opened to African American children. A similar petition submitted to the Boston School Committee by a group of European Americans and African Americans had been summarily denied by the committee.

• By 1840, in Cincinnati, Ohio, three tuition schools for African Americans were being operated. Two of the schools had 65 pupils each and one had 47 pupils. The students paid $3 per quarter. In addition, a school sponsored by the (European American) Ladies Anti-Slavery Society provided instruction for 54 pupils.

• In Washington, D. C., Alexander Cornish established a school for African Americans in his home. Cornish had an average of 40 pupils. Margaret Hill also opened a school for African Americans in Georgetown, D.C.

• *The Black Church:* James W. C. Pennington became pastor of the African Congregational Church in Hartford, Connecticut, and later served as president of the Hartford Central Association of Congregational Ministers, in which he was the only non–European American member. Pennington was elected five times to the General Convention for the Improvement of Free People of Color.

• The 1840 census reported that Cincinnati (Ohio) African Americans had four Sabbath schools with a regular attendance of 310; one Baptist and two Methodist churches with a total membership of 800, a Total Abstinence Temperance society with 450 members, and a Sabbath school or Youth society with 180 members. One-fourth of the city's African American population belonged to temperance organizations, compared with less than a tenth of the European American population.

• *The Arts and Sciences:* Frank Johnson of Philadelphia, an African American, organized an orchestra. Johnson specialized in martial music and would eventually play in England, before Queen Victoria.

• *Black Enterprise:* In the 1840s, A. F. Boston, an African American, took command of the American whaling ship, the *Loper*. The officers and most of the ship's crew were African American.

• The 1840 census reported that Ohio had 17,342 African Americans. 2,255 of these African Americans lived in Cincinnati. The Cincinnati African Americans owned property valued at $209,000 and the African American churches of Cincinnati owned property valued at $19,000. In Cincinnati, a real estate company known as the Iron Chest built homes for African Americans. One of the city's African Americans owned property worth between $12,000 to $15,000. This same person owned seven houses in Cincinnati and 400 acres of land in Indiana.

AFRICA

• In 1840, the French continued their Algerian campaign of conquest. On March 15, the French occupied Cherchell and a series of battles commenced. The battles at Meskiana (March 21), Selson (March 24), and Afroun (March 27) occurred. On May 17, the French occupied Medea and, on June 8, they occupied Miliana.

• In November, Muhammed Ali of Egypt evacuated his troops from Syria.

• Egypt expanded its Sudanese possessions.

• Beke explored Gojjam.

• Sayyid Said moved his court from Oman to Zanzibar.

• The government of India acquired bases in Tadjoura and Zaila (Somalia).

• Pretorius went to war against the Pondo.

• The French obtained territory in Madagascar.

• Beecroft explored the Benin and Niger rivers.

• There was a heroic defense of the fort of Mazagan (February 3–6).
• Around 1840, the Imbangala and the Ovimbundu began to raid each other's caravans.

The Ovimbundu are people who inhabit the central highlands of Angola. The Ovimbundu are today known as the main supporters of the National Union of Angolan Workers (UNITA), and its leader, Jonas Savimbi, who is a member of the group.

EUROPE

• Osifekunde of Ijebu was discovered in Paris.

Osifekunde was born in Warri in 1798. In 1820, he was enslaved and shipped to Brazil. He would spend the next twenty years in Brazil.

Around 1840, Osifekunde went to France with his owner. Osifekunde subsequently lived in Paris employed as a servant.

In Paris, Osifekunde met Marie Armand Pascal d'Avezac-Macaya, who was, at that time, the vice-president of the Société Ethnologique of Paris and a member of numerous geographical societies and associations with interests in Africa and Orient. D'Avezac realized that Joaquin (as Osifekunde was known in France) came from a kingdom which had been identified on maps of the seventeenth and eighteenth centuries but which Europeans knew very little about. D'Avezac interrogated Osifekunde for weeks concerning aspects of his homeland and his native language.

D'Avezac eventually arranged for Osifekunde to return to Africa. However, Osifekunde refused the offer. Osifekunde preferred to remain in servitude under his former owner in Brazil where he could be with his son. Upon his return to Brazil, Osifekunde retreated from the light of history. *See 1798.*

1841

THE UNITED STATES

The summer of 1841 was a very hot summer in Cincinnati, Ohio, as far as race relations were concerned.

In June, an Englishman harbored an escaped slave and refused to turn the slave over to his former owner.

In August, two African Americans killed a German American farmer near Cincinnati and a European American woman was allegedly insulted by two African American men.

On August 29, a street fight between European Americans and African Americans erupted into an anti–African American riot. For five days and nights, African Americans were shot and their homes were burned. The Ohio state militia was called in, and city authorities persuaded 300 African American men to go to jail for their own security. The 300 men complied but only after reaching an understanding that their families would be protected.

Tragically, after these 300 men were released they discovered that the authorities had not upheld their end of the bargain. The wives and children of the 300 African American men had been attacked by the mob. They were beaten and some were raped. Only a handful of the European American participants in this travesty were arrested. None was ever punished.

• 134 slaves on the *Creole*, en route from Richmond to New Orleans by sea, seized control of the ship (after killing one officer) and headed for Nassau in the Bahamas. They were led by Madison Washington, a slave. In the Bahamas, the British government granted the slaves asylum and they were set free (November). Their status was finally settled in 1853 by arbitration between the United States and Britain. The British government agreed to pay $110,000 in compensation for having allowed the slaves to go free. *See 1840.*
• In Atlanta, Georgia, separate Bibles were used for African Americans and European Americans in issuing the oath before giving testimony in court.
• In Boston, the authorities required African Americans mourning the death of President William Henry Harrison to march at the end of the funeral procession.
• President Tyler sent a message to Congress dealing with the suppression of the slave trade (June 1).
• In 1841, the 54 Africans who seized the Spanish slave ship, *Amistad*, returned to Africa. *See 1839.*
• In Florida, Wild Cat was captured, thereby essentially ending the Second Seminole War.

The Capture of Wild Cat

The story of the black Seminoles did not end with the cessation of hostilities between the Seminoles and the United States Army in 1841 (*see 1837*). Indeed, in many respects the story had only begun, and the story essentially became the story of Wild Cat and John Horse.

By 1837, the Second Seminole War had been

waged for two years in the miserable swamps of Florida. Thomas S. Jessup, the general who commanded the American forces, had grown frustrated by his inability to defeat the greatly outnumbered Seminoles. Something had to be done to halt the guerrilla war which had cost so much money and had embarrassed both Jessup and his predecessors.

In 1837, Jessup found a way to end the war. Disregarding the rules of war, he had his men seize several Seminole leaders (including the debilitated Osceola) when they came in to parley under a flag of truce. A Seminole war leader Coacoochee, known to the soldiers as Wild Cat, was among those captured. In years to come, the fate of the black Seminoles would be tied to his.

Wild Cat was the son of a prominent chief and had a mesmerizing effect on those he met. He was a handsome man and a charismatic leader. It is said that Wild Cat could both charm the ladies with a graceful bow just effectively as he could ambush a column of soldiers.

Wild Cat shared a taste for fine clothes and whisky with fellow prisoner John Horse, a black Seminole leader noted for his valor and intelligence. In war, John Horse was coolheaded and deadly accurate with a rifle, while Wild Cat had the unsettling habit of erupting into laughter in the heat of battle. Although darker skinned and taller than the Seminoles, John Horse was a Seminole in both dress and spirit.

Sitting in a prison cell at Fort Marion, with their great leader Osceola dying in faraway South Carolina and betrayed and cut off from their own people, John Horse, Wild Cat and 18 other prisoners of war knew they would have to escape if they were to avoid being executed. After darkness fell, one of the warriors climbed to a high window, using handholds chipped in the cell wall. The warrior worked loose a bar and squeezed through the narrow opening. The others followed, often leaving behind scraped skin on the rough stone of the cell window. The band descended using a makeshift rope to the moat below and escaped into the night.

This dramatic breakout, along with the martyred death of Osceola, inspired many Seminoles to continue with the war. Wild Cat was a key leader in rounding up the Seminoles and encouraging them to continue with the struggle. Less than a month after the escape from Fort Marion, Wild Cat led a force of red and black Seminoles in a major battle against the United States Army 200 miles to the south.

The forces of Wild Cat fought bravely and with desperation. However, despite their courage, the Seminoles were badly outnumbered and pitifully supplied. As casualties mounted, many Seminoles surrendered rather than face starvation. However, Wild Cat fought on. For three additional years, Wild Cat waged his own guerrilla war—a war which would not end until Wild Cat was captured.

Only with the capture of Wild Cat could the Second Seminole War be considered to have ended. The war had lasted seven years and had cost the United States $40 million and the lives of 1,500 soldiers.

It is said that when Wild Cat and two of his followers surrendered to the United States Army they were dressed in the theatrical costumes which they had stolen from a trunk. Dressed as Hamlet, Richard III, and Horatio, these three men represented the tragedy, and the rather pathetic farce, that comprised the Seminole "surrender" to the United States.

- *The Abolition Movement:* Frederick Douglass became a lecturer for the Massachusetts Anti-Slavery Society (August). He also attended a convention of the society which was held in Nantucket. *See 1817.*
- Charles Lenox Remond returned from the World Anti-Slavery Convention with a petition entitled "Address from the people of Ireland." The petition had 60,000 signatures and urged Irish Americans to oppose slavery and racial discrimination.
- J. W. Loguen, a former slave who became a bishop of the African Methodist Church (in 1869), settled in Syracuse, New York, where he was involved with the Underground Railroad in sheltering fugitive slaves.
- *Notable Births:* Grafton Tyler Brown, an African American lithographer and painter, was born in Harrisburg, Pennsylvania.
- Blanche Kelso Bruce, the only African American to serve a full term in the United States Senate during the Reconstruction Era, was born a slave in Prince Edward County, Virginia (March 1).

Blanche Kelso Bruce (1841–1898) was born in Farmville, Prince Edward County, Virginia. A quadroon (a person with one-quarter African blood—one grandparent of African descent), Bruce was taken to Missouri several years before the Civil War. While in Brunswick, Missouri, Bruce learned the printer's trade.

In 1861, Bruce escaped and went to Hannibal, Missouri. In Hannibal, Bruce organized a school.

After the war, Bruce took a two-year course at Oberlin College. After the course, he went to Mississippi.

In 1869, Bruce was made the sergeant-at-arms of the Mississippi State Senate. Bruce held many local positions in Mississippi. At different times, Bruce was a county assessor, a tax collector, a sheriff, a superintendent of schools, and a member of the Levee Board. Bruce also became a wealthy planter and a prominent member of the Republican Party.

In 1874, Bruce was elected to the United States Senate as the senator from Mississippi. He was the only African American to serve a regular term in the United States Senate during the Reconstruction Era. *See 1837: Pinckney Benton Stewart Pinchback.*

After his term as senator, Bruce settled in Washington, D.C., where he became register of the Treasury under President Garfield. In 1889, President Harrison appointed Bruce recorder of deeds for Washington, D.C., and, in 1895, he was recalled to be the register of the Treasury.

- James M. Townsend, the first African American to serve as a member of the Indiana Legislature, was born (August 18).
- *Miscellaneous State Laws:* According to New York law, out-of-state slave owners could not keep their slaves in the state for more than nine months.
- The New York Legislature authorized New York school districts to establish separate schools for European Americans and African Americans.
- In Atlanta (Georgia) courts, African Americans were required to swear on separate Bibles from European Americans.
- A South Carolina law prohibited African American and European American cotton mill hands from looking out of the same window.
- *Publications:* James W. C. Pennington published the *Textbook of the Origin and History of the Colored People. See 1809.*
- James McCune Smith published *A Lecture on the Haytien Revolutions: with a Sketch of the Character of Toussaint l'Ouverture. See 1813.*
- In Brooklyn, New York, *The African Methodist Episcopal Church Magazine,* edited by George Hogarth, began publication.
- The *Sketches of the Higher Classes of Colored Society in Philadelphia* was published. The author of this publication was anonymous but did state in the text that he was African American. If so, this publication

was the first sociological study of book length on the Northern urban African American by an African American.

- Charles L. Reason, an African American and a professor at Central College in New York, wrote an antislavery tribute, *Freedom.* In *Freedom,* Reason catalogued incidents in the world's long struggle for liberty.
- *The Black Church:* In Brooklyn, New York, *The African Methodist Episcopal Church Magazine,* edited by George Hogarth, began publication.
- The introduction of a trained choir at the African Methodist Episcopal Church of Philadelphia caused dissension within the congregation and resulted in a rift in the church.

THE AMERICAS

- In 1841, Afro-Cubans represented 58.5% of the population. Of these, 152,838 were free, and 436,495 were enslaved.

AFRICA

- Marshal Bugeaud was appointed governor of Algeria (January).
- France annexed the islands of Nossi-be and Nossi-Komba, off the coast of Madagascar.
- The Pashalik of Egypt was made hereditary in Muhammed Ali's family.
- The palm oil industry was started in Dahomey (Benin).
- The British Consulate was moved from Muscat to Zanzibar.
- A British diplomatic mission was dispatched to Shoa.
- France obtained Mayotte on the Comoro Islands.

— 1 8 4 2 —

THE UNITED STATES

In 1842, George Latimer was seized in Boston as an escaped (fugitive) slave and was held in custody to allow his "claimer," James B. Grey of Norfolk, Virginia, an opportunity to gather evidence. The people of Boston raised such an outcry against Latimer's imprisonment that the authorities agreed that Latimore would be released for $400. The $400 was promptly raised.

The capture of George Latimore in Boston precipitated the first of several famous fugitive slave cases which would serve to embitter the North and the South (November 17).

Another one of the reasons why this case was notable was that William Lloyd Garrison's magazine published Frederick Douglass' letter on this case. It was Douglass' first appearance in print.

• The United States Senate, at the instigation of John C. Calhoun, voted to exclude African Americans from the army and navy except as cooks, stewards and servants. The House of Representatives never voted on this bill.
• When the African Americans of Philadelphia paraded to celebrate the abolition of slavery in the West Indies, European Americans attempted to break up the parade. The riot ended in the wounding and killing of several people, and the destruction of the New African Hall and the Negro Presbyterian Church.
• The Episcopal Convention of the Pennsylvania Diocese reaffirmed a 1795 vote to exclude representatives from African American churches.
• Alexander Crummell (an African American born in New York in 1819) was ordained an Episcopal minister and later had a parish in New York. *See 1819.*

By 1842, minstrelsy had become a distinctive form of American entertainment. Dan Emmett, with four other European American actors, formed a company to perform black face minstrelsy. Edwin Christy became a star of minstrelsy in this period. Earlier companies included the Virginia Minstrels, Congo Melodists, Ethiopian Serenaders and Georgia Minstrels. All of the companies were made up of European Americans in black face.

• *The Abolition Movement:* Former President John Quincy Adams, in his role as a representative from Massachusetts, submitted a petition to Congress on behalf of his antislavery constituents who believed the time had come to begin a peaceful dissolution of the Union (January 24).
• William Wells Brown, a former slave and a steamboat operator on Lake Erie, ferried 69 escaped slaves across Lake Erie to freedom in Canada. *See 1816.*
• *The Labor Movement:* Violence erupted between Irish American and African American coal miners in Pennsylvania.
• *Notable Births:* Robert C. De Large, a Reconstructionist congressman from South Carolina, was born.

Robert C. De Large (1842–1874) was born a slave in Aiken, South Carolina. With some education, he became a successful planter in South Carolina during the Reconstruction Era. Elected first to the South Carolina State Legis-

lature, De Large subsequently was elected to the United States Congress in 1871.
During his term in office, De Large returned to South Carolina to investigate voting irregularities which occurred during his own election. The House Commission on Elections declared his seat vacant in 1873.
De Large became a Charleston city magistrate in 1873. He would serve in this capacity for only one year. He died in 1874.

• Robert Brown Elliott, a Reconstruction congressman from South Carolina, was born (August 11).

Robert Brown Elliott (1842–1884) was the son of West Indian parents living in Boston, Massachusetts. Elliott was educated abroad in Jamaica, at the High Holburn Academy in London, and at Eton.
Upon returning to the United States, Elliott became the editor of the *Charleston Leader*. He was made a delegate to the South Carolina Constitutional Convention in 1868, and became a member of the State Legislature.
In 1871, Elliott was elected to the United States House of Representatives representing South Carolina. He served two terms in the House. Afterwards, Elliott retired to New Orleans where he practiced law.

• Lucius Henry Hosley, a bishop of the Colored Methodist Episcopal Church, was born.

Lucius Henry Hosley (1842–1920) was born to an African slave, Louisa, and James Holsey, a slave owner. In 1868, Holsey was licensed to preach. He helped to found Paine College in Augusta, Georgia; Lane College in Jackson, Tennessee; Holsey Industrial Institute in Cordele, Georgia; and the Helen B. Cobb Institute for Girls in Banesville, Georgia.
Holsey compiled a *Hymn Book of the Colored Methodist Episcopal Church in America* and published it in 1891. In 1894, Holsey published a *Manual of the Discipline of the Colored Methodist Episcopal Church in America.*

• Charlie Smith, reputed to be the last known slave brought to America, was born in Liberia.
• Josiah T. Walls, a Reconstructionist congressperson, was born.

Josiah T. Walls (1842–1905) was born of free parents in Winchester, Virginia. By 1860, Walls had moved to Florida and had become a successful farmer.
Walls was drafted into the Confederate Army,

was captured, and, by 1865, had become a sergeant-major in the Union Army.

A member of the Florida State Legislature, he was elected to Congress from 1871 to 1877, and advocated support for the Cuban Revolution.

Walls was almost ruined as a planter by severe weather conditions, and accepted the superintendence of a farm at Tallahassee.

• *Notable Deaths:* James Forten, African American abolitionist and chairperson of the First Negro Convention held in Philadelphia in 1817, died in Philadelphia.

• *Miscellaneous State Laws:* The Dorr Rebellion in Rhode Island, which was a political rebellion against the conservative forces controlling the state, led to the drafting of a new state constitution which extended suffrage (the right to vote) to African Americans.

• Maryland law made it a felony for a free African American to "call for, demand, or receive" abolition newspapers.

• *Miscellaneous Cases:* When Edward Prigg had Margaret Morgan, an escaped slave, seized and returned to her owner, Prigg was arrested and convicted of kidnapping. In his defense, his attorney claimed that the 1826 Pennsylvania "personal liberty" statute under which Prigg was convicted was unconstitutional and in conflict with the Federal Fugitive Law of 1793. The United States Supreme Court, in *Prigg v. Pennsylvania*, upheld Prigg's conviction. In the majority opinion written by Justice Story, the court said that the Fugitive Act had to be enforced by federal officials and that state (and state officials) could not be made to act. After this decision, a number of other states adopted "personal liberty" laws.

• *Publications:* One of the notable sidebars to the case of George Latimore, an escaped slave whose plight touched the citizenry of Boston, was that William Lloyd Garrison's magazine published Frederick Douglass' letter on this case. It was Douglass' first appearance in print.

• The *Register*, a Raleigh, North Carolina, newspaper, reported that Allen Jones, a free African American blacksmith, was dragged from his home and whipped by some of the European Americans of Raleigh for having described being tarred and feathered by a Raleigh group to the Anti-Slavery Convention in New York. A town meeting which included many of the more prominent citizens met to protest the whipping and condemned this outrage as a violation of the law.

• The *National Watchman*, a newspaper edited by William G. Allen, an African American, began publication in Troy, New York. Henry Highland Garnet was associated with Allen in this enterprise. *The National Watchman* ceased publication in 1847.

• In 1842, both William Wells Brown and Lunsford Lane published narratives of their lives as slaves.

• *Scholastic Achievements:* The Institute for Colored Youth was incorporated in Philadelphia.

• The Philomathean Institute of New York and the Philadelphia Library Company and Debating Society applied for admission to the International Order of Odd Fellows. They were refused on the basis of race. Subsequently, Peter Ogden, an African American, acquired a charter for an independent lodge, Philomathean No. 646 of New York, the first African American lodge in the United States.

• *The Black Church:* The Sisters of the Holy Family, a Catholic order of African American nuns, was formed in New Orleans by Henriette Delille and Juliette Gaudin.

• *The Arts:* Robert Scott Duncanson (1817–1872) exhibited his paintings at the Western Art Union exhibition in Cincinnati, Ohio.

THE AMERICAS

• The Reverend Hiram Wilson and Josiah Henson established the British and American Manual Labor Institute for Afro-Canadian children in Dresden, Ontario.

• Uruguay emancipated its slaves.

AFRICA

• In 1842, pursuant to the Webster-Ashburton Treaty, the United States and Great Britain agreed to station ships off the African coast to thwart the African slave trade.

• In 1842, Joseph Jenkins Roberts became the first president of the colony of Liberia—a colony created by the American Colonization Society to accept free African Americans and freed slaves from the United States. *See 1809.*

• In August, France occupied Mayotte on the Comoro Islands.

• Treaties between France and Guinea, the Ivory Coast and Gabon were negotiated.

• Skirmishes and open war erupted between the Boers and the British in Natal.

• There was a migration from Sierra Leone to Abeokuta.

Today Abeokuta is an industrial town in western Nigeria.

RELATED HISTORICAL EVENTS

The end of slavery was decreed in Russia, but the decree was largely ignored.

1843

THE UNITED STATES

In 1843, the United States and Great Britain agreed to patrol the west coast of Africa in order to intercept ships which engaged in the illegal slave trade. Between 1843 and 1852, with only sailing vessels employed to pursue the slavers, the United States Navy captured 19 slave ships. Six of the captured ship captains were convicted of violating the law banning the slave trade.

• United States Attorney General Hugh Legare declared that African Americans were neither aliens nor citizens, but were somewhere in the middle. Legare said that African Americans could apply for benefits under the land pre-emption act.

• Henry Highland Garnet made a controversial speech at the National Convention of the Free People of Color in Buffalo, New York, calling for a slave revolt and a general strike (August 22). The National Convention refused to endorse these sentiments, and Garnet was especially criticized by Frederick Douglass. Garnet's popularity fell and his influence waned. *See 1815.*

• Peter Ogden established an African American Oddfellows lodge (Philomethian Lodge No. 646) in New York City. Ogden was a ship's steward who held a card from a lodge in Liverpool, England.

• African Americans participated in a national political gathering for the first time at a meeting of the Liberty Party convention (August 30).

The Liberty Party National Convention included African American delegates, speakers and officials. Henry Highland Garnet (*see 1815*) of New York was a member of the executive nominating committee; Charles B. Ray (*see 1807*) was elected a convention secretary; and Samuel R. Ward (*see 1817*) led the convention in prayer and also addressed the convention. This was the first time that African Americans actively participated in the leadership of a national political party in the United States. The Liberty Party had earlier been endorsed at the National Convention of the Free People of Color in Buffalo, New York, where also the American Colonization Society was denounced and Henry Highland Garnet issued a militant call for slaves to rise up against their oppressors. *See 1815.*

• *The Abolition Movement:* In 1843, a former New York slave named Isabella changed her name to Sojourner Truth. As Sojourner Truth, she became the first African American woman to serve as a lecturer against slavery. After becoming Sojourner Truth, she left New York and began her work as an abolitionist traveling throughout the United States with her message (June 1). *See 1797.*

• James W. C. Pennington, a noted African American abolitionist, represented the State of Connecticut at the World Anti-Slavery Convention at London. In this year, Pennington would also represent the American Peace Convention at the meeting of the World Peace Society in London. *See 1809.*

• *Notable Births:* Richard Henry Boyd, an African American clergyman, was born.

Richard Henry Boyd (1843–1922) was the son of Indiana Dixon, a slave of a planter in Mississippi. Named Dick Gray by his owner, Boyd changed his name to Richard Henry Boyd in 1864. He learned to read in 1865 and, in 1870, Boyd was ordained a Baptist minister.

In 1872, Boyd organized the first Negro Baptist Association in Texas. In 1897, he formed the National Baptist Publishing Board. The National Baptist Publishing Board issued the first series of African American Baptist literature ever published.

Boyd authored a number of church-related publications. *Jubilee and Plantation Songs* and *Pastor's Guide; the Church Directory* were two of Boyd's more prominent publications.

• *Miscellaneous State Laws:* The Massachusetts Legislature, in response to petitions arising out of the Latimer case (see 1842), ignored the Federal Fugitive Law of 1793, and passed a law forbidding state officials from aiding the recapture of fugitive slaves or from using state jails for their imprisonment. The penalty for violation of the state law was either a fine or imprisonment.

• In Vermont, a "personal liberty" law was enacted which prohibited state officials from aiding the recapture of fugitive slaves and carried penalties of up to $1,000 in fines and up to five years of imprisonment for violation of the law.

• On February 24, 1843, the Massachusetts Legislature repealed a 1786 law which prohibited interracial marriages.

• In response to the desires of local citizens, a special Mississippi law was passed to enable Henry Lee, a free African American barber, to live in Vicksburg with his family. Henry Lee was required, however, to practice barbering and no other trade. The same law gave county boards of police the power to make similar exceptions.

• In North Carolina, a law was enacted which prohibited taxes on free African Americans for support of common (public) schools since the African Americans were not allowed to attend the schools. This law was a clarification and codification of the practice that had existed throughout the state for a long period of time.

• A Maryland law prohibited the formation of secret societies by African Americans. Another Maryland law authorized peace officers to search any free African American suspected of having abolition papers provided that the officer use "as little violence to the feelings of such free Negro or mulatto as is compatible."

• *Publications:* In 1843, Martin Robinson Delany began publishing *The Mystery* in Pittsburgh. *See 1812.*

• African Americans in New Orleans began publishing *L'Album Litteraire, Journal des Jeunes Gens, Amateurs de la Litterature*, a monthly review in the French language. The journal included poems, stories, fables and articles.

• *Scholastic Achievements:* In 1843, James Enoch Ambush established a school known as the Wesleyan Seminary.

• *The Black Church:* The Society of Colored People of Baltimore, an organization composed of Catholic African Americans, was organized. In addition to meeting for the purposes of worship, the society also maintained a library (December 3).

• The Oblate Sisters of Providence opened a Catholic school for girls in Baltimore, Maryland. This school later came to be known as Mount Providence Junior College.

• *Black Enterprise:* Norbert Rillieux perfected the multiple vacuum evaporation system which refined the production of sugar and made sugar a much more consummable product.

Rillieux's innovation helped to change the food consumption patterns of the world, influenced the nature of colonial dependency in a major portion of the third world, and helped to expand and perpetuate the institution of slavery in the Western Hemisphere.

THE AMERICAS

• In Haiti, Jean Pierre Boyer was driven into exile by the urban mulattoes and the people of Santo Domingo (the Dominican Republic) declared Santo Domingo to be a separate republic.

• Teixeira E. Sousa, a noted Afro-Brazilian novelist, published the first Brazilian novel, *Filha do Pescador. See 1812.*

AFRICA

• On May 16, Duc d'Aumale was defeated by Abd-el-Kader. Smala, Algeria, was seized.

• Greek and Italian traders began operations in Khartoum (Sudan).

• The Sanusi sect was started in Libya.

• The British Crown resumed the direct control of the Gold Coast (Ghana) settlements.

• The French made further treaties on the west coast of Africa.

• Natal was proclaimed to be a British colony and Basutoland was annexed.

• Orleansville was built.

• Sidi Bel Abbes was founded.

Sidi Bel Abbes is an important communications and trading center in northwestern Algeria, and was the headquarters of the French Foreign Legion until Algeria obtained its independence in 1962.

RELATED HISTORICAL EVENTS

• The Indian Government Act of 1843 abolished the legal status of slavery in India.

1844

THE UNITED STATES

The growing abolitionist movement demonstrated its strength in the 1844 Presidential election. The votes that James G. Birney (of the abolitionist Liberty Party) took away from Henry Clay in the election of 1844 allowed James Polk to win the presidential election.

In New York, James G. Birney, the Liberty Party candidate, so weakened Henry Clay that James Polk carried the state and won the presidential election. *See 1839.*

• The Reverend Moses Dickson of Cincinnati and eleven other African Americans organized the Order of 12 of the Knights and Daughters of Tabor. The purpose of this organization was to rescue slaves and to overthrow the institution of slavery by military means if necessary.

• Jonathan Walker (reportedly a European American) was imprisoned, sentenced to stand in the pillory, and branded on the hand with the letters "SS" for "slave stealer." Walker was overtaken and captured sailing from Pensacola, Florida, for the Bahamas. Part of his cargo was seven escaped slaves.

• L. W. Paine, a European American machinist from Rhode Island who was at the time working in Georgia, was imprisoned for six years for persuading slaves to escape.

• The Committee of Free Colored Citizens sent a petition to the United States Senate protesting the anti–African American remarks made by Secretary of State Calhoun to the British ambassador to the United States. Calhoun had made disparaging remarks concerning the social condition of free African Americans in the Northern states. Dr. James McCune Smith wrote and signed the petition.

• The Methodist Church of the United States split on the issue of whether or not a bishop could hold slaves. The Southern members organized the Southern Methodist Episcopal Church.

• *The Civil Rights Movement:* In Boston, Massachusetts, African Americans began a series of meetings to combat the segregation in the public school system.

• *Notable Births:* Richard Theodore Greener, the first African American to receive a degree from Harvard College, was born.

Richard Theodore Greener (1844–1922) was born in Philadelphia, Pennsylvania. In 1849, his family moved to Boston where, in 1870, Greener became the first-known African American to receive a degree from Harvard College.

Greener taught school and served as principal of Summer High School. For a time, Greener, who was also a lawyer, served in the office of the United States attorney for the District of Columbia. In 1873, Greener became an associate editor of the *New National Era.*

During Reconstruction, Greener held the Chair of Mental and Moral Philosophy and Logic at the University of South Carolina. Greener held this position until 1877 when the university closed its doors to African Americans.

Greener had been admitted to the South Carolina Bar in 1876, and, after leaving the University of South Carolina, became an instructor in the Law Department of Howard University. In 1879, Greener became dean of the Howard University law school.

• Elijah J. McCoy, the inventor of the lubricating cup, was born (May 2).

Elijah J. McCoy (1844–1928) was born in Canada. He moved to Michigan and began to work in 1872 as an inventor.

McCoy was granted over 72 patents during his lifetime. Most of his inventions were related to lubricating appliances for engines. McCoy was a pioneer in the art of steadily supplying oil to machinery from a cup so as to render it unnecessary to stop a machine to oil it.

Many of McCoy's inventions were long in use on locomotives of the Canadian and Northwestern Railroads and on the steamships of the Great Lakes.

During his lifetime, McCoy's name became synonymous with quality machine work. The association of his name to quality led to the creation of an American phrase indicating that an article was genuine and good—that the article was "the real McCoy."

• Charles Nash, a Reconstruction congressman from Louisiana, was born (May 23).

Charles E. Nash (1844–1913) was born in Opelousas, Louisiana. Nash was a bricklayer by trade. During the Civil War, Nash joined the Chasseurs d'Afrique Regiment of the Union Army, and rose to the rank of sergeant major.

After the war, Nash was appointed to be the United States custom inspector for Louisiana. In 1874, he was elected to the House of Representatives.

After serving one term in Congress, Nash returned to Louisiana and became a town postmaster.

• James E. O'Hara, a Reconstruction congressman from North Carolina, was born.

James E. O'Hara (1844–1905) was born of free parents in New York City. O'Hara studied law at Howard University. He was admitted to the Bar in 1873.

During Reconstruction, O'Hara served a term in the North Carolina State Legislature. In 1875, he was a delegate to the North Carolina Constitutional Convention.

O'Hara was elected to Congress in 1882. He served two terms in Congress. During his second term, O'Hara worked on civil rights legislation and for equal access to public accommodations.

After failing to gain a third term, O'Hara practiced law in New Bern, North Carolina.

• John Henry Smyth, a minister to Liberia, was born.

John Henry Smyth (1844–1908) was born in Richmond, Virginia, of a slave father, Sully Smyth. John attended a Quaker school until 1857. At the age of 14, he was admitted to the Pennsylvania Academy of Fine Arts. In 1862, Smyth attended the Institute for Colored Youth.

Smyth taught in Philadelphia public schools until 1865, when he went to England with the intention of studying under Ira Aldridge, the famous African American Shakespearean actor (*see 1805*). However, Aldridge died not long after Smyth arrived in England and Smyth had to change his plans.

In 1869, Smyth returned to the United States and entered Howard University Law School. He graduated in 1872. Upon his graduation, he became a cashier of the Wilmington, North Carolina branch of the Freedmen's Savings and Trust Company of Washington.

In 1874, Smyth began to practice law. The following year, he became a delegate to the Virginia State Constitutional Convention.

On May 23, 1878, Smyth was appointed minister resident and consul general of Liberia. He held this position until 1885.

After his return to the United States, Smyth became editor of the *Reformer*, in Richmond, Virginia. In 1899, Smyth was instrumental in establishing the Virginia Manual Labor School at Hanover.

• *Miscellaneous State Laws:* In Connecticut, state officials were prohibited from arresting escaped slaves. However, they were not to interfere with federal officials who were attempting to do so.
• The new Constitution of New Jersey confined suffrage (the right to vote) to European Americans.
• In North Carolina, the state law prohibited free African Americans from selling alcoholic beverages, except those which they had made themselves. The fine for violation of this law was $10.
• *Publications:* In 1844, Alexander Dumas, the great Afro-French writer, published the immortal *Three Musketeers* and *Count of Monte Cristo. See 1802.*
• In Paris, Le Théâtre-Français produced a play by the African American Victor Sejour entitled *Diegareas. See 1817.*
• *Scholastic Achievements:* George Vashon (1824–1878) received a bachelor's degree from Oberlin College in Ohio.
• In Cincinnati, Ohio, a high school for African Americans was established by the Reverend Hiram Gilmore.

THE AMERICAS

• In 1844, Juan Pablo Duarte, Francisco del Rosario Sanchez, and Ramon Mella led a successful revolt against the Haitians on the eastern portion of the island of Hispaniola and afterwards established the Dominican Republic. *See 1801.*

Historically, there has been racial tension between the residents of the Dominican Republic and Haiti. The residents of the Dominican Republic are primarily brown-skinned or light-skinned mulattoes, while the residents of Haiti are dark-skinned. The mulattoes of Santo Domingo chafed under the control of the dark-skinned Haitians and this antagonism eventually led to the final division of the island in 1844.

The history of the relations between Haiti and the Dominican Republic is instructive as to the nature of racism because it demonstrates that racial discrimination and even racial hatred may not so much be a function of race as it is a function of differentiation. Indeed, at times it seems that racism is a manifestation of some primal need—a primal instinct—of people to be able to perpetuate their particular gene pool to the detriment of a different gene pool—to the detriment of the different people.

If this observation is correct, then it may be impossible to eradicate racism because as long as people are engaged in a struggle to survive, there will always be this tendency to advance the interests of "us" over the interests of "them."

• Placido, an Afro-Cuban and one of Cuba's greatest poets, took part in the Cuban Revolt of 1844. Placido would later be captured and executed.

In 1844, Placido was charged with conspiring against the government and executed without any proof of guilt. The Spanish Govenor had accused Placido of participating in a "racial conspiracy" composed of Afro-Cubans and mestizos. *See 1809.*

AFRICA

In 1844, Joseph Jenkins Roberts, the first president of Liberia, traveled to the United States on a diplomatic mission. He hoped to resolve the dispute concerning Liberia's import tax but the American government avoided taking a stand in defense of Liberia ostensibly because the annexation of Texas had compelled the issue of slavery to the forefront of political debate. Eventually, the American Colonization Society gave up all claims on the Liberian colony and left the African American colonists on their own. *See 1809.*

• The Sudanese administration was centralized.
• France went to war against Morocco.
• On March 6, "The Bond of 1844," a treaty between the British, Fante, and others was negotiated.

The Fante are a coastal people living in the central region of Ghana. By the early 1900s, the Fante dominated the Ghanaian coast from Winneba to the Pra River. Although they were never united as a single entity, the various Fante groups often cooperated in time of danger and their region was the only coastal area not dominated by the Ashanti.

Despite a period of rapprochement between the Ashanti and the Fante, the two groups began competing over control of the coastal-inland trade. Tensions increased when the Fante began providing refuge to Ashanti rebels. The Ashanti responded by declaring war against the Fante. After ten years of war, the Ashanti won.

Not long afterwards, the British arrived in the region and found the Fante natural allies against the Ashanti. In 1844, the Fante leaders signed a treaty with the British by which their region became a British protectorate. Ostensibly this was done to get even with the Ashanti. But in reality it was more akin to being a pact with the devil. Only belatedly did the Fante come to recognize that the "Bond of 1844" essentially relinquished their independence. When they did, they rose up in anger to try to regain their freedom, but they failed.

- A French consulate was opened in Zanzibar.
- The administration of the Cape colony and Natal were combined.
- There were a large number of local uprisings reported in Portuguese Guinea.
- Around 1844, an Arab trading center was set up at Unyanyembe, near Tabora.
- Maulai Abd al-Rahman of Morocco attacked the French in Algeria but was repelled. The French seized the Oudja oasis from Morocco (July 19). The French bombarded Tangier (August 6). At the Battle of Isly, Bugeaud defeated Abd al-Kader. The French also bombarded Mogador (August 15). On September 20, the Convention of Tangiers ended hostilities between France and Morocco. However, in October, the French began a campaign in Algier against the Kabyles.

The Kabyles are a Berber people who live in the Kabylia (al-Qabail) region of Algeria—a mountain range east of Algiers. The name Qbayl (the Arabic word for "tribes") was applied beginning in the 1700s and originally referred to all the Berbers of North Africa.

The inaccessibility of the Kabyle mountains often served as a refuge and formed a basis for resistance, first against the Romans, then the Vandals, the Byzantines, the Arabs, and, in 1844, the French.

EUROPE

- In Paris, Le Théatre-Français produced a play by the African American Victor Sejour entitled *Diegareas*. *See 1817.*
- Alexander Dumas, père, the great Afro-French writer, published *Three Musketeers* and *Count of Monte Cristo*. *See 1802.*

1845

THE UNITED STATES

In 1845, the antislavery "gag rule" was repealed, largely due to the efforts of Congressmen (and ex–President) John Quincy Adams, of Massachusetts, and Joshua Giddings, of Ohio. In 1836, Congress had adopted a "gag rule" which provided that no antislavery petition should be read, printed, committed or in any way acted upon by the House, but should instead be laid upon the table without debate or discussion. This rule was generally considered a direct violation of the Constitution and it was this perceived violation which served as the basis for the repeal.

- Macon B. Allen (1816–1894) became the first African American formally admitted to the bar when he passed the examination at Worcester, Massachusetts (May 3). Allen had practiced law in Maine for the preceding two years.
- Frederick Douglass delivered a commencement address at Western Reserve College which was one of the first African American attempts to scientifically refute racism.
- William Leidesdorff (1810–1848), a noted African American businessman in California, became the United States subconsul for consultation with Mexican authorities.
- An orphanage for African American children was established in Cincinnati by Salmon Chase and other European Americans and African Americans.
- The lyceum in New Bedford, Massachusetts, established a policy which specifically excluded African Americans from membership and allowed them to sit only in the gallery seats. Previously, the African Americans had enjoyed the same privileges as the European Americans. In protest of this discrimination, Ralph Waldo Emerson, Charles Sumner, Theodore Parker and many local abolitionists threatened to boycott the lyceum. Subsequently, these abolitionists

organized a rival lyceum which admitted African Americans on an equal basis.

• *The Abolition Movement:* Several New England African Americans, including Henry Weeden, William C. Nell, Judith Smith, Mary L. Armstead and Thomas Cummings, organized the Freedom Association to assist fugitive slaves.

• *Notable Births:* Edmonia Lewis, a noted African American sculptress, was born.

Edmonia Lewis (1845–1890) was the daughter of a Chippewa mother and an African American father. She was born near Albany, New York.

Edmonia's mother died when she was only three years old. After her mother's death, she lived with her Chippewa aunts in upstate New York, making baskets and embroidering moccasins. During her time among the Chippewa, she was known by her Chippewa name — she was known as "Wildfire."

From 1860 to 1862, with money given to her by her brother, "Sunrise," Edmonia Lewis attended Oberlin College. It was at Oberlin that her interest in sculpting began.

While at Oberlin, Lewis was accused of attempting to poison two European American acquaintances. In a well-publicized trial, she won an acquittal.

Lewis left Oberlin for Boston where she soon frequented abolitionist circles. In 1865, she was introduced to William Lloyd Garrison, the noted abolitionist. While in Boston she received a number of commissions to do busts of prominent people.

In 1870, the Story family of Boston sent Lewis to Italy to study. She was to remain in Europe for most of the remainder of her life.

Like Edward Bannister (*see 1828*), Edmonia Lewis had a successful showing at the Philadelphia Centennial Exposition in 1876. Her *Death of Cleopatra* drew critical praise as "the grandest statue in the exposition." The statue weighed over two tons and stood over twelve feet tall.

Among Lewis' other notable sculptures were *The Marriage of Hiawatha, The Madonna with Infant* and *Forever, Free.* Lewis' portrait busts done in Roman classical style include busts of Lincoln, Longfellow, John Brown, Charles Sumner and William Story.

• *Notable Deaths:* John Tucker, "one of the Negro pioneers" of Indianapolis, Indiana, was attacked and killed on a downtown street by a band of European Americans who were shouting: "Kill the damned nigger!"

Two men were arrested for this murder. One of the arrestees was convicted of manslaughter and sentenced to three years at hard labor. The actual murderer, however, escaped.

• *Miscellaneous State Laws:* Georgia enacted a law which prohibited contracts with African American mechanics regardless of whether they were slave or free.

• *Publications:* The *Narrative of the Life of Frederick Douglass* was published. *See 1817.*

• *Les Cenelles*, an anthology of poetry by Afro-American poets in New Orleans, was published in French and English. *Les Cenelles* contained 82 poems, the work of 17 New Orleans poets, and was 215 pages long. Reviewed in *La Chronique* on January 30, 1848, *Les Cenelles* was the brainchild of Armand Lanusse, a free African American born in New Orleans in 1812. Lanusse himself contributed 16 poems to the anthology. *See 1812.*

• *Scholastic Achievements:* By 1845, African Americans could attend schools with European Americans in Salem, New Bedford, Nantucket, Worcester and Lowell, Massachusetts.

• *The Arts and Sciences:* William Henry Lane, an African American minstrel dancer, received top billing with a European American minstrel company. Lane's stage name was "Master Juba." Lane took his stage name from the African dance, the juba. In 1845, Lane won the title "King of All Dancers" after three challenge contests.

During the second half of the nineteenth century, minstrelsy was the most popular form of American entertainment. In 1844, E. P. Christy had worked out the minstrel formula which companies throughout the country followed. As late as 1919, three large minstrel companies were touring the United States. Performances often included jubilee singers, plantation songs, camp meeting songs, field-hollers and work songs. All of the music was rich in African musical techniques and rhythms.

The music of minstrelsy would lead to a unique American musical contribution — it would lead to a musical form which we today know as "jazz." Minstrelsy was not just the womb of jazz rhythms and techniques, it also provided a training ground for many of the founding African American jazz musicians that were to come. For example: Jack Laine led a minstrel band in New Orleans in 1895; W. C. Handy joined Mahara's Minstrels in 1896 and became the band leader in 1897; Ma Rainey performed with Rainey's Rabbit Foot Minstrels; and Jelly Roll Morton was with the McCabe and Young Minstrels in 1910.

While today minstrel shows are scoffed at because of the derogatory manner in which African Americans were depicted, it should not be ignored that one of the unique African American musical contributions was conceived in such minstrel shows.

THE AMERICAS

• In Cuba, a law was passed which was intended to repress the slave trade in, and to, Cuba.

AFRICA

• In June, the Kabyles (*see 1844*) revolted against the French. On September 22, 450 Frenchmen were massacred in an ambush at Sidi Brahim, Algeria.

• Additional treaties were negotiated between the Portuguese and French concerning West Africa.

• The first schools were established in Cameroon.

• Queen Ranavalona (of Madagascar) declared all foreigners subject to local laws. In response, the Anglo-French interests issued their own ultimatum concerning their status on the island and punctuated the ultimatum by bombarding Tamatave.

RELATED HISTORICAL EVENTS

• Britain declared that it would seize all Brazilian slave ships found at sea. But even with this pronouncement, the slave shipments to Brazil continued. It is estimated that some 20,000 slaves were imported into Brazil in 1845.

1846

THE UNITED STATES

In 1846, the Reverend Moses Dickson of Cincinnati and 11 other African Americans met in St. Louis, Missouri, and formed a secret, militant organization—the Knights of Liberty. Dickson's Knights of Liberty agreed to disperse for ten years to form secret societies to emancipate the slaves. In 1856, by the time of the ten year reunion, there were said to be 47,240 members of the Knights of Liberty. The organization remained secret until 1871 as the Temple and Tabernacle of the Knights and Daughters of Tabor, in Independence, Missouri.

• In 1846, another incident involving an escaped slave arose in Boston, Massachusetts.

When he arrived in Boston, a certain Captain Hannum of the brig *Ottoman* found an escaped slave on board his ship. Captain Hannum set sail with the intentions of returning the slave to captivity. Hannum's ship was followed by a steamer which had been sent out by Boston authorities for the purpose of freeing the slave. Hannum's ship eluded the Boston steamer. This incident outraged the citizenry and a protest committee was formed to combat such activities.

• An abolitionist, Gerrit Smith, attempted to encourage independent farming and voting among African Americans, and offered to distribute 140,000 acres of his own land in upstate New York to 3,000 African Americans, in parcels of 40 to 60 acres. The project failed because much of the land was poor and many African Americans did not have the capital needed to start a farm. By 1848, fewer than 30 families were settled on the land.

Between 1829 and 1846, it was reported that out of the prisoners in the Eastern Penitentiary in Pennsylvania, 14% of the Europeans were pardoned compared to 2% of the African Americans. In the same period, the average sentence for European Americans was 2 years, 8 months, 2 days while for African Americans it was 3 years, 3 months and 14 days.

• *The Abolition Movement:* David Wilmot, a representative from Pennsylvania, proposed the exclusion of slavery from territory acquired from Mexico after the Mexican War, not because of "morbid sympathy for the slave," but for the "cause and rights of white freemen." The Wilmot Proviso was defeated in the Senate.

• *The Labor Movement:* The New England Working Man's Association, organized in 1845, passed a resolution at its convention in Lynn, Massachusetts, expressing concern for African Americans as well as for their own rights.

• *Notable Births:* Jeremiah Haralson, a Reconstruction Era congressman, was born.

Jeremiah Haralson (1846–1916?) was born of slave parents in Muscogee County, Georgia. Moving to Alabama after emancipation, Haralson was elected to the House of Representatives in 1874. Accused of fraud and of maintaining a close friendship with Jefferson Davis, Haralson only served two terms.

Later Haralson moved to Colorado. While in Colorado, Haralson was killed in a hunting accident.

• *Miscellaneous State Laws:* A New Jersey law abolished slavery. However, nonresidents traveling in the state could bring in and take out the "usual number" of household slaves.

• A constitutional amendment to grant equal voting rights to New York African Americans was defeated by popular vote.

• A Kentucky law provided a penalty of imprisonment for enticing slaves to run away or inciting them to rebellion. Another Kentucky law prohibited free African Americans from manufacturing or selling liquor.

• Virginia's Governor Smith proposed to the state legislature that a law be passed whereby each county might have the right to vote upon the question of removing free African Americans from the county. At that time there were approximately 47,000 free African Americans living in Virginia.

• *Publications:* A paper entitled "The Influence of Climate on Longevity, with Special Reference to Life Insurance," by Dr. James McCune Smith, a New York African American, was published. *See 1813.*

• *Scholastic Achievements:* A petition by an interracial group of European Americans and African Americans, led by George Putnam, an African American, was presented to the Boston School Committee. The petition called for the opening of public schools to African Americans. It was refused.

• *The Black Church:* Harrison W. Ellis, an African American from the South, was ordained by the Presbyterian Church as a preacher. Ellis was subsequently sent to Liberia as a missionary.

• The Abyssinian Baptist Church of New York had 424 members. The Reverend Sampson White was pastor of the church.

• *Black Enterprise:* Norbert Rillieux, a Louisiana Creole, patented a vacuum cup which "revolutionized sugar refining methods in that day." *See 1806.*

• David Ruggles constructed a building out of which he operated a center for hydropathic treatments. Known as the "water cure doctor," Ruggles operated his therapeutic center in Northampton, Massachusetts, until his death in 1849.

• William Leidesdorff opened a hotel in San Francisco.

THE AMERICAS

• By 1846, a Baptist church had been established in Toronto, Canada.

• Goncalves Crespo, an Afro-Brazilian poet, was born.

Goncalves Crespo (1846–1883) was educated at the University of Coimbra. Crespo is considered by many to be the finest poet of the Parnassian school and one of the major poets of the Portuguese language. Of his poems, *A Sesta, Na Roca,* and *Cancun,* deal nostalgically with plantation Afro-Brazilians, their earthiness, durability and beautiful women.

AFRICA

• The Ethiopian (Eritrean) port of Massawa (Mits'iwa) was leased by Egypt to Turkey.

• The vicariate of Central Africa and the Galla was created.

• The French began to expand their influence in Madagascar.

• War erupted between the Cape colonists and the Xhosa. In the Natal, segregation began to be imposed.

• The French defeated the Kabyle rebels in Algeria.

• David Livingstone embarked on his first exploration. *See 1813.*

1847

THE UNITED STATES

In 1847, Whigs of both the Northern and Southern wings opposed the annexation of Mexican territory in a party platform. The Southern Whigs, however, denied that Congress had any power to restrict slavery in the Mexican territories. The Southern Whigs succeeded in having the party's Presidential nomination go to Zachary Taylor (*see 1837*), a Southerner and a slaveholder, rather than Henry Clay. Clay stood for compromise on the slavery question.

• The Prince Hall Lodge of Masons in Massachusetts, the First Independent African Grand Lodge in Pennsylvania, and the Hiram Grand Lodge in Pennsylvania formed a National Grand Lodge of Negroes.

• The Independent Order of Good Samaritans and Daughters of Samaria was organized by African Americans and European Americans to promote temperance. In separate district grand lodges, at first, African Americans could vote only on matters which concerned African Americans. However, as the African American membership increased, the European Americans dropped out, and the African Americans eventually gained control of the order. In 1877, an African American was elected Grand Sire.

• Green Flake, Oscar Crosby, and Hank Lay became the first African Americans to settle in the Salt Lake Valley of Utah.

• Robert Morris, of Boston, and George B. Vashon, a graduate of Oberlin, were admitted to the Bar. Vashon also taught classics at New York Central College.

• *The Abolition Movement:* Frederick Douglass was elected president of the New England Anti-Slavery Society. *See 1817.*

• *Notable Births:* John Roy Lynch, a Reconstruction Era congressman, was born.

John Roy Lynch (1847–1939) was born of slave parents in Concordia Parish, Louisiana. For his education, Lynch attended night school. After attending night school, and now in Mississippi, Lynch became a justice of the peace in Adams County in 1869. Later, Lynch was elected to the state legislature where he eventually became Speaker of the House.

Lynch was active in the State Republican Party. He was elected to the House of Representatives from 1873 to 1877 and again from 1881 to 1883.

Lynch was a delegate to the Republican National Convention of 1884 where he presided over the convention proceedings. Appointed fourth auditor of the Treasury in 1889 and United States Paymaster in 1898, Lynch retired in 1911 to private practice as a lawyer.

Lynch published two books, *The Facts of Reconstruction* and *Some Historical Errors of James Ford Rhodes.*

• Isaiah Thornton Montgomery, the founder of Mount Bayou, Mississippi, was born.

Isaiah Thornton Montgomery (1847–1923) was born a slave on the Hurricane Plantation which was owned by Joseph E. Davis, the brother of Jefferson Davis, the president of the Confederacy. At the age of 9, Montgomery worked in his owner's office.

After the Civil War, the plantation of the Davis brothers was turned over to Isaiah's father, Benjamin Montgomery, for $300,000 in bonds. The plantation was operated by Benjamin Montgomery for thirteen years until a court decision returned the land to the Davis heirs.

Isaiah Montgomery founded Mount Bayou on 30,000 acres of land in 1887 in the Mississippi Yazoo delta. Eventually, this primarily agricultural community grew to 3,000 persons and was self-sufficient. In time, Mount Bayou would have its own bank and farming cooperative.

The influence of Mount Bayou also impacted neighboring communities. The formation of the Mount Bayou National Farm Loan Association—an association which insured federal loans—helped to sustain Mount Bayou and the neighboring communities over various seasons of agricultural depression.

Isaiah Montgomery, along with Booker T. Washington, was a founder of the National Negro Business League. Montgomery was the only African American at the Mississippi Constitutional Convention in 1890. Along with President Theodore Roosevelt, Isaiah Montgomery spoke at ceremonies dedicating the Lincoln Memorial at Hodgensburg, Kentucky.

• *Miscellaneous State Laws:* Pennsylvania passed a "personal liberty" law which prohibited state officials from aiding in the enforcement of the 1793 Federal Fugitive Law, and prohibited the use of state jails to incarcerate or detain escaped slaves. Those persons claiming escaped slaves were subject to fine and imprisonment if they attempted violence in reclaiming the slave. Slave owners were also denied the right to transport their slaves through the state.

• In Kentucky, the legislature initiated a petition which called for a more stringent fugitive slave law. This petition would lead to the enactment of the provisions of the Compromise of 1850 which addressed the issue of escaped slaves.

• Missouri law prohibited the instruction of African Americans or mulattoes in reading or writing.

• *Miscellaneous Cases:* The Dred Scott case was initiated in the St. Louis Circuit Court (June 30).

Dred Scott, a slave, filed suit in the St. Louis Circuit Court claiming that his temporary residence in a free territory should have made him a free man. Scott was a semiliterate man whose travels throughout the country—specifically into the free portions of the Louisiana Territory where slavery had been excluded by the Missouri Compromise of 1820, and into free Illinois—formed the basis for the case.

• *Publications:* William Wells Brown published *Narrative of William Wells Brown, a Fugitive Slave. See 1816.*

• Frederick Douglass began to publish his own newspaper, the *North Star* (December 3).

Frederick Douglass (*see 1817*) and Martin Delany (*see 1812*) started the *North Star*, an abolitionist newspaper in Rochester, New York. The paper became the rallying point for African American abolitionists.

• The African Methodist Episcopal Church began publication of *The Christian Herald*, a weekly magazine. In 1852, its name would be changed to *The Christian Recorder*.

• *Scholastic Achievements:* David J. Peck graduated from Rush Medical College in Chicago.

• Louisiana established a common school system for "the education of white youth" to the exclusion of African Americans.

• In Philadelphia of this year, out of the 4,466 African American children, 1,888 were enrolled in schools, 504 were at work or apprentices, and 2,074 were at home.

• *The Black Church:* Quinn Chapel, an African Methodist Episcopal church, was established in Chicago, Illinois.

• The African Methodist Episcopal Church began publication of *The Christian Herald*, a weekly magazine. In 1852, its name would be changed to *The Christian Recorder*.

Black Enterprise: In 1847, there were 20,240 African Americans living in Philadelphia, Pennsylvania. Of these, approximately 57% were Pennsylvania natives. Out of the 11,000 African Americans living in central Philadelphia, some 4,000 were domestic servants. The other 7,000 were mostly laborers, artisans, coachmen, expressmen, and barbers.

The African Americans of Philadelphia paid $6,000 in taxes and owned real estated valued at $400,000. Approximately 8% of the African Americans (some 300) were land owners.

• William Alexander Leidsdorff, an African American businessman, launched the first steamboat to sail in San Francisco Bay. He also built the first hotel in that city and organized the first horse race in California.

William Alexander Leidsdorff was the son of a Danish father and a mulatto mother from the Danish West Indies. Leidsdorff launched the first steamboat on the San Francisco Bay. Leidsdorff was a prosperous businessman and was well known in San Francisco government. He was a member of the city council and of the school board.

Leidsdorff was appointed vice-consul to Mexico under Commodore Stockton's military rule of California during the Mexican War.

AFRICA

• In 1847, Joseph Jenkins Roberts convened a conference at which the new Republic of Liberia was proclaimed and he was elected its first president (July 26). *See 1809.*

• An unsuccessful Anglo-French initiative was taken against the Hova (the Merina) of Madagascar (April).

• Abd el-Kader surrendered to the French in Algeria. Duc d'Aumale became the governor general of Algeria. The French campaigns against the Kabylia resumed.

• Da Silva Porto explored Barotseland.

• The first Spahis were recruited.

• Around 1847, in Ethiopia, the future Emperor Theodore gathered a band of insurrectionists and seized Gondar.

─────── 1 8 4 8 ───────

THE UNITED STATES

Attending the organizational convention of the Free Soil Party in Buffalo, New York, were such prominent African Americans as Samuel R. Ward (*see 1817*), Henry Highland Garnet, (*see 1815*), Charles L. Reason, Henry Bibb, and Frederick Douglass (*see 1817*). Martin Van Buren was chosen as the presidential candidate by the party. Van Buren ran on a platform advocating the exclusion of slavery from the new lands seized from Mexico.

In September, support for the new party was approved by a vote at an African American convention held in Cleveland, Ohio.

In November, both the Free Soil Party and the Democratic Party would lose the election to the Whig candidate, Zachary Taylor (*see 1837*).

• Kentucky demanded that Ohio's Governor Bell extradite 15 persons on the charge of aiding a slave to escape. Bell refused, stating that Ohio law did not construe men as property.

• William and Ellen Craft escaped from slavery in Georgia in one of the most dramatic escapes of the period (December 26).

A Tale of Two Cities

In 1848, the position of African American workers in two cities—Philadelphia, Pennsylvania and Charleston, South Carolina—was chronicled.

In Phildelphia, out of the African American males in the city, 3,358 were 21 years or over. There were 1,581 laborers; 557 waiters, cooks, etc.; 286 mechanics; 276 coachmen, carters, etc.; 156 barbers; 96 in miscellaneous occupations. Out of the 4,249 African American women in the city who were over the age of 21, 1,970 were washerwomen, 486 seamstresses, 786 day workers, 213 in trades, 290 housewives, 156 servants, 173 cooks, 103 ragpickers. These numbers excluded 3,716 live-in servants in European American families.

Out of the 4,798 Philadelphia African Americans who were between the ages of 5 and 20, 1,940 were school children, 1,200 were unaccounted for, 484 were at home, 33 were orphaned, 274 were working at home, 354 were servants, 12 were chimney sweeps, 18 were porters and 230 were apprentices.

In Charleston, the figures for workers in certain occupations were: building trades, 213 slaves, 41 free African Americans; clothing trades, 103 slaves, 329 free African Americans; food trades, 105 slaves, 74 free African Americans; furniture trades, 12 slaves, 1 free African American; nurses and sextons, 3 slaves, 14 free African Americans; transportation trades, 87 slaves, 20 free African Americans; bookbinders, 3 slaves, 0 free African Americans; printers, 5 slaves, 0 free African Americans; navigation (sailors), 101 slaves, 7 free African Americans; unclassified mechanics, 147 slaves, 9 free African Americans; and miscellaneous occupation and servants, 6,576 slaves, 95 free African Americans.

In Charleston, in 1848, slaves as opposed to free African Americans were sailors and plasterers. Boatmen and most of the city's carpenters and coopers were slaves. Free African Americans, as opposed to slaves, could be found as tavern keepers, hotel keepers, milliners and storekeepers.

• *The Abolition Movement:* Captain Drayton and another officer of the schooner *Pearl* were sentenced to 20 years imprisonment for trying to rescue 75 escaped slaves who had fled from Washington, D. C. In 1852, Drayton would be pardoned by President Fillmore.
• The Citizen's Union of Pennsylvania was organized by African Americans to work for first-class citizenship. In 1848, Philadelphia African Americans owned real estate valued at $531,809. This amount did not include church property.
• *Notable Births:* Christopher Harrison Payne, an African American diplomat, was born.

Christopher Harrison Payne (1848–1925) was born in Red Sulphur Springs, Monroe County, Virginia. His mother was the daughter of (and had been the slave of) James Ellison. It was James Ellison who taught Payne's mother how to read and write. Payne's father was a cattle drover.

Between 1861 and 1864, Payne was a body servant in the Confederate Army. After the war, he attended night school in Charleston, West Virginia. In 1868, Payne passed the teacher's examination and received a teacher's certificate.

In 1875, Payne converted to the Baptist faith and, in 1877, he was ordained a Baptist minister. In 1880, Payne became the pastor the Moore Street Baptist Church in Richmond, Virginia. He was appointed a missionary for the eastern division of Virginia in 1883, and on April 1, 1884, he was installed as pastor of the First Baptist Church of Montgomery, West Virginia.

Payne founded the *West Virginia Enterprise* "for the purpose of disseminating correct information about the achievements of the colored people," and later started *The Pioneer* at Montgomery, West Virginia. The weekly, *Mountain Eagle*, was also founded by Payne.

Payne became active in the Republican Party. As a recipient of party patronage, Payne was rewarded with the position of Deputy Collector of Internal Revenue at Charleston, West Virginia.

Between 1889 and 1893, Payne studied law. In 1896, he was admitted to practice in West Virginia.

Payne served as a United States internal revenue agent in 1898 and 1899. In 1903, he was appointed United States Consul to St. Thomas in the Danish West Indies. Payne would remain in this position until 1917, when the islands were purchased by the United States and became known as the Virgin Islands.

After leaving the position as consul, Payne continued to reside on the Virgin Islands and served as a prosecuting attorney and a police judge.

• *Notable Deaths:* Martin Donato, a free African American of St. Landry, Louisiana, died leaving a wife and children, 4,500 arpents (about 3800 acres) of land, 89 slaves and personal property worth $46,000.
• *Miscellaneous State Laws:* A Rhode Island law prohibited state officials from enforcing the 1793 Federal Fugitive Law.
• Virginia law provided the death penalty for advising or conspiring with a slave to rebel. Postmasters were required under penalty of law to give notice of the arrival of insurrectionary books or literature to the authorities so that said material could then be burned.
• A clause of the Illinois Constitution of

1848 which barred the further immigration of African Americans into the state was ratified 2 to 1 by popular vote. This constitutional provision was rarely enforced even though it remained the law until 1865.

• *Publications:* Henry Highland Garnet published *The Past and Present Condition and the Destiny of the Colored Race* in Troy, New York. *See 1815.*

• *Scholastic Achievements:* The president of Harvard College, Edward Everett, announced that an African American applicant would be judged only by his qualifying examinations, and "if the white students choose to withdraw all the income of the College will be devoted to his education."

• California's first school was opened under the direction of a board of education chaired by William Leidesdorff, an African American businessman.

• African American attendance in school in New York City was recorded at 1,375 students.

• A manual labor school for African Americans, later known as Union Literary Institute, was established near Newport, Indiana.

• A Florida law established common schools and gave all taxpayers the right to vote at district meetings, but only European American children could attend the schools.

• *The Arts:* William Henry Lane, an African American minstrel dancer who danced under the stage name of "Master Juba," garnered acclaim for his London performances.

• *Black Enterprise:* An African American blacksmith, Lewis Temple, invented a Toggle harpoon which became the standard harpoon of the American whaling industry.

AFRICA

• Tunis sent a diplomatic mission to London without notifying the Porte (the Turks).

• The first Senegalese deputy was sent to the French National Assembly.

• The sultan of Pate was deposed for asserting independence from Oman.

• Great Britain annexed the territory between the Orange and Vaal rivers for its Cape colony. A new constitution was drafted for the Cape colony.

• Ibrahim Khedive was appointed regent of Egypt during the time of Muhammed Ali's imbecility.

RELATED HISTORICAL EVENTS

• On February 2, the Treaty of Guadalupe Hidalgo was agreed to between the United States and Mexico. Pursuant to the terms of the treaty, Mexico received $15 million, while the United States acquired Arizona, California, Nevada, New Mexico, Utah, and parts of Colorado and Wyoming. Additionally, the annexation of Texas was confirmed.

• In February, Karl Marx and Frederick Ingels issued the *Communist Manifesto.*

• On April 27, slavery was finally abolished in the French colonies.

—————— 1 8 4 9 ——————

THE UNITED STATES

In 1849, the United States Secretary of State, John M. Clayton, stated that passports should not be issued to African Americans and that African Americans would be granted United States protection abroad only when they were in the service of United States diplomats.

• Harriet Tubman escaped from slavery in Maryland (July). During her subsequent career on the Underground Railroad, Tubman would return to the South 19 times, rescuing over 300 slaves. *See 1821.*

• William Wells Brown represented the American Peace Society at the Peace Congress in Paris. *See 1816.*

• In Philadelphia, a gang of European Americans known as the "Killers of Moyamensing" led an armed raid on the African American section of Philadelphia. The state militia was called out to stop the raid. Three European Americans and one African American were killed. Twenty-five people were injured during the raid.

• The first African American gold miner in California was Waller Jackson. Jackson sailed to California via Cape Horn. Originally from Boston, Jackson mined at Downieville in California. Several hundred other African American miners came to California during the gold rush.

• *The Abolition Movement:* The Citizens of Color in Connecticut met in New Haven, Connecticut. The Reverend Beman was named president and S. M. Africanus of Hartford was elected secretary. The organization was formed to protest the disenfranchisement (denial of the right to vote) set forth in Connecticut law for African Americans.

• *Notable Births:* Archibald H. Grimke, Harvard Law School graduate and author of biographies of Charles Sumner and William Lloyd Garrison, was born near Charleston, South Carolina (August 17).

Archibald Henry Grimke (1849–1930) was the son of Henry Grimke, of South Carolina, and

Nancy Weston, a family slave. Grimke attended Lincoln University, receiving his bachelor of arts degree in 1870 and a master of arts degree in 1872. In 1874, Grimke received an LL.B. degree from Harvard Law School.

Between 1883 and 1885, Grimke was the editor of the *Hub* in Boston. At this time, he wrote a series of articles for the *Boston Herald*, the *Boston Traveler* and the *Atlantic Monthly*.

In 1894, Grimke was named consul to Santo Domingo.

Grimke was an active member of the American Negro Academy. He served as the academy's president from 1903 to 1916.

Grimke was a prolific writer. He is especially noted for his biographies. In 1891, he published a biography of the abolitionist William Lloyd Garrison and, in 1892, *The Life of Charles Sumner, the Scholar in Politics* was published. Grimke's other works include *Right on the Scaffold, or the Martyrs of 1822* (1901); *The Ballotless Victim of One-Party Governments* (1913); "The Sex Question and Race Segregation" in *Papers of the American Negro Academy, 1915* (1916); *The Ultimate Criminal* (1915); and *The Shame of America, or, The Negro's Case against the Republic* (1924).

In 1919, Archibald Henry Grimke was awarded the Spingarn Medal by the National Association for the Advancement of Colored People (the N.A.A.C.P.).

• Thomas Ezekiel Miller, a Reconstruction Era congressman, was born.

Thomas Ezekiel Miller (1849–1937) was born of free parents in Ferebeeville, South Carolina. Miller attended public schools and Lincoln University. In 1875, he was admitted to the South Carolina bar.

Miller practiced law in Beaufort, South Carolina. While in Beaufort, he became active in politics. In 1880, he was elected to the State Senate and, in 1889, he was elected to Congress. Miller served one term in Congress.

Miller was elected to the South Carolina Constitutional Convention in 1895. He later served as president of the State Colored College in Orangeburg.

• "Blind Tom," a musical prodigy, was born a slave in Georgia.
• *Notable Deaths:* Morris Brown, a bishop of the African Methodist Episcopal Church, died. *See 1770.*
• *Miscellaneous State Laws:* In Ohio, the legislature repealed the law requiring that African Americans post a bond insuring their good behavior as a prerequisite to admission into the state. Ohio's repeal was the only case of a state repealing such a law before the advent of the Civil War.
• Also in Ohio, the legislature repealed such "black laws" as the ban on African American testimony being allowed in court. Additionally, the legislature passed a law which established publicly supported schools for African American children.
• The Maryland Legislature repealed an 1832 law forbidding the bringing of slaves into the state.
• Virginia law stated that the right to citizenship in the state was confined to free European Americans.
• In Wisconsin, a law was enacted which disenfranchised (took the right to vote from) African Americans.
• *Miscellaneous Cases:* Benjamin Roberts filed the first school integration suit on behalf of his daughter who had been denied admission to the Euro-American schools in Boston. The Supreme Court of Massachusetts rejected the suit and established a "separate but equal" doctrine.

Benjamin F. Roberts sued the city of Boston on behalf of his five year old daughter, Sarah. Roberts asked for damages because the city refused to allow Sarah to attend the European American (but publicly funded) schools. The case was argued by Charles Sumner and Robert Morris, an African American lawyer. However, the Roberts were not successful at the trial court level.

On appeal to the Supreme Court of Massachusetts, the Roberts again lost. Of particular significance for future cases was the principle enunciated by the court. The Massachusetts Supreme Court rejected the Roberts' appeal by establishing a new precedent which permitted exclusion of African Americans when "separate and equal" facilities are made available. This "separate and equal" doctrine would soon find its way into the fabric of American law.

• In 1849, the African Americans of Cincinnati took advantage of a new state law which provided for the school tax collected from African American property to be used for the education of African American children. The African Americans took advantage of this law by electing a board of trustees and forming their own independent school district which employed their own teachers. The city leaders of Cincinnati, upset with the audacity of the African Americans, refused to turn over the tax money to the

African American trustees on the grounds that African Americans were not voters and, therefore, could not be officeholders. The African Americans contested this matter by taking the matter to court. The African Americans eventually won.

• *Publications:* James W. C. Pennington published *The Fugitive Blacksmith: His Early Life* (London 1849). *See 1809.*

• In 1849, Henson published *The Life of Josiah Henson, Formerly a Slave, Now an Inhabitant of Canada as Narrated by himself,* and in 1858 an enlarged edition appeared with an introduction by Harriet Beecher Stowe, under the title *Truth Stranger than Fiction, an Autobiography of the Rev. Josiah Henson See 1789.*

• *Scholastic Achievements:* New York Central College in McGrawville, New York, was founded by the American Baptist Free Mission Society. New York Central College was a co-ed, interracial college—admitting both sexes and both races. William G. Allen, an African American, was appointed to the faculty. However, when Allen subsequently announced his engagement to a European American (white) student, he was forced to flee the community because of the anger exhibited by the townspeople. In 1858, the college went bankrupt and closed its doors in 1861.

• Avery College for Negroes in Allegheny City, Pennsylvania, was established with a $300,000 bequest of the Reverend Charles Avery. Both African Americans and European Americans served on the faculty.

In 1849, the African Americans of Cincinnati took advantage of a new state law which provided for the school tax collected from African American property to be used for the education of African American children. The African Americans took advantage of this law by electing a board of trustees and forming their own independent school district which employed their own teachers. The city leaders of Cincinnati, upset with the audacity of the African Americans, refused to turn over the tax money to the African American trustees on the grounds that African Americans were not voters and, therefore, could not be officeholders. The African Americans contested this matter by taking the matter to court. The African Americans eventually won.

• A "Negro school" abolition organization was set up in Boston, Massachusetts by Jonas Clark and 227 others. The abolition organization tried to have the courts declare separate schools unconstitutional, and to prevent the use of the African American Smith School. Eventually, the abolition organization decided to create its own "integrated" school. A school with both African American and European American students was formed and the students were taught by the Reverend Daniel Foster, an African American preacher.

• Martin R. Delany, an African American from Pittsburgh, Pennsylvania, was admitted to Harvard Medical School. *See 1812.*

• John V. DeGrasse of New York and Thomas J. White of Brooklyn, both African Americans, were allowed to study medicine at Bowdoin College.

• Charles L. Reason, an African American, became a professor of belles lettres and French at Central College, McGrawville, New York, which admitted both European American and African American students.

• *The Black Church:* In Philadelphia, there was one grammar school for African Americans which had an enrollment of 463 pupils and there were two primary schools with 339 pupils. There was also one infant school with 70 infants. The infant school was run by the Pennsylvania Abolition Society. Twenty African American private schools with an enrollment of 300 pupils were also in Philadelphia. The total number of pupils in the African American schools was about 1,300.

• *Black Enterprise:* In 1849, it was reported that 7.4% of the African Americans in Philadelphia County owned property.

• In Columbia, Pennsylvania, William Whipper and Stephen Smith, African Americans, owned a business operation which included an inventory of several thousand bushels of coal and 2,250,000 feet of lumber. The business also had 22 railway cars on the Baltimore to Philadelphia route, stock in the Columbia Bridge valued at $9,000, stock in the Columbia Bank valued at $18,000. Smith also owned 58 houses in Philadelphia and some in Lancaster and Columbia.

AFRICA

• In 1849, under Joseph Jenkins Roberts' leadership, the Republic of Liberia agreed to a commercial treaty with Great Britain. Subsequent visits by Roberts to France and Belgium were instrumental in achieving recognition for Liberia as a sovereign country. *See 1809.*

• In 1849, J. Beecroft was appointed the British consul for Benin and Biafra. During his tenure, Beecroft would unsuccessfully attempt to end the slave trade.

• Courts of equity were established in Nigeria.

• Libreville (the French equivalent of "Freetown"), Gabon was founded for freed slaves.

• Muhammed Abduh (1849–1905), mufti of Egypt and religious reformer, was born.

• Hamburg (German) traders began to operate in Zanzibar.

• Muhammed Ali, the ruler of Egypt, died.

Muhammed Ali (1769–1849), also known as Mehmet Ali, was an Albanian (Greek?) soldier of fortune who made himself the ruler of Egypt.

In 1801, Muhammed Ali was an officer in the Turkish army who was sent to drive the French forces of Napoleon out of Egypt. In the chaos that followed the departure of the French, Muhammed Ali seized the day to take power for himself.

By 1805, Muhammed Ali had established himself as Egypt's ruler. In 1811, he assassinated his Mameluke rivals and secured his hold over the country.

Muhammed Ali was noted for his efforts to modernize Egypt. An outstanding military and political leader, Muhammed Ali's initial focus was on strengthening the military. Having served in the Turkish army, Muhammed Ali knew that his position in Egypt remained secure only as long as his army was able to rebuff the Turks.

To achieve his goal, Muhammed Ali brought in French military experts and modeled his army on that of France. Additionally, Muhammed Ali introduced Western education into Egypt and retained European teachers to teach in his country.

In 1821, Muhammed Ali was retained by the Ottoman sultan to suppress the Greek rebellion. Muhammed Ali commanded the forces which successfully put down the rebellion. Among the rebels was the famous poet Lord Byron and it was during this struggle that Lord Byron died.

As a reward for his services, Muhammed Ali was to receive the Peloponnesus as a reward. However, the combined forces of Great Britain, France and Russia destroyed his fleet at the Battle of Navarino in 1827 and his prize was relinquished forever.

Back in Egypt, Muhammed Ali resumed his modernization efforts. He worked to improve agriculture and he began the transformation from basin irrigation to year-round irrigation. Muhammed Ali also promoted the industrialization of Egypt.

History records that many of Muhammed Ali's reforms did not meet with success. The lack of success may have been due to a too ambitious plan for too little time. However, the lack of success may also have been due to interference from other international players. One player in particular, Great Britain, was hostile to the achievements of Muhammed Ali. Having waged war against the Ottoman Empire for three hundred years, the British feared the creation of a strong state in this key area of the Mediterranean.

Throughout his reign, the British applied pressure upon Muhammed Ali. Finally, in 1841, the British forced Muhammed Ali to accept a limitation on his army. After this time, his army could only be 18,000 strong.

By the time of his death in 1849, the industries Muhammed Ali had introduced and the educational system he had founded had collapsed. The promise of a potentially strong African nation was, for the time, simply not to be.

• The warden zone for the Basuto frontier was established.

Basuto or Basutoland is the former name for the land which is today known as the kingdom of Lesotho. Lesotho is a landlocked kingdom which is entirely surrounded by South Africa.

• Abbas I became the khedive of Egypt.

A "khedive" is the term used to describe a ruler of Egypt during the time of Turkish domination of the country. The "khedive" served as a viceroy (governor) for the sultan of Turkey.

1850

THE UNITED STATES

In 1850, the United States census reported that the African American population was 3,638,808 which comprised 15.7% of the total population. 434,495 African Americans (11.9% of the African American population) were listed as free. More than half of these free African Americans lived in slave states.

Of the 3,204,313 slaves, it was estimated that

400,000 lived in cities and towns, while 2,800,000 lived on farms or plantations (1.8 million on cotton plantations alone).

The slave population in selected states was:

Alabama	342,844
Arkansas	47,100
Delaware	2,290
District of Columbia	3,687
Florida	39,310
Georgia	381,682
Kentucky	210,981
Louisiana	244,809
Maryland	90,368
Mississippi	309,878
Missouri	87,422
New Jersey	236
North Carolina	288,548
South Carolina	384,984
Tennessee	239,459
Texas	58,161
Virginia	472,528
Utah Territory	26

Mulattoes made up 11.2% of the total African American population (one out of every four African Americans in the North was a mulatto). It was estimated that 159,000 mulattoes were free.

The European American population of the South was 6,184,477. Of this number, 76% were farmers owning no slaves. Of the 347,525 who did hold slaves, only 11 owned 500 or more, 254 owned 200 or more, and approximately 8,000 owned 50 or more. In other words, only 7% of the European Americans in the South owned 75% of the slaves.

The census reported that a prime field hand could be sold for approximately $1600, and the main products of slave labor and their commercial value were:

Cotton	$98,603,720
Tobacco	13,982,686
Cane Sugar	12,378,850
Hemp	5,000,000
Rice	4,000,000
Molasses	2,540,179
TOTAL	$136,505,435

It was estimated that the number of slaves involved in producing a commodity was proportionate to the revenue generated by the commodity.

The census also reported that fugitive slaves amounted to 1,011 or 0.0315% of the total slave population.

• A fugitive slave law was passed by Congress as part of the Compromise of 1850. It offered federal officers a fee for captured slaves (September 18).

In 1850, a number of issues continued to fester threatening to cause a permanent rift between the Northern and Southern states. Congress attempted to address these issues by formulating the Compromise of 1850.

The Compromise of 1850 provided that: (1) California would enter the United States as a free state; (2) other land gained from Mexico would be organized into territories with no provision one way or the other on slavery; (3) Texas would receive money in exchange for ceding land to the New Mexico Territory; (4) a more stringent fugitive slave law would be enacted; and (5) the slave trade in the District of Columbia would be abolished.

The Federal Fugitive Slave Law which was enacted as part of the Compromise of 1850 allowed any claimants of runaway slaves to take possession of the suspected slave upon establishing proof of ownership before a federal commissioner. However, no procedural safeguards such as jury trial or a judicial hearing were provided for the suspected slave.

The Federal Fugitive Slave Law provided fines of $1,000 and imprisonment for six months for citizens or officials who failed to aid in the captive of fugitives.

Within 36 hours of passage of the Fugitive Slave Law, 40 Massachusetts African Americans departed for Canada, and the African American population of Columbia, Pennsylvania, dropped from 943 to 437.

The enactment of the Fugitive Slave Law hastened the demise of the Whig Party. The anti–Jacksonian issues that had united Southern and Northern Whig members were no longer binding, while the deliberations of the Compromise of 1850 and the Federal Fugitive Slave Law only served to heighten the differences between the two Whig factions.

With regard to the Fugitive Slave Law, Northern Whigs disapproved of the law. In response to this disapproval, one Southern Whig representative was compelled to remark, "Take secession, nullification and hail disunion as a blessing, rather than yield the Fugitive Slave Law." However, the majority of Southern Whigs were willing to accept slavery limitations as a price for preserving the Union.

Early in 1850, at the Nashville Convention (a nonpartisan gathering of Southern politicians), the Whigs defended the admission of California to the Union as a free state. In contrast, the Southern Democrats opposed admission because slavery was outlawed there. Within the next two years, most Southern Whigs abandoned the Whig Party and transferred their allegiance to the Democratic Party. With their departure, the Whig Party would soon die.

• The first recorded enforcement of the Fugitive Slave Law of 1850 was in September. James Hamlet, a free African American living in New York was seized and accused of being a fugitive slave belonging to Mary Brown of Baltimore. The outraged citizenry of New York raised money on the behalf of Hamlet and, in October, bought Hamlet out from slavery.

• Captain Thomas B. Sullivan estimated that one-half of the American seamen were African Americans. This meant that some 75,000 American seamen were African American.

• The citizens of Lehigh County, Pennsylvania, asked that all African Americans be expelled from the state.

• Returning to the South for the first time since her escape in 1849, Harriet Tubman went to Baltimore and led her sister and two children to freedom.

• An African American Masonic Lodge was organized in Louisville, Kentucky, despite opposition from European Americans.

• By 1850, approximately 960 African Americans had come to California, either as slaves or as free men.

Miscellaneous Census Facts

Ohio had 25,279 African Americans, 3,237 of them living in Cincinnati.

Michigan had 2,500 African Americans.

In Virginia, nearly one out of every five free African Americans lived in towns compared to one out of every ten European Americans.

The free African American population of North Carolina was 27,463 or 3.16% of the total population of the state. 73% of the families in North Carolina owned no slaves, and more than one-half of the slave owners had less than 10 slaves.

Free African Americans in Pennsylvania numbered 53,626 out of a total state population of 2,311,786.

In 1850, it was also estimated that some 20,000 escaped slaves were living illegally in the northern United States.

• *The Abolition Movement:* The Ohio Colored Convention reported the formation of the Colored American League to assist runaway slaves, improve the condition of African Americans and encourage African American communities to establish military companies.

• *The Labor Movement:* New York African Americans formed the American League of Colored Laborers to promote a union of skilled workers, to encourage the practical education of African Americans to assist African Americans in establishing businesses. The first president of the American League of Colored Laborers was Samuel R. Ward. *See 1817.*

• *Miscellaneous State Laws:* A constitutional amendment to grant equal voting rights to New York African Americans was defeated by a popular vote of the people.

• Virginia law placed an annual per capita tax of $1.00 on free African Americans.

• A Vermont law called on the state's attorneys to defend fugitive slaves.

• *Publications:* Daniel Payne published *Pleasures and Other Miscellaneous Poems.* *See 1811.*

Scholastic Achievements: In 1850, the United States census reported that school attendance and adult literacy among African Americans (A. A.) in 16 cities were as follows:

City	Total Free A. A. Population	Free A. A. in School	Illiterate Free A. A.
Boston, MA	2,038	1,439	205
Providence, RI	1,499	292	55
New Haven, CT	989	360	167
Brooklyn, NY	2,424	507	788
New York City	13,815	1,418	1,667
Philadelphia	10,736	2,176	3,498
Cincinnati, OH	3,237	291	620
Louisville, KY	1,538	141	567
Baltimore, MD	25,112	1,153	9,310
Washington, DC	8,158	420	2,674
Richmond, VA	2,369	none	1,594
Petersburg, VA	2,616	none	1,155
Charleston, SC	3,441	68	45
Savannah, GA	686	none	185
Mobile, AL	715	53	12
New Orleans, LA	9,905	1,008	2,279

These literacy figures did not include the almost universal illiteracy among the slaves.

In New York City, it was reported that about the same percentage of European American and African American children attended school.

The census showed that there were 100,591 European Americans in school in North Carolina, but only 217 free African Americans. Additionally, of the 12,048 free African American adults, 5,191 (43%) were literate.

• Lucy Ann Stanton completed Oberlin College's two-year ladies course and received the bachelor of literature degree from Oberlin College (December 8).

• *The Black Church:* Saint Andrew's African Methodist Episcopal Church, the first African Methodist Episcopal church in California, was founded in Sacramento.

• *Black Enterprise:* David Clay, an Ohio African American, advertised his manufactured plows which could be made any size and plow a depth of 8 to 20 inches.

• Around 1850, the potato chip was invented. Among those who lay claim to inventing the chip are two African Americans, Hyram S. Thomas Bennett and Catherine A. Wicks, along with George Crum, an Indigenous American.

THE AMERICAS

The Black Seminoles of Mexico

At the conclusion of the Second Seminole War, the United States sought to relocate the Seminoles to Oklahoma. Gathering up those Seminoles that had been captured, the army transported the Seminoles (including the black Seminoles) up the Mississippi and Arkansas rivers to the Oklahoma Indian Territory. However, this relocation would soon prove to be problematic because the black Seminoles still considered themselves free.

As soon as the black Seminoles arrived at Fort Gibson, agents hired by slave owners were waiting for them to enslave them. Additionally, the Creek, old enemies of the Seminoles, and "civilized" slave keepers in their own right, were ready to enslave the black Seminoles. Many of the black Seminoles were kidnapped and sold into slavery. When the Seminole leaders protested to the government, the government said that despite the military's promise, those black Seminoles who had been slaves before the Second Seminole War remained slaves and could be recaptured.

However, some of the black Seminoles were able to remain relatively free and intact. Under the leadership of John Horse, some 300 black Seminoles stayed together and settled in the village of Wewoka. These 300 black Seminoles were not only together, they were armed. As General Arbuckle, the commanding officer of Fort Gibson noted: "The negroes well know what to expect after being deprived of their arms, and they are not disposed to yield peaceably to any.

Arbuckle's words proved to be prophetic. Not long after settling in at Wewoka, a party of about 200 Creek attacked the town. Promised a bounty of $100 a head by slave hunters, the Creek seized a number of men, women and children. This attack and the prospect of many more, convinced John Horse that his band of black Seminoles must leave the Indian Territory or perish.

As it happened, a number of the red Seminoles were also ready to leave the Indian Territory. The Seminoles had been promised their own land when they surrendered but, when they arrived in the Indian Territory, they discovered that their land allotment was located within the Creek nation.

Realizing that their old enemies now, essentially, controlled them, Wild Cat decided to act. Wild Cat and John Horse got together and decided that the best hope for their people was to find a new homeland — in Mexico.

In the fall of 1849, Wild Cat and John Horse and their Seminole followers broke free. Two hundred strong, the Seminoles warned that they would kill anyone who tried to stop them. John Horse led the black Seminole contingent under the overall command of Wild Cat.

The Seminoles who left with Wild Cat and John Horse left without the permission from either the army or the Indian agent in charge. Their future was uncertain, the Creek might pursue them, the Plains Indians might attack them or the Mexicans might turn them away. All was unknown and all was risked. All was to be given in the quest to be free.

For the next nine months, scattered reports of the whereabouts of the Seminole band were spread across Texas. At one time, the Seminoles were reported on the Texas prairie; another they were seen on the Nueces River; and for a while it was reported that they were encamped for the winter near the Brazos River. Naturally, given the uncertainty of their whereabouts, along with the reputation of the Seminoles, the citizenry of Texas became alarmed.

But the Seminoles were not found, at least not until one day when they just suddenly appeared at Eagle Pass on the Texas side of the Rio Grande. After consulting with the Mexican authorities, the Seminoles were invited to settle on land near the Rio Grande. This they did, first near Piedras Negras and later at Nacimiento.

The cimarrones — the Seminoles — were now in Mexico where slavery was forbidden and where they could be free.

• With the passage of the Fugitive Slave Law of 1850, an exodus of African Americans to Canada occurred. At the end of three months, some 3,000 African Americans had fled to Canada.

• In 1850, what was perhaps the most successful Afro-Canadian settlement was established. In 1850, the town of Buxton was incorporated and populated by the former slaves of William King of Louisiana who had emancipated his slaves and brought them to Canada. The charter for the town stated that the town was established for "the settlement and moral improvement of the colored population of Canada,. . . ."

• In 1850, the Queiroz Law closed down Brazil's principal sources for new slaves.

AFRICA

• The new Cape colony constitution permitted an elected upper house of the legislature.

• Damaraland was explored.

Damaraland is a plateau region of central Namibia and is the homeland of the Damara (Bergdama) people.

• The Gold Coast (Ghana) was separated from Sierra Leone. An executive and legislative council were set up to govern the Gold Coast.

• Hajj Umar attacked Segu (on the River Niger), Kaarta and Massina.

• Barth's expedition reached Bornu (Nigeria), Kano and Kuka.

• Sayyid Said dispatched his troops against Gazi.

• A three-year war between the British and the Khoikhoi began.

1851

THE UNITED STATES

In the wake of the passage of the 1850 Federal Fugitive Slave Law, incidents involving African Americans fleeing slavery dominated 1851.

In Maryland, a certain Mr. Miller was killed on his way back to Nottingham, Pennsylvania, with a free African American girl who had been kidnapped from his house and taken to Baltimore.

In Christiana, Pennsylvania, a slave catcher named Gorsuch was killed by free African Americans when he and his assistants refused to leave the home of Willian Parker, a free African American.

In Boston, Thomas M. Sims was arrested as an escaped slave of Mr. Potter of Virginia. Sims was sent to Virginia on the *United States Acorn,*

despite the protests of such prominent Boston abolitionists as Wendell Phillips and Theodore Parker.

Also in Boston, African American abolitionists rescued a fugitive slave named Shadrach from a courtroom (February), while, in Syracuse, New York, a fugitive slave named Jerry was rescued in the same way (October).

• James Beckwourth discovered a pass through the Sierra Nevadas to the Pacific Ocean which was subsequently named "Beckwourth Pass" (April 26). *See 1798.*

• *The Abolition Movement:* Frederick Douglass split from William Lloyd Garrison on the tactics and strategy to be employed to further the abolitionist movement. In an address before the Annual Convention of the American Anti-Slavery Society, he supported political action and opposed the dissolution of the Union since dissolution would place slaves at the complete mercy of the South. Declaring that the Constitution implied the eventual extinction of slavery, Douglass predicted that slavery would end in violence.

• *The Labor Movement:* The *New York Tribune* reported a clash between African American and European American workers at the Hazel River Works in Culpepper County, Virginia. One African American was killed.

• The Industrial Congress, "a short-lived, national organization of reformers and workingmen," admitted African American delegates to its convention.

• The Mechanics Association of Portsmouth, Virginia, protested the teaching of trades to slaves because slave carpenters, coopers, tradesmen, "degraded" the European American mechanics by their competition.

• New York African Americans formed a committee to welcome the Hungarian revolutionary, Kossuth. George T. Downing, a young African American labor leader, was chosen to make the address of welcome.

• *Notable Births:* Walter H. Brooks, distinguished clergyman, was born (August 30).

• Alberry Whitman, a noted African American poet, was born.

Alberry Whitman (1851–1902) was born a slave. After emancipation, Whitman went to Wilberforce University. At Wilberforce, he came under the influence of Bishop Daniel Payne (*see 1811*). Whitman was widely read and cultivated. His memory was particularly notable.

In 1873, Whitman published his first volume of poetry. It was entitled *Leelah Misled* and was an apolitical volume of verse.

In 1877, Whitman published *Not a Man and Yet a Man* a 20-volume epic. In *Not a Man and Yet a Man*, Whitman relates the story of a mulatto slave who rescues his owner's daughter during an Indian (Indigenous American) uprising. The mulatto slave falls in love with the young woman and the long narrative follows the lovers travails as the slave suffers tribulations which eventually lead him to Canada and his freedom.

In 1884, Whitman published another long narrative poem, *The Rape of Florida. The Rape of Florida* was done in Spenserian stanzas and is focused on the European oppression of the Seminoles. The significance of the poem was that Whitman saw the Seminoles in a position analogous to that of his own people. *See 1813, 1816 and 1837.*

In Whitman's subsequent long poems, *The Octoroon* (1901) and *The Southland's Charm and Freedom's Magnitude* (1902), Whitman showed a preference for mulattoes. Whitman claimed that pure blacks — pure Africans — do not exist. Whitman championed the acceptance of mulattoes into white society.

It is said that Whitman's poetry was the best done by an African American before the advent of Paul Laurence Dunbar.

• *Notable Deaths:* John Brown Russwurm, the first superintendent of schools in Liberia and governor of the African colony of Maryland, died.

• A certain Mr. Miller was killed in Maryland on his way back to Nottingham, Pennsylvania, with a free African American girl who had been kidnapped from his house and taken to Baltimore.

• A slave catcher named Gorsuch was killed by free African Americans in Christiana, Pennsylvania, when he and his assistants refused to leave the home of William Parker, a free African American.

• The *New York Tribune* reported a clash between African American and European American workers at the Hazel River Works in Culpepper County, Virginia. One African American was killed.

• *Miscellaneous State Laws:* A new Virginia constitution provided that slaves henceforth set free would be made slaves again if they remained within the state for more than 12 months.

• A Virginia law imposed upon county sheriffs or sergeants the duty of summoning a special court to hear evidence concerning an escaped slave if the county or corporation court was not in session. This law was enacted to facilitate the recovery of escaped slaves.

• A California law denied African Americans the right to testify in court against a European American.

• The Indiana Constitution of 1851 prohibited the further admission of African Americans into the state. However, violators of this law were seldom prosecuted. The state constitution also denied African Americans the right to vote and excluded them from serving in the militia.

• *Publications:* William C. Nell published *Services of Colored Americans in the Wars of 1776 and 1812,* the first full-length study of the military contributions of African Americans (May). This study would be reissued in a revised form in 1855 under the title of *The Colored Patriots of the American Revolution with Sketches of Several Distinguished Colored Persons to which is Added a Brief Survey of the Condition and Prospects of Colored Americans. See 1816.*

• Frederick Douglass published *Lectures on American Slavery. See 1817.*

• The *Colored Man's Journal,* an African American newspaper, began publication in New York.

• The *Liberty Party Paper* merged with Frederick Douglass' *North Star.*

• *Scholastic Achievements:* Myrtilla Miner, a young European American woman from New York, established an academy for African American girls in Washington, D.C. The school eventually became a college bearing her name.

• *The Arts and Sciences:* The Colored American Institute for the Promotion of the Mechanic Arts and Sciences exhibited work of African American mechanics in Philadelphia in April. There were: portraits by Videll of New York and Wilson of Philadelphia; marine paintings by Bowser; exhibits by Dutere; and exhibits of artificial teeth by a Dr. Rock. Also shown at the convention was an invention by Roberts for replacing derailed cars onto railroad tracks. *The Pennsylvanian* called the convention "the first exhibition of its kind in the U. S."

• Elizabeth Taylor Greenfield, an African American raised by a Quaker woman, sang for the Buffalo Musical Association. At the conclusion of her performance, Greenfield was compared to Jenny Lind and the other great sopranos of the day. Greenfield, who came to be known as the "Black Swan," reportedly had a range of three and a quarter octaves. She would go on to give concerts throughout the United States and Europe.

• *Black Enterprise*: In Detroit, African Americans were credited with owning $30,000 worth of property. There were some 1,000 African Americans in Detroit at the time.

• In Cincinnati, Knight and Bell, African American plasterers, received a contract for plastering the public buildings of Hamilton County.

THE AMERICAS

• The Anti-Slavery Society of Canada was organized to raise money for the relief of slaves and other African Americans fleeing the United States.

• In Colombia, slavery was abolished.

• A cholera epidemic ravaged Jamaica.

AFRICA

• In May and June, a French expedition under the command of General Saint-Arnaud was launched against Little Kabylia.

• The British attacked and occupied Lagos (Nigeria).

• The Egyptian State Railway was begun under the supervision of Robert Stephenson (October).

• Moshesh (Moshoeshoe) greatly enlarged the Basuto Territory.

• The French fleet bombarded the Moroccan ports of Sale and Rabat in revenge for acts of piracy.

• Barth and Overweg explored Lake Chad.

Heinrich Barth (1821–1865) was a German explorer who is deemed by many to have been the keenest European observer of West Africa during the 1800s. Barth's five-volume account of his West African explorations (*Travels and Discoveries in North and Central Africa*) was, until recently, considered to be the most comprehensive and accurate study of West Africa produced during the nineteenth century.

• Cotonou, the main port and business center of Benin, was founded.

RELATED HISTORICAL EVENTS

• The British attempted to curtail the Arab-controlled East African slave trade by negotiating an agreement with the kings of Somalia.

---
1 8 5 2

THE UNITED STATES

In 1852, the first edition of *Uncle Tom's Cabin* was published. The book, which had been serialized in an abolitionist newspaper the year before, sold more than a million copies within six months. According to Harriet Beecher Stowe, "God wrote it. I merely wrote his dictation" (March 20).

The chief character in *Uncle Tom's Cabin* is Uncle Tom, a dignified old slave. *Uncle Tom's Cabin* describes Tom's experiences with three slaveholders. Two of them — George Shelby and Augustine St. Clare — treat Tom kindly. However, the third, Simon Legree, abuses Tom and has him brutally beaten for refusing to tell where two escaped slaves are hiding. Tom dies from the beating.

A subplot of *Uncle Tom's Cabin* concerns the slave family consisting of the characters, George, Eliza and their baby and their flight to freedom in Canada. In one famous episode, Eliza, clutching her baby, escapes across the frozen Ohio River from pursuing slave catchers. Two other characters in the book are Topsy — a mischievous slave girl — and Little Eva, St. Clare's young daughter. The death of Little Eva is another famous episode in *Uncle Tom's Cabin*.

Uncle Tom's Cabin presented a realistic account of American life ten years before the Civil War. Stowe created a vivid picture of Southern life, with Tom being sold from one slave owner to another. *Uncle Tom's Cabin* also described the upper Midwest as seen by George and Eliza as they flee northward into Canada.

Uncle Tom's Cabin is often described as melodramatic and sentimental, but it is more than a melodrama. *Uncle Tom's Cabin* recreates characters, scenes, and incidents with humor and realism. It analyzes the issue of slavery in the Midwest, New England, and the South during the days of the Fugitive Slave Law.

Uncle Tom's Cabin was published on the heels of the Compromise of 1850. The book served to intensify the disagreement between the North and the South which led to the Civil War. Stowe's name was anathema in the South, and many historians believe that the bitter feelings aroused by Stowe's book helped cause the Civil War.

It is important to understand that the images that most people have of the characters in *Uncle Tom's Cabin* are not the way the characters are actually portrayed in the book. After the

Civil War, *Uncle Tom's Cabin* became known chiefly through abridgements of the novel and by plays (particularly George L. Aiken's play) based on the book. However, these versions distorted the original story and characters. By the late 1800s, most people believed that *Uncle Tom's Cabin* dealt primarily with the death of Tom and Little Eva, Topsy's antics, and Eliza's escape. The term "Uncle Tom" as derived from the plays and distortions came to stand for an African American man who, for selfish reasons or through fear, adopted a humble, often self-degrading, manner to gain the favor of European Americans. However, in Stowe's novel, Uncle Tom is portrayed as a brave man who dies rather than betray two fellow slaves.

• Martin R. Delany (*see 1812*) called for the establishment of an African American "Promised Land" in Central or South America. Delany expressed his profound opinion that there was little hope for the improvement of the position of African Americans in the United States.

• Sojourner Truth (*see 1797*), a former New York slave, attended the Second National Women's Suffrage Convention in Akron, Ohio, and delivered her famous "A'int I a woman?" speech.

• Dr. James McCune Smith (*see 1813*), was nominated to serve on a five-man committee to draft a constitution for the "Statistic Institute," of which he became a leading member.

• In 1852, it was reported that Simon Gray, a slave, was the captain of a lumber company flatboat operating on the Mississippi River. Gray was allowed to travel freely as a company agent and lived as though free with his family.

• *The Abolition Movement:* The first edition of *Uncle Tom's Cabin* was published. The book, which had been serialized in an abolitionist newspaper the year before, sold more than a million copies within six months. According to Harriet Beecher Stowe, "God wrote it. I merely wrote his dictation (March 20).

• African Americans applied for jobs at businesses owned by members of the executive committee of the American and Foreign Anti-Slavery Society. Some were rejected, the rest were given menial jobs.

• William Still, an African American, became chairman of the Acting Vigilance Committee of Philadelphia (the Underground Railroad). The purpose of the committee was to aid and harbor escaped slaves and assist them to seek a safe haven in Canada.

• *Notable Births:* Jan E. Matzeliger, an African American inventor, was born.

Jan E. Matzeliger (1852–1889) was born in Dutch Guiana. Matzeliger came to the United States as a young man and served as a cobbler's apprentice, first in Philadelphia, and later in Lynn, Massachusetts.

Although Matzeliger died at the young age of 37, in his brief life his contributions made a "lasting" impact on the leather industry. Matzeliger's "sole machine" was a profound advancement in the shoemaking business. The sole machine was the first machine of its kind. It was capable of performing all the steps required to hold a shoe on its last, grip and pull the leather down around the heel, guide and drive the nails into place, and then discharge the complete shoe from the machine. This invention essentially automated the shoemaking process enabling shoes to be manufactured in mass.

Matzeliger's patent was bought by the United Shoe Machinery Company of Boston, which made millions on the basis of Matzeliger's invention. The company was soon able to expand. It rapidly grew to include 40 subsidiaries and employed tens of thousands of people in its plants.

• George H. White, a congressperson from North Carolina, was born.

George H. White (1852–1918) was born in Rosedale, North Carolina, and was educated at Howard University. White taught in North Carolina and pursued legal studies. He was admitted to the North Carolina bar in 1879.

White gained a reputation as a brilliant lawyer. He was elected to the state legislature in 1880 and, in 1886, became state solicitor.

In 1897, White was elected to Congress. He was reelected in 1899. While in Congress, White spoke as an advocate for equal constitutional rights for African Americans.

• *Miscellaneous State Laws:* A petition from the free African Americans of San Francisco, California, asked for the repeal of the state law provision which prohibited the use of African American testimony against European Americans in court. The petition was denied.

• Delaware law provided for taxation of all property, whether held by European Americans or African Americans, for the support of schools for European American children.

• In Georgia, a bill was introduced to permit the education of slaves as a means of increasing their value. The measure failed in the Georgia Senate.

• Another Georgia law placed a per capita tax of $5 per year on free African Americans.

• In Kentucky, a law was passed which prohibited the immigration of free African Americans into the state on the pain of imprisonment.

• *Publications*: The first edition of *Uncle Tom's Cabin* was published. The book, which had been serialized in an abolitionist newspaper the year before, sold more than a million copies within six months. According to Harriet Beecher Stowe, "God wrote it. I merely wrote his dictation." (March 20) *See 1811.*

• William Wells Brown published *Three Years in Europe* (also known as *The American Fugitive in Europe: Sketches of Places and People Abroad* [1855]). *See 1816.*

• Martin R. Delany published *The Condition, Elevation, Emigration and Destiny of the Colored People of the U.S., Politically Considered. See 1812.*

• The *Alienated American*, an African American publication, began circulation in Cleveland, Ohio, with W. H. H. Day as editor.

• *Scholastic Achievements*: Grace A. Mapps obtained a degree from Central College, McGrawville, New York.

• In Cincinnati, Ohio, some 450 African American children attended school, including 50 in high school.

• Evening schools for African Americans were opened in New York City. One school was for males, the other for females. The combined attendance for the two schools was 379 students.

• *The Black Church*: Henry Highland Garnet was sent as a missionary to Jamaica. *See 1815.*

• There were six African American churches in Cincinnati, Ohio.

• *Black Enterprise*: In Cincinnati, there were 3,500 African Americans. Two hundred of these African Americans were property owners who paid real estate taxes. The assessed value of their property was $500,000.

THE AMERICAS

• Napoleon III issued a decree against the slave trade (March 29).

• The slave trade (as opposed to slavery itself) was completely brought to end in Brazil.

• In 1852, Teixeira Sousa, the noted Afro-Brazilian novelist, published *Maria ou a Menina Rouhada* in Paul Brito's (*see 1809*) magazine, *Marmota Fluminense*. *Maria* was the first novel in Brazilian literature in which Afro-Brazilians were the leading characters. The novel dealt with Afro-Brazilian customs, religion and sorcery. *See 1812.*

AFRICA

• The French captured Laghouat and Ourgla.

Laghouat is a staging post on the Route du Hoggar, 400 kilometers (250 miles) south of Algiers, Algeria.

• A treaty was negotiated between Great Britain and Lagos (Nigeria).

• Al Hajj Umar initiated a jihad from a base in Upper Guinea. The jihad would lead to the establishment of the Tuculor state on Middle Niger.

"Al Hajj" is an Arabic title meaning "the pilgrim." The title is used by Muslims who have made the pilgrimage to Mecca.

• A legislative assembly was convened in the Gold Coast (Ghana).

• At the Sand River Convention, Great Britain formally recognized the Transvaal.

EUROPE

• Alexander Dumas, fils, the son of Alexander Dumas the author of *The Three Musketeers*, had his first play produced. The play, *The Lady of the Camellias* (often called *Camille*), was an overnight success and helped to establish the literary reputation of the younger Dumas. *See 1824.*

RELATED HISTORICAL EVENTS

• In 1852, it was reported that some 200,000 Irish emigrated to the United States, indicating an explosion in the number of Irish immigrants which would not subside for some sixty years.

1853

THE UNITED STATES

Professor Dew of William and Mary College in Virginia, Chancellor Harper of the South Carolina Supreme Court, Senator Hammond of South Carolina, and Gilmore Simms jointly published a book entitled *Pro-Slavery Argument*. In this book, slavery was defended by the authors on several bases. The most profound argument was set forth by Senator Hammond who argued that the European American factory worker of the Northern states was a wage slave. Hammond contended that as a wage slave the European American factory worker was treated callously by the powers that be in industrial society. Hammond then contrasted the treatment of the factory workers with the paternalism exhibited by the slaveholder in the treatment of the slaves. The publication of *Pro-Slavery Argument* was prompted by the success of *Uncle Tom's Cabin* (1852) and the sympathetic audience *Uncle Tom's Cabin* created for the abolition of slavery.

• A Colored Young Men's Christian Association was organized in Washington, D. C. Its first president was Anthony Bowen who worked for the patent office (January 3).

• A *New York Herald* editorial urged the United States government to make the emigration of free African Americans to Liberia more attractive. The newspaper felt that the African American's "racial inferiority" made him a burden on the United States.

In 1853, 783 African Americans were transported to Liberia.

• A planned slave revolt in New Orleans involving 2,500 slaves was averted when a free African American disclosed the plans for the revolt.

• African Americans, led by William C. Nell, petitioned for enlistment in the Massachusetts militia.

• African Americans in Pennsylvania petitioned the State Legislature to secure protection for African Americans when they traveled in slave states.

• In Philadelphia, Robert Purvis, an African American, refused to pay the school tax because his children were excluded from the public school.

• *The Abolitionist Movement:* The Society of Progressive Friends was organized in Pennsylvania to oppose slavery more aggressively than conservative Quakers had wished to do.

• *The Labor Movement:* On July 6, 1853, delegates from several states met and organized the National Council of Colored People in Rochester, New York, to encourage the mechanical training of African Americans.

• Striking Irishmen on the Erie Railroad were replaced with armed African Americans.

• *Notable Births:* George Washington Murray, an African American Congressperson from South Carolina, was born.

George Washington Murray (1853–1926) was born of slave parents in Rembert, South Carolina. He received an education and attended South Carolina University for two years. A teacher by profession, in 1888, Murray was made the Republican Party chairman for Sumter County, South Carolina.

In 1893, Murray was appointed customs inspector for Charleston harbor by President Harrison.

In 1895, Murray was elected to Congress. While in Congress, Murray advocated better educational opportunities for African Americans. Murray left politics after an unsuccessful attempt to lead an African American faction away from the Republican Party.

• *Miscellaneous State Laws:* A Virginia law levied a poll tax on free male African Americans between the ages of 21 and 55. The money was to be used to establish a fund dedicated to the removal (emigration) of free African Americans to Africa.

• An Illinois law prohibited the entry of African Americans and mulattoes into the state. Another Illinois law provided that African Americans could be advertised and sold at public auction if they did not produce certified proof of freedom and post a bond guaranteeing their good behavior.

• Indiana law stated that African Americans should not be taxed for school purposes.

• An Ohio law transferred control of the African American public schools to managers of the European American school system.

• *Miscellaneous Cases:* In the Pennsylvania case of *Foremans v. Tamm*, Tamm, a free African American who had settled on a piece of land and gained title by preemption, sought redress when Foremans, a European American, evicted him. The court held that, although African Americans were without political rights, they did have civil rights and among those civil rights was the right to acquire land by preemption. Judgment, therefore, was for Tamm.

• Anne Douglass, a European American woman from South Carolina, was imprisoned in Norfolk, Virginia, for violating a state law against instruction of African Americans.

• *Publications:* William Wells Brown published *Clotel, or the President's Daughter, A Narrative of Slave Life in the United States,* the first novel by an African American.

Clotel, or the President's Daughter was basically an abolitionist book which told the story of the "mythic" illegitimate daughter of Thomas Jefferson. In the story, Clotel tries to escape slavery but is killed, ironically within the sight of her father's (Jefferson's) house. Much of the text of the book was given over to a detailed description of the "peculiar institution" of slavery of which Brown had firsthand experience.

Because of its content, the *Clotel* was first published in London, England. When *Clotel* was published in the United States in 1867, the story was altered. In the place of Jefferson, an anonymous senator became Clotel's father. *See 1773: Sally Hemings.*

• Frederick Douglass published "The Heroic Slave," a short story based on the real life exploits of Madison Washington, a recaptured escaped slave, who took the lead in seizing the ship on which he was being sent to be sold from Virginia to Louisiana, and regained his freedom by sailing the vessel to Nassau.

• Solomon Northrup's *Narrative of a Slave* (also known as *12 Years a Slave*), one of the most famous of the many narratives written by fugitive slaves, was published.

• *Scholastic Achievements:* Alexander Crummell, an African American Episcopal priest, earned a degree from Queens College, Cambridge University in England. Crummell subsequently went to Liberia.

• In 1853, the board of education of the city and county of New York took over the European American and African American schools of the Public School Society; a Normal School for African American teachers was established; and attendance in African American schools was 2,047.

• *The Black Church:* The Episcopal Convention of the New York Diocese voted to admit representatives from St. Phillip's Episcopal Church (an African American church) after a seven-year battle led by John Jay, a grandson of the first chief justice of the United States Supreme Court.

• *The Arts:* Elizabeth Taylor Greenfield, the African American singer known as the "Black Swan," gave a command performance before Queen Victoria (May 10).

• By 1853, most Southern cities had African American bands, and military parades were usually accompanied by an African American brass band. These bands were composed of free African Americans and house slaves who played European march music in imitation of European American concert bands. However, after the Civil War, when the former field slaves were allowed to join these bands, certain African influences began to be incorporated into the music. These influences would greatly affect the development of such American musical inventions as jazz and rhythm and blues.

THE AMERICAS

• Mary Ann Shadd Cary published the *Provincial Freeman,* a Canadian newspaper published for those African Americans who had fled the United States for Canada after the passage of the Fugitive Slave Law of 1850.

AFRICA

• Leopold of Belgium visited Egypt.
• A British consulate was established in Lagos (Nigeria).
• Ras Kassa (Emperor Theodore of Ethiopia) conquered Gojjam, Begember, Tigrai (Tigre) and Shoa.
• David Livingstone began his trans–Africa expedition.
• Kigeri IV Rwabugiri, the "Mwami" (the king) of Rwanda, came to power. During his reign, the modern-day boundaries of Rwanda would be established.

EUROPE

• By 1853, Portuguese officials had received 2,850,965 pounds in bribes from the British government in an effort to halt the slave trade.

RELATED HISTORICAL EVENTS

• Cecil Rhodes (1853–1902), a British South African financier and statesman, was born.
• Vaccination against smallpox was made compulsory in England.

1854

THE UNITED STATES

The major event of 1854 was the debate concerning, and the enactment of, the Kansas-Nebraska Act. The Kansas-Nebraska Act was proposed by Senator Stephen Douglas of Illinois to encourage the rapid settlement of the West (what is today called the Midwest). As proposed, the act repealed the Missouri Compromise of 1820 which prohibited the establishment of slavery north of a specified line of latitude (36 degrees, 30 minutes). The act permitted slavery above this line by allowing "squatter or popular sovereignty" in Kansas and Nebraska.

The spread of slavery anticipated by the introduction of the Kansas-Nebraska Act, became a clarion call for those opposed to slavery. In Ripon, Wisconsin, lawyer Alvan Bovay proposed the name "Republican Party" for a new political party being organized to fight the spread of slavery as authorized under the Kansas-Nebraska Act (February 4). The Republican Party was created by Free Soilers and Whigs as well as Democrats who were opposed to the extension of slavery.

On May 30, 1854, the Kansas-Nebraska Act was passed. The act repealed the Missouri Compromise and opened Northern (Midwestern) territory to slavery.

On October 16, 1854, in Peoria, Illinois, a former Illinois congressman by the name of Abraham Lincoln made his first public statement in opposition to the extension of slavery in the new territories. In reference to the purpose of the Kansas-Nebraska Act, Lincoln said:

"This ... zeal for the spread of slavery, I cannot but hate. I hate it because of the monstrous injustice of slavery itself. I hate it because it deprives our republican example of its just influence in the world — enables the enemies of free institutions, with plausibility, to taunt us as hypocrites — causes the real friends of freedom to doubt our sincerity, and especially because it forces so many really good men amongst ourselves into an open war with the very fundamental principles of civil liberty — criticizing the Declaration of Independence, and insisting that there is no right principle of action but *self-interest*.

Before proceeding, let me say I think I have no prejudice against the Southern people. They are just what we would be in their situation. If slavery did not now exist amongst them, they would not introduce it. If it did now exist amongst us, we should not instantly give it up. This I believe of the masses north and south. Doubtless there are individuals, on both sides, who would not hold slaves under any circumstances; and others who would gladly introduce slavery anew, if it were out of existence. We know that some Southern men do free their slaves, go North, and become tip-top abolitionists; while some Northern ones go South, and become most cruel slavemasters.

When Southern people tell us they are no more responsible for the origin of slavery, than we; I acknowledge the fact. When it is said that the institution exists; and that it is very difficult to get rid of it, in any satisfactory way, I can understand and appreciate the saying. I surely will not blame them for not doing what I should not know how to do myself. If all earthly power were given me, I should not know what to do, as to the existing institution. My first impulse would be to free all the slaves, and send them to Liberia, — to their own native land. But a moment's reflection would convince me, that whatever of high hope, (as I think there

is) there may be in this, in the long run, its sudden execution is impossible. If they were all landed there in a day, they would all perish in the next ten days; and there are not surplus shipping and surplus money enough in the world to carry them there in many times ten days. What then? Free them all, and keep them among us as underlings? Is it quite certain that this betters their condition? I think I would not hold one in slavery, at any rate; yet the point is not clear enough for me to denounce people upon. What next? Free them all, and make them politically and socially, our equals? My own feelings will not admit of this; and if mine would, we well know that those of the great mass of white people will not. Whether this feeling accords with justice and sound judgment, is not the sole question, if indeed, it is any part of it. A universal feeling, whether well or ill-founded, cannot be safely disregarded. We cannot, then, make them equals. It does seem to me that systems of gradual emancipation might be adopted; but for their tardiness in this, I will not undertake to judge our brethren of the South.

The doctrine of self-government is right — absolutely and eternally right — but it has no just application, as here attempted. Or perhaps I should rather say that whether it has such just application depends upon whether a Negro is *not* or *is* a man. If he is *not* a man, why in that case, he who *is* a man may, as a matter of self-government, do just as he pleases with him. But if the Negro *is* a man, is it not to that extent, a total destruction of self-government, to say that he too shall not govern *himself*? When the white man governs himself this is self-government; but when he governs himself, and also governs *another* man, that is *more* than self-government — that is despotism. If the negro is a *man*, why then my ancient faith teaches me that "all men are created equal;" and that there can be no moral right in connection with one man's making a slave of another.

Slavery is founded in the selfishness of man's nature — opposition to it, is his love of justice. These principles are an eternal antagonism; and when brought into collision so fiercely, as slavery extension brings them, shocks, and throes, and convulsions must ceaselessly follow. Repeal the Missouri Compromise — repeal all compromises — repeal the Declaration of Independence — repeal all past history, you still cannot repeal human nature. It still will be the abundance of man's heart, that slavery extension is wrong; and out of the abundance of his heart, his mouth will continue to speak.

Near eighty years ago we began by declaring that all men are created equal; but now from that beginning we have run down to the other declaration, that for SOME men to enslave OTHERS is a "sacred right of self-government." These principles cannot stand together. They are as opposite as God and mammon; and whoever holds to one, must despise the other.

• Anthony Burns was returned to slavery in Virginia in spite of an attempt by Boston citizens to purchase his freedom for $1200 (June 3).

Anthony Burns, an escaped slave, was captured in Boston, Massachusetts. Despite an attempt by Boston citizens to free him, an escort of 2,000 United States soldiers accompanied Burns through the Boston streets. Burns was later freed, attended college and became a pastor of the Zion Baptist Church in Canada.

• John Mercer Langston was admitted to the Ohio State Bar. Langston's admission was based upon the assessment of the examination committee that Langston had more European blood than African. *See 1829.*
• The United Brothers of Friendship and Sisters of the Mysterious Ten, a benevolent and charitable organization composed of African Americans, was formed in Lexington, Kentucky.
• The Massachusetts Medical Society admitted John V. De Grasse, an African American, as a member of the society. During the Civil War, De Grasse would be one of the eight African Americans who were commissioned as surgeons in the United States Army.

Martin Robinson Delany, in reaction to the Kansas-Nebraska Act, issued a call for a National Emigration Convention.

The convention was held in Cleveland, Ohio, in August. Delegates from eleven states attended what was officially called the National Emigration Convention of the Colored People. Most of these delegates were from Ohio and Pennsylvania. The conveners advocated the establishment of an African American colony with nationalistic aspirations. Another rationale for the creation of this colony would be to escape the racial oppression experienced by so many African Americans.

James Theodore Holly was an instrumental force in organizing this convention and, in the aftermath of the convention, Holly led a group of African Americans who decided to emigrate to Haiti. *See 1812 and 1829.*

• In Ohio, the state Senate expelled an African American editor from his seat in the reporters' section on the grounds that the laws of nature required a strict separation of the races.
• Martin Robinson Delany, the black nationalist associated with the National Emigration Convention who also happened to be a graduate of the Harvard Medical School, distinguished himself for his work during a cholera epidemic in Pittsburgh. *See 1812.*
• *The Abolition Movement:* In April of 1854, antislavery forces organized the New England Emigration Aid Society to settle "free-soilers" in Kansas.
• *Notable Births:* James Bland, a popular African American songwriter, was born.

James Bland (1854–1911) was born of free parents in Flushing, New York. His father, Allen M. Bland, was a college graduate and an examiner in the United States Patent Office.

Bland was educated at Howard University. During his career, Bland wrote over 600 popular songs, among them *Carry Me Back to Ole Virginny*; *Oh, Dem Golden Slippers*; and *In the Evening by the Moonlight.*

• Lucey C. Laney, founder of Haines Institute in Augusta, Georgia, was born (April 13).
• Nat Love (also known as Deadwood Dick) (1854–1921) was born a slave in a log cabin in Davidson County, Tennessee.
• Augustus Tolon, one of the first African American Catholic priests to serve in the United States, was born in Battle Creek, Missouri (April 1).
• *Miscellaneous State Laws:* Connecticut law provided for punishment by fine or imprisonment for falsely and maliciously seizing a free person with the intent to enslave him.
• Rhode Island law forbade state officials from enforcing the 1850 Federal Fugitive Slave Law.
• Vermont law provided penalties of fine and imprisonment for attempting to kidnap a free person to remove him from the state as a slave.
• *Miscellaneous Cases:* An African American woman was dragged out of her seat while protesting the segregated seating on the New York City street cars. The woman took her case to court. One of her attorneys was Chester Arthur, the future President of the United States. The woman won her suit and street car segregation was ended.
• *Publications:* Francis Ellen Harper published *Poems on Miscellaneous Subjects. See 1825.*

• *Scholastic Achievements:* Lincoln University, the first African American college, was chartered as Ashmun Institute in Chester, Pennsylvania (January 1). Ashmun Institute was founded by Presbyterians.

• James Theodore Holly was appointed to the post of public school principal in Buffalo, New York. *See 1829.*

• The *New Bern Atlantic*, of North Carolina, complained of the "notorious fact" that day schools were being operated for the benefit of free African Americans in the town.

• In Norfolk, Virginia, a European American woman was found to be conducting a school for African Americans in defiance of state law.

• The first school for African American children in San Francisco, California, was started in the basement of the St. Cyprian African Methodist Episcopal Church. This school had an enrollment of 23 pupils.

• *The Black Church:* James Augustine Healy was ordained a priest in Paris, France. *See 1830.*

The Healy family was one of the most distinguished families in African American history. In addition to James Healy, two other Healy brothers became ordained Catholic priests: Alexander Sherwood Healy was ordained for the diocese of Massachusetts while Patrick Francis Healy (*see 1834*) became a Jesuit. One of their sisters, Eliza became a nun (Sister Mary Magdalen) and a notable school head, and another brother, Michael Alexander Healy (*see 1839*), became a captain in the United States Revenue Cutter Service, the forerunner to the United States Coast Guard.

The three Healy brothers, James, Patrick and Michael would leave the most indelible marks. James would ascend the Catholic faith hierarchy to become the bishop of Portland, Maine. Patrick would earn a Ph.D. from Louvain University in Belgium and would eventually become the president of Georgetown University. Michael, while serving in the Revenue Cutter Service, would become the de facto chief law enforcement officer in the coastal waters of Alaska. As such, Michael would serve as the model for Jack London's *Sea Wolf* (see also James Michener's *Alaska*).

The factors contributing to the Healys' success was their acknowledgement by their European American father and the relative acceptability afforded to them due to the color of their skin. The Healys were born to an Irish planter (Michael Morris Healy) and a mulatto slave (Mary Eliza Smith) on the Healy plantation near Macon, Georgia. Unlike other plantation owners, Michael Morris Healy genuinely cared for his mulatto children and took pains to see that they received an education. This care and education enabled the Healys to attain a measure of success.

The other reason for the Healys' success was the fact that the color of their skin was more European in appearance than African. While the racial identity of the Healys was not concealed, neither was it widely broadcast. Their fair skinned appearance no doubt contributed in no small measure to the Healys' ability to attain a measure of success which was uncommon for their darker-skinned contemporaries.

• The first school for African American children in San Francisco, California, was started in the basement of the St. Cyprian African Methodist Episcopal Church. This school had an enrollment of 23 pupils.

THE AMERICAS

• Venezuela abolished slavery.
• Jose Do Patrocino, an Afro-Brazilian abolitionist, was born.

Jose Do Patrocino (1854–1905), the son of a priest and an Afro-Brazilian vegetable peddler, was very sympathetic toward slaves from early childhood. He spent his later life as an abolitionist.

In 1877, Do Patrocino published *Motta Coquiero. Motta Coquiero* was a story concerning the murder of a plantation owner as retaliation for a murder he did not commit. Its importance lies in the careful examination of racial tensions and conflicts on a plantation in Brazil among Euro-Brazilians, Afro-Brazilians, and mulattoes.

• Juan Francisco Manzano, the Afro-Cuban poet, died. *See 1797.*

AFRICA

• Abbas I of Egypt was assassinated. He was succeeded by Muhammed Said.
• Louis L. Faidherbe (1818–1889) was appointed the French governor of the French Senegalese settlements.
• Ferdinand de Lesseps was granted a concession to build the Suez Canal.
• Al-Hajj Umar initiated a jihad and seized Bambouk.

Al-Hajj Umar (c. 1794–1864) was a Muslim theologian, political reformer and military leader. He is credited with founding the Tukolor Empire of West Africa and with initiating one of the major West African Islamic revolutionary movements of the 1800s.

• At the convention of Bloemfontein, the Orange Free State was constituted.

1855

THE UNITED STATES

• The New York Liberty Party nominated Frederick Douglass for New York secretary of state, the first time an African American was nominated for a state office.

• A Captain Fountain smuggled 21 slaves out of Norfolk, Virginia, and brought them to freedom in Philadelphia. The slaves were concealed in a cargo of grain in the holds of his ship.

• In a memorial, a group of North Carolina citizens asked the state legislature to authorize the education of African Americans, to allow slaves to marry, and to prohibit the forced separation of slave families.

• As an indictment against the notion that gradual emancipation might eradicate the problem of slavery, it was reported that between 1791 and 1855 the General Assembly of North Carolina had passed 37 acts of emancipation which altogether freed a total of 98 African Americans.

• John Mercer Langston (1829–1897) became the first African American on record to win an elective office when he became town clerk of Brownhelm, Ohio.

• Brigham Young declared that one drop of African blood prevented a man from entering the Mormon priesthood. This edict created a clear distinction between the European American and African American male members of the faith. *See 1827.*

• African Americans in Cincinnati, Ohio, formed the "Attucks Guards," an African American militia.

• *The Abolition Movement:* Frederick Douglass and fellow African American, James McCune Smith, along with Lewis Tappan and Gerrit Smith, called a convention of Radical Political Abolitionists at Syracuse, New York. James McCune Smith presided over the convention. The next year the Political Abolition Party nominated Gerrit Smith for President of the United States and Samuel McFarland for Vice-President.

• *The Civil Rights Movement:* The first convention of California African Americans was held in the Colored Methodist Church of Sacramento in November. Forty-nine delegates attended the gathering. The chairperson for the convention was William

H. Yates of San Francisco. During the convention, the delegates protested against the exclusion of African Americans as witnesses in court against European Americans, and claimed that the approximately 6,000 California African Americans had a combined capital estimated to be 3 million dollars.

• New York African Americans formed a legal rights association and employed Chester A. Arthur and others to defend some of their members who had deliberately violated the segregation rules on public transportation in New York City. The Legal Rights Association was successful in winning a case in which an African American woman was awarded damages for being expelled from a segregated railroad car.

• The Reverend James W. C. Pennington (*see 1809*) of New York refused to leave the Sixth Avenue horsecar in New York City when he was requested to do so. Pennington was thrown off the car. He subsequently sued the horsecar company and won.

• African Americans in New York established the State Suffrage Association to work for the amendment of the New York Constitution to enable African Americans to obtain the right to vote.

• *The Labor Movement:* In 1855, 87% of all gainfully employed African Americans in New York City worked in menial or unskilled jobs. Thus, when European American longshoremen struck to protest wage cuts and attacks on their union, African Americans were recruited to serve as strikebreakers. At Morgan's London Line docks the Irish longshoremen fled when it was discovered that an African American worker was armed. Within a few months, the old workers came back, replacing almost all of the strikebreakers.

• *Miscellaneous State Laws:* Maine, Massachusetts and Michigan passed "personal liberty" laws which prohibited state officials from aiding in the enforcement of the Fugitive Slave laws of 1793 and 1850.

• On April 28, 1855, segregation in Massachusetts schools was abolished by law. The following September, Boston schools were integrated with no incident.

• *Publications:* William Wells Brown published *The American Fugitive in Europe: Sketches of Places and People Abroad,* a revised version of Brown's *Three Years in Europe: or Places I Have Seen and People I Have Met* which was published in 1852. *See 1816.*

• William Cooper Nell published *Colored Patriots of the American Revolution. See 1816.*

• Frederick Douglass published *My Bondage and My Freedom. See 1817.*

• The *Herald of Freedom,* an African American publication, commenced publication in Ohio with Peter H. Clark as editor.

• Mifflin Wistar Gibbs (1823–1915), an African American, established *Mirror of the Times,* an abolitionist newspaper, in San Francisco, California.

• *Scholastic Achievements:* In 1855, there were 3,000 African American children between four and seventeen years of age in New York City, of whom 913 attended public schools, 240 attended an African American orphan asylum school, and 125 attended private schools. In this same year, there were 159,000 European American children between the ages of four and seventeen, of whom 43,858 attended public schools, 2,826 attended public corporate schools, and 17,560 attended private schools. The average attendance was about the same for both groups. However, the proportion of African Americans to European Americans in public schools was about 1 to 40. The money spent by the board of education on school building and sites for African Americans and for European Americans was about $1,000 for African Americans to $1.6 million for European Americans.

• On April 28, 1855, segregation in Massachusetts schools was abolished by law. In September of 1855, Boston schools were integrated with no incident.

• *The Sciences:* By 1855, the system of steam evaporation which was developed by Norbert Rillieux was installed in all the sugar refineries in the southern United States, Cuba, and Mexico. *See 1806.*

• *Black Enterprise:* In 1855, the per capita ownership of property by Ohio African Americans compared favorably with that of Ohio European Americans. African Americans in Cincinnati owned $800,000 worth of property, and in the whole state they owned $5,000,000 worth of property.

• In Philadelphia, African Americans owned $2,655,693 in real and personal property. They paid $9,766.42 in taxes in 1855. 19,000 African Americans owned real property valued at $800,000. By 1855, African Americans had incorporated 108 mutual benefit societies with 9,762 members, and had deposited $28,366 in Philadelphia banks.

THE AMERICAS

• Mary Ann Shadd Cary (1823–1893) became a corresponding member of the African American (and Afro-Canadian) convention movement.

AFRICA

• An Egyptian outpost was set up at Fashoda to monitor the slave trade.

• Ras Kassa was crowned Emperor Theodore II of Ethiopia.

• Beginning in 1855, the first of the Soninki-Marabout wars erupted in Gambia.

Today the Soninki (Soninke) are a people who reside in Mali but because of a Soninki diaspora, the Soninki can be found throughout West and Central Africa.

During the precolonial period, the Soninki accumulated wealth because of their proximity to the desert trade route from North Africa. The Soninki were known for trading salt and cattle for cereals. The Soninki also traded in slaves and were major suppliers of the Atlantic slave trade in the 1700s.

RELATED HISTORICAL EVENTS

• The British attempted to curtail the Arab-controlled East African slave trade by negotiating an agreement with the shah of Persia.

1856

THE UNITED STATES

In 1856, the nation's attention turned towards the upcoming Presidential election and the debate over the issue of slavery. In this year, the Republican Party was formally organized. The Republican Party included members of the Whig and Democratic parties committed to a free-soil policy in the West (today's Midwest). The South interpreted the policy of the Republican Party as being abolitionist.

In Kansas, proslavery groups tried to discourage settlement by "free-soil" advocates. A proslavery group attacked the town of Lawrence. In retaliation, an antislavery band led by John Brown avenged the attack on Lawrence by a military action which came to be known as the massacre of Pottawatomie Creek.

The mounting hostility between proslavery and antislavery factions even reached the hallowed halls of the United States Senate. In 1856, Senator Charles Sumner of Massachusetts was beaten to insensibility in the Senate chambers by Representative Brooks of South Carolina after Sumner severely criticized slavery and the legislators who favored it.

• In 1856, a fair price of a healthy thirty year old African American woman with a child was between $700 and $800. A fertile

African American woman of child bearing age was worth one-sixth to one-quarter more than a woman who was unable to conceive.

• In 1856, mining companies sometimes owned slaves, but in general hired them from their owners for $120 to $200 per year.

In 1856, a truly tragic incident occurred which dramatized the desperation the institution of slavery sometimes created within the minds of the slaves. In this year, in Ohio, a certain Margaret Garner, an escaped Kentucky slave, attempted to kill her children to keep them from being recaptured and returned to slavery. Garner succeeded in killing one of her children, but she and the others were captured and were shipped back to Kentucky. While en route to Kentucky, Garner unsuccessfully tried to drown herself and another child in the river.

For all too many slaves, death was a preferable alternative to slavery.

• In 1856, United States Attorney General Caleb Cushing declared that African Americans did not have the right to apply for benefits under the Land Preemption Act of 1841. *See 1853: Foremans v. Tamm.*

• The Galilean Fishermen, a secret organization, was founded by African Americans in Baltimore.

• A poem by William J Grayson (consisting of over 1,600 lines) was published. Grayson's poem was perhaps the best expression by a Southerner of the Greek Ideal. As perceived by Grayson (and as by many of his Southern contemporaries), slavery allowed for the development of a humane and cultivated society—a society akin to the Golden Age of Greece.

• *The Abolition Movement:* By 1856, there were said to be 47,240 members of the Knights of Liberty, a secret and militant organization formed by African Americans to free the slaves. *See 1846.*

• *The Civil Rights Movement:* The Proceedings of the State Convention of Colored Citizens of the State of Illinois reported the formation by African Americans of the Repeal Association to work for the revocation of the state "black laws."

• *Notable Births:* Timothy Thomas Fortune, an African American newspaperman, was born.

Timothy Thomas Fortune (1856–1928) was born in Marianna, Florida. During Reconstruction, Fortune's father became a state legislator. It is believed that through his father, Fortune met a European American congressman by the name of William J. Purman. Purman was able to secure Fortune a position as a customs inspector in Delaware.

While serving as a customs inspector in Delaware, Fortune also attended Howard University. Upon his graduation in 1881, Fortune went to New York and a year later became editor of the New York *Globe*, an African American weekly. In 1884, Fortune moved to the New York *Freeman*, and later in the year, Fortune published *Land, Labor and Politics in the South.*

In 1885, Fortune published *The Negro in Politics.*

Fortune was an advocate of full equality for African Americans. In 1887, he formed the Afro-American League which worked for full civil rights for African Americans, including the right to vote, an antilynching bill and the equitable distribution of school funds. By 1890, the Afro-American League had representatives in 21 states.

During the 1890's, Fortune became a follower of Booker T. Washington. Fortune edited the *New York Age*, a pro-(Booker T.) Washington publication. Fortune also performed a number of "ghost writing" and public relations functions for Mrs. Booker T. Washington.

While a follower of Booker T. Washington, Fortune maintained tight control over his Afro-American League. He turned aside the efforts of Monroe Trotter and George Forbes to reestablish the league's early egalitarian militancy. Although Fortune helped Booker T. Washington to write Washington's autobiography, Washington began to distance himself from Fortune. Booker T. objected to Fortune's vehement attacks on Trotter and Forbes and frowned upon Fortune's addiction to alcohol.

In 1914, Fortune established the Washington *Sun.* Until a short time before his death in 1928, Fortune directed the publication of *The Negro World*, the house organ of Marcus Garvey's Universal Negro Improvement Association.

• Booker T. Washington, the prominent civil rights leader, was born a slave in Franklin County, Virginia (April 5).

Booker Taliaferro Washington (1856–1915) was the most prominent African American leader of his era. He was born a slave on a plantation in Franklin County, Virginia.

After the Civil War, Washington went to West Virginia and worked in the coal mines. However, while working in the mines, Washington attended night school.

In 1872, Washington enrolled in Hampton

Institute in Virginia. He arrived at Hampton by foot after walking for almost 500 miles.

Washington worked his way through Hampton Institute as a janitor and graduated in 1875. He taught for a brief period in Malden, West Virginia, and then went to Wayland Seminary in Washington, D.C. After his stay at Wayland, he became an instructor at Hampton Institute.

In 1881, Washington was chosen to organize a school for African Americans at Tuskegee, Alabama. To finance this undertaking, Washington was budgeted $2,000. Despite the lack of funds, Washington was able to rapidly develop Tuskegee. At Tuskegee, Washington emphasized industrial training for African Americans. In the first two decades of Tuskegee Institute, over 40 buildings were erected on the campus—most of these were erected by the students themselves.

Washington was an extremely powerful and effective public speaker. He lectured throughout the United States and Europe. In his lectures, Washington stressed that African Americans should not be strident in their struggle for political and social rights. His emphasis on African American quiescence met with a receptive audience in the United States. Booker T. Washington soon became the principal African American spokesman.

Washington summarized his position on the African American's quest for equality in his famous opening speech at the Cotton States Exposition, held in Atlanta, Georgia, in 1895. In this speech, Washington advised African Americans to "cast down your bucket where you are." By this he meant that African Americans should accommodate themselves to the inequities and injustices that prevailed in the South and focus their energies on improving their economic prospects. In Washington's mind, the European American Southerner was the "friend" of the African American and that if African Americans would just concentrate on their economic pursuits, conditions throughout the South, for whites and for blacks, would improve.

Washington's position of placating the powers that be brought him into odds with more militant African Americans such as W. E. B. Du-Bois. However, because his position on racial issues was appealing to European Americans in both the North and the South, Washington was soon cast in the role as the national spokesman for African American causes.

One of Washington's most enduring legacies was his emphasis on economic self-reliance. In 1900, he organized the National Negro Business League.

In 1901, Washington published his classic autobiography, *Up From Slavery*. He also published *The Future of the American Negro* (1899), *Character Building* (1902), *Working With the Hands* (1904), *Tuskegee and Its People* (1905), *Putting the Most into Life* (1906), *Life of Frederick Douglass* (1907), *The Negro in Business* (1907), *The Story of the Negro* (1909), *My Larger Education* (1911), and *The Man Farthest Down; a Record of Observation and Study in Europe* (1912).

• Granville T. Woods, inventor of industrial appliances, was born (April 23).

Granville T. Woods (1856–1910) developed an egg incubator, a system of telegraphing from moving trains, and improvements in electric railways and the phonograph. General Electric and Bell telephone purchased many of his inventions. However, Woods also marketed some of his own inventions through his own company.

• *Miscellaneous State Laws:* Under Virginia law, African Americans were entitled to the right to enslave themselves. By submitting a petition to the legislature, an individual African American could choose his or her own owner. The owner would only be required to pay the court one-half the valuation of the slave.

• Another Virginia law prohibited the selling of poisonous drugs to free African Americans or slaves.

• *Miscellaneous Cases:* In Indiana, an African American man was convicted for violating the state's African American exclusion law by bringing an African American woman into the state in order to marry her. The conviction was upheld in the State Supreme Court.

• In New York, a jury refused to find against a railroad company for expelling an African American minister from a railroad car. The jury's decision was based on the grounds that common carriers were not required to carry persons when it would adversely affect their interests.

• In the Bladen and Robeson counties of North Carolina, maroons (escaped slaves) terrorized the countryside.

• *Publications:* Elymas Rogers, an African American Presbyterian minister, wrote a satire in verse, *The Repeal of the Missouri Compromise Considered.* The author feared that Massachusetts would be forced to obey the Fugitive Slave Law. The poem was filled with references to incidents such as the Brooks-Sumner scandal dealing with the slavery question.

• George Vashon published *Autographs of Freedom* which contained the famous poem *Vincent Oge*. *Vincent Oge* is a romantic narrative about a real life mulatto hero of the Haitian Revolution. This poem is one of the best examples of antislavery poetry. *See 1820.*

• William Wells Brown published *Experience, or How to Give a Northern Man a Backbone,* a dramatic work.

• *Scholastic Achievements:* Wilberforce University was founded by the Methodist Episcopal Church (August 30). Four African Americans, Alfred J. Anderson, the Reverend Louis Woodson, Ishmael Keith and Bishop Daniel Payne *(see 1811)*, and 20 European American men were on the original board of trustees.

• In Kentucky, Berea College was founded. Berea College followed a policy of integration until 1907 when the United States Supreme Court upheld a Kentucky law of 1904 which required segregation of the races.

• On April 28, 1855, segregation in Massachusetts schools was abolished by law. In September of 1855, Boston schools were integrated with no incident.

• In Ohio, African Americans were given control over their schools.

• *Black Enterprise:* African Americans in New England had an estimated $2 million invested in business, not including agriculture, according to a report of the National Convention of Colored Americans in Philadelphia. African Americans in Ohio, Illinois, and Michigan had $1.5 million invested, and, in New York and Pennsylvania, African Americans had $3 million invested. By 1856, African Americans in New York City had $600,000 deposited in savings banks.

AFRICA

• The Cairo-Alexandria railway was completed.

• Sayyid (Seyyid) Said of Zanzibar died. He was succeeded by Sayyid (Seyyid) Majid.

• Pretoria was made the capital of Transvaal.

• The South African Republic was established with Marthinius Pretorius as its first president.

• Natal was chartered as a Crown colony and Indian indentured labor was sought to serve the colony.

• Arab traders reached Urua (in the Shaba region of Zaire).

• In 1856, Joseph Jenkins Roberts was elected the first president of the new College of Liberia. *See 1809.*

RELATED HISTORICAL EVENTS

• The British attempted to curtail the Arab-controlled East African slave trade by negotiating an agreement with the Persian Gulf sheiks and the kings of Somalia.

--------------- 1 8 5 7 ---------------

THE UNITED STATES

The United States Supreme Court declared that Dred Scott, a slave, could not sue for his freedom even though he had been brought into territory where slavery was outlawed, because as a slave he was property and had no right to sue in any circumstance. The court ruling also invalidated the Missouri Compromise, upsetting a delicate balance which had kept peace between free and slave states since 1820. The Dred Scott decision (written by Chief Justice Roger Taney) essentially opened federal territory to slavery and denied citizenship to African Americans (March 6).

Dred Scott and his family were eventually freed by their new owner, Taylor Blow (May 26).

In the wake of the Dred Scott decision, the commissioner of the United States General Land Office announced that since African Americans were not citizens, they could not qualify for public land grants in the West.

In response to these pronouncements, African Americans convened in Philadelphia to denounce the decision. While in Cleveland, the second National Emigration Convention was convened. *See 1812 and 1829.*

As for the South, at the Knoxville Southern Commercial Convention, Edward Bryan of South Carolina presented a motion to annul Article 8 of the Webster-Ashburton Treaty of 1843 in which the United States and Great Britain had agreed to maintain ships off the African coast to suppress the slave trade. The motion was approved 66 to 26, with only delegates from Maryland, North Carolina and Tennessee dissenting.

• *The Civil Rights Movement:* Mifflin Gibbs and John Lester, African American proprietors of a store in San Francisco, protested in an open letter that the tax collector had come to their store and carted off $20 to $30 worth of goods because they had refused to pay a California poll tax on the grounds that they were not allowed to vote and, therefore, should not be compelled to pay a poll tax.

• *Notable Births*: Henry Plummer Cheatham, an African American and a member of Congress, was born.

Henry Plummer Cheatham (1857–1935) was born in Henderson, North Carolina. Cheatham studied law after receiving a bachelor of arts (B.A.) and a master of arts (M.A.) from Shaw University.

Cheatham served as the register of deeds in Vance County from 1884 to 1888 and became principal of the Plymouth State Normal School in 1888.

Cheatham was elected to the House of Representatives twice as a Republican from North Carolina. President McKinley subsequently appointed Cheatham recorder of deeds in Washington, D. C.

From 1901 until his death, Cheatham worked for, and supervised, an African American orphanage in North Carolina.

Miscellaneous State Laws: In the aftermath of the Dred Scott decision, a number of state legislatures passed measures to address the issue of slavery within state boundaries.

In New Hampshire, a state law declared that African descent, previous servitude or color of skin would not serve as disqualifiers for attaining the full rights of citizenship within the state. Additionally, any slave brought in the state by his owner was to be set free, and that the holding of any person as a slave was punishable as a felony (hard labor from one to five years).

In Maine, a law was passed which declared that all slaves brought by their owners into the state were free.

In Ohio, a "personal liberty" law was passed which prohibited the use of the state jails to hold fugitive (escaped) slaves. [This law would be repealed in 1858.]

In Oregon, a clause in the Oregon Constitution which prohibited any further admission of African Americans into the state was ratified by an 8 to 1 majority of the popular vote.

In Wisconsin, African Americans petitioned the state legislature for the right to vote.

Tennessee enacted a law which facilitated the reenslavement of free African Americans.

• *Publications:* James Theodore Holly published A *Vindication of the Capacity of the Negro Race for Self-Government and Civilized Progress*, a lecture based on the history of Haiti. *See* 1829.

• Hinton R. Helper's book, *The Impending Crisis*, was published. Helper, a North Carolina European American, argued that slavery had caused much of the disparity between the economic growth of the North and the South. Almost a million copies of the book were sold.

• Franklin Webb, published (in London) *The Garies and their Friends*. Webb was a member of the free African American population of Philadelphia. Consequently, Webb's concerns were not so much on the issue of slavery but rather with regard to racial discrimination. In *The Garies and their Friends*, Webb dealt with what he perceived to be a caste system which prevented African Americans from advancing themselves economically. The novel also dealt with interracial marriages and job discrimination.

• *Scholastic Achievements:* The New York Society for the Promotion of Education Among Colored Children appealed to a commission appointed by the governor to investigate the city's schools for an improvement of African American education. Charles B. Ray (*see* 1807) was president of the society, and Philip A. White was secretary.

• Wilberforce University awarded its first baccalaureate degree.

• *Black Enterprise:* New York City African Americans paid taxes on real estate worth $1,400,000. The value of the African American churches in the city was $250,000; they had $1,121,000 deposited in savings banks and personal property worth $710,000.

• A free African American in St. Paul's Parish, South Carolina, was said to have 200 slaves, a European American wife and a European American son-in-law.

AFRICA

• The French conquered Grand Kabylia (Algeria).

• The French occupied Dakar.

Today Dakar is the main port and capital of Senegal.

• Al-Hajj Umar besieged Medine.

• Pretorius invaded the Orange Free State. A truce was negotiated by Paul Kruger.

• The *Charles et Georges*, a French slaver, was captured by the Portuguese off the coast of Mozambique. The French filed a protest.

• Richard Burton and J. H. Speke reached Lake Tanganyika from Bagamoyo.

1858

THE UNITED STATES

1858 marked the emergence of Abraham Lincoln as a national figure.

In June, in his acceptance speech for the nomination for senator from Illinois, Lincoln stated:

> A house divided against itself cannot stand. I believe this government cannot endure permanently half *slave* and half *free*. I do not expect the Union to be *dissolved*. I do not expect the house to *fall*, but I *do* expect it will cease to be divided.

During his summer debates with Stephen Douglas (the author of the Kansas-Nebraska Act), Lincoln forced Douglas to alienate many of his Southern supporters with his "Freeport heresy"—a position propounded by Douglas which required popular sovereignty to determine the fate of slavery despite the unlimited right of slavery pronounced in the Dred Scott decision.

In September, during a debate with Douglas, Lincoln denied that he desired to create a political and social equality between African Americans and European Americans. He also adamantly opposed interracial marriage, the enfranchisement of African Americans, and African American political officials. Lincoln noted that

> there is a physical difference between the . . . races which I believe will forever forbid the two races living together on terms of equality.

Later, in October, Lincoln pronounced that the Republican Party was committed to the abolition of slavery. He said:

> We think it is a moral, a social and a political wrong. . . . On the other hand . . . there is a sentiment which treats it as not being wrong. That is the Democratic sentiment of this day.

• United States Attorney General Jeremiah S. Black ruled that a slave could not be granted a patent, on the grounds that a slave was not a citizen and could not enter into an agreement with the government. Neither could a slave assign his invention to his or her owner. For this reason, Jefferson Davis (the future president of the Confederacy) was unable to patent a boat propeller invented by his slave, Benjamin Montgomery. *See 1847: Isaiah Thornton Montgomery.*

• The third National Emigration Convention was held in Chatham, Ontario, Canada. At this convention, Martin Robinson Delany was chosen as the chief commissioner and was designated to explore the valley of the Niger as a possible site for African American emigration. *See 1812.*

• In 1858, a prime slave laborer sold for $800.

• At the Montgomery Convention of 1858, the Georgia delegate Kimbree's resolution to support the opening of the slave trade was rejected 71 to 3. Roger Pryor, editor of the *Richmond South*, expressed the attitude of the delegates when he called the resolution an expression of "an unworthy issue, . . . repugnant to the instincts of Southern chivalry." Although favoring secession if a Republican was elected, Pryor was opposed to secession solely for the purpose of kidnapping "cannibals from Africa." Similar resolutions were defeated by the legislatures of Alabama, Arkansas, Louisiana, Mississippi, South Carolina, and Texas.

• Congress' English bill, enacted in May, broke a deadlock over the acceptance or rejection of the Lecompton Constitution submitted by proslavery forces preparatory to the admission of Kansas as a state. The bill provided for resubmission of the constitution to a popular vote. The constitution was subsequently rejected by the people of Kansas, and Kansas did not become a state until January 1861.

• In Philadelphia, when streetcars were introduced, the street car company allowed African Americans to ride only on the front platform.

• Dr. John S. Rock made a speech in Boston in March. In this speech, Rock expressed his pride in his race. Rock was an abolitionist, a doctor, and the first African American lawyer admitted to practice before the United States Supreme Court.

• *The Abolition Movement:* John Brown rescued eleven slaves in Missouri and took them to Kansas. Upon leaving Kansas, Brown took these slaves to Canada and freedom.

• Twelve European Americans and thirty-four African Americans attended John Brown's antislavery convention in Chatham, Canada (May 8).

• *The Labor Movement:* The Association of Black Caulkers was organized in Baltimore, Maryland. It was one of the first African American labor organizations. It was organized to resist the efforts of European American workers to drive African Americans out of the caulking field (July).

• *Notable Births:* Charles W. Chestnutt, an

African American novelist, was born (June 20).

• Daniel Hale Williams, called the "Father of Negro Hospitals, was born in Hollidaysburg, Pennsylvania (January 18).

Daniel Hale Williams (1858–1931) while born in Hollidaysburg, Pennsylvania, was raised in Janesville, Wisconsin. In Janesville, Wisconsin, Williams was educated at Hare's Classical Academy and received a degree in medicine from Northwestern University in 1883.

Williams later became an anatomy lecturer at Northwestern and served for four years on the Illinois Board of Health. Having begun his medical practice in Chicago in 1883, Williams became concerned that hospitals discriminated against African Americans as interns and nurses. Through his efforts, Provident Hospital in 1891 was established, where African Americans could receive training in hospital work.

In 1893, Daniel Hale Williams conducted the first open-heart surgery under rather primitive conditions.

• *Miscellaneous State Laws:* The Lecompton Constitution, the Kansas Constitution which sanctioned slavery, was rejected by a popular vote of the people of Kansas (August 2).

• In Vermont, a law similar to the law passed in New Hampshire in 1857 was enacted. The Vermont law declared that African descent would not serve as a disqualification from citizenship of the state. The Vermont law freed any slave who entered the state, with or without permission of his master, and made holding another person as a slave punishable by one to fifteen years in prison and up to $2,000 in fines.

• Wisconsin and Kansas passed "personal liberty" laws.

• Ohio repealed its 1857 "personal liberty" law.

• Texas passed a law to facilitate the reenslavement of free African Americans.

• In Virginia, a free African American could not acquire a slave except "by descent" according to Virginia law.

• In California, a law was enacted which prohibited the immigration of additional African Americans or mulattoes into the state. This law would be repealed in 1859.

• A Maryland law prohibited free African Americans and slaves from having or using boats on the Potomac River.

• *Miscellaneous Cases:* In Ohio, 37 citizens of Oberlin and Wellington, Ohio, were indicted for rescuing John Rice who had been captured as a runaway slave by two kidnappers. Some of the defendants were imprisoned pending trial, but the sentences finally imposed were minimal.

• In the Virginia case of *Baily, et. al. v. Poindexter,* the court invalidated a will which allowed slaves to choose between emancipation and being sold at auction. The court invalidated the will because, as property, slaves had no legal capacity to choose.

• *Publications:* William Wells Brown published *The Escape,* the first play written by an African American.

• In 1849, Henson published *The Life of Josiah Henson, Formerly a Slave, Now an Inhabitant of Canada as Narrated by himself,* and in 1858 an enlarged edition appeared with an introduction by Harriet Beecher Stowe, under the title *Truth Stranger than Fiction, an Autobiography of the Rev. Josiah Henson. See 1789.*

• *Scholastic Achievements:* Two African American doctors were graduated from Berkshire Medical School.

• A free school for African Americans was opened in Washington, D.C. by the St. Vincent de Paul Society, an association of African American Catholics, under the direction of Father Walter.

• *The Black Church:* Francis Burns (1809–1863) was made a bishop in the Methodist Episcopal Church for his missionary work in Liberia. Burns was raised in Albany, New York. He served for twenty-four years in Liberia.

• *The Arts:* Thomas Greene Bethune ("Blind Tom") gained national fame as a child piano prodigy.

Thomas Greene Bethune (1849–1909) was born blind and a slave near Columbus, Georgia. His musical talents soon came to the fore and caught the attention of his owner, Colonel Bethune, who had purchased Tom in 1850.

In 1858, Blind Tom made his debut in Savannah, Georgia, and began a musical career that would span four decades.

Blind Tom was noted for his artistry and his ability to recall more than seven hundred piano pieces from memory. Over his career, it is said that he composed over one hundred musical pieces.

AFRICA

• John Hanning Speke (1827–1864) reached the southern end of Lake Victoria.

• Msiri established a trading station for ivory, copper and slaves in Katanga (Zaire).

• The Basuto, Batalpin, Bushmen and

Koranas invaded Transvaal. On September 29, the treaty of Aliwal North was signed which resulted in the Basuto boundaries being redrawn.

1859

THE UNITED STATES

1859 was the year which was dominated by the actions of John Brown.

In August, John Brown met with Frederick Douglass for the last time at an old quarry in Chambersburg, Pennsylvania (August 19).

In October, John Brown and 18 of his followers raided the Federal Arsenal at Harper's Ferry, Virginia (October 17). His purpose was to seize arms with which to free the slaves. A number of African Americans were with Brown. Lewis Sheridan Leary, Dangerfield Newby, John Anthony Copeland, Shields Green and Osborn Perry Anderson were part of Brown's band.

Cornered by a Colonel Robert E. Lee (who soon would have his own fame), an armed confrontation ensued. Osborn Perry Anderson managed to escape, but Lewis Sheridan Leary and Dangerfield Newby were killed while John Anthony Copeland and Shield Green along with John Brown himself were captured.

Brown was tried for his crimes. At his trial, Brown conducted himself bravely and intelligently. Northern efforts were made to have him declared insane, but he was convicted on charges of treason. On December 2, 1859, John Brown was hanged.

John Brown's actions may have ended in failure, but his gallantry in the face of death served to inspire other abolitionists and to aggravate the grievances between the North and the South which would lead to Civil War.

Of John Brown, Ralph Waldo Emerson would say that his death made the gallows "as glorious as a cross" and, during the Civil War, Union soldiers would sing:

> John Brown's body lies a-mouldering in
> the grave,
> But his soul goes marching on.

• In Vicksburg, Mississippi, those favoring the reopening of the slave trade organized the African Supply Association with J. D. B. DeBow as president.
• Rebecca Cox Jackson (1795–1871) established an African American Shaker family in Philadelphia.
• A slave ship, the *Clothilde*, landed its cargo of slaves at Mobile, Alabama.

Between 1859 and 1862, of the 170 American slave expeditions to Africa, 74 departed from New York.

• At the Vicksburg Southern Commercial Convention, a resolution demanding the reinstitution of the slave trade was adopted. Tennessee and Florida opposed the resolution. The delegations from South Carolina and Texas split their vote.
• Abraham Molineaux Hewlitt was named the director of physical culture at Harvard University.
• Martin Robinson Delany sailed to the Niger Valley to explore possible emigration sites for African American emigrants. Delany departed from New York aboard the *Mendi*, a vessel owned by three African merchants. *See 1812.*
• A slaveholders' convention in Baltimore refused to recommend the expulsion of free African Americans from Maryland, despite the protests of many that free African Americans were injuring the business of European American mechanics by monopolizing hotel labor and encroaching on barbering, coach businesses, etc. The majority felt that the labor of free African Americans was essential to the economy of the state. *See 1708.*
• The African Americans of Baltimore, Maryland, paid school taxes of $500. However, their children were excluded from the tax-supported schools.
• A Rhode Island bill to abolish segregation in schools failed by two votes.
• *Notable Births:* George Wylie Clinton, a bishop of the African Methodist Episcopal Zion Church, was born.

George Wylie Clinton (1859–1921) was born in Cedar Creek Township, Lancaster County, South Carolina. He was one of the first African Americans to enroll as a student at the University of South Carolina during the Reconstruction Era. Clinton attended the University of South Carolina from 1874 to 1877. However, Clinton was forced to leave the university in 1877 when legislation was passed which restricted the use of the university to European Americans.

Clinton taught school for 12 years. During this time, he also commenced his study of the law in the office of Allison and Connors in Lancaster County.

In 1879, Clinton was licensed as a preacher of the African Methodist Episcopal Zion Church. In association with his church activities, Clinton edited the *Afro-American Spokesman*. Clinton also helped to start the *Quarterly Review* of the African Methodist Episcopal Zion Church, and was editor of *The Star of Zion*.

In 1896, Clinton was consecrated a bishop of the African Methodist Episcopal Zion Church. Clinton participated in the Southern Sociological Congress, in the work of the Interracial Commission of the South, and also in the work of the Federal Council of the Churches of Christ in America.

• Henry O. Tanner, a world famous African American artist, was born in Pittsburgh, Pennsylvania (June 21).

Henry Ossawa Tanner (1859–1937) was born on June 21, 1859, in Pittsburgh, Pennsylvania. Henry was the son of Benjamin Tucker Tanner (*see 1835*), a bishop in the African Methodist Episcopal Church, and Sarah Tanner. His middle name Ossawa, was derived from Osawatomie, the town in Kansas where in 1856, John Brown launched his antislavery campaign. John Brown's heroic struggle symbolized for many African Americans their quest for freedom. Thus, for Benjamin and Sarah, Ossawa embodied the hope for emancipation.

Soon after Henry's first birthday, Benjamin Tanner was assigned by Bishop Daniel A. Payne (*see 1811*) of the African Methodist Episcopal Church to be a "supply and interim minister" at the prestigious Fifteenth Street Colored Presbyterian Church. The Tanners would remain in Washington for eighteen months.

After a series of posts near Washington, D.C., and in Maryland (and after the publication of Benjamin Tanner's *An Apology for African Methodism* in 1867), the family moved to Philadelphia in 1868. In Philadelphia, Benjamin Tanner became the editor of the African Methodist Episcopal Church's influential newspaper, the *Christian Recorder*. Benjamin Tanner would hold this position until 1884.

Upon his arrival in Philadelphia, Henry attended the Lombard Street School for Colored Students (later known as the James Forten School). He attended this school for two years. After the Lombard Street School, Henry attended the Roberts Vaux Consolidated School for Colored Students (later known as the Roberts Vaux Grammar School).

In 1872, while walking with his father in Fairmount Park, Henry observed an artist at work and became inspired to become a painter. In 1876, his first known work, *Harbor Scene*, was painted in Atlantic City.

In 1877, Henry graduated from the Roberts Vaux Grammar School with a class of ten.

Henry was valedictorian and delivered a valedictory address entitled "Compulsory Education." After his graduation, Henry was apprenticed to a family friend in the flour business, but, by 1878, after a severe illness, he gained his parents' consent to pursue an artistic career.

In 1879, Henry entered the Pennsylvania Academy of Fine Arts and studied under the famed artist, Thomas Eakins. Henry would remain a sporadic student of the academy until 1885.

From 1882 to 1888, Tanner lived with his parents in Philadelphia while working to establish himself in the art world. During this period, he managed to sell illustrations to New York publishers and his work was exhibited at the Pennsylvania Academy of the Fine Arts and the National Academy of Design in New York.

In 1889, Henry went to Atlanta, Georgia, where he worked as an illustrator, photogravure and art instructor at Clark University. In Atlanta, the patronage of Bishop and Mrs. Hartzell was instrumental in encouraging Tanner's belief in his own artistic abilities. It was the Hartzells who purchased a number of Henry's paintings thereby enabling him to go to Europe to study.

After arriving in Paris in 1891, Henry decided to remain in the city. In Paris, he enrolled in the Julien Academy. He would study there off and on for five years.

In 1893, Tanner returned to the United States to recover from a bout with typhoid fever. While in the United States, Tanner was invited to speak at the Congress on Africa which was held at the World's Columbian Exposition in Chicago, Illinois, in August of 1893. Tanner's experience at the congress brought on a racial awareness which had heretofore been lacking in Tanner's work. This increased racial awareness led to Tanner's painting *The Banjo Lesson* (1893), one of Tanner's most recognized pieces, and *The Thankful Poor* (1894) (a painting subsequently purchased by William and Camille Cosby for a record amount for an African American painting).

Henry Tanner's range of artistic subject matter was very broad. He was adept at painting portraits of African American plantation life, European peasant life, landscapes, animals, and Biblical events. In 1896, Tanner's *Daniel in the Lion's Den* (*Daniel dans la Fosse aux Lions*) received honorable mention at the Paris Salon. In 1897, *The Resurrection of Lazarus* (*La Resurrection de Lazare*) was awarded a medal at the

Paris Salon and was purchased by the French government for the Luxembourg Gallery.

In 1898, two events occurred which would have a significant impact on Henry Tanner's life and career. First, Henry traveled to the Holy Land. Second, Henry met his future wife, a European American named Jessie Macauley Olssen. They would marry in 1899 (December 14).

In 1900, Tanner received the Lippincott Prize from the Pennsylvania Academy of Fine Arts for his painting *Nicodemus Visiting Jesus*. Later in the same year, he received the Silver Medal at the Paris Exposition for a second showing of *Daniel in the Lion's Den*.

[*Daniel in the Lion's Den* would also win awards at the Pan-American Exposition in Buffalo (1901) and the Louisiana Purchase Exposition in St. Louis (1904).]

In 1906, Tanner's *Two Disciples at the Tomb* was awarded the Harris Prize by the Art Institute of Chicago for being the most distinguished work of the 1906 art season. The painting was purchased by the art institute and added to its permanent collection. Later in the year, *The Disciples at Emmaus* would be purchased by the French government for 4,000 francs and paired with *The Resurrection of Lazarus* at the Musee du Luxembourg.

In 1915, Tanner's *Christ at the Home of Lazarus* was awarded the gold medal at the Panama-Pacific Exposition which was held in San Francisco.

During World War I, Tanner worked for the American Red Cross in France as an ambulance driver.

In 1921, Tanner's work was shown at the first large all-African American art exhibition. The exhibition was held at the New York Public Library branch at 135th Street—a place now known as the Schomberg Center for Research in Black Culture.

In 1922, a group of African American artists in Washington D.C., established the Tanner Art League to promote African American art and artists.

In 1923, Tanner's father, Benjamin Tanner, died; Tanner was made a chevalier of the Legion of Honor, the highest recognition that the French government bestows on a nonmilitary person; and Tanner returned to the United States (for the last time) with an exhibition of his religious paintings.

On September 8, 1925, Tanner's wife, Jessie Macauley Olssen Tanner, died. The loss of Jessie was a severe blow to Tanner and his artistic career was never the same without her.

In 1927, Tanner was elected a full academician to the National Academy of Design in New York and his *Flight into Egypt (At the Gates)* was awarded a bronze medal at the National Arts Club in New York.

In 1930, Tanner's *Etaples Fisher Folk* was awarded the Walter L. Clark Prize at the Grand Central Art Galleries Members Prize Exhibition in New York.

Henry Ossawa Tanner, perhaps the greatest African American painter, died in his sleep on May 25, 1937, in Paris, France. His artistry paved the way for such African American artists as Romare Bearden, Hale Woodruff and Aaron Douglas.

• *Notable Deaths:* John Brown was hanged at Charles Town, West Virginia (December 2). *See above and 1800.*

• Samuel Cornish, one of the first men to approach the race problem from an economic point of view and one of the founders of *Freedom's Journal*, the first African American newspaper, died at the age of 69.

• *Miscellaneous State Laws:* Georgia law prohibited manumission by will or deed or other means after the death of the owner.

• Louisiana passed a law which facilitated the reenslavement of free African Americans.

• An Arkansas law required free African Americans and mulattoes either to leave the state by the end of the year, or to choose slave owners "who must give bond not to allow such (*African Americans*) to act as free."

• North Carolina prohibited the sale of alcoholic beverages to free African Americans except upon a written statement from a physician or a magistrate which indicated that the alcohol was necessary for medicinal purposes.

• Ohio law denied the right to vote to anyone with a "distinct and visible admixture of African blood." Before this, fair-skinned African Americans had been considered eligible to vote under Ohio law.

• In California, state law once again permitted African Americans to immigrate.

• *Miscellaneous Cases:* In the Ohio case of *Van Camp v. Board of Education of Logan, Ohio*, the court held that separate schools for African Americans were constitutional. The court also held that children who were three-eighths African and five-eighths European and who were regarded as African American in appearance could not attend European American schools. The previous color line had simply been one-half.

• In Philadelphia, a mulatto sued a streetcar company after being thrown off a street-car. He was given a nominal award and the case was appealed. In 1861, the District Court of Philadelphia ruled that a railroad company might lawfully refuse to allow African Americans on its cars.

• In Cincinnati, Ohio, a mulatto woman who was thrown off a street car by the conductor, brought an action for assault and battery—and won.

Publications: Karl Marx quoted in *Das Kapital* a report by the New York *Daily Tribune* of December 20, 1859, about a Grand Union demonstration held in New York under the slogan "Justice for the South." The main speaker was Charles O'Conor, head of the New York Bar Association, who said amid "thunderous applause":

> Now, gentlemen, to that condition of bondage the Negro is assigned by nature. . . . He has strength, and has the power to labor; but the hand which created him denied to him either the intellect to govern or the willingness to work. Both were denied to him. And this nature which deprived him of the will to labor, gave him a master to coerce that will, and to make him a useful and valuable servant . . . useful for himself and for the master who governs him. . . . I maintain that it is not injustice to leave the Negro in the condition in which nature placed him, to leave him in a state of bondage, and the master to govern him . . . nor is it depriving him of any of his rights to compel him to labor in return, and afford to that master just compensation for the labor and talent employed in governing him and rendering him useful to himself and to the society around him.

In addition, O'Conor said:

> It is the duty of the white man to treat him kindly and it is the interest of the white man to treat him kindly. It is not pretended that the master has a right to slay his slave. Why, we have not a right here in the North to be guilty of cruelty and inhumanity to our horses!

The Grand Union demonstration was supported by three former United States presidents and the mayor of New York.

• Perhaps as a reflection of the growing socialist mood, Martin Robinson Delany published "Blake, or the Huts of America" in the *Anglo-African* magazine. "Blake, or the Huts of America" ran in the magazine from January 1859 through July 1859. The serial

focused on slavery as an exploitative labor system. The story's hero tried to organize the slaves for a general insurrection throughout the South, and preached class solidarity. *See 1812.*

• Harriet E. Adams Wilson (c. 1827–1870) published a novel, *Our Nig; or, Sketches from the Life of a Free Black, In a Two Story White House North, Showing That Slavery's Shadows Fall Even There.* This novel depicted the social, racial, and economic oppression experienced by a mulatto woman living in the North.

• Frances Ellen Watkins Harper (1825–1911) wrote "The Two Offers," a short story which appeared in the *Anglo-African* magazine.

• The *Afro-American Magazine*, an African American literary magazine, began publication.

• The *Anglo-African*, an African American magazine began publication in New York.

• *Scholastic Achievements:* In 1859, 1,031 African Americans were enrolled in the public schools in Philadelphia while 331 were in private schools. Additionally, there were four evening schools; 19 African American Sunday schools with 1,667 pupils; and four Sunday schools run as missions of European American churches with 215 pupils.

• *The Black Church:* In 1859, George Bentley, an African American minister from Giles County, Tennessee, debated a European American minister on the principles of baptism. Bentley was deemed the victor in this debate. He would go on to preach to both European American and African American audiences.

• *The Arts and Sciences:* Roderick Badger, a free African American, practiced dentistry in Atlanta, Georgia.

• *Black Enterprise:* In 1859, 352 free African Americans in Charleston, South Carolina, paid taxes on $778,423 worth of real estate. 108 free African Americans owned 277 slaves and paid $12,342.02 in taxes on them.

• Samuel T. Wilcox, an African American who owned a grocery business in Cincinnati, had $59,000 worth of property. Wilcox's business made up to $140,000 per year during the 1850s.

• In Philadelphia, 1,700 African Americans were engaged in various trades and occupations.

• In New York City, African Americans owned real estate with an assessed value of $1,400,000. In addition, African Americans in Brooklyn owned property valued from 1 to 1.5 million dollars.

• *Institution Population:* The report of the

governors of the almshouses in New York City revealed that there were 67,998 European Americans and 2,006 African Americans in such public charitable institutions. As for the penal system in New York, there were 43,115 European Americans and 1,136 African Americans confined in the state's prisons.

AFRICA

• Construction on the Suez Canal began.
• Sayyid Majid of Zanzibar signed a trade treaty with the Hanseatic (German) cities.
• The first railway in the Cape colony was constructed.
• In Ethiopia, Consul Plowden was assassinated and John Bell was shot protecting Emperor Theodore.

1860

THE UNITED STATES

In 1860, the last census to include slaves was taken. In 1860, the United States census reported that there were 4,441,830 African Americans in the United States. This number represented 14.1% of the total population. Of the 4,441,830 African Americans, 3,953,760 were listed as slaves while 488,070 (11%) were designated as free.

In 1860, African Americans represented less than one percent (1%) of the total population of the following states: Maine, New Hampshire, Vermont, Massachusetts, Indiana, Illinois, Michigan, Wisconsin, Minnesota, Iowa, Nebraska, Kansas, Colorado, New Mexico, Utah, Nevada, Washington, and Oregon.

In 1860, African Americans were less than five percent (5%) of the total population of the following states: Rhode Island, Connecticut, New York, New Jersey, Pennsylvania, Ohio, and California.

The percentage of African Americans in the other states was as follows: Missouri (10%); Delaware (19.3%); Maryland (24.9%); Washington, D.C. (19.1%); Virginia (34.4%); North Carolina (36.4%); South Carolina (58.6%); Georgia (44.1%); Florida (44.6%); Kentucky (20.4%); Tennessee (25.5%); Alabama (45.4%); Mississippi (55.3%); Arkansas (25.6%); Louisiana (49.5%); and Texas (30.3%).

Ninety percent (90%) of all African Americans were born in the United States. Thirteen percent of these African Americans were visibly of part–European heritage (i.e., 13.2% of the total African American population were classified as mulattoes).

The number of free African Americans by state was: Maine (1,327); New Hampshire (494); Massachusetts (9,602); Rhode Island (3,952); Connecticut (8,627); Vermont (709); New York (49,005); New Jersey (25,318); Pennsylvania (56,949); Delaware (19,829); Maryland (83,942); Virginia (58,042); North Carolina (30,463); South Carolina (9,914); Minnesota (259); Iowa (1,069); Kansas (189); Georgia (3,500); Alabama (2,690); Mississippi (773); Louisiana (18,647); Tennessee (7,300); Kentucky (10,684); Ohio (36,673); Indiana (11,428); Illinois (7,628); Missouri (3,572); Michigan (6,799); Arkansas (144); Florida (932); Washington, D.C. (11,131); Oregon (128); California (4,086); and Texas (355).

In 1860, forty-four percent (44%) of all African Americans lived in the South where they comprised thirty-seven percent (37%) of the total population. Sixteen percent (16%) of all African Americans lived in urban areas.

Only 2,000,000 out of the 7,000,000 European Americans living in the South owned slaves, and only seven percent (7%) of the total population in the South owned nearly 3,000,000 of the 3,953,760 slaves.

• Two African Americans were selected as jurymen in Worcester, Massachusetts. This was the first record of jury service by African Americans in Massachusetts.
• Barney Ford, an escaped slave, arrived in Colorado. Ford became a successful businessman who is known for building the Inter-Ocean Hotel in Denver. He also became active in politics in the Colorado Territory.

On February 27, 1860, Abraham Lincoln delivered an address on slavery and the framers of the Constitution to an audience of 1,500 at Cooper Union in New York City. In the address Lincoln said:

Let all who believe that "our fathers, who framed the Government under which we live, understood this question [of slavery] just as well, and even better, than we do now," speak as they spoke, and act as they acted upon it. This is all Republicans ask — all Republicans desire — in relation to slavery. As those fathers marked it, so let it be again marked, as an evil not to be extended, but to be tolerated and protected only because of and so far as its actual presence among us makes that toleration and protection a necessity.

A few words now to Republicans. It is exceedingly desirable that all parts of this great Confederacy shall be at peace, and in harmony, one with another. Let us Republicans do our part to have it so. Even though much provoked, let us do nothing through passion and ill temper. Even though the southern people will not so listen to us, let us calmly consider their demands, and yield to them if, in our deliberate view of our duty, we possibly can. Judging by all they say and do, and by the subject and nature of their controversy with us, let us determine, if we can, what will satisfy them.

Will they be satisfied if the Territories be unconditionally surrendered to them? We know they will not. In all their present complaints against us, the Territories are scarcely mentioned. Invasions and insurrections are the rage now. Will it satisfy them, if, in the future, we have nothing to do with invasions and insurrections? We know it will not. We so know, because we know we never had anything to do with invasions and insurrections; and yet this total abstaining does not exempt us from the charge and the denunciation.

The question recurs, what will satisfy them? Simply this: We must not only let them alone, but we must, somehow, convince them that we do let them alone. This, we know by experience, is no easy task. We have been so trying to convince them from the very beginning of our organization, but with no success. In all our platforms and speeches we constantly protested our purpose to let them alone; but this has had no tendency to convince them. Alike unavailing to convince them, is the fact that they have never detected a man of us in any attempt to disturb them.

These natural, and apparently adequate means all failing, what will convince them? This, and this only: cease to call slavery wrong, and join them in calling it right. And this must be done thoroughly—done in acts as well as in words. Silence will not be tolerated—we must place ourselves avowedly with them. Senator Douglas's new sedition law must be enacted and enforced, suppressing all declarations that slavery is wrong, whether made in politics, in presses, in pulpits, or in private. We must arrest and return their fugitive slaves with greedy pleasure. We must pull down our Free State constitutions. The whole atmosphere must be disinfected from all taint of opposition to slavery, before they will cease to believe that all their troubles proceed from us.

I am quite aware they do not state their case precisely in this way. Most of them would probably say to us, "Let us alone, do nothing to us, and say what you please about slavery." But we do let them alone—have never disturbed them—so that, after all, it is what we say, which dissatisfies them. They will continue to accuse us of doing, until we cease saying.

I am also aware they have not, as yet, in terms demanded the overthrow of our Free-State Constitutions. Yet those Constitutions declare the wrong of slavery, with more solemn emphasis, than do all other sayings against it; and when all these other sayings shall have been silenced, the overthrow of these Constitutions will be demanded, and nothing be left to resist the demand. It is nothing to the contrary, that they do not demand the whole of this just now. Demanding what they do, and for the reason they do, they can voluntarily stop nowhere short of this consummation. Holding, as they do, that slavery is morally right, and socially elevating, they cannot cease to demand a full national recognition of it, as a legal right, and a social blessing.

Nor can we justifiably withhold this, on any ground save our conviction that slavery is wrong. If slavery is right, all words, acts, laws, and constitutions against it, are themselves wrong, and should be silenced, and swept away. If it is right, we cannot justly object to its nationality—its universality; if it is wrong, they cannot justly insist upon its extension—its enlargement. All they ask, we could readily grant, if we thought slavery right; all we ask, they could as readily grant, if they thought it wrong. Their thinking it right, and our thinking it wrong, is the precise fact upon which depends the whole controversy. Thinking it right, as they do, they are not to blame for desiring its full recognition, as being right; but, thinking it wrong, as we do, can we yield to them? Can we cast our votes with their view, and against our own? In view of our moral, social, and political responsibilities, can we do this?

Wrong as we think slavery is, we can yet afford to let it alone where it is, because that much is due to the necessity arising from its actual presence in the nation; but can we while our votes will prevent it, allow it to spread into the National Territories, and to overrun us here in these Free States? If our sense of duty forbids this, then let us stand by our duty, fearlessly and effectively. Let us be diverted by none of those sophistical contrivances wherewith we are so industriously plied and belabored—contrivances such as groping for some middle ground between the right and the wrong, vain as the search for a man who should be neither a living man nor a dead man—such as a policy of "don't care" on a question about which all true men do care — such as Union appeals beseeching true Union men to yield to Disunionists, reversing the divine rule, and calling, not the sinners, but the righteous to repentance —

Neither let us be slandered from our duty by false accusations against us, nor frightened from it by menaces of destruction to the Government nor of dungeons to ourselves. LET US HAVE FAITH THAT RIGHT MAKES MIGHT, AND IN THAT FAITH, LET US, TO THE END, DARE TO DO OUR DUTY AS WE UNDERSTAND IT.

• The 1860 Republican Party platform opposed the extension of slavery into the Western territories. The platform called the extension of slavery "revolutionary" and "subversive of the peace and harmony in the country."

• The 1860 Democratic Party platform supported the Dred Scott decision, and opposed the "personal liberty" laws passed to subvert the Federal Fugitive Slave Law of 1850.

• Sylvester Gray, a free African American, petitioned Congress for the return of his land which he had settled in Wisconsin in 1856 in accordance with the Preemption Act of 1841, and on which he had spent $223. Gray had received a letter from the commissioner of the General Land Office revoking his claim on the grounds that he was not a citizen according to the Dred Scott decision.

• The Pony Express began operations in the West. Eastern mails went by railroad to St. Joseph, Missouri, then were picked up by professional riders who, working in relays, delivered letters as far west as San Francisco. Two of the professional riders employed by the Pony Express were African Americans — George Monroe (1843–1886) and William Robinson.

After his stint with the Pony Express, George Monroe went on to become a famous stagecoach driver and gold miner. His name is today memorialized by a meadow (Monroe Meadows) which was named for him in Yosemite National Park.

• Abraham Lincoln was elected President of the United States (November 6).

A New York Republican reported that of the 32,000 New York Republicans who voted for Lincoln, only 1,600 endorsed an amendment to the New York constitution which would have given African Americans the right to vote.

• In his message to Congress on December 4, President Buchanan advocated Constitutional amendments upholding the principles of the fugitive slave acts.

• South Carolina declared herself an "independent commonwealth" (December 18).

Miscellaneous Census Facts

Boston had about 2,000 free African Americans; Philadelphia had 22,185; and New York City had 12,500.

In 1860, prime field hands were selling for $1,000 in Virginia and $1,500 in New Orleans.

The total value of Southern manufactures was estimated to be in excess of $238,000,000. In 1860, the United States produced five million bales of cotton. In 1852, it had produced three million bales and, in 1822, it had produced 1.5 million bales.

• *The Abolition Movement*: The radical abolitionists, Frederick Douglass and Gerrit Smith, refused to support Lincoln for President because Lincoln was not in favor of the complete, immediate abolition of slavery. Douglass wrote in the *Liberator*: "I care nothing about that antislavery which wants to make the territories free, while it is unwilling to extend to me, as a man, in the free states, all the rights of a man."

• By 1860, some 500 African Americans were engaged in traveling from Canada to the South for the purpose of rescuing slaves.

• *The Civil Rights Movement*: By 1860, five states (Massachusetts, Maine, New Hampshire, Vermont and Rhode Island) granted African Americans equal suffrage (voting) rights. However, these five states contained only six percent (6%) of the total African American population located in the North.

• *The Socialist Movement*: Karl Marx thought that the hanging of John Brown would start the American movement of slaves which he considered to be "the greatest event in the world" at that time. "The signal, once given, will make the thing by and by serious — what will then happen to Manchester?" By transferring the headquarters of his "International" from Europe to America, Marx hoped, Communists would be able to activate an African American movement.

• *Miscellaneous State Laws*: Maryland law prohibited the manumission of slaves, and provided for authorization of free African Americans to renounce their freedom and become slaves.

• In Arkansas, a law went into effect which prohibited the employment of free African

Americans on boats or ships navigating the rivers of the state (January 1).

• Virginia law provided for sale into "absolute slavery" of free African Americans convicted of offenses "punishable by confinement in the penitentiary."

• *Scholastic Achievements:* In 1860, 32,629 African Americans in the United States were enrolled in school. The percentage of free African Americans within each state who were literate was: Delaware (26.4%); Washington, D.C. (41.3%); North Carolina (46.6%); Tennessee (46.9%); Maryland (48.9%); Virginia (54.2%); Kentucky (56.2%); Missouri (59%); Texas (61.9%); Alabama (63.8%); Georgia (65.8%); Arkansas (68%); South Carolina (68.5%); Mississippi (71.8%); and Louisiana (71.9%).

• By 1860, twenty-eight African Americans had received degrees from recognized colleges in the United States.

• *Black Enterprise:* In 1860, free African Americans in the South tended to live in urban areas and held property with an estimated value of $25,000,000. 10,689 free African Americans lived in New Orleans, Louisiana, where they worked in such diverse occupations as teachers, jewelers, architects, and lithographers. New Orleans African Americans owned property valued at $15,000,000.

• Free African Americans in Maryland paid taxes on over $1,000,000 worth of real property. Twelve individuals owned property valued at over $5,000 each.

• In Massachusetts, out of 2,929 African American males over 14 for whom an occupation had been indicated, 2,398 (78.4%) had some form of occupation. Of the 484 African American males in Ward 6 of Boston (the ward with the highest concentration of African Americans), 440 (90.9%) had distinct occupations, compared to a percentage of 90.6% of the general population.

• In Boston, Massachusetts, there were 2,000 free African Americans. These African Americans were engaged in almost 100 different occupations, including paper hanging, photography, engraving, tailoring, quarrying, and other trades. African Americans in Boston also practiced such professions as law, teaching, dentistry and the ministry.

• The total value of real property owned by free African Americans in North Carolina was $480,986. The total value of personal property owned by free African Americans in North Carolina was $564,657, for a total of $1,045,643. This meant that the per capita wealth of each African American was $34

but the per capita wealth of each African American property owner was $287.

• In North Carolina, there were 1,048 free African American farmers. Approximately fifty percent of them owned some land. David Reynolds of Halifax County owned $3,000 worth of land. Thomas Blacknall of Franklin County had $6,000 worth of land and owned three slaves. At the time, $100 worth of land was deemed to be "adequate for farming purposes."

• In all of North Carolina, there were eight free African American slave owners with a total of 25 slaves. In 1830, there had been 191 free African American slave owners, with a total of 620 slaves.

• Of the 3,287 free African Americans in Charleston, South Carolina, 371 were taxpayers. These free African Americans had an estimated $1,000,000 worth of real estate and 389 slaves.

AFRICA

• War broke out between Morocco and Spain. Spain gained Santa Cruz de Mar Pequena while Ceuta and Melilla were made free ports.

• A treaty of peace was negotiated between France and al-Hajj Umar concerning their interests near Senegal.

• Mbarak bin Rashid al-Mazrui became the wali of Gazi. He would often find himself in rebellion against Zanzibar.

• British Kaffraria was made into a Crown colony.

• The Cape Parliament demanded secession from Britain.

• Indentured laborers from India arrived to work in the Cape colony.

• Beginning in 1860, a slave trade began to develop in the northern and eastern parts of the Congo.

EUROPE

• George Polgreen Bridgetower, the violin virtuoso for whom Beethoven composed the *Kreutzer* sonata, died in Peckham, London, England (February 29). *See* 1779.

1861

THE UNITED STATES

In 1861, the slave states formed what was to be a new nation. It was called the Confederate States of America. In February, Jefferson Davis became the president of the Confederate States of America. In his inaugural address (delivered in Montgomery, Alabama), Davis endorsed slavery "as necessary to self-preservation."

The Confederate States adopted a constitution that resembled the United States Constitution in language and most of its provisions and which even prohibited the African slave trade (March 11). The Confederate Constitution counted slaves as three-fifths of a person for the purpose of representation and taxation, prohibited an external slave trade, and advocated the protection of the institution of slavery and the "right of property in Negro slaves."

On March 21, the vice-president of the Confederacy, Alexander Stephens, claimed that the new government "rests upon the great truth that the Negro is not equal to the white man, that slavery, subordination to the superior race, is a natural and normal condition . . . our new Government, is the first in the history of the world, based upon this physical, philosophical, and moral truth."

• Kansas became the thirty-fourth state of the Union, with a constitution that outlawed slavery (January 29).

• Robert Smalls watching preparations for the attack on Fort Sumter, said "this, boys, is the dawn of freedom for our race" (April 10).

In 1861, Confederate authorities pressed Smalls into the service of the Confederate Navy. He became a member of the crew of the *Planter*. In 1862, in the absence of Confederate officers, Smalls navigated the *Planter* into the line of the blockading federal squadron outside Charleston harbor. The federal forces, upon receiving the *Planter*, made Smalls a pilot in the United States Navy, commissioned him a captain, and then promoted him to commander. *See 1839.*

• The Civil War began as Confederate forces attacked Fort Sumter (April 12).

• Lincoln issued a proclamation calling for 75,000 volunteers from the states (April 15). African American volunteers were not accepted when the first call for troops was made.

Frederick Douglass' editorial in *Douglass' Monthly*, called for a harsher war and said:

Let the slaves and free colored people be called into service, and formed into a liberating army, to march into the South and raise the banner of emancipation among the slaves.

After the fall of Fort Sumter, many African Americans volunteered for the army, but were refused enlistment.

As a poignant footnote to history, it must be noted that James Stone, a light skinned escaped slave, enlisted in the First Fight Artillery of Ohio (August 23). Stone, whose wife was a European American woman, passed himself off as a European American man. Fighting for the Union in Kentucky--the state in which Stone had been enslaved—Stone contracted a service-related illness and died from it in 1862. After his death, Stone's true racial identity became known. Stone is notable not only for this act but also because he may have been the first African American to fight for the Union during the Civil War having done so almost two full years before African Americans were authorized to join Union forces.

• Nicholas Biddle, a sixty-five year old former slave, became the first-known African American to be a casualty of Civil War hostilities when he was wounded while accompanying troops from Pennsylvania as they marched through Baltimore (April 18).

• Clara Barton, along with five young African American women, gave aid to the wounded in the passage through Baltimore (April 21).

• In Virginia, Brigadier General Benjamin F. Butler refused to return three escaped slaves as they were "contraband of war" (May 24). Butler was the first Union officer to declare that slaves who fell into Union hands would be confiscated since Confederate forces used them in building defenses. Butler utilized the escaped slaves for construction. Butler's decision soon became Union policy.

• General George B. McClellan, Ohio Department, issued orders to suppress any African American attempts at insurrection (May 26).

• Negro Mass Meeting offered to raise an army of 50,000 men and that the women would serve as nurses, etc. (May 31).

• On July 22, the United States Senate resolved that the Civil War was "not waged . . . for any purpose . . . of overthrowing or interfering with the rights or established institutions of . . . southern States."

• After the defeat of the Union forces at the first Battle of Bull Run in July, Lincoln ordered that a corps of 50,000 African Americans be organized by the Quartermaster Department of the Army. Sensitive to the feelings of the border states, Lincoln opposed statements on slavery and the arming of African Americans. The army subsequently used nonenlisted African Americans in the Quartermaster, Commissary, Medical and Engineer Services. African Americans also served in the Union Army as pioneers, scouts, laborers, hostelers, teamsters, wagoners, carpenters, masons, laundresses, hospital attendants, fortification, highway and railroad builders, longshoremen and blacksmiths. They also served as servants and orderlies to officers from 1861 to the end of the war.

• In New York, African Americans formed a military drill club, but the police disbanded it. The governor of New York specifically rejected the services of three regiments of African American volunteers.

• On August 6, Congress passed the Confiscation Act which declared that any property used with the owner's consent to aid in insurrection became the lawful subject of prize and capture. If that property consisted of slaves, the slaves were to be freed. Taking advantage of this act, General John Fremont (once the expeditionary commander of the legendary James Beckwourth [see 1798]) proclaimed from his headquarters in Missouri that slaves from all owners who take up arms against the Union shall be "declared free men." But President Lincoln requested a modification of Fremont's extension of the act toward an emancipation of slaves. This the general declined to do and he was therefore removed from the army. One of Fremont's successors, General Henry W. Halleck, would customarily evict escaped slaves from the camps under his command.

• On September 25, the Secretary of the Navy, Gideon Wells, authorized the enlistment of African Americans into the navy, under the same forms and regulations as applied to other enlistments. However, the African Americans could achieve no higher rank than "boys" and were to be paid at a compensation of $10 per month and one ration a day.

• In the campaign against the Hatteras Forts, escaped slaves served as gun crews on Union boats.

• In October, the War Department refused the offer of a Michigan African American, Dr. G. P. Miller, to organize "5,000 to 10,000 freemen to take any position that may be assigned to us." Similar offers from other African American groups were also refused.

• The Union officer, Major General John A. Dix, would not allow fugitives within his lines. However, James H. Lane, an abolitionist senator from Kansas, and then Brigadier General in the Union Army, encouraged slaves to flee to his state and fight with Union troops.

• In October, Thomas A. Schott, the acting secretary of war, directed Brigadier General Thomas W. Sherman, commanding the expedition to the Southern coast, to avail himself "of the services of any persons, whether fugitives from labor or not, who may offer them to the National Government." These escaped slaves were to be employed "in such services . . . as you may deem most beneficial to the service; this however not being a general arming of them for military services." General Sherman never acted on this authorization.

• On the island of Hilton Head, South Carolina, escaped slaves were employed by the Union forces to grow cotton for sale by the Treasury Department.

In 1861, the average price in gold of a 20 year old male slave in the Confederacy was $1,050. By 1865, the average price had fallen to $100.

• The Confederacy used African Americans as teamsters, hospital attendants, railroad bridge and road repairment, and in arms factories, in the iron mines and for building and repairing defenses. The government at first hired slaves from their masters, but when owners appeared reluctant to part with their slaves, the slaves were requisitioned by the army for military purposes.

• Independent Confederate states were recruiting free African Americans. Tennessee authorized the use in military services of all free males of color between the ages of 15 and 50. This conscription was often done without prior notice. African American women were conscripted by Confederate forces for camp and hospital service.

• The state of Kentucky granted a charter to the United Brothers of Friendship and Sisters, a benevolent and charitable organization composed of African Americans.

• William C. Nell was appointed post office clerk in Boston. Nell, thereby, became the first African American to hold a civil service position in the federal government.

• *Miscellaneous State Laws:* North Carolina prohibited free African Americans from acquiring slaves.

• *Publications:* Martin Robinson Delany published an official report on his exploration of the Niger Valley for possible African American emigration sites. *See 1812.*

• *Scholastic Achievements:* Mary Smith Kelsick Peake (1823–1862), a free African American, began teaching African American youths at Fort Monroe, Virginia, and, on September 17, she opened a school in

Hampton, Virginia—a school which would form the basis for Hampton Institute. Peake was financially supported by the American Missionary Association in a humanitarian effort to educate freed slaves. Peake died of tuberculosis on February 22, 1862.

• Blanche K. Bruce established a school in Hannibal, Missouri. *See 1841.*

• With the permission of General Butler, the American Missionary Association opened a school for freedmen in Tennessee. Shortly thereafter, the American Missionary Association established schools on plantations, and in Hampton, Norfolk, Portsmouth and Newport News.

THE AMERICAS

• In 1861, there were 11,413 Afro-Canadians.

• In 1861, James Theodore Holly, of New York, led a group of African American emigrants to Haiti. Embarking from Philadelphia, the emigrant contingent numbered 2,000. By the time their ship arrived in Port-au-Prince, only a third of the original 2,000 survived. *See 1829.*

• James Theodore Holly, formerly of New York, was consecrated Bishop of Haiti by the Episcopal Church. *See 1829.*

• At the Dominicans' request, from 1861 to 1865, Spain governed the Dominican Republic in order to protect it from the Haitians. *See 1801.*

• In 1861, Cuba's population was 43.2% Afro-Cuban. Among the Afro-Cubans, 232,493 were free and 370,553 were enslaved.

AFRICA

• The British bombarded Porto Novo.

Today Porto Novo is the administrative capital of Benin.

• A British protectorate of Lagos was proclaimed.

• The Arabs were expelled by the British from Zanzibar.

• Radama II, the king of the Merina, came to power. On September 12, a treaty with France was negotiated.

• The American College for Girls was opened in Cairo, Egypt.

RELATED HISTORICAL EVENTS

• Great Britain declared that it would remain neutral with regard to the American Civil War.

1862

THE UNITED STATES

In 1862, Abraham Lincoln replied to Horace Greeley's editorial in the New York *Tribune* in which Greeley questioned Lincoln's objectives in the war by saying:

As to the policy I "seem to be pursuing" as you say, I have not meant to leave anyone in doubt.

I would save the Union. I would save it the shortest way under the Constitution. The sooner the national authority can be restored; the nearer the Union will be "the Union as it was." If there be those who would not save the Union, unless they could at the same time save slavery, I do not agree with them. If there be those who would not save the Union unless they could at the same time destroy slavery, I do not agree with them. My paramount object in this struggle is to save the Union, and is not either to save or to destroy slavery. If I could save the Union without freeing any slave I would do it, and if I could save it by freeing all the slaves I would do it; and if I could save it by freeing some and leaving others alone I would also do that. What I do about slavery, and the colored race, I do because I believe it helps to save the Union; and what I forbear, I forbear because I do not believe it would help to save the Union. I shall do less whenever I shall believe what I am doing hurts the cause, and I shall do more whenever I shall believe doing more will help the cause. I shall try to correct errors when shown to be errors; and I shall adopt new views so fast as they shall appear to be true views.

I have here stated my purpose according to my view of official duty; and I intend no modification of my oft-expressed personal wish that all men everywhere could be free.

However, as time would soon show, the freedom of the slaves and the salvation of the Union were to be indivisably linked.

• On March 6, President Lincoln recommended to Congress a gradual, compensated emancipation of the slaves.

• In Cincinnati, visiting abolitionist Wendell Phillips was pelted with eggs and rocks after he called for emancipation of slaves to be made one of the goals of the Civil War. The official purpose of the war at this stage was to end the rebellion, not to abolish slavery (March 24).

• In March, military commanders were forbidden to return escaped slaves.

• The United States Senate passed Lincoln's proposal for a bill abolishing slavery in the District of Columbia (April 4). The bill became effective on April 16. Compensation of not more than $300 was awarded for each slave and $100,000 was allotted for the emigration of freedmen to Haiti or Liberia.

• In April, Congress passed Roscoe Conkling's resolution that the United States cooperate with any state adopting a plan of gradual emancipation and compensation.

• In May, the House of Representatives failed to pass a law to confiscate and free all slaves belonging to the rebel forces.

• Robert Smalls, an African American Union war hero, sailed an armed Confederate steamer, the *Planter* out of Charleston, South Carolina, and presented the ship to the United States Navy (May 13).

In 1861, Confederate authorities pressed Robert Smalls into the service of the Confederate Navy. He became a member of the crew of the *Planter*. In 1862, in the absence of Confederate officers, Smalls navigated the *Planter* into the line of the blockading federal squadron outside Charleston harbor. The federal forces, upon receiving the *Planter,* made Smalls a pilot in the United States Navy, commissioned him a captain, and then promoted him to commander. *See 1839.*

• Lincoln nullified a proclamation issued by General David Hunter which freed the slaves in Georgia, Florida and South Carolina.

• Slavery was outlawed in United States territories (June 19). President Lincoln signed a bill abolishing slavery in the territories in June. In July, a measure became law, setting free all slaves of masters disloyal to the United States.

• Lincoln recommended aid to states abolishing slavery (July 14).

• Congress authorized Lincoln to employ "persons of African descent" and to use them in any way necessary in the Confiscation Act which was passed on July 16. More specifically, on July 17, in the Militia Act, Congress authorized the President to employ African American troops. If a volunteer was a slave, his family was to be set free. The pay for African American troops was set at $7 ($3 less than that of his European American counterparts). In protest against the discrepancy in pay between European Americans and African Americans, the 54th Massachusetts Regiment (composed of African Americans) served a year without pay rather than accept discriminatory wages.

Despite the Confiscation Act, Union generals in the field made their own policy about escaped slaves. In west Tennessee, General Grant appointed John Eaton to take charge of escaped slaves. Eaton, and General Butler of Louisiana, leased abandoned plantations to Northern sympathizers and hired out the ex-slaves—but, of course, the ex-slaves were not paid for these services.

• The first regular African American troops were enlisted at Leavenworth, Kansas (July 17).

The First South Carolina Volunteers are reported to have been the first African American soldiers to be organized to fight in the Civil War. The First Carolina Volunteers were followed by the First and Second Kansas Colored Volunteers, a contingent which fought a skirmish in Clay County, Missouri. Additionally, the First Regiment Louisiana Native Guards were mustered into the army on September 27.

However, despite their efforts, these early enlistments were disavowed by the government and the groups were officially disbanded.

• On July 22, Lincoln presented a draft of a general emancipation proclamation to his Cabinet. However, he delayed issuing the proclamation because he agreed with Secretary of State Seward that the proclamation should only be issued after a Union military victory to avoid being seen as an act of desperation.

• In August, Lincoln held a meeting with prominent African Americans and urged them to support colonization.

• On August 6, Lincoln refused the offer of two African American regiments from Indiana and told them that he was "not prepared to go the length of enlisting Negroes as soldiers." Lincoln said he would employ all African American men as laborers, but would not promise to make soldiers of them.

• The radicals in Congress pressed for a change in the official government policy towards the use of African American troops.

• Although the new secretary of war, Edwin M. Stanton, gave no support to Major General David Hunter's First South Carolina Volunteers, he authorized Brigadier General Butler to plan for five companies of African Americans; gave General O. M. Mitchell the right to use African Americans as guards and scouts in Alabama; and, on August 25, appointed General Rufus Saxton to recruit up to 5,000 African Americans at the same pay as European Americans (although the equal pay provision was never to be honored).

• On September 22, Lincoln issued a preliminary emancipation proclamation which was to take effect on January 1, 1863. This proclamation would free all the slaves in the states where people were in rebellion.

• Returning to the South (New Orleans) during the Civil War, in 1862, P. B. S. Pinchback created the Corps d'Afrique, a unit composed of African American troops for the Union Army. Pinchback resigned in September of 1862 over racial difficulties but, subsequently, he was commissioned to raise a company of African American cavalry. *See 1837.*

• The defenses of the city of Corinth, Mississippi, built in preparation for the battle of October 1862 were primarily the work of African Americans. The African Americans involved were organized into squads of 25 each and commanded by army personnel.

• Acting on Lincoln's suggestion in his annual message to Congress (December 1), Congress appropriated $500,000 for the colonization of slaves of rebellious masters, and authorized the exchange of diplomatic representatives with Haiti and Liberia.

• In December, General Saxton, commanding the Department of the South, issued a general plan for dealing with escaped slaves. According to the plan, abandoned lands were to be used for the benefit of the ex-slaves. Two acres were to be allotted for each working member of a family. Tools were to be furnished by the government. Corn and potatoes were to be planted for personal use. Cotton was to be planted for government use. Since only a small amount of land was available, the superintendents appointed were not always interested in the project. Eventually, the government would sell much of the seized land.

• During 1862, while the issue of the use of African American troops was being debated, some Union generals, nevertheless, utilized African Americans in such roles as guides, scouts and even spies. Many others were used to perform heavy labor or to serve as cooks and teamsters. However, in these supporting capacities, the African Americans were rarely armed.

• By the end of 1862, the following African American regiments had been organized: The 1st, 2nd and 3rd Regiments of Louisiana Native Guards. General Saxton's reorganized 1st South Carolina Volunteers (already commended for bravery in coastal raids), and the unofficial 1st Kansas Colored Volunteers.

• African American pickets successfully protected contraband camps from Confederate attacks on St. Simon Island off the coast of Georgia, and again on St. Helena Island, South Carolina.

• In 1862, the National Freedman's Relief Association was formed in New York. The Contraband Relief Association was founded shortly afterwards in Cincinnati (later changing its name to the Western Freedmen's Aid Commission). The Friends Association for the Relief of Colored Freedmen was founded in Philadelphia. The Northwestern Freedmen's Aid Commission was founded in Chicago. In 1865, all of these organizations would be combined into the American Freedmen's Aid Commission.

• In 1862, in the South, the labor shortage was so acute that most states authorized the impressment of African Americans.

• During the conduct of the war, captured African Americans were hanged or made to work in irons. The Confederate War Department outlawed Union generals who armed African Americans. If captured, these generals were to be executed.

• *The Labor Movement:* European American workers in the North resisted the use of African Americans as laborers because African Americans were often used as strikebreakers and European Americans feared competition would depress wages. In a minor riot in New York, African American women and children who were employed in a tobacco factory were mobbed. In New Jersey, agitation resulted when African Americans were employed on the Camden and Amboy Railroad.

• The American Seamen's Protective Association was founded by William M. Powell, an African American in New York City.

In 1850, it was estimated that half of the 25,000 American seamen were persons of African descent. After the creation of the American Seamen's Protective Association, it was reported (in 1870) that 3,500 African American seamen were headquartered in New York City.

• *Notable Deaths:* Anthony Burns, Baptist clergyman whose capture as a fugitive slave caused a riot in Boston, died (July 27).

• *Miscellaneous State Laws:* To stop slaves from escaping, many Southern states strengthened patrol laws by cancelling exemptions from patrol, requiring them to be made more often, imposing fines and/or prison for failure to patrol. Several states moved their African Americans to the interior, away from Union lines. North Carolina moved more that 2,000 slaves.

• *Scholastic Achievements:* Charlotte Forten, African American poet and teacher, arrived in St. Helena, South Carolina, to teach African Americans (October 29).

• Beginning in 1862, Wilberforce University

came under the control of African Americans, the first such college in the United States.

• The Morrill Land Grant College Act was passed, providing federal funds for state universities. Generally, the funds were used only for European American institutions. However, after the war, Hampton Institute received one third of the grant for the State of Virginia and Chaflin College and Alcorn in Mississippi also received funds.

• Mary Jane Patterson graduated from Oberlin College. She was the first African American female college graduate in the United States.

• *The Black Church:* The First African Methodist Episcopal Church was established at New Bern, North Carolina (December 27).

THE AMERICAS

• The gradual abolition of slavery in Paraguay was completed.

AFRICA

• Liberia was recognized as a free nation by the United States.

• William Balfour Baikie (1825–1864) visited Bida, Kano and Zaria.

Today Kano is a trading city of the Hausa people of northern Nigeria and is the third largest city in Nigeria after Lagos and Ibadan.

• Richard Francis Burton (1821–1890) visited Benin.

• France purchased Obock for 10,000 Maria Theresa dollars.

• An Egyptian expedition against Ethiopia was halted by a smallpox epidemic.

• Emperor Theodore of Ethiopia requested the creation of an alliance with Queen Victoria against the Muslims. His request was refused. In the wake of the rejection, the British consul and other Europeans were imprisoned.

• A chamber of commerce was established in Khartoum.

RELATED HISTORICAL EVENTS

• J. W. Colenso, the bishop of Maritzburg, South Africa, publicly denied the authority of the Pentateuch.

• Louis Botha, a South African statesman and soldier, was born.

1863

THE UNITED STATES

After a long deliberation, President Abraham Lincoln issued the Emancipation Proclamation, declaring that slaves in rebel states were free. The Emancipation Proclamation became effective on January 1, 1863. The proclamation actually freed all slaves except those in states or in parts of states that were not in rebellion. Exceptions to the proclamation included thirteen parishes in Louisiana, West Virginia, and seven counties of eastern Virginia (including the cities of Norfolk and Portsmouth). In essence, some 800,000 slaves were not covered by the Emancipation Proclamation.

Thomas Wentworth Higginson, a New Englander then in South Carolina leading a regiment of African Americans, wrote that when an American flag unfurled at a meeting held to announce the proclamation,

> there suddenly arose a strong male voice (but rather cracked and elderly), into which two women's voices instantly blended, singing, as if by an impulse that could no more be repressed than the morning note of the song-sparrow—"My Country, 'tis of thee, Sweet Land of Liberty, of thee I sing! (January 1).

• The War Department authorized the recruitment of African American troops. Colonel E. A. Wild, Brigadier General Daniel Ullmann, Governor Andrew of Massachusetts, the governor of Rhode Island, and General Nathaniel P. Banks were specifically authorized to recruit African Americans. Out of this authorization, the 54th Massachusetts Volunteers was the first African American regiment raised in the North (January 26). This unit would achieve more widespread fame 126 years later as the subject of the feature film titled "Glory."

• In February, after much debate, Thaddeus Stevens' bill calling for 150,000 African American soldiers, or 150 regiments, was passed in the House, 83 to 54. The Senate did not act on the bill, considering it unnecessary in light of the 1862 Militia Act.

• Two African American infantry regiments, the First and Second, South Carolina, captured and occupied Jacksonville, Florida, causing panic along the Southern seaboard (March 10).

• The Confederate Congress passed a resolution which branded African American troops and their officers criminals thereby allowing captured African American troops to be put to death or enslaved (May 1).

The treatment of prisoners of war by the South was rather direct. All African American prisoners captured in Jackson, Louisiana, were shot. Stories abounded of hangings, enslavements and forced labor on chain gangs. James Seddon, Confederate Secretary of War, advised Lieutenant General E. Kirby Smith that European American officers of African American troops, when captured, were to "be dealt with red-handed in the field, or immediately thereafter."

- President Lincoln warned of retaliatory action if the Confederates were to continue to murder or enslave captured African American soldiers.
- In May, the War Department's General Order No. 143 fully organized and centralized control of African American troops as the United States Colored Troops (USCT). From this point on, African Americans were mustered into the army directly.

At the Battle of Port Hudson, Captain André Cailloux, a well-to-do free African American of New Orleans, led his men in battle. With a shattered left arm, Cailloux encouraged his troops for the final attack. Cailloux died running ahead of them, crying "Follow me," in French and then in English.

- The 54th Massachusetts Volunteers, the first African American regiment raised in the North left Boston to fight in the Civil War (May 28).

General Ullman remarked of his African American troops:

They are far more in earnest than we. I have talked with hundreds of them. They understand their position full as well as we do. They know the deep stake they have in the issue . . . that, if we are unsuccessful they will be remanded to a worse slavery than before. They also have a settled conviction that if they are taken, they will be tortured and hung. These impressions will make them daring and desperate fighters.

- The Bureau for Colored Troops was established to administer the affairs of the United States Colored Troops (USCT). Major Charles W. Foster was appointed to oversee the administrative matters of the corps.
- In the last stages of the Battle of Vicksburg, eight African Americans manning the siege works were killed by a Confederate mine.
- Eight African American regiments played an important role in the siege of Port Hudson which, with the fall of Vicksburg, gave the Union control of the Mississippi River and cut the Confederacy into two sections (July 9).

By July of 1863, thirty African American regiments had been federalized, and the President and government were officially committed to their use. Most African Americans served in the infantry. However, there were some in the cavalry, engineering units, and in batteries of light and heavy artillery. By the end of the war, these African American units had participated in 449 engagements of which 39 were major battles of the war.

Only four combat regiments of African Americans were never federalized and, therefore, never became a part of the United States Colored Troops. These four regiments were the 29th Regiment of Connecticut Volunteer Infantry, the 5th Regiment of Massachusetts Cavalry, and the 54th and 55th Regiments of the Massachusetts Volunteer Infantry.

On March 25, 1863, Brigadier General Lorenzo Thomas, as a representative of the War Department, began traveling through the Mississippi Valley to recruit officers and men for the United States Colored Troops, and to investigate the arrangements for existing troops and contraband camps. Generals Halleck and Grant gave their support for the recruitment and use of African American troops. Meanwhile, Frederick Douglass wrote articles calling for volunteers.

A Major George L. Stearn was appointed by Governor Andrew of Massachusetts and became second only to General Thomas as a leading recruiter of African American troops. However, in stark contrast to General Thomas, Major Stearn opposed impressment (conscription), offered enlistment bounties and established schools for his African American troops.

War Department General Order No. 144 established a careful system of examining boards to choose officers for African American regiments. The boards were uniformly severe and almost forty percent (40%) of the applicants were rejected during the war. In general the officers of the United States Colored Troops were better than their counterparts in the regular army.

The War Department discouraged African Americans from becoming officers and only 75 to 100 were appointed. Three-quarters of the African American officers could be found under the command of General Butler in Louisiana. A battery of light artillery from Kansas was unique in that all three of its officers were African Americans.

The highest ranking African American officer of the war was Lieutenant Colonel Alexander

T. Augusta. Augusta was appointed "surgeon of the United States Colored Troops" in 1863. Later Dr. Augusta was transferred from his unit when his two European American assistant surgeons complained to the President about serving under an African American officer.

• The New York City Draft Riots were the bloodiest in American history (July 13–17).

In 1863, New York City was controlled by the New York Democratic Party. The New York Democratic Party was strongly opposed to the Civil War. The leader of the party, Boss Tweed, was a major antiwar spokesman.

The Democratic governor of New York, Horatio Seymour, denounced the Conscription Act passed by Congress early in 1863 as unconstitutional. Under the act, conscription (compulsory military service) was to begin in July. The act permitted a man to buy his way out of the draft by paying $300.

The ability to pay as a way of avoiding the draft was deemed to be discriminatory against the newly arrived and impoverished Irish immigrants. The Irish were further angered by their belief (based upon historical practice) that once the slaves were set free they would flood the city, thereby taking away the jobs typically held by the Irish. From the perspective of the Irish, they were being compelled to risk their lives fighting a war which could only lead to their being permanently unemployed.

The passage of the Conscription Act caused a great deal of friction to develop between the Irish American and African American communities. On July 13, riots broke out in New York City. Any African Americans found by the rioters were severely beaten, often to death. The African American orphan asylum was burned to the ground.

The riots lasted through July 17. 1,200 lives were lost. Two million dollars ($2,000,000) worth of damage was done to property. Along with the homes of African Americans, the townhouses and brownstones of the wealthy were also sacked and burned.

• The 54th Massachusetts Volunteers made a charge on Fort Wagner in Charleston Harbor, South Carolina. At least one member of the all–African American regiment won the Congressional Medal of Honor for his bravery (July 18).

On July 18, despite poor rations, a forced march the day before and a general state of fatigue, the 54th Massachusetts Colored Infan-

try led the ill-planned assault on Fort Wagner. The unit suffered about forty-two percent (42%) casualties.

Sergeant William H. Carney, of Company C, 54th Massachusetts Colored Infantry, was awarded the Congressional Medal of Honor for his bravery in the Battle of Fort Wagner, South Carolina. When the standard bearer was killed, Carney picked up the regimental colors and led the attack to the fort. Carney was badly wounded on two occasions during the fighting.

William Harvey Carney (1840–1908) was born in Norfolk, Virginia. He was able to receive some education and later settled in New Bedford, Massachusetts, where he was employed as a seaman.

On February 17, 1863, Carney enlisted in the army and became a member of the 54th Massachusetts Colored Infantry. He rose to the rank of sergeant and commanded Company C.

Carney earned his medal of honor only five months after he joined the army when, at the battle for Fort Wagner, the color bearer was wounded. Carney, despite being wounded, sprang forward and seized the flag before it slipped from the bearer's grasp, an act of gallant, albeit futile, bravery.

After Fort Wagner, Carney was discharged from the army because of the wounds he had received.

For "various reasons," Carney's medal of honor was not issued until May 23, 1900.

Upon Carney's death in 1908, the flag at the Massachusetts state capitol was lowered to half mast in tribute to this brave man.

• Robert Blake, serving on the U.S.S. Marblehead, was awarded the Navy Medal of Honor for his part in routing the enemy off Legareville in the Stono River.

Robert Blake, an African American powder boy aboard the USS Marblehead, was awarded the Naval Medal of Honor for "conspicuous gallantry, extraordinary heroism, and intrepidity at the risk of his own life."

• As an experiment in colonization, 500 African Americans were sent to Cow Island, Haiti. The experiment failed badly. President Lincoln was forced to send a ship to bring the emigrants back to the United States.
• In October, at the contraband camp at Pine Bluff, Arkansas, a group of untrained African Americans repulsed a Confederate attack on the camp. Five were killed and 12 were wounded. The captain of the camp reported that they deserved "the applause of their country and gratitude of the soldiers."

Throughout the war, departmental and divisional commanders varied in their use of African American troops. In the trans–Mississippi West, they generally served in combat, for example at Cabin Creek, Indiana Territory and Baxter Springs. In the departments of Tennessee and of the South, they did fatigue detail, had little time to drill, and were often treated unfairly. Along the Atlantic Coast, both situations existed.

Despite successive official orders and investigations, many African American troops continued to be treated unfairly by their officers and division commanders.

In September, the Commissioner for the Organization of Colored Troops reported to the secretary of war that "the colored men here are treated like brutes; any officer who wants them, I am told, impresses on his own authority; and it is seldom that they are paid ... one was shot."

The 65th United States Colored Infantry recruited in Missouri, was sent in December to Benton Barracks, without any hats or shoes, thinly clad, without proper feeding provisions. 100 soldiers died in the first two months.

Brigadier General Q. A. Gillmore, in command of the Department of the South, reported that African American troops, detailed for fatigue duty, had been employed in one instance at least to prepare camps and perform menial duty for white troops.

The commanding officer of the 14th United States Colored Infantry wrote,

it behooves the friends of this movement [the use of African Americans as soldiers] to secure a favorable decision from the great tribunal, public opinion. This cannot be done by making laborers out of these troops; ... [it is] degrading to single out colored troops for fatigue duty while white soldiers stand by.

• The conditions in federal refugee camps for freed slaves were generally horrendous. The mortality rate in these camps averaged approximately twenty-five percent (25%).

With an acute labor shortage, the Confederate government passed a General Impressment Law which allowed Confederate authorities to conscript slave laborers for government and military purposes. However, planters often refused to obey the law because they feared the loss of their slaves to the government.

In Kentucky, slave owners voiced opposition to the recruitment of slaves, fearing the loss of their slaves to the army.

• Susie King Taylor (1848–1912), an African American woman, became a nurse in the United States Army and served with the First Regiment of the South Carolina Volunteers.

Susie King Taylor (1848–1912) was born a slave on a plantation near Savannah, Georgia. In 1902, Taylor's Civil War memoirs were published. *Reminiscences of My Life in Camp* is the only comprehensive written record of life and activities of African American army nurses during the Civil War.

• Alexander T. Augusta was commissioned as a medical officer in the Union Army.

Alexander T. Augusta (1825–1890) was born a free person in Virginia. After serving a medical apprenticeship in Philadelphia, Augusta went to Trinity Medical College in Toronto, Canada, where he graduated in 1856.

In 1863, Augusta joined the Union forces and was commissioned with the initial rank of major but was soon promoted to lieutenant colonel.

In 1865, Augusta became the director of the newly created Freedman's Hospital which was located on the grounds of Howard University.

In 1868, Augusta became a demonstrator of anatomy at Howard University Medical School and, in 1869, Augusta received an honorary degree from Howard University.

• *Notable Births:* Charles "Buddy" Bolden, a prominent jazz musician, was born.

Charles "Buddy" Bolden (1863–1931) was born in New Orleans. Bolden grew up amid the brass band craze, playing cornet. In 1897, he organized the first jazz band and for seven years he was considered the "King of Jazz" in New Orleans.

Horns were the favorite instruments of New Orleans African Americans because they were easily carried in parades and because they were inexpensive.

Bolden's first band consisted of cornet, trombone, clarinet, guitar, string bass and drums. Bolden's musical accomplishments were notable because neither Bolden nor his band members could read music.

One of Bolden's noted protégés was Bunk Johnson.

• Kelly Miller, author and educator, was born (July 18).

• Dr. Mary Church Terrell, the first president of the National Association of Colored Women, was born (September 23).

• *Miscellaneous State Laws:* In its constitution, West Virginia provided for separate schools for African Americans.

• *Publications:* William Wells Brown published *The Black Man, His Antecedents, His Genius and His Achievements. See 1816.*

• *Scholastic Achievements:* In 1863, Daniel Alexander Payne purchased Wilberforce University and served as president of the university for thirteen years. *See 1811.*

• Sarah J. (Smith) Thompson (later to be known as Sarah Garnet) was appointed principal in the New York City public school system.

• The New England Freedmen's Aid Society established schools in South Carolina (in towns and on plantations). In 1863, 5,000 African Americans attended these schools. General Banks established a public education system in the Department of the Gulf. By the end of 1864, there were 95 schools, 162 teachers, 9,571 day students and 2,000 evening students.

• *The Black Church:* Saint Francis Xavier Church in Baltimore, Maryland, became the first exclusively African American Catholic parish in the United States when the church was purchased by its African American congregation (October 10).

• Henry McNeal Turner was appointed to the post of army chaplain by President Lincoln. He was assigned to the First Regiment of Colored Troops. *See 1834.*

AFRICA

• Egypt came under the control of Khedive (Viceroy) Ismail. Sultan Abdul Aziz of Turkey visited Egypt.

• The Baker expedition met up with Speke at Gondokoro.

• The British went to war against the Ashanti (Asante).

• Al-Hajj Umar captured Timbuktu and established his capital at Hamdillahi.

• Dakar was founded.

Today Dakar is the main port and capital of Senegal.

• Napoleon III of France refused the appeal of Emperor Theodore of Ethiopia for assistance in his struggle against the Muslims.

• The Holy Ghost Fathers were established in Zanzibar.

• Ismail Pasha became the khedive of Egypt.

• The Boulaq Museum (later known as the Egyptian Museum) was founded.

RELATED HISTORICAL EVENTS

• The Union forces defeated the Confederate forces at the Battle of Gettysburg.

• The British attempted to curtail the Arab-controlled East African slave trade by negotiating an agreement with the king of Mukalla.

• Bishop Colenso was ostracized and censured for heresy by the South African Anglican bishops.

1864

THE UNITED STATES

In the February election held in the Louisiana Territory (which was then largely under Union control), African Americans were denied the right to vote. The Louisiana Constitutional Convention, composed of delegates elected by European American votes in Union-controlled areas, was held in April. At the convention, the delegates abolished slavery by a vote of 72 to 13, but appealed to Congress for compensation. After the intervention of the governor and the Union commanding general, the convention did not categorically exclude African Americans from voting.

In October, the Louisiana State Legislature, also elected from Union territory, met. The Legislature abolished slavery but refused to grant the right to vote to African Americans and prohibited interracial marriages.

As the Louisiana situation aptly indicated, just as the struggle against slavery had been virtually won, the struggle for equality had yet to begin. It would be one hundred years before African Americans in Louisiana could be legally guaranteed their right to vote, and their right to marry whomever they pleased.

• Despite the hatred of African Americans shown during the July, 1863 New York City Draft Riots, the residents of New York City cheered at the parade of its African American regiment, the 20th United States Colored Troops.

• The Battle of Fort Pillow, famous for the massacre of African American troops after the surrender of the Union forces, occurred (April 12).

• Congress passed a bill equalizing, for the first time, the pay, arms, equipment and medical services of African American troops.

Despite the efforts of the War Department, reports of ill-treatment, equipment of the poorest kind, inadequate medical personnel, and excessive fatigue duty continued to be made by the officers commanding African American regiments.

In the North, there were African American physicians. However, only eight were appointed as surgeons in the army, and, of these eight, six were attached to hospitals in Washington, D.C., while the other two remained in African American regiments for only a very short time.

Sergeant William Walker, an African American in the 3rd South Carolina Volunteers, was shot by order of a court martial for having led the men of his company to stack arms and to refuse to serve until the agreement under which they had enlisted—an agreement for equal pay—was met. At least three other African American soldiers were executed for similar protests, and over twenty members of the 14th Rhode Island Heavy Artillery were jailed.

Lieutenant Colonel Augusta, an African American surgeon for the United States Colored Troops, found it necessary to tell Senator Henry Wilson that the army paymaster at Baltimore had "refused to pay him more than $7 per month"—the pay that an African American enlisted man would receive. Augusta rejected the insulting pay. A letter from Senator Wilson to the secretary of war dated April 10, 1864, resulted in an order two days later to the paymaster general to compensate the lieutenant colonel according to his rank.

In mid-June of 1864, Congress in its Army Appropriations Bill finally addressed the inequities associated with the pay of African Americans. The bill authorized the same enlistment bounty for African Americans and European Americans. Equal pay was made retroactive to January 1, 1864, for "all persons of color who were free on the 19th day of April, 1861." This last condition caused many African Americans (with the tacit approval of their superior officers) to lie about their status in 1861. In Massachusetts, Governor Andrews simply had the state legislature pay the difference in wages irrespective of status.

- At Petersburg, Virginia, in June, the African American division under the command of General W. F. Smith attacked the fort and made a mile-wide gap in the Confederate defenses.
- The fugitive slave laws were repealed (June 28).
- In July, a federal law was enacted which enabled Northern states to recruit in occupied areas of the South.

- In July, the federal government entitled the families of African Americans who had been killed in the war to pensions. No provision had been made previous to this bill.
- At Wolf River Bridge, Tennessee, in December, the 2nd Regiment of West Tennessee Infantry of African Descent, was formally commended by its commander.
- In December, the 25th Corps was organized as an all–African American regiment. The regiments usually did fatigue duty in the encampment around Richmond, Virginia.

As more African Americans became involved in the battles of the Civil War, opportunities arose in which a number of African Americans displayed exceptional valor.

In a duel between the USS *Kearsarge* and the CSS *Alabama* off the coast of France, an African American sailor, Joachim Pease, displayed "marked coolness," and won the Congressional Medal of Honor (June 19).

John Lawson and James Mifflin, African American loaders on the *Hartford* and *Brooklyn*, respectively, won Congressional medals of honor for their part in the Battle of Mobile Bay.

Between May 1864 and April 1865, most African American troops were used in the campaign against the army of Northern Virginia. At the Battle of Chaffin's Farm in September, 14 of the 37 Congressional Medal of Honor winners were African American.

Sergeant Major Thomas Hawkins of the 6th United States Colored Troops was awarded the Medal of Honor for rescuing the regimental colors from the enemy at the Battle of Deep Bottom, Virginia.

Sergeant Decatur Dorsey of the 39th United States Colored Troops took the colors and led the men in his unit against the Confederates at the Battle of Petersburg, Virginia.

The following African Americans were awarded the Congressional Medal of Honor for valor at the Battle of New Market Heights:

Private William H. Barnes
38th United States Colored Troops

First Sergeant Powhatan Beaty
5th United States Colored Troops

First Sergeant James H. Brownson
5th United States Colored Troops

Sergeant Major Christian Fleetwood
4th United States Colored Troops

Private James Gardiner
Company I, United States Colored Troops

Sergeant James Harris
38th United States Colored Troops

Sergeant Alfred B. Hilton
4th United States Colored Troops

Sergeant Major Milton M. Holland
5th United States Colored Troops

Corporal Miles James
5th United States Colored Troops

First Sergeant Alexander Kelly
6th United States Colored Troops

First Sergeant Robert Pinn
5th United States Colored Troops

First Sergeant Edward Radcliff
38th United States Colored Troops

Private Charles Veal
4th United States Colored Troops

• In May, African Americans at Port Royal, South Carolina, participated in a meeting which elected delegates to the Republican National Convention. Robert Smalls and three other African Americans were among the delegates, but were denied seats.

• President Lincoln's conservative stand on Reconstruction caused radical abolitionists such as Frederick Douglass to endorse John C. Fremont's candidacy for the Presidency.

In June of 1864, the Wade-Davis Bill was passed in Congress in opposition to President Lincoln's Reconstruction policies. The Wade-Davis Bill declared that the Confederate states were no longer states within the Union but rather that they held the status of territories. As territories, Congress would establish the conditions upon which the Confederate states would be readmitted to the Union.

Among the provisions which the Union Republicans wanted to impose upon the Confederate states as a condition for readmission was the abolition of slavery. (Although the issue of the right to vote by African Americans was not addressed.) President Lincoln, who was unwilling to commit himself to a specific Reconstruction plan, and believing that Congress did not have the constitutional power to abolish slavery, utilized the pocket veto to defeat the bill.

• At the Republican convention in June, which took place in Baltimore, the plank supporting the abolition of slavery was written into the party platform.

• In the Presidential election of 1864, over sixty percent (60%) of the seats in both Houses of Congress were won by Union Republicans.

In 1864, the leaders of the Confederacy found themselves in a quandary. Needing more troops, a resolution was introduced and passed by the Confederate governors which authorized the use of slaves as troops. Jefferson Davis opposed this resolution but, in desperation, it was passed nonetheless.

Meanwhile, due to the shortage of manpower, the Confederate government sought to impress 20,000 slaves as laborers. However, the slave owners, fearing that the impressment would lead to the eventual divestment of their "property" refused to cooperate.

Elsewhere in the South, the status of captured African American troops essentially stalemated prisoner exchange negotiations. Since the South considered captured African American troops to be property, irrespective of their prior status, the exchange of Confederate men for African American soldiers was virtually nonexistent. The Civil War would be over before any African American prisoners of war were to be released.

In April, Confederate General Buford promised to execute all African American troops that were captured. Confederate General Hood threatened to execute the officers and men of the African American regiments if their commanders did not capitulate. These promises and threats only served to strengthen the resolve of the African American Union troops.

Nevertheless, throughout 1864, Confederate officers reported the execution of captured African American troops. Near Lewisburg, Tennessee, two Union officers were murdered and another officer wounded and left for dead. Their war crime was simply that they commanded African American troops.

However, perhaps the worst atrocity committed by the Confederacy in furtherance of their captured African American soldier policy was the incident at Fort Pillow, Tennessee. On April 12, 1864, at Fort Pillow, Tennessee, a Confederate cavalry force under Major General Nathan B. Forrest, captured Fort Pillow. Fort Pillow was garrisoned by African American troops. A massacre ensued. Approximately 300 soldiers, many of them already wounded, plus women and children, were killed.

• *The Civil Rights Movement:* In October, the National Negro Convention in Syracuse, New York, called for African American suffrage. Among the delegates were: Frederick

Douglass and George L. Ruffin. Ruffin was to become the first African American to sit as a judge on the Massachusetts bench.

• In December, a bill forbidding discrimination in the hiring of mail carriers was passed by the Congress.

• *The Socialist Movement:* Karl Marx wrote to President Lincoln from London and assured him of the solidarity of the European workers in the battle to abolish slavery in America. According to the minutes of the International Workers Association, Lincoln answered "in a more than formal way."

• *Notable Births:* Although he himself was not certain of the actual date, George Washington Carver, the great African American scientist, traditionally considered July 12, 1864, to be his birthdate.

George Washington Carver (1864–1943) was kidnapped at the age of 2 and separated from his mother. Carver worked his way through high school. After high school, he applied to Simpson College in Indianola, Iowa. After many rejections, he was finally accepted to the college and became its first African American student.

Carver concluded his college education at Iowa Agricultural College in Ames, Iowa. In 1894, Carver received a bachelor of arts degree and, in 1896, he received a masters of arts degree. Upon his attaining his masters degree, Carver joined the faculty of the college — the first African American faculty member.

Later in 1896, Carver accepted the invitation of Booker T. Washington and joined the faculty at Tuskegee Institute. Washington was concerned about the agricultural economy of the South and about how the African American farmer might produce successful crops. With Washington's assistance, Carver focused his research on such Southern staples as sweet potatoes and peanuts.

During the course of his career, Carver developed some 300 products from the peanut. Such products such as dyes, plastics, soap, ink and many others now in common use. Carver also developed new products from sweet potatoes, wood shavings and cotton stalks.

Carver was frequently honored for his discoveries but he seldom reaped any of the financial rewards associated with them. Over and over again, Carver was exploited by Southern commercial firms which made millions off his discoveries. And yet despite this exploitation, Carver never became bitter. In his life, he possessed a rather saintlike quality. He was beloved by everyone he encountered.

In 1917, Carver was made a Fellow of the Royal Society of Arts in London. In 1923, he received the Spingarn Medal. In 1939, he was awarded the Theodore Roosevelt Medal for Distinguished Research in Agricultural Chemistry. In 1940, the International Federation of Architects, Engineers, Chemists and Technicians gave him a citation.

In his life, George Washington Carver received several honorary degrees from various universities. The farm near Diamond Grove, Missouri, where he was born is now maintained as a national monument by the United States government.

• John W. Boone (aka "Blind Boone"), a noted musical prodigy was born in Miami, Missouri.

• Richard B. Harrison, a featured actor who created the role of "De Lawd" in *Green Pastures*, was born (August 28).

• Charles Young, an African American West Point graduate who held the highest rank (colonel) of any African American military officer in his time, was born.

• *Miscellaneous State Laws:* The Maryland constitution was amended to abolish slavery (July 7).

• In Arkansas, an antislavery state constitution was drawn up and accepted by the European American electorate.

• *Publications:* The New Orleans *Tribune* began publishing as the first daily African American newspaper in French and English (October 14).

• *Scholastic Achievements:* Solomon G. Brown (1829–1903) became an assistant at the Smithsonian Institution.

Solomon G. Brown (1829–1903) had little formal education but a great deal of work experience. As a young man, Brown worked for Samuel F. B. Morse, the inventor of the telegraph. In 1852, Brown accompanied Joseph Henry, a Morse associate, when Henry became the first secretary of the Smithsonian Institution.

Brown became an indispensable worker who prepared most of the illustrations for scientific lectures until 1887.

• The first public school system for African Americans opened in the District of Columbia.

• By 1864, the American Missionary Association had 3,000 African Americans enrolled in its schools with a faculty of 52 teachers. At least five of the 52 teachers were African Americans. These schools were in Virginia.

In North Carolina, another 3,000 students were enrolled in, and 66 teachers worked in, the American Missionary Association schools.

• Rebecca Lee (Crumpler) (1833–?) was awarded a medical degree from the New England Female Medical College in Boston. Lee would establish her medical practice in Richmond, Virginia.

• Benjamin William Arnett, an African American, became a teacher in Fayette County, Pennsylvania.

• The African Methodist Episcopal Church established Western University in Kansas.

• *Black Enterprise:* At Davis Bend, Mississippi, 25 miles south of Vicksburg, federal officials seized six plantations and settled African Americans on the land. By the end of 1864, seventy-five (75) African Americans were living and working on the former plantations. These African Americans raised crops which gave them profits up to $1,000 each after repaying credit advanced by the government. In 1865, 1,800 resettled African Americans ended the year with a total cash balance of $159,200.

THE AMERICAS

• The United States recognized Haitian sovereignty. Haitian General Fabre Geffrard subsequently introduced his plan to bring "industrious men of African descent from the United States."

• Buenaventura Baez became the dominant political figure in the Dominican Republic.

AFRICA

• Sudanese troops mutinied at El Obeid.

• Sharif Abd al-Rahman of Morocco decreed that Jews were entitled to equality in Moroccan society.

• The British defeated the Ashanti and annexed southern Ghana.

• Al-Hajj Umar was assassinated. He was succeeded by Ahmadu Sefu.

EUROPE

• Thomas Morris Chester (1834–1892), an African American, served as a correspondent for a major newspaper, the *Philadelphia Press* during the Civil War. A previous editor of the *Star of Liberia*, Chester's dispatches covered a period of time from August 1864 through June 1865. His dispatches included reports on African American troop activity around Petersburg and Richmond, Virginia.

Thomas Morris Chester (1834–1892) was born in Harrisburg, Pennsylvania. He studied at Alexander High School in Monrovia, Liberia,

and then at the Thetford Academy in Vermont. After the Civil War, Chester read law with a Liberian lawyer. Liking the law, he moved to England and spent the next three years at Middle Temple in London.

In April 1870, Chester became the first-known Anglo-African to be admitted to practice before the English courts.

——— 1865 ———

THE UNITED STATES

On January 31, 1865, the House of Representatives passed the Thirteenth Amendment to the United States Constitution. The Senate had already approved the amendment. The Thirteenth Amendment abolished slavery. It reads:

Amendment XIII

Section 1. Neither slavery nor involuntary servitude, except as a punishment for crime whereof the party shall have been duly convicted, shall exist within the United States, or any place subject to their jurisdiction.

Section 2. Congress shall have power to enforce this article by appropriate legislation.

Upon passage by the Thirty-eighth Congress, the amendment was submitted to the states for ratification. In a proclamation of the secretary of state dated December 18, 1865, the Thirteenth Amendment was declared to have been ratified by the legislatures of twenty-seven of the thirty-six states and was, therefore, the law of the land. The states which ratified the Thirteenth Amendment, and the dates of ratification, are as follows*:

Illinois	February 1, 1865
Rhode Island	February 2, 1865
Michigan	February 2, 1865
Maryland	February 3, 1865
New York	February 3, 1865
Pennsylvania	February 3, 1865
West Virginia	February 3, 1865
Missouri	February 6, 1865
Maine	February 7, 1865
Kansas	February 7, 1865
Massachusetts	February 7, 1865
Virginia	February 9, 1865
Ohio	February 10, 1865
Indiana	February 13, 1865
Nevada	February 16, 1865
Louisiana	February 17, 1865
Minnesota	February 23, 1865

In March 1995, the state of Mississippi, after 130 years, ratified the Thirteenth Amendment, the last to do so.

Wisconsin	February 24, 1865
Vermont	March 9, 1865
Tennessee	April 7, 1865
Arkansas	April 14, 1865
Connecticut	May 4, 1865
New Hampshire	July 1, 1865
South Carolina	November 13, 1865
Alabama	December 2, 1865
North Carolina	December 4, 1865
Georgia	December 6, 1865

The legislatures for the following states ratified the Thirteenth Amendment after December 6, 1865:

Oregon	December 8, 1865
California	December 19, 1865
Florida	December 28, 1865
Iowa	January 15, 1866
New Jersey	January 23, 1866
Texas	February 18, 1870
Delaware	February 12, 1901
Kentucky	March 18, 1976

The Arkansas State Legislature adopted the Thirteenth Amendment by unanimous vote, and, in Alabama, the legislature passed the amendment by a vote of 75 to 15 with the following proviso:

Be it further resolved, that this amendment to the Constitution of the U.S. is adopted by the Legislature of Alabama, with the understanding that it does not confer upon Congress the power to legislate upon the political status of freedmen in this state.

• General Lee said that it was "not only expedient but necessary" that the Confederate Army use African American slaves as soldiers (January 11).

A bill was introduced in the Confederacy which would permit the voluntary enlistment of slaves in the Confederate Army with freedom guaranteed at the end of hostilities. This bill was buried in a committee.

However, General Robert E. Lee desperately needed additional soldiers and made a plea for African American troops. In response to General Lee's plea, the State of Virginia passed a resolution which allowed the army to enlist slaves if agreeable settlement was made with the slave's owner. After Virginia passed this resolution, the House and Senate of the Confederacy allowed the army to enlist African Americans. The Confederate resolution stipulated that no change was to be made in the slave–slave owner relationships and that the slaves were to receive the same pay and rations as the European American troops.

On March 13, Confederate President Jefferson Davis signed a bill allowing the Confederate States to fill their military quota by using slaves, but the number of slaves recruited was not to exceed twenty-five percent (25%) of the able-bodied male slave population between the ages of 18 and 45. This measure came too late to help the Confederacy. However, on the eastern seaboard a number of slaves were recruited and were mustered into Confederate service (March 24).

• John S. Rock became the first African American to practice before the United States Supreme Court (February 1).
• Martin Robinson Delany received a commission as a major in the Union Army and was ordered to Charleston, South Carolina where he served as an army physician. Delany was the first African American to achieve the rank of major in the regular United States Army. *See 1812.*
• On February 12, Henry Highland Garnet preached a sermon in the House of Representatives commemorating the passage of the 13th Amendment. Garnet was the first African American to preach in the Capitol. *See 1815.*
• The first three drafts of the Reconstruction Bill, introduced in the House of Representatives on January 16, February 21, and February 22, all limited the right to vote to European American males, although one draft did give African American soldiers the right to vote.
• Four companies of the 54th United States Colored Troops became the first African Americans to participate in an inaugural parade (March 4).
• After much debate, Congress passed a bill giving freedom to wives and children of African American soldiers in Union service (March 13).
• Aaron Anderson, a landsman on the U.S.S. *Wyandanch*, was awarded the Navy Medal of Honor for bravery at Mattox Creek (March 17).
• With the Civil War at a virtual end, Confederate General Robert E. Lee surrendered his army to Union General Ulysses S. Grant at Appomattox Court House in Virginia (April 9).

During the Civil War, 178,895 African Americans served with the Union Army. This number represented approximately ten percent (10%) of the total Union forces.

It is estimated that 3,000 African Americans were killed in battle. However, more than 26,000 died from disease associated with the war.

There were 14,887 African Americans who were deserters. This number represents about seven percent (7%) of the total desertions.

Between November, 1864, and April, 1865, more than 49,000 African Americans enlisted into Union service. 4,244 of these African American enlistees were from Confederate states.

On July 15, 1865, the 123,156 African Americans serving in the Union Army were assigned as follows:

120 infantry regiments	98,938
12 heavy artillery regiments	15,662
10 batteries of light artillery	1,311
7 cavalry regiments	7,245

• President Lincoln was shot and mortally wounded by John Wilkes Booth while attending the comedy "Our American Cousin" at Ford's Theater in Washington, D.C. (April 14). The President died the following morning.

At 7:22 A.M., Abraham Lincoln died from wounds received when shot at Ford's Theater Washington D.C. by the actor John Wilkes Booth (April 15).

In Lincoln's funeral procession, the Irish Immigrant Organization refused to march with African Americans. The New York City Council refused to allow African Americans to march. It was only due to the intervention of the police commissioner, that a place in the procession was assigned to African Americans. Police protection was necessary to insure the safety of the African American marchers.

• On May 4, Joseph Smith III, the son of the Mormon prophet Joseph Smith, had a revelation that African Americans were truly equal and not banned from the priesthood. This was accepted into the doctrine of the Reorganized Church of the Latter Day Saints, which soon had many African American members. However, it was not the position of the regular Mormon Church located in Salt Lake City, Utah, which continued to deny the priesthood to African Americans.

• Two white regiments and an African American regiment, the 62nd USCT, fought the last action of the Civil War at White's Ranch, Texas. Sergeant Crocket, an Afro-American, is believed to have been the last man to shed blood in the war (May 13).

Juneteenth

Lincoln issued the Emancipation Proclamation on January 1, 1863, and Confederate General Robert E. Lee surrendered to Union General Ulysses S. Grant on April 9, 1865. However, the last battle of the Civil War took place in Texas and did not conclude until May 15, 1865.

Union Major General Gordon Granger with 1,800 soldiers arrived in Galveston on June 18, 1865, to take command of the District of Texas. The next day, June 19, from his headquarters in the Osterman Building at the corner of Strand and 22nd streets, the lives of countless Texans, starting with a quarter of a million African Americans changed.

The African Americans were, for the first time, informed that in accordance with Lincoln's Emancipation Proclamation, they were set free. For the African Americans of Texas it was a time of celebration.

The next year, African Americans in Texas remembered June 19 as their own emancipation day and celebrations were organized. From Galveston to the Red River, former slaves marched and celebrated. Newspaper accounts in Houston reported that thousands of American flags waved as the African Americans paraded down Main Street to the uplifting music of a brass band.

The first official Texas Emancipation Day was celebrated on June 19, 1869. Lottie Brown was named the first "Juneteenth Queen."

After Reconstruction, the day lost its official state sanction. However, for the better part of the 1900s, African Americans in Texas continued to celebrate the unofficial holiday by gathering together at parks for picnics, barbecues, baseball games and reunions.

Although the popularity of Juneteenth waned during the 1960s, local groups kept the Juneteenth tradition alive. After the showing of the television program *Roots* in 1977, interest in African American history and culture revived, and the interest in the Juneteenth holiday received new life.

In 1979, the Texas Legislature made June 19 "Black Heritage Day"—an official Texas holiday. Since that time, Juneteenth has become a symbolic holiday for African Americans throughout the nation.

• President Andrew Johnson announced his Reconstruction plan (May 29).

President Johnson followed the ideas on Reconstruction outlined in the Wade-Davis Bill, but he followed Lincoln in insisting that Reconstruction was the function of the president.

In 1865, Arkansas, Louisiana, Tennessee, and Virginia already had governments loyal to the

United States. President Johnson recognized them as legal and legitimate.

In May and June of 1865, President Johnson also appointed governors in North Carolina, Mississippi, Georgia, Texas, Alabama, South Carolina, and Florida. By the end of 1865, these governors had convened state conventions which nullified secession, abolished slavery, and repudiated debts.

In May of 1865, President Johnson issued his Amnesty Proclamation which granted amnesty to all Confederates who took the oath of allegiance to the United States. The exceptions to the Amnesty Proclamation were those individuals who were: (1) civil and diplomatic officers of the Confederacy; (2) Confederates who left United States judicial posts; (3) officers above the rank of colonel in the army, or lieutenant in the navy; (4) Confederates who left Congress; (5) Confederates who left the armed services of the United States; (6) Confederates who mistreated war prisoners; (7) Confederates who fled the United States; (8) Confederates who attended West Point or the Naval Academy; (9) Confederates who were governors of Confederate states; (10) Northerners who fought for the South; (11) persons whose taxable property value was over $20,000.

By mid–1866, because of President Johnson's liberal view on amnesty, very few Confederates remained unpardoned. Indeed, the former Confederate States would send to the Thirty-ninth Congress such men as Alexander Stephens, the former vice president of the Confederacy, and four former Confederate generals, five Confederate colonels, 6 Confederate Cabinet officers and 58 former Confederate congressmen.

• 1,800 African Americans were settled on confiscated plantations in Davis Bend, Mississippi. By the end of the year, they had a cash balance of $159,200. Despite the wishes of Stevens and Sumner, land confiscation and redistribution to African Americans was never authorized by Congress. Thus, no real land reform was carried out. When President Johnson pardoned the owners of plantations such as those at Davis Bend, the land was returned to them.
• General Sherman issued Special Field Order No. 15, by which the South Carolina and Georgia sea islands, south of Charleston, and the abandoned lands along the rivers for a distance of 30 miles inland were to be used for the settlement of African Americans on plots of not more than 40

acres. General Rufus Saxton was appointed Inspector of the settlements. In January 1866, President Johnson removed Saxton and most of the land was returned to its original owners.

The Freedmen's Bureau was established as part of the War Department. The commissioner of the bureau was to be appointed by the president, with the consent of the Senate. The commissioner had the authority to "control all subjects relating to refugees and freedmen." The commissioner could set aside abandoned tracts of land up to 40 acres to be leased to freedmen at a low rent, giving them the right to buy the land at the end of three years.

As part of the Freedmen's Bureau's authorizing legislation, Union Army officers would be used as assistant commissioners, and the secretary of war could issue provisions, clothing and fuel to the freedmen and refugees.

The Freedmen's Bureau established schools, hired teachers, made provisions for transportation, issued food and clothing and with an expenditure of over $2,000,000 treated 450,000 medical cases.

Due to the efforts of the Freedmen's Bureau, the death rate of freed slaves was reduced from a high of thirty-eight percent (38%) in 1865 to a little more than two percent (2.03%) in 1869.

• Edward G. Walker and Charles L. Mitchell were elected to the Massachusetts House of Representatives thus becoming the first African Americans elected to an American legislative assembly.
• From 1865 to 1877, Robert Small, an African American Civil War hero, served in the South Carolina state militia, rising to the rank of major general. *See 1839.*
• The Ku Klux Klan was organized in Tennessee.
• Michael Augustine Healy was appointed to the United States Revenue Service, the forerunner to the Coast Guard. *See 1839.*
• James Lewis received an appointment as inspector of customs for the Port of New Orleans.

When the Union troops occupied New Orleans in 1862, James Lewis (1832–1914) abandoned the Confederate ship on which he was serving as a steward, raised two companies of African American soldiers, and led the First Regiment of the Louisiana National Guard during the battle of Port Hudson.

After the Civil War, Lewis became active in Louisiana politics and received a number of federal appointments.

• Alexander T. Augusta, an African American, became the director of the Freedmen's Hospital which was located on the grounds of Howard University.

• In December 1865, Thaddeus Stevens submitted a plan to the Republican caucus which (1) claimed Reconstruction as the business of Congress; (2) regarded the President's steps as provisional; (3) postponed consideration of admission of members from Southern states; (4) suggested a joint committee of fifteen be appointed to study conditions in the Confederate States. A resolution creating the joint committee passed the House of Representatives by a vote of 129 to 35, with 18 abstaining. It was subsequently passed by the Senate in February of 1866.

The Stevens Plan was not a great deviation in Congressional policy. Congress had, in fact, followed a policy independent of the Reconstruction plans of Presidents Lincoln and Johnson by forbidding Virginia, North Carolina, South Carolina, Georgia, Florida, Alabama, Mississippi, Louisiana, Texas, Arkansas, and Tennessee representation in the Electoral College.

• *The Civil Rights Movement:* An African American convention held in Raleigh, North Carolina, adopted resolutions for the repeal of discriminatory laws, for proper wages, protection and education.

• An African American convention in Charleston, South Carolina, protested the results of the state constitutional convention. *See Miscellaneous State Laws, below.*

• *Notable Births:* Timothy T. Fortune, journalist and founder of the New York *Age*, was born (October 3).

• Matthew A. Henson, an African American explorer who accompanied Peary to the North Pole, was born in Charles County, Maryland (August 8).

• Adam Clayton Powell, Sr., the famed pastor of the Abyssinian Baptist Church, was born.

Adam Clayton Powell, Sr., (1865–1953) was born in Franklin County, Virginia. As a youth, Powell worked his way through Rendville Academy in West Virginia by working in the neighboring coal mines. He graduated in 1885.

Three years after his graduation from the Rendville Academy, Powell entered the Wayland Seminary in Washington, D.C. In 1892, he became pastor of his first church, the Ebenezer Baptist Church in Philadelphia. A year later, Powell accepted the post of minister at the Immanuel Baptist Church in New Haven, Connecticut. He would hold this position until 1908.

While in New Haven, Powell gained a reputation as a lecturer and writer. In 1895, he published *Souvenir of the Immanuel Baptist Church.* Powell lectured all over the East Coast and in California.

Powell also tried to organize the New Haven African Americans to become a political force, but factionalism and jealousy of Powell destroyed the effort.

In November 1908, Powell became pastor of the Abyssinian Baptist Church in New York City. One of his first political acts in New York was to lead a campaign to force the city to rid the area (40th Street on the West Side) in which the church was then located of the prostitutes who infested the locale.

In 1910, Powell joined the newly formed National Association for the Advancement of Colored People and was appointed to its Finance Committee. Powell remained active in community work, trying to convince European American merchants in African American neighborhoods to hire African American help and trying to have a Harlem Community Center built.

By 1920, Powell had become a figure of national prominence. His sermons were often published in pamphlet form, and he made over $1,200 from the sale of *Watch Your Step* and *The Valley of Dry Bones.*

In 1932, Powell was nominated as a Presidential elector-at-large by the Republican Party of New York.

In 1937, Powell retired from the pulpit and was succeeded by his son, Adam Clayton Powell, Jr.

• *Notable Deaths:* James McCune Smith, an abolitionist writer considered by some to be the most scholarly African American of his time, died.

Miscellaneous State Laws:

The Black Codes

With the demise of slavery, the states of the former Confederacy sought new legislative ways to control African Americans without resorting to abject enslavement. These states developed what have become known as the Black Codes.

The Black Codes were regulations written into the state constitutions that regulated the lives of African Americans. Generally, the Black Codes relegated the freed slaves to virtual slavery if not legal slavery.

Under the Black Codes, any African American convicted of vagrancy was made subject to a period of indefinite servitude. Any African American child that was separated from its parents could be subjected to a period of indefinite servitude. African Americans could come into court as witnesses only in cases in which African Americans were involved.

Under the Black Codes, access to land was limited, and the right to bear arms was forbidden. African American employment, which was previously, relatively unlimited, was limited to contract labor under the Black Codes.

Some of these codes were so onerous that the Southern states were compelled to repeal them under pressure from the North.

- The South Carolina Constitution provided that no African American could enter the state unless, within twenty days after arrival, the African American put up a bond of $1,000 to ensure his good behavior. An African American had to have a special license for any job except as a farmer or a servant. The license included an annual tax of from $10 to $100. African Americans were prohibited from manufacturing or selling liquor. Work licenses were granted by a judge, revocable on complaint, and in case of revocation, the penalty was a fine double the amount paid for the license, half of which went to the informer.
- South Carolina created special courts for African Americans. The local magistrate was commissioned and "especially charged with the supervision of persons of color in his neighborhood, their protection, and the prevention of their misconduct."
- The Mississippi Constitution required every African American to submit evidence annually from the mayor or member of the police board proving that he had a lawful home and means of employment.
- The property provision of the Mississippi Black Codes provided that African Americans were prohibited to rent or lease land, except in incorporated towns or cities, in which places the corporate authorities controlled the land.
- In a Louisiana Black Code, all agricultural workers were required to make contracts with employers during the first ten days of each January; workers could not leave their employers until the contract expired; refusal to work would be punished by forced labor on public works. African Americans were required to work ten hours daily in summer and nine hours daily in winter.
- In South Carolina, the rules for contracting African American servants to European American employers were as follows: Employers were allowed to work servants under 18 "moderately." A servant over the age of 18 could be whipped on judicial authority. The wages and time period for the servants had to be specified in writing. Sunday and night work were forbidden. Unauthorized attacks on servants and the provision of inadequate food to servants were prohibited. The wages to be paid a servant were to be approved by a judge. Failure to make contracts was made a misdemeanor, punishable by fine. Farm labor was required from sunrise to sunset, with intervals for meals. Visitors were not allowed without the employer's consent. Enticing away another's servants was punishable by fine. To sell farm products without the written consent of the employer was forbidden. The contract between the European American employer and the African American servant had to be in writing, witnessed by European Americans and certified by a judge (invariably another European American). Any European American could arrest any African American that the European American saw commit a misdemeanor.
- Mississippi and Florida enacted laws segregating public transportation.
- Texas passed a law requiring every train to have special cars for freed slaves, but it did not specifically prohibit African Americans from riding in other cars.
- Wisconsin rejected a proposal to allow African Americans to vote. Minnesota and Connecticut also voted against African American suffrage.
- *Publications:* George Moses Horton published *Naked Genius*, a volume of poetry. In this book, Horton lampooned Jefferson Davis, the former president of the Confederacy for attempting to escape the Union forces by dressing up as a woman. One poem in the book, "The Slave," expresses Horton's bitterness on being a slave. *See 1797.*
- *Scholastic Achievements:* Fisk University opened (April 20).
- Patrick Henry Healy became the first African American to earn the Doctor of Philosophy (Ph.D.) degree when he passed his final examination in Louvain, Belgium (July 26).
- The American Missionary Association founded Atlanta University at Atlanta, Georgia.
- Francis Louis Cardozo was named principal of the Avery Normal Institute in Charleston, South Carolina.

Francis Louis Cardozo (1837–1903) was born in Charleston, South Carolina, of a Jewish father and a mulatto mother. Cardozo was educated abroad and, after the Civil War, became very active in Reconstruction politics. Cardozo would come to hold several government positions including secretary of state for South Carolina.

• The American Baptist Home Mission helped establish Virginia Union University and Shaw University in Raleigh, North Carolina.
• Howard University was founded as Howard Seminary in Washington, D. C. (November 20).

In 1865, one in every twenty African Americans could read and write. By 1900, one in every two African Americans could read and write.

• *The Black Church:* In 1865, there were 250,000 members of the African Methodist Episcopal Church in the South.
• Daniel Alexander Payne published *The Semi-Centenary of the African Methodist Episcopal Church in the U.S.A. See 1811.*
• *The Arts:* Charles Hicks, an African American, organized the Georgia Minstrels. In 1882, the Georgia Minstrels became part of Callender's Consolidated Spectacular Colored Minstrels.
• *Black Enterprise:* In 1865, various assessments were made concerning the economic health of African Americans.
• In Cincinnati, African Americans owned taxable property valued at a half million dollars.
• In New York, African Americans had invested $755,000 in African American–owned businesses. In Brooklyn (a separate municipal entity at that time), African Americans had invested $76,000 in African American businesses. In New York, African Americans owned $733,000 in unencumbered property. In Brooklyn, they owned $276,000 in unencumbered property and, in Williamsburg, $151,000.
• According to the June 1865 census, there were 16,509 freedmen in Memphis, Tennessee, of which only 220 were indigent. For the previous three years, 1863 to 1865, the African American poor and indigent had been essentially supported by African American benevolent societies who contributed $5,000 for the support of the African American poor.
• The Chesapeake Marine Railroad and Dry Dock Company was founded in Baltimore. It was an African American–owned company and it employed over 300 African American mechanics—men who were normally discriminated against in the Baltimore

shipyards. The Chesapeake Marine Railroad and Dry Dock Company would record a profit for 12 years.

In 1865, an estimated 100,000 of the 120,000 artisans in the South were African Americans. However, by 1890, the skilled African American worker had been eliminated as competition for Southern whites.

THE AMERICAS

• By 1865, there were an estimated 40,000 persons of African descent living in Canada. The census of 1861 had counted approximately 11,000 persons of African descent living in Canada. The more than threefold increase in the Afro-Canadian population was essentially due to escaped slaves leaving the United States during the Civil War.
• Riots erupted in Jamaica.
• The Dominican Republic reasserted its independence from Spain.
• Massillon Coicou, an Afro-Haitian poet, was born.

Massillon Coicou (1865–1908) was born in Port-au-Prince, Haiti, and was educated at Frères de l'Instruction Chrétienne and Lycée Petion.

Like many of the prominent Caribbean and Latin American literary figures, Coicou was also a politician. He was in the Cabinet of President Thiresias S. Sam and served as the Haitian minister to Paris.

Coicou founded the literary intellectual magazine *L'Oeuvre* and wrote two collections of poetry, *Les Poésies Nationales* (1891) and *Impression et Passion* (1902). *Les Poésies Nationales* was a work full of enthusiasm for Haiti and Coicou's revolutionary idealism, while *Impression et Passion* was more thoughtful, more meditative poetry.

In 1904, *Dessalines Liberté*, the best of Coicou's dramatic works was published. The theme of *Dessalines Liberté* was Haitian independence. *Dessalines Liberté* premiered in Paris and became a classic of the Haitian théatre.

Coicou spent his last years as a popular, outspoken professor of philosophy at the most prominent lycée in Port-au-Prince. Coicou's popularity and outspokenness led to his being executed by a firing squad in 1908.

AFRICA

• The Sudanese cotton industry was greatly expanded.

One of the consequences of the American Civil War was the temporary disruption of American cotton production. This disruption enabled the new African (Sudanese) cotton industry to expand in order to fulfill the European demand for cotton.

• Emperor Theodore II of Ethiopia made an unsuccessful attempt to oust Menelik, the Muslim, from Shoa.

• The British Kaffraria was incorporated into the Cape.

• The Orange Free State-Basuto War was waged.

• Cetewayo became the acknowledged leader of the Zulu.

EPILOGUE

Slavery did not end in 1865. Nor did it end in 1886 when Cuba eliminated the patronato system or in 1888 when Brazil outlawed the practice. Slavery as an institution would survive for another hundred years.

In the context of an accurate portrayal of history, it is important to understand that slavery persisted well into the 20th century and that it continued to devastate the lives of millions of Africans long after African Americans had ostensibly been set free.

After 1865, while a number of rogue European and American slavers continued to ply their trade, the predominant perpetuators of African slavery were Arabs and Africans themselves.

While it is true that the African slave trade after 1865 never reached the proportions of the 1700s or the early 1800s, nevertheless, it cannot be ignored that the evil still thrived in many parts of the world. The horror, while lessened, was still a horror. Misery was still fostered. The thousands of deaths were still an unconscionable waste of human life.

At the end of 1865, there was still a great deal to be done before the enslavement of Africans was to be discontinued.

While it was not comparable to the continuing enslavement and genocidal killing that was occuring in Africa, the plight of the freed slaves in the United States did reveal that the end of slavery did not necessarily mean that the slaves were free.

African Americans were discovering that freedom from bondage did not necessarily mean freedom from servitude. As African Americans all too quickly learned, freedom from bondage did not mean equality of opportunity or equality in the exercise of civil rights. In essence, while African Americans could say that they were "free" the word had little meaning if it was not accompanied by the benefits and privileges of citizenship.

It was to this struggle for citizenship that the next one hundred years of the African American experience would be devoted. For the next one hundred years, the quest for freedom would be a quest for civil rights.

BIBLIOGRAPHY

Three years ago, I read William Loren Katz's *Black Indians: A Hidden Heritage*. For me it was an eye-opening book and for as long as I live I shall remember a line which appears on page 9 of the book. Quoting a student of African American and Indigenous American heritage, it read: "If you know I have a history, you will respect me."

As I have journeyed down the road which has led to the creation of this book, I have discovered what is, perhaps, a more profound truth. For me, and hopefully for others like me, I believe that the more accurate assessment is: "If I know I have a history, I am more likely to respect myself. And if I respect myself, I am more likely to respect others."

Katz's book, along with my 1990 Canadian trip, were the initial impetus for writing this book. However, along the way I have encountered a number of other helpful guides. Among the more essential have been Peter M. Bergman and Mort N. Bergman's *The Chronological History of the Negro in America*; Ellen Irene Diggs's *Black Chronology*; G. S. P. Freeman-Greenville's *The Chronology of World History*; Amiram Gonen's *The Encyclopedia of the Peoples of the World*; and Antony Mason, Anne Mahon, and Andrew Currie's *World Facts & Places*. I am also indebted to a number of dictionaries (*World Book, Webster's New Collegiate*) and sets of encyclopedias (*World Book, Funk & Wagnall's, Encyclopaedia Britannica, Webster's New World*) which have provided concise answers to questions which always seemed to crop up in the preparation of this text.

The following is a listing of some of the more significant resources relied upon in the preparation of this book:

Afro-American Encyclopedia (North Miami, Fla.: Educational Book Publishers, 1974).

Ashe, Arthur R., Jr. *A Hard Road to Glory: A History of the African American Athlete 1619–1918* (New York: Warner Books, 1988).

Bergman, Peter M., and Mort N. Bergman. *The Chronological History of the Negro in America* (New York: New American Library, 1969).

Carruth, Gorton. *What Happened When* (New York: Harper & Row, Publishers, 1989).

Chronicle Publications, *Chronicle of America* (New York: Chronicle Publications, 1988).

Coe, Michael D. *Mexico* (New York: Praeger Publishers, 6th printing, 1972).

Cowan, Tom, and Jack Maguire. *Timelines of African American History: 500 Years of Black Achievement* (New York: Perigee Books, 1994).

Crim, Keith, editor. *Dictionary of World Religions* (San Francisco: Harper & Row, 1989).

Davidson, Basil. *Africa in History* (New York: Collier Books, 1991).

Diggs, Ellen Irene. *Black Chronology* (Boston: G.K. Hall, 1983).

Dor-Ner, Zvi. *Columbus and the Age of Discovery* (New York: William Morrow, 1991).

Durant, Will, and Ariel Durant. *The Story of Civilization: The Age of Louis XIV* (New York: Simon & Schuster, 1963).

Encyclopaedia Britannica, Inc. *The Annals of America* (Chicago: Encyclopaedia Britannica, 1968).

Everett, Susanne. *History of Slavery* (Secaucus, N.J.: Chartwell Books, 1991).

Frankin, John Hope. *From Slavery to Freedom: A History of Negro Americans* (New York: Vintage Books, 1969).

Freeman-Greenville, G. S. P. *The Chronology of World History* (Totowa, N.J.: Rowman and Littlefield, 1978).

Fuentes, Carlos. *The Buried Mirror* (New York: Houghton Mifflin, 1992).

Gonen, Amiram, editor. *The Encyclopedia of the Peoples of the World* (New York: Henry Holt, 1993).

Harris, Joseph E. *The African Presence in Asia* (Evanston, Ill.: Northwestern University Press, 1971).

Henry Ossawa Tanner (an art catalogue prepared by the Philadelphia Museum of Art, 1991).

Heyerdahl, Thor. *Kon Tiki: Across the Pacific by Raft* (New York: Rand McNally, 1950).

_____. *The Ra Expeditions*, translated by Patricia Crampton (Garden City, N.Y.: Doubleday, 1971).

The History of Tobacco. Associated Press — *Daily Republic* (Fairfield, Calif.: newspaper, August 28, 1994).

Hoover, Mildred Brooke, Hero Eugene Rensch, Ethel Grace Rensch, William N. Abeloe (revised by Douglas E. Kyle). *Historic Spots in California* (Stanford, Calif.: Stanford University Press, 1990).

Illustrated History of South Africa (Pleasantville, N.Y.: Reader's Digest Association, 1988).

Irwin, Graham W. *Africans Abroad* (New York: Columbia University Press, 1977).

Jefferson, Thomas. *Writings* (Library of America, 1984).

Katz, William Loren. *Black Indians: A Hidden Heritage* (New York: Atheneum, 1986).

Koning, Hans. *Columbus: His Enterprise* (New York: Monthly Review Press, 1976).

Kunitz, Stanley J., and Vineta Colby, editors. *European Authors: 1000–1900* (New York: H. W. Wilson, 1967).

Lincoln, Abraham. *Speeches and Writings 1832–1858* (Library of America, 1989).

_____. *Speeches and Writings 1859–1865* (Library of America, 1989).

Lipschutz, Mark R., and R. Kent Rasmussen. *Dictionary of African Historical Biography* (Berkeley: University of California Press, 1986).

Logan, Rayford W., and Michael R. Winston, editors. *Dictionary of American Negro Biography* (New York: W. W. Norton, 1982).

Magill, Frank N., editor. *Masterpieces of African-American Literature* (New York: HarperCollins, 1992).

Mason, Antony, Anne Mahon, and Andrew Currie. *World Facts & Places* (London: Tiger Books International, 1993).

Mazrui, Ali. *The Africans: A Triple Heritage* (Boston: Little, Brown, 1986).

Meyer, Michael C., and William L. Sherman. *The Course of Mexican History* (New York: Oxford University Press, 1991).

Murray, Jocelyn, editor. *Cultural Atlas of Africa* (New York: Facts on File, 1981).

Parker, Geoffrey, ed. *The World: An Illustrated History* (New York: Harper & Row, 1986).

Ploski, Harry A., and James Williams. *The Negro Almanac: A Reference Work on the African American* (Detroit: Gale Research, 1989).

Robinson, Francis, ed. *The Cambridge Encyclopedia of India* (Cambridge, England: Cambridge University Press, 1989).

Rogers, J. A. *World's Great Men of Color* (New York: Macmillan, 1972).

Sadie, Stanley, editor. *The New Grove Dictionary of Music and Musicians* (London: Macmillan, 1980).

Sertima, Ivan Van. *They Came Before Columbus: The African Presence in Ancient America* (New York: Random House, 1976).

Sloan, Irving. *The American Negro: A Chronology and Fact Book* (Dobbs Ferry, N.Y.: Oceana Publications, 1968).

Smith, Jessie Carney. *Black Firsts: 2,000 Years of Extraordinary Achievement* (Detroit: Gale Research, 1994).

Smithsonian Institution. *Handbook of North American Indians,* volume 5; William Sturtevant, general editor; David Damas, volume editor (Washington, D.C.: Smithsonian Institution, 1984).

Thurston, Herbert, S. J., and Donald Attwater. *Butler's Lives of the Saints* (New York: P. J. Kenedy & Sons, 1956).

Thybony, Scott. "Against All Odds, Black Seminole Won Their Freedom" (*Smithsonian*, August 1991).

Time-Life Books. *Voyages of Discovery* (Richmond, Va.: Time-Life Books, 1989).

Tomb Treasures From China: The Buried Art of Ancient Xi'an (curated by the Kimball Art Museum, Fort Worth, Texas, and the Asian Art Museum of San Francisco: 1994).

Trager, James. *The People's Chronology* (New York: Henry Holt, 1992).

United States Code Annotated, Constitution of the United States, Amendments 7 to 14 (Saint Paul, Minn.: West, 1987).

Utley, Robert M., and Wilcomb E. Washburn. *Indian Wars* (New York: American Heritage, 1977).

Wade, Harold, Jr. *Black Men of Amherst* (Amherst, Mass.: Amherst College Press, 1976).

Waldman, Carl. *Atlas of the North American Indian* (New York: Facts on File, 1985).

Winks, Robin W. *The Blacks in Canada* (Montreal: McGill-Queen's University Press, 1971).

INDEX

In an effort to make this index as easy to use as possible, after each entry there are two references. The first reference is to the year in which the entry appears. The second reference, in parentheses, is to the specific page on which the entry appears.

Names that are European in origin are inverted and thus alphabetized by the last name of the individual. Names that are African, Arabic, or Asian are not inverted. Thus, "Muhammed Ali" appears in this index under the letter "M."